Rentz's
STUDENT AFFAIRS PRACTICE
IN HIGHER EDUCATION

ABOUT THE EDITOR

NAIJIAN ZHANG is Professor of Higher Education Counseling/
Student Affairs at West Chester University of Pennsylvania. He received a B.A. in English from Xi'an Foreign Languages University,
an M.A. in College Student Personnel and an M.A. in Counseling
and Guidance from Bowling Green State University, and a Ph.D. in
Counseling Psychology and Student Personnel Services from Ball
State University. He has held positions of Acting Chair and Graduate Program Coordinator in the Department of Counselor Education at West Chester University of Pennsylvania. Previous administrative positions were held in the Division of Student Affairs at Ball
State University (Indiana). He is recipient of Travel Award from
American Psychological Association (APA), Outstanding Research
Award, and Outstanding Service Award from ACPA. He has served
on the editorial board of the *Journal of College Counseling*. He is also
a licensed psychologist in Pennsylvania.

Fourth Edition

Rentz's
STUDENT AFFAIRS
PRACTICE IN
HIGHER EDUCATION

Edited by

NAIJIAN ZHANG & ASSOCIATES

CHARLES C THOMAS • PUBLISHER, LTD.
Springfield • Illinois • U.S.A.

Published and Distributed Throughout the World by

CHARLES C THOMAS • PUBLISHER, LTD.
2600 South First Street
Springfield, Illinois 62794-9265

© 2011 by CHARLES C THOMAS • PUBLISHER, LTD.

ISBN 978-0-398-07964-2 (hard)
ISBN 978-0-398-07965-9 (paper)
ISBN 978-0-398-07966-6 (ebook)

Library of Congress Catalog Card Number: 2010024595

With THOMAS BOOKS *careful attention is given to all details of manufacturing and design. It is the Publisher's desire to present books that are satisfactory as to their physical qualities and artistic possibilities and appropriate for their particular use.* THOMAS BOOKS *will be true to those laws of quality that assure a good name and good will.*

Printed in the United States of America
MM-R-3

Library of Congress Cataloging in Publication Data

Rentz's student affairs practice in higher education / edited by Naijian Zhang
& Associates. – 4th ed.
        p. cm.
    Includes biographical references and index.
    ISBN 978-0-398-07964-2 (hard)–ISBN 978-0-398-07965-9 (pbk.)
    1. Student affairs services–United States. I. Rentz, Audrey L. II. Zhang,
Naijian. III. Title.

LB2343.S7936 2011
378'194–dc22   2010024595

ABOUT THE CONTRIBUTORS

CATHY AKENS is Assistant Vice President for Student Affairs and Assistant Professor in Higher Education at Florida International University. She received a B.A. from University of Toledo, an M.A. in College and University Administration from Michigan State University, and an Ed.D. in Higher Education from Florida International University. She previously served as Director of Residential Life and held other administrative positions at Florida International University and Bowling Green State University. She is a past Chair of ACPA's Commission for Housing and Residential Life and served as a member of the Editorial Board for the *Journal of College and University Housing.*

TREY AVERY is a Consulting Associate with Keeling & Associates (K&A), holds a Bachelor of Arts in American Cultural Studies from Fairhaven College at Western Washington University, where he was a peer health educator. Since joining K&A in 2006, he has worked on many projects related to student health programs and services for institutions and professional organizations in higher education in the United States and Canada. He is beginning graduate studies in neuroscience and education in New York City in 2010.

IRVIN W. BRANDEL has held the positions of Director, Associate Director, Training Director, and Psychologist at the Counseling Center of the University of Akron. He was also Director of the Career Placement Services concurrently for three years. He received an M.A. degree in College Student Personnel from Michigan State University and a Ph.D. in Counseling from the University of Akron. He has served on the Executive Board of the Association of Counseling Center Training Agencies, the Accreditation Board of the International Association of Counseling Services (IACS), and as a site visitor for the American Psychological Association and IACS. He is an Emeritus member of the Association of University and College Counseling Center Directors.

V. BARBARA BUSH is an associate professor of higher education at the University of North Texas. She holds a Ph.D. in higher education administration from Claremont Graduate University and a master of education degree in college student personnel from Indiana University. Prior to her academic career, she served in various student affairs positions including director of student activities and programs at California State University and dean of students at Scripps College, Claremont California. She has presented papers at the national and international conferences, published articles relating to financial aid and other student services at community colleges, and coedited a book on African American women students.

D. STANLEY CARPENTER is Professor and Chair of the Educational Administration and Psychological Services Department at Texas State University, San Marcos. He holds a B.S. in Mathematics from Tarleton State University, an M.S. in Student Personnel and Guidance from Texas A&M-Commerce, and a Ph.D. in Counseling and Student Personnel Services from the University of Georgia. He has served as the Executive Director of the Association for the Study of Higher Education (ASHE) and as Editor/Chair of the ACPA Media Board, as well as on the NASPA Board of Directors. He has received awards for teaching (Texas A&M's College of Education), scholarship (Senior Scholar of ACPA, 2000; SACSA's Melvene Hardee Award), and service (Distinguished Service Award from ASHE; Esther Lloyd Jones Award from ACPA).

JENNIFER STEVENS MADOFF DICKSON, M.P.H., Dr. P.H., is Consultant and Director of Research for Keeling & Associates (K&A) and serves as Adjunct Lecturer in Narrative Medicine in the Department of Medicine (College of Physicians and Surgeons) and as Associate Research Scientist in the Department of Sociomedical Sciences (Mailman School of Public Health) of Columbia University in New York City. She leads K&A's research, writing, and professional development projects.

MARY F. HOWARD-HAMILTON is Professor in the Department of Educational Leadership, Administration, and Foundations, Higher Education Program at Indiana State University. She received her B.A. and M.A. degrees from The University of Iowa and a Doctorate of Education, Ed.D. from North Carolina State University. She has received the "Robert S. Shaffer Award" for Academic Excellence as a Graduate Faculty Member from NASPA and the Standing Committee for Women "Wise Women Award" from ACPA at the ACPA/NASPA 2007 joint convention.

R. MICHAEL HAYNES is the Assistant Vice President for Student Life Studies at Tarleton State University in Stephenville, Texas. He served as an assistant director of financial aid at the University of North Texas, and as the director of financial aid at the University of North Texas Health Science Center. He holds a bachelor of business administration degree from Baylor University and a master of science and a Ph.D. in higher education from the University of North Texas. His research interest includes participation in higher education by underrepresented groups. His work has been presented at the Texas Association of Student Financial Aid Administrators and the Association for the Study of Higher Education conferences.

DON HOSSLER is the Executive Associate Dean for the School of Education at Indiana University Bloomington. He is a Professor of Educational Leadership and Policy Studies and also serves as the Coordinator of the Higher Education and Student Affairs graduate programs. Other positions that he has held include the Vice Chancellor for Enrollment Services for Indiana University, Bloomington; the Associate Vice President for Enrollment Services for the seven campuses of the Indiana University system; and Chair of the Department of Educational Leadership and Policy Studies. His areas of specialization include college choice, student persistence, student financial aid policy, and enrollment management.

RICHARD P. KEELING is Principal and Senior Executive Consultant for Keeling & Associates (K&A), a comprehensive higher education consulting firm based in New York City. He received a B.A. in English from the University of Virginia and an M.D. from Tufts University School of Medicine. Before founding K&A, he served as Executive Director of University Health Services and Professor of Medicine at the University of Wisconsin-Madison and as Director of the Department of Student Health and Associate Professor of Medicine at the University of Virginia. He is a past-president of the American College Health Association and served two terms as Editor of the *Journal of American College Health.* Through K&A, he has worked with more than 75 colleges and universities to strengthen health-related services for students.

MARIE LINDHORST earned her A.B. in Religion from Vassar, her Master of Divinity from Yale, and her Ph.D. in Educational Theory and Policy from Penn State. She was a university chaplain and faculty member at Wesleyan University, Colgate University, and Lycoming College before coming to Penn State in 1989. Since 2002, she has been the Associate Director of the Division of Undergraduate Studies at The Pennsylvania State University.

JOHN WESLEY LOWERY is an associate professor of Student Affairs in Higher Education at Indiana University of Pennsylvania. He received a B.A. in Religious Studies from the University of Virginia, an M.Ed. Student Personnel Services from the University of South Caroline, and earned his Ph.D. from Bowling Green State University in Higher Education Administration. He is also an affiliated consultant with the National Center for Higher Education Risk Management (NCHERM) and previously served on the faculty at Oklahoma State University and University of South Carolina where he earned his master's. He also coordinated student affairs programs at both institutions. His previous administrative positions include Director of Residence Life at Adrian College and University Judicial Administrator at Washington University in St. Louis.

FIONA J. D. MACKINNON, Ph.D. retired from Bowling Green State University, Department of Higher Education and Student Affairs as an Associate Professor Emeritus. While at Bowling Green she held the positions of Associate Dean in the College of Education and Human Development, Department Chair of Educational Foundations and Inquiry, Provost Associate, and Chair of Faculty Senate. In 1996, she was appointed Senior Fulbright Scholar at Beijing Normal University in Beijing, People's Republic of China. Over her 45-year career in academia and student affairs, she has served in the Career Center and Adult Learner Services at Penn State University, the College of Technology at Southern Illinois University at Carbondale, the Counseling Center and President's Team Leadership Akron Grant at the University of Akron, Counseling Services at Syracuse University, Assistant Dean of Students at The Ohio State University, and Assistant Dean of Women at Denison University.

VICKIE ANN McCOY is an Assistant Professor in the Department of Counselor Education at West Chester University of Pennsylvania. She received her B.A., M.S.Ed., and M.A. degrees from Monmouth University in New Jersey where she spent several years as the Coordinator of Counseling and Testing Services for Students with Disabilities. She earned her Ph.D. in Counseling Psychology from The University of Southern Mississippi where she served as the Behavioral Medicine Coordinator for the University Counseling Center and received the "Bill W. Shafer Memorial Award" for University Counseling Center Service.

JEFF NOVAK is the Associate Director of Housing and Residence Life at the University of Central Florida. He received a B.S. degree in Psychology, an M.Ed. degree in Student Personnel in Higher Education, and Ed.S. degree in Mental Health Counseling from the University of Florida. Additionally, he received his Ed.D in Educational Leadership from the University of Central Florida. He has been active in ACUHO-I and in the SEAHO region for the last 13 years while at University of Central Florida, East Carolina University, and the University of Florida. He is the past chair of the ACUHO-I program committee and has served as the state of Florida representative on the SEAHO Governing Council.

KEITH B. O'NEILL is a doctoral student in the Higher Education Administration program at Bowling Green State University (OH). He earned his B.A. and M.Ed. from Loyola University (IL). Previous administrative positions were held at Loyola University and Saint Xavier University (IL). He has been active in the National Association of Student Personnel Administrators, the Ohio Association of Student Personnel Administrators, and Sigma Pi Fraternity.

WANDA I. OVERLAND is the Vice President for Student Life and Development and Affiliated faculty member in the Higher Education Administration Program at St. Cloud State University (Minnesota). Prior to assuming her current position, she served as the Associate Vice President for Student Affairs and Dean of Students at Bowling Green State University and held other student affairs administrative positions at North Dakota State University. She received her B.S. and M.S. at North Dakota State University and Ph.D. in Higher Education Administration from Bowling Green State University (Ohio).

AUDREY L. RENTZ is Professor Emeritus of Higher Education and Student Affairs at Bowling Green State University (Ohio). She received her A.B. from the College of Mount St. Vincent (Mathematics), M.S. from The Pennsylvania State University (Counselor Education), and Ph.D. in Counseling, Personnel Services and Educational Psychology from Michigan State University. She has served on the editorial boards of *Initiatives* (NAWE), *The Journal of College Student Development* (ACPA), and *The Journal of Psychological Type* (JPT). She was honored by OCPA as the recipient of the Philip A. Tripp Distinguished Service Award.

MARGARET L. SARNICKI is a Program Coordinator in the Division of Student Life and Development at St. Cloud State University (Minnesota). Previously, she was the Director of Adult and Continuing Education at Simpson College (Iowa). She received her B.S. from Minnesota State University–Mankato and is a candidate in the Higher Education Administration M.S. program at St. Cloud State University.

LISA SEVERY is the Director of Career Services at the University of Colorado, Boulder. Before moving to Colorado, she worked at the University of Florida for seven years in various career counseling roles. She received a B.A. in psychology from Indiana University and an M.A. and a Ph.D. in Counselor Education from the University of Florida. Lisa has coauthored two books: *Making Career Decisions that Count* with Darrell Luzzo and *Turning Points: Managing Career Transitions with Meaning and Purpose* with Jack and Phoebe Ballard. She has been designated a Master Career Counselor and honored with many awards including both the NCDA Merit and Presidential Awards. She is a Nationally Certified Counselor and a Licensed Professional Counselor in Colorado.

BETTINA C. SHUFORD currently serves as the Interim Associate Vice Provost for Academic Affairs at Bowling Green State University. She previously served as the Assistant Vice President for Student Affairs and Director of the Center for Multicultural and Academic Initiatives on the same campus. Prior to coming to BGSU, she held positions in residence life, and served as an Assistant Dean of Students and Director of Minority Student Affairs at the University of North Carolina at Greensboro. She received her bachelor's degree in psychology from North Carolina Central University, her master's in Guidance and Counseling from the University of North Carolina at Greensboro, and her doctorate in Higher Education Administration from Bowling Green State University.

EDWARD G. WHIPPLE is Vice President for Student Affairs and adjunct Associate Professor of Higher Education and Student Affairs at Bowling Green State University in Ohio. He received a B.A. from Willamette University (OR), an M.A.T. from Northwestern University, and his Ph.D. from Oregon State University. Previous student affairs administrative positions were held at Montana State University–Billings, the University of Alabama–Tuscaloosa, Texas Tech University, and Iowa State University. He has published a number of articles and book chapters related to student affairs programs and services. He has served in leadership position at the national level with the National Association of Student Personnel Administrators, the Association of Public and Land-Grant Universities, the Association of Fraternity Advisors, and Phi Delta Theta International Fraternity.

ERIC R. WHITE received a B.A. in History from Rutgers University and an M.A. and a Ph.D. in Counseling Psychology from the University of Pennsylvania. He is the Executive Director of the Division of Undergraduate Studies and Associate Dean for Advising at The Pennsylvania State University. He has served as president of NACADA (2004–2005) and the Association of Deans and Directors of University Colleges and Undergraduate Studies (1993). He is also an Affiliate Assistant Professor of Education at Penn State and the recipient of NACADA's Virginia N. Gordon Award for Excellence in the Field of Advising and Penn State's Administrative Excellence Award.

PREFACE

The fourth edition of *Rentz's Student Affairs Practice in Higher Education* has been designed for both Master's- and Doctoral-level students completing graduate courses in the areas of college student personnel, college student affairs, college student development, higher education administration, and/or student affairs counseling. This edition was also designed to assist practitioners who may not have sufficient background knowledge in these fields and student affairs professionals who may use the book for continuing professional development. Finally, this edition may be quite useful to experienced student affairs practitioners and administrators who desire a reference book which systematically describes the development (particularly trends and patterns) of student affairs function, its practice methods, and program models in higher education.

The mission in writing *Rentz's Student Affairs Practice in Higher Education, Fourth Edition*, is to:

- Provide the reader with a solid foundation in the historical and philosophical perspectives of college student affairs development
- Assist the reader in understanding the major concepts, mission, and purpose of student affairs' practice, methods and program models
- Enable the reader to conceptualize the theme, or the fundamental framework of student affairs administration, its roles and functions in higher education
- Start the new professional on the journey toward skilled student affairs practice
- Facilitate the reader's comprehension of the trends and issues of each respective division of student affairs in higher education

The fourth edition of *Rentz's Student Affairs Practice in Higher Education* follows a similar pattern of organization as the previous edition. However, six chapters have been completely rewritten. The new chapters are Chapter 4 "Academic Advising," Chapter 5 "Career Services," Chapter 10 "Residence

Halls," Chapter 12 "Financial Aid," Chapter 13 "Student Health Centers," and Chapter 14 "Afterward." In these chapters, the most recent information on student development and student affairs practice in each area is included.

Taking over the editorship of this book has been a challenge. First, both Dr. Audrey Rentz and Dr. Fiona MacKinnon were my professors when I was a graduate student in the College Student Personnel Program at Bowling Green State University 20 years ago. They remember very well where I was back then. I still remember that I knew little about student affairs in the United States since I came from China, a country where the profession of student affairs does not exist. Second, all the chapter authors in the previous edition were their colleagues, thus a connection and a working relationship had already been built before the actual writing of the book. As the Editor of this fourth edition, I personally do not know any of the authors who contributed to the third edition and thus, I do not have the advantage of an existing working relationship. Third, some of the previous authors have passed away, retired, or chosen not to continue to write their chapters for various reasons. Therefore, identifying qualified and competent new authors became the most challenging task in the process of developing this edition.

In addition to the nine returning experts from the previous edition, fourteen new experts from the field of student affairs joined me on this project. The authors of the fourth edition offer the reader a clear picture of student affairs in U.S. higher education. Chapter 1 "Philosophical Heritage of Student Affairs" presents a brief introduction to the major philosophical schools of thought and philosophical beliefs about U.S. higher education and student affairs and an understanding of how these philosophical beliefs have affected student affairs practice. Chapter 2 "Student Affairs: A Historical Perspective" describes the origins of student affairs, its theoretical development, and the major events in the field from the 1600s to the present. Following these two chapters are the 11 chapters pertaining to the function areas of student affairs: Chapter 3 "From Admissions to Enrollment Management," Chapter 4 "Academic Advising," Chapter 5 "Career Services," Chapter 6 "Counseling Centers," Chapter 7 "Student Conduct," Chapter 8 "Multicultural Affairs," Chapter 9 "Orientation," Chapter 10 "Residence Halls," Chapter 11" Student Activities," Chapter 12 "Financial Aid," and Chapter 13 "Student Health." All of these chapters basically contain the following sections: Introduction, History, Definition, Purpose and Goals, Administration and Organizational Structure, Programs and Services, Staffing, Models, Professional Development, Entry Level Qualifications, Technology, Issues and Trends, and References. Three major issues, which are woven into the majority of these chapters, are the current economic downturn, the increasing use of technology, and the plethora of diversity issues that have affected student affairs and its practice. Chapter 14 "Afterword" presents the overall issues and challenges facing student affairs in higher education as a profession now and in the future.

I have been fortunate in securing the collaboration of knowledgeable experts who have performed admirably. I wish to express my gratitude to all contributing authors, to my colleague, Dr. Vickie Ann McCoy, and to my graduate assistant, Kara Baxter, who have provided me with great assistance in the preparation of this edition. My special gratitude goes to Dr. Fiona MacKinnon who offered me her experience and expertise in editing the third edition. Finally, I'm deeply grateful to Dr. Audrey Rentz who was my thesis advisor and mentor while I was a graduate student in the College Student Personnel Program at Bowling Green State University between 1990 and 1993. Her support and guidance were both personally and professionally empowering. I sincerely hope that the *Rentz's Student Affairs Practice in Higher Education* will continue to be of value to students, practitioners, and researchers in the area of student affairs practice.

I would also like to invite anyone who has read or used this book to send me the feedback and suggestions for the Fifth Edition at nzhang@wcupa.edu.

NAIJIAN ZHANG

CONTENTS

Rentz's
STUDENT AFFAIRS PRACTICE
IN HIGHER EDUCATION

Chapter 1

THE PHILOSOPHICAL HERITAGE
OF STUDENT AFFAIRS

Stanley Carpenter

Og, our mythical Neolithic ancestor, had a problem. To be sure, he and his tribe had lots of problems, but this was the most vexing yet. Although they did not know it or even construct the problem that way, the issue really was that their brains were too big and too differentiated. Having a good brain was an advantage and necessary for survival. Og's people were not very big or very fast compared to other animals. They were not particularly strong or keen of sight, smell, or hearing. But they could think and plan and remember. The problem was that this ability to conceptualize caused them to wonder–to need to know, to speculate, and to be unhappy when they did not have answers. Perhaps it was something poignant, like the death of a child, or just the mundane cycle of the seasons that first elicited a search for a larger meaning to life, but whatever it was, the quest could have soon led to depression, insanity, and death for the members of the tribe and therefore the tribe itself.

Thus was philosophy invented or, as some would say discovered, in an attempt to supplant powerlessness with knowledge. It did not matter that the knowledge was "incorrect" (in modern terms)–simply that it explained otherwise terrifyingly uncertain and uncontrollable things like fire and rain, death and birth. It was necessary to have something to believe and to strive to learn more.

Over time, a tribal culture developed, encompassing all the beliefs, knowledge, and skills that made the group unique and contributed to survival. The culture was inculcated into the children by formal and informal means in a process of education not materially different than what is in place today. As the tribe became a village, then a city, then a sovereign state, philosophical knowledge grew and differentiated. Eventually, it became necessary to attend to the higher learning of some members to prepare them to lead, to teach, and to press the search for new knowledge. Student affairs professionals are the direct descendants of early educators and hence heir to a long tradition of thinking and writing about educational philosophy. The purpose of this chapter is to examine the impact of philosophy generally and several specific philosophical positions upon higher education and the practice of student affairs work.

WHAT IS PHILOSOPHY?

At first all learning was philosophical. The word "philosophy," from the Greek *philosophia,* literally means love of wisdom or learning. Only in the past 200 years has there occurred a separation of "natural philosophy" (or sciences such as chemistry and physics), "mental philosophy" (or psychology), and "moral philosophy" (political science, economics, and sociology, for example) from the general concept (Brubacher, 1982). For thousands of years, the study of philosophy was the same as advanced learning, a wide-ranging intellectual quest. The knowledge explosion and specialization have changed that, but philosophy is still a broad and deep field.

Philosophy is a poorly understood term. People begin sentences with "My philosophy on that is . . ." and proceed to give unsupported opinions, sometimes inconsistent with their behaviors or facts. Philosophy can be thought of as simply a general approach to the world or it can be a process of disciplined inquiry. Gracia (1992) captured it this way:

Philosophy may be interpreted . . . :

I.   . . . as a set of ideas or beliefs, concerning anything that an ordinary person may hold.
II.   . . . as a view of the world, or any of its parts, that seeks to be accurate, consistent, and comprehensive.
III. . . . as a discipline of learning.
   A. Activity whereby a view of the world or any of its parts, that seeks to be accurate, consistent, and comprehensive, is produced.
   B. Formulation, explanation, and justification of rules by which the production of a view of the world, or any of its parts, that seeks to be accurate, consistent, and comprehensive, is produced (philosophical methodology). (p. 56)

This chapter will concern itself primarily with the second meaning (a view of the world), but with elements of the third (a discipline of learning). The reader should be concerned with applying the information presented (a view of the world), using the proper methods (through the discipline), to modify his/her beliefs in such a way that they are accurate, consistent, and comprehensive.

The Three Great Questions of Philosophy

Originally, philosophy was concerned with virtually all knowledge, but in modern times it has come to consist of three main (very large and important) questions: What is real? How do we know? What is of value?

Ontology

Ontology is concerned with the ultimate question of existence. Some people also call it metaphysics (literally "beyond physics"). All people since Og's tribe have hungered to know what was real and what was ephemeral. Is the universe friendly, neutral, or malevolent? Is there order in the universe, or only probabilistic chaos? Is physical existence real or is only our intellect, the goings-on in our minds, real? What is life? Is there a God or some other supernatural entity? Is this all there is?

Clearly, such questions are overwhelming and demand a systematic and satisfying answer. Just as clearly, they call for speculation, at least in the early stages of theory building and maybe for a long time after that. Every action taken by an individual, every decision, every thought will be colored by beliefs about the nature of reality.

Ontology can be usefully broken up into other areas of questions (Johnson, Collins, Dupuis, & Johansen, 1969). Anthropology concerns the nature of the human condition. Are people innately good or evil? What is the relation between the mind and the body? Is there a soul or spirit and does it have precedence over the worldly flesh of the body? Do humans have free will?

Cosmology involves the study of the nature and origins of the universe including questions about time, space, perceptions, and purpose. Theology considers questions of religion. Is there a God? More than one God? A "good" God or an indifferent one? Is God all-powerful? All-knowing? Some ontological theories depend heavily upon theological theories.

Teleology, or the study of purpose in the cosmos, cuts across the other areas mentioned. Is the universe a chance event or is there some larger purpose? Much of what troubled Og's tribe, and continues to trouble humankind, is the province of ontology.

Epistemology

Epistemology examines the nature of knowledge itself, sources of knowledge, and the validity of different kinds of knowledge. Generally, knowledge can be gained from sensory perception (empirical knowledge); revelation (knowledge from a supernatural source or being); from an authority or by tradition; reason, logic, or intellect; or by intuition (non-supernatural insight, not resulting from reason). These sources of knowledge are all subject to criticism. What is truth? Is truth subjective or objective, relative, or absolute? Is there truth external to human experience? Can finite beings understand infinite truth?

Different philosophies have very different epistemologies. One fundamental issue is whether truth is unchanging or varies with the situation or the individual. Clearly hinging upon the answer to this question is whether truth can be "discovered" or "constructed." Some philosophers hold that some truths are self-evident and do not need to be proven. These might be called Truths. Others reject this notion out of hand, suggesting that there is no truth except that leading from experience and that context is paramount. Speculations and theories about the origin and nature of reality and the ways that knowledge may be best gathered lead quickly to choices.

Axiology

Axiology, the third great question of philosophy, concerns values. Values necessitate choices—and choices require evaluating options. What is good? What is beautiful? Individuals, communities, countries, and societies may develop systems of value based upon their philosophies, and when value systems conflict, tension develops. The impact of philosophy on personal and professional behavior is most clear in the process of valuing. What someone believes and thinks is likely, although not certainly, a determinant of action.

Axiology is divided into ethics and aesthetics. Ethics is the study of proper behavioral choices. What is moral? Are ethics contextual or absolute? Is there a connection between what is believed to be right and proper action? Is the good of the societal unit superior to the good of the individual? Who has the right to set ethical standards? Are the laws of society subordinate to the laws of a supernatural entity, such as God? What is the proper relationship between teacher and student? These (and many others) are all questions of ethics.

Professions develop more or less enforceable, formal and informal codes of ethics, based upon shared philosophies. It is incumbent upon the practitioner to learn to apply these ethics in such a way that clients are best served and to participate in ongoing dialogue to update the ethics of the profession.

Aesthetics involves questions about beauty and art. What is beautiful? Is there some ideal that is impossible to attain? Is beauty affected by individual experience, are there absolute standards, or should experts be called upon to judge what is excellent and what is not? Who is to choose? The phrase "beauty is in the eye of the beholder" suggests that the finger painting of a four-year-old is beautiful to some, but the world art market suggests otherwise. Aesthetics allows discussion of such choices and values.

Educational Philosophy

Philosophy as a general discipline is often applied to smaller areas. There exists, for example, a lively literature on the philosophy of science, the philosophy of law, and the philosophy of education.

Educators need to study educational philosophy to undergird their practice. But because of the unique place of education in the culture, the distinction between the general and the specific is not easy in the case of education. Education is the very transmission of the culture and all accumulated knowledge, in such a way that the student is equipped to continue learning and eventually contribute to the whole. In this sense, education is philosophy in action, a point most clearly made by Dewey (1916) when he defined philosophy as the general theory of education.

The educational implications of assuming that humans must somehow overcome their sensory impressions in order to use their intellect or reason to understand reality, for example, are far-reaching. An alternate view is that experience is the only worthwhile learning. Two different educators, holding such disparate philosophies, would be unlikely to agree on any coherent curriculum. This is just one example of differing viewpoints, taken from epistemology. There are many more epistemological examples available, to say nothing of ontological considerations and questions of value. Obviously, everything done in the name of education has a basis in some philosophical notion and/or "teaches" some philosophical tenet to the student.

In a pluralistic society such as the U.S., philosophical differences between and among teacher and student, college and teacher, school and parent, college and society at large, and any permutation of these can and do cause great conflict. This is not necessarily bad, especially at the college and university level where a certain amount of conflict and challenge of views contributes to learning; nevertheless, to the extent that education is an intentional activity, educators and institutions should examine and be aware of their philosophical bases. Practices inconsistent with espoused views and beliefs are confusing at best and may be damaging.

In a nutshell, this is why we study educational philosophy. Professionals have an obligation to learn and know more than techniques and approaches to problem solving. Only by studying and applying underlying premises and deeply held assumptions can a practitioner of student affairs hope to bring insight to a novel problem, a "different" student, a new situation. If a person holds one view and an institution another, conflict is likely; if neither knows what the other believes, then conflict is certain and may not be easily resolved. Student affairs professionals cannot always tell what an institution truly believes, but they can and should always determine their own educational philosophies.

MAJOR PHILOSOPHICAL SCHOOLS

Student affairs and higher education practices are based upon a variety of different philosophies. Therefore, it is necessary to acquaint the reader with a basic understanding of several influential Western schools of thought that have had the most impact upon U.S. education: idealism, realism, neo-Thomism, pragmatism, and existentialism. A treatment of Eastern philosophies and other thinking is beyond the scope of this book.

Idealism

Plato offered the basis of idealism, the notion that the "Real" world is accessible only through reason, in his writing on the teaching of Socrates and through his own work. The thinking here is that the world as perceived by humans is transient, changeable, always becoming but never quite finished, and hence deceptive. The real world is perfect, not needing and not having physical manifestation. Thus, the idea of a chair is more important, a higher order of reality, than the chair which is seen or sat upon.

Ontologically, reality depends upon a superordinate Mind which is capable of conceiving Reality in its Ideal state. Humans possess a spark of this Mind and can communicate with the Real world through (and only through) reason and intellect. Material existence, the things of the flesh, inhibits this communication and reason, and things of the flesh are not to be trusted. Truth is unchanging and permanent, infinite, and ultimately unknowable. Since humans are finite, they can know about the Truth, but can never know all. The ethical goal is to live a moral life, defined as following the will of the Mind or of the universe. Some people (such as teachers, priests, and political leaders) are closer to the Ideal than others and they should be heeded. Beauty is defined as an approximation of the Ideal, usually the Divine. Idealism allows, almost requires, a supernatural entity and is therefore very compatible with religion. Later thinkers have worked out Idealistic philosophies without the use of a God, but they are largely unsatisfying.

Educationally, Idealism posits that each individual should be helped to actualize the spark of the Ideal that is within. However, the test of the actualization is correspondence with the Ideal, much of which has already been "discovered" over the years. Hence, students are taught using materials that have stood the test of time and societal examination. The Great Books are used and the primacy of the state is emphasized. The assumption is that a consensus Ideal is a better approximation than an individual conception. Idealism is one of the cornerstones of a conservative approach to curriculum and education emphasizing essential truths.

Realism

Aristotle was not satisfied with the Platonic view that sensory data were distorted and not to be trusted. He believed instead that observed reality is the only Reality. That is, the universe exists without a mind standing behind it and whether humans perceive it or not. Natural laws are permanent and unchanging and humans can discover them through the use of their minds. If there are things that are not yet understood, then there simply has not been enough research.

Truth, then, is external and independent of knowledge. Epistemologically, Realism uses inductive logic. The observer gathers particular bits of knowledge and fits them into theories, propositions, and laws according to the rules of science. Truth is completely knowable and may be judged by its correspondence with reality. Values and beauty result from conformance with the Laws of Nature. That is good which allows people to live in accordance with nature, the so-called moral law, and that is beautiful which reflects natural harmony. Human nature is everywhere the same and a distinction is made throughout between the natural and the accidental. The essential nature of anything does not change, even though some variations may be noted (Brubacher, 1982).

Educationally, Realism calls for the student to be acquainted with rational methods of observation and logic. Hence, science and mathematics have a large place in the curriculum. However, the traditional humanities are important as well, because there are natural ways for society to function and the student needs to be made aware of the best thinking to date. Students are not left to learn what they think they want to know, since this would take away time from what they should be learning, what is already known. After all, it is inefficient for students to arrive at their own conclusions about that which is already known, let alone the fact that no one can be expected to contribute to new knowledge without a grounding in research to date. Realism is also, clearly, a foundation for conservative educational thinking, with its reliance upon knowledge external to the student.

Neo-Thomism

St. Thomas Aquinas saw much to like in both Idealism and Realism. On the one hand, Aristotle's ideas were very persuasive, grounded in common sense, and seemed to reflect human experience. On the other hand, it was necessary to bring into account the known (to Roman Catholics like Aquinas) existence of a supernatural being (God). The solution was to combine the two, retaining the duality between mind and body proposed by Plato, but assigning faith a preeminent role over reason. That is, humans were free to observe the material world in scientific, logical ways with the proviso that when reason contradicted the revealed truth of religion, then reason was simply faulty. Much of Realism is inherent in Neo-Thomism, so much that some call this philosophy religious realism (Kneller, 1964). The basic notion is that there is no inherent conflict between faith and reason, so long as it is understood that God is perfect and therefore faith is preeminent.

Aquinas lived in the 13th century (the philosophy was originally called Thomism), but his ideas have endured so strongly that the Roman Catholic Church acknowledges this philosophy as its official position (Johnson et al., 1969) and it is the basis of much of Catholic education. There are also lay philosophers who subscribe to Neo-Thomism, with their axiology being based upon a rationally derived and unchanging moral law that is not supernaturally based.

Education for Neo-Thomists consists of teaching the perennial truths derived from faith and reason. Because humans have free will, the student must be taught the discipline of learning and encouraged to make good choices. Knowledge and values are permanent and unchanging and the purpose of learning is to live by rational and moral standards. The student is educated in a moral atmosphere that forms the framework for knowledge. Again, time honored and established methods and materials form the bases of the curriculum.

Pragmatism

Pragmatism defines reality as the sum total of human experience. That is true which is proven useful after careful investigation and analysis. Pragmatism represents a major break with the other philosophies thus far considered in that it rejects the idea of permanent, unchanging truth. Although it has roots in the empiricist tradition developed from Realism, Pragmatism, as explicated by Charles Sanders Peirce, John Dewey, and William James, suggests that even so-called natural "laws" are not eternal.

Indeed, for Pragmatism, reality is defined by the interaction of humans with nature. While nature has an objective, albeit changeable, existence, it has no real meaning except as it relates to human experience. Speculation about the infinite or supernatural is idle, by definition, since it cannot be verified by human means. Pragmatic epistemology does not allow humans to simply make up truth; rather, truth is determined using the experimental method. As a problem is confronted, data are gathered, hypotheses generated, mental testing conducted, and finally solutions implemented. The best or most workable solution is the truth—for these circumstances, using these data collection methods. Given that things change, techniques improve, and different approaches give different answers, this truth is temporary and not absolute. For example, based upon everything scientifically known, the sun will very likely rise in the morning. But it is possible for conditions to change and, therefore, dawn is never a certainty. Values are relative and situational, chosen through a logical process. That does not mean that morality changes willy-nilly, but that there are no absolute precepts, always true and never violated. Morals are not handed down from some higher authority, but rather decided by individuals and groups, by agreement and consensus if possible, in a dynamic process. Pragmatism is thought to require democracy for best use.

The student is thought of as an integrated whole, thoroughly involved in his or her own education. Since experience is the only determiner of reality, the student should be allowed to learn whatever is of interest. Abstract concepts are important, but should be studied later in the education, rather than earlier, so that the student develops a lively style of experiencing and then organizing the experiences from the beginning. This project method should allow for the education of the biological, the psychological, and the social aspects of the student. The teacher or other educator should not be ascendant, but rather facilitative. The curriculum and materials used should be flexible and learner-centered. Readiness and enthusiasm are keys to learning and teaching.

Existentialism

Jean Paul Sartre wrote that "existence precedes essence" (1947, p. 18). This simple phrase is fraught with meaning. The fact of "being" carries with it the awful truth that humans are only and totally what they make of themselves by their own choices. The universe exists and the order that science finds is present, but these facts matter only as backdrop for the confrontation that is inevitable in the life of every person. People find themselves when they become truly aware of their condition in an indifferent universe which has no purpose and in which they are doomed to die.

Truth is that which each individual concludes in a passionate encounter with the self and the choices available. There is complete freedom because of the indifference of nature, the absence of rules; there is complete responsibility because no one else chooses or, if some choice is forcibly imposed, the individual chooses his/her response. The human condition causes "*Angst*," searching for meaning in a meaningless world, possessing freedom and aware of finitude or existential dread. Knowledge is gained in an active way, involving both thinking and feeling. Existentialism does not allow detached analysis. Information is less important than what the person does with the data. Values are meaningless unless chosen. However, freedom does not imply anarchy; a commitment to freedom for self leads inevitably to a conception of freedom for all. Responsibility for choices that restrict the freedom of others is its own kind of limit. Additionally, true freedom is the freedom to commit to others in an authentic relationship. Still, the fundamental value of existentialism is to be true to oneself.

The existentialist educator walks a tightrope between encouraging freedom and bridling immature choices. Students must be confronted with the reality of the human condition and must take responsibility for their choices. The educator must also interact with the students in an authentic way, modeling mature behavior and attending to his/her own growth. The educator stimulates student involvement with learning on a personal level, a commitment to understanding, not to following the crowd or bowing to expert opinion. Every person in any situation is treated with dignity and respect, even if some behaviors are not tolerated.

Humanities, literature, art, and history (Kneller, 1964) are heavily utilized since they reflect the struggles of people to understand their own existence. Students also undertake a careful study of traditional knowledge in order to grasp the world in which they live. The student makes the subject matter his/her own by seeking out interpretations (for example, in historical accounts) and considering counterconclusions. Education is an active process and never ends.

A BRIEF PHILOSOPHICAL HISTORY OF HIGHER EDUCATION

The history of higher education is, in some sense, a history of thought and therefore a history of philosophy. This section of the chapter treats philosophical influences upon Western higher education from the Greeks through the present.

As ancient Greece was settled and city-states established, the life of the mind began to take on more importance. The democratic assemblies put a premium on erudition and persuasion. The Sophists, itinerant teachers, were among the first to meet this need. They focused on utilitarian education–they were not concerned about the ends to which logic and rhetorical skills were turned (Domonkos, 1977). This moral relativism caused a countermovement to use the discipline of learning to attain ethical wisdom and absolute truth. Chief among the philosophers engaged in this quest were Socrates and his student Plato. Most importantly, they each established schools for the edification of both teachers and students. To all intents and purposes, these institutions are the precursors of modern colleges and universities. Plato was an Idealist and believed that only the elite, defined as the intellectually able and educated, should be allowed to rule. Not surprisingly, his notion of education was focused on reason and ideas, a striving for knowledge that was absolute and unchanging. Plato's student, Aristotle, on the other hand, did not distrust sensory data, but rather sought to organize it according to logical and scientific principles. Aristotle did believe that truth is unchanging, as seen above in the discussion of Realism, and he advocated a search for the Laws of Nature. These ideas, along with other minor philosophical schools and some attention to law and medicine, dominated higher education through the fall of Rome.

During the so-called Dark Ages, higher education was essentially the domain of clerics in the Christian West, but there were thriving academic communities among the Jews, Moslems, and the Byzantines. In fact, it is through contact with these other cultures that interest in the ancient Greek philosophies re-emerged to challenge the rather sterile, faith-based notions of the Church hierarchy. The history of all of the early institutions of higher education in the West is too extensive to go into here.

The best of the early universities was the University of Paris, which housed lively philosophical debate around theology and the conflict between religious Idealism and Aristotelian Realism until the University found it necessary to succumb to Church doctrine in order to gain Papal support in a struggle against the Parisian authorities. But this debate was not confined to Paris and raged on. St. Thomas Aquinas successfully joined Realism and religion (see above) and his ideas of reason and science as permissible but subservient to faith became the philosophy of the Church and more specifically the universities and schools. Consequently, most of the great discoveries of science for hundreds of years took place independently of the universities, in the academies or as a result of private patronage of great thinkers.

Even the onset of the Reformation, the ecclesiastical revolt against the Roman Catholic Church, did not materially change the philosophy of higher education. Universities were intellectual captives of whoever their sponsors were, whether state governments or state religions, usually both. But the Reformation had allowed the camel's nose under the tent of Catholic theological hegemony. Sect after sect sprang up, eventually leading to the notion that no one group owned the truth. This fertile climate spawned thinkers who came to speculate about the place of the supernatural in their conceptions of the universe and humankind. Writers and philosophers in this Enlightenment, such as Locke and Voltaire, and the people they influenced, notably Benjamin Franklin and Thomas Jefferson, spoke of inalienable rights and contracts between the rulers and the governed. Effectively, they were seeking the natural laws of society, just as scientists were discovering the natural laws of physics, astronomy, chemistry, and biology. Knowledge and education were becoming too important to be dominated by religious authorities. The power of ideas was beginning to manifest itself.

Still, the colleges and universities were reflective of the society and by and large the society was pietistic. If education was too important to be dictated by the church, it was certainly too important to be left to professors, and so there evolved an uneasy equilibrium between lay control and teacher autonomy. In England, higher education was primarily for the elite, intellectually and/or financially, who were being groomed for ecclesiastical and political leadership. They were provided a classical liberal arts education with little science and much orthodox theology. Their spiritual growth and social progress were monitored as heavily as their intellectual progress. They were taught to strive for the Ideal.

This model of education was lifted whole cloth and set down in the American Colonies. All of the original nine Colonial colleges were sectarian except the University of Pennsylvania (then the College of Philadelphia) and all followed the British model. Standards for behavior, for learning, and for spiritual development were absolute and individuality was not brooked. But new ideas were brewing. In the later part of the Colonial period and much more so in the early Federal period of the United States, there was a proliferation of colleges, mostly sectarian, but some state sponsored. At first, these were much the same as those that had gone before, but market forces, increased specialization of disciplines, and the onrush of scientific discovery began to engender diversity and differentiation (Potts, 1977). To counter this drift toward the secular, and worse, the nonclassical, the faculty of Yale published the Yale Report in 1828. This was the first formal statement of the philosophy of higher education in the U.S. (Brubacher & Rudy, 1976) and held that the traditional, classical curriculum was the only way to provide higher learning to students because of its emphasis upon mental discipline (based upon faculty psychology) and its steadfast refusal to accord status to the transitory, the ephemeral, the worldly—in other words economically or scientifically useful knowledge which could be learned elsewhere. The Yale Report was influential for decades, but its very publication signaled the beginning of the end for strictly Idealist higher education.

Realism, in the form of science, empiricism, and practicality was pushing its way into the curriculum. The latter half of the 19th century saw the advent of the German model university, the bastion of research and academic freedom to teach and to learn. The Morrill Act of 1862 led to the creation of a distinctly U.S. style institution, the land grant university, with its curious combination mission of research, teaching, and service. As secular and current course content displaced religious and ancient knowledge, pressure to focus upon the intellect only increased. The out of class habits of students, the extracurricular activities, the sports they engaged in, these were distractions from the "real" business of education. However, the U.S. was still a moralistic nation and was not about to surrender its young men (and certainly not its young women!) to colleges and universities unconcerned about anything but their minds. Hence, institutions took on obligations that had not existed in other parts of the world, the role of parents without true control, a concern for the out of class behavior of students in ways that were unconnected to the curriculum (as opposed to the earlier British model).

Twentieth Century Philosophical Influences on U.S. Higher Education

As the twentieth century began, the hegemony of Realism, embodied as Newtonian science, was cracking as had Idealism before it. To be sure, the receiving of intellectual knowledge was still the primary role of students, but Pragmatism and later Existentialism were making inroads in almost all disciplines and hence working their way into the thinking of those guiding colleges and universities. Until the early 1960s, the dominant philosophical mode for colleges and universities was still a focus upon intellectualism tied to an almost formless attitude of *in loco parentis*.

In many ways, the conflict boiled down to one of epistemology. Is the student to be educated about the truth or does the educated student participate in shaping the truth? Is the content of a liberal education more or less constant or does it change in relation to context?

On the one hand are the essentialists, variously identified as rationalists, rational humanists, neo-humanists, or perennialists, among other labels. Philosophers and educators in these categories of opinion did not all hold the same beliefs, differing in views about the nature of knowledge, the existence of God, and the importance of reason versus revelation. Nevertheless, they united in their opposition to the corrupting influences of the vocational and the worldly on higher education. Thorstein Veblen's (1918) assertion of the value-free nature of research was one example, but the best known advocates of this position in the early twentieth century were Robert Maynard Hutchins (1936) and Mortimer Adler (1951). Both men extolled the virtues of intellectual excellence to be gained by the assiduous study of the Great Books, the so-called Western Canon. This kind of study and education were thought to prepare the mind in the best way for any field of endeavor. Indeed, these ideas were timeless and essential. Furthermore, education without moral content was considered useless. Hutchins and Adler were ostensibly secular in their suggestions, but their ideas resonate clearly with the views of the religious perennialists. Truth is something that does not change: it needs to be discovered and once discovered must be learned by each succeeding generation. Ideas that have stood the test of time are to be returned to again and again. Fundamental to this viewpoint is the conception of the mind as separate from the body–knowledge uncontaminated by experience.

On the other hand were the pragmatic naturalists, the experimentalists, the instrumentalists, the progressivists, and the reconstructionists. Such thinkers as John Dewey (1937), Sidney Hook (1946), and Alfred North Whitehead (1929) thought that the split of intellect from the world, of theory from practice, was wrong. Liberal education is and should be based in the context of the time and the place and reason should be informed by passion and emotion. Humans are whole and must be educated as such. Experience and rationality should be used as means rather than ends to help solve the problems of society. Indeed, the reconstructionists dared to dream of utopian goals and sought to involve education in their plans. Truth, in this conception, is something that works and is meaningful to each individual in different ways.

Considerations of philosophy were largely settled on the side of the pragmatic by the influx of students after World War II. Returning soldiers had little patience for the parental function of colleges and the nation needed technically trained graduates. The early stirrings of the civil rights movement and the unrest of the 1960s refocused the philosophical lens on higher education. For most schools, the parental role perished in the fiery heat of the social revolution of the 1960s and the aftershocks in the 1970s. Of course, Roman Catholic and many other sectarian institutions continued to adhere to a neo-Thomist view, but in most colleges students experience a mishmash of philosophical influences. Young (2003), writing about this very topic (although using a slightly different classification of philosophies), suggests that no complete philosophy of student affairs could fit within any one system of thought because student affairs, learning, and higher education are influenced by all of these groups of ideas.

Colleges are by turns moralistic in some regulations, scientific in some attitudes and services, existential in their assigning of responsibility for learning, and withal pragmatic. The typical institution harbors individuals in important faculty and administrative positions who exercise great authority and firmly believe in each of the major philosophies. And the school that acts consistently on only one of the philosophies is rare and probably sectarian.

It is not a long leap from the pragmatic viewpoint to that of existentialism, postmodernism, critical theory, and constructivism (Lincoln, 1989), all central to the current understanding of students, learning, and higher education in society. If knowledge is not external and unchanging, if it is defined as what is workable based upon experience, and if the society is working toward democracy, then who is to define truth? If one conception of truth is just as good as any other, then truth ceases to be universal and becomes intensely individual. Reality is constructed rather than discovered. Not only are the mind and the body not separated, but they are one with context. Pluralism, as opposed to assimilation to the dominant culture, is cultivated and acted upon. As should be immediately clear, these ideas have drastic implications for higher education and student affairs. For just one example, it is increasingly well understood that students interact with their various environments, socially, psychologically, physically, and in other ways as they attempt to cope, create, and make sense of their potentially multiple identities (Abes, Jones, & McEwen, 2007; Chavez, Guido-DiBrito, & Mallory, 2003). What does a "set" theory have to say to a first generation, Latino, gay student from the Midwest that is useful or reliable? It seems clear that some parts of some theories or past ideas will work with adjustments for situation and context and with full cooperation of the student, but only by taking all the attendant circumstances into account.

EDUCATIONAL PHILOSOPHY AND STUDENT AFFAIRS

For the first two hundred years or so, higher education in the U.S. largely followed an Idealist model. Education was thought of as mental discipline and things of the flesh were to be conquered so they did not get in the way. Young people (students) especially needed help to control their impulses, what with all that energy and all those hormones. Faculty psychology dictated, and spiritual needs reinforced, that students should invest all their resources into training their intellects and moderating their base desires. To this end, educators controlled living and eating arrangements and arranged curricula in such a way as to leave little free time and less discretionary behavior. Since humans were felt to be flawed and incapable of innate understanding of absolute, eternal truths without restraint and focus on reason, colleges took on a parental role.

The explosion of science and specialization, coupled with a growing democratic mindset and the influx of German ideas of higher education, eroded this position by the latter part of the nineteenth century. In the Realist mode, depending as it did upon the mind-body split articulated by Descartes and others, things of the flesh did not really matter. Professors and researchers at the new universities were quite simply not interested in anything but knowledge and did not care to participate in students' out of class lives. Again, truth was conceived as external to humans, something to be discovered and understood rationally. Human nature was not thought to be inherently negative or positive, simply not relevant to learning and thinking.

Still, higher education as an institution is known for its inertia and the graduate and research universities required a feeder system of undergraduate colleges. Accordingly, the U.S. developed a model unique in the world. Excellent universities, conducting state of the art research, were joined with undergraduate colleges that continued to follow the British model. U.S. society was not prepared to abandon adolescents to their impulses, even if faculty members felt they had better things to do. The necessity of traveling long distances to attend colleges, the relative youth of U.S. students, the essentially Christian character of the nation, and hundreds of years of tradition in higher education contributed to the need to regulate student conduct on campus. Thus, in rough strokes, was born the student affairs worker.

Philosophically, *in loco parentis* provided not only a framework for Idealistic rules in order to bring the student into compliance with age old social mores, but also provided an outlet for emotional and psychological needs unmet, and properly so, in the classroom. The roots of the services and control models of student affairs, then, are in the essentialist philosophical tradition. Knowledge is something absolute that the students must accommodate themselves to. Since they needed help to do this, and since faculty were increasingly unwilling to provide this help, it was necessary to hire a new kind of educator.

By the beginning of the twentieth century, early student affairs workers were filling much of the parental role of the colleges, thereby relieving the faculty of the task. Colleges and universities were growing and becoming more complex organizationally, requiring other administrators and managers as well. Additionally, psychology was finding its niche as the "science" of human behavior, particularly with the testing movement. The idea was that people were suited to certain careers and that systematic counseling would help with a match. Cowley (1957) held that the field was dominated by these three types of student affairs workers well into the 1950s—humanitarians, administrators, and counselors, each with a role, but rather uncoordinated.

The Student Personnel Point of View (1937)

Confusion about the field of student affairs and its goals for students are reflected in the first and second statements of the Student Personnel Point of View (SPPV) (American Council on Education, 1983a). In the 1937 statement, there is a clear emphasis on coordination with the academic enterprise with the goal of ensuring the maximum improvement of the student, the meeting of potential. Emphasis is also placed on scientific research to learn how to better serve institutions and students. In fact, the SPPV would be unremarkable philosophically except for its insistence on the impact of education on the "whole student." While this is grounded in a rational humanist context, overtones of existentialism and pragmatism are clearly present and the student is presumed to have a role in his/her own education—a radical notion at the time.

The Student Personnel Point of View (1949)

The revised SPPV (American Council on Education, 1983b) is philosophically much more straightforward in its pragmatic approach. Democracy and social reconstruction are presented as the bases for education. There are nods toward standards of conduct and self-control. The clinical findings of the social sciences are not left out, but problem solving is clearly preferred as a goal. Again, the student is responsible for his/her own education, but enrichment and facilitation are coming to the fore instead of simply services.

Student Development

The radicalism of the 1960s disturbed the uneasy equilibrium that student affairs had reached with the academic establishment. Obviously, societal standards were in flux and could hardly be transmitted wholesale. Students were demanding an increasing amount of attention—the role of education had to shift. The student affairs response was to counsel a focus on the person rather than on the course content. Colleges were to teach students rather than subject matter. In fact, the argument went, if the focus is really to be on the whole student, then human development principles must be applied across the curriculum and the extracurriculum (Brown, 1972; Miller & Prince, 1976). Furthermore, the student is in control of what is to be learned and what is to be valued. The university was to be construed as a place where learning was facilitated, where the student learned to make choices and understand that every choice has consequences that must be considered and accepted. *In loco parentis,* dead in a legal sense since the 1960s, died in a practical sense in the 1970s, despite recent attempts to revive it.

The student development model, with its underpinnings in the self-confrontational struggle of existentialism and the utilitarian foundation of pragmatism, changed student affairs practice completely. The merging of the goals of the academic and the "other" education recognizes that, to the student, college is a seamless web of growth and development. All aspects of education are interdependent—one cannot be accomplished without the others being in place. Focus on the student means that wellness, support for nontraditional students, alcohol awareness, learning assistance, and many other areas are not only just as essential as housing, financial aid, counseling, and student activities, but are crucial if optimum learning is to occur. Student affairs educators stop being purveyors and become facilitators and consultants. Colleges do not pronounce appropriate choices for students, but rather propose them for the students to choose from–and sometimes not even that.

A student development focus does not mean that values are abandoned by institutions or student affairs professionals, but that expectations are clearly stated up front in such a way that students can make good choices for themselves. Likewise, science is not forsaken; rather, student development theory is based on research into developmental psychology, causing some controversy among practitioners who have to reconcile somewhat lockstep conceptualizations with undeniable student uniqueness. Finally, student development capitalizes upon diversity, celebrating and enhancing differences as necessary and educational.

It may seem that existentialism and pragmatism give too much authority to the individual to be used as bases for transmitting a culture. However, pragmatism has a strong emphasis on the social, with an acknowledgement that the individual lives in a group and that growth for all is a goal. Existentialism emphasizes self-confrontation and acceptance of responsibility for choices. This responsibility is understood to include the impact of personal choices on other free beings. Rights for one are rights for all and must be respected.

The 1987 National Association of Student Personnel Administrators (NASPA) Statement

In 1987, NASPA published "A Perspective on Student Affairs: A Statement Issued on the 50th Anniversary of the Student Personnel Point of View." This paper acknowledged articulately the growing diversity of U.S. higher education, but also strongly emphasized the place of institutional mission in education. Under the label of shared assumptions, the perspective statement argues for the preeminence of the academic mission for higher education and that student affairs should not compete with, or substitute for, the academic mission. Instead, student affairs enhances and supports the principal goals of colleges and universities. Other parts of the statement go on to reiterate (1) the notion of the whole, unique student; (2) the importance of involvement in learning; (3) the crucial nature of environmental; and (4) personal factors in education. Philosophically, the perspective statement is a mixed bag, with a seeming nod toward essentialism (the emphasis on cognitive learning), an expression of existentialist tenets (worth and uniqueness of the student), and recognition of pragmatism (importance of involvement, environment, and diversity). This is partially because the statement was not intended to be a philosophical tract, but rather a political statement, and therefore it tried to be all things to all people. Still, to the extent that the statement represented the mainstream of student affairs leadership, there was a clear turn toward institutions and academic content as foci, at the expense of emphasis on students and their choices.

The "Reasonable Expectations" Statement

A document entitled "Reasonable Expectations: Renewing the Educational Compact between Institutions and Students" was published by NASPA in 1995 (Kuh, Lyons, Miller, & Trow, 1995). While not strictly philosophical in tone, it takes the form of an examination of the Pragmatic contract between colleges and universities and their students. The focus is on mutual respect and high expectations going in both directions, with integrity and communication strongly emphasized. There is an existential recognition of choice and responsibility and a bias toward action and involvement. While the statement is careful to be vague with regard to underlying ontological and epistemological beliefs, presumably so that many and varied institutions are covered, idealist and realist educators would be hard pressed to follow all the tenets espoused. Similarly, although the statement is aimed at the broader institution, it is clear that professional student affairs workers are best able to provide the interface called for between the college and students.

The "Student Learning Imperative" (SLI)

The SLI was published by ACPA in 1994. Ostensibly, it is a call to change student affairs practice so that there is more focus on "student learning and personal development" (ACPA, 1994, p. 1). However, the document makes no clear differentiation between these two aims and student development, at one point calling all three terms ". . . inextricably intertwined and inseparable" (p. 1). Philosophically, the statement leans toward the essentialist, with its insistence on ". . . educationally-purposeful activities" (p. 2). Presumably, some activities are more important for learning than others and student affairs professionals, along with other institutional agents, know which are which and should guide students accordingly. One way to learn about appropriate activities for students is scientific research. To be sure, process is emphasized, the seamless nature of education as perceived by the student is recognized, and a holistic approach is advocated in the SLI. Withal, however, the tone suggests that student affairs has failed in some way(s) and needs to get on the academic productivity bandwagon and help institutions and students become more efficient learners. Student affairs is relegated to a ". . . complementary mission" (p. 2), involving more emphasis on learning theory and assessment. This is an apparent abrogation of existentialism as a fundamental base of student affairs practice and pulls back from Pragmatism, as well.

Principles of Good Practice

In 1996, the presidents of NASPA and ACPA jointly commissioned a committee, co-chaired by Elizabeth Whitt and Greg Blimling to draft a statement and inventories to assess good practice, with a report being issued in 1997 (ACPA & NASPA, 1997). Concepts espoused were active learning, high expectations, collaboration, effective resource use, inquiry-based practice, and community. Holistic emphasis and diversity were clear assumptions and the report breaks no really new ground but serves as a cogent and coherent restatement of modern student affairs values and practices. Philosophically, learning and development are conceived to be the responsibility of the student interacting with a caring and intentional institution in which all parties were working toward a positive learning setting.

Powerful Partnerships

The American Association for Higher Education (AAHE) combined with ACPA and NASPA to publish *Powerful Partnerships: A Shared Responsibility for Learning* in 1998 (Joint Task Force on Student Learning, 1998). The report is a far-reaching prescription for reform of higher education that envisions the application of learning research and theory being applied by boundary spanning academic and student affairs professionals. This vision is truly powerful, encompassing students, faculty, student affairs professionals, and other staff in the context of external stakeholders including parents, boards, and governmental parties among others. Cutting edge programs are highlighted and principles of diversity, student agency, supportive environments, and intentional development are implicitly and explicitly emphasized. Students and institutions are considered to be linked in a common enterprise–that of full learning and development. Cognitive learning is not privileged over holistic development; instead the two are seen as mutually necessary. This statement virtually epitomizes the philosophical notions of pragmatism and existentialism, allowing also for a crucial role to be played by institutional mission.

Learning Reconsidered

In 2004, NASPA and ACPA published *Learning Reconsidered: A Campus-wide Focus on the Student Experience* (NASPA & ACPA, 2004). Meant to do nothing less than transform higher education as it has been previously understood, it is the most philosophically sophisticated of the many reports and documents that have shaped student affairs. Assumptions and points of view are made explicit and the tenets of pragmatism, existentialism, postmodernism, and constructivism (among others) are fully integrated into the thinking. A few select quotes should suffice to give the reader an idea of the tone and tenor of this breakthrough guide.

> *Learning Reconsidered . . .* is also an introduction to new ways of understanding and supporting learning and development as intertwined, inseparable elements of the student experience. It advocates for transformative education–a holistic process of learning that places the student at the center of the learning experience (p. 1). . . . we are all, as colleagues and educators, now accountable to students and society for identifying and achieving essential student learning outcomes and for making transformative education possible and accessible for all students.

> *Learning Reconsidered* defines *learning* as a comprehensive, holistic, transformative activity that integrates *academic learning* and *student development,* processes that have often been considered separate, and even independent of each other. . . . We do *not* say *learning and development* because we do not want to suggest that learning and student development are fundamentally different things, or that one does, or could, occur without the other. . . . Here we work to bring our terminology, and our way of understanding what student affairs professionals contribute to student outcomes, in line with the findings of current learning research and with our own empirical observations about how learning (as a complex integrated process) occurs among today's students. (p. 2)

Clearly, this document changes our conversation and thinking if it is taken seriously. At the heart of the statement are the two philosophical stances most apparent in and central to student affairs practice, pragmatism and existentialism. Assertions about responsibility of the student and the educator, accountability, empirical usefulness, and change to fit the real circumstances are all manifestly philosophical in character. Any serious student of student affairs philosophy must consider this document and take account of its importance.

The Search for a Student Affairs Philosophy Goes On

The several statements noted here are not the only attempts to codify the philosophical tenets of student affairs. Knock, Rentz, and Penn (1989) detailed significant influences on student affairs' philosophical heritage, arguing that professional practice had moved past rationalism and neo-humanism into pragmatism and existentialism as the basis of student development. Whitt, Carnaghi, Matkin, Scalese-Love, and Nestor (1990) asserted that emergent paradigm thinking (Lincoln & Guba, 1985) and the complexities of practices and diversity in higher education made a unified philosophy of student affairs impossible to divine—indeed, unwise and inappropriate. Context and cultural considerations should be paramount.

Manning (1994) has introduced liberation theology into the mix and in 1996 also debunked the myth that student affairs has no philosophy, asserting that pragmatism and existentialism are inherent in most current thinking and practice. Young has examined the values of student affairs several times in work that has clear philosophical underpinnings, notably in a special issue of the *Journal of College Student Development* on the ethos of scholarship as a guiding model for student affairs practice (Young, 2001) and in a chapter in 2003 that situates the values on the field in a philosophical context. Young's consistent theme is that student affairs core values serve both the causes of individuation and community. He also calls for a recognition of the tension between traditional higher education, with all its worth and faults and a more modern conception of the needs of the current world.

Several articles in the same issue of the *Journal of Student Development* have philosophical implications, but the most relevant is that of Evans and Reason (2001) whose extensive analysis of many of the documents explored above (and others) concludes with the identification of several underlying themes which suggest that learning, conceived broadly as development, has been the focus of the student affairs field all along. She also highlights appreciation of diversity, holism, and student self-responsibility, as well as accountability. She argues that there is little new under the sun, but it is always useful to restate our core goals. What is new in the Evans analysis is a call for advocacy and activism on campus. She believes that the time has come for student affairs workers to push harder for critical aspects of social justice and other student needs on campus. Evans characterizes this new role as going past Deweyan pragmatism, but it may well be a natural extension of an evolving philosophy of the student affairs field.

Clearly, it can be argued that pragmatism and existentialism, taken seriously, imply that student affairs workers should examine campus conditions and work to change those that adversely affect students and/or do not facilitate optimum development and learning for everyone in the community. But it is not clear what course of action should be taken. Hirt (2007) points out the discontinuity between the student development narrative and the corporate and knowledge production based on the faculty at many universities and then illustrates how a set of student affairs principles (a proxy for student development) could be "recast" (p. 258) to more closely reflect the narratives that academic administrators and faculty have adopted. Since the corporate university is a fact of life, student affairs must be compatible with the dominant discourse if it wishes to accomplish its work with students. Hirt is not calling for a different outcome than Evans, but a different strategy. Again, it's a matter of philosophy.

Abes (2009) does a remarkable job of wrestling with methodological difficulties attendant to studying students' identity development in an inequitable environment. One of the complications is that a student's identity has to be negotiated with the social, emotional, and psychological milieu, so that analyzing data from even the most sophisticated and aware respondent is dicey, at best. Abes finds herself in a theoretical (and philosophical) borderland, where consistency must sometimes be discarded (or at least worked around) for pragmatic and heuristic reasons. This article is an accessible case study of how a professional comes to grips with philosophical challenges.

Choice and Responsibility

A careful reading of all the statements and assertions detailed above (and of others not mentioned) leads to the position that sufficient evidence exists to determine that student choice is a *sine qua non* for quality in higher education. Students inarguably make choices as individuals. They decide which classes to attend, what to study, which activities to become involved in. By their choices, students determine the level of benefit that will be derived from college and its attendant milieu. Students decide which choices work for them, which consequences they are willing to undergo. In short, students are in charge of their own lives.

While professional judgment is and should be exercised in matters of curriculum and in student affairs practice, students cannot be coerced to follow such advice. Students create their own meaning based on their own phenomenological world. This philosophical stance is largely existentialist, with a generous helping of pragmatism. But, principally, it revisits the distinction made earlier in this chapter about the nature of truth. It is argued here that truth, as we understand it in student affairs practice, is largely constructed by individuals rather than located outside human experience, waiting to be discovered or divined or revealed. The goal of student affairs practice is to facilitate the process of collecting information, undergoing experiences, and making meaning by students. Along the way, student affairs professionals may advise, suggest, cajole, and counsel, but they may not live, know, or choose for the students. Nor can any institution.

BUILDING A PERSONAL PHILOSOPHY OF STUDENT AFFAIRS

This chapter has focused on the philosophical heritage of student affairs and higher education and the importance of philosophy in the formulation of policy and programming. It has been argued that the philosophical terrain of colleges and universities is hotly contested and uncertain. In such loosely coupled organizations, multiple missions exist, multiple actors behave with varying motivations, and multiple choices must be made. For the professional to navigate successfully in these seas, he or she must have reference points, guiding stars to chart a course. A knowledge of one's personal philosophy helps provide such direction.

In developing or examining a personal and professional philosophy the following questions may be considered:

- What is the place of humans in the universe? Are people here to fulfill God's purpose, at the whim of an uncaring supernatural power, as the result of chance, as the ultimate in existence, or does it even matter why? Are people inherently of value or do they need to earn value? Do behaviors matter more than simple existence? Do humans have free choice or is their behavior predetermined by fate, science, or God?
- Does the universe exist in some objective sense external to the understanding of humans? Is reality for any person only what he or she perceives it to be? Is there some larger purpose to creation that is unknown or unknowable?
- Is truth unchanging and eternal, either in an infinite, supernatural way or an immutable, scientific way? Are there discoverable laws of nature? Is truth what works or makes sense to individuals or communities or societies? What is the best way to determine truth, the scientific method, experience, reason, or revelation and intuition?
- Are the laws of God more important than the laws of the society or the country? Is the greatest good for the greatest number a measure of behavior or policy? Are individual rights preeminent? Are people free to act in any way that pleases them? Does any person owe any obligation to any other person or state or the world? What is the nature of responsibility?
- Is beauty in the eye of the beholder? Are there objective standards for art or music or love? Do some people know what is best and most beautiful for other people?
- How can cultural standards be best defined? Should children be given instruction on the tried and true best ways to think and live or should they be given the tools of critical thought and left to create their own

worlds? Is it better to educate for mastery or understanding or even something else? Do appropriate educational practices differ depending on the subject matter and the age of the student?

The answers and the search for answers to these and hundreds of other similar questions influence actions, thoughts, and behaviors for everyone every day. Philosophers in all fields of endeavor have tried to create consistent, coherent systems to help make large and small decisions, but ultimately it comes down to the individual to choose and to act on the choices. But even the choices that are perceived to be available as options are circumscribed by individual circumstances, education, religion, and custom.

No philosophy or set of beliefs is prescribed here. However, it is strongly urged that every student affairs professional make a continuing and intentional effort to understand his or her own worldview. Expediency and reaction are tempting and too easy. Professionalism demands active thought and thoughtful action.

REFERENCES

Abes, E. S. (2009). Theoretical borderlands: Using multiple theoretical perspectives to challenge inequitable power structures in student development theory. *Journal of College Student Development, 50,* 141–156.

Abes, E. S., Jones, S. R., & McEwen, M. K. (2007). Reconceptualizing the model of multiple dimensions of identity: The role of meaning-making capacity in the construction of multiple identities. *Journal of College Student Development, 48,* 1–22.

Adler, M. J. (1951). Labor, leisure, and liberal education. *Journal of General Education, 6,* 175–184.

American College Personnel Association (ACPA). (1994). *The student learning imperative: Implications for student affairs.* Washington, DC: American College Personnel Association.

American College Personnel Association (ACPA) and National Association of Student Personnel Administrators (NASPA). (1997). *Principles of good practice for student affairs.* Retrieved from http://www.acpa.nche.edu/ pgp/principle.htm.

American Council on Education. (1983a). The student personnel point of view: A report of a conference on the philosophy and development of student personnel work in colleges and universities. In G. L. Saddlemire & A. L. Rentz (Eds.), *Student affairs–A profession's heritage: Significant articles, authors, issues and documents* (American College Personnel Association Media Publication No. 25, pp. 74–87). Carbondale: Southern Illinois University Press. (Original work published 1937).

American Council on Education. (1983b). The student personnel point of view. In G. L. Saddlemire & A. L. Rentz (Eds.), *Student affairs–A profession's heritage: Significant articles, authors, issues and documents* (American College Personnel

Association Media Publication No. 25, pp. 122–140). Carbondale: Southern Illinois University Press. (Original work published 1949).

Brown, R. D. (1972). *Student development in tomorrow's higher education–A return to the academy.* Washington, DC: American College Personnel Association.

Brubacher, J. S. (1982). *On the philosophy of higher education.* San Francisco: Jossey-Bass.

Brubacher, J. S., & Rudy, W. (1976). *Higher education in transition.* New York: Harper & Row.

Chavez, A. F., Guido-DiBrito, F., & Mallory, S. (2003). Learning to value the "other": A framework of individual diversity development. *Journal of College Student Development, 44,* 453–469.

Cowley, W. H. (1957). Student personnel services in retrospect and prospect. *School and Society,* Jan., 19–22.

Dewey, J. (1916). *Democracy and education.* New York: Macmillan.

Dewey, J. (1937). President Hutchins' proposals to remake higher education. *Social Frontier, 3,* 103–4.

Domonkos, L. S. (1977). History of higher education. *International Encyclopedia of Higher Education* (pp. 2017–2040). San Francisco: Jossey-Bass.

Evans, N. J. with Reason, R. D. (2001). Guiding principles: A review and analysis of student affairs philosophical statements. *Journal of College Student Development, 42*(4), 359–77.

Gracia, J. J. E. (1992). *Philosophy and its history: Issues in philosophical historiography.* Albany, NY: State University of New York Press.

Hirt, J. B. (2007). The student affairs profession in the academic marketplace. *NASPA Journal, 44*(2), 245–264.

Hook, S. (1946). *Education for modern man.* New York: Dial.

Hutchins, R. M. (1936). *The higher learning in America.* New Haven, CT: Yale University Press.

Johnson, J. A., Collins, H. W., Dupuis, V. L., & Johansen, J. H. (1969). *Introduction to the foundations of American education.* Boston: Allyn and Bacon.

Joint Task Force on Student Learning. (1998). *Powerful partnerships: A shared responsibility for learning.* Retrieved from http://www.aahe.org/teaching/ tsk_frce.htm.

Kneller, G. F. (1964). *Introduction to the philosophy of education.* New York: John Wiley & Sons.

Knock, G. H., Rentz, A. L., & Penn, J. R. (1989). Our philosophical heritage: Significant influences on professional practice and preparation. *NASPA Journal, 27*(2), 116–22.

Kuh, G., Lyons, J., Miller, T., & Trow, J. A. (1995). *Reasonable expectations: Renewing the educational compact between institutions and students.* Washington, DC: National Association of Student Personnel Administrators (NASPA).

Lincoln, Y. S. (1989). Trouble in the land: The paradigm revolution in the academic disciplines. *Higher education: Handbook of theory and research, 5,* 57–133. New York: Agathon Press.

Lincoln, Y. S., & Guba, E. (1985). *Naturalistic inquiry.* Beverly Hills, CA: Sage.

Manning, K. (1994). Liberation theology and student affairs. *Journal of College Student*

Development, 35(2), 94–97.

Manning, K. (1996). Contemplating the myths of student affairs. *NASPA Journal, 34*(1), 36–46.

Miller, T. K., & Prince, J. S. (1976). *The future of student affairs.* San Francisco: Jossey-Bass.

NASPA, & ACPA. (2004). *Learning reconsidered: A campus-wide focus on the student experience.* Washington, DC: National Association of Student Personnel Administrators & American College Personnel Association.

National Association of Student Personnel Administrators (NASPA). (1987). *A perspective on student affairs.* Washington, DC: Author.

Potts, D. B. (1977). 'College Enthusiasm!' as public response, 1800–1860. *Harvard Educational Review, 47*(1), 28–42.

Sartre, J. P. (1947). *Existentialism.* New York: Philosophical Library.

Veblen, T. (1918). *The higher learning in America.* New York: D. W. Huebsch.

Whitehead, A. N. (1929). *The aims of education and other essays.* New York: Macmillan.

Whitt, E. J., Carnaghi, J. E., Matkin, J., Scalese-Love, P., & Nestor, D. (1990). Believing is seeing: Alternative perspectives on a statement of professional philosophy for student affairs. *NASPA Journal, 27*(3), 178–84.

Young, R. B. (2001). A perspective on the values of student affairs and scholarship. *Journal of College Student Development, 42*(4), 319–337.

Young, R. B. (2003). Philosophies and values guiding the student affairs professio. In S. Komives & D. Woodard (Eds.) *Student services: A handbook for the profession* (4th ed., pp. 89–106). San Francisco: Jossey-Bass.

Chapter 2

STUDENT AFFAIRS:
AN HISTORICAL PERSPECTIVE

AUDREY L. RENTZ AND MARY HOWARD-HAMILTON

The student personnel movement constitutes one of the most important efforts of American educators to treat . . . college and university students as individuals, rather than entries in an impersonal roster. . . . In a real sense this part of modern higher education is an individualized application of the research and clinical findings of modern psychology, sociology, cultural anthropology, and education to the task of aiding students to develop fully in the college environment. (American Council on Education, 1949, p. 110)

INTRODUCTION

Seeds of the student personnel movement lie quite naturally within the American system of higher education and yet are also influenced by the larger society outside the walls of academe. A description of the history of student personnel requires a description of this educational context. Thus, this chapter begins with an overview of American higher education from its early colonial period until the mid-1800s. Events leading up to the early 1900s are generally thought of as catalysts for the development of student personnel work. In broad terms, these catalytic factors are the evolving and changing nature of American society, the expanding pluralism of higher education, and the differing educational philosophies that shaped higher education's mission. Material describing student personnel work is organized according to the widely held perception that student personnel work experienced three major movements or stages as it progressed to its present form of practice known as student affairs. Each movement or period of growth reflects a somewhat different philosophy, mission, and style of interaction or practice with students. Significant statements of principle and practice as well as personalities that helped define and operationalize practice for each movement are identified. These movements are: (1) student personnel work (late 1800s to mid-1960s), (2) student development (mid-1960s to late 1980s), and (3) the contemporary emphasis on student learning. Because of the limited nature of this chapter, the reader is encouraged to consult Komives and Woodard's (2003) text *Student Services: A Handbook for the Profession* for complete statements of principles and values that are only highlighted here.

COLONIAL HIGHER EDUCATION (1636–1780)

Responsibility and concern for the whole student, described by the concept *in loco parentis,* is linked to the earliest colonial college, Harvard. Chartered in 1636 by its Puritan founders, this English-American institutional prototype was created to mirror Emmanuel College, Cambridge University (Thelin, 2004). The goal was to bring about a *translatio studii,* the transference of Old World higher learning to the new colonies (Brubacher & Rudy, 1958). The founders were motivated to build institutions *pro modo Academarium in Anglia* ("according to the manner of universities in England") (Brubacher & Rudy, 1958, p. 3). The English models were "organized residential associations . . ." founded ". . . for the purpose of inculcating specific patterns of religious belief and social conduct" (Pierson, cited in Brubacher & Rudy, 1958). Curriculum, student discipline, degree requirements, and policies reflected those of Emmanuel College. The bachelor of arts was the initial degree with a concentration in ministerial preparation. For Harvard's clerical faculty (dons), the education of the intellect was viewed as secondary in importance to the salvation of an individual soul. These dons, deeply committed to their faith and to their students, labored to achieve Harvard's aim, that "Every one shall consider the mayne End of his [sic] life & studyes, to know God & Jesus Christ, which is Eternall life" (Harvard College Records, cited in Brubacher & Rudy, 1958, p. 8). Early entrance requirements reflected a classical concept of a liberal education:

> When any Schollar is able to read Tully or such like classicall Latine Authour ex temporare, and make and speake Latin verse and prose *Suo (out aiunt) Marte,* and decline perfectly the paradigms of Nounes and verbes in the Greeke toungue, then may hee bee admitted into the Colledge, nor shall any claim admission before such qualification. . . . (Colonial Society of Massachusetts, cited in Brubaker & Rudy, 1958, p. 12)

Once admitted, young (aged 11–15) male students' lives, in and out of the classroom, were rigidly controlled and supervised by paternalistic dons. Daily visits to student rooms, meals taken in common, and strictly supervised chapel services and classes were thought to help guard the young students against temptations of sin. The hope was that these "gentleman/scholars" might learn to serve as examples of Puritan piety and civility. A somewhat sarcastic analysis of these early paternalistic efforts saw them as "a persistent emphasis on extracurricular religion and also a considerable snooping into the lives of the students" (Cowley, cited in Mueller, 1961, p. 51). And yet, for the early Harvard scholars, the college level-educated man was viewed as a member of the long line of succession from the early prophets and apostles.

In subsequent years, members of other religious sects (e.g., Anglicans, Calvinists, and Dutch Reform) were motivated to establish institutions to promote their set of Christian values and to prepare literate, college-educated clergy. Duplication of the English collection of like colleges became less important as unsolvable factors mitigated against it as a goal. In comparison to England, colonial campuses were separated by rugged terrain and a lack of satisfactory transportation. In addition, both the founders and the local community residents most often lacked adequate financial resources. As a result, subsequent institutions were less similar to their Emmanuel prototype than Harvard and offered degrees somewhat broader in scope. Among these early institutions and their purposes were William and Mary (1693) to prepare piously educated youth and spread Christianity among the Indians; Yale (1701) to prepare youth for employment in the public state and the church; College of Philadelphia (1740), Princeton (1748), Kings College (1754), and College of Rhode Island (Brown) (1764) to provide education of Baptist ministers who previously lacked formal preparation; Dartmouth (1769) and Queens College (1770) to prepare youth in languages, liberal and applied arts, and sciences for ministerial and other civic roles.

While institutional purposes varied, *in loco parentis* was constant. At Yale, for example, 16 required chapel services weekly, four voluntary noon prayer sessions, and frequent revival gatherings were meant to help students experience "distinct effusions of the Holy Spirit" (Cowley, cited in Mueller, 1961). During these early formative years, these institutions were private, limited to young male students, residential, and staffed by clerical or lay male faculty and administrators.

Matriculation was a challenge for all colleges during this period. Thelin (2004) noted that there was very little emphasis on completing degrees and most students left within a year or two after their arrival on campus. "College students probably constituted less than 1% of the population" (Thelin, 2004, p. 20). The modest enrollments left colleges with an average of 10 students in a class. "At the College of William and Mary so few undergraduates petitioned for graduation that in 1768 a new governor of Virginia, Lord Bote-tourt, resolved to provide both a push and a pull to the conferring of bachelor of arts degree" (Thelin, 2004, p.20). The governor provided prize money for degree candidates who left wealthy and powerful after completing their studies.

A unique hallmark of the colonial system of higher education was the close and personal relationship between its faculty and students. It did not take long for certain campus and societal events to change this orientation. Historians frequently cite the Harvard food riot of 1766, labeled the "butter rebellion" as one such event. Triggered partly by the presence of rancid butter in the warm Spring dining commons and probably more by the repressed volatile behavior of male students, this outburst escalated to such an extent that several deaths were recorded. Subsequently, dons were less willing to continue to worship, eat, and live alongside their youthful students. This personal interest in the whole student and the attitude of *in loco parentis* would not reappear on American campuses for almost another 275 years.

THE PLURALITY OF HIGHER EDUCATION INSTITUTIONS (1780–1865)

An Overview

As the number of collegiate institutions increased, the profile of the American system of higher education as male-centered, private, paternalistic, and residential was considered to be permanent. From approximately 1780 to the outbreak of the Civil War in 1862, a number of societal needs emerged that can be linked to major changes in this profile. Several of these major changes are introduced here. Curricular offerings were expanded by the creation of the elective system. Professional education was enhanced with the establishment of graduate institutions using the older Germanic institutions of scientific thought as prototypes. Degree programs increased as different types of institutions were established to offer curricula in response to expanding societal demands for lawyers, accountants, physicians, merchants, scientists, elementary and secondary schoolteachers, engineers, and farmers trained in the application of technology and science.

Numbers of enrolled students grew as women were accepted as students and later served as faculty members. In addition, women were called upon to fulfill local community needs for hundreds of public elementary and high school teachers. Closely allied to the growing number of women in higher education was the development of a number of women's institutions. Previously private male institutions faced new competition from the creation of land grant institutions, women's colleges, state-supported public institutions, traditional denominational or church-related institutions, and coeducational campuses. Cheyney College in 1830 marked the beginning of black institutions established to provide education for a group of minority people for whom such opportunities had been almost nonexistent. As the profile of higher education changed, leaders of American institutions intensely debated the significance of each new feature while trying both to maintain tradition and to respond to society's changing needs. During this same period, many students reacting to negative campus environments moved off campus. In so doing, they created a somewhat parallel collegiate structure that eventually included student debate clubs, literary societies, housing arrangements, and athletic groups. This resulting structure later became known as the extracurriculum and thrived for many years (Brubacher & Rudy, 1958). These major changes in the profile of American higher education are frequently considered as antecedents of a movement that by the mid-twentieth century had become student personnel work.

Curricular Innovations

Curricular innovations were viewed as one of two kinds: vertical expansion or lateral expansion. The founding of Johns Hopkins (c. 1876) as the first graduate institution represented what Brubaker and Rudy (1958) referred to as a vertical expansion of the American curriculum. Perhaps a more important development was the lateral expansion of the curriculum, the creation of the elective system, an idea that ignited considerable controversy. Advocated by Thomas Jefferson, this innovation gave rise to an examination of several key questions that would dramatically alter the future profile of higher education. At the center of many debates were such fundamental questions as "Should higher education be 'practical' or 'liberal,' a means to an end or an end in itself? Were the 'new' studies (such as science) more important than the 'old' studies (such as the classics)? Should the college be predominantly secular or religious in orientation? Should it aim to be aristocratic, and train the elite, or . . . seek to attain a democratic all-inclusiveness?" (Brubacher & Rudy, 1958, pp. 96–97). In the middle of what was probably the most significant educational controversy of the nineteenth century, Yale President Jeremiah Day undertook a bold and defining role. On behalf of his faculty, Day published the Yale Report of 1828, providing an authoritative statement about Yale's future. The document, ". . . became a classic statement in defense of the old order" (Rudolph, 1990, p. 130). "The thorough study of the ancient languages was the only proper system for a college" (Brubacher & Rudy, 1958, p. 101). The case to preserve Yale's classical and narrow curriculum "was made with such finality that not until the next generation would another band of reformers assail the old course of study" (Rudolph, 1990, p. 131).

Not all higher education leaders agreed. Their response was the creation of yet another type of higher education institution. They founded independent schools whose purpose was to teach nonclassical subjects. Among such institutions were the United States Military Academy at West Point (1802); Rensselaer Polytechnic Institute, where initially in 1824 teachers were prepared to instruct both "sons and daughters of local farmers and mechanics in the art of applying science to husbandry, manufactures, and domestic economy" (RPI Annual Register as cited in Brubacher & Rudy, 1958); the United States Naval Academy (1845); and later the Massachusetts Institute of Technology in 1865. As a result, the variety and the breadth of academic degree programs available multiplied. The young nation continued to mature and as it did, colleges and universities consistently responded to the constantly changing society outside their walls.

The effects of secularization and industrialization were experienced not only outside the ivy-covered walls of the academy, but also within. Male students attended public colleges and universities whose status was confirmed by the 1819 decision in the Dartmouth College case providing that state legislatures may not exert governance or control over such institutions. Similarly, Thomas Jefferson in 1825 established the University of Virginia as the first state-supported but not state-governed institution. The traditional, somewhat narrow, liberal arts curriculum of the colonial colleges was no longer the only curriculum offered.

Lincoln's endorsement of the Morrill Land Grant Acts of 1862 and 1864 affirmed the importance and the permanence of public higher education (Thelin, 2004). These laws to bring about "the liberal and practical education of the industrial classes in the several pursuits and professions of life" (Solomon, 1985, p. 44) set aside acres of public lands in states on which institutions would be built to provide instruction in agriculture, mining, military, and mechanical arts. The result was the development of a large system of agricultural and mechanical colleges, referred to as "utilitarian institutions" or "aggie schools" (Mueller, 1961, p. 52), hence the "A & M" in the name (Thelin, 2004). Their curricular offerings combined concentrations in liberal arts with practical education. Additionally, these legislative acts required states either to admit black students to existing colleges or to provide separate but equal educational facilities for them. Thus, two systems of higher education, historically black and predominantly white, separate but equal, existed side by side (Roebuck & Murty, 1993).

As different types of curricular offerings were created, various institutional settings emerged. From 1850 to 1870, several prototypes of higher education institutions emerged: the private women's college, the religiously oriented coeducational college, the private women's coordinate colleges, the secular coeducational institutions (both public and private), and the public single-sex vocational institution (Solomon, 1985).

Womens' Participation in Higher Education

> Women's education has been a cause of debate for centuries. The advocates of women's education have been few, the enemies many. The arguments against it have included women's immorality, their transcendental virtue, their fragile bodies, and feeble minds. If taught to read, women will give themselves to promiscuity; if they go to college, they will never bear children. (*Better Than Rubies,* 1978, jacket cover)

Phyllis Stock reminds us that "women often gain in status and power in society, not with the advent of a new social structure, but with the breakdown of an old one" (Stock, 1978, p. 26). The validity of this observation would be demonstrated repeatedly as American society and its system of higher education evolved. Women were allowed to assume greater and more powerful roles and responsibilities simply because those roles and responsibilities previously assumed by men became unattended. The young nation's needs for teachers at the elementary, secondary, and collegiate levels added considerable weight to the proponents of access for women into higher education.

As early as 1776, the words of Abigail Adams written to her husband, President John Adams, expressed her views concerning the need to educate women. Those words, still quoted by contemporary authors, became a clarion call to all women:

> If you complain of neglect of Education in sons, What shall I say with regard to daughters, who every day experience the want of it. With regard to the Education of my own children, I find myself soon out of my depth, and destitute and deficient in every part of Education. (as cited in Solomon, 1985, p. 1)

Undergraduate study, formerly considered by many a "forbidden world" to women (Solomon, 1985, p. 1), was now becoming a reality. Women's colleges shared a common purpose with their female seminary predecessors. They perceived their mission to be to educate women so that female graduates might be better prepared to assume roles within the domestic sphere, as wives and mothers and, only if needed, as school teachers (Solomon, 1985). Within several years, granting women access to colleges and universities was viewed as an appropriate and proper way to address societal needs.

With female boarding schools, academies, and seminaries serving as a foundation, women were quickly educated to become teachers and in turn established and taught at colleges for women with a curriculum that varied from high school courses to that equal to neighboring male four-year colleges and universities. Mount Holyoke, established by Mary Lyon in 1836 as a seminary, became one of the earliest women's institutions and served as a model for others in the Midwest, the West, and the South (Solomon, 1985). Other women's institutional pioneers were Emma Willard, founder of Troy Seminary in Troy (New York) in 1821, and Catherine Beecher, who started Hartford Seminary (Connecticut) in 1828 (Rudolph, 1990). The pace quickened and in 1836, Georgia Female College (Wesleyan) offered a curriculum that combined both secondary and collegiate courses. Mary Sharp College (Tennessee) in 1853 went one step beyond the usual course offerings by offering a curriculum that emphasized Latin, Greek, and higher mathematics (Solomon, 1985). In 1837, an alternate form of higher education emerged when in an evangelical community Oberlin College (Ohio) became the first coeducational undergraduate institution to allow four women to enroll. Ultimately, "coeducation . . . became the dominant mode, as early feminists had hoped, . . . but women's colleges did not perish" (Solomon, 1985, p. 43). The profile of American higher education would from here forward always include women.

Once admitted, women were able to pursue the traditional baccalaureate degree program or receive a diploma following completion of a special Ladies Course (Rudolph, 1990, p. 311). Women's presence brought with it a new concern for those responsible for campuses. Worried about the perceived dangers of having women on Oberlin's predominantly male campus, President Charles Finney said ". . . you will need a wise and pious matron with such lady assistants as to keep up sufficient supervision" (Holmes, cited in Mueller, 1961, p. 53).

Several pioneer public women's colleges were founded in the post-Civil War years by religiously motivated persons: Vassar (New York) in 1865; Wellesley (Massachusetts) and Smith (Massachusetts) in 1875; and Bryn Mawr (Pennsylvania) in 1884, patterned after Johns Hopkins University, was awarding graduate degrees by 1888 (Rudolph, 1990). In addition, the Women's College of Baltimore (Maryland), opened in 1884 and, sponsored by the Methodist Conference, held similarly high standards for academic rigor as its Virginian Presbyterian-sponsored neighbor Randolph-Macon College for Women (Virginia). The former is today's Goucher College (Solomon, 1985). "By 1860 at least forty-five institutions offered collegiate degrees to women" (Thelin, 2004, p. 83). These institutions had very unique names such as female seminary, literary institute, and academy (Thelin, 2004).

By 1882, with coeducation flourishing, the lady matrons and principals had proven that their existence had merit. Citing improved relationships between male and female students, it was observed that "there is comparative freedom from the dangers and conditions ordinarily incident to college life" (Holmes, cited in Mueller, 1961, p. 53). These lady principals, later titled Deans of Women, were given administrative and disciplinary functions when appointed by institutional presidents.

As the nineteenth century ended, yet another aspect of higher education was added. Several Catholic girls' schools moved toward collegiate status. The Academy of the Sacred Heart at Manhattanville (New York) became a college in 1900 and Washington Trinity College was founded in the same year (Rudolph, 1990). The Catholic system of higher education developed single-sex and later parallel coeducational institutions.

The Beginnings of Black Institutions

The profile of American higher education was to be altered yet again. This time the enhancement came with the establishment of black institutions in the North. Cheyney College opened in 1830, and both Lincoln College and Wilberforce University were established in 1856 by the Methodist Episcopal Church (Hill, 1984; Ricard & Brown, 2008; Roebuck & Murty, 1993; Thomas & Hirsch, 1987; Thomas & Hirsch, 1989). Alexander Lucius Twilight was the first recorded black graduate of Middlebury College in 1823 (Ranbom & Lynch, 1987, Fall 1988, Winter). In the South, black students were restricted in their pursuit of higher education because collegiate education had previously been "declared" illegal (Fleming, 1984; Hill, 1984; National Advisory Committee on Black Higher Education and Black Colleges and Universities, 1979; Thomas & Hirsch, 1989). In 1860, there were approximately four million black slaves in America, with more than 90 percent living in the South. In each southern state except one, black slaves and free blacks were excluded from formal instruction, which helps explain why over 90 percent of the southern black population was illiterate in 1860. Before the Civil War, the number of blacks who had received undergraduate degrees from American colleges and universities did not exceed 28 (Roebuck & Murty, 1993). Two perceptions formed the basis of the rationale for not educating Blacks: (1) the intellectual inferiority of blacks, and (2) once educated, blacks would "get out of their place" and inevitably become competitors of whites within economic, political, and sexual spheres (Goodenow, 1989, p. 152).

In the years after 1865, with the passage of the Thirteenth Amendment abolishing slavery, Virginia Union, Shaw University (1865), and Howard University (1867) marked the beginning of formal black higher education institutions (Rambon & Lynch, 1987, Fall 1988, Winter). Alcorn College, the recipient of federal land grant funds was the first Black land grant college (Rambon & Lynch, 1987, Fall 1988, Winter). From 1866 to1890, 16 of the historically black public colleges in existence today were created. Hampton

University, considered one of the most influential institutions in the history of black education, was established in 1868 in Virginia (Roebuck & Murty, 1993). The decision of the U.S. Supreme Court in *Plessy v. Fergusson* in 1896 made constitutional "separate but equal" schools and Harvard awarded the first honorary degree to a black scholar, Booker T. Washington (Rambon & Lynch, 1987, Fall 1988, Winter, p. 17). These early historically black institutions served an important function within the larger system of colleges and universities, and their courageous students made possible prototypes for additional institutions in the years ahead.

ANTECEDENTS OF STUDENT PERSONNEL WORK

Most new educational and societal movements arise as a reaction against a situation or an outcome that becomes perceived as undesirable. Such was the case as a series of issues in American higher education and American society influenced the development of student personnel and supported its transition from an early emphasis on *in loco parentis* to today's focus on student learning. To what set of needs were the early proponents of student personnel work responding? What factors helped to create the positions and roles they assumed as the movement grew on college and university campuses? Who were the early pioneers? And what did they bring to the evolving movement that provided it with stability, strength, and a sense of common mission? An exact date for the beginning of student personnel remains a matter of conjecture among historians. W. H. Cowley reminds us that the practice of (student) personnel enjoyed a long history and was characteristic of much earlier systems of higher education: ". . . what might be called Alma Maternal ministrations to students had characterized the universities of the Middle Ages. . ." (cited in Williamson, 1949, p. 16). Efforts on the part of students to move away from the campus' narrow classical curriculum and the emphasis on piety and discipline led ultimately to the establishment of debate clubs, literary societies and eventually the Greek-letter social fraternity movement.

> In a sense, the literary societies and their libraries, the clubs, journals and organizations which compensated for the neglect of science, English literature, history, music and art in the curriculum–this vast developing extracurriculum was the student response to the classical course of study. It helped to liberate the intellect on the American campus. It was an answer to the Yale Report of 1828, an answer so effective that by the end of the century at Yale itself there would be a real concern over which was really more fundamental, more important, the curriculum or the extracurriculum. (Rudolph, 1990, p. 144)

Between 1825 and 1840, so popular were student groups that several national Greek-letter social fraternities were created from former debating societies and drinking clubs: Kappa Alpha, Theta Delta Chi, Sigma Phi, Delta Phi, Chi Psi, and Psi Upsilon (Rudolph, 1990). According to Rudolph ". . . Greek-letter fraternities were intended to bring together the most urbane young men on campus into small groups that would fulfill the vacuum left by removal from the family and the home community. . ." (Rudolph, 1990, p. 146). In addition, they "offered an escape from the monotony, dreariness, and unpleasantness of the collegiate regimen . . . and from the dormitory with its lack of privacy" (Rudolph, 1990, pp. 146–147).

A Period of Intellectualism (1855–1890)

The profile of higher education would not remain inviolate for long. This time change came in the form of an educational philosophy that espoused a much narrower mission for American higher education. Its existence and influence came about as a result of our society's need for scientific and technical professionals prepared in the hard sciences: mathematics, physics, astronomy, and so forth. As more and more American and European faculty, educated in German universities, joined American college and university faculties, they introduced the educational philosophy known as intellectualism. Generally speaking, this school of thought placed primary emphasis on the training of the intellect; the rational mind was valued above all else. Also associated with this school of thought was the concept of academic freedom represented by two words: *lernfreiheit* and *lehrfreiheit*. The first term implied that students were to be free of administrative control and regulation. They could travel from campus to campus, and could live wherever they chose. The latter term conveyed a faculty member's right to engage freely in research or scientific inquiry and to report research conclusions or findings without fear of reprisals (Rudolph, 1990). With the primary focus on rational development, other aspects of students' social, psychological, physical, and spiritual development were devalued. The years when intellectualism was in favor were later known as the period of Germanic influence, approximately 1855 to 1890. Faculty and student roles were redefined. Increasingly, faculty found it both necessary and desirable to devote considerable time to the pursuit of scientific research in addition to teaching, and had little time or concern for student life outside the classroom.

The previous interest and value associated with the residential aspect of many colleges and universities all but disappeared. Yale was the only campus to maintain its position of endorsing a residential setting. The personal quality of student-faculty interactions that had marked American higher education changed dramatically. Institutional or administrative attitudes toward students shifted as well. Earlier handbooks that contained excessively stern rules of student conduct were replaced by pamphlets that were considerably thinner and set forth more liberal rules. Higher education's previous definition of the student had cast him as an adolescent. This perception changed so that the student came to be viewed more as an adult. Male students were perceived to be capable of solving their own problems, academic, religious and social, as they saw fit. "Overweening paternalism gave way to almost complete indifference" (Cowley, 1937, p. 221). Harvard, in 1886, altered its class attendance policies to require only that juniors and seniors pass examinations. Male students left campuses to initiate student-governed off-campus living accommodations and to develop out of class activities. Intercollegiate athletic programs were initiated with a crew race between Harvard and Yale in 1852 and a football game between Princeton and Rutgers in 1869. Later these intercollegiate programs included baseball and track (Brubacher & Rudy, 1976; Rudolph, 1990). By the 1870s, a major element of higher education had taken form, an array of activities referred to as the "era of the extracurriculum."

> In the extracurriculum the college student stated his case for the human mind, the human personality, and the human body, for all aspects of man that the colleges tended to ignore in their single-minded interest in the salvation of souls. In the institutions of the extracurriculum college students everywhere suggested that they preferred the perhaps equally challenging task of saving minds, saving personalities, saving bodies. On the whole the curriculum would still be intact, and compulsory chapel was only beginning to give way. But in the extracurriculum the students erected within the gates a monster. Taming it would now become as necessary a project as the long-delayed reform of the curriculum itself. (Rudolph, 1990, p. 155)

The Pioneer Deans (1870–1920)

From approximately 1875 to 1930, the undergraduate student body increased nearly 30-fold (Brubacher & Rudy, 1958). Presidents were concerned about their ability to administer an ever-growing institution while also assuming responsibility for student life issues. Presidents increasingly endorsed the need for an administrator to coordinate or supervise students. Others voiced a concern for women students on previously predominantly male campuses, while some spoke out publicly against the previous devaluing of the residential component. In 1889, President Gilman at Johns Hopkins established the first system of faculty advisers by appointing Professor E. H. Griffin as the "chief of the faculty advisers" and announcing that "in every institution there should be one or more persons specifically appointed to be counselors or advisers of students" (Cowley, 1949, p. 20).

Presidents became critical of the prevailing philosophy of intellectualism and its hands-off attitude toward students. Responding to both faculty persuasion and parental pressures, Harvard's President Charles Eliot recommended to his Board of Overseers that this most recent wave of treating students impersonally be challenged. Previous policies governing student attendance should be reinstated. It was a time when university governance became a very complex responsibility. As a consequence of all segments of an institution reporting to the president and the growing size and scope of the extracurriculum, Eliot appointed Professor Ephraim Gurney in 1870 as the first college dean. Although the position was considered academic, Gurney's task, in addition to regular teaching, was to relieve Eliot of the responsibility of student discipline. Later in 1891, when the dean's position was reorganized into two separate offices, LeBaron Russell Briggs, age 35 and already a respected professor of English, assumed those duties related to students considered to be nonacademic: discipline, registration and records, and various other aspects of students' lives outside the classroom (Brown, 1926).

Briggs is generally regarded as the earliest dean of students, and the "official sponsor of undergraduates" (Brown, 1926, p. 95; Brubacher & Rudy, 1958; Mueller, 1961). His appointment was part of Eliot's call for a new system of student discipline, a system that would emphasize self-discipline and a developed sense of self-responsibility (Morison, 1930). Briggs's attitude toward dealing with student discipline was evident in the goals he established for his deanship: "(1) To help the student disciplined, and not merely to humiliate him [sic]; (2) to make it easy for the faculty to do its work; and (3) to develop a sentiment among the students which would render discipline less and less necessary" (Brown, 1926, p. 101). In 1897, he organized a group of 60 upperclassmen to assume responsibility for meeting and assisting entering students, "to stand ready in time of need . . . [as] unpretentious counselor(s)" (Brown, 1926, p. 127). Briggs served in the deanship until his retirement from Harvard in 1925.

"Everywhere two types of deans made their appearance: 'academic deans' of colleges or special faculties . . . and 'dean of students' . . . whose concern was with the extracurricular life of undergraduates" (Cowley, 1937, pp. 224–225, cited in Brubacher & Rudy, 1958, p. 322). The University of Chicago's President William Harper was among the first to argue for a resurgence of on-campus living. Greek-letter social group members slowly returned to campuses. Clubs and student organizations flourished and the campus "became an arena in which undergraduates erected monuments not to the soul of man but to man as a social and physical being" (Rudolph, 1990, pp. 136–137). Rudolph's observation reflects the new priority assigned to total human development of students that would help usher in the early stages of student personnel work. Following the years of the Germanic influence, the role of the extracurriculum had come full circle: administrators now valued its existence on their campuses. The effects of this student-established extracurriculum were vast:

> The extracurriculum which these young men developed–the agencies of intellect, the deeply embedded social system, the network of organized athletics– would become the repositories of their power. Through the extracuriculum the student arrived at a position of commanding importance in the American college. By opposing the literary societies, journals, and other clubs to the curriculum, by opposing the fraternities to the collegiate way, and by setting up in the athletic hero a more appealing symbol than the pious Christian, the students succeeded, although not really intentionally, in robbing the college professor of a certain element of prestige and of a sizable area of authority. (Rudolph, 1990, p. 157)

By 1882, the increasing numbers of matrons, wardens, and lady principals had successfully convinced academic administrators of their value within the collegiate environment. Although male and female students dined together, "relations between them are such that there is comparative freedom from the dangers and conditions ordinarily incident to college life" (Holmes, 1939, p. 9). Historians generally concur that at the University of Chicago in 1892, the hiring of Alice Freeman Palmer, former president of Wellesley, constituted the appointment of the first dean of women. At the same time, Marion Talbot, a friend of Palmer's, was appointed assistant dean and assistant professor of domestic sciences (Solomon, 1985). Talbot later replaced Palmer as the first full-time dean of women. Educated in Latin, Greek, and modern languages abroad, she received her B.A .and M.A. from Boston University, and later a B.S. from the Massachusetts of Technology, majoring in sanitation, the field that later evolved into home economics. Talbot cofounded the American Association of University Women in 1881 and convened female colleagues to help establish the National Association of Deans of Women in 1916 (Fley, 1979). No one could claim that Talbot fit that times' narrow stereotype of a woman dean. From the late 1920s until and early 1930s, she served as acting president of Constantinople Women's College in Turkey (Fley, 1979). The first African American woman to serve as a Dean of College Women was Lucy Diggs Slowe at Howard University appointed in 1922 (Solomon, 1985). During her 15-year tenure, Slowe founded two organizations, the National Association of College Women and the Association of Advisors to Women in Colored Schools.

These women deans' responsibilities spanned far beyond the single charge of supervising women's behavior. Their goal was to "champion the intellectual and personal ambitions of young women" (Knock, 1985, p. 31). To achieve this, they recognized that additional educational preparation was needed. Teachers College at Columbia University offered the first M.A. degree program and Diploma of Dean of Women in 1914. An early handbook entitled *The Dean of Women* and written by Dr. Lois Kimball Mathews, Dean of Women at the University of Wisconsin, was published in 1915 and served as an initial text (Lloyd-Jones, 1949). Enrolled women studied

> the hygiene of childhood and adolescence, . . . biology as related to education including sex education, . . . educational psychology, . . . history of the family, . .. sociology, educational sociology; philosophy of education, . . . management of the corporate life of the school, . . . problems of administrative work, . . . the psychology of religion, and a practicum. . ." (Lloyd-Jones, 1949, pp. 262–263)

The University of Illinois claims the first recorded appointment of a dean of men when Thomas Arkle Clark accepted the position in 1901(Cowley, 1937; Rhatigan, 2009). Eight years before he had been appointed dean of undergraduates and assistant to the president. A former student of L. R. Briggs, the first student personnel dean at Harvard in 1890, Clark made contributions primarily in the arena of discipline (Rhatigan, 2009). By 1919, the number of men who held the position of dean on college and university campuses had grown significantly. In that same year, a group from the Midwest decided to formalize their relationship across institutional lines and established the National Association of Deans of Men (NADM).

These student personnel pioneers, male and female, valued the uniqueness and the individuality of each student. They were committed to the holistic development of students and held an unshakeable belief in each student's potential for growth and learning. These core values would become the foundation of future statements and documents that would define the new field's mission and goals.

As the availability of on-campus living facilities grew, the number of students enrolled in higher education increased dramatically. Administrative staffs increased dramatically. During the early 1900s, college and university campuses were being served by large numbers of student personnel practitioners: deans of men, students, and women; registrars; counselors; vocational guidance counselors; placement counselors; residence hall directors, admissions, food and health service staffs; and coordinators and advisors of student organizations and activities (Rudolph, 1990). All were devoted to providing programs and services required to help students derive the maximum benefit from their undergraduate experience, both in and out of the classroom.

Some historians perceive student personnel as emerging solely as a reaction to the dominant German-based intellectualism and its resulting impersonal attitude toward students. However, other factors can also be viewed as causal. W. H. Cowley (1949) explains his viewpoint regarding the rise of student personnel work:

> The usual explanation . . . is that scientific psychology led to the application of research findings to the problems of military, of industry, and of education. . . . But it struck me that for student personnel work at least three other considerations were antecedent to scientific psychological research: first, secularization of education; second, the increase in student populations beginning about 1870; and third, the attacks upon the intellectualistic impersonalism imported by American Ph.D.s trained in Germany. (p. 16)

The Emergence of Student Personnel and Its Associations (1916–1936)

As early student personnel professionals gathered to talk about their evolving field, discussions inevitably turned to the need for a standard definition, a set of criteria to guide practice, and a statement of values to help clarify the new field's role on campuses. What would later be known as the Student Personnel Point of View, a statement of core values and principles of student personnel work, evolved from such a conference of college personnel officers from Purdue University and Wabash College in 1929, in cooperation with the American Council on Education and the Personnel Research Foundation of New York. During that meeting, J. A. Humphreys (Dean of Personnel Services, Oberlin College) proposed five guiding principles to serve as the foundation of student personnel work:

1. Personnel work is, and should be, first of all an idea rather than a tangible organization. It stands for individualization in college education. Personnel work among college students consists of those activities or procedures which have as their objective assisting the individual student.
2. The logical outcome of this principle is the idea that there should be brought to bear on all student problems, either individual or group situations, the point of view which concerns itself with the individual student. The application of established policies and the forming of new ones ought to be made with reference to individual needs. After all the college exists for the student and not the student for the college.
3. Specific personnel problems arise out of situations, not out of a clear sky.
4. Every member of the faculty, every administrative officer and assistant is a personnel officer in the sense that responsibility for serving the individual student rests upon all those who come in contact with the students.
5. College personnel work is not an activity set off apart from the educative process of the college. True personnel work functions as a part of the educative process. (Humphreys, 1930, pp. 11–12.)

Elements of the preceding can be found in the following definition offered by Clothier two years later, now considered a classic, as he wrote for the Committee on Principles and Functions of the American College Personnel Association:

> Personnel work in a college or university is the systematic bringing to bear on the individual student all those influences, of whatever nature, which will stimulate him [*sic*] and assist him [*sic*], through his [*sic*] own efforts, to develop in body, mind and character to the limit of his [*sic*] individual capacity for growth, and helping [*sic*] to apply his [*sic*] powers so developed most effectively to the work of the world. (Clothier, 1931, p. 10)

Small meetings at neighboring campuses brought student personnel deans together to discuss common issues and concerns. These efforts resulted in the creation of three early student personnel professional associations: as cited previously, (1) the deans of women established the National Association of Women Deans (NAWD) in 1916, which became the National Association of Women in Education (NAWE); (2) the deans of men convened the National Association of Deans of Men, (NADM) in 1919; and (3) the deans of men in conjunction with the early deans of students created today's National Association of Student Personnel Administrators (NASPA). Members of the National Association of Placement Secretaries, established in 1924, later changed their name in 1931 to the American College Personnel Association (ACPA). In the early 1950s, a conglomerate of professionals within education established the American Personnel and Guidance Association (APGA), which was later renamed the Association for Counseling and Development (Mueller, 1961). For information about professional associations of interest to specific student affairs practitioners, such as orientation, financial aids, student activities, and so on, the reader is advised to consult appropriate chapters within this book.

Not only was the new field not readily understood, but also academic administrators were dubious about its proper place on a campus. Esther Lloyd-Jones suggested the appropriate role and administrative location for the division or the field within institutional governance. She proposed that student personnel be considered a separate but equal partner to the other two main divisions (instructional and operational) of college and university administration (Lloyd-Jones, 1994).

Two years later, Cowley, in *The Nature of Student Personnel Work* (1936), attempted to bring order to the existing confusion surrounding the amorphous nature of the evolving field by providing a rather detailed discussion of many of the definitions in use. Rejecting several, claiming they were too inclusive, and disregarding others because they were too restrictive, he offered his own definition. At the same time, he sought to differentiate the new field from guidance and personnel work and from the broader concept of education, already an area of some misunderstanding among many practitioners. "Personnel work constitutes all activities undertaken or sponsored by an educational institution, aside from curricular instruction, in which the student's personal development is the primary consideration" (Cowley, 1936, p. 65). He continued,

> The personnel point of view is a philosophy of education which puts emphasis upon the individual student and his [sic] all-round development as a person rather than upon his [sic] intellectual training alone and which promotes the establishment in educational institutions of curricular programs, methods of instruction, and extra-instructional media to achieve such emphasis. (Cowley, 1936, p. 65)

The Student Personnel Point of View (1936)

As noted earlier, numerous definitions and terms were being used interchangeably not only by practitioners, but also by administrators and faculty trying to understand this new movement's purpose. Clearly, an authoritative statement of principles and practice was needed. The Executive Committee of the American Council on Education (ACE) convened a group of professionals in Washington, D.C., in April 1936 to clarify the "so-called personnel work, the intelligent use of available tools, and the development of additional techniques and processes" (American Council on Education, 1937, p. 67). In attendance were F. F. Bradshaw, W. H. Cowley, A. B. Crawford, L. B. Hopkins, E. Lloyd-Jones, D. G. Paterson, C. G. Wrenn, and others, with E. G. Williamson serving as chair. Their deliberations resulted in the document entitled *The Student Personnel Point of View*. This constituted the first statement of philosophy, purpose, and methods of practice that formed the foundation for the field's future growth and put appropriate emphasis on students. (The reader is encouraged to consult: http://www.naspa.org/pubs/files/StudAff_1949.pdf and http://www.bgsu.edu/colleges/library/cac/sahp/word/THE%20STUDENT%20PERSONNEL.pdf for a complete copy of the documents). It is significant that in the initial paragraph of the 1937 statement, labeled Philosophy, committee members affirmed the concept of holism as the fundamental assumption that would guide future practice:

> One of the basic purposes of higher education is the preservation, transmission, and enrichment of the important elements of culture–the product of scholarship, research, creative imagination, and human experience. It is the task of colleges and universities so to vitalize this and other educational purposes as to assist the student in developing to the limits of his [*sic*] potentialities

and in making his [*sic*] contribution to the betterment of society. This philosophy imposes upon education institutions the obligation to consider the student as a whole-his [*sic*] intellectual capacity and achievement, his [*sic*] emotional make-up, his [*sic*] physical condition, his [*sic*] social relationships, his [*sic*] vocational aptitudes and skills, his [*sic*] moral and religious values, his [*sic*] economic resources, his [*sic*] aesthetic appreciations. It puts emphasis, in brief, upon the development of the student as a person rather than upon his [*sic*] intellectual training alone. (American Council on Education, 1937, p. 76)

Twenty-three separate student personnel services were identified, from interpreting institutional objectives and opportunities to prospective students and their parents, to "keeping the student continuously and adequately informed of the educational opportunities and services available to him [*sic*]" (American Council on Education, 1937, p. 70). Coordination was cited as a key concept that the committee believed should be implemented not only within individual institutions, but also between student personnel work and instruction, between student personnel work and business administration, and between higher education and secondary education. The communication of information about students, among all those who worked with them, was viewed as beneficial for students and their development.

Illustrative of the need for student personnel work is the following perception of students held by personnel counselors in a report to their administrative supervisors at a large urban university in 1938:

1. Our students are markedly lacking in social skills, the ability to meet people and to get along with them. They frequently feel ill at ease in a social group and cannot engage in conversation in other than argumentative fashion.
2. Our students are constantly being frustrated by financial difficulties, by their immaturity, by their social awkwardness and by their lack of practical and social experience. (Rudolph, 1990, pp. 86–87)

The Student Personnel Point of View (1949)

Both national and individual priorities changed during the years of World War II, 1939 to 1945. America's involvement in this war to end all wars began in 1941 and demanded sacrifices from all segments of society. The value of the individual lessened as the country's spirit of patriotism grew. Economic goals were defined by a war machine or war production mentality. The manufacture of ammunition, equipment, airplanes, uniforms, and health supplies was geared toward the success of the war effort fought on two continents. While thousands of young men were drafted and others enlisted, food and other commodities were rationed at home to ensure that military troops would be fed and well supplied. Americans believed that this war was a struggle to prove the superiority of democracy, and their goal was to liberate those countries and peoples who had been oppressed by ruthless enemies. In 1945, with the defeat of Hitler's European military effort and the explosion of atomic bombs on Nagasaki and Hiroshima, Japan surrendered. America's long war effort came to an end.

In the period following World War II, values and priorities reverted to the previous peacetime attitude. Families, now able to think about today and to plan for tomorrow, worked to provide material goods for their children that a few years ago were scarce or unavailable. Individual needs and comforts were highly valued. The Serviceman's Readjustment Act of 1944 (the GI Bill) provided funds for direct college costs and subsistence that allowed returning veterans to pursue a college education. College and university enrollments swelled. The American undergraduate student body was becoming somewhat less homogeneous. Student services and programs previously planned for large groups of homogeneous students (e.g., freshmen) were in need of revision. In 1949, with higher education booming, the Committee on College Personnel of the American Council on Education released a revision of the 1936 SPPV document. The goals of higher education were expanded and now reflected the interconnectedness of the world at peace. Among the new goals, three are of particular significance:

1. Education for a fuller realization of democracy in every phase of living;
2. Education directly and explicitly for international understanding and cooperation;
3. Education for the application of creative imagination and trained intelligence to the solution of social problems and to the administration of publications. (American Council on Education, 1949, p. 108)

Paragraphs that described student needs and services for the first time described higher education's awareness of its new types of students–married, veteran, and international.

From these two seminal documents (1937 and 1949), a set of fundamental assumptions arose that would guide professional practice for years. Many professionals believed these assumptions represented the spirit of student personnel practice. Certainly they reflected post-World War II democratic values. They were

1. Individual differences are anticipated and every student is recognized as unique;
2. Each individual is to be treated as a functioning whole;
3. The individual's current drives, interests, and needs are to be accepted as the most significant factor in developing a personnel program appro-

priate for any particular campus (Mueller, 1961, p. 56);

4. Teaching, counseling, student activities and other organized education-al efforts should start realistically from where the individual student is, not from the point of development at which the institution would like to find the hypothetical student; and

5. The student is thought of as a responsible participant in his [sic] own development and not as a passive recipient of an imprinted economic, political or religious doctrine or vocational skill. (American Council on Education, 1949, p. 109)

Student Personnel Practice

Student personnel work continued to flourish during the 1940s and 1950s. Professionals believed they understood the needs of students. They planned and offered services and programs to help students function effectively, not only on the campus but also later in society. Practice was motivated by the spirit of the SPPV, and techniques were grounded in principles from sociology, psychology, philosophy, and anthropology intermingled with educational administration, and guidance. Practitioner roles were varied, including caring parent, adviser, programmer, counselor, and disciplinarian. Students were free to choose to consult or use available student services or to decide to participate in programmatic offerings.

Higher education administrators became aware that several services offered to students were being duplicated, in part because of the dual organizational structure of the two offices of dean of men and dean of women. Standards of practice were not always consistent across these administrative lines, and neither were the educational requirements and backgrounds of those supervising these offices. Nevertheless, practitioners believed that the extracurriculum provided opportunities for students to learn a variety of skills as they moved toward personal and social maturity. The distance between student affairs and the academic side of the campus increased. Programs and services were viewed as extras, extracurricular, and not necessarily linked to the curriculum. Always the aim was to help individual students grow and develop as fully functioning human beings able to survive, thrive, and contribute to society.

With the Russian launch of *Sputnik* in 1957, the United States experienced a new and pressing need for scientifically and technically prepared individuals. The race to demonstrate America's prowess and commitment to space exploration and travel had begun. Increased federal funds were channeled into higher education at an unprecedented rate to ensure the availability of science-oriented programs, students, and teachers. Large numbers of high school students who had demonstrated superior intellectual abilities, were encouraged to pursue degrees in the hard sciences. The National Education Defense Acts provided funding for the professional development of elementary and high school teachers. Undergraduate student enrollments swelled as students flocked to universities to study science and the new computer technology. Other high school graduates, desiring to avoid the military draft linked with the developing Vietnam War, enrolled as well, viewing the college campus as a safe refuge.

STUDENT DEVELOPMENT

In contrast to the prevailing attitudes of tranquility and pride that marked the 1950s, the decade of the 1960s was characterized by turmoil, upheaval, and confrontation. Some years later this period was referred to as the age of student activism, the years of civil disobedience, and the downfall of *in loco parentis*. Many student affairs administrators found themselves in difficult situations. They perceived a conflict among their multiple roles. They desired (1) to be advocates for students, (2) to be sensitive to student needs, (3) to help students learn to navigate bureaucratic organizations and participate in social causes, and (4) to serve as counselors and advisors. At the same time, however, they were being told by their institutional presidents to control student behavior. With exploding student enrollments, large classes, an increased use of graduate teaching assistants, and residential overcrowding, undergraduate students began to react to a deep sense of impersonalism they believed was invading higher education. In addition, the use of new computerized technology to efficiently process class registrations and other institutional procedures seemed to strip them of their personal identities as they became known only by their student identity card and number. Discontent escalated as students viewed undergraduate coursework as irrelevant to the solution of major contemporary societal issues. "Flower power," "take time to smell the roses," "do not fold, staple, or mutilate" and other chants filled the campus air along with shouts of demonstrators protesting the involvement of universities in federally funded research programs to assist military operations. Institutions struggled with federally imposed affirmative action quotas, increasingly diverse and somewhat less prepared students, and funding reductions imposed by state legislatures and institutional boards of trustees. Student affairs administrators were viewed as members of middle management. The specific nature of their roles varied from campus to campus, depending on the background and priorities of the president they served.

These same personnel professionals found themselves involved in debates about whether their field was secondary to or complementary to the academic mission of an institution. The purpose or need for student personnel work, now referred to as student affairs, was being viewed with less certainty than ever before. Following the years of turbulence, riots, sit-ins accompanying student activism, and the burning and looting of several major cities during the Civil Rights movement, college and university administrations began to reevaluate their thinking and orientation toward students and the nature of the student-institution relationship.

Institutional perceptions of students changed as did student affairs professionals' roles. Concepts of confrontation, *in loco parentis,* and meritocracy were replaced by encounter, collaboration, and egalitarianism. The attitude of professional practice moved from reactive to proactive, from an orientation of separate student services to a view of the undergraduate years as a continuous developmental sequence. Students were now thought of as adults, albeit as young adults still experiencing a critical period of growth and development. Institutional policies, based on this new view of students, were more liberal. Students were given seats on governing boards, and student advisory committees were established in many areas of the campus.

For student personnel itself, it was also a time of upheaval, turbulence, and confusion. Annual professional conference attendees heard speeches questioning future configurations of the field or even its continued existence. In 1964, ACPA President Cowley entreated conferees to support and utilize a newly created organization, the Council of Student Personnel Associations in Higher Education (COSPA). He hoped this group would present a unified voice of student affairs to legislators and academic administrators. ACPA President Barbara Kirk described the field as experiencing an "identity crisis" (Kirk, 1965, as cited in Rentz, 1994, p. 202), a period of questioning, self-doubt, and concern about the role future student personnel professionals would play in higher education. Adding to this uncertainty was a reordering of priorities by some institutions that suggested that unless student affairs professionals could quantitatively document their effectiveness with students, future budget allocations would be greatly reduced or nonexistent. Accountability from the corporate world had entered higher education. Hoping to provide leadership and consistency, ACPA President Ralph Berdie responded to the question "What is student personnel work?" during his presidential address.

> (It) is the application in higher education of knowledge and principles derived from the social and behavioral sciences, particularly psychology, educational psychology, and sociology. Accepting this definition student personnel work is different but not apart from other persons in higher education. Neither is it the exclusive responsibility of any one or several groups of persons in colleges and universities. The student personnel worker is the behavioral scientist whose subject matter is the student and whose socio-psychological sphere is the col-

lege. A primary purpose . . . is to humanize higher education, to help students respond to others and to themselves as human beings and to help them formulate principles for themselves as to how people should relate to one another, and to aid them to behave accordingly. . . . Another purpose . . . is to individualize higher education. We recognize the presence and significance of individual differences and hope to structure the education of each individual accordingly. (Berdie, 1966, as cited in Rentz, 1994, pp. 211–212)

The Move toward a Developmental Perspective: COSPA

Discussions among two groups of professionals meeting independently focused on the same topic: assessing the status of student personnel work and conceptualizing its future role and mission. One group in 1968, composed of representatives of various student personnel associations, was known as the Committee on Professional Development of the Council of Student Personnel Associations in Higher Education (COSPA). Their task was to prepare a statement on guidelines for professional preparation. Committee members (Grant, Saddlemire, Jones, Bradow, Cooper, Kirkbride, Nelson, Page, and Riker) concluded that to do so required that they first revisit the SPPV documents of 1937 and 1949. Keystones emerged to direct the committee's thinking. Notice the subtle shift from the previous student personnel perspective to what would become known as student development:

1. The orientation to student personnel is developmental.
2. Self-direction of the student is the goal of the student and is facilitated by the student development specialist.
3. Students are viewed as collaborators with the faculty and administration in the process of learning and growing.
4. It is recognized that many theoretical approaches to human development have credence, and a thorough understanding of such approaches is important to the student development specialist.
5. The student development specialist prefers a proactive position in policy formulation and decision-making so that a positive impact is made on the change process. (Commission of Professional Preparation of COSPA, 1975, as cited in Rentz, 1994)

Identifying the clientele (students as individuals, groups, or organizations) and functions (administrator, instructor, and consultant) of student development specialists, the committee proposed competencies to be mastered during professional preparation programs. The former student personnel worker, a generalist, was now considered more of a specialist. This new professional role of educator implied an area of expertise that could be defined as the "process" by which growth, learning, and development occur and could be facilitated. For a more thorough description, see A. L. Rentz (Ed.) *Student Affairs: A Profession's Heritage* (1994).

The growing diversity of the student body suggested that previous services and programs, designed for a more homogeneous student body, be evaluated and perhaps redesigned. Additionally, new research data describing development within various minority student groups began to appear in the literature. Student personnel practitioners were being introduced to a new understanding of student growth: the developmental perspective.

Student development became a separate movement within student affairs. It had its supporters and its critics. It emerged as a reaction to a perceived negative situation, the devaluing of student personnel on many campuses: "The old approach, student personnel work, was subtly or directly denigrated as inappropriate and outmoded" (Bloland, Stamatakos, & Rogers, 1994, p. 6). Student development

> . . . quickly captured the imagination of a number of student affairs professionals as a way of adding credibility and validity to the work of administrators and practitioners responsible for organizing, guiding, and facilitating the out-of-class education and development of college students. (Miller, Winston, & Mendenhall, 1983, p. 11)

Support for this new movement spread, as evidenced by the title of Burns Crookston's article published in 1976 "Student Personnel–All Hail and Farewell!"

The T.H.E. Project

A second task force chartered by ACPA in 1968 was given the title, Tomorrow's Higher Education (T.H.E.) Project. The goal of this project was described in the resulting monograph *Tomorrow's Higher Education: A Return to the Academy* by Robert Brown:

> The THE Project is an attempt to reconceptualize college student personnel in a way that will serve to provide a measure of creative input from our profession toward the shaping of higher education in the future. By reconceptualization we mean the systematic reconstruction of our fundamental conceptions as to the specific roles, functions, methods and procedures that will characterize future practice. (Brown, 1972, p. i)

Reviewing the literature on the impact of the college experience on students, Brown (1972) identified five key student development concepts:

1. Student characteristics when they enter college have a significant impact on how students are affected by their college experience.
2. The collegiate years are the period for many individual students when significant developmental changes occur.
3. There are opportunities within the collegiate program for it to have a significant impact on student development.
4. The environmental factors that hold the most promise for affecting student developmental patterns include the peer group, the living unit, the faculty, and the classroom experience.
5. Developmental changes in students are the result of the interaction of initial characteristics and the press of the environment. (pp. 33–35)

In addition to these concepts, three families of theories were considered germane to the foundation of the movement: (1) cognitive theories, describing intellectual and moral development; (2) psychosocial theories, describing personal and life cycle development; and (3) the person-environment interaction theories, explaining the ecology of student life (Miller et al., 1983). From these theory families, three core student development principles emerged: (1) human development is both continuous and cumulative; (2) development is a matter of movement from the simpler to the more complex; and (3) human development tends to be orderly and stage-related (Miller et al., 1983, pp. 13–14). Publication of Brown's monograph in 1972 completed Phase I of the T.H.E. Project. A second group was commissioned by ACPA to complete Phase II: model building. Completed in 1974, their process model for operationalizing student development identified three major steps or functions that should guide future practice: (1) goal setting, (2) assessment, and (3) strategies for student development. Strategies to facilitate student development, or human growth and development, were defined as teaching, consultation, and milieu management.

As discussions continued, by 1976, the concept of student development was understood as "the application of human development concepts in postsecondary settings so that everyone involved can master increasingly complex developmental tasks, achieve self direction, and become interdependent" (Miller & Prince, 1976, p. 3). Student development educators, now the preferred term, perceived everyone on campus as members of the academic community. All individuals were also viewed as collaborators and learners in an institution-wide developmental process of growth. This new educator emphasis was an attempt to locate student affairs professionals within the academic side of the institution. Professional practice strategies were reconceptualized and labeled intentional interventions in students' lives to promote human growth and development. "Intentionality" implied that goal setting had occurred and was a collaborative act with students rather than for students. Student development educators now had the ability to assess developmental levels (psychosocial, cognitive, moral, and so on), to design environments and interventions (experiences or programs), and to help students move through a particular developmental sequence of tasks. In addition, student development educators believed they were capable of facilitating more effective classroom learning by sharing their process ideas and strategies with faculty to improve teaching. On a broader scale, the goal of higher education was to be student development.

The 1987 NASPA Statement

The field's shift to student development was neither smooth nor quick. Depending on an institution's mission and the orientation of its president, student affairs practitioners implemented student personnel work, student development, or some combination of the two during the 1980s. As more students graduated from preparation programs that emphasized student development and professionals attended conferences emphasizing student development themes, discussions about the nature of practice surfaced again. The key issue now was student diversity. Existing theories had not been developed on data gathered from diverse student populations.

As 1987 approached, 50 years of student affairs practice had been recorded. To commemorate the anniversary of the Student Personnel Point of View, NASPA President Chambers in 1986 appointed Art Sandeen as Chair of the Plan for a New Century Committee. The product was "A Perspective on Student Affairs: A Statement Issued at the 50th Anniversary of the Student Personnel Point of View" (1987) and revealed ". . . what the higher education community can expect from student affairs. . ." (Sandeen et al., 1994 p. 635). The document served "as a stimulus for discussion and debate within higher education and student affairs . . . to foster a renewed understanding and appreciation of the contributions student affairs professionals make to institutions of higher education and the students they serve" (Sandeen et al., 1994, p. 636). Identified within its pages are the core assumptions the committee hoped would guide future student affairs practice. These were:

The academic mission of the institution is preeminent; Each student is unique; Each person has worth and dignity; Bigotry cannot be tolerated; Feelings affect thinking and learning; Student involvement enhances learning; Personal circumstances affect learning; and Out-of-class environments affect learning (Sandeen et al., 1994, pp. 635–636). These assumptions are reminiscent of the core values and beliefs described by pioneer student personnel practitioners decades earlier.

Student Development Practice

Because several of the contributing authors to this book are specialists within specific areas of student affairs practice, a thorough discussion of the application of student development theory to practice is not deemed appropriate for this chapter. The reader is encouraged to consult particular pages of interest.

What is significant to note is that during this stage in the evolution of student affairs, practice stressed the assessment of developmental levels as described by theorists such as Chickering and Reisser, Perry, Kohlberg, and subsequent contributions of Helms and Cass, to name a few. The impact on student growth associated with the interaction between the student and the student's environment was not only recognized and confirmed, but also led student development educators to attempt to create positive environments that would provide the requisite ratio of challenge and support. These theories therefore were useful because they allowed practitioners the opportunity to identify specific pathways or road maps of students' movement toward maturity. Student development educators' ability to define specific goals for their programmatic efforts, or intentional interventions, was enhanced by an understanding of these theories. Researchers who developed these theories viewed growth, development, and learning almost synonymously, thus the entire academic community was perceived as one whose goal was the personal growth and development of each of its members.

FOCUS ON STUDENT LEARNING

As with previous movements within student affairs, student development has had its supporters and its critics. An important critique of the movement by Bloland, Stamatakos, and Rogers is contained in the 1994 monograph, *Reform in Student Affairs: A Critique of Student Development:*

> Our argument is not with student development per se. It is rather with our fellow professionals . . . who failed to exercise their critical faculties to raise questions about student development, to slow down the headlong pace of its engulfment of the field of student affairs, and to examine alternatives and options as they presented themselves. (Bloland et al., 1994, p. x)

Essentially, these three seasoned professionals examined, challenged, and highlighted *student development* as a reform movement, the application of its theories, and the problems that were part of the student growth process as an extention to the field of student affairs (Bloland et al., p. xi, 1994). Suggesting a new paradigm, they proposed "the student affairs profession again takes its cue from the central educational mission of higher education and views the learning process as integral to the implementation of that mission" (p. 103). Included among final recommendations were:

1. Cease identifying with the student development model as the wellspring or philosophical underpinning of the field of student affairs. . . .
2. Return to the general principles so cogently expressed in the Student Personnel Point of View (ACPA, 1949), clearly placing academic and intellectual development at the center of the student affairs mission.
3. Re-emphasize the primacy of learning as the cardinal value of higher education and employ learning theory, conjointly with student development theory, as an essential tool for planning experiences and programs that will enhance the learning process.
4. Clearly identify with the institutional educational mission for unless student affairs takes its cue from the mission and goals of higher education, it has no function except the provision of support services; any educational outcomes it may claim are purely accidental. (p. 104)

In 1993, ACPA President Schroeder convened a group of leaders in higher education to consider how student affairs might enhance its role relative to student learning and personal development. Members of The Student Learning Imperative Project included A. Astin, H. Astin, P. Bloland, K. P. Cross, J. Hurst, G. Kull, T. Marchese, E. Nuss, E. Pascarella, A. Pruitt, M. Rooney, and C. Schroeder. Their deliberations produced the document, "The Student Learning Imperative: Implications for Student Affairs . . . , "intended to stimulate discussion and debate on how student affairs professionals can intentionally create the conditions that enhance student learning and personal development" (American College Personnel Association, 1994, p. 1). In addition, project members perceived the present as yet another period of major transformation precipitated in part by the continued increase in diversity in higher education, the eroded public confidence, the effects of accountability being imposed by external constituencies and the new importance attached to positive educational environments. Committee members proposed five characteristics student affairs divisions committed to student learning and personal development should exhibit:

1. The student affairs division mission complements the institution's mission, with the enhancement of student learning and personal development being the primary goal of student affairs programs and services;
2. Resources are allocated to encourage student learning and personal development;
3. Student affairs professionals collaborate with other institutional agents and agencies to promote student learning and personal development;

4. The division of student affairs includes staff who are experts on students, their environments, and teaching and learning processes; and

5. Student affairs policies and programs are based on promising practices from the research on student learning and institution-specific assessment data. (American College Personnel Association, 1994, pp. 2–5)

While many professionals perceived this new emphasis on student learning, which sometimes included the concept of teaching, as a major paradigmatic shift from previous goals and values, others viewed it simply as another evolutionary stage in the dynamic development of student affairs. Certainly, teaching and learning are, and always have been, central to the mission of American higher education. In 1954, Lloyd-Jones and Smith coauthored *Student Personnel Work as Deeper Teaching,* a conceptualization of student personnel as fundamentally educative in nature. Almost 20 years later, Brown issued his call for a "return to the academy" (Brown, 1972). One must wonder about the efficacy of that return to the academy. Being so much inside its walls, student affairs professionals may find themselves looking over their shoulders at students' growth and development in areas other than intellectual. To do so would not be consistent with the core values and beliefs espoused by early pioneer deans and practitioners. In addition, members of the academic side of the institution may well perceive student learning as their prerogative and responsibility. Assuming this, future student affairs practitioners may find themselves realigned with tasks associated with the maintenance of students. The purpose of student affairs as extracurriculum or cocurriculum has been and obviously will continue to be debated into the foreseeable future. Such discussions and reassessments may lead to the ambiguous realm of noncurriculum.

The student affairs profession has been continuously challenged and transformed throughout its history. As we begin the second decade of the new millennium there are new issues faced by those who must balance the traditions of the field with the rapidly changing roles of higher education in our society. Sandeen and Barr (2006) present the following questions for student affairs professional to ponder (p. vii): (1) where should student affairs be placed within the organizational structure of the institution? (2) how should student affairs help students learn about diversity? (3) how can student affairs attract and retain a diverse staff? (4) how do sources of revenue affect student affairs? (5) what is the role of student affairs in non-traditional settings? (6) what is the role of student affairs assessment? (7) who has responsibility for the lives of students? and (8) how should professional associations serve student affairs?

The college and university campus today is extremely complex with administrators in charge of areas such as enrollment management and first-year programs. New institutional policies have been created to manage technological plagiarism and cyber harassment. Today's administrator is closely connected to the president of the institution as well as the parents who are constantly hovering vicariously, via technology, around the campus. This type of access and knowledge about these critical issues facing the profession places administrators in the perfect position, much like the founders of the field, to improve the campus environment for all students. McClellan and Stringer (2009) cogently state that "it will be up to each of us, working in conjunction with our campus communities and other stakeholders, to determine the most appropriate responses to the challenges and opportunities that changes present to us" (p. 624). History has taught us that our profession has withstood many turbulent times because of the will, resolve, and focused determination of our prescient visionaries who have passed an unprecedented legacy to us.

<h1 style="text-align:center">REFERENCES</h1>

American College Personnel Association. (1994). The student learning imperative: Implications for student affairs. Retrieved from http://www.housing.berkeley.edu/student/ACPA_student_learning_imperative.pdf.

American Council on Education. (1994). The Student Personnel Point of View (1937). In A. L. Rentz (Ed.), *Student affairs: A profession's heritage* (pp. 66–78). Lanham, MD: University of America Press.

American Council on Education. (1994). The Student Personnel Point of View (1949). In A. L. Rentz (Ed.), *Student affairs: A profession's heritage* (pp. 108–123). Lanham, MD: University of America Press.

Berdie, R. (1966). Student personnel work: Definition and redefinition. *Journal of College Student Personnel, 7,* 131–136.

Bloland, P., Stamatakos, L. C., & Rogers, R. R. (1994). *Reform in student affairs: A critique of student development.* Greensboro, NC: ERIC Counseling and Student Services Clearinghouse.

Brown, R. D. (1972). Student development in tomorrow's higher education. Student Personnel Series, No. 16. Washington, DC: American Personnel and Guidance Association.

Brown, R. W. (1926). *Dean Briggs.* New York: Harper.

Brubacher, J. S., & Rudy, W. (1958). *Higher education in transition.* New York: Harper & Row.

Brubacher, J. S., & Rudy, W. (1976). *Higher education in transition* (3rd ed.). New York: Harper Collins.

Clothier, R. C. (1931). College personnel principles and functions. In A.L. Rentz (Ed.), *Student affairs: A profession's heritage* (pp. 9–18). Lanham, MD: University of America Press.

Commission of Professional Preparation of COSPA. (1994). Student development services in post secondary education (1975). In A. L. Rentz (Ed.), *Student affairs: A profession's heritage* (pp. 428–437). Lanham, MD: University of America Press.

Cowley, W. H. (1936). The nature of student personnel work. In A. L. Rentz (Ed.), *Student affairs: A profession's heritage* (pp. 43–65). Lanham, MD: University of America Press.

Cowley, W. H. (1937, April). A preface to the principles of student counseling. *The Educational Record, 18*(1), 217–234.

Cowley, W. H. (1949). Some history and a venture in prophecy. In E. G. Williamson (Ed.), *Trends in student personnel work.* Minneapolis, MN: University of Minnesota Press.

Fleming, J. (1984). *Blacks in college.* San Francisco: Jossey-Bass.

Fley, J. (1979). Student personnel pioneers: Those who developed our profession. *National Association of Student Personnel Administrators Journal, 17,* 23–39.

Goodenow, R. K. (1989). Black education. In C. R Wilson & W. Ferris (Eds.), *Encyclopedia of southern culture.* Chapel Hill, NC: University of North Carolina Press.

Hill, S. (1984). The traditionally black institutions of higher education: 1860 to 1982. Washington, DC: U.S. Department of Education.

Holmes, L. (1939). *A history of the position of dean of women in a selected group of co-educational colleges and universities in the United States.* New York: Teachers College, Columbia University.

Humphreys, J. A. (1930). Techniques of college personnel work. In J. E. Walters (Ed.), *College personnel procedures: Proceedings of Purdue-Wabash conference of college personnel officers* (pp. 11–13). Lafayette, IN: Purdue University.

Kirk, B. A. (1965). Identity crisis–1965. *Journal of College Student Personnel, 6,* 194–199.

Knock, G. H. (1985). Development of student services in higher education. In M. J. Barr, L. A. Keating, & Associates, *Developing effective student services programs* (pp. 15–42). San Francisco: Jossey-Bass.

Komives, S. R., & Woodard, D. B. (2003). *Student services: A handbook for the profession* (4th ed.). San Francisco: Jossey Bass.

Lloyd-Jones, E. (1949). The beginnings of our profession. In E. G. Williamson (Ed.), *Student personnel work* (pp. 260–263). Minneapolis, MN: University of Minnesota Press.

Lloyd-Jones, E. (1994). Personnel administration (1934). In A. L. Rentz (Ed.), *Student affairs: A profession's heritage* (pp. 19–26). Lanham, MD: University of America Press.

Lloyd-Jones, E., & Smith, M. R. (1954). *Student personnel as deeper teaching.* New York: Harper.

McClellan, G. S., & Stringer, J. (2009). *The handbook of student affairs administration.* San Francisco: Jossey Bass

Miller, T. K., & Prince, J. S. (1976). *The future of student affairs.* San Francisco: JosseyBass, Inc.

Miller, T. K., Winston, R. B., Jr., & Mendenhall, W. R. (1983). *Administration and leadership in student affairs.* Muncie, IN: Accelerated Developments.

Morison, S. E. (1930). *The development of Harvard University since the inauguration of President Eliot 1869–1929.* (pp. Lxviii–lxix). Cambridge, MA: Harvard University Press.

Mueller, K. H. (1961). *Student personnel work in higher education.* Boston: Houghton Mifflin.

National Advisory Committee on Black Higher Education and Black Colleges and Universities. (1979). Black colleges and universities: An essential component of a diverse system of higher education. Washington, DC: Department of Education.

Ranbom, S., & Lynch, J. (1987, Fall 1988, Winter). Timeline: The long, hard road to educational equity. *Educational Record, 46,* 16–17.

Rentz, A. L. (Ed.). (1994). *Student affairs: A profession's heritage.* Lanham, MD: University Press of America.

Rhatigan, J. J. (2009). From the people up: A brief history of student affairs administration. In G.S. McClellan & J. Stringer (Eds.), *The handbook of student affairs administration* (pp. 3–18). San Francisco: Jossey Bass.

Ricard, R. B., & Brown, M. C. (2008). *Ebony towers in higher education: The evolution, mission, and presidency of historically black colleges and universities.* Sterling, VA: Stylus.

Roebuck, J. B., & Murty, K. S. (1993). *Historically black colleges and universities: Their place in American higher education.* Westport, CT: Praeger.

Rudolph, F. (1990). *The American college and university: A history.* Athens, GA: University of Georgia Press.

Sandeen, A., & Barr, M. J. (2006). *Critical issues for student affairs: Challenges and opportunities.* San Francisco: Jossey Bass.

Sandeen, A., Albright, R. L., Barr, M. J., Golseth, A. E., Kuh, G. D., Lyons, W., & Rhatigan, J. J. (1994). A perspective on student affairs: A statement issued on the fiftieth anniversary of the student personnel point of view (1987). In A. L. Rentz (Ed.), *Student affairs: A profession's heritage* (pp. 635–636). Lanham, MD: University Press of America.

Solomon, B. M. (1985). *In the company of educated women.* New Haven, CT: Yale University Press.

Stock, P. (1978). *Better than rubies: A history of women's education.* New York: G. P. Putnam's Sons.

Thelin, J. R. (2004). *A history of higher education.* Baltimore, MD: Johns Hopkins University Press.

Thomas, G. E., & Hirsch, D. J. (1987). Black institutions in U.S. higher education: Present roles, contributions, future projections. *Journal of College Student Personnel, 27,* 496–503.

Thomas, G. E., & Hirsch, D. J. (1989). Blacks. In A. Levine (Ed.), *Blacks in higher education: Overcoming the odds.* Lanham, MD: University Press of America.

Williamson, E. G. (1949). *Trends in student personnel work.* Minneapolis, MN: University of Minnesota Press.

Chapter 3

FROM ADMISSIONS TO ENROLLMENT MANAGEMENT

DON HOSSLER

The admissions office is usually the point of first contact between prospective students and the student affairs division as well as the entire campus. Both the 1937 *Student Personnel Point of View* and its 1949 revision place the function of the admissions office within the purview of student affairs (American Council on Education, 1937, 1949). On many campuses, however, admissions offices are not even part of student affairs divisions but rather are housed in divisions of academic affairs or institutional advancement. An increasingly common organizational structure locates admissions offices within separate enrollment management organizations.

The concerns of student affairs divisions should involve all aspects of students' college experience—from the point of initial contact to the point of graduation. The trend in recent years to separate admissions offices from student affairs divisions is part of the warrant for this chapter, which examines the development of the field of admissions and traces admissions into the emerging concept of enrollment management. Whereas the admissions function has primarily been to attract and admit college students, enrollment management is concerned with the entirety of the students' college experience. The first part of this chapter defines admissions work and presents a history of the admissions field. The second part of the chapter defines enrollment management and explores this organizational concept.

ADMISSIONS–THEN AND NOW

The Roles of Admissions Officers

Swann (1998) identified the following admissions officer roles:

1. Processing applications and credentials;
2. Analyzing the processing and reporting analysis to internal and external parties;
3. Distributing admissions, scholarship, and financial aid materials to the constituent schools and prospect lists and presenting program sessions about the institutions at those feeder schools;
4. Conducting preview programs and tours at the institution; and
5. Counseling visitors to appropriate referral resources within the institution (advisors and student personnel sources such as housing, financial aid, and testing. (p. 35)

The purpose of the admissions process is to help students make a successful transition from high school to college as well as to recruit students for specific colleges and universities (Swann & Henderson, 1998). Thus, it is important for admissions officers to understand the needs of traditional and nontraditional college students and to know their institution. In this way, an institution's admission officer can help students make the best possible college choice decision while at the same time recruiting students well suited to that institution. Like most functions in student affairs divisions, the admissions function has a long history in American higher education. Its formal history, however, is relatively short.

The Admissions Officer as Gatekeeper or Salesperson

The history of the admissions field in American colleges and universities is difficult to unravel because our understanding of it has been shaped by two competing images of the admissions officer. One image is of an Ivy League admissions officer who, along with a faculty admissions committee, decides who will be invited to "join the club" with a coveted offer of admission on "Bloody Monday."[1] The other image is of a salesperson trying to attract prospective students to a college or university so that its budget will be balanced, its doors will remain open, and its faculty will be happy. The history of the admissions function using one image of the admissions officer would

---

1. This is the term used for the Monday in April when all highly selective colleges send notices of acceptance or rejection to new student applicants.

look quite different from the history using the other image. Thelin (1982) has described these two contrasting images of the admissions officer as "the gate-keeper" and "the headhunter." Both images, actually, are accurate for various time periods in American higher education as well as for different types of institutions of higher education.

The role of the office of admissions in early American colleges can be traced to that of the medieval university's "major beadle" (Smerling, 1960), succeeded by the university archivist (Lindsay & Holland, 1930), and later the registrar. The role of faculty members or administrators in these positions was to track the progress of enrolled students and to determine whether prospective students, or new applicants, had the right background for admission to the institution. For the early American college, the right background frequently meant the student had a modicum of proficiency in the English language and was of good moral character. At more selective institutions of the time, students were expected to have some knowledge of Latin and Greek (Broome, 1903; Rudolph, 1962). In any case, most colleges in early America had preparatory schools attached to them so that students who did not meet the admissions requirements could acquire the necessary skills for admission (Brubacher & Rudy, 1997; Rudolph, 1962).

Not all colleges, however, could just passively wait for students to arrive for their admissions test. The American Dream included equal access to education and upward mobility. During the nineteenth century's westward expansion, every town aspired to greatness. The presence of a college in a town was viewed as a clear signal to current and prospective residents that the town was becoming a major center and a good place to live. As a result, colleges were created at a rapid rate. In the early 1870s, for example, England had four universities for a population of 23,000,000, while the state of Ohio had 37 colleges for a population of 3,000,000 (Rudolph, 1962). Many of these colleges consisted of one to three faculty members and probably did not even have a building. Frequently, the education offered by these institutions was at the preparatory level.

In these institutions, however, we find the forerunner of the other image of the admissions officer: the salesperson. The faculties and staffs at most early American colleges were small, frequently consisting of the president and just one or two additional faculty members. The president taught classes as well as performing all of the roles now associated with positions such as the chief fundraiser, the academic dean, the dean of students, and the registrar. Rudolph's (1962) history of American higher education is replete with stories of college presidents traveling through the countryside trying to attract the sons (and it was only sons during most of the eighteenth and nineteenth centuries) of farmers and the emerging merchant class. There simply were not enough potential college students to support the large number and variety of colleges that had been established in the United States. As a result, many institutions of higher education had to be creative in devising new ways to attract students.

Nowadays, new entrants in the college student affairs field view marketing efforts and financial aid strategies–like telemarketing, prepaid tuition plans, or guaranteed cost plans–as new ideas that have emerged because of rising college costs and competition for students. Yet, many early American colleges also had to devise creative marketing and recruitment strategies. In the mid-1800s, several colleges sold advance tuition payments to acquire revenues that they planned to invest in endowments so as to offset future instructional costs as well as to provide immediate support for faculty and instruction. Unfortunately, these early colleges could not afford to invest the money and had to spend the money on current needs. When the new prepaid students arrived the money was gone and in some cases the colleges were also gone, having been forced into bankruptcy. The surviving institutions, like Dickinson and DePauw, lost large amounts of money–up to more than two dollars for each dollar raised (Rudolph, 1962).

Even the mass-marketing techniques of today are not entirely new. In 1893, one state university had sufficient funds and political clout to send out brochures to every school superintendent in the state describing the virtues of attending the institution. Superintendents throughout the state were fined $50 if the university brochures were not posted in their high schools (Thelin, 1982). The entrepreneurial activities of these struggling colleges to attract students are part of the history of the salesperson image of the admissions field. Although the first dean of admissions was not appointed until the early part of the twentieth century, the need was certainly there for a guiding professional.

The Emergence of the Admissions Field

The tension between the images of the gatekeeper and the salesperson continued into the twentieth century even as the professional admissions field began to emerge. Prior to the actual appointment of the first deans of admissions in the 1920s, two important trends emerged that would shape the role of the admissions officer. By the end of the nineteenth century, many colleges and universities had become concerned about the lack of standardization in the preparation of high school students. Institutions of higher learning could make few assumptions about the skills and academic training of college applicants.

In response to this problem, in 1870, the University of Michigan sent teams of faculty out to visit high schools to improve the level of instruction and articulation between colleges and high schools. Other states followed suit, and in 1894, the North Central Association Commission on Accreditation and School Improvement was formed to standardize high school curricula. Although the University of Michigan was the first university to employ this process, the precedent for regional associations had already been set in 1885 with the creation of the New England Association of Schools and Colleges (Brubacher & Rudy, 1997).

Along with the creation of associations to improve education at the high school level, standardized testing also emerged as a way to improve high school education and to standardize the "chaotic entrance requirements" employed by colleges and universities (Brubacher & Rudy, 1997). The Regents exam (created in 1878) was the first such effort. In the 1890s, a meeting of the Association of the Colleges and Secondary Schools of the Middle States and Maryland led to the establishment of the College Entrance Examination Board, later renamed the College Board. With the creation of standardized tests by the College Entrance Examination Board, many colleges and universities slowly abandoned their own entrance exams and came to rely on one standardized test.

The emergence of the accreditation associations and standardized testing had an important impact on the admissions function. It was now easier to determine who was prepared for college (although the criteria for admissions varied), and it was also easier to compare the quality of entering students. Standardization forever changed the dialogue on institutional quality and prestige and formalized the tension between the role of the gatekeeper and that of the salesperson. Now admissions officers could use objective criteria to compare not only the number of students enrolled but also the quality of those students enrolled.

The use of objective criteria in admissions practice did not become widespread until the 1930s even though the first deans of admission were hired in the 1920s. It was during the 1930s that the concept of selective admissions was formally articulated (Thresher, 1966). The concept of selective admissions helped to further entrench the concept of institutional prestige based on selectivity. However, the emergence of elite, highly selective institutions such as Harvard, Yale, and Stanford is still a relatively recent phenomenon.

The onset of the Great Depression led to a downturn in college applicants. As a result, the 1930s was an era of the salesperson—not the gatekeeper. The subsequent entry of the United States into World War II also depressed college applications, and it was not until the end of the war that the gatekeeper function reemerged.

With the large numbers of veterans (GIs) returning to college after World War II and the subsequent rise in enrollments because of the baby boom generation, the 1960s and 1970s are often referred to as the "Golden Age" of American higher education (Jencks & Reisman, 1969). During this time, even some admissions officers at many well-known but less prestigious private colleges and universities as well as many public institutions were able to function as gatekeepers. Nevertheless, it would be a mistake to think of this as having been an era of gatekeeping for all admissions officers. The rapid growth of public four-year and two-year colleges had a major impact on admissions officers at smaller and lesser-known private institutions. As a result, many private colleges and universities had to actively market themselves and recruit students to maintain enrollments (Thresher, 1966).

The Admissions Officer Today

By the beginning of the 1970s, colleges and universities were preparing for a predicted decrease of traditional-age college students estimated to be as high as 42 percent before the end of the twentieth century (Hossler, 1986). Institutions began to implement for-profit business techniques to maintain or increase student enrollments as college administrators shifted from the "bullish" student enrollment market of the 1950s and 1960s to the "bear" market of the 1980s and 1990s. These developments set the stage for the emergence of the admissions officer of today and for the concept of enrollment management.

While continuing to function primarily as salespersons at nonselective institutions, admissions officers have in many cases become hybrids of both the gatekeeper and the salesperson. Even at the most selective institutions, where gatekeeping continues to play an important role, admissions officers have also had to become salespersons to attract a sufficient number of high ability students with the other attributes desired by prestigious colleges and universities, such as geographic representation, minority representation and talents in areas like music, leadership, and athletics.

Starting in the 1970s, admissions offices began to use marketing techniques such as improved publication materials, targeted mailing strategies, and tele-marketing techniques to attract larger numbers of students. At the same time, senior-level administrators began to utilize strategic planning techniques also borrowed from business. Strategic planning incorporates market research so that organizations can better understand their clients and the institution's position in relation to competitors. This push toward marketing laid the foundation for the development of enrollment management, discussed later in this chapter.

To track and communicate with prospective students, admissions officers are now using marketing techniques like targeted mailings, telemarketing, electronic communications, and Internet formats that require admissions officers to analyze students' backgrounds and attitudes to identify the best potential markets. Personalized communication techniques, in both print and electronic media, are also hallmarks of modern marketing. These developments have required admissions officers to become more analytical than before as well as more skilled in computer technologies. For admissions officers serving as salespersons, the adoption of these techniques and skills has become essential for institutional well-being.

The 1990s and the first decade of the twenty-first century have seen greater emphasis among admissions officers on pricing and student financial aid as well as on sophisticated marketing techniques. Whereas 10 years ago new marketing techniques such as direct mail and telemarketing were thought to be key to successful student recruitment, many admissions directors now believe that newly developed enrollment modeling approaches to setting tuition costs and to awarding financial aid are the most important elements of successful new student recruitment. Pricing and student aid may have arguably become the most important and one of the most controversial parts of student recruitment. Many admissions directors report they now spend more time with vice presidents of business on financial aid issues than on any other aspect of their job.

The emergence of the modern admissions office, with its emphasis on marketing, electronic technology, pricing, and student financial aid, has separated admissions officers from other student affairs areas that have strong counseling or student development orientations. As a result, many professionals in the field of admissions do not think of themselves as student affairs personnel (Hossler, 1986; Hossler, 2007). However, as will be seen in the next section of this chapter, while admissions and student affairs staff have become part of enrollment management efforts, the connections between admissions and student affairs work is once again becoming apparent.

ENROLLMENT MANAGEMENT–ORIGINS AND IDEAS

The Changing Admissions Context

With the predicted declines in the numbers of traditional-age college students, college and university administrators became interested in student retention as well as student recruitment. Student attrition was a frequent topic of inquiry during the late 1970s and 1980s, and research in this area has continued (Bean, 1980; Braxton, 2000; Noel, Levitz, & Saluri, & Associates, 1985; Pascarella & Terenzini, 2005; Tinto, 1993). Student affairs administrators often found themselves assigned the responsibility for developing institutional retention programs. In addition to this line of retention research, a growing body of research has emerged on the topics of student college choice that demonstrates the impact of financial aid on recruitment and retention (Brooks, 1996; Hossler, Braxton, & Coopersmith, 1989; Hossler, Schmit, & Vesper, 1998; McDonough, Antonio, Walpole, & Perez, 1998; Paulsen, 1990; Scannell, 1992; St. John, Paulsen, & Starkey, 1996).

The converging interests in attracting and retaining new students provided the impetus for the emergence of the enrollment management concept. On some campuses, student affairs divisions began to play key roles in enrollment management activities. Yet, while enrollment management has provided an integrating framework for institutional efforts to more directly influence student enrollments than previously, enrollment management as a formal concept is relatively new and has little history to document.

A number of conceptual frameworks have been suggested as the organizational basis for student affairs divisions (McClellan & Stringer, 2009), and enrollment management can be viewed as one more such framework. To help familiarize student affairs professionals with the conceptual framework of enrollment management, the second part of this chapter sets out to accomplish the following:

1. Define enrollment management.
2. Examine the evolution of enrollment management.
3. Discuss enrollment management as a concept.
4. Examine enrollment management as a process.
5. Consider organizational enrollment management models.
6. Explore the role of student affairs in enrollment management.
7. Discuss ethical issues related to enrollment management.
8. Consider the professional preparation needs of enrollment managers and the future of enrollment management.

Defining Enrollment Management

On many campuses the term *enrollment management* has acquired potency as denoting a systematic institutional response to issues related to student enrollments. Yet for student affairs professionals to utilize the enrollment management concept they must first understand it well. Enrollment management has become associated at most institutions with a diverse set of efforts by colleges and universities to exert more control over the characteristics or the size of their enrolled student body. In this scenario, the images of the gatekeeper and the salesperson are still relevant. Within the enrollment management perspective, however, institutions are concerned not only about the characteristics and total number of new students but also about the characteristics and total number of all enrolled students.

Enrollment management has been defined in a number of ways, but in each definition students are the fundamental unit of analysis. Enrollment management is not just an organizing concept—it is a process that involves the entire campus.

> Enrollment management is both an organizational concept as well as a systematic set of activities designed to enable educational institutions to exert more influence over their student enrollments and total net tuition revenue derived from enrolled students. Organized by strategic planning and supported by institutional research, enrollment management activities concern student college choice, transition to college, student attrition and retention, and student outcomes. These processes are studied to guide institutional practices in the areas of new student recruitment and financial aid, student support services, curriculum development and other academic areas that affect enrollments, student persistence, and student outcomes from college. (Revised in 2001 from Hossler, Bean, & Associates, 1990)

The evolution of this new concept can now be examined with this definition of enrollment management in mind. Later in this chapter, process elements of an enrollment management system are examined, followed by a discussion of organizational models. These sections further enhance our understanding of enrollment management.

The Evolution of Enrollment Management

Although the term and perhaps the concept of a comprehensive enrollment management system first emerged in 1976, enrollment management as a process had been developing for many years prior to that. An examination of the evolution of admissions and financial aid offices along with other areas of student affairs, nonprofit marketing in higher education, and research on student college choice and student persistence demonstrates that the enrollment management concept represented the convergence of developments in each of these areas. This convergence made it possible to productively analyze the complex and comprehensive nature of the competitive college admissions process.

It is difficult to determine whether the competitive nature of college admissions in recent decades caused the advances in marketing techniques for higher education or whether the emergence of nonprofit marketing made possible the increasing sophistication of collegiate recruitment activities. It is equally difficult to determine whether the emergence of differentiated financial aid and pricing activities were the products of competition for students or if research on student college choice and the effects of aid and price on college choice have resulted in up-to-date, effective aid and pricing policies. Additionally, research on student attrition, the impact of college on students, and institutional retention programs that are often tailored to meet the needs of specific student populations such as nontraditional adult students, transfer students, or minority students has helped to advance the research base that informs enrollment management efforts.

While determining the precise genesis of the enrollment management concept is difficult, it is clear that the declining numbers of traditional-age students along with the overbuilding of colleges and universities to accommodate veterans and baby boomers created a set of internal and external constraints that required college administrators to be more attentive to student enrollments. The emergence of the concept of enrollment management has, thus, been tied to environmental pressures to which institutions of higher education have been forced to respond.

When it first appeared, what made the enrollment management concept new was not the development of new marketing techniques or new retention strategies. Rather, it was the organizational integration of functions like academic advising, admissions, financial aid, and orientation into a comprehensive institutional approach designed to enable college and university administrators to exert influence over the factors that shape enrollments.

Research and scholarship in applied fields frequently lag behind new developments in these fields. Scholars and educational observers sometimes find themselves in the position of following institutional trends by describing emerging developments, thus formalizing them. In 1976, Maguire used the term *enrollment management* to describe his efforts to attract and retain students at Boston College. One of the first times the term appeared in the professional literature was in a *College Board Review* article by Kreutner and Godfrey (1981) that described a matrix approach to managing enrollments developed at California State University at Long Beach. Since these early publications, a spate of books, book chapters, monographs, and articles have been published on the topic of enrollment management.

The concept and process of enrollment management continue to evolve. As institutions' enrollment management systems mature, they maintain their focus on marketing and recruitment while giving more attention to student retention, student learning, and college rankings (Black, 2001). Undoubtedly, enrollment management systems will continue to change and develop in response to the needs of individual institutions.

ENROLLMENT MANAGEMENT–THE CONCEPT

Although definitions and a sense of the history of enrollment management provide some perspective, they do not provide a sufficient understanding of enrollment management. Hossler and Hoezee (2001) suggested that continuous, long-term success in the field of enrollment management rests on the following theories and concepts:

1. Resource dependency theory,
2. Systems theory,
3. Revenue theory and revenue maximization,
4. Enrollment management as courtship, and
5. Students as institutional image and prestige.

Resource Dependency Theory

No theoretical construct provides a better understanding of the emergence of the field of enrollment management or a better focal point for enrollment managers than resource dependency theory. Through the lens of resource dependency theory, enrollment managers are able to understand how colleges and universities respond to the demographic, budgetary, competitive, and public policy changes taking place around them (Pfeffer & Salancik, 1978; Tolbert, 1985). Pfeffer and Salancik (1978) note that resource dependency theory is a means for analyzing the relationships between organizations and the external environment in which they operate. Because they are not self-sufficient, most organizations are heavily dependent on the external environment for the resources for their continuing survival. For-profit organizations operate under some constraints, but they can try developing new markets and new sources of support as they see fit. Nonprofit organizations, operating under different constraints, have less geographic mobility, less control over their product, and a difficult external environment because of their distinctive role in society (Clark, 1983).

Because there is uncertainty in the environments of universities and colleges, institutions seek to acquire additional resources by structuring their relationships to establish unique connections with the external environment. Resource dependency theory helps enrollment managers to continually ask, "What are the scarce resources for my campus associated with student enrollments?" These scarce resources include (1) the number of students enrolled, (2) the total net revenue generated by the number of students enrolled, (3) the diversity of enrolled students, and (4) the academic characteristics of the students enrolled (Hossler & Hoezee, 2001).

Systems Theory

For enrollment managers, an important feature of systems theory is its explanation of closed and open systems of organizations. Organizations with closed systems focus inwardly and are primarily concerned with what happens within their unit. Organizations with open systems, in contrast, have a constant interchange between the organization or units within the organization and the external environment.

Levels of collegiality and informality which are other features that vary across organizations also distinguish institutions of higher education. While open, decentralized characteristics can minimize an institution's closed-system tendencies, these same characteristics can foster independence in administrative units that can create opportunities for closed system thinking within the individual units. Senge (2006) observed that successful modern organizations require open systems and high levels of communication among units throughout the organization. To effectively influence student enrollments, enrollment managers and their unit members must recognize their interdependence and frequently share information, goals, and strategies.

A complex array of factors influence the success of enrollment management efforts: the institution's mission, types of majors, relative emphases on teaching and research, location, tuition and financial aid policies, student-faculty ratio, student body demographic profile, selectivity in admissions, quality of student life, and student recruitment and retention programs—as well as state and federal policies and the condition of the economy. Therefore, enrollment managers must approach their task from an open systems perspective. Because enrollment management involves many organizational units on campus, it requires high degrees of collaboration and *interdependence*. An open systems approach with high levels of communication is fundamental to this profession.

Revenue Theory

The increasingly common practice of providing campus-based financial aid to help recruit and retain students has accentuated and made visible the role of enrollment management in providing revenue to run colleges and universities. In his classic book, *The Costs of Higher Education,* Bowen (1980) puts forth a revenue theory that is just as practical today as it was nearly three decades ago and that along with current work in revenue maximization provides one of the key conceptual underpinnings for enrollment management.

Bowen observed that without the profit motive of for-profit businesses, institutions spend as much money as is available to achieve their goals. Thus, costs follow revenues—an idea counter to some budgeting practices. Bowen's "rules of thumb" are the following:

1. The dominant goals of institutions are educational excellence, prestige, and influence.
2. In quest of excellence, prestige, and influence, there is virtually no limit to the amount of money an institution could spend for seemingly fruit-

ful educational ends.

3. Each institution raises all the money it can.
4. Each institution spends all the money it raises.
5. The cumulative effect of the preceding four rules is toward ever-increasing expenditures.

It is beyond the scope of this chapter to discuss Bowen's laws in detail, but the primary emphasis of his revenue theory of higher education bears repeating: The goal of an institution of higher education is to use all resources available to maintain and preferably to enhance the institution's prestige and influence. This goal should not be lost on enrollment managers. At most institutions the efforts of enrollment managers *can never do enough* to help their institution achieve this goal. If enrollments have increased, then the focus will shift to quality or to diversity so the campus can further enhance its perceived excellence. If enrollment demand curves look solid, efforts are likely to emerge to reduce campus-based financial aid to increase net tuition revenue—which in turn frees up more funds for laboratories, library holdings, and faculty salaries. For enrollment managers, Bowen's observations are simultaneously normative, descriptive, strategic, and frustrating: No matter how successful enrollment management efforts have been, they are never enough. Given the use of campus-based financial aid to help achieve enrollment goals, revenue theory leads naturally to its companion concept—revenue maximization.

Revenue Maximization

As in all organizations with operating expenses, maximizing revenue, minimizing costs, and substituting inputs while monitoring the quality of the output and opportunity costs are common among the administrative practices at colleges and universities. Like all budget administrators, enrollment managers have three options for generating more funds for their organizations: (1) growing more dollars, (2) maximizing the return from a budgeted dollar, and (3) minimizing costs. Growing dollars can be quite difficult. To maximize dollars strategy sessions that bring together relevant administrators from offices ranging from admissions, financial aid, marketing, and orientation are a common way to maximize dollars by reviewing the returns on investment for every dollar spent. For example, some institutions find that simple, inexpensive, black-and-white brochures and reply cards to prospective students are nearly as effective as more costly full-color brochures and reply cards.

Another way for enrollment managers to enhance resources has been found in the practice of tuition discounting. Conceptual leads for this practice can be found in Robert Cross's book, *Revenue Management* (1997). Cross was an early pioneer in financial strategy in the airline industry. Instead of charging a flat fee for each seat on an airplane, variable costs were made available, largely based on the time of the purchase decision. The rationale behind this strategy is related to fixed, variable, and marginal costs-ideas that are the foundation for tuition discounting.

In his examination of the cost structure of operating a college, Breneman (1994), an economist and a former president of a small college, understood clearly that overhead and salaries were fixed costs and represented a sizable portion of the operating budget. He also knew that some classrooms were filled to capacity and others had empty chairs. In this context, institutions may provide some students (who exhibit certain characteristics of value to the institution) a financial aid award-basically a discount-to encourage their conversion from admitted to enrolled students. More recently, Bontrager and Brown (2008) present a detailed overview of the strategic use of financial aid and how it can be linked to institutional financial plans. They demonstrate how tuition discounting can be used for a range of purposes-from enhancing institutional prestige to improving access for low-income students to increasing institutional net tuition revenue. Like revenue theory, revenue maximization is one of the major foundations of current enrollment management practices.

Enrollment Management as Courtship

Recruitment and retention efforts are likely to be successful if they are conceptualized in the following ways: How can we convey to prospective students-or to current students-that this campus would be a good fit for them? How can we encourage students to spend more time with us? Hossler and a number of his colleagues have proposed that recruitment and retention activities along with many other aspects of the enrollment management process have an apt metaphor in courtship (Abrahamson & Hossler, 1990; Hayek & Hossler, 1999; Hossler, 2000; Hossler, Schmit, & Vesper, 1998). Hayek and Hossler (1999) elaborated on this concept, noting that the best way to convey a sense of courtship in interactions with prospective students is to continually increase the degree of personalization and timeliness-and that personalization and timeliness might indeed be the essential attributes of both successful courtship and successful recruitment. When applied to students who frequently reevaluate their decision to attend the college where they are enrolled, the courtship strategy for retention is productive and transparent.

Although no institution of postsecondary education can compromise its academic standards just to court students, given the importance of student life, student services, and out-of-class contact with faculty, a welcoming and personalized style of exchanges with enrolled students can enhance student persistence. These elements of courtship–timeliness and personalization–provide a clear conceptual road map to help guide the recruitment and retention efforts of enrollment managers.

Rankings and Students as Institutional Image and Prestige

The visibility and impact of college rankings and ratings have steadily increased in the past two decades and, unfortunately, are likely to become not less but greater in the years ahead. While most enrollment managers are not fond of rankings, they are aware that their impact on students, parents, college presidents, boards of trustees, and faculty governance groups is greater than ever and unlikely to diminish.

Although most enrollment managers and other campus administrators know they can ill afford to ignore rankings publications, many college administrators and faculty fail to realize the extent to which it is students who define their colleges and universities for many internal and external audiences. Descriptors such as *small, large, selective, nonselective, diverse, prestigious, national,* or *regional* describe not only the institution but also the enrolled student body, their high school class ranks or test scores, their national or local recruitment, and so forth. An effective enrollment management system constantly monitors the institution's image in the enrolled student body as well as its image in published rankings to determine how these images are affecting recruitment and retention efforts.

ENROLLMENT MANAGEMENT–THE PROCESS

To develop a comprehensive enrollment management system, a diverse set of functions and activities must be formally or informally linked. Functional areas that must be linked range from admissions, financial aid, career planning and placement, to new student orientation. Equally important are activities such as student outcomes assessments and retention efforts that must be linked to policy decisions in areas such as admissions, financial aid, or curriculum.

Planning and Research

The enrollment management process begins with institutional planning, and institutional planning begins with a discussion of the institutional mission statement. Most authors on strategic planning call next for an objective assessment of the external and internal environment (Bryson, 2004), including external social trends, such as reductions in state and federal student financial aid or increasing numbers of adults enrolling in higher education; and internal strengths and weaknesses, such as the need for new campus buildings, the skill gaps of some administrators, or the lack of an academic major favored by high school graduates. Following this environmental assessment, planning involves the development of goals and objectives taking into consideration the institution's mission, its internal strengths and weaknesses, and its external environment.

A planning process such as the one outlined in this chapter cannot be undertaken without institutional research and evaluation. Not all campuses can afford a full-time institutional research office, but even small campuses should have a faculty member or an administrator who conducts institutional research projects. Information provided by institutional research guides the planning process and establishes a context for policy decisions in areas ranging from admissions to student activities.

Attracting Applicants and Matriculants

To attract applicants likely to matriculate, an effective enrollment management program requires the cooperation of several campus offices. Marketing and recruitment units are typically located in the admissions office. However, institutional research efforts provide needed information about student characteristics that help the admissions office determine what types of students are most likely to be interested in coming to the campus. Marketing research can also provide insights into the type of information in which students and parents will be most interested. Tuition levels, or the "sticker price," and targeted financial aid packages play an important role in determining whether a student will apply for admissions to an institution and will matriculate (Hossler & Hoezee, 2001). Indeed, financial aid directors have become key actors in all enrollment management efforts. The financial aid and admissions offices should coordinate financial aid awards with other courtship activities to attract the quality and number of students the institution is seeking. The admissions and financial aid offices represent the admissions management subsystem of an enrollment management system.

Influencing the Collegiate Experience

In an enrollment management system, once students arrive on campus their collegiate experiences become the focus of attention. The comprehensiveness of enrollment management systems means these systems are concerned with the students' experiences during their entire tenure at the institution. Successful integration into the campus environment has a positive impact on students' satisfaction and persistence.

The admissions officers in an enrollment management system are just as concerned about the matriculated students' subsequent success at the institution as they are about the number of students they recruit. Hossler, Bean, and Associates (1990), for example, suggested that admissions officers be evaluated on the basis of how many matriculates persist rather than on the number of students they recruit. An enrollment management system encourages student affairs officers to create a campus environment that will retain as well as attract students. The work of Kuh and his colleagues in student engagement in college has demonstrated the importance of the college experience in both in-class and out-of-class learning (Kuh, Kinzie, Schuh, & Whitt, 2005; Kuh, Schuh, Whitt, & Associates, 1991). Pascarella and Terenzini (2005) provided evidence that formal and informal faculty contact has a positive impact on student satisfaction and perceptions of the college environment, demonstrating that both faculty and administrators have central roles in an enrollment management system.

Orientation and Enrollment Management

An effective and comprehensive orientation helps students at the point of transition into the college experience to adjust to the intellectual norms, social norms, and physical features of the campus. Orientation programs are a key part of an enrollment management system. Pascarella (1986) recommends viewing orientation as an opportunity for new students' "anticipatory socialization" and the creation of new student expectations closely approximating the campus environment and norms. With such orientation experiences, students are likely to find meaning and satisfaction in their collegiate environment (Hossler, Bean, & Associates, 1990). Patton, Morelon, Whitehead, and Hossler (2006), however, find that the extant research on retention interventions and other transition programs points intended to enhance student persistence to be of uneven quality or at least the empirical evidence of their efficacy is scant

Academic Advising and Enrollment Management

Many new college students have their first advising session during orientation. Faculty involvement in these extended orientation and advising programs, or in small freshman seminars, can encourage student-faculty interaction. Several campuses have begun to take advantage of the linkages between orientation and advising to develop extended orientation and advising programs. "University 101," an orientation and advising course offered at the

University of South Carolina, is an example of an approach linking advising and orientation (Upcraft, Gardner, & Barefoot, 2004).

Course Placement and Enrollment Management

The diversity among college students today has resulted in wide variation in student interests, experiences, and skills. This is especially true of two-year colleges and open-admission four-year institutions, where some matriculants enter with minimal academic skills while others are eligible for honors programs. These multiple factors have increased the importance of academic advising and course placement. An enrollment management system should include academic assessment tests to facilitate appropriate course placement. Helping students to select the courses that will challenge them but not overwhelm them is a function of orientation and advising during the critical first year. Students who do not fare well academically are less likely to persist.

Student Retention and Enrollment Management

Many colleges and universities assign retention activities to a committee which too often ensures that retention will not receive adequate attention. As committee assignments change and new members rotate on and off the committee, it is difficult to develop a coherent, coordinated set of activities. Within the enrollment management perspective, retention is usually not the direct responsibility of one office–unlike functional areas like admissions or orientation–but, rather, it cuts across many of the institution's functional areas and divisions. As part of an enrollment management plan, precisely because so many organizational variables can affect student attrition, only one administrative office should oversee student retention programming and research, just as admissions or student activities are the assigned task of identifiable administrators. The critically important role of student retention in maintaining enrollments requires that this be the responsibility of one specific office and that an administrator be assigned to coordinate retention data collection, analysis, as well as making sure that programs are planned, implemented, and evaluated in a coherent, coordinated manner.

While the retention officer is an integral element of the enrollment management system, no individual should be held personally accountable for attrition rates, as the issue is too complex for one office or officer to "control." Nevertheless, creating an administrative office to monitor student attrition and develop retention programs ensures that the institution will continue to address student persistence.

Academic Support Services and Enrollment Management

Many colleges continue to admit underprepared students. To help these students succeed, campuses have established academic support offices offering a wide range of services including study skills workshops, reading assistance, writing labs, test-taking workshops, and tutoring in specific subject areas. In their review of published evaluations of successful retention programs, Patton and her colleagues (2006) found that academic support programs have a positive impact on student persistence. Academic support professionals are part of the enrollment management staff.

Because the admissions office can identify underprepared students during the admissions process, it is in the best position to inform the academic support office of these students' academic needs. Academic support offices monitoring the academic success of students are in a unique position to provide continual feedback to the admissions office regarding student academic success. If few underprepared students eventually succeed, the institution may not be spending recruiting and financial aid dollars wisely or it may not be providing adequate academic support services.

Career Services and Enrollment Management

A significant part of college experience is career preparation. Students are very aware of the competitive nature of the job market, and career concerns have become one of the most important considerations for college students from the time they select an institution until the time they graduate. Institutions perceived as helping to place their graduates in good jobs after graduation will be in a position not only to attract new students but also to retain current students. Part of the job turnover model of student attrition developed by Bean (1980; 1983) posits that the deemed practical value of a college degree, i.e., the likelihood of getting a desirable job after graduation, has a positive effect on student persistence. In an enrollment management system, an effective career planning and placement office helps students to establish linkages between their academic and vocational goals and to secure desirable positions after graduation.

Other Roles of Student Affairs in Enrollment Management

Enhancing the quality of student campus life facilitates recruitment and retention and supports the enrollment management mission. Career services, academic support, and orientation are among an array of student services found on most campuses, usually in the student affairs division. Depending on the type of institution and campus, intramural and intercollegiate athletics, residence life, and Greek affairs can greatly enhance the quality of life on campus.

Student participation in intramurals, student government, or Greek affairs may also enhance student development and student persistence. Upcraft et al. (2004), Kuh and his colleagues (1991, 2005), and Pace (1991) assert that student involvement in cocurricular and extracurricular activities plays an important role in determining the range and quality of student outcomes as well as in influencing student persistence. The goals of facilitating student development and managing student enrollments may not be in conflict but instead may be mutually reinforcing goals in some areas of student life. Using the theory of student involvement as a conceptual basis, through careful planning and evaluation student affairs officers can develop programs that encourage student involvement, enhance student development, and increase student persistence.

The Faculty Role in Enrollment Management

The role of faculty in the enrollment management system is undeniably important, and it is a mistake for any enrollment manager to overlook it. Faculty quality and reputation, for example, are important factors in where students decide to go to college (Hayek & Hossler, 1999; Hossler, Schmit, & Vesper, 1998). Speaking directly to the issue of faculty quality is complicated and risky for administrators, however. At best, they are likely to be disregarded, and at worst they will alienate the faculty and reduce their own effectiveness with them. Faculty should, nevertheless, be aware—or be made aware—of the impact they have on student enrollments.

In the areas of marketing and student recruitment, the institution's academic image and available majors may determine where students decide to go to college. With an institutional lens from marketing research, faculty can see how prospective students perceive them. Faculty may discover, for example, that prospective students' negative image of certain academic programs discourages them from enrolling. Information such as this can be the impetus for academic program changes that would be difficult for administrators to require.

Student-faculty interaction has a significant impact on student outcomes and student persistence. Enrollment managers should play an educative role with the faculty in this area. On many campuses, faculty already understands the connection between enrollments and institutional health. On these campuses, acquainting faculty with research establishing the impact of faculty on students and the role of academic programs in college choice is likely to increase receptiveness to enrollment management activities. Many commuter institutions as well as research universities, however, do not have a strong tradition of faculty involvement with students. Faculty who are not concerned about student enrollments will be difficult to convince to seek out opportunities for student-faculty interaction, yet students at these institutions can surely benefit from greater contact with faculty.

Enrollment management begins with planning and research. Marketing and recruitment of students follow. The student collegiate experience has an impact on student retention and graduation. A comprehensive enrollment management plan does not stop with graduation, but rather strengthens its cyclical capacities with a broad perspective. Student outcomes studies including regular assessments of alumni experiences and attitudes can provide institutions with useful information. The enrollment management systems perspective provides the imagery of the wide-angle lens that enables colleges and universities to see and understand the entire collegiate experience and its long-term effects.

ORGANIZING FOR ENROLLMENT MANAGEMENT

One of the most common questions from campus administrators is, "How should we organize to most effectively influence our student enrollments?" Solving the enrollment issues on a campus, of course, is not just a matter of establishing a position for a senior enrollment manager or "czar of enrollment management." Organizational life is seldom that simple.

Enrollment management organizations typically include some elements of a matrix organization and some elements of a senior management role. Figure 3.1 displays the central elements of an enrollment management effort typically included within an enrollment management organization and those areas less likely to be within the direct purview of a senior enrollment officer. Areas outside the direct control of the enrollment manager require a matrix approach to management. Both of these elements—the enrollment management division and the enrollment management matrix—are briefly described below.

	Influence Area		
Improvement Programs	Academic Programs	Service	Program Development
	Control Area		
Campus Life	Records	Financial Aid	Budgeting
	Enrollment Management (EM) Approach		
Student Activities	EM & Market Research	Admission & Recruitment	Academic Policy
Housing	Registration	Advising	Placement
Retention	Instiutional Marketing		Alumni

Figure 3.1. The Scope of Enrollment Management.

The Enrollment Management Division

In the past decade, the employment of one senior-level administrator with authority over the major offices connected with enrollment management efforts has become the norm at most colleges and universities. The advantages of such an organizational model are apparent. One vice president directs each of the principal components of the system and speaks with formal authority on enrollment issues in all policy decisions. Cooperation, communication, and resource allocation are dealt with from a system-wide perspective.

Establishing a comprehensive enrollment management organization can be problematic. Administrators do not often gladly give up the responsibility for offices that have been under their control. Philosophical differences may arise when career planning or student activities professionals find themselves reporting to someone with the title of enrollment manager–a title that does not sound very "developmental." In addition to these potential problems, Leslie and Rhoades (1995) note that the number of administrators at colleges and universities has been increasing for several decades while the number of faculty members has remained constant. Many faculty members are concerned about the growth of administrative "empires" and would react negatively to the creation of a new vice-president. Thus, the potential benefits and liabilities of an enrollment management division should be weighed carefully before implementing this model.

The Enrollment Management Matrix

The factors that influence students' matriculation and persistence decisions are too complex for any college or university administrator to control. Even the senior enrollment manager with wide-ranging authority must coordinate the activities of other units in the organization and convince other senior campus administrators of the benefits of cooperating to achieve enrollment goals. Key campus administrators who can influence recruitment and retention are often not part of a formal enrollment management organization. In such instances, it helps to have in place a formal or informal enrollment management matrix.

In the enrollment management matrix model, key administrators in units such as residence life, academic advising, career planning, or student activities–units not normally part of a formal enrollment organization–are invited to participate in meetings focusing on student recruitment, success, and graduation. The senior enrollment manager functions in this situation somewhat like an enrollment management coordinator, relying more on cooperation and persuasion and less on hierarchy and authority.

To make the matrix model work, however, the senior enrollment manager must be regarded as an influential campus-level administrator empowered to make important decisions. This ensures a noticeable impact on organizational structure and campus resources as well as cooperation and communication among the appropriate offices. The head of this matrix is thus able to become deeply involved in all elements of an enrollment management system. The enrollment management matrix process can also educate other campus administrators about enrollment management issues and garner support across a wide array of campus stakeholders.

Student Affairs in the Enrollment Management Framework

Just as the expertise of a biologist is in living organisms and the professional expertise of a business officer is in managing money, the specialized expertise of student affairs personnel is in students. It follows, then, that the unit of analysis in student affairs work and in enrollment management is *students*.

In classical models of student affairs organizations, all of the administrative elements of an enrollment management system (excluding curriculum and teaching) fall under the student affairs umbrella—admissions, financial aid, orientation, career planning and placement, student activities, and alumni affairs. Although some offices, especially admissions and financial aid, are frequently housed in areas outside of student affairs, there can be little doubt that student affairs professionals can play an important role in an enrollment management system. On some campuses, student affairs staff members may be responsible for student retention or for conducting student outcomes research. On other campuses, student affairs has very little input as a formal, direct enrollment management division.

Conversely, in other instances, student affairs divisions have included admissions, financial aid, and registration and records for many years. At times, these areas have felt unwanted. Missions such as student development and student engagement as the *raison d'être* for most offices of student affairs can sometimes make enrollment-related offices feel unwanted because they lack a developmental orientation or a formal educational mission. The enrollment management concept, however, provides an administrative framework that makes these offices an important part of a student affairs division.

Student affairs professionals on some campuses may consider the marketing emphasis in the enrollment management concept incompatible with a student development perspective. Student affairs professionals rightly pride themselves in putting students first. Moreover, the implications of putting students first are clearer in traditional student affairs divisions than they are in enrollment management divisions. As Hossler (2007) has noted that when students have a variety of choices of which institution to attend and when it is unclear which campus will provide the best fit, putting students first can be a more complex proposition within enrollment management organizations. If we believe that student development and student engagement result in increased student growth and satisfaction, however, then enrollment management and student development need not be in conflict. Increasing student development and engagement should enhance student persistence. The enrollment management concept need not replace existing philosophies for student affairs divisions. It can, in fact, be used along with other frameworks within a comprehensive student affairs division.

ETHICAL ISSUES IN ENROLLMENT MANAGEMENT

Numerous campus-based and public policy concerns are rife with ethical issues for admissions and enrollment professionals. The most pressing topics include the following: recruitment ethics, the role of standardized testing, the use of merit-based financial aid, the impact of college rankings publications, and the use of technology.

Recruitment Practices

During the recruitment process there are always temptations to misrepresent the way a campus is portrayed to increase the likelihood that more students will matriculate. Admissions folklore is replete with stories of admissions representatives who have told prospective students that they could earn a degree in a major the campus did not offer or that the campus used aerial photographs to make a campus look closer to a desirable mountain resort, lake, or beach. A major public university, for example, fell under heavy criticism for electronically inserting pictures of students of color in existing photographs to make their campus appear to be more diverse. Written publications should accurately describe the location of the campus, the academic offerings, and the composition of the student body. Unethical recruitment practices are unfair to students and can harm both the institution and the entire higher education system. This can cause the general public, students, and their families to lose confidence in the mission and purpose of American higher education.

Standardized Tests and Admissions

Results from tests such as the SAT and ACT have long been among the application requirements for admission to colleges and universities. With such an important role in the admissions process at most institutions, standardized tests have been key determinants of the composition of student bodies and have thereby exerted a profound influence on the character of institutions. Yet, questions have arisen about what the SAT measures and the extent to which it should be emphasized in college admissions decisions.

There are competing interpretations of the correlation between SAT scores and grades and other measures of collegiate success. Some critics have charged that the correlation is so modest as to make the SAT practically worthless ("SAT I", 2007). Others point out that the SAT is second only to high school class rank in predictive strength (Gehring, 2001). Most importantly, perhaps, these tests have been roundly criticized because of persistent racial/ethnic differences in test scores and the effects these tests can therefore have on campus diversity when test scores affect admissions decisions. Among the critics of using SAT and ACT scores in college admissions are a number of college presidents, including a former president of the University of California (Atkinson, 2001), and many business leaders, who have called for less emphasis on the SAT and more on factors important in business success—such as integrity, communication, and leadership skills (Gehring 2001).

The most commonly suggested alternative to the use of standardized test scores in admissions decisions is "holistic review" of student applications. However, it seems likely that such assessments would be expensive and filled with unknown biases that are different but not necessarily more benign than any biases in the SAT. Moreover, new ways to use SAT and ACT scores have been developed that account for students' differing opportunities and circumstances. Goggin (1999) has suggested a "merit-aware" approach that would focus not on absolute scores but on students' scores relative to peers in their own high schools. St. John, Simmons, and Musoba (2002) have simulated admissions decisions and found it possible to use a "merit-aware" model to increase diversity without having race as an explicit criterion in the admissions decision.

The role of the SAT and other standardized tests in admissions is a contentious topic with no ready resolution in sight. Recent rulings by the United States Supreme Court in the University of Michigan affirmative action cases (*Gratz v. Bollinger,* 2003; *Grutter v. Bollinger,* 2003) have helped to clarify but not to settle the issue of the appropriate role of standardized tests and other criteria in admitting students. The court ruled in favor of holistic admissions reviews but did not establish a well-defined role for standardized tests.

Merit-Based Campus Financial Aid

As already noted in this chapter, financial aid has become a powerful tool for addressing a variety of often competing institutional goals such as excellence, access, diversity, and revenue enhancement. The 1990s saw a sharp increase in the use of merit-based scholarships across all institutional types. Between 1988 and 1996, the number of nonneed-based scholarship recipients at public four-year schools increased over 160%, while the average award amount nearly tripled. This large increase in institutional aid went disproportionately to funding the higher education of middle- and upper-income students rather than those with demonstrated need (Redd, 2000). This use of financial aid to attract the best and the brightest without regard to need has come to be called tuition discounting (Loomis-Hubble, 1991). Redd (2000) defines tuition discounting as a form of institutionally-funded grants designed to attract specific groups of undergraduates to help them pay all or a portion of their tuition and fee charges to increase the probability that these students will attend the institution offering the grant.

While conceptually similar to the academic merit and athletic scholarships that have been used for decades, the widespread use of discounting has added a new element of expensive competition to the admissions landscape. Discounting has caught on precisely because it has been effective. However, as bidding wars escalate among schools all competing for the same small pool of the "best and the brightest," there is a danger of further concentration of resources on those who need them least, squeezing the neediest students out of the market entirely.

Although discounting may be rational and efficient for each school acting alone, the sum of the actions can perversely lead to a market of discounts so steep that discounting ceases to enhance revenue, fails to increase diversity and/or class quality, and ultimately diverts resources from other critical areas. Redd (2000) calls this scenario "discounting toward disaster." In the short term, tuition discounting can help recruit the more desirable students from the existing applicant pool, providing a marginal boost to measures of incoming student quality, enhancing diversity, or increasing revenue. However, as discounts rise to levels as high as 45 percent to 50 percent of tuition revenue at some private colleges, this level of funding cannot help but reduce an institution's ability to adequately fund the faculty and other vital student support services. This is a complex issue, and it behooves all senior campus administrators including student affairs professionals to grapple with the details and understand the issues.

The Impact and Uses of College Rankings

During the past three decades, published rankings of colleges and universities such as *U.S. News & World Report's America's Best Colleges* have come to play a major role in shaping much of the discourse on the quality of colleges and universities and related concepts. Although a number of higher education scholars have criticized them, these rankings publications have become increasingly important among students and families, boards of trustees, senior campus administrators, and alumni. The principle criticism is that they primarily measure inputs variables such as SAT scores, institutional selectivity, or faculty characteristics rather than what students actually gain during their college experience, i.e., outcomes measures (Hossler & Hoezee, 2001; Pascarella, 2001).

The pressures of rankings are forcing more and more campuses to seek ways to improve their own rankings. In this context, many campus administrators focus on admissions selectivity. This can lead to an intense focus on the finite number of students with high GPAs and high-standardized scores, which in turn leads to spiraling competition for top students, reflected in ever-larger merit-based scholarship programs. Hossler (2001b) has described a number of unethical practices that have arisen in this context, for example, some institutions encourage inadmissible students to apply so they can reject these students, use early decision programs to increase yields, and misreport admissions statistics.

Seeking to counterbalance the impact of rankings, many scholars and observers of higher education in the U.S. have suggested that the kinds of data collected by the National Survey of Student Engagement (NSSE) represent much more useful information about the quality of college experience than rankings provide (Confessore, 2003; Hossler, 2001a; Pascarella, 2001). NSSE asks students how they spend their time in academic and out-of-class activities while attending college, measures the extent to which students are engaged in their college experiences, and asks students to estimate their cognitive and noncognitive growth as a result of their college experiences. Efforts like NSSE provide data on the actual experiences of students rather than indirect measures of institutional quality.

ELECTRONIC TECHNOLOGY IN ENROLLMENT MANAGEMENT

The proliferation and growing use of electronic enrollment management tools such as large electronic student databases, e-mail, the Internet, YouTube, and Facebook—while having great benefits—raise a host of privacy issues that are gaining more and more attention. Offices such as financial aid or registration and records now have large databases stored electronically with personal information protected by privacy laws. Regularly, however, electronic hackers find ways to get through electronic security barriers and access institutional databases. The same databases can also be accessible to other kinds of hacking. The well-publicized event in which an Ivy League admissions professional hacked into the electronic admissions files of a competitor Ivy League school (Barbaro, 2002) reveals the fragility of the systems and highlights the legal issues associated with the new uses of electronic tools in enrollment management.

The Internet is at least as liable to carry false information as print materials are. Web sites such as YouTube and Facebook have grown rapidly because they are viewed to be less susceptible to the manipulation of professional marketing and have less editorial control. Colleges and universities can undermine the confidence that prospective students place in these sites as well as in their institutions if they attempt to manipulate information from these trusted third-party sources.

The Preparation and Training of Enrollment Managers

Currently, few formal preservice training programs specifically designed to prepare enrollment managers exist. The University of Miami has offered a master's degree in enrollment management for several years. Other universities and professional organizations have tried to offer the master's degree and certificate program in enrollment management but with limited success. The American Association of Collegiate Registrars and Admissions Officers (AACRAO), ACT, the College Board, and the National Association of Student Personnel Administrators (NASPA) have all played leadership roles in offering professional development opportunities for aspiring and practicing enrollment managers; but to date, there has not been sufficient support or sustaining interest to develop a number of graduate programs focused exclusively on enrollment management.

Leadership positions in enrollment management systems are typically assigned to mid- or senior-level administrators who may have already served as the chief student affairs officer or the director of admissions or financial aid. Occasionally, the position is filled by a faculty member or a director of institutional research. The enrollment management concept has gained recognition and acceptance, but it continues to be difficult to find professionals with the necessary skills and background. The career opportunities in this area, as well as in related entry-level areas such as admissions and financial aid, should continue to be strong for the foreseeable future. The demand for professionals in new student orientation and student retention is not as strong, but these areas also provide a sound background for enrollment managers. Entry-level student affairs professionals should attempt to have a range of experiences in the work areas outlined.

In 1989, when the first edition of this chapter was published, the enrollment management concept was too novel to assertively predict the future of what was then a new organizational model. However, 20 years have passed—sufficient time to make it possible to assess the future of enrollment management. Competition among colleges and universities has not abated. Not all campuses use the term *enrollment management* for their efforts to recruit and retain students, but the use of research and evaluation in admissions, financial aid, and retention programs is widespread and is not likely to disappear. Organizational linking, either through a matrix model or a more centralized model, is now common practice of such offices as admissions, financial aid, career planning, and other areas of student affairs. Student enrollments account for 60 to 80 percent of all revenues on most campuses, bonding the health and vitality of institutions of higher education to their ability to attract and retain students. A senior campus enrollment officer has become the norm on many campuses and the stakes around student enrollment have become so great that it is hard to imagine the function of the enrollment manager disappearing any time soon.

Even student affairs professionals not attracted to the concept of enrollment management should be aware of it because so many of the functions within a student affairs division are potentially part of an enrollment management system. In the future, student affairs professionals may find themselves in enrollment management leadership roles or support roles on many campuses. Student affairs divisions that choose to become involved with this new concept can be an integral element of any enrollment management system.

ENROLLMENT MANAGEMENT RESOURCES ON THE INTERNET

The American Association of Collegiate Registrars and Admissions Officers (http://www.aacrao.org) has emerged as one of the leading professional organizations in the field of enrollment management.

ACT (http://www.act.org) and the College Board (http://www.collegeboard.com), like AACRAO, provide services, issue publications, and host conferences.

The National Center for Education Statistics (http://nces.ed.gov) is one of the best sources of data on enrollment trends, financial aid patterns, and retention statistics and studies. Successful enrollment management relies heavily on data and the analysis of data.

Postsecondary Education Opportunity (http://www.postsecondary.org), a monthly research letter, provides a host of interesting statistics and trend data enrollment managers can use to understand trends at their institutions. The information can also enable enrollment managers to better explain to other senior campus administrators regional and national trends affecting student enrollments at individual campuses.

REFERENCES

Abrahamson, T. D., & Hossler, D. (1990). Applying marketing strategies in student recruitment. In D. Hossler & J. P. Bean (Eds.), *The strategic management of college enrollments* (pp. 100–118). San Francisco: Jossey-Bass.

American Council on Education. (1937). The student personnel point of view, 1937. Retrieved from NASPA-Student Affairs Administrators in Higher Education Website at http://www.naspa.org/pubs/files/StudAff_1937.pdf.

American Council on Education. (1949). *The student personnel point of view, 1949.* Retrieved from NASPA-Student Affairs Administrators in Higher Education Website at http://www.naspa.org/pubs/files/StudAff_1949.pdf.

Atkinson, R. C. (2001, February 18). *Standardized tests and access to American universities.* The Robert H. Atwell Distinguished Lecture, delivered at the 83rd annual meeting of the American Council on Education, Washington, DC. Retrieved from http://www.ucop.edu/ucophome/commserv/sat/speech.html.

Barbaro, M. (2002, July 30). Princeton apologizes for Web breach. *The Washington Post,* p. A3.

Bean, J. P. (1980). Dropouts and turnover: The synthesis and test of a causal model of student attrition. *Research in Higher Education, 12*(2), 155–182.

Bean, J. P. (1983, Winter). The application of a model of turnover in work organizations to the student attrition process. *The Review of Higher Education, 6*(2), 129–148.

Black, J. (Ed.). (2001). *The strategic enrollment management revolution.* Washington, DC: American Association of Collegiate Registrars and Admissions Officers.

Bontrager, B., & Brown, G. (2008). Integrating enrollment and budget planning: The SEM planning model. In B. Bontrager (Ed.), *SEM and institutional success: Integrating enrollment, finance, and student access* (pp. 59–84). Washington, DC: Association of Collegiate Registrars and Admissions Officers.

Bowen, H. R. (1980). *The costs of higher education: How much do colleges and universities spend per student and how much should they spend?* San Francisco: Jossey-Bass.

Braxton, J. M. (Ed.). (2000). *Reworking the student departure puzzle.* Nashville, TN: Vanderbilt University Press.

Breneman, D. W. (1994). *Liberal arts colleges: Thriving, surviving, or endangered?* Washington, DC: The Brookings Institution.

Brooks, S. H. (1996). Econometric modeling of enrollment behavior. *Journal of Student Financial Aid, 26*(3), 7–17.

Broome, E. C. (1903). *A historical and critical discussion of college admission requirements.* New York: Macmillan.

Brubacher, J. S., & Rudy, W. (1997). *Higher education in transition: A history of American colleges and universities* (4th ed.). New Brunswick, NJ: Transaction Publishers.

Bryson, J. M. (2004). *Strategic planning for public and nonprofit organizations: A guide to strengthening and sustaining organizational achievement* (3rd ed.). San Francisco: Jossey-Bass.

Clark, B. R. (1983). *The higher education system: Academic organization in cross-national perspective.* Berkley, CA: University of California Press.

Confessore, N. (2003, November). What makes a college good? *The Atlantic, 292*(4),

118–126.

Cross, R. G. (1997). *Revenue management: Hard-core tactics for market domination.* New York: Broadway Books.

Gehring, J. (2001, May 9). SAT said to be reliable predictor of college success. *Education Week.* Retrieved from http://www.edweek.org/ew/articles/2001/06/13/40act.h20.html.

Goggin, W. (1999, May 30). A "merit-aware" model for college admissions and affirmative action. *Postsecondary Education Opportunity Newsletter, 83,* 6–12.

Gratz v. Bollinger, 539 U.S. 244 (2003).

Grutter v. Bollinger, 539 U.S. 306 (2003).

Hayek, J., & Hossler, D. (1999, April). The information needs of prospective students: I want what I want when I want it. Paper presented at the annual meeting of the American Association of Collegiate Registrars and Admissions Officers, Charleston, SC.

Hossler, D. (1986). *Creating effective enrollment management systems.* New York: College Entrance Examination Board.

Hossler, D. (2000). Effective admissions recruitment. In G. H. Gaither (Ed.), *Promising practices in recruitment, remediation, and retention* (New Directions for Higher Education 108, pp. 15–30). San Francisco: Jossey-Bass.

Hossler, D. (2001a, September/October). Everybody wants to be no. 1: A look at college rankings (Part 1). *Indiana Alumni Magazine,* 26–29.

Hossler, D. (2001b, November/December). Everybody wants to be no. 1: A look at college rankings (Part 2). *Indiana Alumni Magazine,* 22–26.

Hossler, D. (2007). Putting students first in college admissions and enrollment management. In G. L. Kramer & Associates (Eds.), *Fostering student success in the campus community* (pp. 101–119). San Francisco: Jossey-Bass.

Hossler, D, Bean, J. P., & Associates. (1990). *The strategic management of college enrollments.* San Francisco: Jossey-Bass.

Hossler, D., Braxton, J. M., & Coppersmith, G. (1989). Understanding student college choice. In J. C. Smart (Ed.), *Higher education: Handbook of theory and research* (Vol 5, pp. 231–288). New York: Agathon Press.

Hossler, D., & Hoezee, L. (2001). Conceptual and theoretical thinking about enrollment management. In J. Black (Ed.), *The strategic enrollment management revolution* (pp. 57–72). Washington, DC: American Association of Collegiate Registrars and Admissions Officers.

Hossler, D., Schmit, J., & Vesper, N. (1998). *Going to college: How social, economic, and educational factors influence the decisions students make.* Baltimore: Johns Hopkins University Press.

Jencks, C., & Reisman, D. (1969). *The academic revolution.* Garden City, NY: Doubleday.

Kreutner, L., & Godfrey, E. S. (1980-81, Winter). Enrollment management: A new vehicle for institutional renewal. *College Board Review, 118,* 6–9, 29.

Kuh, G. D., Kinzie. J., Schuh, J., & Whitt, E. J. (2005). *Student success in college: Creating conditions that matter.* San Francisco: Jossey-Bass.

Kuh, G. D., Schuh, J., Whitt, E., & Associates. (1991). *Involving colleges: Successful approaches to fostering student learning and development outside the classroom.* San Francisco: Jossey-Bass.

Leslie, L. L., & Rhoades, G. (1995, March/April). Rising administrative costs: Seeking explanations. *Journal of Higher Education, 66*(2), 187–211.

Lindsay, E. E., & Holland, O. C. (1930). *College and university administration.* New York: Macmillan.

Loomis-Hubble, L. (1991). *Tuition discounting: The impact of institutionally funded financial aid.* Washington, DC: National Association of College and University Business Officers.

Maguire, J. (1976, Fall). To the organized go the students. *Bridge Magazine, 39*(1), 16–20.

McClellan, G. S., & Stringer, J. (Eds.). (2009). *The handbook of student affairs administration* (3rd ed.). San Francisco: Jossey-Bass.

McDonough, P. M., Antonio, A. L., Walpole, M., & Perez, L. X. (1998). College rankings: Democratized college knowledge for whom? *Research in Higher Education, 39*(5), 513–533.

Noel, L., Levitz, R. S., Saluri, D., & Associates. (1985). *Increasing student retention.* San Francisco: Jossey-Bass.

Pace, C. R. (1991). *The undergraduates.* Los Angeles: University of California at Los Angeles, Higher Education Research Institute.

Pascarella, E. T. (1986). A program for research and policy development on student persistence at the institutional level. *Journal of College Student Personnel, 27,* 100–107.

Pascarella, E. T. (2001). Identifying excellence in undergraduate education: Are we even close? *Change Magazine, 33*(3), 19–23.

Pascarella, E. T., & Terenzini, P. (2005). *How college affects students: Vol. 2 A third decade of research.* San Francisco: Jossey-Bass.

Patton, L. D., Morelon, C., Whitehead, D. M., & Hossler, D. (2006). Campus-based retention initiatives: Does the emperor have clothes? In E. P. St. John & M. Wilkerson (Eds.), *Reframing persistence research to improve academic success* (New Directions for Institutional Research 130, pp. 9–24). San Francisco: Jossey-Bass.

Paulsen, M. B. (1990). *College choice: Understanding student enrollment behavior* (ASHE-ERIC Higher Education Reports No. 6). Washington, DC: ERIC Clearinghouse on Higher Education and The George Washington University.

Pfeffer, J., & Salancik, G. R. (1978). *The external control of organizations: A resource dependence approach.* New York: Harper & Row.

Redd, K. E. (2000). Tuition discounting: A view from the financial aid office. *NASFAA Journal of Student Financial Aid, 30,* 27–37.

Rudolph, F. (1962). *The American college and university: A history.* New York: Vintage Books.

SAT I: A faulty instrument for predicting college success. (2007, August 20). FairTest. Retrieved from http://www.fairtest.org/index.htm.

Scannell, J. J. (1992). *The effect of financial aid policies on admission and enrollment.* New York: College Board.

Senge, P. M. (2006). *The fifth discipline: The art and practice of the learning organization.*

New York: Random House.

Smerling, W. H. (1960). The registrar: Changing aspects. *College and University, 35*(2), 180–186.

St. John, E. P., Paulsen, M. B., & Starkey, J. B. (1996). The nexus between college choice and persistence. *Research in Higher Education, 37*(2), 175–220.

St. John, E. P., Simmons, A. B., & Musoba, G. D. (2002). Merit-aware admissions in public universities: Increasing diversity. *Thought & Action, 17*(2), 35–46.

Swann, C. C. (1998). Admissions officer: A profession and a career. In C. C. Swann & S. E. Henderson (Eds.), *Handbook for the college admissions profession* (pp 29–36.). Washington, DC: American Association of Collegiate Registrars and Admissions Officers.

Swann, C. C., & Henderson, S. E. (Eds.). (1998) *Handbook for the college admissions profession.* Washington, DC: American Association of Collegiate Registrars and Admissions Officers.

Thelin, J. R. (1982). *Higher education and its useful past: Applied history in research and planning.* Cambridge, MA: Schenkman.

Thresher, B. A. (1966). *College admissions and the public interest.* New York: College Entrance Examination Board.

Tinto, V. (1993). *Leaving college: Rethinking the causes and cures of student attrition* (2nd ed.). Chicago: University of Chicago Press.

Tolbert, P. S. (1985). Institutional environments and resource dependence: Sources of administrative structure in higher education. *Administrative Science Quarterly, 30*(1), 1–13.

Upcraft, M. L., Gardner, J. N., & Barefoot, B. O. (Eds.). (2004). *Challenging and supporting the first-year student: A handbook for improving the first year of college.* San Francisco: Jossey-Bass.

Chapter 4

ACADEMIC ADVISING

ERIC R. WHITE AND MARIE J. LINDHORST

INTRODUCTION

Academic advising has been around since the founding of universities in the United States. Academic advising is defined as a relationship between a student and a college representative, for the purpose of crafting a program of study which helps the student take advantage of all curricular and cocurricular opportunities. The academic advising practice has grown from an informal *in loco parentis* association to a flourishing profession. Though the curriculum was once relatively limited, the electives nonexistent, and the student body homogenous in nature, this formerly straightforward practice has developed into a complex field grounded in a rapidly expanding curriculum, a multitude of higher education options, and an increasingly diverse student body (Rudolph, 1962).

Now, it is recognized that significant learning occurs outside of the classroom, laboratory, and studio. One of the most obvious locales where learning occurs is in the academic advisor's office. Students continue to demand quality academic advising to help them with their educational plans, to assure that they are making adequate progress toward their degrees, and to assist them in meeting their educational goals within a reasonable time frame. To meet this demand, institutions have hired full- and part-time professional staff members to augment the work that was once solely within the faculty's purview (Self, 2008).

This cadre of both faculty and professional staff advisors forms the basis for a professional organization—the National Academic Advising Association (NACADA) which is devoted exclusively to the advancement of academic advising. Since its founding in 1979, NACADA has endorsed standards for the profession; promulgated theories; encouraged the creation and dissemi-

96

nation of new knowledge about the field; supported practitioners in their work with regional, national, and international conferences; and catalogued best practices. It is now an organization of over 10,000 members (Goetz, 2004).

Given the growing complexity of our institutions of higher education and their curricula, the diversity of the current student body, and the societal need to provide as much access as possible to higher education to all who can benefit, the institutional response has been to expand upon a system of academic advising that had been in place officially since the last quarter of the nineteenth century. Since then the approaches to academic advising have taken many forms and have been influenced by the mission and the culture in which the practice has been conducted. Covering a time span which has moved from academic advising as an undefined practice, to one that had definition but was unexamined, to its current state as defined and examined (Frost, 1991), academic advising has taken its place in the higher education community as a student-oriented practice that can respond to the particular demands of the twenty-first century students of higher education.

This chapter is divided into five topics: History of Academic Advising, Definitions of Academic Advising, Administrative and Organizational Structures, The Use of Technology in Advising, and Current Issues in Academic Advising.

HISTORY OF ACADEMIC ADVISING

The origins of academic advising in the U.S. go back to the very first institutions of higher education established in the United States' colonial period. To understand how academic advising functions at U.S. colleges and universities in the twenty-first century, two historical strands need to be examined. These two strands—the ever changing curriculum and the relationship of faculty to students—have influenced both the need for academic advising and the dialog surrounding who should be the providers of advising (Frost, 2000).

The first academic advisors in the colonial period, although not identified by this title, were faculty members who most often lived in residence with their students. These faculty members oversaw all aspects of their charges' lives and, in fact, established the practice of serving *in loco parentis*. As long as the curriculum remained relatively unchanged and the types of students entering institutions of higher education were relatively homogenous, there was no compelling reason to modify how academic advising was delivered.

However, as the curriculum started to expand and electives were introduced; as faculty began to identify with specific disciplines and organized themselves around a departmental structure; and as the doors to higher education began to slowly open wider; the leaders of higher education saw the need to make organizational changes to the provision of advising. The once informal system became more organized as cadres of academic advisors, chosen primarily from the faculty ranks, were established (Brubacher & Rudy, 1968).

The rationale for college presidents to conceive of and to implement academic advising systems was provided by the introduction of electives into the curriculum in the last quarter of the 19th century, coupled with the notion that students, without faculty advice, could not be trusted to make cogent decisions about their course of study. The president of Johns Hopkins University, Daniel Coit Gilman, is credited with the establishment of the first system of faculty advisors in 1876. In 1889, President Gilman appointed Edward Herrick Griffin "Chief of Faculty Advisors." At the same time, Hopkins' publications were articulating the role for these advisors (White & Khakpour, 2006).

While the need to formalize a structure to deliver academic advising was being introduced into colleges and universities, simultaneously the faculty members were moving away from their traditional roles where they oversaw all aspects of a college student's experience. An era of specialization was beginning as offices of "Deans of Men and Women" were created to replace faculty members who could not and did not necessarily want to take on all aspects of a student's college experience (such as discipline, moral development, and cocurricular activities).

Although differentiations of responsibilities were starting to take hold by the turn of the twentieth century, academic advising was still not recognized and had not yet achieved status as a distinct endeavor separate from counseling and psychological interventions. This may have been the case because faculty members were still the primary sources of academic advice, while the non-academic experiences were tended to by counselors who arrived on campuses as part of the mental hygiene and vocational guidance movements of the early twentieth century (Frost, 2000).

The post-World War II period is recognized as a transformative moment for higher education in the U.S. with the passage of the GI Bill, resulting in the enrollment of over 2.25 million veterans in more than 2,000 colleges and universities. The impact of these students on the college scene required a reexamination of the processes of student orientation to higher education, academic advisement, and provision of programs and services beyond an ever-expanding curriculum (Thelin, 2004).

U.S. colleges and universities were committed to assuring that these veterans were able to take advantage of their educational benefits. The huge influx of these veterans placed incredible demands on colleges and universities, and necessitated the hiring of specifically trained professionals to help these students match their abilities and interests to the vast array of educational opportunities available. In the post-World War II decade, it was clear that the solution was to establish an expanded cadre of academic advisors on U.S. college and university campuses.

The question of who would oversee the delivery of academic advising depended upon local campus history and culture. Community colleges often relied on a traditional guidance model emulating the high school organizational configuration and placed the delivery of advising within the auspices of student affairs units. Other colleges and universities, taking the cue from the descriptor "academic," housed advising responsibilities within the offices of academic deans. Some institutions moved the responsibility around depending on the inclination of leadership and evolving local trends (King, 2008).

In 1972, the *Journal of College Student Personnel* published "A developmental view of academic advising as teaching" (Crookston, 1972). This article provided the advising community with the theoretical framework to move away from the typical advising practices of helping students register for classes, regardless of whether or not these courses were appropriate for a particular student's circumstances. In effect, the Crookston article gave the advising community a chance to abandon a "prescriptive" approach to advising, or at least to acknowledge that academic advising was something more. Advisors saw in the Crookston article the chance to articulate a new vision for their work: one more developmental and holistic in scope and one that moved the practice of advising closer to professional status.

By 1977, the first national conference on academic advising was held in Burlington, Vermont, partially in an attempt to bring advisors together to discuss only the topic of academic advising. Two years later, the National Academic Advising Association was formed with 429 charter members (Cook, 2009). Today the association has over 10,000 members and is one of the fastest growing student-oriented professional organizations in the nation.

In 1981, the Educational Resources Information Center (ERIC) formally designated "academic advising" as a descriptor. ERIC thus provided the practice of academic advising with far larger public recognition, allowing for more concentrated and effective searches for information and the ability to spread programmatic efforts related to academic advising more quickly (Cook, 2009).

A number of additional events advanced the recognition of academic advising as a field unto itself. NACADA issued its first Journal in 1981. The publication of *Developmental Academic Advising* (1984), as a follow-up to the Crookston article, gave practitioners in the field their first comprehensive resource covering all aspects of academic advising. In 1986 NACADA, collaborating with the Council for the Advancement of Standards in Higher

Education, endorsed the Standards and Guidelines for Academic Advising thus giving the profession a tool to articulate its mission and programmatic efforts and the basis for either establishing new advising programs or altering existing ones (Goetz, 2004).

Additional resources, such as Grites' (1979) *Academic Advising: Getting Us through the Eighties* and Gordon's (1992) *Handbook on Academic Advising,* continued to delineate the purpose and value of academic advising. In 2000, the first edition of the *Academic Advising Handbook* (Gordon & Habley, 2000) was printed. This edition saw tremendous distribution and served as an informal textbook for the field. In response to the rapidly changing zeitgeist in higher education in the early twenty-first century and the consequent changes in academic advising, the second edition of the *Academic Advising Handbook* was published in 2008 (Gordon, Habley, & Grites, 2008).

As higher education faces the challenges of the twenty-first century, academic advising has responded by building upon the academic foundations of advising and adopting the language of instruction, specifically the notion of learning outcomes. Such an approach is consistent with other student- oriented practices that responded to the call from Richard Keeling (Keeling 2004; 2006) in the *Learning Reconsidered* monograph series, produced collaboratively by NASPA and ACPA. These monographs have called for a renewed focus on the learning aspects of all co-curricular activities.

Using the language of instruction, the National Academic Advising Association adopted a Concept of Academic Advising Statement in 2006. The preamble to the Concept of Academic Advising Statement indicates where advising should position itself in the 21st century and more specifically, procedures for working as effectively as possible with students so that they can achieve success.

> Academic advising is integral to fulfilling the teaching and learning mission of higher education. Through academic advising, students learn to become members of their higher education community, to think critically about their roles and responsibilities as students, and to prepare to be educated citizens of a democratic society and a global community. Academic advising engages students beyond their own world views, while acknowledging their individual characteristics, values, and motivations as they enter, move through, and exit the institution. Regardless of the diversity of our institutions, our students, our advisors, and our organizational structures, academic advising has three components: curriculum (what advising deals with), pedagogy (how advising does what it does), and student learning outcomes (the result of academic advising). (NACADA, 2006)

Academic advising is comprised of a series of historical strands: its faculty-based foundations, the introduction of a developmental perspective, and the adoption of an instructional and learning outcomes focus. These strands, when woven together, more clearly represent the work of academic advising as a student-centered and consequently a learner-centered profession within higher education.

DEFINITIONS OF ACADEMIC ADVISING

Throughout the history of academic advising, the core purposes and goals of advising have included the development of student maturity and conscious academic decision-making. From early attempts to create academic advising systems at The Johns Hopkins University and at Harvard (Frost, 2000; Rudolph, 1990), through the expansion of advising efforts throughout the twentieth century, the importance and complexity of student educational choices have been at the heart of the distinctive role of academic advisors. Though often imperfectly implemented and frequently critiqued (Hopkins, 1926; Robertson, 1958), advising was understood to play a critical role in the academic experience of college students.

In recent decades, attempts to define academic advising have been influenced by critiques of the faculty-student relationship, the rise of holistic understandings of college student development, and an emphasis on student learning (Crookston, 1972; Laff, 2006; Lowenstein, 1999; Robertson, 1958). Most recently, efforts to define advising have focused on the broad educational objectives in the advising relationship (NACADA, 2006) and the significance of academic advising as a scholarly practice and field distinct from student personnel professions (Schulenberg & Lindhorst, 2008).

By the 1960s, academic advising (as practiced generally by faculty) was widely critiqued as clerical and prescriptive in nature, responding in only the most rudimentary way to the needs of students for assistance with their academic planning, and often consisting of the imposition of curricular requirements (Raskin, 1979). In response, the work of Crookston (1972) and O'Banion (1972) argued for the application of student development theory to the work of academic advising. "Developmental advising" was distinguished from earlier prescriptive or clerical models by its appreciation for the whole student and a level of personal engagement with advisees regarding their educational plans. According to O'Banion (1972), academic advising involved helping students not only choose and schedule courses, and decide on an academic major, but also explore life and vocational goals. Definitions of academic advising in response to these theories emphasized the role of advisors in promoting a student's general development (Creamer & Creamer, 1994).

More recently, definitions of academic advising have moved toward a focus on advising as teaching and on student learning outcomes. For Lowenstein (1999, 2000, 2005) and others, academic advising is best understood and defined as teaching focused on the student's understanding and navigation of higher education institutions and their curricula. In 2006, the National Academic Advising Association (NACADA) published the "Concept of Academic Advising" which made this teaching/learning focus more clear:

> Academic advising, based in the teaching and learning mission of higher education, is a series of intentional interactions with a curriculum, pedagogy, and a set of student learning outcomes. Academic advising synthesizes and contextualizes students' educational experiences within the frameworks of their aspirations, abilities and lives to extend learning beyond campus boundaries and timeframes. (NACADA 2006, p. 1)

Building on this teaching focus and reflecting the broader higher education emphasis on student learning (Barr & Tagg, 1995), academic advisors have carried on a significant discussion about what advisors teach and what advisees learn (Hemwall & Trachte, 2005; Kelley, 2008; Lowenstein, 2005). Recent attempts to define academic advising have also emphasized the complexity of higher education, curricula, and student educational decisions in an effort to further clarify the distinctive arena and contribution of the field.

> . . . the description of academic advising clearly includes helping students understand academic disciplines and ways of thinking, helping them develop their sense of themselves, teaching them how to respond to academic experiences, facilitating their self-interpretation through personal transformations, and helping them make sense of their education as more than choosing courses or majors. (Schulenberg & Lindhorst, 2008, p. 49)

These efforts to define advising beyond its most rudimentary elements of helping students choose courses and plan their curriculum will certainly continue as the profession and its scholarship continue their evolution.

ADMINISTRATIVE AND ORGANIZATIONAL STRUCTURES

The organizational structure of academic advising programs is almost as varied as the types of higher education institutions in the United States. While some programs are deliberately designed and implemented, others exist in their current configuration based only on historical precedent, administrative inclinations, or financial considerations. Some programs are driven by explicitly articulated mission statements while others exist to respond to the immediate advising needs of students.

With the publication of the Standards and Guidelines for Academic Advising by the Council for the Advancement of Standards in Higher Education (CAS, 1986), the profession laid the ground work to establish and maintain a quality academic advising program by adhering to certain standards. Specifically, academic advising programs need to have mission statements which declare their purpose. In addition, academic advising programs need to articulate clearly their delivery models, so that the goals of the programs are in line with their mission statements.

To understand the administrative and organizational structure of academic advising programs, a number of conditions need to be taken into account:

1. What configuration is used to deliver academic advising?
2. Who is delivering academic advising?
3. How do advisors interact with students?

The organizational models for academic advising have been classified as centralized, decentralized, and shared (Habley, 1983). In the decentralized model, academic advising is provided at the departmental level, most often by faculty and sometimes with staff. In this model, there may or may not be any centralized coordination. Essentially, the advisors operate almost exclusively within the departmental realm. In comparison, the centralized model puts all the delivery of academic advising into a single unit such as an advising or counseling center. This unit often has a director or dean who oversees a staff of advisors. Typically, all advising is delivered from one location and is not distributed throughout the campus.

The shared model is a combination of centralization and decentralization. For example, first-year and second-year students may be advised in a centralized advising center. After a major is declared, the student is then reassigned to a departmental advisor. While the model might dictate a particular structure, who delivers the actual academic advising is independent of the model, except for the model identified as faculty-only, in which the delivery personnel and the model are the same.

The selection of academic advisors on any particular campus, like the organizational structure, is driven by many variables. Institutions with long histories of using faculty as academic advisors, particularly those schools that pride themselves on promoting a close working relationship between faculty and students, continue to use faculty as advisors. However, these colleges sometimes have a coordinator of advising, and this person can be drawn from the faculty ranks. However, this is not always the case. A coordinator of advising in a faculty-only model college may have always been an administrator with no higher education teaching experience, but with a professional background in managing an academic advising program (King, 2008).

As the work of academic advising has become more specialized, as faculty have chosen not to advise, and as administrators have moved advising responsibilities from faculty to staff for a variety of reasons, the professional academic advisor or counselor has come onto the scene. The choice of advisor versus counselor as a title is an institutional preference. Some institutions prefer to have counselors (that is, individuals with counseling credentials) performing advising duties because they believe that the responsibilities of academic advisors require the skills that come with counselor training and credentials.

Other institutions often use the term *advisor* with the descriptor *academic.* In this case, the credentials may be any master's degree (including a degree in counseling or college student affairs) as a minimum requirement. Those institutions that do not specify a particular master's degree believe that the inherent qualities and skills that an academic advisor needs to have can be acquired through an advanced degree and appropriate work experiences. Currently, there are only two master's degree programs in academic advising, offered online from Kansas State University and Sam Houston State University, although several universities are beginning to offer master's level courses in the foundations of academic advising.

While the most recent Standards and Guidelines for Academic Advising from the Council for the Advancement of Standards in Higher Education (CAS, 2009) calls for a master's degree (although allowing for a bachelor's degree and significant appropriate work experience), institutions have run the gamut from using clerical staff and office managers as the primary deliverers of academic advising to individuals with doctoral and postbaccalaureate professional degrees. Having academic advisors with doctoral and advanced postbaccalaureate degrees raises the visibility of the profession and sets up the expectation that academic advising transcends mere course scheduling and assistance with registration. The availability of individuals with doctoral degrees as academic advisors brings the field full circle to the time when only faculty provided advising and the issue of necessary preparation to be an advisor was not even considered (Self, 2008).

Other personnel who provide academic advising include graduate students and peer advisors. For a variety of reasons, such as cost savings, financial assistance, and cocurricular experiences, some advising programs have decided to use such persons. Using graduate students as academic advisors provides departments with necessary personnel to fulfill the academic advising obligations. In addition, these advising assistantships provide the funding that graduate students need to pursue their education. In some cases, these graduate students are the primary deliverers of advising, while in other cases, they may work under the auspices of a faculty advisor or a departmental coordinator. Peer advisors (undergraduates) may or may not be compensated for their work, but can find the experience informative as they contemplate their professional futures. No doubt, there are some professional advisors who got their start as peer advisors (Self, 2008).

The obvious disadvantage to using students is the need for continual training and supervision. Both graduate and undergraduate students come and go and do not represent a steady employment pool. As some students are entering the peer advisor ranks, others are leaving. This revolving door means that permanent staff members have to be assigned the responsibility for selecting these advisors, training them, and providing quality supervision. While graduate stipends do not always rise to the level of a professional staff salary and undergraduates work for either minimal salary, credits, or as volunteers, the coordinators of advising programs who use such personnel have to weigh the balance between a cost-saving measure and the time commitment of a permanent staff member. While permanent staff may also need continuous training and supervision, one of the advantages of permanent staff members is their relative permanency. For any academic advising administrator this advantage has to be juxtaposed against the finances of the advising operation (Self, 2008).

The long standing approach to academic advising has been the one-on-one interview. However, other approaches to advising students have been introduced and have shown themselves to be effective. Academic advising with students in groups has now become common place, and there are particular times when group advising may be a more effective approach than the standard one-on-one model (King, 2008). Traditional orientation programs either provided during the summer or in the days immediately preceding the start of a semester now contain group advising sessions. These sessions may constitute a time when students are exposed to the language of academic advising in higher education, the institution's academic policies and procedures, and an opportunity to plan and perhaps even officially register for their first semester of enrollment (Fox, 2008).

Extending immediately beyond orientation, academic advising has become a component for first-year seminars. Content can range from a continuation of materials presented during orientation, including how to use the institution's technology resources for advising and the registration process, to establishing advising e-portfolios that students can maintain for their entire tenure at their chosen school. At times, these first-year seminars are even taught by the student's advisor thus serving to create a unique bond between advisor and student (King, 2008).

When residence halls exist on campus, academic advising has sometimes moved to the student residences. In this case, advisors are given offices in the residence halls, and students can have convenient access to their advisors. Advisors may be permanently housed in these offices or they may spend a defined percentage of their work week here. In either case, the thrust of this approach is to make advising as accessible as possible. This approach allows advisors to work with groups of students in the residence hall in addition to seeing students individually (King, 2008). These group approaches provide the advisor with the opportunity to convey information to many students at a single time, rather than repeating information to one student after another. Residence halls also serve as a location for group academic advising programming conducted by advisors who do not have residence hall offices (Schein, 1995).

As senior capstone courses become more prevalent, the opportunity to deliver academic advising in group settings to students in these types of courses has become more prevalent as well. The capstone course allows students to look back and examine their educations and also to look forward to post-baccalaureate experiences. It is time to hear from alumni, for example, who are in the world of work and able to discuss their transition from college to the workforce. Students can also learn what is most valued in the world of work and what skills they may need to enhance.

Group academic advising can also be provided to students who represent "special" populations. Such groups include honor students, exploratory and undecided students, students considering over-subscribed majors that require more than the minimally established entrance-to-major requirements, students who represent a uniquely defined outreach population, and students on warning or academic probation. The value of group academic advising goes beyond efficiency. Advising students in groups can help students to know that they are not alone (King, 2008). This might be the case for undecided students, for example, who may believe, most times erroneously, that every other student is either enrolled in a major or can articulate a major goal. Group academic advising allows students to share their concerns, so that some of the anxieties of being associated with a "special" population on campus can be alleviated (King, 2008; Woolston & Ryan, 2007).

No matter who provides academic advising or in what configuration, the responsibility for academic advising has to be placed somewhere within the institution's organizational structure. Where the responsibility lies is not dictated by any established mandate (Campbell, 2008). Each institution decides for itself, based on a variety of reasons such as historical precedent, administrative preference, philosophical and theoretical leanings. In fact, there can even be movement across administrative units as institutions adjust their delivery of academic advising based upon some analysis of where it is believed advising might function most effectively. The delivery of academic advising can be moved between student affairs and academic affairs administration if advising is perceived to be either a student-centered activity best placed in the student affairs realm or in the academic affairs side of the house if the full force of the adjective *academic* is to be emphasized. In fact, with the establishment of units such as enrollment management, academic advising programs have been moved there to reflect the current issues of admissions, the retention of students, and the role that academic advising plays in these areas (Campbell, 2008).

There are proponents for placing the responsibility for academic advising within all three of these areas. Proponents for each approach have their own rationales: the history of advising rests on the academic side, is provided often by faculty, involves the academic rules of the institution and thus should be the responsibility of academic affairs. Or, academic advising is all about student development, and the skills needed to be a competent advisor are acquired or enhanced in college student affairs and counseling programs (Nutt, 2009). Enrollment Management units lay claim to the administration of academic advising asserting that advising starts with the admission process and extends throughout the students' educational experience where students may come and go from the institution, change majors, seek enrollment to oversubscribed majors and fail out, and then seek re-enrollment. All of these unique transition points are the concern of such units (Habley, 2004).

Regardless of where the responsibility for the delivery of an academic advising program is housed (and there may be other unique organizational configurations beyond the three previously mentioned), the ultimate test of the effectiveness of such programs is not necessarily their administrative homes, but rather whether or not the mission, goals, and objectives of the programs are met (Campbell, 2008). Where that can happen may change over time and it is not unusual to have this responsibility change, even more than once.

THE USE OF TECHNOLOGY IN ACADEMIC ADVISING

The impact of technology on academic advising has been significant. While there were originally some pockets of resistance (fears of being replaced by the technology was the typical response), generally the academic advising community has responded positively to the advances in technology and has indeed embraced technology to alleviate the weight of the routine aspects of the work and as a mechanism to create new advising paradigms (White & Leonard, 2003).

Starting with websites, the academic advising community learned quickly that such tools "push" information out to students in a timely fashion, and that with diligent upkeep, information can always be current since the capacity to update immediately is a hallmark of the Web. Advising websites are now ubiquitous and take many forms: advising handbooks, course descriptions, curricular plans, advising indexes, college and university catalogs (Leonard, 2008).

The introduction of student information systems has allowed advisors to access information about students. These systems, either purchased or home grown, provide advisors immediately with the information necessary to conduct advising sessions and have eliminated the need to maintain paper files on students. These systems have also provided advisors with the mechanism to introduce their advising notes into the database, and consequently allow for the sharing of advising notes within the advising community. While having such notes available has been very useful to advisors, it has also created the need to establish protocols for the nature of advising notes and how they are to be entered, maintained, shared, and interpreted within the advising community (Leonard, 2008).

These databases have now become interactive so that students are able to add courses, drop courses, and even withdraw from a college or university via a simulation of an academic advising interview, thus assuring that all students will be provided with consistent and expert-developed advising exchanges. Functions such as the Grade-Point Average Target (GPA) application, once done manually, can now be done electronically. This application is useful for students who may need to know what kinds of grades they must make to keep a scholarship, earn a fellowship, enter a particular major, or simply to make adequate academic progress toward a degree (Leonard, 2008; McCauley, 2000).

One of the most important technological advances for advising has been the introduction of the degree audit, which is an electronic major checklist (McCauley, 2000). Having access to student courses and their fit with any curriculum within the institution has not only saved advisors many manual labor hours working through transcripts and assured that no errors have been created, but also saved on duplicate copies for students and advisors. The degree audit, now available online within seconds both to students and to advisors, has allowed students to easily explore majors and to see how past course work can be reconfigured into new majors. It is especially useful for undeclared and exploratory students and for students considering changing majors. Databases that include the potential of academic credits to transfer to and from institutions have also assisted the advising community in providing up-to-date information. The availability of such information has given advisors more time to discuss substantive transfer issues such as the appropriateness of the transfer and an assessment of the educational plans which might call for a transfer of institutions (McCauley, 2000).

Webinars, also called web casts and web conferences, have become useful tools for the professional development of academic advisors. For communicating among themselves or with their advisees, academic advisors now have available instant messaging, social networking sites, e-mail, listservs, course management systems, podcasts, cell phones, and blogs (Leonard, 2008).

The use of technology in academic advising will continue as academic advisors mold the current tools to their own purposes, and begin the development of new technology-based approaches (Leonard, 2008). It is anticipated that the next generation of academic advisors will be even more comfortable with advising technologies. Current students have come to expect that the latest technologies will be applied to their advising experiences. The extent to which technological approaches to advising continue to be useful is limited only by our own imaginations. Despite this embrace of technology, however, the need for the one-on-one interview does not seem to have diminished. In fact, in a world that has come to depend on immediate communication, the high-touch, high-tech paradigm continues to be relevant (White, 2005).

Online Technology Resources

The National Academic Advising Association maintains an online Clearinghouse of Academic Advising Resources. This central location within the NACADA Web site is for the collection, organization, storage, and dissemination of information and resources to assist academic advisors. The section of the site dealing specifically with technology can be accessed at the URL: http://www.nacada.ksu.edu/Clearinghouse/AdvisingIssues/Technology.htm. This page includes nonendorsed commercial sites, a list of best practices in technology at colleges and universities, articles pertinent to technology in advising, and a bibliography.

Within NACADA's commission structure, the Technology in Advising Commission helps academic advisors and advising administrators to understand the impact that technologies such as the web, e-mail, degree audits, online registration, and student information systems have on academic advising. This commission also seeks to serve as a central resource and clearinghouse for information about innovations and issues in academic advising technology. Through the commission's electronic discussion forum (TEC ADV-L), NACADA members are encouraged to engage in discussions related to the uses of technology in advising. Other venues to discuss technology in advising include *The Mentor*–an electronic journal devoted to academic advising topics at http://www.psu.edu/dus/mentor and the listserv ACADV–an electronic information exchange for professionals interested in all advising topics.

CURRENT ISSUES IN ACADEMIC ADVISING

Academic advising shares many of the challenges that face higher education in the twenty-first century as advisors interact with students. American high schools continue to provide uneven results in terms of academic skills, but increasing numbers of students enter college, with both high expectations and low levels of academic engagement (Keup & Kinzie, 2007). As a consequence, higher education institutions enroll large numbers of students whose basic academic skills need remediation, and whose goals for their education are often unclear. These students represent a bewildering diversity of preparation, characteristics, and life conditions (Kennedy & Ishler, 2008). The costs of higher education have continued to rise, creating financial barriers for a significant number of students. Some students who begin college don't complete a degree, and many others leave college with significant student loan debt (Kennedy & Ishler, 2008). The academic skills and achievements of those who do finish their degrees have come under some criticism (U.S. Department of Education, 2006). Out of a focus on student learning and in response to calls for greater accountability, higher education institutions and accrediting bodies have sharpened their focus on learning outcomes assessment (e.g., MSCHE, 2005).

Because the focus of academic advising is on the ways in which students make academic choices and implement their educational plans, advisors work at the intersection of many of these issues (Schulenberg & Lindhorst, 2008). Advisors need to understand higher educational institutions and work to interpret the institutions to these various students. They need to know the curriculum and determine how to teach its logic to students for whom the disciplines may be indecipherable. Advisors need to know their students and create advising strategies that maximize the chances the students will be able to make informed choices and navigate the institution's complexity. As described below, some of the current issues in the field reflect these challenges, as academic advisors seek to more clearly understand their students, define educational objectives in advising, assess student learning outcomes, develop and apply theories to inform practice, and implement a research agenda to nourish the field's responses to this complex practice and context.

Understanding Students

Like practitioners in other areas of higher education, academic advisors face the challenge of working with a great diversity of students with unique needs (Kennedy & Ishler, 2008). Academic advisors have noted that the advising relationship and the academic choices of their advisees may be affected by personal, social, cultural, and economic factors (Hunter & Kendall,

2008). An emerging field of scholarship in advising addresses the advising needs of students of color, nontraditional students, students with disabilities, LGBT students, and athletes, among other categories (Harding, 2008). In addition, the scholarship of academic advising addresses the particular advising challenges for students in various academic areas (e.g., students pursuing business, education, or engineering majors) or with particular academic needs (Steele & McDonald, 2008). Scholarship and interest groups within the profession examine advising issues and strategies related to students who are first generation, honors, undecided or exploratory, or "at-risk" because of weak preparation (Harding, 2008).

In all of these areas, advisors seek to increase their understanding of the characteristics of students in these special groups as learners and decision-makers (Appleby, 2008). Advisors, like other higher education professionals, need to understand the particular challenges these students may face in the classroom and in the institution generally. The choices students are prepared to make may be affected by their self-interpretation and their life conditions, as well as the institution's responses to their characteristics and needs (Self, 2007). Of consequence for advisors, the advising relationship may be affected by the interpersonal dynamics between the advisor and students whose life experiences and perspectives may be different from those of the advisor.

This scholarship also addresses the advising strategies that might be employed with certain groups of students to enhance the advising relationship. Harding (2008) notes that part of the challenge with many special groups of students lies in the coordination of academic advising with student support programs. For example, advisors not only need to appreciate the particular issues facing student athletes which will affect their academic decisions and progress, but also need to coordinate with athletic counselors to provide a coherent engagement with the individual student. Academic advisors need to understand how they relate systemically to other offices that also address the particular challenges of special populations of students.

Educational Objectives and the
Assessment of Student Learning Outcomes

Academic advising has participated in the recent focus within higher education on student learning. As academic advisors began to discuss the role of advisors as teachers (Lowenstein, 1999), they also began to participate in the broader discussion of student learning outcomes. What do academic advisors teach? What do advisees learn? How are the educational objectives of advisors for their students different from the educational objectives of other educators, including those in student personnel fields? What will advisees know, be able to do, and value, as a result of academic advising? These questions have sparked a broad discussion in the field (Appleby, 2008; Lowenstein, 2005).

This focus on teaching and learning within advising also provides the background for a focus on assessment that has increasingly centered on the measurement of student learning outcomes. For several years, the National Academic Advising Association has sponsored an Assessment of Academic Advising Institute at which academic advisors and advising administrators can increase their understanding of assessment tools and strategies. It is a part of a broader commitment to the assessment of advising programs and student learning outcomes within the profession (McGillin & Nutt, 2007).

While assessment tools have existed for some time in the academic advising field, they typically involved an assessment of program delivery and advisor behaviors, often in the form of student satisfaction surveys (e.g., Winston & Sandor, 1984). More recently, though advisor and program effectiveness are still the subjects of assessment efforts (Cuseo, 2008; Troxel, 2008), there has been a strong focus on an elaboration of educational objectives (set in the context of the advising unit's mission) and student learning outcomes that can be measured (CAS, 2005; McGillin & Nutt, 2007; Schuh, 2008). While many formulations of these possible outcomes of academic advising have been grounded in more general statements about student development (CAS, 2005) and include possible outcomes in all areas of student life, more recent efforts to define outcomes specific to academic advising have focused on areas such as awareness of the curriculum, academic disciplines, and the nature of student educational choices and experiences (McGillin & Nutt, 2007). These outcomes include skills in self-evaluation, specific awareness of majors, degree requirements (e.g., knowledge of general education requirements), academic opportunities such as education abroad and undergraduate research, facility with Web resources such as degree audit systems, and an understanding of university policies such as entrance to major requirements (McGillin & Nutt, 2007).

This focus on learning outcomes for academic advising has nourished broader assessment efforts and an outreach to educate students about the advising relationship. The idea of an advising syllabus has gained much currency, as a vehicle by which academic advisors can let students know what the advisor can teach them and what they should learn through the relationship (Appleby, 2008). In the advising syllabus, the advisor can begin to teach students about the nature of the educational choices they will need to make, the information and awareness that will be crucial for those decisions, and the expectations that the advisor has for what students will achieve through this relationship. The syllabus sets the advising relationship squarely in the teaching and learning context (Appleby, 2008).

Informing Practice with Theory and Research

As the numbers of professional academic advisors have expanded in recent years, the field has begun to develop a body of scholarship that supports its practice and expresses the unique insights of academic advising as an academic field of inquiry (Schulenberg & Lindhorst, 2008). The National Academic Advising Association (2009) has made the development of research and scholarship a priority for its members, identifying critical areas for research, providing grants and resources, and offering workshops to support members' research work. As part of that scholarship, efforts to articulate and create theoretical perspectives that inform the practice of academic advising continue at a significant pace (NACADA, 2009). Advisors have often used theories and research insights from related fields such as career and psychological counseling and student personnel to describe, understand, and improve advising practice, as many have noted (Hagen & Jordan, 2008; Schulenberg & Lindhorst, 2008). Current efforts in the field have focused on the development of new theory, and scholarship focused more specifically on academic advising as a unique practice and field (Schulenberg & Lindhorst, 2008).

Because academic advisors need to know about students, the field has made extensive use of general theories about student development which inform many fields in higher education, to understand the student as a whole person making educational decisions (Williams, 2007). More recently, the teaching-learning paradigm has been extensively used to understand the advising relationship, with a focus on the student's intellectual engagement and academic decision-making (Hemwall & Tracte, 2005). Further, theories from other fields (e.g., narrative theory, social norms theory) have been applied to advising to provide insight into the advising exchange (Demetriou, 2005; Hagen & Jordan, 2008).

Academic advising practitioner-scholars conduct research on a range of topics relating to students, higher education institutions, curriculum, and the larger educational objectives of higher education, as well as the broad social and cultural contexts in which advisors work. Research into student characteristics, how students make academic decisions, how they engage with institutions and curricula, and how specific technologies and interactions might be used in advising are at the forefront of researchers' concerns (NACADA, 2009). Increasingly, the areas of research in advising address a multiplicity of topics, including the creation of general and local histories of advising units, comparative studies of advising in other countries, the significance of general education, and broad examinations of higher education and curriculum (Schulenberg & Lindhorst, 2008). A robust conversation about the nature of academic advising itself is another feature in the profession's theory and research agenda as it continues into the twenty-first century (Schulenberg & Lindhorst, 2008). In a growing professional field, this scholarly work supports improved practice and contributes to general higher education scholarship.

REFERENCES

Appleby, D. C. (2008). Theoretical foundations of academic advising. In V. N. Gordon, W. R. Habley, & T. J. Grites (Eds.), *Academic advising: A comprehensive handbook* (2nd ed.) (pp. 85–102). San Francisco: Jossey-Bass.

Barr, R., & Tagg, J. (1995). From teaching to learning: A new paradigm for undergraduate education. *Change, 27*(6), 12–25.

Brubacher, J. S., & Rudy, R. (1968). *Higher education in transition.* New York: Harper & Row.

Campbell, S. (2008). Vision, mission, goals, and program objectives for academic advising programs. In V. N. Gordon, W. R. Habley, & T. J. Grites (Eds.), *Academic advising: A comprehensive handbook* (2nd ed.) (pp. 229–241). San Francisco: Jossey-Bass.

Cook, S. (2009). Important events in the development of academic advising in the United States. *NACADA Journal, 29*(2), 18–40.

Council for the Advancement of Standards in Higher Education (CAS). (1986). *CAS standards and guidelines for student services/development programs.* Washington, DC: Consortium of Student Affairs Professional Organizations.

Council for the Advancement of Standards in Higher Education (CAS). (2005). *Academic advising: CAS standards and guidelines.* Retrieved from http://www.nacada.ksu.edu/Clearinghouse/Research_Related/CASStandardsForAdvising.pdf.

Council for the Advancement of Standards in Higher Education (CAS). (2009). *CAS professional standards for higher education* (7th ed.). Washington, DC: Author.

Creamer, D. G., & Creamer, E. G. (1994). Practicing developmental advising: Theoretical contexts and functional applications. *NACADA Journal, 14*(2), 17–24.

Crookston, B. B. (1972). A developmental view of academic advising as teaching. *Journal of College Student Personnel, 13,* 12–17.

Cuseo, J. (2008). Assessing advisor effectiveness. In V. N. Gordon, W. R. Habley, & T. J. Grites (Eds.), *Academic advising: A comprehensive handbook* (pp. 369–385). San Francisco: Jossey-Bass.

Demetriou, C. (2005). Potential applications of social norms theory to academic advising. *NACADA Journal, 25*(2), 49–56.

Fox, R. (2008). Delivering one-to-one advising skills and competencies. In V. N. Gordon, W. R. Habley, & T. J. Grites (Eds.), *Academic advising: A comprehensive handbook* (pp. 342–355). San Francisco: Jossey-Bass.

Frost, S. H. (1991). *Academic advising for student success: A system of shared responsibility.* (ASHE-AAHE Higher Education Report No. 3, pp. 3–8). Washington, DC: The George Washington University School of Education and Human Development.

Frost, S. H. (2000). Historical and philosophical foundations for academic advising. In V. N. Gordon & W. R. Habley (Eds.), *Academic advising: A comprehensive handbook* (pp. 3–17). San Francisco: Jossey-Bass.

Goetz, J. J. (2004). In F. McKinnon & Associates (Eds.), *Rentz's student affairs practice in higher education* (pp. 89–107). Springfield, IL: Charles C Thomas.

Gordon, V. N. (1992). *Handbook of academic advising.* Westport, CT: Greenwood Press.

Gordon, V. N., & Habley, W. R. (Eds.). (2000). *Academic advising: A comprehensive handbook.* San Francisco: Jossey-Bass.

Gordon, V. N., Habley, W. R., & Grites, T. J. (Eds.) (2008). *Academic advising: A comprehensive handbook* (2nd ed.). San Francisco: Jossey-Bass.

Grites, T. J. (1979). *Academic advising: Getting us through the eighties,* American Association for Higher Education Resources Information Center (AAHE-ERIC, Higher Education Research Report No. 7). Washington, DC: American Association for Higher Education.

Habley, W. R. (1983). Organizational structures of academic advising: Models and implications. *Journal of College Student Personnel, 24*(6), 535–540.

Habley, W. R. (Ed.). (2004). *The status of academic advising: Findings from the ACT Sixth National Survey.* (NACADA Monograph Series, No. 10, pp. 93–95). Manhattan, KS: National Academic Advising Association.

Hagen, P. L., & Jordan, P. (2008). Theoretical foundations of academic advising. In V. N. Gordon, W. R. Habley, & T. J. Grites (Eds.), *Academic advising: A comprehensive handbook* (2nd ed., pp. 17–35). San Francisco: Jossey-Bass.

Harding, B. (2008). Students with specific advising needs. In V. N. Gordon, W. R. Habley, & T. J. Grites (Eds.), *Academic advising: A comprehensive handbook* (pp. 189–203). San Francisco: Jossey-Bass.

Hemwall, M. K., & Trachte, K. (2005). Academic advising as learning: 10 organizing principles. *NACADA Journal, 25*(2), 74–83.

Hopkins, L. B. (1926). *Personnel procedure in education: Observations and conclusions resulting from visits to fourteen institutions of higher learning.* Washington, DC: American Council on Education.

Hunter, M. S., & Kendall, L. (2008). Moving into college. In V. N. Gordon, W. R. Habley, & T. J. Grites (Eds.), *Academic advising: A comprehensive handbook* (pp. 142–156). San Francisco: Jossey-Bass.

Keeling, R. P. (Ed.). (2004). *Learning reconsidered: A campus-wide focus on the student experience.* Washington, DC: National Association of Student Personnel Administrators–Student Affairs Administrators in Higher Education.

Keeling, R. P. (Ed.). (2006). *Learning reconsidered 2: Implementing a campus-wide focus on the student experience.* Washington, DC: National Association of Student Personnel Administrators–Student Affairs Administrators in Higher Education.

Kelley, B. (2008). Significant learning, significant advising. *NACADA Journal, 28*(1), 19–28.

Kennedy, K., & Ishler, J. C. (2008). The changing college student. In V. N. Gordon, W. R. Habley, & T. J. Grites (Eds.), *Academic advising: A comprehensive handbook* (pp. 123–141.). San Francisco: Jossey-Bass.

Keup, J. R., & Kinzie, J. (2007). A national portrait of first-year students. In M. S.

Hunter, B. McCalla-Wriggins, & E. R. White (Eds.), *Academic advising: New insights for teaching and learning in the first year* (pp. 19–38). Columbia, SC: University of South Carolina, National Resource Center for the First-Year Experience and Students in Transition.

King, M. C. (2008). Organization of academic advising services. In V. N. Gordon, W. R. Habley, & T. J. Grites (Eds), *Academic advising: A comprehensive handbook* (pp. 242–252). San Francisco: Jossey-Bass.

King, N. S. (2008). Advising delivery: Group strategies. In V. N. Gordon, W. R. Habley, & T. J. Grites (Eds), *Academic advising: A comprehensive handbook* (pp. 279–291). San Francisco: Jossey-Bass.

Laff, N. S. (2006). Teachable moments: Advising as liberal learning. *Liberal Education, 92*(2), 36–41.

Leonard, M. J. (2008). Advising delivery: Using technology. In V. N. Gordon, W. R. Habley, & T. J. Grites (Eds), *Academic advising: A comprehensive handbook* (pp. 292–306). San Francisco: Jossey-Bass.

Lowenstein, M. (1999). An alternative to the developmental theory of advising. *The Mentor, 1*(4). Retrieved from http://www.psu.edu/dus/mentor.

Lowenstein, M. (2000). Academic advising and the "logic" of the curriculum. *The Mentor, 2*(2). Retrieved from http://www.psu.edu/dus/mentor.

Lowenstein, M. (2005). If advising is teaching, what do advisors teach? *NACADA Journal, 25*(2), 65–73.

McCauley, M. (2000). Technological resources that support advising. In V. N. Gordon & Wesley R. Habley (Eds.), *Academic advising: A comprehensive handbook* (pp. 238–248). San Francisco: Jossey-Bass.

Middle States Commission on Higher Education. (MSCHE). (2005). *Assessing student learning and institutional effectiveness: Understanding middle states expectations.* Retrieved from http://www.msache.org/.

McGillin, V., & Nutt, C. (2007). Assessment of advising: Measuring teaching and learning outcomes outside the classroom. In M. S. Hunter, B. McCalla-Wriggins, & E. R. White (Eds.), *Academic advising: New insights for teaching and learning in the first year.* Columbia, SC: University of South Carolina, National Resource Center for the First-Year Experience and Students in Transition.

NACADA. (2006). *NACADA concept of academic advising.* Retrieved from http://www.nacada.ksu.edu/Clearinghouse/AdvisingIssues/Concept-Advising.htm.

NACADA. (2009). *Research agenda.* Retrieved from http://www.nacada.ksu.edu/Clearinghouse/Research_Related/researchagenda.htm.

Nutt, C. (2009, April). Is academic advising an academic affairs or student affairs function [Web log message]? Retrieved from http://www.nacada.ksu.edu/web/index.php/blogs/charlie.

O'Banion, T. (1972). An academic advising model. *Junior College Journal, 42*(6), 62–69.

Raskin, M. (1979). Critical issue: Faculty advising. *Peabody Journal of Education, 56*(2), 99–108.

Robertson, J. H. (1958). Academic advising in colleges and universities: Its present state and present problems. *The North Central Association Quarterly, 32*(January),

228–239.

Rudolph, R., (1962). *The American college and university.* New York: Random House.

Rudolph, F. (1990). *The American college and university: A history* (2nd ed.). Athens, GA: University of Georgia Press.

Schein, H. (1995). University residence halls in the academic advising process. In R. E. Glennen & F. N. Vowell (Eds.), *Academic advising as a comprehensive campus process* (NACADA Monograph Series, No. 2, pp. 115–120). Manhattan, KS: National Academic Advising Association.

Schuh, J. H. (2008). Assessing student learning. In V. N. Gordon, W. R. Habley, & T. J. Grites (Eds.), *Academic advising: A comprehensive handbook* (pp. 356–368). San Francisco: Jossey-Bass.

Schulenberg, J., & Lindhorst, M. (2008). Advising is advising: Toward defining the practice and scholarship of academic advising. *NACADA Journal 28*(1), 43–53.

Self, C. (2007). Advising lesbian, gay, bisexual, and transgender first-year students. In M. S. Hunter, B. McCalla-Wriggins, & E. R. White (Eds.), *Academic advising: New insights for teaching and learning in the first year* (pp. 213–221). Columbia, SC: University of South Carolina, National Resource Center for the First-Year Experience and Students in Transition.

Self, C. (2008). Advising delivery: Professional advisors, counselors, and other staff. In V. N. Gordon, W. R. Habley, & T. J. Grites (Eds.), *Academic advising: A comprehensive handbook* (pp. 267–278). San Francisco: Jossey-Bass.

Steele, G. E., & McDonald, M. L. (2008). Moving through college. In V. N. Gordon, W. R. Habley, & T. J. Grites (Eds.), *Academic advising: A comprehensive handbook* (pp. 157–177). San Francisco: Jossey-Bass.

Thelin, J. R. (2004). *A history of American higher education.* Baltimore: The Johns Hopkins University Press.

Troxel, W. (2008). Assessing the effectiveness of the advising program. In V. N. Gordon, W. R. Habley, & T. J. Grites (Eds.), *Academic advising: A comprehensive handbook* (pp. 386–395). San Francisco: Jossey-Bass.

U.S. Department of Education (2006). *A test of leadership: Charting the future of U.S. higher education.* Retrieved from http://www.ed.gov/about/bdscomm/list/hiedfuture/reports/final-report.pdf.

White, E. R. (2005, February). Academic advising and technology: Some thoughts. *Academic Advising News 28*(1). Retrieved from http://www.nacada.ksu.edu/AAT/NW28_1.pdf.

White, E. R., & Leonard, M. J. (2003). Faculty Advising and Technology. In Gary L. Kramer (Ed.), *Faculty advising examined: Enhancing the potential of college faculty as advisors.* Bolton, MA: Anker.

White, M. R., & Khakpour, P. (2006). The advent of academic advising in America at the Johns Hopkins University. *The Mentor, 8*(4). Retrieved from http://www.psu.edu/dus/mentor/.

Williams, S. (2007). *From theory to practice: The application of theories of development to academic advising philosophy and practice.* Retrieved from http://www.nacada.ksu.edu/Clearinghouse/AdvisingIssues/Theories.htm.

Winston, R. B., Jr., Miller, T. K., Ender, S. C., & Grites, T. J. (Eds.). (1984).

Developmental academic advising. San Francisco: Jossey-Bass.

Winston, Jr., R. B., & Sandor, J. A. (1984). Developmental academic advising: What do students want? *NACADA Journal, 4*(1), 5–13.

Woolston, D., & Ryan, R. (2007). Group advising. In P. Folsom & B. Chamberlain (Eds.), *The new advisor guidebook: Mastering the art of advising through the first year and beyond* (NACADA Monograph Series, No. 16, pp. 119–123). Manhattan, KS: National Academic Advising Association.

Chapter 5

CAREER SERVICES

Lisa Severy

INTRODUCTION

What does it mean to be an educated person? What are the goals for college graduates after graduation? What responsibility does the university have to alumni post-graduation? What role should faculty play in the professional, post-graduation development of students? Why do people go to college? Many colleges and universities have been grappling with these questions for years. In a global sense, they represent questions about the ultimate worth and value of the education provided. From an outcomes perspective, they represent the bottom line for students (and parents) in terms of what exactly they get for their time and money investments. In a national poll conducted by *The Chronicle of Higher Education* in 2003 which assessed public opinions on higher education, respondents indicated that the most important role for a college is preparing undergraduates for a career (Selingo, 2003). These questions also represent the scope and mission of career services centers in higher education. Founded mostly by single staff members challenged with the task of job placement, career services have grown and evolved along with colleges and universities to represent the breadth and depth of personal, academic and professional development.

A general description of a Career Services department can be hard to describe as colleges and universities define this type of department, including what are essential components and how to measure success, in very different ways. From varied structures (e.g., career services by discipline or centralized), varied reporting lines (e.g., in individual colleges, in academic administration or student affairs), and varied program offerings (e.g., counseling, credit-based career classes, experiential education, academic testing, job fairs, and placement), the definition of a "typical" can be elusive (Bechtel,

119

1993). These differences will be described later in this chapter, but it is important to know that everything discussed here may look very different depending on the campus and its priorities.

Unlike some student services such as health care centers, mental health counseling, or student housing, the career services department seems to be an ever-changing entity with a different menu of services every five to ten years, even within the same institution. As one of the bridges between the world of academia and the world of work, an unbendable organization and selection of services for career services would ultimately break and be unable to serve the needs of the institution. In other words, with a constantly changing student population and a constant shifting in terms of demands from the marketplace, an adaptable, changing career center is imperative.

Most career professionals recognize that the placement model has out-lived its usefulness (Lucas, 1986; Rayman, 1993; Wessel, 1998). Although some cringe at the "p" word, it is important to acknowledge its place in history. The placement model worked well with small numbers of graduates joining a stable, life-long career path, usually with the same company. Those career paths no longer run a straight course, and most graduates will leave their first jobs within one to three years. If every "placed" graduate returned to his or her alma maters for career services, institutions would be unable to accommodate the sheer number of requests. A 1999 U.S. Department of Labor report, titled "Futurework–Trends and Challenges for work in the 21st Century," found that young people would hold an average of nine jobs before the age of 32. David Birch (1990) expanded this idea in his article titled "The Coming Demise of the Single-Career Career" by predicting that today's college graduates can expect to have three to five careers with ten to twelve jobs before they retire.

Newer models of career services have, therefore, adapted to more accurately reflect the needs of graduates (Casella, 1990; Wessel, 1998). Like the old cliché, career services professionals are teaching people to fish for a life-time rather than providing fish for a day. The shift from a placement model to a professional development model has also opened the door for career development activities that span the academic tenure, rather than meeting people only on the way out (Casella, 1990; Wessel, 1998). Job placement spread to internship placement, which opened the door to career planning and so on.

In the early days of career services up until quite recently, it was not uncommon to see lines of students wrapped around the block, simply waiting to physically sign up for interview slots. The process at that time was tedious for both career service staff and students seeking opportunities. Technological advances in data storage and referral helped to alleviate many of these issues (Harris-Bowlsbey & Sampson, 2005). Today, students can log on to their job searching accounts at 2 a.m., read job descriptions from employers coming to campus, submit their resumes, and schedule interviews. This "no walls career center" helps to meet the needs of students at their own pace and in their preferred mode. At the same time, this high-tech approach has not replaced the need for high touch assistance (NACE, 2008, April). Now that the burden of managing an intensely detailed system has been given to computers, career services staff have more time to meet with students. Career counselors and coaches focus on more developmental tasks and skills such as decision making, resume writing, interviewing and professional skills. Whether online or in person, students have more access than ever before to programs and services designed to help them plan and prepare for their futures.

This emphasis on career and personal planning reflects role of work in our culture. When students meet each other for the first time, the next question after a name exchange is generally "What's your major?" After graduation, that question changes slightly to "What do you do?" So much personal identity is wrapped up in professional identity that focusing on one without the other seems ludicrous. Work has been described as people's connection to the world outside of themselves. In that sense, it could be argued that career service departments are higher education's connection to the world outside of academia.

HISTORY

Placement

As long as there have been institutions of higher education, there has been career placement. In the beginning, these services were provided directly by faculty and administrators, often through the network of friends and acquaintances (Blaska & Schmidt, 1977; Lucas, 1986; Wessel, 1998). This "old boys' network" of male faculty and male students providing placement in an employment situation constituted a rite of passage, a transformation from student to colleague, under the sponsorship of the principal professor (Blaska & Schmidt, 1977; Lucas, 1986; Wessel, 1998). This informal system served students and institutions well for years. Over time, however, professional demands on faculty in terms of teaching and research began to overshadow this important function. Also, as faculty members became more insulated to the university and less connected with those outside of academia, the breadth and depth of the network suffered. As the student population grew in number and diversity, the role of mentoring and advocacy outside of the classroom moved further away from individual faculty members. In response to student demand for assistance, colleges and universities began taking a more centralized role in career assistance (Blaska & Schmidt, 1977; Lucas, 1986; Wessel, 1998).

Formal placement activities emerged from two main paths. In some instances, groups of faculty and administrators began forming committees to help students meet their professional goals (Blaska & Schmidt, 1977; Lucas, 1986; Wessel, 1998). Early examples include the Oxford University Committee on Appointments in 1899 and Yale University's in 1919. This development coincided with the larger vocational development movement, pioneered by Frank Parsons in the early 1900s (Baker, 2009; Lucas, 1986). At the same time, teacher placement emerged as a formal endeavor (Lucas, 1986). Many career centers at colleges and universities today trace their roots back to early teacher placement programs (Blaska & Schmidt, 1977).

In 1924, the National Association of Appointment Secretaries, the first professional organization for practitioners in this field was established (Blaska & Schmidt, 1977; CAS, 2006). In 1931, that organization changed its name to the American College Personnel Association (ACPA), widely recognized today as a leading organization not only for career development practitioners, but for all student affairs professionals. In 1940, the Association of School and College Placement became the first comprehensive, national association for career services, which later became the College Placement Council, and still later grew into the National Association of Colleges and Employers (NACE, 2009, January).

The role of career planning and placement grew in importance after World War II as the demands by employers for educated employees and the great number of veterans returning to school put placement efforts at the forefront of the higher education issues (Blaska & Schmidt, 1977; CAS, 2006). In 1944, 429 colleges and universities partnered with the Veteran's Administration to establish counseling services (Blaska & Schmidt, 1977; Lucas, 1986; Wessel, 1998). In the following year, the first *Occupational Information Handbook* was published by the Veteran's Association in partnership with the Vocational Rehabilitation and Educational Service as well as the Bureau of Labor Statistics (Blaska & Schmidt, 1977; Lucas, 1986; Wessel, 1998). These partnerships and increased demand for services brought the greatest period of growth for placement offices. By 1950, most colleges and universities offered some form of placement service. As with most growing professional fields, the need to associate and network with other practitioners sparked new professional associations. In 1957, the College Placement Council was formed and served as a clearinghouse for research and publications including the *Directory of College Placement Offices, A Manual for Campus Recruiting,* and *The Fundamentals of College Placement* (Blaska & Schmidt, 1977; Lucas, 1986; Wessel, 1998).

Profound cultural changes surrounding the civil rights movement, the Vietnam War, the women's movement, and the student activism forced colleges and universities to examine their missions and greater role of higher education (Blaska & Schmidt, 1977; Lucas, 1986; Wessel, 1998). At that time, the scope of practice for career services broadened to include the entire career planning process. Once focused exclusively on transition from college to work, career center staff shifted their focus to include the entire career development process. Some form of this balanced model of career placement and career planning can still be seen in most career centers today.

Since the move toward career development and planning, the most significant changes within career service departments have been in technology. On-campus recruiting and job posting automation started with a student employee in the career center at Texas A & M, Erik Mulloy. Mulloy developed software to simplify the university's intense interview scheduling process which he later grew into a complete systematic automation system for career services. This first system called 1st Place! was launched by Mulloy's new company, Academic Software, in 1987 (CSO, 2009). Mulloy ran Academic Software until 1999 and had more than 600 university clients. Mulloy returned to the field in 2001 when he founded Career Services Office (CSO) Research. Frequent mergers, buy-outs, and discontinuation of service by vendors have made the provision of these types of systems somewhat volatile. Current technology will be discussed later in the chapter.

The introduction of Academic Software brought about a huge cultural shift for career centers. No longer tied to a labor intensive recruiting system, more resources could be dedicated to one-on-one counseling interventions. Career centers of today try to integrate their two roles of career counseling and job placement in alignment and support of institutional goals (Hoff, Kroll, MacKinnon, & Rentz, 2004). Several factors have impacted this integrative approach including:

- The restructuring and downsizing of business and industry
- The increasingly global economy
- The change from an industrial economy to a service-oriented economy
- The end of the cold war focus on defense
- The growth of small and medium size companies with smaller volume hiring needs
- The increased debt carried by college students and graduates
- The diversity of students attending college
- The decreasing federal and state support for higher education

Understanding the history and cultural context of career services will help to better understand the theories guiding practice and the changes that have precipitated change.

Career Planning

"Placement" services focused specifically on the process by which a student's skills, education, preferences, and abilities matched the requirements of a particular job or profession (Rayman, 1999). The expansion into "career planning" incorporated the three-part model originally proposed by Frank Parsons including a thorough understanding of self, knowledge of the world of work, and a logical assessment of the fit between the two (Baker, 2009, DeBell, 2001). This shift from the personal to the professional blurred formerly clear lines and distinctions between the internal, psychological focus of counseling centers and the personal focus of career counselors (Hackett, 1993). Some colleges and universities merged these functions, but over time, the need for separate services became clear. What began as a simple matching or brokering services between institutions of higher education and employers evolved into a comprehensive support and development service (Casella, 1990; Wessel, 1998). Rather than focusing solely on graduates transitioning to the world of work, career planning services now focus on professional needs throughout a student's tenure, from choosing a major to selecting a graduate school (Freeman, 1994). In looking at the human resource allocations within career centers, the incorporation of programs designed to help students gain an understanding of themselves, their interests, abilities, values, goals, balanced those solely focused on placement (NACE, 2009, March).

With one foot in the world of work and one foot in academia, career planning professionals are in a unique position to inform the academy about changes graduates should expect from new positions (Bechtel, 1993; Casella, 1990; Wessel, 1998). At the same time, employer relations specialists work closely with employers to help them develop, train, and retain new graduates (Casella, 1990; Wessel, 1998). Career service departments also serve a unique role within the university, often serving as the primary corporate relations department on campus.

PURPOSES AND GOALS

Every college and university has its own unique identity, mission, and purpose and so does every career center. To provide some consistency, the Student Affairs profession has developed core principles that guide practice, including practice within career centers. The Council for the Advancement of Standards (CAS), a consortium of professional associations in higher education, provides standards of practice for a number of student services, including career services. In the sixth edition of its *Professional Standards for Higher Education* (2006), CAS outlines the core mission of career services:

. . . to assist students and other designated clients through all phases of their career development. In addition, the mission of career services is

- To provide leadership to the institution on career development concerns
- To develop position relationships with employers and external constituencies
- To support institutional outcomes assessment and relevant research endeavors.

As institutions and models of service vary, CAS recommends the inclusion of eight key components that involve helping students and others to:

- Develop self-knowledge related to career choice and work performance
- Obtain educational and occupations information to aid career planning and to develop an understanding of the world of work
- Select suitable academic programs and experiential opportunities
- Take personal responsibility for developing job search competencies
- Gain experience through student activities community service, student employment, research or creative projects, cooperative education, internships, and other opportunities
- Link with alumni, employers, professional association, and others to provide opportunities to explore the world of work
- Prepare for finding suitable employment by following established career development practices
- Seek desired employment opportunities or entry into appropriate educational, graduate or professional programs.

In 1993, Jack Rayman edited an important handbook for the New Directions in Student Services series that examined *The Changing Role of Career Services*. In his concluding remarks, Rayman (1993) outlined ten imperatives for career centers:

1. We must acknowledge the lifelong nature of career development and initiate programs and services that enable and encourage students to take responsibility for their own career identity.

2. We must accept and embrace technology as our ally and shape its use to free staff time for those tasks that require human sensitivity.

3. We must continue to refine and strengthen our professional identity and that of career services within the academy.

4. We must acknowledge and accept that individual career counseling is at the core of our profession, and endeavor to maintain and enhance the centrality of individual career counseling in the career development process.

5. We must not forget cooperative relationships with faculty, advising professionals, other student affairs professionals, administrators, and student groups to take advantage of the "multiplier effect" that such cooperative relationships can have in furthering our goal of enhanced student career development.

6. We must redouble our efforts to meet the changing career development needs of an increasingly diverse student body.

7. We must accept our position as the most obvious and continuing link between corporate America and the academy, but we also must maintain our focus on career development and not allow ourselves to be seduced into institutional fundraising at the expense of quality career services.

8. We must acknowledge and accept that on-campus recruiting as we have known it is a thing of the past and develop alternative means of facilitating the transition from college to work.

9. We must resolve the ambiguities that exist about our role in delivering alumni career services and solicit from our alumni associations the resource support necessary to provide those services.

10. We must advocate more effectively for resources to maintain and increase our role in facilitating student career development within the academy, and we must become more efficient and innovative in our use of existing resources. (p. 101)

In his review of his ten imperatives, Rayman (1999) found that all ten had remained remarkably relevant; with a special emphasis on the importance of technology and the continuing need focused on the alumni dilemma. As Rayman notes, "satisfied, successfully employed alumni are more likely to be generous and supportive alumni"(p. 182).

Developing a comprehensive strategic plan has become an essential component of a successful career center to ensure that the above goals are accomplished particularly in response to a climate of constant change in higher education and the employment marketplace.

ADMINISTRATION AND ORGANIZATIONAL STRUCTURES

Organizational Models

Although most college and university campuses have some type of career service, not all have approached this task in the same way. Generally speaking, there are two main structures: "centralized" and "decentralized." The "centralized" career center is usually housed within a campus-wide administrative group like student or administrative affairs. In the Career Services Benchmark Survey (2009, January) from the National Association of Colleges and Employers (NACE), over 68 percent of respondents indicated that they report to the Division of Student Affairs, with another 19 percent reporting to Academic Affairs. The main advantage to a centralized career center is that one office covers the breadth of opportunities on campus and in all kinds of industries (Herr, Rayman, & Garis, 1993). For example, companies or organizations seeking interns or employees can go to one place on campus to connect with the entire university. At the same time, students seeking services are not limited by their academic area but are free to explore many varied opportunities. There are, of course, disadvantages to a centralized model, mostly in that it is very difficult for one campus career center to have an intricate knowledge of the entire campus and, therefore, some centralized career centers feel somewhat disconnected from the specific faculty and student groups (Herr, Rayman, & Garis, 1993). Additionally, staffing within centralized career services does not always grow at the same rate as enrollment, making it difficult to provide service at appropriate levels.

The decentralized career center is part of the administration of a particular school or college within the university and is, therefore, more intricately involved at the academic level (Herr, Rayman, & Garis, 1993). This model addresses the very issue of disconnection between the center and the specific faculty and student groups, helping career center staff to be more closely connected to faculty, staff and employers in a particular area as well as more aligned with a particular college's goals and needs. Of course the trade-off is accessibility. For example, if one employer would like to meet multiple constituencies, he or she must make multiple trips to campus and connect with various offices. Another disadvantage to the decentralized model involves repetition of services and much higher costs. Having multiple career centers on one campus is very expensive and requires a great deal more human resources than a centralized campus. For example, the University of Colorado at Boulder has one career center that serves the entire campus. At the University of Texas at Austin, there are 14 different career centers, each with its own budget and staff. From a resource perspective, the centralized model is much more efficient. Many universities have implemented hybrid approaches that bridge both models and ameliorate their relative disadvantages, including satellite offices, consortiums of all campus career services offices, and liaison models.

According to the latest *State of the Profession: Career Services Benchmark Survey* (January, 2009) from the National Association of Colleges and Employers (NACE), most universities offer primarily centralized service delivery models rather than decentralized models. Of those schools participating, over 88 percent defined themselves as a centralized service. As colleges and universities struggle to provide more services with fewer resources and funding, centralized career services may offer an advantage in terms of efficient use of human resources, office space, equipment, technology costs, and convenience for students and employers.

Reporting Structure

As career and professional development crosses so many areas of student development, it is not surprising that reporting structures vary and reporting structure trends change constantly. Most centralized career services are housed with the division of student affairs, with many career center directors reporting directly to the division head (vice chancellor or vice president) or to the dean of students. According to a recent National Association of Colleges and Employers (NACE) survey, over two-thirds of the respondents reported being a part of the division of student affairs (2009, January). Being housed within the division of Student Affairs increases referrals between career services and other student-related services (Hoff, Kroll, MacKinnon, & Rentz, 2004). In addition, being a part of the student development program from orientation through graduation helps the service gain recognition (Hoff et al., 2004). This integration into Student Affairs is somewhat different from the early years of career centers when most directors reported directly to the president or provost (Herr, Rayman, & Garis, 1993). Being structured within a particular discipline enhances the relationship with faculty in that college, which also helps to build a strong resource base (Herr, Rayman, & Garis, 1993). Other reporting structure examples include a reporting line to the Dean for Undergraduate Education or into Enrollment Management. Such reporting structures often foster greater connection to all of the academic units as well as enhanced funding because of the connection to the educational enterprise. As institutions of higher education become more complex, reporting structures continue to vary and a typical reporting structure is difficult to define.

Regardless of structure or reporting line, key components must be available to career service personnel in order to run an effective practice. Shea (1995) summarized these components:

- Faculty support, acceptance, referral, and buy-in,
- Career professionals with a good understanding of general student development principles and a good working relationship with other Student Affairs practitioners,
- Support from upper administration on the value of career services for the university as well as for individual students and graduates, and
- Funding in accordance with expected outcomes.

Funding

Regardless of reporting lines or organizational structure, career center funding comes from a combination of four main sources: institutional funds, direct revenue, donations, and student fees (Herr, Rayman, & Garis, 1993). First, most career centers receive some money directly from the institution, either through a general fund allocation or from the reporting structure in which they reside. Many career centers also raise their own auxiliary funds through career fairs, partnerships with campus departments, premium services, or testing services. In addition, companies who work closely with career centers often donate funds to help with special projects, sponsor events, or showcase their organization through naming opportunities. Some career centers also receive money directly from students. This may be in the form of fee-for-service, such as charging students a certain amount to register with the online system, or a student fee charged directly with tuition. Most career centers use a combination of these four revenue streams. That diversification may help career centers weather changes. For example, if revenues from career fairs declines in a particular year, a director may be able to ask for a small increase in the student fee to compensate.

TYPES OF SERVICES

As mentioned throughout this chapter, the types of programs and services offered by college and university career centers vary greatly. There are, however, some key services that tend to define a campus career center and can be found in most settings. The Council for the Advancement of Standards in Higher Education (CAS) has outlined four core programs within career services (2006, p. 87-91): Career Counseling, Information Resources on Careers and Further Study, Opportunities for Career Exploration through Experiential Education, and Job Search Services.

Of course, with so much diversity in terms of structure and funding, it should not be surprising that there are significant differences between schools in terms of how these standards are met. Career center staff members are creative, innovative, and dynamic, allowing themselves continually to create entirely new programs as well as to adapt older services to meet the changing needs of students and employers. There are, however, a set of core services that tend to be a part of every career program. In the Career Services Benchmark Survey for Four-year Colleges and Universities (2009, January) conducted by the National Association of Colleges and Employers (NACE), more than 75 percent of respondents offered some type of:

- Career Counseling by Appointment
- Career Fairs
- Professional & Skill Development Workshops
- Assistance with Employer-Offered Internships
- Career Counseling by Drop-in
- Assistance with Academic Internships
- On-Campus Interviewing & Recruiting

In addition, some career centers also offer:

- Career Planning Courses for Academic Credit
- Career Libraries (Online or Physical)
- Credentials Storage & Referral
- Alumni Services
- Testing Services
- Student Employment.

According to NACE, in the last ten years, some service delivery trends have impacted many career centers. First, many career centers have dropped their print libraries and moved towards online resources only (2009, January). Occupational information changes so frequently that many resources seemed out-of-date before they even hit the shelves. Also, as print libraries take up a great deal of facility space, some organizations were able to expand the number of staff offices by closing libraries. Second, many career centers have outsourced their credentials and recommendations file services to third-party vendors like Interfolio (NACE, 2009, January). Now students and alumni can open and manage their credentials files anytime with a variety of payment methods. This outsourcing has saved staff time and helps to alleviate long-term record storage problems. Finally, the accessibility and flexibility of the service increased the level of customer service available to students.

Service to alumni has been an increasing dilemma for colleges and universities, especially as economic changes have thrown many graduates into career transition. It seems that just about every article related to surviving a lay-off encourages people to contact their alma maters for assistance and they certainly have! Some colleges and universities have free services for alumni either through their career center or the alumni relations department (NACE, 2009, January). While this is a great way of staying connected to and supporting alumni, it can also cause great strain on the existing services for current students. At the other end of the spectrum are centers that are completely closed to alumni. Usually, these centers have limited resources that must be dedicated solely to students or they are funded by a student fee. In between these extremes are a range of set-ups including those centers serve alumni on a fee-for-service basis. For example, some offer access to job postings free or on a subscription fee basis while they charge a market or sliding scale rate for counseling. There are also programs that offer services to recent graduates free (within a year or two of graduation) and charge older alumni. While there is no industry standard for the provision of career services for alumni, it is clear that the issue continues to grow more challenging. In fact, many students and parents attending college admissions fairs are asking about career services for students and continuing support upon graduation. According to a 2008 survey by the *Chronicle of Higher Education,* over half of the freshman surveyed indicated that they based their choice of where to attend school on whether or not the school's graduates get good jobs, an almost 3 percent increase over the 2006 survey (Hoover, 2008).

While complete chapters could be included for each type of career service offered, theories behind them, and variations offered throughout the country, the following core services will be covered in more detail: career counseling (including vocational assessment and computer assisted career guidance systems), career courses for credit, occupational information, experiential education (including cooperative education, internships, and student employment), and on-campus recruiting (including career fairs and information sessions).

Career Counseling and Vocational Assessment

While career counseling paradigms and theories guide how an individual practices, three components tend to be common to all. Generally speaking, these components are self-knowledge, knowledge of the world of work, and decision-making skills (DeBell, 2001). Career counselors working with college students and new graduates use early decisions (choosing a major, finding an internship, interviewing for an entry-level position) as a learning tool for a life-time of self career management (Whiston, 2000). By empowering students to effectively manage their own career transitions, career services professionals are planting seeds for future growth (Heppner & Johnston, 1993). Now that a plethora of information is available at the touch of a button, counselors must not only guide students in where to find the best, most accurate information, but also how to sort and integrate relevant details (Gardner, 1998).

According to the CAS Professional Standards for Higher Education (2006), colleges and universities must, ". . . offer career counseling that helps students and other designated clients at any stage of their career development to:

- Understand the relationship between self-knowledge and career choice through assessment of interests, competencies, values, experience, personal characteristic, and desired lifestyles
- Obtain and research occupational, educational, and employment information
- Establish short-term and long-term career goals
- Explore a full range of career and work possibilities
- Make reasoned, informed career choices based on accurate self-knowledge and accurate information about the world of work. (p. 88)

Vocational assessment is one of the major components of career counseling and has been a part of the career counseling profession since its inception. Career counselors often encounter questions like, "where can I get one of those tests that will tell me what I should be?" While vocational assessment tools offer a great deal of information to students in the "self-knowledge" phase of professional development, the overreliance on testing and the tendency for students to put too much weight on the results, makes some counselors wary (Davidson, 2001). Vocational assessments, including norm-referenced instruments, are often well-researched, reliable, and valid (Herr, Rayman, & Garis, 1993). They can be administered individually or in large groups, making them a very effective and efficient intervention. In fact, many of these tools were developed in a time when large groups of people were entering the job market at once, making quick assessments essential (Lucas, 1986). At the same time, these instruments are often criticized in that comparison to a norm group may not account for individual differences and the limited scope of the instruments may encourage students to narrow down choices too quickly.

Vocational assessment has been theorized in two different ways. Most early vocational assessment and some current models are based on a reductionist model. The intent of these assessments is to separate various aspects of the self into small, measureable components. For example, the Holland Code model sorts people into six categories of career interest, thus making it easier for people to find coordinating work settings (Herr, Rayman, & Garis, 1993). Some newer models, on the other hand, advocate for a more holistic approach to building self-knowledge with counselors and clients working together to paint a complete picture (Savickas, 1992). For example, the narrative approach to career counseling asks individuals to reflect on past experiences and themes to help develop and write the next chapter of a person's self story.

The most popular vocational assessment tools currently used by career counselors include the *Myers-Briggs Type Indicator* (MBTI), *Do What You Are, the Strong Interest Inventory, the Campbell Interest & Skills Survey,* and *Strengths Quest* (NACE, 2009, January; Whitfield, Feller, & Wood, 2009). The MBTI was developed 1943 by Katherine Cook Briggs and her daughter, Isabel Briggs Myers, (Myers, McCaulley, Quenk, & Hammer, 1998). Based mostly on the writings and philosophies of Carl Jung, the MBTI indentifies a person as having one preference or the other on four specific criteria: Introversion or Extroversion, Sensing or Intuition, Thinking or Feeling, and Judging or Perceiving (Myers at al., 1998). These preferences are determined by comparing the tester against a large norm group. The combination of these four preferences places a person in one of sixteen personality types. Career counselors use this information to help a client explore what type of work situation might be a good fit.

Do What You Are is a modernized personality type finder based on the best-selling career book by Paul Tieger and Barbara Barron (2007). Using the client's response to realistic scenarios, the system creates a personality profiles using the same four preferences as the MBTI (Tieger & Barron, 2007). These profiles are then linked to potential career paths and college majors (Do What You Are, 2009). This link with college-specific information makes this instrument particularly popular in collegiate career centers.

The Strong Interest Inventory is designed to measure a client's interests in a range of occupations, work activities, leisure activities, and school subjects (Donnay, Morris, Schaubhut, & Thompson, 2005). These interests are then compared with large norm reference groups (Donnay et al., 2005). Results indicate where a student's interests cluster and how these interests compare with satisfied and successful professionals in various fields. The interest clusters are based on the work of John Holland, who identified six general interest categories and comparable work task categories: Realistic, Investigative, Artistic, Social, Enterprising, and Conventional (Donnay et al., 2005).

The *Campbell Interest & Skills Survey* (CISS) is similar to the *Strong Interest Inventory* in that its occupational orientations generally correspond with Holland's RIASEC themes. The CISS categorizes the interest clusters slight differently and actually splits one of Holland's categories into two unique groups: Adventuring & Producing (Realistic), Analyzing (Investigative), Creating (Artistic), Helping (Social), Influencing (Enterprising), and Organizing (Conventional) (Campbell, Hyne, & Nilsen, 1992). Some counselors prefer these new terms for their current students. In addition, the CISS includes a skills-based self-assessment designed to measure a client's confidence in a certain area (Campbell et al., 1992). Counselors can use this information to determine if a lack of confidence may be impacting a student's interest or preference in a certain area (Severy, 2009).

StrengthsQuest is a relatively new addition to vocational assessment in collegiate career services. Developed by the Gallup organization, *StrengthsQuest* (2006) is based on the work of Donald Clifton, Edward Anderson, and Laurie Schreiner. *StrengthsQuest* builds on basic concepts of positive psychology and the power of focusing on strengths rather than deficits (Clifton, Anderson, & Schreiner, 2006). *StrengthsFinder* is the assessment instrument that helps clients rank order 34 distinct strengths. Identifying professional opportunities that benefit from a client's unique combination of strengths can help him or her make both short-term and long-term decisions. As the *StrengthsQuest* system involves a great deal of research as well as a plethora of tools for clients to use while in college and as a graduate, it is quickly becoming very popular with college career counselors (Clifton et al., 2006).

In addition to these instruments, there are other tools available for counselors who want to help students increase their self-knowledge through process, rather than comparison with large norm groups. These tools have been used for years, beginning with card sorts and continuing through creative activities like career collages. These informal assessment tools often promote greater client ownership of the career planning process, increased reflection and self-discovery, and they are offered at little to no cost (Niles & Harris-Bowlsbey, 2009). New tools that combine these two approaches by providing systematic assessment for allowing individuals to explore and create their own pathways are also emerging. These new models include Mark Savickas' narrative career counseling model and the *True Path from Turning Points* (Savickas, 1992; Turning Points, 2009). Mark Savickas (1992, 1995) advocates for the use of story-telling and theme identification to help clients understand who they are in the world and how they want to relate to the world through work. Through a counseling interview, Savickas asks clients to summarize their themes and think about how these themes may play out in the world of work.

True Path from Turning Points (2009) is a collection of both traditional and narrative-based interventions. It is designed to help people identify personal themes of significance and success and then how to translate those personal stories into professional stories. These professional stories can then be turned into marketing materials such as resumes.

Career Counseling

If any service helps to define a career center, it has to be career development and career counseling. According to the NACE survey (2009, January), 93 percent of respondents offer career counseling. Career counselors and coaches provide help to students at all levels and across multiple disciplines. Each student a counselor sees will present a new set of circumstances, challenges, and opportunities. Some students need formal counseling and others need assistance with job related skills. Others may need coaching to help them develop confidence as they progress towards their goals. Presenting concerns that clients bring to career counselors range dramatically from internal, deeply personal issues to professional skill and confidence building. According to Zunker (2002), "Career counseling includes all counseling activities associated with career choices over a life space. In the career counseling process, all aspects of individual needs (including family, work, and leisure) are recognized as integral parts of career decision-making and planning" (p. 9).

Is career counseling personal counseling? Over the years, there has been a great deal of debate on this topic (Hackett, 1993). Although some clients with more pressing clinical and developmental issues may be referred to a campus counseling center, these issues often play a role in career development dilemmas. Therefore, career counselors must have the clinical skills necessary to address the diverse needs of clients in crisis. In the CAS Standards for Higher Education (2006), the guidelines for career counseling include the reminder that counselors must, ". . . recognize that students' career decision making is inextricably linked to additional psycho-social, personal, developmental, and cultural issues and beliefs" (p. 88).

As with most professions, career counselors are supported and guided by an association of colleagues in a professional association. These organizations help to identify and outline competencies required by professionals in the field. Many career counselors in college and university career centers are members of the National Career Development Association (NCDA), a division of the American Counseling Association (2009). NCDA defines career counseling as the process of assisting individuals in the development of a life-career with focus on the definition of the worker role and how that role interacts with other life roles (1997). NCDA has established a set of minimum competency standards necessary to effectively perform the role of career counselor (1997). NCDA recognizes professional career counselors as those with a master's degree or higher who demonstrate the knowledge and skills in career development that generalist counselors might not possess. The NCDA (1997) minimum competencies include skills and knowledge in the following areas:

- Career Development Theory
- Individual & Group Counseling
- Individual & Group Assessment
- Information Resources
- Program Promotion, Management, and Implementation
- Coaching, Consultation, and Performance Improvement
- Diverse Populations
- Supervision
- Ethical & Legal Issues
- Research & Evaluation
- Technology

In this extensive list of competencies, the program promotion, management, and implementation component differentiates career counseling from other types of counseling services on college campuses.

Along with these competencies, other sets of skills are important for career counselors. For example, in addition to individual and group counseling, college career counselors develop programs, workshops, and presentations to engage students at every level of their professional development. Some of these programs focus on specific skills such as building a resume, interviewing, or networking; while others focus on larger concepts like panels of employers or alumni who work in different industries and workshops on developing students' career passion. Many career counselors point to this diversity of task, from meeting with clients to planning and presenting large scale programs and career conferences, as a source of great excitement and satisfaction.

In addition to the National Career Development Association, many career counselors are members of the Career Development Commission within the American College Personnel Association (ACPA). Unlike NCDA which is an organization for career counselors from all settings and all age groups, the Career Development Commission of ACPA serves career counselors specifically working within higher education (ACPA, 2009). Career counselors can expand their professional skills and better their practice by participating in these organizations and attending conferences.

Professional career counselors must stay current with trends in career development and the world of work and use various tools to do so. For example, many career centers subscribe to the *Campus Career Counselor* newsletter. Edited by Peter Vogt and Pamela Braun, the *Campus Career Counselor* (2009) is the only national publication geared specifically towards college and university career services practitioners. It provides information about programs across the country, resource reviews, and summaries of the latest information and research in the field. In addition, there is also phenomenal research being done by Phil Gardner at Michigan State University's Collegiate Employment Research Institute (CERI, 2009).

Computer-Assisted Career Guidance Systems

Computer-assisted career guidance systems (CACGS) have been used in college and university career centers since the 1960s (Harris-Bowlsbey & Sampson, 2001, 2005; Iaccarino, 2000). Those who developed the first systems were generally theorists and educators looking to operationalize their models of career development, choice, and decision-making (Harris-Bowlsbey & Sampson, 2001; 2005). They hoped that these new systems would help clients gain self-knowledge and knowledge of the world of work, while facilitating solid decision-making (Iaccarino, 2000). Early CACGS included the Education and Career Exploration System, the System for Interactive Guidance and Information, and the Information System for Vocational Decisions (Harris-Bowlsbey & Sampson, 2001, 2005). Some of these early systems never reached the general population in that they were too complex for the computer systems available at the time. By the 1970s, they were replaced by more simple models that were more manageable and accessible (Harris-Bowlsbey & Sampson, 2001, 2005). These systems continued to be used through the 1970s-1980s as stand-alone units and into the 1990s as stand-alone and networked systems. With the introduction of the internet, a more direct mode of service delivery became available and more CACGS moved in that direction (Harris-Bowlsbey & Sampson, 2001, 2005).

Early research on computer-assisted career guidance programs (CACGS) indicated that use of these systems increased self-knowledge, occupational knowledge, knowledge of the needs for a career plan, and career decidedness (Harris-Bowlsbey & Sampson, 2001, 2005). At the same time, research found that CACGS were most effective when used in conjunction with individual or group career counseling (Niles & Garis, 1990).

According to a National Association of Colleges and Employers (NACE) survey, almost 52 percent of college and university career centers provide access to computer-assisted career guidance systems (CACGS) for their students (NACE, 2009, January). Of those, more than 85 percent used one of three products or systems: SIGI/SIGI PLUS, DISCOVER, and Focus (NACE, 2009, January).

Career and Life Planning Classes

Perhaps the most effective method for integrating career planning and professional development into the campus environment is to embed it right into the curriculum (Halasz, 2000; Oliver & Spokane, 1988). Many colleges and universities offer classes for academic credit. Unfortunately, according to the Career Services Benchmark Survey of Four-Year Colleges and Universities conducted by NACE, only about a third of career centers are able to offer credit career classes (2009, January). Career classes vary in scope from career exploration and decision making to career theory (Halasz, 2000). Research on the efficacy of credit-based career classes indicates that students who participate in these classes have higher career decidedness, change majors with less frequency, have higher attrition rates, and graduate in a shorter time period than students who do not take these courses (Niles & Garis, 1990; Oliver & Spokane, 1988;). These outcomes may be confounded by the fact that most of these courses are elective and the students who choose to take them may also be more engaged in college in general, but the impact that these integrated courses have on student success cannot be ignored (Halasz, 2000). Some colleges and universities have been successful in mandating early career development coursework while others have integrated the curriculum into other mandatory classes. Several universities, including Colorado State University and the University of Central Florida, have enjoyed success in incorporating career development content into First Year Experience programming, such as Freshman Seminars. Only time will tell if this trend will help to bolster overall retention goals for colleges and universities.

Information Resources

As mentioned earlier, some career centers have closed their physical libraries recently in efforts to save space and resources, as well as to keep information up to date. As an alternative to print libraries, most career centers point students to quality career information on their websites or provide subscription access to comprehensive online career libraries. Perhaps the most widely used and most accessible resource is the online Occupational Outlook Handbook (OOH), the modern version of the occupational information first collected when the field began (Bureau of Labor Statistics, 2009). The OOH includes information on 400 different types of jobs collected by the US Bureau of Labor Statistics and is revised every two years (Bureau of Labor Statistics, 2009). Each entry includes information about the training and education requirements of the job, earnings, job prospects, job descriptions, and working conditions. Although not all of the occupations outlined in the OOH require a college degree, the website (http://www.bls.gov/OCO/) provides a solid starting point for career-related information. In addition to the OOH, other free websites (Monster, JobWeb, HotJobs) and subscription service sites (WetFeet, Vault) are also available to provide information on companies, salaries, and job searching skills.

Experiential Education Programs

Although there is a great deal of variation in employer expectations, generally speaking, employers are drawn to candidates based on the combination of three key components: education/training, skills, and experience (CAS, 2006; Herr, Rayman, & Garis, 1993). There are many ways to gain important professional experience and leadership skills. Experiential education programs embrace this by offering students the opportunity to learn out in the world to compliment their classroom experiences. Experiential education happens all over campus, like in labs or in study abroad programs. Within career services, these generally take the form of internship and cooperative education programs. Research indicates that students who participate in these types of programs are more likely to graduate and more likely to graduate sooner that those who do not (Wolff & Tinney, 2006). In addition, internship and other experiential education programs can help students to be more marketable, to develop networks of professionals in specific companies and fields, and can help students hone their career choices. Finding a good career fit is just like shopping for a pair of jeans–it often helps to try on a few pair to see which ones fit best.

According to the NACE 2008 Experiential Education Survey, companies draw 40 percent of their full-time hires from their intern programs. This trend is increasing. In the 2001 survey, just over 35 percent of interns were converted to full-time employees whereas in 2008, more than half were. In another survey conducted in 1998, 88 percent of the recruiters surveyed indicated that related work experience as either important or very important (Reardon, Lenz, & Folsom, 1998).

According to the 2006 CAS Standards, "Experiential learning programs enable students to integrate their academic studies with work experiences and career exploration" (p. 89). Although most people think of internships, experiential education may take many forms including cooperative education (full-time, paid experiences over multiple semesters), service learning, volunteer opportunities, research projects, or student employment. In terms of career service benchmarks, only about 18 percent of career centers manage student employment on their campuses as most of these programs are managed through the office of financial aid (NACE, 2008, March).

Internships may take many forms, and coordinating an internship program can be complicated. There are two sides of the internship equation, the employer who provides the experience and may or may not provide monetary compensation, and the academic department which may be involved in supervising the experience and may or may not choose to grant academic credit. Each of these groups has requirements that may conflict with each other and at times the student may be caught in the middle. For example, a company may require an unpaid intern to be receiving academic credit in order to do an internship. That student may be trapped if his or her academic department decides that the experience does not meet the requirements of that program. Internship coordinators in career centers work closely with academic departments and with employers to minimize these conflicts and create systems that work for everyone. They may also spend a good deal of time networking with employers to develop and provide more internship opportunities.

Many experiential education coordinators belong to professional associations including the Cooperative Education and Internship Association (CEIA, 2009) or the National Society for Experiential Education (NSEE, 2009). Being a member of these organizations and participating in professional development opportunities help staff members increase their skills and understand more about other successful programs.

ON-CAMPUS RECRUITING AND CAREER FAIRS

The opportunity for students and employers to meet face-to-face has continued to be a core function of career services, even as technology becomes more a part of the industry (Stewart, 1993). Some theorists such as Donald Casella and Roger Wessel describe the progression of the career services industry as starting with placement, moving to career planning, and now emerging as a networking paradigm (Casella, 1990; Wessel, 1998). The networking paradigm focuses attention on the career center's role of bringing together students, alumni, employers, and university faculty and staff in all aspects of professional development. On-campus recruiting and career fairs are the most traditional ways in which career centers provide these groups opportunities to network.

In the NACE Career Services Benchmark survey (2009, January), almost 94 percent of respondents indicated that they provide career fairs. In addition, 75 percent of those surveyed offer formal on-campus recruiting programs, a number that increases significantly with the size of the school. Of those schools with enrollment over 20,000 students, 98 percent have on-campus recruiting programs.

As with most everything else in career services, career fairs tend to vary greatly between schools. From large, all-major fairs for all industries, to small, specialized fairs for one discipline only, the concept of "career fair" is hard to define. Generally, fairs offer the opportunity for companies to set-up displays that provide information about their organization and their hiring goals. They usually bring small give-away items that students can keep. Students attend the fair to gather general information or to network directly with recruiters in organizations they are targeting for their search (Stewart, 1993). Students have expressed some frustration with an employer trend to not accept resumes at career fairs. Usually these companies have extensive online recruiting systems that they are required to use for applicants, but students well-prepared for the fair do not like to hear that they should apply online. Career counselors can help by making students aware of this trend and assuring them that the face-to-face interaction makes it much more likely for the application to be noticed once it is received through the system. Career fairs are generally revenue-generating for career centers. According to the NACE Benchmark Survey (2009, January), more than 88 percent of respondents charge employers for space at career fairs.

On-campus interviewing programs provide the opportunity for employers to meet and interview multiple candidates in one day or on one visit to campus (Herr, Rayman, & Garis, 1993). Most schools use some type of automated system for on-campus interviewing that allows employers to describe an opportunity, students to apply, employers to select candidates, and candidates to sign-up for a specific interview appointment time. Generally on-campus interviews are considered screening interviews, and successful candidates are usually invited for a second interview on site with the company.

Career service professionals who work as event planners with career fairs or who manage on-campus recruiting systems are considered specialists in employer relations. By helping students navigate the system and helping employers connect with candidates, they provide a valuable bridge between academia and the world of work. Many employer relations professionals belong to the National Association of Colleges and Employers (NACE) or one of four regional associations, the Eastern Association of Colleges and Employers (EACE), the Southern Association of Colleges and Employers (SACE), the Midwest Association of Colleges and Employers (MidwestAce) and the Mountain-Pacific Association of Colleges and Employers (MPACE). These associations are unique in that they bring together both sides of the recruiting equation with career service professionals on one side and corporate university relations departments on the other. Educational resources and annual conferences provide the opportunity for practitioners to learn from each other and for continued dialogue on the best way to connect students and employers.

TECHNOLOGY

While career centers today may look remarkably similar to career centers in the 1960s, with a strong combination of career counseling, experiential education, and employer relations programs, the infrastructure behind the scenes is entirely different. As late as the mid-1990s, students were still sharing resumes with employers using a complicated disk system. While that was certainly easier than lining up for interviews every morning, the introduction of a web-based system changed the way students and employers connect forever. In the Career Services Benchmark Survey from NACE (2009, January), 96.4 percent of respondents indicated that they used an online job postings system and over half indicated that they used online interview scheduling.

As the career services industry has a history of emerging, declining, or merging of online recruiting systems, it can be difficult to describe the current marketplace. Generally speaking, each system has the capability for employers to post jobs and interview schedules and for students to search jobs, apply online, and sign up for interviews once selected (Herr, Rayman, & Garis, 1993). Most systems also provide a detailed reporting system to make it easy to report on every function of the system. Most systems also include event management capabilities, mentoring systems, online portfolios, consortium capabilities, customer relationship management tools, surveying functions, and other value-added services. For schools that want to add a system or change from their current system to a new one, the process of assessing differences can be labor intensive. The choice really comes down to three criteria: the functionality of the system, the level of customer service provided, and the philosophy of the vendor. In addition to a few small systems and schools that use home-grown tools, there are about four major vendors of complete career services office management systems available in the market: NACElink/Symplicity, CSO, and Experience.

Despite early hopes that the NACElink project would help to assuage vendor market volatility and place control of these systems with the nonprofit professional association, the new partnership with Symplicity has confused some practitioners. In addition, most systems, including NACElink, have a dual revenue model with services for both schools and employers. While some believe this model helps to bring students and employers together and leverages aggregated career center relationships, others feel the demands of the system take away the personal touch provided by the career center itself. It can also put the organization in a difficult position if the needs of one customer do not align with the needs of another. At this point in time, the only vendor that does not have a financial relationship with employers is CSO Research, providers of the Interfase system.

CONSORTIA

One of the many benefits of the online career service management systems has been the capability of building partnerships and consortia between schools. By banding together into a consortium, schools can allow employers the opportunity to post jobs and internships to one system that automatically feeds all the schools in that consortium Many different consortia have developed over time from small regional internship consortia to systems like NACElink with schools around the country. Large consortia tend to be revenue-generating by charging organizations to post positions at multiple schools. NACElink and Experience all generate revenue for themselves using this model. Other consortia are managed by the schools directly involved and carry no fee to either the schools or the people posting positions. Regardless of structure, consortia of schools give employers the flexibility of sharing opportunities locally, regionally, and nationally.

QUALIFICATIONS FOR CAREER SERVICES EMPLOYMENT

It is difficult within one chapter to provide details on all of the intricacies, politics, diversity, and opportunities that a department of career services can provide. With the range of services provided for students and employers, it takes people of all backgrounds, experience, and skills to make a successful team. The Council for the Advancement of Standards in Higher Education (CAS) Professional Standards for Higher Education (2006) notes that career center staff, ". . . must, in combination, have the competencies necessary to perform the primary functions. The primary functions are program management and administration, program and even administration, career counseling and consultation; teaching/training/educating; marketing/promoting/outreach; brokering/connecting/linking; and information management" (p. 92).

Career counselors in career centers at colleges and universities generally have master's degrees in counseling, higher education, student personnel services or a related field (Greenberg, 2001). According to the Career Services Benchmark Survey (2009, January) from NACE, about a third of respondents indicated that their counselors were certified with most of those certifications coming from the National Board of Certified Counselors (NB CC). Some counselors are also licensed counseling practitioners within their state. Entry-level counseling positions also require some experience in higher education, usually through an internship at a college career center (Greenberg, 2001).

Professionals in other positions within career services, including employer relations staff, internship coordinators, event planners, IT personnel, and administrative staff come from all different backgrounds and levels of experience. Many have master's degrees in their respective fields and most have experience in recruiting either from the college side of the equation or from human resources. According to the Career Services Benchmark Survey (2009, January) from NACE, "The master's degree is the most commonly held degree by directors, assistant and associate directors, career counselors, and internship coordinators while career information/library specialists, along with marketing, recruiting, and technical coordinators are most likely to hold bachelor's degrees" (p. 12).

According to the CAS Professional Standards for Higher Education (2006), career center leaders must,

- Articulate a vision for their organization
- Set goals and objectives based on the needs and capabilities of the population serviced
- Promote student learning and development
- Prescribe and practice ethical behavior
- Recruit, elect, supervise, and develop others in the organization
- Manage financial resources
- Coordinate human resources
- Plan, budget for, and evaluate personnel and programs
- Apply effective practices to educational and administrative processes
- Communicate effectively
- Initiate collaborative interaction between individuals and agencies that possess legitimate concerns and interests in the functional areas (p.91).

In addition to these internal functions of managing and leading, the career center staff and directors are also responsible for representing career services to other constituents including administrators, parents, employers, and the media. As full members of the higher education community, most career service directors have master's degrees and a growing number also have doctorates (NACE, 2009, January).

CHALLENGES AND OPPORTUNITIES

In a Sept. 2003 article in *The Chronicle of Higher Education,* Jane Wellman and Thomas Ehrlich examined the recent trend towards outcome and accountability in higher education. "'Accountability for performance is today's mantra in higher education," they wrote. "Whether defined to mean greater attention to student learning, enhanced efficiency and productivity, or public evidence about institutional results, it is being hotly discussed by state higher-education commissions, governing boards, accreditation organizations, and colleges and universities throughout the country."

Although not all outcome studies focus on employment after graduation or placement in graduate school, some proponents of specific outcomes criteria focus on these measurements as the "value added" components parents and students should be aware of in the college selection process. In fact, the Career College Association, representing private career colleges and training programs, has lobbied Congress to compel schools to publish annual outcomes reports. In an April 2003 *Chronicle* article, reporter Stephen Burd explains that CCA recommends that ". . . factors such as job-placement rates, average starting salaries, graduate- and professional-school admissions data, passage rates of students on competency tests or certification exams, student and alumni satisfaction surveys, and employer-satisfaction surveys could be considered."

This continuing focus on outcomes and accountability has elevated career services to an interesting role on campus. Some career centers find themselves responsible for statistical outcomes data. Where are our graduates going after graduation? What are they doing? How many are unemployed or underemployed? Are they successful in their chosen fields? Although these types of questions have been asked of career service professionals for years, they are now taking on an entire new importance. Unfortunately, these numbers are notoriously difficult to collect with any accuracy, unless a university is willing to invest a great deal of money in the outreach to and follow-up of students. Even then, the pacing of the study can be complicated. The National Association of Colleges and Employers (NACE) collects this information in its Salary Survey, a publication cited by many media outlets. Unfortunately, the sample numbers for each major and degree are so small that the overall data is not very reliable. At some colleges and universities, Career Services conducts these surveys in partnership with institutional research. Because the data is important and is requested by students, faculty, parents, and administrators, Career Services can be seen as a value-added partner to academic departments and institutional administrators who need such data for assessment and planning as well as accreditation and other external reviews.

In the United Kingdom, outcome studies, called "Destination of Leavers of Higher Education" (previously known as First Destination Survey), are now statutory mandates and are often run out of career service offices. While that has brought more attention to the issue and more funding to meet those mandates, the surveys take criticism for the usefulness of the data. For example, the law requires that the surveys be conducted within six months of graduation. Many students in the UK actually take a year off after college and, therefore, are both difficult to reach and probably not working within the career they intend to pursue long-term. In reporting the results of this survey, many schools caution that by the time the report comes out, many of the students surveyed will have moved on to the next stage in their careers. While some in the United States lobby for similar mandates as the only way to ensure the funding and other resources to make such a large scale project work, others are wary of over-legislating what should be specific to each varied campus. In other words, what might be feasible and would provide good information at a small liberal arts college may place undue burden with sketchy information at a large school with 40,000 or more students.

At other colleges and universities, career service offices are asked to do more than reflect the outcomes of higher education. In fact, they are much more intricately involved in determining what the goals of that education should be. Facilitating a reflective process, career services helps to gather information about the needs of employers and filters that information back to curriculum committees and other academic planners. In this way, career services' staff members help to shape the very nature of academia by commenting on the demands of the marketplace. Rather than an older model of helping students to package and market their academic credentials, professional experience and personal skills, this new model asks career services to provide more to the content of that package. Another area of assessment is the measurement of student learning and development outcomes related to career development. According to CAS (2006), Career Services (CS) must identify relevant and desirable student learning and development outcomes and provide programs and services that encourage the achievement of those outcomes. Examples of outcomes that are promoted through career development include realistic self-appraisal, enhanced self-esteem, clarified values, effective career choices, and achievement of personal goals.

Without a doubt, it is an exciting and often challenging time to be a career counselor on a college or university campus. With changing demands from administration, potential employers and an evolving student population, doing things the way they have always been done is no longer an option. How each campus chooses to address these issues varies as a reflection of its history and respective constituencies' demands. For example, the University of Colorado at Boulder includes an on-campus testing as part of the office. Students looking to pursue graduate programs can take the required tests on campus rather than having to go to an off-site testing service.

Keeping up with the changing needs of multiple constituencies is not always easy. With the breadth and depth of services offered through career service offices, there is usually some overlap on campuses that can be threatening. For example, internship programs are notoriously tricky for career services. Internships take many forms across campus and take place in numerous arenas. Some disciplines require experiential education, some may simply recommend it, and others may have no program at all for gaining work-related experience. As such, some internships are offered specifically through a department, some can be found through on-campus recruiting, and others are more for self-directed students who create their own experiences. Trying to integrate these varying opportunities into a centralized internship program brings out the territorial nature in many departments. Perhaps these offices want to "reserve" opportunities for their students alone or maintain a close relationship to the sponsoring company or organization, but whatever the cause, it can quickly cause deterioration of campus relationships. Opening the door toward communications while allowing campus groups to control their own information helps to strike a balance to meet the needs of the entire campus.

Another common struggle involves marketing and public relations. It is common to hear practitioners at professional development meetings complaining about the stereotype that services are provided only for students in business and engineering disciplines. In fact, many industries are looking for students in diverse disciplines and are searching for students with varying skill sets. The impression that only business engineering students are marketable creates a self-fulfilling prophecy wherein students expect to find no opportunities and, therefore, stop looking. Encouraging students to engage with Career Services early in their academic careers can help students expand their understanding of real demands in the workplace. To accomplish the goals of engaging students earlier and more often, many career centers have added a full-time staff person responsible for marketing their programs. A director's nightmare is hearing from a recent graduate who finally comes in for assistance and says, "Wow! I didn't even know you guys were here!"

Even with all the struggles, career services centers are fast-paced dynamic environments that serve both institutions and students. By continuing to open dialogues with various stakeholders both on and off campus, career services staff sit in a unique position of helping to address the "what" and "why" questions the chapter began with as they relate to higher education.

REFERENCES

ACPA: American College Personnel Association. (2009). Available: http://www2.myacpa.org/.

Baker, D. B. (2009). Choosing a vocation at 100: Time, change, and context. *The Career Development Quarterly, 57*(3), 199–206.

Bechtel, D. S. (1993). The organization and impact of career programs and services within higher education. In J. R. Rayman (Ed.), *The changing role of career services* (pp. 23–36). San Francisco: Jossey-Bass.

Birch, D. L. (1990). The coming demise of the single-career career. *Journal of Career Planning and Employment, 50*(2), 38–40.

Blaska, B., & Schmidt, M. R. (1977). Placement. In W. T. Packwood (Ed.), *College student personnel services* (pp. 368–421). Springfield, IL: Charles C Thomas.

Burd, S. (2003, April). Will congress require colleges to grade themselves? *Chronicle of Higher Education, 49*(30), p. A27.

Bureau of Labor Statistics. (2009). *Occupational outlook handbook, 2008–2009.* Retrieved from http://www.bls.gov/OCO/.

Campbell, D. P., Hyne, S. A., & Nilsen, D. L. (1992). *CISS: Campbell Interest & Skill Survey manual.* Minneapolis, MN: NCS Pearson, Inc.

Campus Career Counselor. (2009). *About us.* Retrieved from http://www.campus careercounselor.com/about,htm.

Casella, D. A. (1990). Career networking- The newest career center paradigm. *Journal of Career Planning and Employment, 50*(4), 33–39.

CEIA–Cooperative Education & Internship Association. (2009). *About us.* Retrieved from http://www.ceiainc.org.

CERI–Collegiate Employment Research Institute (2009). *About us.* Retrieved from http://ceri.msu.edu/about.html.

Clifton, D. O., Anderson, E. C., & Schreiner, L. A. (2006). *StrengthsQuest: Discover and develop your strengths in academics, career, and beyond.* New York: Gallup Press.

Council for the Advancement of Standards in Higher Education. (2006). *CAS professional standards for higher education* (6th ed.). Washington, DC: Author.

CSO. (2009). *Our team.* Retrieved from http://www.csoresearch.com/company/?sub =founder.

Davidson, M. M. (2001). The computerization of career services: Critical issues to consider. *Journal of Career Development, 27*(3), 217–228.

DeBell, C. (2001). Ninety years in the world of work in America. *The Career Development Quarterly, 50*(1), 77–88.

Do What You Are. (2009). Available: http://www.bridges.com/us/prodnserv/dwya/ Bridges Transitions, Inc.

Donnay, D. A. C., Morris, M. L., Schaubhut, N. A., & Thompson, R. C. (2005). *Strong Interest Inventory manual: Research, development, and strategies for interpretation.* Mountain View, CA: CPP, Inc.

Freeman, J. (1994). *A vision for the college placement center: Systems, paradigms, processes, people.* Westport, CT: Praeger.

Gardner, P. D. (1998). Are college seniors prepared to work? In J. N. Gardner & G. Van der Veer (Eds.), *The senior year experience: Facilitating integration, reflection, closure, and transition* (pp. 60–78). San Francisco: Jossey-Bass.

Greenberg, R. (2001). In search of career services professionals. *Journal of Career Planning and Employment, 61*(3), 45–48.

Hackett, G. (1993). Career counseling and psychotherapy: False dichotomies and recommended remedies. *Journal of Career Assessment, 1*(2), 105–117.

Halasz. T. J. (2000). Career planning workshops and courses. In D. Luzzo (Ed.), *Career counseling of college students* (pp. 157–172). Washington, DC: American Psychological Association.

Harris-Bowlsbey, J., & Sampson, J. P. (2005). Use of technology in delivering career services worldwide. *The Career Development Quarterly, 54*, 48–56.

Harris-Bowlsbey, J., & Sampson, J. P. (2001). Computer-based career planning systems: Dreams and realities. *The Career Development Quarterly, 49,* 250–260.

Heppner, M. J., & Johnston, J. A. (1993). In J. R. Rayman (Ed.), *The changing role of career services* (pp. 57–78). San Francisco: Jossey-Bass.

Herr, E. L., Rayman, J. R., & Garis, J. W. (1993). *Handbook for the college and university career center.* Westport, CT: Greenwood Press.

Hoff, K. S., Kroll, J., MacKinnon, F. J. D., & Rentz, A. L. (2004). Career services. In F. J. D. MacKinnon & Associates (Ed.), *Rentz's student affairs practice in higher education* (pp. 108–143). Springfield, IL: Charles C Thomas.

Hoover, E. (2008). Colleges face tough sell to freshman, survey finds. *Chronicle of Higher Education, 54*(21), p. A1.

Iaccarino, G. (2000). Computer-assisted career-guidance systems. In D. Luzzo (Ed.), *Career counseling of college students* (pp. 137–156). Washington, DC: American Psychological Association.

Lucas, E. B. (1986). College career planning and placement centers: Finding their identity. *Journal of Career Development, 12*(1), 9–17.

Myers, I. B., McCaulley, M. H., Quenk, N. L., & Hammer, A. L. (1998). *MBTI manual: A guide to the development and use of the Myers-Briggs Type Indicator.* Palo Alto, CA: CPP, Inc.

NACE–National Association of Colleges and Employers. (2008, March). *NACE 2008 experiential education survey: Executive summary.* Bethlehem, PA: National Association of Colleges and Employers.

NACE–National Association of Colleges and Employers. (2008, April). *Strategic plan.* Retrieved from http://www.naceweb.org.

NACE–National Association of Colleges and Employers. (2009, January). *2008 career services benchmark survey for four-year colleges and universities.* Bethlehem, PA: National Association of Colleges and Employers.

NACE–National Association of Colleges and Employers. (2009, March). *About us.* Retrieved from http://www.naceweb.org.

NCDA–National Career Development Association. (1997). *Career counseling competencies.* Retrieved from http://www.ncda.org.

NCDA–National Career Development Association. (2009). *NCDA mission statement, NCDA history and purpose.* Retrieved from http://www.ncda.org.

Niles, S. G., & Garis, J. W. (1990). The effects of a career planning course and a computer-assisted guidance program (SIGI PLUS) on undecided university students. *Journal of Career Development, 16*(4), 237–248.

Niles, S. G., & Harris-Bowlsbey, J. (2009). Assessment and career planning. In S. G. Niles & J. Harris-Bowlsbey, *Career development interventions in the 21st century* (pp. 158–190). Upper Saddle River, NJ: Pearson Education, Inc.

NSEE–National Society for Experiential Education. (2009). Retrieved from http://www.nsee.org/.

Oliver, L. W., & Spokane, A. R. (1988). Career-intervention outcome: What contributes to client gain? *Journal of Counseling Psychology, 35*(4), 447–462.

Rayman, J. R. (1993). Concluding remarks and career services imperatives. In J. R. Rayman (Ed.), *The changing role of career services* (pp. 100–108). San Francisco:

Jossey-Bass.

Rayman, J. R. (1999). Personal perspectives: Career services imperatives for the next millennium. *The Career Development Quarterly, 48*(2), 175–184.

Reardon, R., Lenz, J., & Folsom, B. (1998). Employer ratings of student participation in non-classroom-based-activities: Findings of a campus survey. *Journal of Career Planning and Employment, 58*(4), 36–39.

Savickas, M. L. (1992). New directions in career assessment. In D. H. Montross & C. J. Shinkman (Eds.), *Career Development Theory & Practice* (pp. 336–355). Springfield, IL: Charles C Thomas.

Savickas, M. L. (1995). Constructivist counseling for career indecision. *Career Development Quarterly, 43*(4), 363–373.

Selingo, J. (2003, May). What Americans think about higher education. *The Chronicle of Higher Education, 49*(34), p. A10.

Severy, L. E. (2009). Campbell Interest & Skills Survey (CISS) review. In E. Whitfield, R. Feller, & C. Wood (Eds.), *A counselor's guide to career assessment instruments* (5th ed.). Broken Arrow, OK: National Career Development Association.

Shea, D. D. (1995). Merging career and experiential education centers: A perspective. *Journal of Career Planning and Employment, 55*(2), 29–35.

Stewart, R. A. (1993). Placement services. In J. R. Rayman (Ed.), *The changing role of career services* (pp. 37–56). San Francisco: Jossey-Bass.

Tieger, P. D., & Barron, B. (2007). *Do what you are: Discover the perfect career for you through the secrets of personality type.* New York: Little Brown.

Turning Points. (2009). *About us.* Retrieved from http://www.TurningPointsResearch .org.

U.S. Department of Labor. (1999). Futurework: Trends and challenges for work in the 21st century. *Occupational Outlook Quarterly, 44*(2), 31–37.

Wellman, J. V., & Ehrlich, T. (2003, August). Re-examining the sacrosanct credit hour. *Chronicle of Higher Education, 50*(5), p. B16.

Wessel, R. D. (1998). Career centers and career development professionals of the 1990s. *Journal of Career Development, 24*(3), 163–177.

Whitfield, E. A., Feller, R., & Wood, C. (2009). *A counselor's guide to career assessment instruments* (5th ed.). Broken Arrow, OK: National Career Development Association.

Whiston, S. (2000). Individual career counseling. In D. Luzzo (Ed.), *Career counseling of college students* (pp. 137–156). Washington, DC: American Psychological Association.

Wolff, M., & Tinney, S. (2006, May) *Applied learning as a best practice model: A strategy for higher education student success.* Research report presented at the annual meeting of the Association of Institutional Research, Chicago, IL.

Zunker, V. G. (2002). *Career counseling: Applied concepts of life planning* (6th ed.). Florence, KY: Wadsworth.

Chapter 6

COUNSELING CENTERS

NAIJIAN ZHANG, IRVIN W. BRANDEL AND VICKIE ANN MCCOY

INTRODUCTION

Ever since the origin of US colleges, counseling has served as a function of facilitating students' learning and development (Hopkins, 1926, as cited in Williamson, 1961). The demands of college students in terms of their needs for support during a time of social, academic, and personal growth has lead to counseling services becoming specialized units of student affairs divisions on US college and university campuses. In the past century, college and university counseling centers have developed into an integral part of the student personnel work (Williamson, 1961). Counseling center staff members have played a crucial role in the process of higher education and student affairs. However, the role of the counseling center may still be vague to many members of the campus community, even those in the student affairs field. This chapter will attempt to demystify and illuminate the nature and characteristics of the higher education counseling center.

IIISTORY

College counseling at its inception would more accurately have been called student advising. These early counselor/advisors were generally members of the faculty and the college president (Gibson et al., 1983). In 1889, Johns Hopkins University appointed a "Chief of Advisors," thus beginning the trend in higher education of specifically designating an individual to

---

Note: The authors would like to acknowledge the contributions of Dr. Elizabeth Yarris to this chapter. Dr. Yarris was the sole or co-author of this chapter in the earlier editions of this text.

function in the capacity of student advisement. Harvard University quickly followed with the appointment of a "Dean of Student Relations" in 1890 (Gibson et al., 1983). In 1910, Princeton University opened the first campus mental health service (Kadison & DiGeronimo, 2004). A variety of influences led to the need for more specialized "counselors" and these were the student personnel workers of the late nineteenth and early twentieth century (Davis & Humphrey, 2000).

As colleges and universities continued to expand in both numbers and services, the development of land-grant colleges, the elective curriculum, and a renewed emphasis on technological and scientific education presented US educators and their students with new challenges (Yarris, 1996). The college and university environments were ripe for developments which addressed the personal, as well as the academic needs of their students.

Three major events coincided to establish the first centers of professionally trained counselors. The first of these was the development of psychometrics during World War I (Schneider, 1977). The second was the beginning of the Mental Hygiene movement toward prevention and cure, which is often considered to have begun in 1909 with the publication of Clifford Beers' *A Mind that Found Itself* (Tyler, 1969). The third influence was Frank Parsons' 1906 publication of *Choosing a Vocation,* in which he proposed a model of counseling which focused on the need for helping young people to find suitable places in the world of work (Tyler, 1969). The convergence of these three events led to the appearance of the earliest counseling centers on a few college campuses after World War I. They also led to the rise of the counseling profession and to a counseling center specialty area within student personnel work (Berk, 1983; Hedahl, 1978; Tyler, 1969).

These three threads can be seen throughout the historical development of counseling centers, and in today's centers, as weaving together the fabric of three essential functions of counseling: to measure and assess, to facilitate wise choices and decisions, and to promote adjustment or mental health (Tyler, 1969). While student mental hygiene clinics were created at Princeton University, the University of Wisconsin, Washburn College, the U.S. Military Academy, Dartmouth College, Vassar College, and Yale University between 1910 and 1925 (Farnsworth, 1957, cited in Davis & Humphrey, 2000), the earliest separate unit organized to offer professional educational and vocational guidance appears to be the University Testing Bureau, which began at the University of Minnesota in 1932 (Hedahl, 1978). The service emphases of this unit were psychometrics and facilitation of vocational choice. Most colleges had no professional counselors on campus at this time.

Following World War II, there were many veterans who used their government subsidies to attend college. They were monitored by guidance bureaus funded by the Veterans Administration (VA). The efforts of the VA were primarily aimed at vocational and psychological assessment of the returning veterans. Over the years, fewer veterans were attending college and as a result, the VA removed their services from college campuses. The colleges and universities took over the services formerly provided by the VA and the modern counseling centers were born (Forest, 1989).

The following decade from 1945 to 1955, has been called a time of "transition and professionalism" (Heppner & Neal, 1983). Just as the VA was pulling out of the college counseling business, the field of psychology was experiencing the development of counseling psychology as a specialty area within the American Psychological Association. On campuses where such counseling psychology departments functioned, their faculty members often became involved in the growth and development of the campus counseling center (McKinley, 1980). It was during this same time period in the early 1950s that annual meetings of college counseling center directors began.

Some of the growth and development during this period, and into the 1960s, paralleled changes within the field of counseling psychology (Whiteley, 1984), which is a trend that has continued into the 1990s (Sprinthall, 1990; Tyler, 1992). Then, the third phase of attention to personal adjustment and mental health began to emerge as a major emphasis in many centers during this period. The field of counseling psychology, and counseling centers themselves, began a trend away from exclusively vocational guidance to a broader, developmental form of personal counseling (Berk, 1983). As counseling centers established protocol for assisting with a variety of student concerns, the need for specialized training for providers increased. With this new emphasis on the personal, as well as the vocational, needs of students, college counseling began to develop an identity that was separate and distinct from other student affairs divisions (Hodges, 2001).

The decade of 1960–1970 was a time of social unrest, student activism and idealism, "encounter groups," and draft counseling. During this time period, college and university counseling centers were faced with the duality of simultaneous consolidation and expansion. (Heppner & Neal, 1983; Lamb et al., 1983). This duality was further evidenced by the simultaneous, and often conflicting, demands for responsiveness to social concerns, calls for relevance to the goals of higher education and increasing budgetary constraints (Forman, 1977). Expectations of centers expanded to include outreach, consultation, and crisis intervention. An emphasis on preventative and developmental activities was gaining momentum in many centers. Even from within the profession (Warnath, 1971, 1973), criticism was leveled at counseling centers that were practicing in a medical model, viewing the student as "sick" and "in need of treatment," and serving only a small select group of students in long-term counseling and psychotherapy. While this perspective did have its adherents, they were being more openly questioned and challenged. The decade ended dramatically and tragically, as in May of 1970, four students were killed by National Guard troops on the campus of Kent State University, and two students were killed by police on the campus of Jackson State University. These events caused many individuals involved in higher education to re-examine priorities and policies, and counseling centers were no exception.

The 1970s were a period of reassessment of the role of counseling centers (Lamb et al., 1983). Fortunately for the field, groundwork had already begun for constructive change. A proposal from Morrill, Ivey, and Oetting in 1968 (cited in McKinley, 1980) pointed the way toward needed changes in the functions of college and university counseling centers. They proposed that counseling centers become the heart of campus student development by moving out into the campus to create programs to prevent problems, mobilizing community resources for mental health, and redefining the counseling center role within a developmental framework (McKinley, 1980). This important work legitimized for many centers the movement to a more developmental theoretical model. A task force of counseling center directors kept the momentum in this direction by developing guidelines (Kirk et al., 1971), which distinguished between remedial and developmental/preventive services.

This distinction among services and the concept of a human development center came into clearer focus through a conceptual scheme called the "cube" (Morrill, Oetting, & Hurst, 1974). The "cube" was a model for organizing the expanding role of counselors' specified targets (individual, primary group, associational group, and institution or community); purposes (remedial, preventive, or developmental); and methods (direct, consultation and training, or media) for intervention on a college campus (McKinley, 1980). It was also in the 1970s that the related concept of "campus ecology" emerged. This concept emphasized the interrelationship between students and their environment. At this time, the concept of "campus environment" as the counseling center client began, and the counselors were charged with the task of attending to the campus environment (e.g., Aulepp & Delworth, 1976; Conyne et al., 1979). In addition to these changes, other influences on counseling center development in the 1970s included external accrediting bodies, related professional organizations and even the center directors themselves (Lamb et al., 1983). Finally, legal requirements for licensure or certification of psychologists, social workers, and counselors affected the changing role of counseling centers in the 1970s.

In the 1980s, counseling centers continued to grow and develop with ever expanding roles and functions (Heppner & Neal, 1983). They were, at most campuses, established as important members of the student affairs team. However, throughout the 1980s and continuing into the 1990s, many campuses were dealing with two major phenomena. The first of these was declining enrollment and the correlating decrease in resources, and the second was an increase in student demand for psychological services and an accompanying increase in the perceived severity of student problems (Gallagher et al., 1995, Gallagher et al., 2001). It was a time of "doing more with less." The centers of the 1980s and 1990s also began to vary in design from campus to campus. At some campuses, services such as testing, career counseling, and training were part of the mission of the counseling center, while at other campuses these services were shared with or assigned altogether to another office (Stone & Archer, 1990). In particular, these decades saw many placement offices assume much of the traditional career assessment and career counseling which was once the exclusive responsibility of counseling centers.

Adding to the pressures and challenges for counseling centers in these decades were worries about managed health care, mergers, and outsourcing (Gallagher et al., 1995–2001; Hodges, 2001; Whitaker, 1997; Widseth et al., 1997). The dominant theme was the growing insufficiency of funding for higher education, and college and university administrators focused considerable energy on ways to conserve resources. Managed health care represented a potential way to limit the expenses of campus health services and counseling centers. Likewise, mergers of student affairs offices were another administrative way to save resources. The concern about mergers was widespread enough that the 2000 International Association of Counseling Services, Inc. (IACS) Standards include a new section on mergers (Boyd et al., 2003). The most common mergers, proposed and/or carried out, were counseling centers with health services or with career planning and placement services, with the former being the more common. This threat of outsourcing and/or merging was taken very seriously by center leadership, and numerous creative efforts were undertaken to quell such efforts. These efforts included the increased development of internships in counseling centers (Boggs & Douce, 2000), and the attainment of accreditation for centers and for internships. Training became an increasingly important aspect of centers, especially at larger institutions, since the staff size could be increased with significantly less expense than adding licensed staff. Additionally, counseling center directors became more involved in utilizing client data and evaluations in research which supported the value of counseling center services (Archer & Cooper, 1998; Bishop, 1995; Guinee & Ness, 2000; Turner & Berry, 2000; Wilson et al., 1997). They also developed, through their professional organization, The Association of University and College Counseling Center Directors (AUCCCD) and the AUCCCD Research Consortium, which was designed to create a database on the impacts of university and college counseling centers (Archer & Cooper, 1998).

The concern about campus ecology of the 1970s led most centers to be concerned about their integration into and involvement within the campus

community (Guinee & Ness, 2000). Now centers were more and more involved with training resident advisors, consulting with faculty and other administrators, providing outreach programs, and training. A second major
concern of this time period, the increase in student demand for services and
in the severity of student problems, began to put enormous and unrealistic
demands on centers. They were doing more things with more people, while
at the same time, seeing larger caseloads with more disturbed students
(Guinee & Ness, 2000). In 1990, Stone and Archer published a landmark article on the counseling centers of the 1990s. In it, they recommended many
steps that centers should take to address this myriad of challenges that had
befallen them (Stone & Archer, 1990).

By the 1990s, centers were also increasingly involved in major campus
tragedies, in effect, making the campus and local communities the client
(Davis & Humphrey, 2000). It became more and more common for centers
to reach out to the campus community with services and support after student and faculty suicides, homicides, and major events such as accidents,
severe storms, and fires (Archer & Cooper, 1998; Stone, 1993). In September
of 2001, the terrorist attacks on New York and Washington D.C. also motivated centers to provide resources to their campus communities for students,
faculty, and staffs who were frightened, disturbed, and confused by these
world affairs (Grayson & Commerford, 2002; Raskin, Fenichel, Kellerhouse,
& Shadick, 2002). These resources and strategies were shared with one another via the Counseling Center Directors Listserv and the AUCCCD Listserv. Schwitzer (2003) outlined a conceptual model for designing counseling
center responses to large scale traumatic incidents in response to indications
that most psychotherapists have limited experience dealing with large scale
catastrophic incidents, and college and university counseling centers today
need to be prepared for crisis events such as terrorist attacks, war, and local
catastrophes.

Following the disturbing fatal shootings that occurred at Northern Illinois
University and Virginia Tech, where students with records of mental-health
problems went on killing sprees, college administrators nationwide have
been pumping more money and resources into efforts to prevent similar tragedies on their campuses. These efforts include updating emergency-alert systems, refining crisis-management plans and greater collaboration between
counseling center mental-health staffs and other groups on campuses to identify at-risk students (Farrell, 2008). Voelker (2007) cites these incidents of violence as rationales for the need for closer monitoring of mental health in college students and questions if colleges even have the resources and ability to
handle the mental health needs of their students and suggests that counseling centers need to seek other resources. The International Association of
Counseling Services, a nonprofit accrediting organization, recommends that

colleges have a ratio of one counselor for every 1,500 full-time-equivalent students. The average ratio, according to 2007 data, was one counselor per 1,969 students, and 85 percent of counseling centers reported that more students were arriving at their centers with significant histories of mental-health issues (Farrell, 2008). According to the Association of University and College Counseling Center Directors' 2007 annual survey (Rando, Barr, & Aros 2007). One-third of college counseling centers have added at least one new staff member, and 15 percent have received a larger budget. Also, 63 percent of those centers now have psychiatrists on staff in addition to counselors, which is a 5 percent increase over the previous year.

In addition to the new wave of concerns resulting from traumatic and violent events, counseling center staff must also cope with the day-to-day challenges of serving the Millennial Generation (born 1982-present) who share the following attributes: special, sheltered, confident, team-oriented, achieving, pressured, and conventional (Howe & Strauss, 2000). Endres and Tisinger (2007) would add plugged-in to this list of attributes as they describe the challenges of counseling students who are often digitally distracted. Counseling center staff will need to revise protocols to address serving a cohort of students who are constantly wired and connected and whose activities revolve around their cell phones, iPods, laptops, TVs, and gaming consoles (Cohen & Rosenzweig, 2006).

DEFINITION

Mission, Goals, and Purposes

A study by Whiteley et al. (1987) reported that the majority of four-year postsecondary institutions have a counseling center located on the campus, whose primary mission and function is to serve the needs of students (Corazzini, 1995). According to the Accreditation Standards of the International Association of Counseling Services, Inc. (IACS), "Counseling services are an integral part of the educational mission of the institution and support the mission in a variety of ways, such as consultation, teaching, preventive and developmental interventions, and treatment" (Boyd et al., 2003). Centers provide counseling services to address students' stress from personal, academic, and/or career pressures that may interfere with their attaining the educational opportunities available to them (Boyd et al., 2003). The roles of college counselors are varied. Certainly, their primary function is advocacy for students and their needs, but they also participate in program development, teaching and consultation to assist the faculty and improve the campus environment. They are also responsible for facilitating and promoting psychological and emotional growth and development across the spectrum of campus life (Boyd et al., 2003).

Most centers provide services in the three general categories of remedial, preventative, and developmental services, as conceptualized by the "cube" model (Morrill et al., 1974). Remedial services include solving existing problems and crisis intervention. Preventive services are designed to aid the student in avoiding difficulties. Examples of preventative services are providing study and anxiety management skills. Developmental services are designed to aid the student in his/her normal developmental tasks. Career planning, groups addressing relationship issues, and assertiveness training are examples of developmental services.

The proportion of attention that should be given to each of these purposes is a common and ongoing issue, both at individual centers and for the field at large. Few, however, would disagree with Demos' and Mead's (1983) statement that:

> Personal counseling and therapy should be based on a developmental and clinical foundation—that is, counselors should be well-versed in both developmental psychology and diagnosis and assessment procedures. Since a focus on any single theoretical background is too narrow, professional staff should be diverse in their training and background. Consultation services are important, but they are supplementary to counseling services, which are the primary function of the center. (p. 6)

Demos and Mead (1983) assert that "a direct contact of students and counselors in counseling interactions, individual or group, is the major function of the psychological counseling center" (p. 7).

Many current issues, including the possible impact of health care reform, have added to the long-standing debate over the ratio of direct service to the preventive and developmental functions of outreach and consultation (Yarris, 1996). In practice, it is difficult to avoid a large proportion of direct and remedial service, however, many centers have found that utilizing brief models of therapy (Cooper & Archer, 1999), group work, videotapes, self-help materials (Guinee & Ness, 2000), computer programs, and other creative programming efforts can create some relief from large caseloads. However, as is the case with most areas of student affairs, counseling centers experience certain times of the year when the demand for their services, particularly individual counseling, peaks. Finding the balance between developmental and clinical approaches, and viewing them as complementary rather than mutually exclusive, is the challenge for counseling centers (Davis & Humphrey, 2000).

It is becoming increasingly common for counseling centers to include some level of commitment to the advancement of multiculturalism and the appreciation of human diversity (Guinee & Ness, 2000). Efforts to reach out to underserved populations such as ethnic minorities, the physically and emotionally challenged, and gay, lesbian, bisexual, and transgendered students have been undertaken at many centers (Archer & Cooper, 1998; Davis & Humphrey, 2000). These efforts might also include outreach presentations regarding diversity, mediation of campus conflicts related to diversity issues, and integrating diversity issues into the training that may take place at the center (Boggs & Douce, 2000).

In the early 1990s, both Bishop (1990) and Stone and Archer (1990) recommended that counseling center staffs use more consultation services and renew their emphasis on prevention over remediation. Stone and Archer also recommended that centers not give up the career counseling function, that outreach and consultation be continued within limits, and that centers should learn to value diversity, including seeking out diverse staff members and trainees, among other recommendations.

ADMINISTRATION AND ORGANIZATIONAL STRUCTURE

Administration

Since counseling center work by nature is often confidential, there are often fewer acknowledgements of achievement, and both the campus wide and public perceptions can be faulty (Likins, 1993). Add to this the fact that the services offered by counseling centers often do not dovetail well with administrative structure (Schoenberg, 1992) and may even have a somewhat ambiguous role in the organizational flowchart of the institution. Further problems may arise because of the intricacies of having multiple, and often conflicting, responsibilities to the student/client, the institution and the profession (Gilbert 1989). Autonomous is a common adjective used to describe counseling centers. Although the relationship to other units within the institution will vary based on organizational structure and individual campus needs and history, the counseling service should be administratively neutral to preserve students' perceptions that information disclosed in counseling sessions will not affect other academic or administrative decisions (Boyd et al., 2003).

Counseling services are typically housed in the student affairs unit and work closely with academic units, other student service offices, campus and community medical services, community mental health services, as well as with faculty and administrators. Some colleges and universities have both an independent counseling center and a mental health unit that are part of student health services (Boyd et al., 2003). Other institutions have one or more training clinics, usually aligned with the departments of counseling and/or counseling psychology, that provide some services by trainees as part of their graduate training. On most campuses, the independent counseling center is the only service-oriented center focusing on preventative and developmental services, as well as remedial services.

Many campuses have separate academic advising centers, career placement centers, sexual assault services, alcohol education and prevention offices, learning support centers, and women centers. It can become very complicated for students to determine where to go for counseling-related services on their campuses. For example, it is possible for the coordinator of sexual assault services to report directly to the counseling center at some institutions, while reporting to health services or campus safety at others (Gallagher et al., 1994). This is especially true for smaller institutions, but the degree of overlap and cooperation between these various centers and services varies from institution to institution. Gallagher et al. (1998) found 19 percent of counseling centers surveyed to be administratively linked to a student health service. Of those centers that were administratively linked to a student health service, 34 percent of the counseling center directors reported to the student health service director and 31 percent of the student health service directors reported to the counseling center director (Gallagher et al., 1998). A smaller number of mergers have connected career placement services with counseling centers.

A great deal of a counseling center director's time must be spent in developing and maintaining a strong working relationship with her/his immediate supervisor and other relevant campus administrators (Davis & Humphrey, 2000). Frequent changes in administrative personnel and structure, a phenomenon not uncommon in student affairs, force directors to feel a regular need to educate or re-educate supervisors to the design and work of the center. Reconfigurations of the center's model, mission, and charge add to the challenge of maintaining productive relationships with college and university administrators.

Financial Support

Financial support for college and university counseling centers is pivotal because insufficient funds can cause low quality service for students. Four major sources have been identified as the financial backbone of the counseling center: budgetary funding from the institution, mandatory fees from students, fees collected from students, and private and federal grants (Rando, Barr, & Aros 2007). Although concerns regarding possible reduction of funding from the institution have remained among counseling center directors since the early 1990s (Gallagher et al., 1994), the budgetary increases from the institutions since the beginning of this century appear to be the trend, particularly after the Virginia Tech shootings incident (Gallagher & Taylor, 2008). For example, 21 percent of counseling centers have received additional funding due to the increased focus on counseling services after the Virginia Tech Shootings (Gallagher & Taylor, 2008), and according to the results of the Counseling Center Directors Survey from 2000 to 2005, the percentage of counseling centers that increased their staff salaries ranged from 50.4 percent (Gallagher, 2002) to 78 percent (Gallagher et al., 2005). In addition, 29.2 percent of counseling center directors reported that their costs budget was increased and this number was 10 percent up from 2003 (Gallagher et al., 2005). The majority of those counseling center directors who did not report an increase in funding remarked that their budget at least remained the same.

In spite of the fact that the financial support has either increased or remained the same, 63 percent of 230 counseling center directors surveyed reported budget as one of the major stressors in the role as director (Gallagher & Taylor, 2006). Moreover, 16 percent of 339 counseling center directors surveyed reported pressure from their institutions to be more self-supporting (Gallagher et al., 2004). This figure is up 3 percent from those who reported such pressure in 2001 (Gallagher et al., 2001) and down 3 percent from those directors who reported such pressure in 1994 (Gallagher et al., 1994). One of the major financial sources for college and university counseling centers is mandatory fees, for example, 44 percent of counseling centers are supported by mandatory fees which include 23 percent from students health fees, 18 percent from a student life fee, and 3 percent from a counseling center fee (Gallagher & Taylor, 2008). Although this figure is down 3 percent and 2 percent in 2007 and 2006 respectively, it has increased steadily since 2000.

Charging students a fee for personal counseling at college and university counseling centers appears to be an upside down V shape in the past 18 years. At the beginning of the 1990s, less than 4 percent of counseling centers charged students a fee for personal counseling; up until 1996, this reached the peak of 17.2 percent. However, since then, there has been a gradual decline, with 7.4 percent of centers charging such a fee in 2008 (Gallagher & Taylor, 2008). Less than 20 percent of centers generate some income by charging students for services such as career testing, structured groups, psychological testing and assessment, consultation, workshops, teaching, and psychiatry (Rando, Barr, & Aros, 2007). Only 2.5 percent to 5 percent of centers collect third-party payments (Gallagher et al., 2005; Gallagher & Taylor, 2008).

In addition to the aforementioned financial support avenues, counseling centers also innovatively obtain funding from federal and private grants and contracts for their expenses. For example, 21.9 percent of counseling directors reported that their centers received funding from either grants or contracts (Rando, Barr, & Aros, 2007). This grant or contract money can be used for hiring student workers, treating chronically suicidal clients, or walk-in services from insurance company (Gallagher et al., 2005). Grant money may also be used for educational outreach programs such as alcohol and tobacco cessation, sexual assault, or violence prevention.

Although funding increases for college counseling centers appear to be steady in the twenty-first century, pressures and concerns regarding falling short on financial resources remain a pressing issue for both counseling center directors and counselors (Gallagher et al., 2004; Smith et al., 2007). These pressures and concerns may be due to the increased needs of mental health care from college students. As the economy cycles to its down turn, the stabilization of funding to provide appropriate counseling services particularly for students with severe issues can become a major challenge for the college counseling centers (Meadows, 2000).

Physical Facilities

Counseling services should be centrally located, physically separate from administrative offices, campus police, and judicial offices, and readily accessible to all students, including those who are physically challenged (Boyd et al., 2003). IACS Standards (Boyd et al.) recommend individual sound-proofed offices with a telephone, an interoffice communications system, audio or video recording equipment, and furnishings that create a relaxing environment for students. Today's counseling centers also require access to computers and other appropriate equipment to support record keeping, research, and publication activities; technical resources for media presentations, and other adjuncts to treatment (Boyd et al.). A reception area that provides a comfortable and private waiting space and a central clerical area where all client records are kept secure are recommended for all centers (Boyd et al.). Also necessary are areas to house library resources, areas suitable for individual and group testing, and for group counseling and staff meetings (Boyd et al.). Centers with a training program will also require audio and visual recording facilities as well as facilities for direct observation (Boyd et al.).

Technology

Counseling centers, like all other departments on the college and university campus, have been greatly impacted and influenced by technology.

Counseling center directors, counselors, and all other personnel in the twenty-first century at college and university counseling centers increasingly have become dependent upon computers even though the use of modern technology is relatively recent (Baier, 1993). According to the University and College Counseling Center Directors Annual Survey in 2007, counseling centers have used computers in a variety of ways such as scheduling (79% of counseling centers), electronic mail (83.7% of centers), database on services/activities (69.4% of centers), maintaining clients case notes (60.9% of centers), online service (49% of centers), programs to output clinicians caseloads and turnover rates (33.9% of centers), billing (9.6% of centers), and others (5.8% of centers) (Gallagher & Taylor, 2007). Apparently the increase of technology use by the counseling centers has been significant in the past 15 years, e.g., only 34 percent of counseling centers reported computer use in 1993 (Gallagher et al., 1994). Along with the trend of new technology development, the most recent IACS Standards (2000) also emphasize the basic understanding and appropriate use of technology within counseling centers. Particularly the IACS application contains appropriate user and system security measures for client records. For example, confidential information should not be transmitted via e-mail and cordless or cellular phones. When electronic mail is used to communicate with clients or transmit information, inherent risks to technology must be explained to clients and informed consent must be obtained from clients (Boyd et al., 2003). When a fax machine is used, a system must be developed to safeguard the material from unauthorized access (Boyd et al., 2003). Most importantly, technical support personnel must be provided with training regarding securing confidential information (Boyd et al., 2003).

Listservs for various interest groups, including center directors, clinical directors, and training directors are becoming essential tools in the operation of counseling centers. In 2001, most directors (90%) surveyed reported being on a directors listserv, and both seeking assistance (71%), and benefiting from the assistance they received (91%) from the listserv (Gallagher et al., 2001). The creation of websites for counseling centers is also becoming a common phenomenon, with most centers now having some form of homepage.

PROGRAMS AND SERVICES

Range of Services

The programs and services offered by a counseling center will depend upon the size and type of institution, the model of the center, the orientation of the director, and the services offered elsewhere on campus (Yarris, 1996).

Some counseling centers will provide services to faculty, staff and members of the community (Gallagher et al., 1994). While it is common to provide consultation and referral to non-students, the number of centers providing direct services to faculty, staff, and members of the community is decreasing.

IACS standards require the following program functions: (a) individual and group counseling and therapy services that are responsive to student needs; (b) crisis intervention and emergency coverage either directly or through arrangements with other resources; (c) outreach programming focusing on the developmental needs of students; (d) consultation services with members of the university community; (e) referral resources; (f) research services; (g) program evaluation of services; and (h) training and professional development experiences for staff, interns, practicum students, and others in the university community (Boyd et al., 2003). Centers with larger staffs, centers at public institutions, and those accredited by IACS were most likely to provide this wide range of functions (Whiteley et al., 1987). During the fall and winter terms, full-time counselors spend 62 percent of their time on direct service, which includes individual/group counseling, intakes, assessment, crisis-intervention, and workshops; 20 percent of time on indirect service which includes supervision, RA/peer/clinical training, consultation, case conferences, case notes, and workshops; 14 percent of time on administrative services which include staff business meetings, center management, and professional development; and 4 percent of time on other activities which include research, training, etc. (Gallagher & Taylor, 2008).

Career counseling, historically a cornerstone of university and college counseling centers, appears to be part of the price of keeping up with the increased demand for psychological services. As recently as 1994, 67 percent of centers provided career counseling (Gallagher et al., 1994). In 2005, 67 percent of centers reported that career counseling takes place primarily in a separate office, 22 percent reported that it takes place in the counseling center, and 6.3 percent reported that it was shared equally by the two offices (Gallagher et al., 2005). The percentage of this equally shared service of career counseling has dropped from the 13 percent that was reported in 1999 (Gallagher et al., 1999). Over the past 10 years, responsibility for career counseling has been moved out of 20.4 percent of counseling centers, while only 1.1 percent of counseling centers have gained this responsibility (Gallagher et al., 2005). The wisdom of such changes in counseling services delivery systems has been seriously questioned (e.g., Guinee & Ness; Stone & Archer, 1990). The debate on whether or not to provide career counseling in the counseling center will, undoubtedly, continue on many fronts and for many years to come.

To deal with the increased requests for individual service, many centers are limiting the number of individual sessions that are available (Gallagher et al., 1994; Magoon, 1994; Stone & Archer, 1990). In 2007, 52 percent of centers have set limits on the number of client sessions (Gallagher & Taylor, 2007), an 8 percent increase since 2001 (Gallagher et al., 2001). The trend toward establishing session limits is growing and appears to be a common response to the increase in demand for services (Bishop, 1995; Stone & McMichael, 1996). Instead of longer-term counseling and therapy, many counseling centers offer referrals to appropriate group programs in lieu of or in addition to individual services (Stone & McMichael, 1996). Also, the use of group counseling may be a direct response to the fact that 97 percent of counseling center directors reported that the number of students with significant psychological problems become a growing concern (Gallagher & Taylor, 2007). These groups can be either therapeutic groups aimed at remediation or psychoeducational groups aimed at fostering student development and preventing problems. Though groups are reported to be effective in the literature, many counseling center directors have reported that it is difficult to fill groups (Gallagher et al., 1994).

In an effort to serve a larger portion of the student body, many counseling centers have turned toward outreach programming as a way to provide preventative services to students who might not otherwise seek traditional counseling services (Boyd et al., 2003). Some common outreach programs include issues such as study skills, time management, assertive communication, responsible decision making, and the prevention of problems associated with sexual offenses, alcohol/drug abuse, and technology addiction. The target population of prevention programs might also be the parents of students, as it is becoming more common for representatives of the counseling center to meet with groups of parents of new students to discuss student development, typically during a student orientation period.

Direct service to students (individual and group counseling, intakes, assessment, crisis intervention, psychoeducational groups, and workshops) accounted for 62 percent of counseling center staff time (Gallagher & Taylor, 2008), but in smaller centers, direct service might fill all available time (Gallagher et al., 1994). Indirect service (supervision, RA/peer clinical training, consultation, outreach) accounted for 20 percent of staff time (Gallagher & Taylor, 2008). Most centers (67%) offer some type of self-help materials such as books or audio tapes (Gallagher et al., 1994; Guinee & Ness, 2000).

Counseling center staffs often function as consultants who summarize and interpret the needs of students and advocate on their behalf to institutional faculty, staff, and administrators (Boyd et al., 2003). Consultation frequently refers to helping others respond to a student problem; however, there is also consultation activity that focuses on organizational dynamics. Consultation must be done with a commitment to protecting confidentiality, and this is not always easy. Deans and vice presidents may interpret their need to know as more important than the student's right to confidentiality (Gallagher, 2001). Centers many have ongoing consultative relationships with campus police, residence life, and academic or athletic departments. There has been an increase in the amount of time centers are spending on outreach and consultation (Guinee & Ness, 2000).

Crisis intervention usually refers to a situation that requires immediate attention for students who are experiencing acute emotional distress, who are perceived to be a danger to self or others, or who are in need of immediate hospitalization (Boyd et al., 2003). The majority (76%) of centers provide on call services for student emergencies, and 69 percent of centers consider this to be a part of the job responsibility and thus offer no additional compensation (Gallagher et al., 2001). Beepers and cell phones are increasingly employed during on-call hours. Many centers have at least one representative who participates on a campus crisis team. In 2008, 76 percent of counseling center directors noted a greater interest in the development or redesign of interdepartmental crisis management teams (Gallagher & Taylor, 2008).

An additional program, especially in larger counseling centers, is that of training. In addition to the training of paraprofessionals (e.g., Resident Advisors), many centers are involved in pre-professional training programs. These may include practicum placement for master's and doctoral level graduate students in fields such as Counseling Psychology, Clinical Psychology, Counseling and Guidance, and College Student Personnel. A more formal and structured training program exists in centers providing pre-doctoral and/or postdoctoral internships in professional psychology, especially if the training program is approved by the American Psychological Association (APA) (Yarris, 1996). In 1997, 19 percent of centers had an APA accredited predoctoral internship program and 64 percent reported that their training program had been increased within the last five years (Gallagher et al., 1997). In 2007, 37 percent of counseling centers had predoctoral trainees while 20 percent of center directors reported that they had postdoctoral trainees (Rando et al., 2007). The campus community often relies upon the counseling center staff to provide training to non-counseling professions (e.g., training faculty and others to respond well to students in trouble and to make appropriate referrals).

Most counseling centers have some type of testing services available. These might include use of instruments such as interest inventories, personality assessments, or the administration of national testing programs such as the SAT, ACT, and GRE (Yarris, 1996). While these can be important aspects of the center's mission, and well integrated into the functioning of the center, it is a far cry from the centers of the 1930s and 1940s, where testing was often the most prominent service.

Many centers have a variety of learning support activities. Some centers do academic advising, many provide study skills programs and services, many center staff members teach orientation and study skill courses, and some centers provide study tables and/or tutors. As counseling professionals, center staffs are expected to maintain ongoing advocacy, evaluation and accountability tasks as outlined by professional guidelines of their field (Boyd et al., 2003; Guinee & Ness, 2000; Stone et al., 2000).

Types of Problems

Historically, researchers and practitioners have tried to categorize and predict the types of problems that higher education students would bring to counseling centers. Understanding and expecting certain student concerns in advance allows center staff to be better prepared to assist. A review of the literature since 1910, when Princeton University opened the first campus mental health service, indicates that the anticipated student concerns have changed dramatically over the past century. While center personnel are still concerned with the traditional issues pertaining to academic and social adjustment, they are also managing greater psychological pathology (both emerging and chronic) and increasing concerns related to our current zeitgeist.

Early student concerns were summarized by Williamson (1939) as pertaining to social maladjustments, speech adjustment, family conflicts, student discipline, educational orientation and achievement, occupational orientation, and finances. While these are certainly still concerns for twenty-first century students, there are many additional concerns for the current generation, many of which are developmental in nature. Late adolescence and early adulthood are difficult times which can bring difficulties associated with the challenges of mastering new developmental tasks such as: (a) adjusting to a new environment; (b) choosing a major and planning for a future career; (c) establishing an identity separate from parents; (d) learning time management and study skills appropriate to higher education; (e) establishing intimate relationships; (f) exploring sexual identity; and (g) values clarification (Yarris, 1996). Likewise, many more nontraditional age students are attending colleges and universities and they are bringing new sets of challenges which correspond to later stages of development. Counselors need to be mindful of changing demographics and consider the varying presenting issues that might relate age, gender, academic major, ethnicity, previous history, cohort and ability level.

The fact that the college years are stressful is well documented and it appears that stress among college students is increasing (Dunkel-Schetter & Lobel, 1990). Not surprisingly, many studies report academics, career planning, social issues (including romantic relationships), family concerns (including a family history of alcohol abuse), and financial concerns as the most frequent presenting problems on college campuses (e.g., Bertocci et al., 1992; Carney et al., 1990; Dunkel-Schetter & Lobel, 1990; Heppner et al., 1994). Other studies reported increasing student concerns with drug and alcohol use, eating and weight, sexual assault and harassment, various forms of violence, and AIDS (Bertocci et al., 1992; Roark, 1993; Stone et al., 2000). Today, college students also confront new challenges associated with internet/electronic addiction, electronic sexuality (sexting), cutting/self-mutilation, and sleep deprivation (Kadison & DiGeronimo, 2004).

Unexpected crisis events also happen to college students. Examples include the following: (a) death or suicide of a friend or family member; (b) chronic illness in a family member, friend, or self; (c) parents' divorce and remarriage; (d) sexual assault; (e) legal problems and pending jail terms; (f) disability from a car accident or other traumatic event; and (g) various types of harassment, including being stalked (Yarris, 1996). Global crises also impact college students.

The current zeitgeist contributes to the concerns of recent cohorts of college students. Hotelling (1995) cites the number of ways in which events of our modern society have contributed to feelings of vulnerability in students: exposure to increased violence; uncertainty over functioning in a more diverse environment; fearing the loss of affirmative action, and economic pressure to choose a major or a four-year degree program that is not wanted. Additionally, Kadison and DiGeronimo (2004) cite our culture of fear in the aftermath of 9/11/01 and the subsequent terrorist activity and wars as contributing to student concerns. These concerns are heightened by recent events of campus violence that force students to acknowledge that the campus is not a refuge and adolescents are not invulnerable. Though financial issues have already been cited as a standard concern for this age group, recent changes in the stability of the U.S. economic condition are expected to exacerbate this concern for the current cohort. Surveys of graduate students, who are generally older than traditionally aged students, found similar concerns (Bertocci, at al., 1992; Hodgson & Simoni, 1995). Vye, Scholljegerdes, and Welch (2007) point out that the current cohort of college students has lived through terrorist attacks, natural disasters, school shootings, health crises, and financial peril, not to mention that they are living in what Twenge (2000) has been labeled the Age of Anxiety.

Over the past 20 years, there have been increasing reports of larger numbers of students who arrive on campus with chronic problems in addition to the expected developmental issues, crisis situations, and environmental stressors. Recent studies have documented examples which include issues such as learning disabilities, inherited biochemical imbalances/depression, unmedicated compulsive behaviors, or hallucinations, and eating disorders (Gallagher et al., 1994; Guinee & Ness, 2000; Stone & Archer, 1990). In the 1980s, there was an increase in the number of students who came to counseling centers for help with eating disorders, while in the 1990s, there has been an increase in problems caused by childhood physical or sexual abuse (Gallagher et al., 1994; Stone & Archer, 1990). Such chronic concerns combine with the unavoidable stresses of campus life, to facilitate increasing feelings of depression and anxiety, thoughts of suicide, substance abuse, somatic problems, interpersonal difficulties, and difficulty in concentrating on academic work (Heppner et al., 1994; Miller & Rice, 1993).

In addition to understanding the unique challenges that students bring, counseling center staff can also examine the changing patterns of use in counseling center services. Patterns of use in the 1970s and 1980s research indicated that between 10 percent and 25 percent of students used the Counseling Center (Heppner & Neal, 1983). In 1997, Magoon found 10 percent of students at large schools and 14 percent of students at small schools were clients at counseling centers. Earlier reports indicated that students were more likely to come to the center for career planning, negotiating the system, and coping with financial and academic concerns (Carney et al., 1979), but then came to view the counseling center as an appropriate place to discuss personal and interpersonal concerns (Heppner & Neal, 1983). In the 1990s there were numerous reports of increased requests for counseling services (Guinee & Ness, 2000). In the 2008 annual survey, counseling center directors reported that 9.0 percent of enrolled students sought counseling in the past year, which represents approximately 310,000 students from the surveyed schools. However, 29.6 percent (almost one million) were seen by counselors in other contexts (workshops, orientations, classroom presentations, etc.) (Gallagher & Taylor, 2008). In the same survey, 95 percent of center directors also reported a trend of greater number of students with severe psychological problems on their campuses.

In addition to the aforementioned presenting issues, there are demographic factors that also impact the utilization of higher education counseling centers. Some factors such as gender and culture may impact student utilization of counseling centers. Female students are more likely to use counseling services than men, white students are more likely than racial/ethic minority students to use counseling services, and domestic students are more likely than international students to see a counselor for their academic, social, and personal problems (Hyun, Quinn, Madon, & Lustig, 2006; Zhang & Dixon, 2003).

The above patterns of use refer to students who come to a counseling center requesting counseling. Other patterns of use have not been so well described in the literature but include such outreach activities as counseling center staff going to a residence hall to discuss with students and staff the impact of a homicide in the hall (Waldo et al., 1993), or mobilizing a community-wide support and counseling effort after a campus tragedy (Archer & Cooper, 1998; Stone, 1993).

In 2008, 95 percent of counseling center directors reported a significant increase in severe psychological problems of their students (Gallagher & Taylor, 2008). Some authors (Sharkin, 1997; Erickson Cornish et al., 2000) have empirically examined these perceptions, and their findings challenge the notion that the pathology is more severe. However, they do agree that some types of psychological disturbances are not uncommon in college populations, some small increases in the numbers of severely distressed students have been documented, and the perception of counseling center directors of an increase in pathology is long-standing and consistent. In order to manage the perceived increasing number of students with severe psychological problems, many centers have undertaken steps such as increasing the amount of time training faculty and others to respond in a helpful way to students in trouble and to make appropriate referrals (68%), serving on a campus-wide Student Assistance Committee (62%), increasing training for staff in working with difficult cases, providing psychoeducational assistance on center websites (55%), expanding external referral networks (48%), increasing counseling center staff (42%), increasing psychiatric consultation hours (32%), increasing part-time counselors during busy time of year (26%), increasing training for staff in time-limited therapy, and providing psychologically-oriented articles for the student newspaper (Gallagher & Taylor, 2008). Though many higher education administrators continue to debate the level of responsibility that the institution has toward student mental health, particularly in an increasingly stressed financial climate, most experts would agree that the institution as a whole benefits from strong mental health services (Kadison & DiGeronimo, 2004).

STAFFING

The 2000 IACS Standards state that, "The human resources necessary for the effective operation of a counseling service depend, to a large degree, on the size and nature of the institution and the extent to which other mental health and student support resources are available in the area" (Boyd et al., 2003, p. 175). IACS guidelines recommend minimum staffing ratios of one full-time equivalent (FTE) professional staff member to every 1,000 to 1,500 students and require hiring practices that are consistent with the goals of equal opportunity and affirmative action (Boyd et al., 2003). Gallagher & Taylor, (2008) approximates the ratio of FTE mental health professionals to FTE students to be 1:3557 at large schools (>15,000) and 1:918 at small schools (<2,500).

Traditionally, a campus counseling center staff is comprised of profession-al individuals who emerged from a variety of disciplines, specialties and training levels and paraprofessional support staff which may include practi-ca/internship students. There appears to be a growing trend at larger centers toward developing multidisciplinary staffs, which utilize psychologists, social workers and/or counselors, and psychiatrists on the same staff. This is par-ticularly beneficial if the center has a training program, because it allows the trainees to have exposure to several fields and the opportunity to witness the collaborative efforts across fields of specialization. Credentials for entry level professional staff are reviewed in a section below.

In 2008, the majority of counseling center directors (63%) held a doctoral degree and the number of directors who held a master's degree was rela-tively small (22%) (Gallagher & Taylor, 2008). Also in 2008, 42 percent of directors identified themselves as counseling psychologists, 23 percent as clinical psychologists, about 15 percent as professional counselors, and 7 per-cent as social workers (Gallagher & Taylor, 2008). Directors who oversee a larger staff, run a center in a public institution and/or head a center accred-ited by IACS are more likely to have doctoral degrees (Whiteley et al., 1987). IACS standards for accreditation recommend that the director should have an earned doctorate and equivalency criteria are recommended for non-doc-torate directors (Boyd et al., 2003).

There is a definite shift in the numbers of females employed as profes-sionals in counseling centers and employed as directors. Gallagher & Taylor, (2008) reported that 55 percent of directors responding to the annual survey were female, as compared to 19 percent in 1982. Between 1989 and 1995, newly hired, doctoral female staff out numbered newly hired doctoral males nearly two to one, and at the master's degree level, it was nearly three to one (Affsprung, 1997). Similarly, 68 percent of all paid professional staff mem-bers in counseling centers in 2006 were female (Gallagher & Taylor, 2006), prompting 35 percent of directors to indicate that they were finding it increasingly difficult to hire qualified male staff members (Gallagher et al., 1999). It appears that the majority of counseling center staff of the future will be women (Affsprung, 1997).

Magoon (1994) reported that the number of center directors who hold aca-demic rank in large institutions has been on the decline since 1980. How-ever, in that same year, approximately half of the center directors surveyed by Gallagher et al. (1994) still held academic rank. The 2000 IACS standards state the expectation that "Salaries, benefits, and career advancement oppor-tunities should be commensurate with those of others in the institution with similar qualifications and responsibilities and comparable professionals in other institutions of higher education in the region" (Boyd et al., 2003, p. 175).

Those centers with a predoctoral internship training program typically designate a staff member as Training Director and many larger centers delegate responsibilities to Directors of Clinical Services, Evaluation and Research, Career Services, and Outreach and Consultation. Additionally, some centers that offer testing services have a psychometrician on staff and many centers have a psychiatrist either on staff or available for consultation. In 2005, 35 percent of campuses reporting had a psychiatrist in the counseling center, 14 percent had a psychiatrist in the student health service, 8 percent had a psychiatrist in both the counseling center and the student health service, while 36 percent reported having no access to a psychiatrist except as a private referral (Gallagher et al., 2005).

Since support staff play important roles in students' impressions of the counseling service, they should be selected carefully and receive training not only in the operation of the service but also in issues regarding confidentiality and the limits of their functioning (Boyd et al., 2003). Further, the 2000 IACS Standards insist, "Student-workers must not have access to client files and confidential office records and should not be involved with client scheduling" (Boyd et al., 2003, p. 174).

MODELS

The model of a counseling center is determined in part by the types of programs and services expected from the center; the philosophy of the director; and the philosophy and practical pressures on other key administrators. Other concepts related to the model of any given center are staff size; accreditation status of the center (Boyd et al., 2003; Whiteley et al., 1987); similar services available on campus or in the community; the professional training programs on campus and their relationship to the center; the relationship between student health services and the center; the relationship with the center and service assignments of a career placement office; the relationship with academic advisors and whether advising is centralized or decentralized; and the location and extent of services available for sexual assault and alcohol and drug abuse prevention and treatment.

In the 1960s, vocational guidance was the cornerstone of most counseling centers. In 1970, Oetting and associates (1970) reported that the "original counseling center" still followed a *vocational guidance model* with a primary emphasis on testing and vocational choice. The aforementioned survey (Oetting et al., 1970) also identified six other models of counseling centers: personnel services model, academic affairs model, psychotherapy model, training model, research model, and traditional counseling model. Oetting et al. (1970) reported that the "traditional" model was found among those centers whose directors had formed the original counseling center directors' organization and functioned as a separate campus agency, providing vocational counseling, short-term treatment of emotional problems, and some longer term counseling. Service to clients was the primary orientation, although some intern and practicum training experiences existed (Yarris, 1996). Among the models identified during the 1970s, this traditional model was evaluated most positively by counselors, resident assistants, faculty, students, and administrators (Gelso et al., 1977).

Following the work of Oetting et al. (1970), the next major effort to characterize types of counseling centers was a survey conducted in the 1980s (Whiteley et al., 1987). The authors were able to identify five primary types of centers. The macrocenter (21% of the sample) provided a broad range of services with an extensive number of both counseling and career-related services, testing, and special functions such as outreach and training. The career-oriented center (16%) offered minimal counseling and related services and focused on career planning and placement assistance. The counseling oriented center (29%) was similar to the macrocenter but focused more on personal counseling functions and less on career services. The general purpose center (20%), which was more likely to be found at private schools, provided a more general level of services, with more responsibilities similar to those of a dean of students (e.g., responsibilities and services related to student organizations, fraternity and sorority advising). The microcenter (15%) provided some counseling services and a minimal level of other services (Yarris, 1996). For those interested in counseling models used in community colleges, Coll (1993) provides that discussion.

In a rapidly changing social environment, with limited resources and increasing demands, there has been a tendency to focus on counseling center issues, functions, and/or models that address economic concerns (Bishop, 1990; Keeling, & Heitzmann, 2003; Steenbarger, 1995; Stone & Archer, 1990) and student retention issues (Sharkin, 2004; Van Brunt, 2008). Crego (1990), for example, admonished counseling center leaders to move beyond "simply adding programs, balancing programs, and . . . prioritizing programs" (p. 609), and notes that counseling centers continue to employ a model designed for the white, middle-class, full-time, traditional-aged, self-directed student (Yarris, 1996). The diversity and changing needs of college students must not be ignored as new models and approaches to the design of counseling centers are explored (Resnick, 2006).

One attempt to reconceptualize models of counseling center functioning suggested "rounding out the cube" (Pace et al., 1996). According to Pace et al. (1996), the original cube presented the counseling center as an independent and fixed structure with a closed uni-directional system and decision-making that was primarily internal. The cube concept did not address resource allocation and it implied a non-collaborative style. Pace et al. (1996) proposed a "global" model for counseling centers that has an "interactive" cube that focuses on the institution as a system; is interdependent with the system; is a living system rather than a fixed structure; is multi-directional; makes decisions in consultation with the campus community; strives for a homeostatic balance of resources and services; and collaborates with the university community as equals (Yarris, 1996). This interactive network conceptualization was further endorsed by Boyd et al. (2003) because it more closely mirrors the accreditation standards set forth by the International Association of Counseling Services (IACS).

PROFESSIONAL DEVELOPMENT

IACS Standards identify professional development as an essential dimension of a counseling program and recommend release time and budget resources be provided to staff for such purposes (Boyd et al., 2003). Counseling center personnel are further directed by the professional standards of IACS, to participate in professional organizations; attend local, state, and national conferences; take part in in-service training; engage in scholarship and leadership within their field; and become involved in relevant community activities (Boyd et al., 2003).

Professional organizations provide opportunities for collegial interaction, professional development, collection and dissemination of information, contributions through publications, presentations, and committees, as well as the establishment and maintenance of standards.

The Association for University and College Counseling Center Directors (AUCCCD) is the primary professional affiliation for directors of centers (Gallagher et al., 2001). This organization is primarily concerned with the functioning of counseling centers as integral parts of collegiate institutions (Archer & Bingham, 1990). The annual AUCCCD Conferences have been used to establish guidelines, review accountability issues, develop clearinghouses for the dissemination of innovative counseling programs, and to formulate constructive responses to the challenges facing counseling centers (Yarris, 1996).

In 1994, Magoon reported that many counselors affiliated with campus counseling centers chose the American Psychological Association (APA), as their primary professional affiliation and many were also involved with Division 17 (Counseling Psychology), which has a special interest group focused on counseling centers, and the American College Personnel Association (ACPA). Commission VII (Counseling and Psychological Services) of ACPA is a very active organization of a wide range of professionals interested in counseling and psychological services in community colleges, colleges, and universities. According to Magoon (1994), affiliation with the American Counseling Association (ACA) (formerly the American Personnel and Guidance Association) has declined, especially among staff of larger institutions. ACA does have a division dedicated to college counselors, American College Counseling Association (ACCA) which has seen resurgence in recent years. ACA is also reported to be the most popular national association for community college counselors (Coll, 1993). Some counseling center staff members are also active in their state psychological or college personnel associations and 3 percent are affiliated with the American College Health Association (Gallagher et al., 1994).

Those centers that provide predoctoral internship training often are affiliated with the Association of Counseling Center Training Agencies (ACCTA) and the Association of Postdoctoral and Psychology Internship Centers (APPIC). In addition to their specific annual meetings, these organizations, as well as AUCCCD, frequently meet at the annual conventions of APA and ACPA. It is important to note that in these rapidly changing times, traditional methods of professional communication, such as publications and meetings, have been augmented by use of electronic communication (Yarris, 1996). Centers that provide such pre- and postdoctoral training of counseling center personnel will need to provide training that allows professionals to become well versed in the briefer therapies, crisis intervention, group work, consultation and outreach, the theory and practice of career and student development, and those public health issues that are relevant to a college population, as well as multicultural, research, and evaluation competencies (Bishop, 2006).

The International Association of Counseling Services, Incorporated has developed standards that are used for the formal accreditation of college and university counseling programs (Boyd et al., 2003). Approximately half of the centers from institutions of over 15,000 are accredited by IACS (Gallagher et al., 1994).

Periodicals that publish articles on issues, theory, and research relevant to counseling services include *The Counseling Psychologist, The Journal of Counseling Psychology,* and *Professional Psychology: Research and Practice* which are journals of the American Psychological Association. Also relevant are the Journal of College Student Development (ACPA), the *Journal of Counseling and Development* (ACA), the *Journal of Multicultural Counseling and Development* (ACA), *The Journal of College Student Psychotherapy,* the *Journal of College Counseling* (JCC), the *Chronicle of Higher Education,* journals published by state organizations and the newsletters of professional organizations (Hood & Arceneaux, 1990; Stone & Lucas, 1991). Although counseling center directors report that research activities become problematic due to heavy service demands (Stone & Archer, 1990), a survey of counseling-relevant journals found that counseling center-related authors, participants, and topics were well represented in the literature (Stone & Lucas, 1991).

In addition, various data banks are available such as the AUCCCD Data Bank collected by Dr. Vivian Boyd at the University of Maryland, AUCC-CD Survey of Counseling Center Director coordinated by Robert Rando at Wright State University, and the National Survey of Counseling Center Directors collected by Dr. Robert Gallagher at the University of Pittsburgh. The Research Consortium of Counseling and Psychological Services in Higher Education was organized by Dr. David Drum at the University of Texas (Drum, 1995).

Finally, it is the responsibility of all professionals in counseling and higher education administration to continue in the development of their professional skills and understanding, particularly in light of changing student culture and needs (Davis & Humphrey, 2000). In some states, it is a legal requirement for professionals to demonstrate continuing education in order to remain licensed in their professional fields. Such continuing education credits might come from attendance at workshops aimed at a specific issue (such as a conference on counseling persons living with HIV and AIDS), and/or from relevant presentations at conventions such as those of ACPA, APA, AUCCCD, ACA, and ACCTA. Such licensure requirements are the topic of much recent discussion as state regulatory boards struggle to adapt adequately to emerging professional issues related to professional mobility, temporary practice across jurisdictional boundaries, distance learning/counseling, disciplinary actions and the proposed competency assessment of newly licensed professionals (DeMers, Van Home, & Rodolfa, 2008).

ENTRY-LEVEL QUALIFICATIONS

In reviewing the history of student services staff, Hood and Arceneaux (1990) indicated that counseling center staffs were the first to obtain the necessary training, professional organization affiliations and accreditation/licensure to be considered "professionals" in their field. Yarris (1996) summarized a survey (Gallagher et al., 1994) of 310 counseling center directors and found that about 85 percent of the centers have a licensed psychologist on staff, while 32 percent reported staffs who were licensed MSWs, and 51 percent have a certified professional counselor. For colleges and universities with an enrollment of over 15,000, almost 97 percent reported having licensed psychologists on the staff. A doctoral degree in clinical or counseling psychology has been the most typical educational requirement, especially for staff of centers at larger four-year colleges and universities. Vespia (2007) surveyed counseling center directors at small colleges (500-4000 students) and found that 9 percent employed psychiatrists with MD's, 48 percent of centers employed staff with doctoral degrees in counseling/clinical psychology; 11 percent of centers hired staff with doctoral degrees in other related areas; 77 percent of centers employed professional counselors with masters degrees in counseling/clinical psychology; 26 percent of centers hired professionals with masters degrees in other related areas; and 68 percent reported staffs who were licensed. In many centers, an entry-level staff member is expected to be licensed or license-eligible, which means having completed a doctoral program that is either accredited by the American Psychological Association or otherwise fulfilling the state requirements to be admitted to the licensing examination. This includes a year-long, predoctoral internship and at least one year of supervised postdoctoral experience. Larger centers may require or prefer a psychologist with an APA approved internship. A similar process is required to become a licensed Social Worker or a Certified Professional Counselor (Yarris, 1996).

IACS Accreditation Standards for University and College Counseling Centers (Boyd et al., 2003) state that professional staff should have at least a master's degree from disciplines such as counselor education, counseling psychology, clinical psychology, psychiatry, and social work. Doctoral-level staffs are expected to be licensed and certified to practice within their specialty and nondoctoral staffs are encouraged to seek a similar credential. Appropriate course work and supervised experience in the counseling of college-aged students are required. Those who have administrative responsibilities or who supervise the clinical work of others must hold a doctorate or have an appropriate master's degree and experience in the training of other professionals. A psychiatrist holds a medical degree and has completed a residency in psychiatry. Finally, standards of practice require competence in working with human differences (American Psychological Association, 1995) and freedom from prejudice with respect to race, religion, age, sex, sexual orientation, or physical challenge (Boyd et al., 2003).

As previously mentioned, many college counseling center staff members identify with the field of counseling psychology (Phelps, 1992); however, several sources predict that an increasing number of master's level counselors and social workers will be employed in college counseling centers (Baron, 1995; Hotelling, 1995; Toth, 1995). As mentioned above, more counseling centers are moving toward multidisciplinary staffs.

ROLE AND APPLICATION OF STUDENT DEVELOPMENT THEORY AND THE STUDENT LEARNING IMPERATIVE

The history of counseling centers has paralleled that of the field of counseling psychology (Sprinthall, 1990; Tyler, 1992; Whiteley, 1984). Given that the distinguishing feature of counseling psychology is its emphasis on development and life planning (Tyler, 1992), counseling centers began with an inherent focus on student development (Yarris, 1996). In contrast to therapy which is generally presumed to be a remedial service, "Counseling, as it began, was a service for everybody" as "We are all faced with the necessity of choosing how we will live our lives" (Tyler, 1992, p. 343). As Stone & McMichael (1996) point out, "Internally, mental health policy relating to counseling centers has been shaped historically by a student-need based philosophy including the SPPV student development point of view (American Council on Education, 1937), and more recently by formulations related to college student development (e.g., Chickering, 1969) and wellness and health promotion.

In addition to the emphasis on choices throughout the lifespan, counseling psychology was also an outgrowth of the psychological study of individual differences (Tyler, 1992). Thus, counseling center staff members are prepared to work with not only the traditionally aged college student, but also adult learners and students from diverse backgrounds (Yarris, 1996).

In the 1970s and 1980s, college counseling centers placed heavy emphasis on identity and function as student development centers (McKinley, 1980). As mentioned above in the Types of Problems section, most counseling centers are designed to aid students in the major developmental tasks of late adolescence and early adulthood. During this time, many counselors on campuses were committed to student development and campus ecology (Aulepp & Delworth, 1976; Conyne et al, 1979; Hurst, 1978). Relevant research demonstrates that the counseling needs of students vary according to class level, age, sex, and race of the student (Carney et al., 1990); that minority and underrepresented students may be less likely to utilize services (Brinson & Kottler, 1995); and attention to developmental struggles and needs is a prerequisite to good counseling or therapy with college students (Whitaker, 1992). Most counseling centers are excellent examples of the application of student development theory.

However, some who counsel college and university students are questioning the current meaning of "normal" developmental issues, given the evidence of more and more dysfunctional and pathological families, and traumatic childhood and adolescent experiences. Thus, as Stone and Archer (1990) conclude, "the developmental issues for many of our students include learning to overcome serious psychological problems" (p. 546). Yarris (1996) summarized several studies supporting the position that early life experiences can complicate the resolution of the expected developmental tasks of the college student. For example, White and Strange (1993) found that an unwanted childhood sexual experience had significant effects on subsequent psychosocial tasks of intimacy and career planning in a sample of college women. Similarly, typical college students' experimentation with new behaviors, as they experience physical, sexual, psychological, identity, and moral development, can increase risk of serious problems with substance abuse, violence, and exposure to HIV infection (Rivinus & Larimer, 1993; Triggs & McDermott, 1991).

It is also true that counseling centers are outstanding examples of the application of the Student Learning Imperative. The increased focus on student learning and personal development, the collaboration with fellow educators, the experience-based and research-based expertise of counseling center staff regarding student characteristics, and the increase in data-based outcome evaluations and assessment data are all congruent with the Student Learning Imperative. Efforts on many campuses have long existed and continue to exist to include counseling centers as contributors to seamless learning/second curriculum environments (Kahn et al., 1999). Another growing trend, and further evidence of counseling centers' resonance with the Student Learning Imperative, is the effort of centers to conduct research and evaluation that demonstrate the relationship between counseling outcomes and student learning (Schwitzer & Metzinger, 1998).

ISSUES AND TRENDS OF THE TWENY-FIRST CENTURY

Issues

The 1990s also brought to our awareness a new problem known as internet addiction. Many students are spending inordinate amounts of time in internet sites, including chat rooms and sexually oriented sites. This and other problems, such as alienation and isolation related to reliance on information technology, will continue in the twenty-first century. As new technological advancements are discovered, new human problems as a result of the advancements are likely to occur. Due to the increase in the numbers of students requesting help, and the seriousness of their problems, there is great concern and debate over managing these demands in the future (Stone & Archer, 1990). Among the major concerns expressed by counseling center directors are (1) an increased number of students with severe psychological problems which have led to various concerns for counselors such as burnout, shortages during peak times, decreased focus on student normal developmental concerns, and ending too many cases prematurely; (2) increase in crisis counseling; (3) finding referral for students needing long-term help; (4) increased demand for services with no increase in resources; (5) increase in self-injury reports (e.g., cutting, etc. to relieve anxiety); (6) administrative issues related to the handling of students with severe psychopathology; (7) increase in number of students with eating disorders; (8) boundary issues with administration; (9) inadequate number of clerical staff; (10) increase in sexual assault cases; (11) not enough technical support; and (12) an increase in waiting lists for counseling services (Gallagher & Taylor, 2008). All of these concerns are likely to continue into the next 15 or 20 years due to the current economy down turn.

To cope with these increased service demands, college and university counseling centers have implemented the following actions: (a) increasing the amount of time training faculty and others to respond in a helpful way to students in trouble and to make appropriate referrals; (b) serving on a campus-wide Student Assistance Committee; (c) increasing training for staff in working with difficult cases; (d) providing psychoeducational assistance on center websites; (e) expanding external referral networks; (f) increasing psychiatric consultation hours; (g) increasing part-time counselors during busy time of year; (h) increasing training for staff in short term therapy; and (i) providing psychologically-oriented articles for the student newspaper (Gallagher & Taylor, 2008). Other attempts to cope with demand include increasing psychiatric hours; providing more mandated suicide assessment; providing gatekeeper training to students, faculty and staff; extending evening hours; and making more use of peer education groups (Gallagher & Taylor, 2008).

Both legal and ethical issues will continue to be a high priority for counseling centers, and they are and will continue to become increasingly complex (Archer & Cooper, 1998). Guidelines of professional organizations and state laws suggest or require standards for professional practice (e.g., American College Personnel Association, 2006; American Counseling Association, 2005; American Psychological Association, 2003). However, lawsuits filed by students and parents against individual practitioners, centers, and universities are becoming more common. According to the counseling center director's survey there have been 23 lawsuits against college and university counseling centers in the past six years (Gallagher & Taylor, 2006, 2008; 2005, 2004, 2003; Rando et al., 2007). Among all the legal and ethical issues, confidentiality has been most frequently identified as a source of ethical dilemmas for psychologists, counselors, and social workers (Archer & Cooper, 1998; Pope & Vetter, 1992). Survey research shows that clients and the general public share the belief that confidentiality is crucial in counseling relationship (Kremer & Gesten, 2003) and counseling professionals are ethically obligated to keep client information confidential, however, this may not be a legal privilege in all circumstances (Archer & Cooper, 1998). In many, but not all, states there is a legal privileged communication between client and psychologist, counselor, or social worker, however, this is typically viewed in the legal profession as a judicial rather than legislative privilege. Therefore, psychologists, counselors, and social workers can claim privileged communication, but there is no guarantee that all courts will honor the claim. In short, there are five main exceptions to confidentiality, and these exceptions occur in (1) cases that a client is potentially suicidal and dangerous to self, (2) cases in which a client is considered harmful to others, (3) cases of minor or elder abuse, (4) certain legal proceedings in which a client's records may be subpoenaed, and (5) requests by insurance companies for review of clients' diagnosis records and benefits of services. Regardless, counseling center professionals are ethically bound to protect the client confidentiality.

Issues of confidentiality and other legal and ethical issues have also become more complex due to modern technology, HIV and AIDS third-party payments, and a societal increase in violence and terrorism. Confidentiality and adherence to a student development model is threatened in modern counseling centers by complications arising from insurance reimbursement models and other health care models which use psychiatrists to diagnose and third-party payments to supplement the budget (Crego, 1995; Gilbert, 1994). While these models may permit university counseling centers to provide more in depth services in a cost efficient way, the possibility of records reviews and imposed session limits raise ethical questions about long-term therapy relationships in a college counseling center context (Lilly-Weber, 1993).

As the number of students with serious emotional problems increases, so does the risk of behavioral disturbances (Dannells & Stuber, 1992). Over the past 20 years, counseling center staffs have become the campus frontline in intervening with students who come to the attention of others on campus as needing help. In this role, conflicting loyalties and confidentiality dilemmas arise (Amada, 1993; Gilbert, 1989). Some counseling directors are ambivalent about the recent trend toward increasing requests for counseling centers to provide mandated counseling and assessment (Margolis, 2000; Stone & Lucas, 1994). Other challenges to confidentiality are the increased need to notify others of potential suicidal or homicidal behavior, the need to report child and elder abuse, and questions about whether the unprotected sexual activity of a person living with HIV constitutes reportable harm to others (Gallagher et al., 1994). Increased use of electronic communication has resulted in IACS and many individual centers developing policy statements which inform students that counseling center staff will not respond to personal problems by email.

In addition to the aforementioned challenges associated with increased demand for services, college counseling centers also must address underutilization issues pertaining to populations who have been historically difficult to reach such as international students, ethnic minority students, and many students who plan to harm/kill themselves or others (e.g., Atkinson et al., 1990; Brinson & Kottler, 1995; Oropeza et al., 1991; Shea, 1995).

Violence and hate crimes have been a major challenge to college and university counseling center professionals. In the 2006 survey, more than 30 percent of counseling center directors believes that incidents of violence against students have increased in the past five years (Gallagher & Taylor, 2006). Although college students were victimized by violent crime at a lower rate than were nonstudents at the same age, the average number of students who experience violent crimes is inconceivable (e.g., 526,000 per year) (U.S. Department of Justice, 2003). The Virginia Tech massacre in 2007 and the Northern Illinois University campus shootings in 2008, which totaled 38 deaths and many wounded, shocked the nation. Sixty percent of centers in 2000 saw obsessive pursuit cases, in which 50 persons were injured and five persons were killed; and 30 percent of schools surveyed reported a student suicide in 2000 (Gallagher et al., 2001). Although the suicide rate among college students is less than among Americans aged 15 to 24 who are not in college, suicide is still the second leading cause of death (after accidents) for college students (Shea, 1995). One in 12 college students makes a suicide plan (Kadison & DiGeronimo, 2004); and among the 284 surveyed counseling centers center directors, there were reports that 118 students had committed suicide (Gallagher & Taylor, 2008). Federal legislation such as the Campus Security Act requires colleges to publish crime statistics and to actively respond to the needs of victims of campus violence (Garland & Grace, 1993). On Tuesday, February 4, 2009, the U.S. House of Representatives passed legislation, the Center to Advance Monitor and Preserve University Security (CAMPUS) Safety Act, to create a center for college campus safety. Although the numbers of homicides on and around college and university campuses are small, the impact of such disasters on the campus community is far reaching and requires immediate and expert intervention (Allen, 1992).

There has been an increase in the number of counseling centers that evaluate their services (Magoon, 1995; Guinee & Ness, 2000). In this time of increasing competition for resources, evaluation, accountability and strategic planning are necessary for centers to receive the resources they require (Guinee & Ness, 2000; Stone & Archer, 1990).

Finally, Guinee and Ness (2000), who researched how well centers have responded to Stone's and Archer's recommendations for the 1990s, conclude that centers have been very active in responding to the challenges of the 1990s and in following the recommendations of Stone and Archer (1990).

Further, the authors conclude, "Counseling center directors and their staff must make critical decisions on where their agency's priorities will lie and their resources and energies will be directed. We hope that future studies will enable counseling center staff to increasingly examine when and how counseling centers can make changes that will enhance the vitality and security of the agency in the years to come" (Guinee & Ness, 2000, p. 279).

Trends

The issues of mental health at colleges and universities are paralleled with the changes in higher education. In the first decade of the twenty-first century, colleges and universities in the United States have been comprised of more women, members of underrepresented groups, students with disabilities, non-traditional students, students from low social-economic families, and part-time students. Consequently, college and university counseling centers are confronted with the complex puzzle of cultural diversity (Hodges, 2001). Besides outsourcing and commercializing its services (e.g., facilities management, business services, and student services), most institutions of higher education are employing a new contingent workforce of part-time/adjunct, full-time, nontenure track faculty, and graduate students (Kirp, 2002). Issues that the college and university counseling centers had in the later twentieth century such as demands for services and shortage of resources will continue to exist in the twenty-first century. Therefore, the following trends identified by Davis and Humphrey (2000) seem likely for counseling centers in the twenty-first century.

First, there will be more students with more complex problems than in the past. The explosion in technological advances, the increase in acts of random violence (e.g., Virginia Tech Massacre, Northern Illinois University shooting) and hate crimes, the instability of global economies, and the terrorist acts of September 11, 2001, have left many people throughout the world confused distressed, frightened, and anxious. There can be little doubt that college students will continue to experience increased stress and psychological symptoms. The continuing need for counseling centers on campuses of the future seems certain (Archer & Cooper, 1998). How these centers will be designed, administered, and financed remains the mystery.

Second, there will be an increasingly diverse student body. According to the statistics by the U.S. Department of Education (2007) minorities made up 33 percent of the U.S. population in 2005; between 2005 and 2020, the minority population is expected to increase by 32 percent, compared to 4 percent for the White population; and it is predicted that minorities will represent 39 percent of the total population by then. More than half of U.S. public school children in the South come from low-income families. During the 2006–2007 school year, 54 percent of students in 15 Southern states qualified for free or reduced lunches. Three states outside the South–California, New Mexico, and Oregon–also have a majority of public school students living in poverty (Viadera, 2007). This demographic change will definitely impact American higher education and present new challenges to college and university counseling centers.

Third, there will also be greater use of internet based and interactional technologies in service delivery by counseling centers. Fifty-five percent of center directors report that they provide psychoeducational assistance on center websites to address the increase of students with serious psychological problems (Gallagher & Taylor, 2008) and 49 percent of counseling centers offer online services (Rando et al., 2007). Other services provided via internet and interactional technologies include survey, assessment, webpage of information, and online groups (Rando et al., 2007). The use of internet and interactional technologies for counseling services will increase as those born in the 1990s enroll in college.

Fourth, there will be an increase in the demand for accountability in the face of limited resources. The number of college students in need of psychological services in counseling centers, is rising sharply. That is partially because of new psychotropic prescription medications that allow many students to attend college who might not have been able to in the past (Blom & Beckley, 2005). According to the 2007 National College Health Assessment, completed by 20,507 students at 37 colleges and universities, almost 43 percent of college students have psychological problems such as depression, anxiety, eating disorders, and seasonal affective disorders. Ninety-five percent of directors report that the recent trend toward greater number of students with severe psychological problems continues to be true on their campuses. The pressure on counselors to manage this increasingly complex case load has led to various concerns, for example, staff burnout problems, shortage during peak times, decreased focus on students with normal developmental problems, need to end too many cases prematurely, and increased worry about liability issues (Gallagher & Taylor, 2008). To deal with the increasing demands, counseling centers may use briefer therapies, creatively manage waiting list, improve efficiency of scheduling clients to avoid missing appointments, increase group counseling, establish emergency procedures separately, provide staff training on assessment and referral procedures, and institute automatic termination policies (Murphy & Martin, 2004). Furthermore, all counseling services should develop an informed consent statement that accurately describes whatever limits to counseling and confidentiality that exist on that particular campus (Bishop, 2006).

Besides the aforementioned four trends identified by Davis and Humphrey (2000), current debates focus on what is necessary to survive in a rapidly changing world and uncertain economic times, while retaining a commitment to the counseling center mission of serving students. It appears institution decision makers prefer a counseling center that is a specialized kind of mental health service that is valued in increasingly broader ways on the campus instead of a long-term treatment facility (Bishop, 2006). Counseling center staff members need to be well versed in the briefer therapies, crisis intervention, group work, consultation and outreach, the theory and practice of career and student development, multicultural issues, research, evaluation, and those public health issues that are relevant to a college population (Bishop, 2006).

Another noticeable trend is that there is an increase in female and minority staff and an increase in the time spent on outreach and consultation (Gallagher & Taylor, 2008; Guinee & Ness, 2000; Rando et al., 2007). This is because the U.S. higher education system has graduated more women than men and the number of minority doctoral graduates has been the highest ever (National Opinion Research Center, 2007). Also, the greatest changes during the 1990s included the integration of counseling services with the campus, the high quality of training, and the variety of services provided (Guinee & Ness, 2000). This trend tends to continue in the twenty-first century.

The impetus of potential outsourcing and mergers seems to be waning, although 16 percent of counseling centers have been fully integrated within a health service (Rando et al., 2007). In 2001, 97 percent of center directors reported that outsourcing/privatization of the counseling center had not occurred and did not seem likely (Gallagher et al., 2001). Likewise, significantly more centers reported increases rather than decreases in staff and budget, particularly after the Virginia Tech shootings (Gallagher & Taylor, 2008; Gallagher, Weaver-Graham, & Taylor, 2005; Rando et al., 2007).

It is expected that counseling centers will continue in the trends toward hiring both a multidisciplinary staff and more part-time staff members. In the mid-1990s, there were slight trends toward counseling centers merging with Student Health or losing the career counseling function. The former trend seems to be decreasing. Many strongly believe that the trend toward a medical model with third party reimbursement needs to be reversed to make way for a return to a more comprehensive developmental approach (e.g., Crego, 1990, 1995). Others argue that in order to survive, counseling centers must compete in a managed care market (e.g., Drum, 1995; Steenbarger, 1995). Dr. Thomas Magoon, a former counseling center director with a long history of professional involvement, recommended that counseling centers need to be seen as part of the university academy and that research is the key to building that bridge (Dressel, 1995). Magoon also recommended that counseling center staff need to be active in professional organizations, especially at the state level where laws governing psychology are being made.

Despite all of the uncertainty about the future, it seems very clear that in complex times college counseling centers can be a key factor in managing crisis, assisting in recruitment and retention, and reducing liability risks (Bishop, 2006). With increased reliance on technology, and staggering amounts of information available at one's fingertips, human contact will become increasingly important. Counseling centers must not lose sight of their greatest asset, the ability of staff to sit down face to face with students and build trusting and supportive working alliances.

TECHNOLOGY RESOURCES

The following list may prove useful as examples of counseling center and counseling center information websites:

Positions in Counseling Centers

http://www2.kumc.edu/people/llong/picc/
http://www2.kumc.edu/people/llong/picc/list.asp

University and College Counselor Resources

http://www.collegecounseling.org/resources/links.html

Mental Health Licensure Resources

http://www.mentalhelp.net/poc/view_doc.php?type=doc&id=2589&cn=145

The Counseling Center Village

http://ub-counseling.buffalo.edu/ccv.html

Counseling Centers on the Internet

http://ub-counseling.buffalo.edu/centers.html

The Virtual Pamphlet Collection

http://www.dr-bob.org/vpc/

AUCCCD Website

http://www.aucccd.org/

IACS Website

http://mason.gmu.edu/~iacs/

Counseling Center Listservs

http://ccvillage.buffalo.edu/Village/Staffdev/lists.html

Clearinghouse for Structured/Thematic Groups and Innovative Programs

http://www.utexas.edu/student/cmhc/chindex.html
http://www.cmhc.utexas.edu/clearinghouse/index.html

REFERENCES

Affsprung, E. H. (1997). Gender demographics of college counseling center hiring 1989–1995. *Journal of College Student Psychotherapy, 11*(3), 5–11.

Allen, R. D. (1992, November). The counseling center director's role in managing disaster response. *Commission VII Counseling Psychological Services Newsletter, 19*(2), 4–5.

Amada, G. (1993). The role of the mental health consultant in dealing with disruptive college students. *Journal of College Student Psychotherapy, 8,* 121–137.

American Health College Association. (2007). *National college health assessment: Reference group executive summary, fall 2007.* Retrieved from American Health College Association National College Health Assessment Web Site: http://www.acha-ncha.org/docs/ACHA-NCHA_Reference_Group_ExecutiveSummary_Fall2007.pdf.

American Psychological Association. (1995). *Ethical principles of psychologists and code of conduct.* Washington, D.C.: American Psychological Association.

Archer, J., & Cooper, S. (1998). *Counseling and mental health services on campus: A handbook of contemporary practices and challenges.* San Francisco: Josey-Bass.

Archer, J., & Bingham, R. (1990). *Task force on organizational structure.* Proceedings of the 39th Annual Conference of the Association of University and College Counseling Center Directors, p. 119.

Atkinson, D. R., Jennings, R. G., & Liongson, L. (1990). Minority students' reasons for not seeking counseling and suggestions for improving services. *Journal of College Student Development, 31,* 342–350.

Aulepp, L., & Delworth, U. (1976). *Training manual for an ecosystem model: Assessing and designing campus environments.* Boulder, CO: Western Interstate Commission for Higher Education.

Baier, J. L. (1993). Technological changes in student affairs administration. In M. J. Barr and Associates, *The handbook of student affairs administration.* San Francisco: Josey-Bass.

Baron, A. (1995, March). *Transforming the academy: A counseling center perspective.* Paper presented at the meeting of the American College Personnel Association, Boston.

Berk, S. E. (1983). Origins and historical development of university and college counseling. In P. J. Gallagher & G. D. Demos (Eds.), *Handbook of counseling in higher education* (pp. 50–71). New York: Praeger.

Bertocci, D., Hirsch, E., Sommer, W., & Williams, A. (1992). Student mental health needs: Survey results and implications for service. *Journal of American College Health, 41,* 3–10.

Bishop, J. B. (1990). The university counseling center: An agenda for the 1990s. *Journal of Counseling and Development, 68,* 408–413.

Bishop, J. B. (1995). Emerging administrative strategies for college and university counseling centers. *Journal of Counseling and Development, 74,* 33–38.

Bishop, J. B. (2006). College and university counseling centers: Questions in search of answers. *Journal of College Counseling, 9*(1), 6–19.

Blom, S. D., & Beckley, S. L. (2005). 6 major challenges facing student health problems. *The Chronicle of Higher Education, 51*(21), pp. B25, B26.

Boggs, K. R., & Douce, L. A. (2000). Current status and anticipated changes in psychology internships: Effects on counseling psychology training. *The Counseling Psychologist, 28*(5), 672–686.

Boyd, V., Hattauer, E., Brandel, I., Buckles, N., Davidshofer, C., Deakin, S., Erskine, C., Hurley, G., Locher, L., Piorkowski, G., Simono, R., Spivack, J., & Steele, C. (2003) Accreditation standards for university and college counseling centers. *Journal of Counseling and Development, 81*(2), 168–177.

Brinson, J. A., & Kottler, J. A. (1995). Minorities underutilization of counseling centers' mental health services: A case for outreach and consultation. *Journal of Mental Health Counseling, 17*(4), 371–385.

Carney, C. G., Peterson, K., & Moberg, T. F. (1990). How stable are student and faculty perceptions of student concerns and of a university counseling center? *Journal of College Student Development, 31,* 423–428.

Carney, C. G., Savitz, C. J., Weiscott, G. N. (1979). Students' evaluations of a university counseling center and their intentions to use its programs. *Journal of Counseling Psychology, 26,* 242–249.

Cohen, D., & Rosenzweig, R. (2006, February 24). No computer left behind. *Chronicle of Higher Education, 52*(25), pp. B6, B8.

Coll, K. M. (1993). *Community college counseling: Current status and needs* (Series No. 10). Alexandria, VA: International Association of Counseling Services, Inc.

Conyne, R. K., Banning, J. H., Clack, R. J., Corazzini, J. G., Huebner, L. A., Keating, L. A., & Wrenn, R. L. (1979). The campus environment as client: A new direction for college counselors. *Journal of College Student Personnel, 20,* 437–442.

Cooper, S., & Archer, J. (1999). Brief therapy in college counseling and mental health. *Journal of American College Health, 48*(1), 21–28.

Corazzini, J. G. (1995, March). Counseling centers have a future. *Commission VII Counseling & Psychological Services Newsletter, 21*(3), 8.

Crego, C. A. (1990). Challenges and limits in search of a model. *The Counseling Psychologist, 18,* 608–613.

Crego, C. A. (1995, March). The medicalization of Counseling Psychology: Managed care vs. developmental models in university and college counseling centers. *Commission VII Counseling & Psychological Services Newsletter, 21*(3), 9.

Dannells, M., & Stuber, D. (1992). Mandatory psychiatric withdrawal of severely disturbed students: A study and policy recommendations. *NASPA Journal, 29,* 163–168.

Davis, D. C., & Humphrey, K. M. (Eds.). (2000). *College counseling: Issues and strategies for a new millennium.* Alexandria, VA: American Counseling Association.

DeMers, S., Van Home, B., & Rodolfa, E. (2008, October). Changes in training and practice of psychologists: Current challenges for licensing boards. *Professional Psychology: Research & Practice, 39*(5), 473–479.

Demos, G. D., & Mead, T. M. (1983). The psychological counseling center: Models and functions. In P .J. Gallagher & G. D. Demos (Eds.), *Handbook of counseling in higher education* (pp. 1–22). New York: Praeger.

Dressel, J. L. (1995, July). Commission VII: A historical perspective. *Commission VII Counseling Psychological Services, 22*(l), 3–4.

Drum, D. J. (1995, March). Paper presented at the meeting of the American College Personnel Association, Boston.

Dunkel-Schetter, C., & Lobel, M. (1990). Stress among students. In H. L. Pruett & V. B. Brown (Eds.), *Crisis intervention and prevention* (New Directions for Student Services, No. 49, pp. 17–34). San Francisco: Jossey-Bass.

Endres, J., & Tisinger. D. (2007). Digital distractions: College students in the 21st century. Retrieved from http://www.nacada.ksu.edu/clearinghouse/Advising Issues/Digital-Distractions.htm.

Erickson Cornish, J. A., Riva, M. T., Cox Henderson, M., Kominars, K. D., & McIntosh, S. (2000). Perceived distress in university counseling center clients across a six-year period. *Journal of College Student Development, 41*(1), 104–109.

Farrell, E. (2008, February 29). Counseling centers lack resources to help troubled students. (Cover story). *Chronicle of Higher Education, 54*(25), pp. A1, A28.

Forest, L. (1989). Guiding, supporting, and advising students: The counselor role. In U. Delworth & G. R. Hanson (Eds.), *Student services: A handbook for the helping professions* (pp. 265–283). San Francisco: Jossey-Bass.

Forman, M. E. (1977). The changing scene in higher education and the identity of counseling psychology. *The Counseling Psychologist, 7,* 45–48.

Gallagher, R. P. (2002). *National survey of counseling center directors* (Series No. 8L). Alexandria, VA: International Association of Counseling Services, Inc.

Gallagher, R. P., Bruner, L. A., & Weaver-Graham, W. (1994). *National survey of counseling center directors* (Series No. 8D). Alexandria, VA: International Association of Counseling Services, Inc.

Gallagher, R. P., Christofidis, A., Gill, A. M., & Weaver-Graham, W. (1996). *National survey of counseling center directors* (Series No. 8F). Alexandria, VA: International Association of Counseling Services, Inc.

Gallagher, R. P., Gill, A. M., & Goldstrohm, A. L. (1997). *National survey of counseling center directors* (Series No. 8G). Alexandria, VA: International Association of Counseling Services, Inc.

Gallagher, R. P., Gill, A. M., & Goldstrohm, A. L. (1998). *National survey of counseling center directors* (Series No. 8H). Alexandria, VA: International Association of

Counseling Services, Inc.

Gallagher, R. P., Gill, A. M., Goldstrohm, S. L., & Sysko, H. B. (1999). *National survey of counseling center directors* (Series No. 8I). Alexandria, VA: International Association of Counseling Services, Inc.

Gallagher, R. P., Gill, A. M., & Sysko, H. B. (2000) *National survey of counseling center directors* (Series No. 8J). Alexandria, VA.: International Association of Counseling Services.

Gallagher, R. P., Sysko, H. B., & Zhang, B. (2001). *National survey of counseling center directors* (Series No. 8K). Alexandria, VA: International Association of Counseling Services, Inc.

Gallagher, R. P., & Taylor, R. (2006). *National survey of counseling center directors* (Series No. 8P). Alexandria, VA: International Association of Counseling Services, Inc.

Gallagher, R. P., & Taylor, R. (2007). *National survey of counseling center directors* (Series No. 8Q). Alexandria, VA: International Association of Counseling Services, Inc.

Gallagher, R. P., Weaver-Graham, W., Christofidis, A., & Bruner, L. A. (1995). *National survey of counseling center directors* (Series No. 8E). Alexandria, VA: International Association of Counseling Services, Inc.

Gallagher, R. P., Weaver-Graham, W. & Taylor, R. (2005). *National survey of counseling center directors* (Series No. 8O). Alexandria, VA: International Association of Counseling Services, Inc.

Gallagher, R. P., Zhang, B., & Taylor, R. (2004). *National survey of counseling center directors* (Series No. 8N). Alexandria, VA: International Association of Counseling Services, Inc.

Garland, P. H., & Grace, T. W. (1993). *New perspectives for student affairs professionals: Evolving realities, responsibilities and roles.* (ASHE-ERIC Higher Education Report No. 7). Washington, DC: The George Washington University, School of Education and Human Development.

Gelso, C. J., Birk, J. M., Utz, P. W., & Silver, A. E. (1977). A multigroup evaluation of the models and functions of university counseling centers. *Journal of Counseling Psychology, 24,* 338–348.

Gibson, R. L., Mitchell, M. H., & Higgins, R. E. (1983). *Development and management of counseling programs and guidance services.* New York: MacMillan.

Gilbert, S. P. (1989). The juggling act of the college counseling center: A point of view. *The Counseling Psychologist, 17,* 477–489.

Gilbert, S. P. (1994, August). Practicing ethically in managed care treatment settings. *Commission VII Counseling Psychological Services Newsletter, 21*(1), 2–4.

Grayson, P., & Commerford, M. (2002, December). September 11, 2001: New York City Perspective. *Journal of College Student Psychotherapy, 17*(2), 3–15.

Guinee, J. P., & Ness, M. E. (2000). Counseling centers of the 1990s: Challenges and changes. *Counseling Psychologist, 28*(2), 267–280.

Hedahl, B. M. (1978). The professionalization of change agents: Growth and development of counseling centers as institutions. In B.M. Schoenberg (Ed.), *A handbook and guide for the college and university counseling center* (pp. 24–39). Westport, CT: Greenwood.

Heppner, P. P., Kivlighan, D. M., Good, G. E., Roehlke, H. J., Hills, H. I., & Ashby,

J. S. (1994). Presenting problems of university counseling center clients: A snap-shot and multivariate classification scheme. *Journal of Counseling Psychology, 41,* 315–324.

Heppner, P. P., & Neal, G. W. (1983). Holding up the mirror: Research on the roles and functions of counseling centers in higher education. *The Counseling Psychologist, 11,* 81–98.

Hodges, S. (2001). University counseling centers at the twenty-first century: Looking forward, looking back. *Journal of College Counseling, 4*(2), 161–173.

Hodgson, C. S., & Simoni, J. M. (1995). Graduate student academic and psycholog-ical functioning. *Journal of College Student Development, 36,* 244–253.

Hood, A.B., & Arceneaux, C. (1990). *Key resources on student services: A guide to the field and its literature.* San Francisco: Jossey-Bass.

Hotelling, K. (1995, March). *Environmental change and students at risk: Implications for counseling centers.* Paper presented at the meeting of the American College Personnel Association, Boston.

Howe, N., & Strauss, W. (2000). *Millennials rising: The next generations.* New York: Vintage Books.

Hurst, J. C. (1978). Chickering's vectors of development and student affairs pro-gramming. In C.A. Parker (Ed.), *Encouraging development in college students* (pp. 113–127). Minneapolis, MN: University of Minnesota Press.

Hyun, J. K., Quinn, B. C., Madon, T., & Lustig, S. (2006). Graduate student mental health: Needs assessment and utilization of counseling services. *Journal of College Student Development, 47*(3), 247–266.

International Association of Counseling Services, Inc. (2000). Accreditation stan-dards for university and college counseling centers. Retrieved from http://www.iacsinc.org/Accreditation%20Standards.htm#B.6.

Kadison, R., & DiGeronimo, T. F. (2004). *College of the overwhelmed: The campus men-tal health crisis and what to do about it.* San Francisco: Jossey-Bass.

Kahn, J. S., Wood, A., & Wiesen, F. A. (1999). Student perceptions of college coun-seling center services: programming and marketing for a seamless learning envi-ronment. *Journal of College Student Psychotherapy, 14*(1), 69–80.

Keeling, R., & Heitzmann, D. (2003, Fall). Financing Health and Counseling Services. *New Directions for Student Services, 103,* 39–58.

Kirk, B. A., Johnson, A. P., Redfield, J. E., Free, J. E., Michel, J., Roston, R. A., & Warman, R. E. (1971). Guidelines for university and college counseling services. *American Psychologist, 26,* 585–589.

Kirp, D. L. (2002, March 15). Higher Ed Inc.: Avoiding the perils of outsourcing. *Chronicle of Higher Education, 48*(27), pp. B13, B14.

Kremer, T. G., & Gesten, E. L. (2003). Managed mental health care: The client's per-spective. *Professional Psychology: Research and Practice, 34*(2), 187–196.

Lamb, D. H., Garni K. F., & Gelwick, B. P. (1983). *A historical overview of university counseling centers: Changing functions and emerging trends.* Unpublished manuscript.

Likins, P. (1993). The president: Your master or your servant? In M. J. Barr & Associates, *The handbook of student affairs administration* (pp. 83–92). San Francisco: Jossey-Bass.

Lilly-Weber, J. (1993, November). Should survivors of sexual abuse be treated for this issue at college and university counseling centers? *Commission VII Counseling Psychological Services Newsletter, 20*(2), pp. 3, 5.

Magoon, T. M. (1994). *College and university counseling center directors' data bank.* Unpublished manuscript, University of Maryland, College Park.

Magoon, T. M. (1995). *College and university counseling center directors' data bank.* Unpublished manuscript, University of Maryland, College Park.

Magoon, T. M. (1997). *College and university counseling center directors' data bank.* Unpublished manuscript, University of Maryland, College Park.

Margolis, G. (2000). Late drops, deadlines and depression. *Journal of College Student Psychotherapy, 14*(4), 3–8.

McKinley, D. (1980). Counseling. In W. H. Morrill, J. C. Hurst, with E. R. Oetting & others, *Dimensions of intervention for student development* (pp. 175–187). New York: Wiley.

Meadows, M. E. (2000). The evolution of college counseling. In D. C. Davis & K. M. Humphrey (Eds.), *College counseling: Issues and strategies for a new millennium* (pp. 15–40). Alexandria, VA: American Counseling Association.

Miller, G. A., & Rice, K. G. (1993) . A factor analysis of a university counseling center problem checklist. *Journal of College Student Development, 34,* 98–102.

Morrill, W. H. , Oetting, E. R. , & Hurst, J. C. (1974) . Dimensions of counselor functioning. *Personnel and Guidance Journal, 52,* 354–359.

Murphy, M. C., & Martin, T. L. (2004). Introducing a team-based clinical intake system at a university counseling center: A good method for handling client demand. *Journal of College Student Psychotherapy, 19*(2), 3–13.

National Opinion Research Center. (2007). *Survey of earned doctorates.* Retrieved from http://www.norc.org/projects/Survey+of+Earned+Doctorates.htm.

Oetting, E. R., Ivey, A. E., & Weigel, R. G. (1970). *The college and university counseling center.* Student Personnel Series No. 11. Washington, DC: American College Personnel Association.

Oropeza, B. A. C., Fitzgibbon, M., & Baron, A. (1991). Managing mental health crises of foreign college students. *Journal of Counseling and Development, 69,* 280–284.

Pace, D., Stamler, V. L., Yarris, E., & June, L. (1996). Rounding out the cube: Evolution to a global model for counseling centers. *Journal of Counseling and Development, 74*(4), 321–325.

Phelps, R. E. (1992). University and college counseling centers: One option for new professionals in counseling psychology. *The Counseling Psychologist, 20*(1), 24–31.

Pope, K. S., & Vetter, V. V. (1992). Ethical dilemmas encountered by members of the American Psychological Association: A national survey. *American Psychologist, 47,* 397–411.

Rando, R., Barr, V., & Aros, C. (2007). *The association for college and university counseling center directors annual survey.* Alexandria, VA: International Association of Counseling Services, Inc.

Raskin, R., Fenichel, A., Kellerhouse, B., & Shadick, R. (2002, December). In the Shadow of the World Trade Center: A View of September 11, 2001, from a

College Counseling Center. *Journal of College Student Psychotherapy, 17*(2), 17–38.

Resnick, J. (2006, February). Strategies for implementation of the multicultural guidelines in university and college counseling centers. *Professional Psychology: Research & Practice, 37*(1), 14–20.

Rivinus, T. M., & Larimer, M. E. (1993). Violence, alcohol, other drugs and the college student. *Journal of College Student Psychotherapy, 8,* 71–119.

Roark, M. L. (1993). Conceptualizing campus violence: Definitions, underlying factors, and effects. *Journal of College Student Psychotherapy, 8,* 1–27.

Schneider, L. D. (1977). Counseling. In W. T. Packwood (Ed.), *College student personnel services* (pp. 340–367). Springfield, IL: Charles C Thomas.

Schoenberg, B.M. (Ed.). (1992). *Conceptualizations: Counseling center models* (Series No. 9). Alexandria, VA: International Association of Counseling Services, Inc.

Schwitzer, A. (2003, December). A framework for college counseling responses to large scale traumatic incidents. *Journal of College Student Psychotherapy, 18*(2), 49–66.

Schwitzer, A. H., & Metzinger, T. (1998). Applying the student learning imperative to counseling center outcome evaluation. *Journal of College Student Psychotherapy, 13*(2), 71–92.

Sharkin, B. S. (1997). Increasing severity of presenting problems in college counseling centers: A closer look. *Journal of Counseling & Development, 75*(4), 275–281.

Sharkin, B. (2004, Fall2004). College counseling and student retention: research findings and implications for counseling centers. *Journal of College Counseling, 7*(2), 99–108.

Shea, C. (1995, June 11). Suicide signals. *The Chronicle of Higher Education,* pp. A35, A36.

Smith, T. B., Dean, B., Floyd, S., Silva, C., Yamashita, M., Durtschi, J., & Heaps, R. A. (2007). Pressing issues in college counseling: A survey of American College Counseling Association members. *Journal of College Counseling, 10,* 64–78.

Sprinthall, N. A. (1990). Counseling psychology from Greystone to Atlanta: On the road to Armageddon? *The Counseling Psychologist, 18,* 455–463.

Steenbarger, B. (1995, March). Managed care and the future of university counseling centers. *Commission VII Counseling & Psychological Services Newsletter, 21*(3), 2–4.

Stone, G. L. (1993). Psychological challenges and responses to a campus tragedy: The Iowa experience. *Journal of College Student Psychotherapy, 8,* 259–271.

Stone, G. L., & Archer, J. (1990). College and university counseling centers in the 1990s: Challenges and limits. *The Counseling Psychologist, 18,* 539–607.

Stone, G. L., & Lucas, J. (1991). Research and counseling centers: Assumptions and facts. *Journal of College Student Development, 32,* 497–501.

Stone, G. L., & Lucas, J. (1994). Disciplinary counseling in higher education: A neglected challenge. *Journal of Counseling and Development, 72,* 234–238.

Stone, G. L., & McMichael, J. (1996). Thinking about mental health policy in university and college counseling centers. *Journal of College Student Psychotherapy, 10*(3), 3–27.

Stone, G. L., Vespia, K. M., & Kanz, J. E. (2000). How good is mental health care on college campuses? *Journal of Counseling Psychology, 47*(4), 498–510.

Toth, M. (1995, March). *Transforming the academy: A counseling center perspective.* Paper presented at the meeting of the American College Personnel Association, Boston.

Triggs, J., & McDermott, D. (1991). Short-term counseling strategies for university students who test HIV positive: The case of John Doe. *Journal of College Student Development, 32,* 17–23.

Turner, A. L., & Berry, T. R. (2000). Counseling center contributions to student retention and graduation: A longitudinal assessment. *Journal of College Student Development, 41*(6), 627–636.

Twenge, J. M. (2000). The age of anxiety? Birth cohort change in anxiety and neuroticism. *Journal of Personality and Social Psychology, 79,* 1007–1021.

Tyler, L. E. (1969). *The work of the counselor* (3rd ed.). Englewood Cliffs, NJ: Prentice-Hall.

Tyler, L. E. (1992). Counseling psychology–why? *Professional Psychology: Research and Practice, 23,* 342–344.

U.S. Department of Education. (2007). *Status and trends in education of racial and ethnic minorities.* Retrieved from U.S. Department of Education–Institute of Education Sciences Web Site: http://nces.ed.gov/pubs2007/minoritytrends/ind_1_1.asp.

U.S. Department of Justice. (2003). *College students victimized less than non-students according to new Justice Department study.* Washington D.C. Retrieved from U.S. Department of Justice–Bureau of Justice Statistics Web Site: http://bjs.ojp.usdoj.gov/content/pub/press/vvcs00pr.cfm.

Van Brunt, B. (2008, May). Retention and college counseling centers. *Recruitment & Retention in Higher Education, 22*(5), 1–3.

Vespia, K. M. (2007). A national survey of small college counseling centers: Successes, issues, and challenges. *Journal of College Psychotherapy, 22*(1), 17-40.

Viadera, D. (2007, October). Low-income students are public school majority in South, study finds. *Education Week.* Retrieved from Education Week Web Site: http://www.edweek.org/ew/articles/2007/10/30/10poor_web.h27.html?print=1.

Voelker, R. (2007, June 6). Campus tragedy prompts closer look at mental health of college students. *JAMA: Journal of the American Medical Association,* pp. 2335–2337.

Vye, C., Scholljegerdes, K., & Welch, I. D. (2007). *Under pressure & overwhelmed: Coping with anxiety in college.* Westport, CT: Praeger.

Waldo, M., Harman, M. J., & O'Malley (1993). Homicide in the university residence halls: One counseling center's response. *Journal of College Student Psychotherapy, 8,* 273–284.

Warnath, C. F. (1971). *New myths and old realities: College counseling in transition.* London: Jossey-Bass.

Warnath, C. F. (1973). *New directions for college counselors: A handbook for redesigning professional roles.* San Francisco: Jossey-Bass.

White, K., & Strange, C. (1993). Effects of unwanted childhood sexual experiences on psychosocial development of college women. *Journal of College Student Development, 34,* 289–294.

Whitaker, L. C. (1992). Psychotherapy as a developmental process. *Journal of College Student Psychotherapy, 6,* 1–23.

Whitaker, L. C. (1997). The influence of managed care. *Journal of College Student*

Psychotherapy, 12(2), 23–40.

Whiteley, J. M. (1984). Counseling psychology: A historical perspective (Special issue). *The Counseling Psychologist, 12*(1), 3–109.

Whiteley, S. M., Mahaffey, P. J., & Geer, C. A. (1987). The campus counseling center: A profile of staffing patterns and services. *Journal of College Student Personnel, 28,* 71–81.

Widseth, J. C., Webb, R. E., & John, K. B. (1997). The question of outsourcing: the roles and functions of college counseling services. *Journal of College Student Psychotherapy, 11*(4), 3–22.

Williamson, E. G. (1939). *How to counsel students.* New York: McGraw-Hill.

Williamson, E. G. (1961). *Student personnel services in colleges and universities.* New York: McGraw-Hill.

Wilson, S. B., Mason, T. W., & Ewing, M. J. M. (1997) Evaluating the impact of receiving university-based counseling services on student retention. *Journal of Counseling Psychology, 44*(3), 316–320.

Yarris, E. (1996). Counseling. In A. L. Rentz (Ed.), *Student affairs practice in higher education* (pp. 143–174). Springfield, IL: Charles C Thomas.

Zhang, N., & Dixon, D. (2003). Acculturation and attitudes of Asian international students toward seeking psychological help. *Journal of Multicultural Counseling and Development, 31,* 205–222.

Chapter 7

STUDENT CONDUCT

John Wesley Lowery

INTRODUCTION

A college or university is a *disciplined* community, a place where individuals accept their obligations to the group and where well-defined governance procedures guide behavior for the common good. (Carnegie Foundation for the Advancement of Teaching, 1990, p. 37)

Student conduct is a timely, complex, and controversial subject. It is timely because now, perhaps more than at any other time in the history of American higher education, campuses are still in search of civility based on shared values while they are simultaneously concerned about violence and disregard for others' rights (Carnegie Foundation, 1990; Paterson & Kibler, 2008). It is complex because it has many different and seemingly competing dimensions, including philosophical, legal, legislative, educational, and organizational issues. And it is controversial because it resides at the interface of community needs and individual liberties.

HISTORY

The history and evolution of college student discipline in America is reflective of the development of the institutions of higher education themselves (Smith, 1994). In colonial colleges, the president and faculty exerted total control over students' behavior as part of the strict moral, ethical, and

The author would like to acknowledge the contributions of Dr. Mike Dannells to this chapter. Dr. Dannells was the sole or lead author of this chapter in each of the earlier editions of this text and generously allowed the use of those chapters as a starting point for the current edition.

religious training that, along with the classical curriculum, was the accepted role and mission of the institution. Garland and Grace (1993) noted, "Discipline was *the* student affairs approach of this period. . ." (p. 3). To control and mold the character of young colonial students, most of whom were in their early to mid-teens, extensively detailed codes of behavior and harsh penalties including public confessions and ridicule, fines, and corporal punishment, were commonly and liberally employed (Smith, 1994). The handling of more serious disciplinary matters was shared with the trustees, while the president often delegated less serious offenses to faculty (Leonard, 1956; Schetlin, 1967; Smith & Kirk, 1971). But students did not accept this system completely without question. A number of institutions struggled with student riots which President Ashbel Green of Princeton attributed to this rigid system of student discipline (Rudolph, 1990, Thelin, 2004).

Discipline became less paternalistic during the late 1700s and into the 1800s with the rise of the public university, the broadening of the university's mission, the increasing secularization and pluralism of higher education in general, and increasing enrollments. Punishments became milder, with corporal punishment almost disappearing; trustee participation in conduct matters declined; and counseling of student offenders emerged. Several institutions also began to experiment with systems of student self-governance during this period (Bruce, 1920; Smith, 1994; Wagoner, 1976, 1986). As the president became increasingly occupied with an expanding curriculum, fiscal and administrative matters, and external relations, specialists were chosen from the faculty to deal with nonacademic conduct of the students (Leonard, 1956; Schetlin, 1967; Thelin, 2004).

In the years following the Civil War, the introduction of the German university model, with its disregard for all but the intellectual growth of students, and the demands of the Industrial Revolution on faculty for development of their academic disciplines, resulted in a major shift away from rigid behavior control to greater emphasis on self-discipline and self-governance (Brubacher & Rudy, 1968; Durst, 1969; Schetlin, 1967). More humanitarian and individualized methods of discipline were used, and more democratic systems involving student participation developed concurrent with student governments and honor systems (Smith, 1994). Student discipline encountered new challenges with the increasing attendance of women at colleges and universities; "supervising such daring activities as unmarried young men and women dining together in a campus dining hall" (Fenske, 1989, p. 30) complicated the administration of student discipline of the time.

By the turn of the century, the first deans of men and women had been appointed "to relieve administrators and faculties of problems of discipline" (ACE, 1937, p. 2); and during the early 1900s, these positions were established on most campuses. LeBaron Russell Briggs, one of the first student affairs professionals, found student discipline to be an important part of his job when he was appointed Dean of Harvard College in 1891 (Brown, 1926; Fley, 1974). These early deans expanded both the philosophy and the programs of discipline in higher education. Idealistic and optimistic about the kinds of students they could develop, they approached discipline with the ultimate goal of self-control or self-discipline, and they used more individualized, humanistic, and preventative methods. Hawkes and Hawkes (1945) noted that the dean was not "a police officer in academic costume" (p. 186) and argued that discipline is more than then rigid enforcement of the rules which demanded a consideration of the individual student. The concept of the student as a whole began to develop (Durst, 1969), and counseling as a form of corrective action became popular (Fley, 1964).

Discipline became an unfortunate point of separation between the early deans and the emerging student personnel specialists (Appleton, Briggs, & Rhatigan, 1978; Knock, 1985). While they had many purposes and approaches in common, the "personnel workers tended to view the deans' disciplining of students as antithetical to their developmental efforts" because they regarded the "dean's role as a disciplinarian only in the sense of punishment. This view, of course, separated the 'punishing' dean from the 'promoting' personnel worker" (Knock, 1985, pp. 32-33). As higher education expanded under the philosophies of meritocracy and egalitarianism, the campus student body became larger and more heterogeneous, resulting in increased disciplinary work for the dean, while the personnel worker "became the specialist in human development" (Knock, p. 33). Thus, the unfortunate schism widened as the dean was perceived as the "bad guy," interested more in control and punishment, while the student development specialist was viewed more positively as the true promoter of student interests and growth (Appleton et al., 1978). Rhatigan (2000) recently reminded us of the truly humanistic orientation of the early deans.

After World War II and the influx of veterans into colleges and universities, campus facilities and regulations were tested by the large number of older and more worldly students who "could not digest the traditional palliatives served up by the dean to justify student conduct regulation and discipline" (Smith & Kirk, 1971, p. 277). But a widespread crisis was avoided because veterans' overriding vocational orientation kept them preoccupied with academics. While they may have had little time for the dean's discipline, they also had little time or interest in revolting against it. However, a small number of institutions experienced protests by veterans and other students against the paternalistic rules of the period (Lowery, 1998c).

Throughout the 1950s and 1960s, disciplinary affairs became less punishment and control-oriented, more democratic, and more focused on education and rehabilitation. Professionally trained counselors were delegated more responsibility, and disciplinary hearing boards composed of both staff and students were established (Sims, 1971). One of the factors that contributed significantly to this change was the emergence of the student protest movement on campus starting in 1964. Mario Savio, the leader of the Free Speech Movement at Berkeley, spoke forcefully about the connection between the Free Speech Movement and the Civil Rights Movement as well as new student expectations regarding campus rules and policies:

> Last summer I went to Mississippi to join the struggle there for civil rights. This fall I am engaged in another phase of the same struggle, this time in Berkeley. The two battlefields may seem quite different, but this is not the case. The same rights are at stake in both places–the right to participate as citizens in a democratic society and the right to due process of law. We are asking that our actions be judged by committees of our peers. We are asking that regulations ought to be considered as arrived at legitimately only from a consensus of the governed. (Warshaw & Leahy, 1965, p. 27)

The 1960s and 1970s were characterized by increased student input into disciplinary codes and processes, broadened legal and educational conceptions of students' rights and responsibilities, and the introduction of due process safeguards in the hearing of misconduct cases. These developments may be attributed to several factors: more older students, the lowered age of majority, an increasingly permissive society, the civil rights movement, the realization of the power of student activism and disruption on many campuses, and court intervention in the disciplinary process (Gibbs, 1992; Smith, 1994).

This court intervention which begins with *Dixon v. Alabama State Board of Education* (1961), coupled with genuine concern for students' constitutional rights, led many colleges and universities in the 1960s to establish formal, legalistic "judicial systems" for the adjudication of misconduct and the determination of sanctions. This movement caused concern that such adversarial systems, borrowed from our system of criminal justice, focused primarily on the mechanism of the disciplinary process to the detriment of the educative purpose (Dannells, 1978; Gehring, 2001). The literature of the last three decades and contemporary practice of student conduct administration reflect a renewed and continuing interest in the reintegration of the concept and goals of student development within the framework of campus conduct systems designed to protect the legal rights of students and to educate all students involved in the process (Ardaiolo, 1983; Caruso & Travelstead, 1987; Dannells, 1997; Gehring, 2001; Greenleaf, 1978). The overzealous adoption of criminal-like proceedings seems to have faded (Dannells, 1990), in favor of a balanced approach designed to insure fairness, protection of the educational environment, *and* learning (Bracewell, 1988). But the courts' interventions of the 1960s began the still on-going tension between the student development approach and the legalistic approach to discipline (Lake, 2009; Lancaster & Cooper, 1998; Smith, 1994).

Another indication of the development of student conduct as a specialization within student affairs was the establishment of Commission XV: Campus Judicial Affairs and Legal Issues of the American College Personnel Association in the early 1970s and the founding of the Association for Student Judicial Affairs (ASJA) in 1987. The rapid expansion of ASJA, which is now the Association of Student Conduct Administration (ASCA), in the years following its founding was a clear signal that student conduct administration had become a distinct area of specialization in student affairs. Longitudinal research on student conduct administration also reflects this trend (Dannells, 1990, 1991; Lowery & Dannells, 2009). As Lancaster and Waryold (2008) noted, student conduct was "finding our voice as a profession" (p. 280).

DEFINITION, PURPOSE, AND SCOPE OF STUDENT CONDUCT

Probably no other specialty area in student affairs has engendered so much debate, disagreement, and dissension (Fley, 1964). As Appleton et al. (1978) put it, "the subject of discipline has been one of the most pervasive and painful topics in the history of student personnel administration" (p. 21). It raises fundamental questions about the goals of higher education, the role of student personnel work within it, and our view of students.

Much of the controversy and disagreement about student conduct relates to its several meanings and purposes. Within the context of college student personnel work, discipline may be variously defined as: (1) *self-discipline,* or that virtue which may be regarded as the essence of education (Appleton et al., 1978; Hawkes, 1930; Mueller, 1961; Seward, 1961; Wrenn, 1949); (2) *the process of re-education* or rehabilitation (Appleton et al., 1978); or (3) *punishment* as a means of external control of behavior (Appleton et al., 1978; Seward, 1961; Wrenn, 1949).

Authority to Discipline and the Student-Institutional Relationship

Closely related to the purpose of student discipline is the matter of the institution's authority to do so. Seven different theories defining the institution's source of power to discipline its students and describing to some degree the nature of the student-institutional relationship have been identified (Dannells, 1977), but only three—the doctrine of *in loco parentis,* the contract theory, and the educational purpose theory—merit description.

In loco parentis, literally "in the place of a parent," is a common law doctrine, which views the institution as taking the role of the parent with respect to all student conduct. In this view, the institution is presumed to know best the needs of students and is vested with great latitude in the disciplinary process (see *Gott v. Berea College,* 1913). As such, this doctrine was once used as the justification for paternalistic, informal, and sometimes arbitrary use of power to discipline (Hoekema, 1994; Ratliff, 1972), even though, according to Appleton et al. (1978) "its formalization into the law occurred long after the original relationship was abandoned in practice" (p. 25). Ever since its application to the college disciplinary situation, this doctrine has been problematic; it has been criticized as impractical, erroneous, and misleading as a viable educational concept (Penney, 1967; Ratliff, 1972; Strickland, 1965). Today, while vestiges of paternalism may still exist in the reaffirmation of concern for the whole student as reflected in student development theory and practice (Gregory & Ballou, 1986; Parr & Buchanan, 1979; Pitts, 1980), the doctrine of *in loco parentis* as a legal description of the student-institutional relationship is generally considered to be inappropriate, untenable, intolerable, or simply dead (Grossi & Edwards, 1997; Henning, 2007; Nuss, 1998).

Contract theory defines the relationship of the student and institution as a contractual one, the terms of which are set forth in the institution's catalogue, other publications, and oral addenda. Students enter the contract by signing the registration document and paying fees, and thereby accepting the conduct rules and academic regulations. Violations of the rules may then be met with those measures enumerated as sanctions in the contract. This theory was once restricted largely to private institutions and to academic affairs; but now, with the lowered age of majority, older students, increasing consumerism, and the general litigiousness in our society, it is seeing increasing acceptance and application to all student-institutional relationships (Barr, 1988; Grossi & Edwards, 1997; Hammond, 1978; Shur, 1983, 1988). By analogy, students at public institutions also have another type of contract with the institution, a contract created by the United States Constitution as well as the state constitutions.

Educational purpose theory views the student-institutional relationship as an educational one, thereby limiting disciplinary control to student behavior adversely affecting the institution's pursuit of its educational mission. Given that the institution's *raison d'etre* is education and that this is the reason for its relationship with students, this view is considered by many to be the only realistic and justifiable basis for student discipline (Callis, 1967, 1969; Carnegie Commission, 1971; National Education Association, 1971; Penney, 1967; Van Alstyne, 1966). It stems from the premise that the academy is a special place, with a special atmosphere in which educators attempt to fashion an environment "where dialogue, debate, and the exchange of ideas can proceed unfettered . . . [and] in which there is concern about preserving the sanctity of the classroom and protecting academic freedom" (Gehring & Bracewell, 1992, p. 90). This theory allows the institution to discipline students for the purpose of maintenance of order or in furtherance of its educational objectives vis-à-vis an individual student or group of students. It protects the institution from unwanted court intrusion by recognizing that the courts have historically adopted a policy of nonintervention or judicial restraint in matters which are legitimately part of the educational enterprise (Ardaiolo, 1983; Travelstead, 1987). Furthermore, the educational purpose theory serves to remind us of the inherent superiority of achieving student discipline through proactive means, especially in the face of a permissive society (Georgia, 1989).

For a new and creative model of the legal relationship of the institution and its students, the "facilitator university," the reader is referred to Bickel and Lake (1999). Lake (2009) has expanded upon the application of this facilitator model to student conduct.

Extent of Institutional Jurisdiction

Two basic questions arise with respect to the extent of the institution's jurisdiction: (1) Should it apply internal sanctions, seek external (i.e., criminal) sanctions, or both where institutional rules and criminal law both apply (Stein, 1972)? (2) Should the institution concern itself with students' off-campus behavior? Concerning both questions the recent trend, in keeping with the educational purpose theory of discipline, is that internal actions are appropriate in all cases, whether on-or off-campus behavior is involved, where the institutional mission is affected. The courts have clearly supported this extension of institutional authority to include off-campus behavior (*Hill v. Michigan State University*, 2001; Kaplin & Lee, 2006; *Krasnow v. Virginia Polytechnic Institute*, 1977). Dannells' (1990) research on changes in the practice of disciplinary affairs over the period 1978 to 1988 showed a significant increase in the number of institutions that concerned themselves with the off-campus behavior of students. Follow-up research in the 2007–2008 academic year indicated additional significant increases over the next twenty years in the number of institutions which addressed off-campus behavior (Lowery & Dannells, 2009). The question of the application of criminal law is essentially a separate matter, especially in dealing with students who are legal adults and when the criminal act is of a serious nature (Sims, 1971; Stein, 1972).

Double jeopardy is an issue related to jurisdiction. On occasion students have argued that, for the same act, to be both disciplined by their institution and tried for a criminal offense constitutes double jeopardy. However, it is well established that double jeopardy applies only to the two criminal proceedings for the same offense and not to a criminal proceeding and college disciplinary action for the same offense (Fisher, 1970; Kaplin & Lee, 2006; *Paine v. Board of Regents,* 1973; Rhode & Math, 1988). Nonetheless, it is recommended that the institution avoid the mere duplication of criminal punishments by emphasizing the educational approach of its proceedings and subsequent response (Ardaiolo & Walker, 1987; Fisher, 1970; Stoner & Lowery, 2004).

Due Process

Due process, while a flexible concept (Bracewell, 1988; Gehring, 2001; Janosik & Riehl, 2000; Lowery, 2008; Stoner & Lowery, 2004) related to time and circumstances (Ardaiolo, 1983), may be defined as "an appropriate protection of the rights of an individual while determining his [her] liability for wrongdoing and the applicability of punishment" (Fisher, 1970, p. 1). It is a constitutional right granted by the Fifth Amendment with respect to action by the federal government and by the Fourteenth Amendment with respect to state action. The well-established standard used by the courts when questions of due process have arisen in the context of student discipline is that of *fundamental fairness* (Ardaiolo, 1983; Bakken, 1968; Buchanan, 1978; Fisher, 1970; Footer, 1996; Young, 1972). It is important to recognize that only students at public colleges and universities have a constitutional right to due process. At private institutions, the contracts that exist between the student and the institution define the rights and responsibilities of students (Kaplin & Lee, 2006, Lowery, 2008; Stoner & Lowery, 2004).

Procedural due process refers to the individual's rights in the adjudication of an offense. That which is "due," or owed, to insure fairness in any given circumstance will vary with the seriousness of the alleged offense and with the severity of the possible sanction. Substantive due process relates to the nature, purpose, or application of a rule or law. Again, applying the standard of fairness, rules must be clear and not overly broad, they must have a fair and reasonable purpose, and they must be applied in fairness and good faith (Young, 1972).

Since 1960, there have been many court cases on due process in disciplinary proceedings, especially dismissal hearings. Prior to that time, under a combination of *in loco parentis* and contract theories, the courts generally assumed the college to be acting fairly and in the best educational interests of all concerned. But the civil rights movement, during which some students were summarily dismissed from college because of their participation in civil rights demonstrations, prompted significant legal and philosophical changes

(Ardaiolo, 1983; Bakken, 1968; Bickel, 2008; Dannells, 1977). In the land-mark case, *Dixon v. Alabama State Board of Education* (1961), the court ruled, on the basis of an analogy of education as property (thus bringing dismissal from a state college under the due process clause of the Fourteenth Amendment), that a student has a constitutional right to notice and a hearing. The *Dixon* court went on to recommend several procedural safeguards to insure fairness in such cases: the notice should give specific charges; the hearing should consider both sides of the case; the accused should be informed about witnesses against them and the nature of their testimony; the student should have a chance to present a defense; the findings of the hearing should be reported to the student; and the "requirements of due process are met in dismissal hearings where the rudiments of fair play are followed" (Dannells, 1977, p. 249).

Numerous court decisions since *Dixon* established it as precedent and further specified the procedural due process safeguards for dismissal and other serious conduct hearings from public institutions. All of the procedural safeguards required in criminal proceedings are not required in student conduct hearings (Carletta, 1998; Correnti, 1988; Gehring, 2001; Gehring & Brace-well, 1992; Kaplin & Lee, 2006; Lowery, 2008; Shur, 1983, Stoner & Lowery, 2004), and no one particular model of procedural due process is required (Bracewell, 1988; Buchanan, 1978; Lowery, 2008; Travelstead, 1987; Zdziarski & Wood, 2008). The court in *Esteban v. Central Missouri State College* (1969) observed, "School regulations are not to be measured by the standards which prevail for criminal law and for criminal procedure" (p. 1090).

In the area of substantive due process, several principles for public institutions are well established (Arndt, 1971; Buchanan, 1978; Kaplin & Lee, 2006; Lowery, 2008): (1) Colleges have the authority to make and enforce rules of student conduct to maintain discipline and order. (2) Behavioral standards, including rules applied to off-campus behavior, must be consistent with the institution's lawful purpose and function. (3) Rules must be constitutionally fair, reasonable, and not capricious or arbitrary. (4) The code of conduct should be written and available for all to see. (5) The constitutionally guaranteed rights of students can be limited to enable the institution to function, but blanket prohibitions are not permitted. (6) A rule must be specific enough to give adequate notice of expected behavior and to allow the student to prepare a defense against a charge under it. Vague or overly broad rules, such as general proscriptions against "misconduct" or "conduct unbecoming a Siwash College student," have not been upheld (Gehring & Bracewell, 1992).

The courts have not required private institutions to meet these due process standards because they are not engaged in state action and therefore do not fall under the Fourteenth Amendment (Buchanan, 1978; Carletta, 1998; Kaplin & Lee, 2006; Lowery, 2008; Stoner & Lowery, 2004; Shur, 1983, 1988). The analogy of education as a property right has not been extended to private schools, and their relationship with their students is still considered largely contractual. Thus, despite many projections in the 1970s that the courts would abolish the public-private distinction in disciplinary matters, the private institution still legally has more latitude in defining and adjudicating student misconduct (Carletta, 1998; Correnti, 1988; Lowery, 2008; Shur, 1983, 1988). But procedural reforms tend to become normative in higher education; many private colleges now contract with their students to provide the basic due process protections expected in public institutions and having done so, they are contractually required to follow their own rules and procedures (Carletta, 1998, Lowery, 2008; Pavela, 1985, 2000, 2006c; Shur, 1983, 1988; Stoner, 1998; Stoner & Cerminara, 1990; Stoner & Lowery, 2004). Furthermore, since the 1960s the courts have more critically examined this contractual relationship and applied similar standards of review to those applied to other contracts between unequal parties.

The courts have generally distinguished between academic dismissal and dismissal for misconduct (Rhode, 1983; Rhode & Math, 1988), although this dichotomy "may be very difficult to apply in fact" (Ardaiolo, 1983, pp. 17–18). In the landmark case of *Board of Curators of the University of Missouri v. Horowitz* (1978), the U.S. Supreme Court placed limitations on the due process procedures required in academic dismissal situations. Instead of a hearing, the student need only be informed of the particular academic deficiencies and of the consequences of those shortcomings (e.g., dismissal) should they not be remedied. Once this warning has occurred, the decision-making person or body must then make a "careful and deliberate" decision based on "expert evaluation of cumulative information" (p. 79). The court noted that this process is "not readily adapted to the procedural tools of judicial or administrative decision making" (p. 79) and declined to enter this academic domain. It should be emphasized that this case involved the academic evaluation of a student and was not a matter of academic misconduct, such as cheating or plagiarism, where an allegation of wrongdoing is made and fact-finding is central to the disciplinary process. That distinction may be blurred and problematic in cases where it is difficult to distinguish misconduct (e.g., plagiarism) from poor scholarship (Travelstead, 1987) or where standards of dress, personal hygiene, or interpersonal conduct are the focus of evaluation in professional/clinical training. The courts have indicated that in cases involving faculty allegations of academic dishonesty, rather than academic deficiency, students should be afforded the same rights as students in other disciplinary cases (Kaplin & Lee, 2006; Kibler, 1998).

Constitutional Protections of Student Rights

Another general issue is the extent to which the institution can prescribe students' behavior. In the area of students' constitutional rights at public institutions, four principles are well established:

1. The institution cannot put a blanket restraint on students' First Amendment rights of freedom of assembly and expression, but it may restrain assembly and expression which will substantially interfere with its educational and administrative duties (Bird, Mackin, & Schuster, 2006; Gibbs, 1992; Kaplin & Lee, 2006; Mager, 1978; Pavela, 1985; Schuster, Bird, & Mackin, 2008; Sherry, 1966; Young, 1970).
2. The institution cannot restrict, prohibit, or censor the content of speech, except for extraordinarily compelling reasons, such as someone's safety (Kaplin & Lee, 1997; Mager, 1978; Pavela, 1985; Sherry, 1966). The special problem of hate speech will be addressed later in this chapter.
3. The college cannot apply its rules in a discriminatory manner (Sherry, 1966).
4. Students are protected by the Fourth Amendment from unreasonable searches and seizures (Bracewell, 1978; Fisher, 1970; Keller, 1985; Parrish, Fern, & Dickman, 1998; Smith & Strope, 1995; Young, 1970).

Student Misconduct: Sources and Responses

What constitutes misconduct is a function of the goal of student discipline and of the nature and number of rules and regulations which follow (Foley, 1947; Seward, 1961; Williamson, 1956, 1961; Williamson & Foley, 1949; Wrenn, 1949). Other institutional factors that influence the frequency and nature of student misconduct include the full array of campus environmental conditions. It is understandable why residential campuses with largely traditional-aged student populations have greater disciplinary caseloads than commuter/nonresidential campuses given the significant additional time that students spend on campus and in the residence halls.

Intrapersonal sources of student misconduct may be categorized as pathological or nonpathological. Nonpathological misbehavior may be viewed as stemming from lack of information or understanding or from inadequate or incomplete development, once referred to as immaturity or adolescent mischievousness and excess energy (Williamson, 1956). Pathological origins of student behavior have become of greater interest and concern as serious psychopathology among college students seems to be on the rise, at least insofar as it is manifest in such behaviors as sexual harassment, acquaintance rape, other forms of dating violence, alcohol abuse, and "stalking" (Gallagher,

Harmon, & Lingenfelter, 1994). However, the increasing concern for behaviors which stems from pathological origins has not been accompanied by a significant increase in the frequency of the types of disciplinary cases one might expect (Dannells, 1991).

Institutional responses may be categorized as punitive, rehabilitative (educational or developmental are more popular terms today), or environmental (actions aimed at external sources of misconduct). The extent to which a given sanction is best categorized as punitive, or developmental, is a matter of philosophy and purpose. While sanctions may be viewed as punitive in the immediate-particularly by the recipient-they are a proper and effective developmental or therapeutic tool for much of the problematic behavior of traditional-aged college students, many of whom are still learning to manage impulses (Frederickson, 1992). In *Esteban v, Central Missouri State College* (1968), the court commented on the educational nature of the disciplinary process:

> The discipline of students in the educational community is, in all but the case of irrevocable expulsion, a part of the teaching process. In the case of irrevocable expulsion for misconduct, the process is not punitive or deterrent in the criminal law sense, but the process is rather the determination that the student is unqualified to continue as a member of the educational community. Even then, the disciplinary process is not equivalent to the criminal law processes of federal or state criminal law. (p. 628)

Sanctions commonly employed include various forms of "informative" disciplinary communications, such as oral and written warnings or admonitions, often accompanied by a reference to more severe sanctions to follow if problems continue; disciplinary probation; denial of relevant privileges or liberties, such as restrictions on participation in extracurricular activities or the use of facilities, often used as a condition of probation; restitution, or monetary compensation for damage or injury; fines; denial of financial assistance (now thought to be rare); and actions that affect the student's status, such as suspension (the temporary dismissal of the student for either a finite period or indefinitely) and expulsion (permanent dismissal). In recent years, many campuses have added to the range of disciplinary sanctions (Bostic & Gonzalez, 1999), often by adding community service and other educational sanctions, but the actual use of disciplinary sanctions and rehabilitative actions appears to have changed little (Dannells, 1990, 1991).

Institutional responses involving rehabilitation or intentional human development include counseling, referral for medical or psychiatric care, and the assignment of a civic or public service project designed to enhance appreciation or awareness of personal responsibility. Disciplinary counseling may involve a professionally trained counselor; other professionals within the institution, such as an administrator or a faculty member associated with the campus conduct system or with the residence hall program; or extra-institutional assistance from parents, clergy, social workers, or other helping professionals.

Actions aimed at sources of misbehavior external to the student include changing living arrangements and finding financial assistance or employment. Other possible responses are academic assistance, such as tutoring or learning skills development, and policy revision, where the "misconduct" is more a function of outmoded or unnecessarily restrictive rules.

The choice of institutional response in a disciplinary situation is affected by a number of considerations: one's views on changing human behavior, the institution's educational mission as reflected in the nature and extent of its behavioral standards, the degree of divergence between those standards and those of its students, the behavior itself, what kinds of information about the accused are judged to be important (Janosik, 1995), the array of responses established in policy, and the creativity of the decision-maker(s).

Conflict Resolution

In addition to formal adjudication of cases, there has been growing attention to the development of a broader spectrum of resolution options in dealing with student conduct (Schrage, 2009; Schrage & Thompson, 2009; Willenbrock, 2009). Schrage (2009) described the various resolution options included within this spectrum, "Resting on an educational focus and placing value on diversity and cultural competence, the Spectrum Model incorporates mediation from a social justice framework, but also offers conflict coaching, facilitated dialogue, restorative justice practices, and shuttle diplomacy/negotiation" (p. 23). Meditation has been proposed in the literature as a viable component for many years (Fischer & Geist Giacomini, 2006; Serr & Taber, 1987; Sisson & Todd, 1995; Warters, 2000; Zdziarski, 1998). More recently, restorative justice has emerged as another approach to conflict resolution and sanctioning that deserves mention here. It is an alternative to punishment-oriented process that emphasizes student accountability and community healing. Students who are found responsible for code violations or criminal behavior on campus are expected to acknowledge responsibility by apologizing, making restitution, and working to restore damage done to the fabric of the community (Karp, 2004; Karp & Allena, 2004; Sebok, 2006; Warters, Sebok, & Goldblum, 2000). Often these new models for resolving student conduct are grounded in social justice theory (Holmes, Edwards, & DeBowes, 2009; Lopez-Philips & Trageser, 2008). Forums such as mediation, conflict coaching, and restorative justice are not intended to replace formal adjudication completely, but instead offer a broader area of options to student conduct administrations and institutions in responding to student conduct. A full examination of these approaches is beyond the scope of this chapter and readers seeking more information are encouraged to see Schrage and Giacomini (2009) and Karp and Allena (2004).

ADMINISTRATION AND ORGANIZATION

The administration of student conduct may be divided into three areas: (1) the roles and functions of student affairs professionals in student conduct; (2) the nature and scope of campus conduct systems; and (3) the handling of disciplinary records. Research findings have been consistent in one important respect; from campus to campus there is substantial heterogeneity in approaches to student discipline (Dannells, 1978, 1990, 1997; Durst, 1969; Dutton, Smith, & Zarle, 1969; Lancaster, Cooper, & Harman, 1993; Lowery & Dannells, 2009; Ostroth & Hill, 1978; Steele, Johnson, & Rickard, 1984). Institutional factors influencing the nature of a campus' system include its educational philosophy/mission; its size, type of control (public or private), and residential character (Lancaster et al., 1993); the needs of the community; and the extent to which governance is shared with students (Ardaiolo & Walker, 1987).

Roles and Functions of Student Affairs
Professionals in Discipline

Student affairs professionals may be charged with a broad range of roles and functions related to the disciplinary process. At one end of the continuum, they may function in the role of an ombudsman or mediator, independently and informally facilitating the resolution of conflicts and handling minor complaints. This approach has the advantage of brevity, keeping the problem at the lowest possible level of resolution; and it provides an educational, nonadversarial alternative for settling differences in certain situations (Hayes & Balogh, 1990; Serr & Taber, 1987; Sisson & Todd, 1995). At the other end of the spectrum there may be a specialist—often called a hearing officer or student conduct officer—charged with the responsibility of the total disciplinary system, including orchestrating the workings of one or more tribunals or boards, handling all disciplinary records, and investigating and preparing cases in more serious matters. The main advantages of this model are expertise and freeing other staff from the disciplinary function. Continuity, equity, and improved management of the process are also arguments for the specialist (Steele et al., 1984). Specialized student conduct officers are uncommon in smaller colleges; Steele et al. found that of the 18 schools (12% of their respondents) which reported conduct officers, ten were large (10,000 + students) institutions. Lancaster et al. (1993) found that commuter, public, and large institutions are significantly more likely to have student conduct specialists.

The most common model is that of a middle-level student affairs professional, most often associated with the dean of students office or the office of residence life, who administratively handles relatively minor violations and presents serious cases to a hearing board for final disposition. At larger institutions and those with residential student bodies, responsibility for relatively minor violations of student code by residential students in the halls may be delegated to hall directors or other residence life staff. For many years at smaller and private institutions, the dean of students had and continues to retain major responsibility for adjudicating student misconduct (Dannells, 1978, 1990; Lancaster et al., 1993; Ostroth, Armstrong, & Campbell, 1978; Steele et al., 1984).

Student affairs professionals involved in student conduct programs may function as educators in several ways. As coordinators, advisors, and trainers of members of campus conduct boards, they have opportunities to encourage the development of students along moral, ethical, and legal lines (Boots, 1987; Cordner & Brooks, 1987, Pavela, 2008; Waryold, 1998). Working with students whose behavior is in question, they may, through a combination of teaching and counseling techniques, help students gain insight and understanding about their behavior and responsibilities. Furthermore, student conduct officers can contribute to the intellectual climate of the institution not only by helping to preserve a safe and educationally conducive atmosphere (Boots, 1987), but also by leading the entire campus community in the process of defining and disseminating a behavioral code which represents a set of shared beliefs and values about the educational environment and the student's responsibilities within it (Dannells, 1997; Pavela, 1985, 2006a, 2006b, 2006c, 2006d).

Caruso (1978) defined the important roles of the student discipline specialist in terms of the basic student personnel functions outlined by Miller and Prince (1976). *Goal setting* is important for keeping the discipline system in accord with the broader institutional goals, for working developmentally with the individuals, and for designing outcomes-oriented training programs for student judicial boards. *Assessing student growth* can provide important, yet frequently lacking, evaluative information about the efficacy of the disciplinary process for all of the students involved. *Instruction* may take the form of teaching credit or noncredit courses as educational sanctions on topics such as anger management, may involve student leadership training and judicial board member education, or may take the form of offering "mainstream" coursework in a collaborative or team-teaching approach with another academic unit in subjects such as moral development, legal aspects of higher education, parliamentary procedure, or one of various life skills like parent effectiveness. *Consultation* includes working with the campus policy committees, conduct boards, and paraprofessionals in the residence halls, and assisting academic units with the administration of academic misconduct cases. *Environmental management* involves any response to a behavior problem which is designed to reduce or eliminate conditions that contribute to the problem, such as the placement of residence hall fire protection equipment, campus lighting, and the sale and distribution of alcoholic beverages on the campus. The last is the important function of *program evaluation* through which the discipline program may study itself for purposes of improvement and justification of resources.

Disciplinary counseling is another basic function of the educational approach to discipline. Williamson (1963) defined it as "sympathetic but firm counseling to aid the individual to gain insight and be willing to accept restrictions on his [or her] individual autonomy and behavior" (p. 13). Frequently cited objectives of disciplinary counseling include rehabilitation and behavior change, insight, maturation, emotional stability, moral judgment, self-reliance, self-control, and understanding and accepting responsibility for and consequences of personal behavior (Dannells, 1977). The counseling techniques of information giving (teaching) and confrontation are central to the "helping encounter in discipline" and may be employed throughout the disciplinary process (Ostroth & Hill, 1978).

The Nature and Scope of Campus Judicial Systems

Like the roles and functions of the student affairs professional in discipline, campus judicial systems vary greatly depending on those key institutional factors (philosophy, size, etc.) cited previously. Smaller and private institutions tend to have more informal, centralized systems, while larger and public schools tend toward the more formal, legalistic, and decentralized/specialized model (Dannells, 1978, 1990; Lancaster et al., 1993; Steele et al., 1984). Campus judicial systems may differ on the extent of their authority and responsibility; the differentiation between criminal and campus codes and procedures and between academic and non-academic misconduct; how specifically behavior is defined and proscribed; the due process rights accorded the student at both the prehearing and the hearing phases of the adjudicatory process; the availability and application of sanctions, conditions, appeals, and rehabilitative actions; the nature and extent of student input into the code of conduct; the level of student involvement in the process of adjudication; and the availability of alternative adjudicative mechanisms (Ardaiolo & Walker, 1987; Baker, 2005).

Research conducted during the past 40 years revealed the following trends about the administration of student discipline (Bostic & Gonzalez, 1999; Dannells, 1978, 1990; Durst, 1969; Dutton et al., 1969; Fitch & Murry, 2001; Leslie & Satryb, 1974; Lowery & Dannells, 2009; Ostroth et al., 1978; Steele et al., 1984; Van Alstyne, 1963; Wilson, 1996):

1. In the 1960s, there was a dramatic increase in student input into conduct rules and procedures and the adjudication of misconduct (judicial boards). This trend continues to shape student judicial affairs and student involvement remains high on most campuses.
2. There has been a similar trend in the provision of both procedural and substantive due process mechanisms, starting with a major shift toward more legalistic processes and leveling in more recent years. More formal, legalistic procedures can be expected for cases that may result in dismissal, while more informal processes are used with minor cases.
3. Milder sanctions are more often employed than stiffer penalties. Warnings, both oral and written, and disciplinary probation have been and continue to be the most common responses to student misconduct.
4. Disciplinary counseling continues to be the most common rehabilitative action, but over the years it is increasingly more likely to take place in either a disciplinary specialist's office or in the counseling center, especially in larger institutions. At smaller colleges, the disciplinary function, including post-hearing counseling, continues to be performed in the dean of students' office.
5. While most institutions do not anticipate changes in their programs, those that do indicate a need for change and suggest that it should be in the direction of streamlining and simplifying their processes and making their hearings less legalistic.
6. Diversity continues to characterize the administration of disciplinary affairs.

Drawing upon the CAS Standards for Judicial Services, the Statement of Principles of the Association of Student Judicial Affairs, and the research base on the subject, Lancaster et al. (1993) offered the following model for organizing and administering the disciplinary function:

1. Assign, as a primary responsibility, all disciplinary administration to a single staff member, even where multiple hearing bodies exist.
2. Place this staff member in a direct reporting relationship to the president or chief student affairs officer.
3. Create a philosophy for this staff member's practice and for the disciplinary system that fosters a developmental approach to discipline.

4. Create a formal training and assessment procedure, supported by appropriate documentation, for judicial officers and other regular participants. (p. 118)

The Management of Disciplinary Records

The Family Educational Rights and Privacy Act (FERPA; also known as the Buckley Amendment) of 1974 was intended to protect the privacy of student records by limiting their release to third parties and guaranteeing students' right of access to their own education records. However, the protections of education records have never been absolute. For example, the legislation has always allowed institutions to share information with school officials who possess a legitimate educational interest or the parents of a dependent student (Baker, 2008a; Gregory, 1998; Lowery, 1998a, 2008).

Prior to FERPA and the lowering of the age of majority, college students' parents were routinely notified of their sons' or daughters' disciplinary records, and student records, including disciplinary files, were available to other agencies and prospective employers. Within a few years after the passage of "Buckley," Dannells (1978) found that the great majority of respondent institutions conformed to the law by keeping students' academic and disciplinary records confidential. Four-fifths of colleges kept their disciplinary records separate from other student records, and very few made them available to outside agencies or prospective employers without the student's consent. Only 8 percent reported releasing records to parents. Parents were notified of their student's involvement in the disciplinary process by 37 percent of the respondents if the student was a minor, but 30 percent indicated they did not notify parents regardless of the student's age. Little change in these practices was found in a follow-up study conducted ten years later (Dannells, 1990).

There was considerable debate in the 1990s about the privacy protections provided to student disciplinary records as part of a larger concern about campus crime (Gregory, 1998; Lowery, 1998a, 2004). Since the passage of the federal Higher Education Amendments (HEA) of 1998, "parental notification" has also become a significant issue in the administration of campus discipline (Lowery, 2000; Palmer, Lohman, Gehring, Carlson, & Garrett, 2001).

The Higher Education Amendments (HEA) of 1998 altered FERPA to permit, but do not require, colleges and universities to notify parents of students who are under the age of 21 at the time of the notification (Gehring, 2000; Lowery, 2000, 2005) that the student has violated institutional rules or local, state, or federal laws relating to the possession or use of alcohol or a controlled substance (Inter-Association Task Force, n.d.; Kaplin & Lee, 2000;

Lowery, 2000). Institutional responses to this and subsequent federal guidelines have varied depending on size, type, nature of the student body, institutional philosophy, and state law (Lowery, Palmer, & Gehring, 2005; Palmer et al., 2001; Palmer, Lowery, Wilson, & Gehring, 2003; Sluis, 2001). Lowery, Palmer, and Gehring (2005) found that 45.8 percent of the respondents to their survey had parental notification policies in place. However, parental notification policies were more common at private college and universities (55%) than public institutions (40%). Guidelines for the formulation of such policies have been developed by the Association of Student Judicial Affairs and the Inter-Association Task Force on Alcohol and Other Substance Abuse Issues.

The Student Right-to-Know and Campus Security Act of 1990 amended FERPA to allow disclosure of the outcome of campus disciplinary proceeding to the victim of an alleged crime of violence or nonforcible sex offense, and a subsequent change to the Clery Act required this notification in sexual assault cases (Lowery, 1998a, 2000; U.S. Dept. of Education, 2005). Two years later, Congress amended the Clery Act to require victim notification in sexual assault cases (Higher Education Act Amendments of 1992) which the U.S. Department of Education has ruled in responding to several complaints must be unconditional and subsequently included language to that effect in the Notice of Final Rule for FERPA (U.S. Department of Education, 2008). The HEA of 1998 also amended FERPA and the Campus Security Act with respect to reporting the outcome of disciplinary proceedings against a student alleged to have committed a crime of violence or a nonforcible sex offense. The outcome of such a proceeding may now be reported to the public when the student is found responsible of these charges. In such cases, state open public record laws and privacy protections will influence how much and to whom information may be released by public institutions (Gehring, 2000; Kaplin & Lee, 2000; Lowery, 1998a, 2000, 2007, 2008). Most recently, the Higher Education Opportunity Act of 2008 amended FERPA to require victim notification in violent offenses, other than sexual assault, when a written request is made.

In recent years, student charges of unfairness in campus judicial proceedings and allegations that institutions are using the campus judicial system to hide campus crime have prompted considerable interest, especially among journalists, in opening such hearings to the public (Gregory, 1998; Lowery, 1998a). In January 1995, the U.S. Department of Education issued final rules that amended FERPA which clarified that disciplinary proceedings and subsequent actions **are** education records. The state supreme courts of Georgia and Ohio have ordered the release of student disciplinary records under state open records laws in *Red & Black Publishing Company v. Board of Regents* (1993) and *State ex rel The Miami Student v. Miami University* (1997), respectively. However, the U. S. Court of Appeals for the 6th Circuit ruled that FERPA prevented the release of student disciplinary records as ordered by the *Ohio Supreme Court in United States v. Miami University* (2002).

STUDENT CONDUCT AND STUDENT DEVELOPMENT THEORY

Seemingly in reaction to the perceived excessive proceduralism following the *Dixon* case, the student affairs profession in the last several decades has shown renewed interest in the educational nature of discipline and the application of student development to the conduct of disciplinary affairs. Not only is there concern for protection of the individual's rights and of the institution itself, but there appears to be a growing realization of the primacy of the educational value in the disciplinary function. This is not to suggest that meeting students' legal rights and fostering their development are incompatible, which they are not (Greenleaf, 1978), but rather that the increasingly adversarial nature of the process became a significant drain on and distraction to those charged with administering campuses' disciplinary system. It became more difficult to find that proper balance necessary to the survival of the Student Personnel Point of View (Caruso, 1978). With the growing body of theory, research, and literature on cognitive, moral, and ethical development, there appears to be increasing interest in its application to the disciplinary setting (Boots, 1987; Healy & Liddell, 1998; Patton, Howard-Hamilton, & Hinton, 2006; Saddlemire, 1980).

Student conduct is, and always has been, an excellent opportunity for developmental efforts. The traditional dean of students knew this but operated without the benefit of formal developmental theories, especially those emphasizing moral and ethical growth which lend themselves to the disciplinary process. Much of discipline involves teaching (Ardaiolo, 1983; Ostroth & Hill, 1978; Travelstead, 1987) and counseling (Foley, 1947; Gometz & Parker, 1968; Ostroth & Hill, 1978; Stone & Lucas, 1994; Williamson, 1963; Williamson & Foley, 1949). By the application of developmental theory, the individual may be better understood and counseling/developmental interventions may be more scientifically and accurately fashioned (Boots, 1987).

Various developmental theories have been applied to the disciplinary process and its impact on the individual student (e.g., see Boots, 1987; Greenleaf, 1978; Ostroth & Hill, 1978; Smith, 1978), and certain common elements and objectives of the different views and approaches are noted in the literature. These include: (1) insight as a commonly stated objective and means to further growth in the individual "offender" (Dannells, 1977); (2) self-understanding or clarification of personal identity, attitudes, and values, especially in relation to authority, for both the student whose behavior is in question and also for students who sit on judicial boards (Boots, 1987; Greenleaf, 1978; Harper, Harris, & Mmeje, 2005); (3) goals of self-control, responsibility, and accountability (Caruso, 1978; Pavela, 1985; Travelstead, 1987); (4) the use of ethical dialogue in both confronting the impact of the individual's behavior and its moral implications and examining the fairness of rules (McBee, 1982; Pavela, 1985; Smith, 1978); and (5) there appears to have been an extension of the scope and goals of student discipline to a broader objective of moral and ethical development as it relates to contemporary social issues, such as prejudice, health and wellness, sexism, racism, and human sexuality (Baldizan, 1998; Dalton & Healy, 1984).

In a survey of counseling center directors, Stone and Lucas (1994) found the following frequencies of goals for disciplinary counseling: assessment/evaluation, 28 percent; behavior change, 27 percent; student insight, 16 percent; education, 10 percent; establishment of appropriate goals, 5 percent; and "other," 14 percent. When asked to identify "reference material that the respondent would recommend for counseling center staff in working with disciplinary referrals" (p. 235), none of the counseling center directors offered developmental theory/theorists. This lack of reference to developmental theory may be taken as evidence of the oft-bemoaned theory-to-practice gap in student affairs, and may lend credence to the critiques of the usefulness of student development theory in our practice (e.g., see Bloland, Stamatakos, & Rogers, 1994).

Nonetheless, the weight of authority is clearly in keeping with Boots' (1987) assertion that developmental theory can be a "proactive part of the total educational process" (p. 67). Dannells (1991) provided an example of how that might be done:

> For example, in working with a student involved in disruptive behavior and underage drinking at a residence hall party, the student affairs professional may render an informal assessment (King, 1990) of the student's level of moral reasoning at Level I (preconventional morality), Stage 2 (relative hedonism) using Kohlherg's (1969) model. Concurrently, using Chickering's (1969) theory, the student may be viewed as struggling with developing interpersonal competence and managing emotions. This may be a common diagnosis that would lend itself to a group intervention focusing on the campus regulations about alcohol, the reasons for them, and the ways that students can be socially engaged without using alcohol. (p. 170)

Developmental theory is also useful for thinking about the relative maturity level of students (Thomas, 1987) and about the positive outcomes for all students. Chickering and Reisser (1993) explained:

Students may learn about community values and ethical principles when they either violate the conduct code or serve in judicial systems. The latter case represents an opportunity to develop integrity. In hearing cases, reviewing disciplinary procedures, and determining sanctions, students consider moral dilemmas in a concrete way. . . . By serving on hearing committees, students also benefit from watching faculty members, administrators, and staff members grapple with the arguments. The need for rules has not disappeared. . . . The challenge now is engaging students to take more responsibility for maintaining a safe and positive learning environment, becoming aware of the institution's code of conduct, and respecting the processes of enforcing and amending regulations. (p. 448)

CURRENT ISSUES IN STUDENT CONDUCT

Balancing Legal Rights and Educational Purposes

Following the *Dixon* decision in 1961, many institutions, private and public, rushed to establish disciplinary systems affording students their "due" protections. Some overreacted, went far beyond the court's requirements, and became "mired in legalistic disputes" (Lamont, 1979, p. 85). Critics of this "creeping legalism," or proceduralism, argued that it has undermined the informal and uniquely educational aspect of the disciplinary process in higher education; it has resulted in costly, complex, and time-consuming processes; and it places the student and the institution in an unnecessarily adversarial relationship (Dannells, 1977, 1997; Gehring, 2001; Pavela, 1985; Travelstead, 1987). Gehring (2001) noted, "The 'creeping legalism' described by Dannells (1997) has gone far beyond what the courts have actually required in order to provide students with due process. Institutions have unnecessarily formalized their procedures" (p. 477). Judging from the frequency of the reminders in the literature, it would appear student affairs administrators need to be periodically reminded that "due process" is, in fact, a flexible concept which allows for the less formal/legalistic disposition of most disciplinary cases, especially when the penalty or outcome is less than dismissal (Ardaiolo, 1983; Bracewell, 1988; Gehring, 2001; Pavela, 1985; Travelstead, 1987). As Bracewell (1988) pointed out, "[i]n less than two decades, colleges and universities have accommodated this legal concept [due process] in their regulations and disciplinary procedures" (p. 275), but "[a] strange amalgam of legalism and counseling was created" (p. 274). This "strange amalgam," and the struggle between the two opposing forces that created it, continue to challenge many student affairs professionals engaged in disciplinary work (Smith, 1994). The findings of Bostic and Gonzalez (1999) suggest a reconciliation of the tension between legalism and developmentalism may be developing in the profession although legalistic language can still be found in codes of student conduct (Martin & Janosik, 2004).

Demands for More Supervision of Students

Some may find it ironic that not long after the celebration of the twenty-fifth anniversary of the "Joint Statement on Rights and Freedoms of Students" (see generally Bryan & Mullendore, 1992), and "[h]aving moved from strict control over student conduct to treating students as adults subject to much less control, institutions now are being pressed to take more responsibility for students' behavior" (Pavela, 1992, p. Bl). According to Pavela (1992), the same consumer-protection movement that aided the progress for students' rights left students with concurrent liabilities, including taking more responsibility for themselves and making it more difficult for them to hold colleges responsible for injuries suffered at the hands of other students. He observed that student-consumer protection statutes, like the Crime Awareness and Campus Security Act,

> Frequently go well beyond setting guidelines for reporting information to students; they often contain explicit or implicit requirements that specific disciplinary policies like restrictions against underage drinking be adopted, enforced, and monitored by colleges to protect students and members of the public. (pp. B1-2)

Pavela pointed out that besides legislation, other social and economic forces have conspired to pressure colleges to take greater responsibility for their students' behavior, whether on or off-campus, "at the worst possible time" (p. B2). He called on deans and presidents to take the creative lead in setting and enforcing standards of student behavior that will result in more responsible and civil student conduct.

Pavela's charge came at a time when concerns for campus crime and student safety may have been at an all-time high. Sloan (1994) reviewed the findings of the 1990 U.S. Congressional Hearings on Campus Crime and reported that from 1985–1989, campus crime steadily increased, over 80% of campus crime involved students as both perpetrators and victims, and 95% of campus crime involved the use of alcohol or other drugs. More recently, the U.S. Department of Education Office of Postsecondary Education (2001) conducted research based upon the crime statistics that institutions submitted on-line in 2000. In compliance with the Higher Education Amendments of 1998, the U.S. Department of Education Office of Postsecondary Education submitted a report to Congress regarding crime on campus. The report concluded,

The campus crime statistics collected by the U.S. Department of Education suggest that our nation's college campuses are safe. In nearly every category of crime for which data were collected, college campuses showed lower incidence of crime than comparable data for the nation as a whole. (p. 13)

While "[m]ost studies of campus crime show that colleges are safer than the communities around them" (Lederman, 1995, p. A41), a *Chronicle of Higher Education report* (Lederman, 1995) showed a "continuing increase in the number of violent crimes" on campuses with enrollments over 5000 (p. A41). With such reports, the pressure continues for institutions to respond with preventative measures, criminal prosecution, and disciplinary action.

On-going Concerns about Academic Misconduct

In addressing this issue, it is important to distinguish between academic *evaluation* and academic *misconduct.* Academic evaluation refers to evaluative judgments, typically made by faculty, about the student's performance in a course or in the course of a professional training program. The courts have been reluctant to hear cases involving such professional judgments. In the determination of such decisions, including a decision to dismiss on the basis of academic deficiencies, students need not be afforded the same due process safeguards required in disciplinary cases. The landmark case in this area is *Board of Curators of the University of Missouri v. Horowitz* (1978).

Academic misconduct refers to violations of rules of academic honesty or integrity, such as cheating on tests or plagiarism "that involve students giving or receiving unauthorized assistance in an academic exercise or receiving credit for work that is not their own" (Kibler 1993a, p. 253). The standards of due process in cases of academic misconduct are generally the same as those in nonacademic, or social, misconduct.

Academic misconduct, as it represents deviance from and erosion of the core value of academic integrity, has always been of concern in higher education; but in recent years the concern has grown even though empirical evidence of the increasing incidence of cheating is lacking (McCabe & Bowers, 1994). Estimates of the extent of cheating by college students vary widely. May and Loyd's (1993) review of research done in the 1980s found that "between 40% and 90% of all college students cheat" (p. 125). Kibler (1993b) observed that cheating occurs on most, if not all, campuses; and that although it is difficult to prove it is actually increasing, "it is generally agreed that academic dishonesty is a serious issue for all segments of higher education" (p. 9).

The causes of academic misconduct and the many possible solutions to it are complex and beyond the scope of this chapter. However, one general approach deserves mention. As Gehring (1995) has pointed out,

> [b]oth NASPA's "Reasonable Expectations" and ACPA's "Student Learning
> Imperative" call for greater cooperation between student affairs and faculty
> affairs to enhance student learning. One area in which this can take place is
> that of fostering academic integrity. There are many issues involved in breach-
> es of academic integrity–institutional environments, expectations, rules and
> regulations, moral reasoning and legal rights and responsibilities. Student
> affairs practitioners have expertise in many of these issues and could use that
> knowledge to assist faculty in improving the campus climate relative to aca-
> demic integrity. (p. 6)

For student affairs professionals to assert their expertise into what many
faculty consider their exclusive domain will not be easy. Faculty tends to
ignore formal academic dishonesty policies and procedures (Aaron &
Georgia, 1994; Jendrek, 1989). Despite its unpleasantness, faculty has a
strong sense of duty in this area and possesses more expertise when poor
scholarship confounds the problem. But as Gehring (1995) noted, many faculty do not understand the differences between academic judgments and
misconduct decisions requiring due process, "something student affairs practitioners have been instructed in for the past 35 years" (p. 6). Drinan and
Gallant (2008) identified several factors which have contributed to student
affairs professionals playing a larger role in academic integrity issues in
recent years:

> (1) adoption of honor system that are historically student-run with minimal fac-
> ulty involvement; (2) complaints by students that faculty judge and adjudicate
> misconduct within the classroom domain without providing students proper
> due process; (3) faculty fears of litigation, time-consuming procedures, or neg-
> ative effectives on student academic and career futures that led them to ignore
> misconduct; and (4) faculty denial and anger. (pp. 259-260)

As Bracewell (1988) observed, the processes and procedures normally managed by student affairs professionals are ideally suited to the adjudication of
academic dishonesty. Baker (2008b) has identified several common approaches for the organization of institutional responses to academic dishonesty.

Disciplinary Counseling

As previously defined, disciplinary counseling is one possible rehabilitative or educational response to student misconduct. It has a long history in
the literature on student discipline (see, for example, ACE, 1937, 1949;

Gometz & Parker 1968; Snoxell, 1960; Williamson, 1956, 1963; Williamson & Foley, 1949; Wrenn, 1949) and was a commonly accepted practice since 1900. But with the rise of professional mental health centers on campuses, administrators charged with the responsibility for discipline began sending students for counseling as a form of rehabilitation, often as a condition of continued enrollment and often with the expectation that the counselor would make some report on the progress of the student's development of insight and perhaps forecast the student's future behavior. By definition, disciplinary counseling is mandatory, or nonvoluntary, unless one supports the argument that the student can always choose dismissal rather than accept counseling, in which case it is, at least, coercive.

Referrals for disciplinary counseling appear to be increasing, and disciplinary counseling is widely practiced (Consolvo & Dannells, 2000; Dannells, 1990, 1991; Stone & Lucas, 1994) despite being highly controversial on two main points: ethics and efficacy. Almost half (48%) of the counseling center directors surveyed by Stone and Lucas (1994) responded that counseling centers should not do disciplinary counseling citing primary reservations as ethics (involving issues of coercion, confidentiality, and role conflicts) and management and effectiveness issues. Stone and Lucas concluded there is considerable confusion, ambivalence, and ambiguity about disciplinary counseling in the minds of counseling center directors. They called for a distinction between disciplinary *therapy* and disciplinary *education,* while admitting that such "sharply drawn conceptual differences often disappear in practice" (p. 238).

Amada (1993, 1994) strenuously objected to mandatory disciplinary psychotherapy for college students on several counts, including that it "distorts and undermines the basis for corrective disciplinary action" (1993, p. 128); it is "often motivated by fanciful and naive notions about psychotherapy" (1993, p. 129); it is "unequivocally a coercive measure that serves to instill in the student resentment toward the therapist and therapy itself" (1993, p. 129); it lacks confidentiality; it is probably in violation of the laws that protect persons with handicaps from discriminatory treatment; and it "tends to transfer the responsibility and authority for administering discipline from where it rightly belongs–the office of the designated administrator–to where it does not belong–the offices of counselors and therapists" (1993, p. 130). He concluded that disciplinary therapy is definitely unethical.

In a study of the policy and practice of disciplinary counseling at four-year institutions, Consolvo and Dannells (2000) confirmed that its existence as policy has increased while significant issues of policy articulation and organizational and ethical conflict surround it. For example, they determined that in almost three out of ten institutions, the counseling center director and the primary judicial officer did not agree that they engaged in its practice; one in five respondents agreed that there were significant organizational conflicts; one in four agreed that it posed ethical problems; and they found considerable disagreement about the goals of disciplinary counseling. Consolvo and Dannells recommended various educational/developmental alternatives to disciplinary counseling.

First Amendment Issues

By the late 1980s, there was growing concern in higher education about the rising tide of racial incidents on campus. A number of institutions sought to address this concern by adopting policies that prohibited certain forms of racist speech that came to be commonly referred to as Hate Speech Codes. The courts rejected on First Amendment grounds the Hate Speech Codes adopted by several prominent public institutions including the University of Wisconsin (*UWM Post v. Board of Regents,* 1991) and the University of Michigan (*Doe v. University of Michigan,* 1989) (O'Neil, 1997). The fundamental constitutional defect of both of these policies lay in their vagueness and overbreadth (Bird, Mackin, & Schuster, 2006; Downs, 2005; Heumann & Schurch, 1997; Hodges, 1996; Paterson, 1994, 1998; O'Neil, 1997; Schuster, Bird, & Mackin, 2008; Silverglate & Lukianoff, 2003). A number of authors also charged that Hate Speech Codes were antithetical to the free exchange of ideas at any institution of higher education, public or private (Downs, 2005, Hentoff, 1992; Kors & Silvergate, 1998; Silverglate, French, & Lukianoff, 2005). While few institutions have explicit hate speech codes today, the courts have recently invalidated sexual harassment and other harassment and discrimination policies on the same grounds (*Bair v. Shippensburg Univ.,* 2003; *DeJohn v. Temple,* 2008).

The problems associated with Hate Speech Codes reach far beyond their mere legal implications. The People for the American Way (1991) warned,

> Schools looking for a shortcut through the First Amendment toward the difficult goal of fighting intolerance forget the obligation to foster a climate of acceptance and open debate. In fact, such a shortcut is an abdication of this responsibility, a white flag that says, muffling the worst about and among us is the best we can do. (p. 25)

The more significant question raised by the People for the American Way and others was whether Hate Speech Codes actually improved the racial climate on campus (O'Neil, 2003). Faced with mounting concerns, some institutions developed approaches that did not involve the same constitutional problems. At the same time that Wisconsin and Michigan were developing their Hate Speech Codes, the University of South Carolina developed the

Carolinian Creed as a positive expression of institutional values in response to the growing problem of intolerance and incivility (Lowery, 1998b; People for the American Way, 1991; Pruitt, 1996).

PROFESSIONAL ASSOCIATIONS

Professionals engaged in the disciplinary process on their campuses would likely find benefit in membership in at least four professional associations: (1) The Association for Student Conduct Administration (formerly the Association for Student Judicial Affairs) exists exclusively to address issues faced by administrators of student conduct systems; (2) The American College Personnel Association has a commission structure which includes the Commission for Student Conduct & Legal Issues (formerly Commission XV, Campus Judicial Affairs and Legal Issues); (3) The Center for Academic Integrity which focuses specifically on institutional responses to academic dishonesty; and (4) The National Association of Student Personnel Administrators addresses leadership and professional growth opportunities for senior student affairs officers and others who are charged with disciplinary responsibilities.

ENTRY-LEVEL QUALIFICATIONS

The Council for the Advancement of Standards (CAS, 2006), in its Standards and Guidelines for Student Conduct Programs, requires that professional staff members in judicial programs and services "hold an earned graduate degree in a field relevant to the position they hold or must possess an appropriate combination of education credentials and related work experience" (p. 316). And a "qualified member of the campus community must be designated as the person responsible for student conduct programs" (p. 317). Qualifications for this designated individual are also provided:

The designee should have an educational background in the behavioral sciences (e.g., college student affairs, psychology, sociology, student development including moral and ethical development, higher education administration, counseling, law, criminology, or criminal justice).

The designee and any other professional staff member in the student conduct programs should possess (a) a clear understanding of the legal requirements for substantive and procedural due process; (b) legal knowledge sufficient to confer with attorneys involved in student disciplinary proceedings and other aspects of the student conduct services system; (c) a general interest in and commitment to the welfare and development of students who participate on boards or who are involved in cases; (d) demonstrated skills in working with decision making processes and conflict resolution; (e) teaching and consulting skills appropriate for the education, advising, and coordination of hearing bodies; (f) the ability to communicate and interact with students regardless of race, sex, disability, sexual orientation, and other personal characteristics; (g) understanding of the requirements relative to confidentiality and security of student conduct programs files; and (h) the ability to create an atmosphere where students feel free to ask questions and obtain assistance. (p. 317)

TECHNOLOGY

Student affair professionals interested in student conduct affairs might find the following websites of interest.

Association for Student Conduct Administration
    http://www.theasca.org
    ASCA is the leading professional organization for student judicial affairs professionals. The website contains valuable information for those interested in this field including the association's Statement of Ethical Principles and Standards of Conduct. The website includes additional resources in a members only area.

Campus Legal Information Clearinghouse
    http://counsel.cua.edu/
    Campus Legal Information Clearinghouse is a joint effort between the American Council on Education (ACE) and The Catholic University of America's Office of General Counsel to provide access to a comprehensive range of resources and information relating to legal issues in higher education.

Center for Academic Integrity
    http://www.academicintegrity.org/
    The Center for Academic Integrity was established to promote academic integrity and response effectively to academic dishonesty. The website includes additional resources in a members-only area.

Council on Law in Higher Education
    http://clhe.org/
    The Council on Law in Higher Education focuses on law and policy

issues in higher education. The website includes additional resources in a members only area.

Inter-Association Task Force on Alcohol and Other Substance Abuse Issues
http://www.iatf.org/
The Inter-Association Task Force on Alcohol and Other Substance Abuse Issues is a coalition of organizations committed to address alcohol and other substance abuse issues on campus. The website includes extensive resources related to address these issues.

Restorative Justice Online
http://www.restorativejustice.org/
The International Centre for Justice and Reconciliation sponsors this newsletter which promotes the application of restorative justice principles to various community settings.

THOMAS: Legislative Information on the Internet
http://thomas.loc.gov/
THOMAS: Legislative Information on the Internet is a project of the Library of Congress and includes extensive legislative information including search databases of pending legislation.

U.S. Department of Education, Campus Security
http://www.ed.gov/admins/lead/safety/campus.html
The U.S. Department of Education's Campus Security website contains useful legislative and regulatory information regarding the Jeanne Clery Disclosure of Campus Security Policy and Campus Crime Statistics Act.

U.S. Department of Education's Family Policy Compliance Office
http://www.ed.gov/policy/gen/guid/fpco
The U.S. Department of Education's Family Policy Compliance Office website contains useful legislative and regulatory information regarding the Family Educational Rights and Privacy Act.

U.S. Department of Education's Higher Education Center
for Alcohol and Other Drug and Violence Prevention
http://www.edc.org/hec/
The U.S. Department of Education's Higher Education Center for Alcohol and Other Drug and Violence Prevention website contains extensive resources related to address these issues on campus.

THE FUTURE OF JUDICIAL AFFAIRS

The future of the disciplinary function in student affairs is inextricably tied to the futures of student affairs and of higher education. Innumerable influences will come to bear on those institutions, rendering futurism a risky and perhaps foolish enterprise. But as Sandeen and Rhatigan (1990) said, the "difficulty of accurate forecasting has never deterred people from the effort" (p. 98).

It is tempting to refer the reader to the section on current issues in disciplinary affairs and forecast more of the same. In many instances that strategy might well prove accurate, but there are some new, some different, and some continuing trends and indicators to consider in thinking about the future of disciplinary work in higher education.

The Changing Legal and Legislative Environment

With the growing recognition and acceptance that the academy is a part of the "real world" and a microcosm of the greater society, the student-institutional relationship has become increasingly viewed as a consumer business, one subject to many of the same contractual expectations and constraints as any other seller-buyer or landlord-tenant, relationship. Society, students, and even some students' parents no longer expect institutions of higher education to act on a vague set of social or parental rules in disciplinary matters. In particular, older students have little tolerance for paternalistic policies and processes. Instead, they wish to know exactly what is expected of them as adults. This has undoubtedly influenced many institutions to review carefully catalogues and other official documents, including codes of conduct, which may be considered part of the enrollment contract. This trend will continue, and it will benefit those who administer their campus disciplinary system to closely review their rules and methods to ensure they are treating students like the adults they legally are.

Related to this is the projection (Hodgkinson, 1985; Kuh, 1990) that in addition to the increasing average age of future students, more will be part-time and more will be attending commuter institutions in urban settings. Since most student misconduct involves traditional-aged students in residential settings, this would suggest that the relative incidence of student misconduct should decrease over time. Alternatively, increasing pressure to get good grades may lead to higher rates of academic dishonesty. Both hypotheses are ripe for future research.

Forecasting the future regulatory and legal issues for student affairs, Fenske and Johnson (1990) noted seven crucial issues, two of which are most directly relevant for disciplinary affairs. One is that "[s]tudent affairs professionals will be increasingly involved in balancing the constitutional rights of students with the elimination of prejudice and harassment and the promotion of tolerance" (p. 133). The second is that "[c]ourt rulings and state laws on liability will require closer monitoring of on-campus and off-campus social events where alcohol is served, as well as increased willingness to take action against illegal drug and alcohol abuse" (pp. 133-134). Both of these issues have implications for codes of conduct and their enforcement.

A third significant issue that has emerged over the course of the last two decades is a rapid expansion of the federal legislation impacting student judicial affairs. In addition to the changes to FERPA included in the Higher Education Amendments of 1998 previously discussed, the Campus Security Act was also amended to require that institutions include statistics for students referred for disciplinary action, but not arrested, for alcohol, drug, and weapons law violations (Lowery, 1998a, 1999, 2000, 2006). The Higher Education Opportunity Act of 2008 with provisions including victim notification, fire safety, missing students, peer-to-peer file sharing, and sanctions for alcohol violations has additional significant implications for student conduct practice.

According to Bickel and Lake (1999), there has been a fundamental shift in the way the courts have viewed liability claims against universities. After the demise of *in loco parentis,* the courts moved into an era in which colleges and universities were seen to have no duty whatsoever to students described as the "Bystander Era." However, Bickel and Lake have documented an emerging trend in which the courts are moving away from the "Bystander Era" into a new era of duty for institutions in relationship to their students.

The Continuing Need for Program Evaluation

Like any other student affairs program, student conduct programs should be periodically and systematically evaluated to ensure that they are effectively meeting their established objectives (CAS, 2006; Emmanuel & Miser, 1987; Janosik & Stimpson, 2009; Schuh & Upcraft, 2001; Zacker, 1996). Those objectives should be defined in terms of measurable outcomes statements and evaluated on the basis of pre-established criteria and processes. The various components of the program, such as its publications, training program for judicial board members, consistency of sanctions and procedures and practices, as well as the personnel involved in the execution of the program, should be included in a comprehensive review. Methods of evaluation will vary according to the nature and needs of the individual program, but may include interviews, direct observation, written reports, surveys, community feedback, task force review, questionnaires (Emmanuel & Miser, 1987), and student portfolios (Zelna, 2002; Zelna & Cousins, 2002). It must be acknowledged, however, that scientific research in the area of student discipline has been and will continue to be problematic because of difficulties in identifying and controlling variables, in gathering data from recalcitrant program participants, and in meeting legal and ethical requirements for confidentiality and informed consent. Few outcomes studies, like that of Mullane (1999) and Howell (2005), are found in the literature. Likewise, research on the effectiveness of judicial systems, like that of Fitch and Murry (2001), are rare. Readers seeking a review of research in the student conduct area are encouraged to see Stimpson and Stimpson (2008) as well as Swinton (2008).

The Search for Common Values

Many institutions have recently engaged in lengthy processes to clarify institutional values as they are reflected in such documents as mission statements, codes of conduct, and academic integrity policies. Many institutions have yet to approach this formidable set of tasks, but they must, and most will do so.

The increasing diversity of the many constituents on campuses makes the task of finding and implementing common values more challenging. Cultural differences can be expected to complicate the disciplinary function; consensus about what constitutes acceptable behavior may no longer be taken for granted. Thus, it is all the more important that colleges and universities which for some time have not reviewed their codes of conduct do so, and in so doing to involve students, faculty, and staff from diverse backgrounds to ensure a set of behavioral principles as widely accepted as possible.

The apparent increase in, and the new or renewed concern about, student cheating may prove an important and useful ground for the collaboration of academic affairs and student affairs leaders. Codes of conduct should include clear policy statements on academic integrity that are acceptable to faculty, understandable to students, and enforceable for faculty and the administrators who are responsible for student conduct systems.

Garland and Grace (1993) listed twelve "potential focal points for collaboration between academic affairs and student affairs" (p. 62). At least four of them fall directly within the area of student discipline or have direct implications for it. They are:

- Manage disciplinary problems from a unified rather than a unilateral approach for consistency in response.
- Respond to alcohol and drugs on campus to prevent personal and academic debilitation.
- Respond to increased violence on campus.
- Respond to increased psychopathology, balancing the needs of troubled students and the community. (Garland & Grace, 1993, p. 62)

The Profession and Discipline

Student discipline has been, and perhaps should continue to be, a topic of professional concern and debate because it is such a dramatic reflection of our attitudes and assumptions about the nature of our students, our relationship to them, and our role in their development. There was a period in our profession's history when the subject was all but ignored, a source of embarrassment to be apologetically dispatched and forgotten in favor of more glamorous and "positive" functions.

After a careful analysis of the undergraduate experience at American colleges and universities, Ernest Boyer (1987), then President of the Carnegie Foundation for the Advancement of Teaching, wrote:

> What we found particularly disturbing is the ambivalence college administrators feel about their overall responsibility for student behavior. Most of the college leaders with whom we spoke had an unmistakable sense of unease—or was it anxiety? Many were not sure what standards to expect or require. Where does the responsibility of the college begin and end? Where is the balance to be struck between students' personal "rights" and institutional concerns? . . . Unclear about what standards to maintain and the principles by which student life should be judged, many administrators seek to ignore rather than confront the issues. (p. 203)

Student affairs leaders, particularly those charged with the responsibility for discipline, must actively and positively embrace that responsibility and stimulate the dialogue on campus necessary to ensure that it is not ignored or dispatched halfheartedly and, ultimately, poorly.

Student Discipline, the Core Curriculum, and Liberal Education

Those concerned with student behavior and judicial systems should find encouragement in the widespread efforts in higher education to develop an integrated core curriculum which reaffirms the traditional principles of a liberal education and which may help create a climate on campuses where the development of the whole person, including the moral aspect, is once again paramount. This movement suggests exciting possibilities for student affairs professionals to "return to the academy" (Brown, 1972).

Many institutions are considering team-taught, interdisciplinary subject matter which will challenge an increasingly materialistic, aphilosophic, and career-oriented student body. Might there not be a place for a course entitled "Student Rights and Responsibilities in the College and the Community"? Such a course could be approached from a myriad of combinations of the different disciplines of law, political science, sociology, psychology, education, and philosophy (ethics) and could include the campus' chief discipli-nary/judicial officer. In this way, the subject of student conduct and moral/ethical development could be considered within the broader context of civic responsibility and community involvement. Thus, the moral dia-logue inherent in a developmental approach to discipline (Pavela, 1985) could be brought to the classroom with the student affairs professional as an integral part of the teaching/ learning partnership and process.

REFERENCES

Aaron, R., & Georgia, R. T. (1994). Administrator perceptions of student academic dishonesty. *NASPA Journal, 31,* 83–91.

Amada, G. (1993). The role of the mental health consultant in dealing with disrup-tive college students. *Journal of College Student Psychotherapy, 8,* 121–137.

Amada, G. (1994). *Coping with the disruptive college student: A practical model.* Asheville, NC: College Administration Publications.

American Council on Education (ACE). (1937). *The student personnel point of view* (American Council on Education Studies, Series 1, Vol. 1, No. 3). Washington, DC: Author.

American Council on Education (ACE). (1949). *The student personnel point of view* (Rev. Ed.). American Council on Education Studies, Series 6, Vol. 13, No. 13. Washington, DC: Author.

Appleton, J. R., Briggs, C. M., & Rhatigan, J. J. (1978). *Pieces of eight.* Portland, OR: National Association of Student Personnel Administrators.

Ardaiolo, F. P. (1983). What process is due? In M. J. Barr (Ed.), *Student affairs and the law* (New Directions for Student Services No. 22; pp. 13–25). San Francisco: Jossey-Bass.

Ardaiolo, F. P., & Walker, S. J. (1987). Models of practice. In R. Caruso & W. W. Travelstead (Eds.), *Enhancing campus judicial systems* (New Directions for Student Services No. 39, pp. 43-61). San Francisco: Jossey-Bass.

Arndt, J. R. (1971). Substantive due process in public higher education: 1959–1969. *Journal of College Student Personnel, 12,* 83–94.

Bair v. Shippensburg Univ., 280 F. Supp. 2d 357 (M.D. Pa. 2003).

Baker, T. R. (2005). *Judicial complaint resolution models for higher education: An adminis-trator's reference guide.* Horsham, PA: LRP Publications.

Baker, T. R. (2008a). Navigating state and federal student privacy laws to design edu-cationally sound parental notice policies. *New Directions for Student Services, 122,* 81–101.

Baker, T. R. (2008b). Processing academic dishonesty complaints: How higher edu-cation institutions systematize caseload management. *Journal of Student Conduct Administration, 1,* 61–74.

Bakken, C. J. (1968). *The legal basis of college student personnel work* (Student Personnel Monograph Series No. 2). Washington, DC: American Personnel and Guidance

Association.

Baldizan, E. M. (1998). Development, due process, and reduction: Student conduct in the 1990s. In D. L. Cooper & J. M. Lancaster (Eds.), *Beyond Law and policy: Reaffirming the role of student affairs* (New Directions for Student Services No. 82, pp. 29–37). San Francisco: Jossey-Bass.

Barr, M. J. (1988). Conclusion: The evolving legal environment of student affairs administration. In M. J. Barr & Associates, *Student services and the law* (pp. 347–353). San Francisco: Jossey-Bass.

Bickel, R. D. (2008). A commentary on the history of constitutional due process in the context of student discipline. *Journal of Student Conduct Administration, 1,* 6–13.

Bickel, R. D., & Lake, P. F. (1999). *The rights and responsibilities of the modern university: Who assumes the risks of college life?* Durham, NC: Carolina Academic Press.

Bird, L. E., Mackin, M. B., & Schuster, S. (Eds.). (2006). *The First Amendment on campus: A handbook for college and university administrators.* Washington, DC: NASPA.

Bloland, P. A., Stamatakos, L. C., & Rogers, R. R. (1994). *Reform in student affairs. A critique of student development.* Greensboro, NC: ERIC Counseling and Student Services Clearinghouse, University of North Carolina.

Board of Curators of the University of Missouri v. Horowitz, 435 U.S. 78 (1978).

Boots, C. C. (1987). Human development theory applied to judicial affairs work. In R. Caruso & W. W. Travelstead (Eds.), *Enhancing campus judicial systems* (New Directions for Student Services No. 39, pp. 63–72). San Francisco: Jossey-Bass.

Bostic, D., & Gonzalez, G. (1999). Practices, opinions, knowledge, and recommendations from judicial officers in public higher education. *NASPA Journal, 36,* 166–183.

Boyer, E. L. (1987). *College: The undergraduate experience in America.* New York: Harper & Row.

Bracewell, W. R. (1978). An application of the privacy concept to student life. In E. H. Hammond & R. H. Shaffer (Eds.), *The legal foundations of student personnel services in higher education* (pp. 24–33). Washington, DC: American College Personnel Association.

Bracewell, W. R. (1988). Student discipline. In M. J. Barr & Associates, *Student services and the law* (pp. 273–283). San Francisco: Jossey-Bass.

Brown, R. D. (1972). *Student development in tomorrow's higher education—A return to the academy.* Washington, DC: American College Personnel Association.

Brown, R. W. (1926). *Dean Briggs.* New York: Harper.

Brubacher, J. S., & Rudy, W. (1968). *Higher education in transition.* New York: Harper & Row.

Bruce, P. A. (1920). *History of the University of Virginia 1819-1919* (Vol. 2). New York: Macmillan.

Bryan, W. A., & Mullendore, R. H. (Eds.). (1992). *Rights, freedoms, and responsibilities of students* (New Directions for Student Services No. 59). San Francisco: Jossey-Bass.

Buchanan, E. T., III. (1978). Student disciplinary proceedings in collegiate institutions–Substantive and procedural due process requirements. In E. H. Hammond & R. H. Shaffer (Eds.), *The legal foundation of student personnel services in higher edu-

cation (pp. 94–115). Washington, DC: American College Personnel Association.

Callis, R. (1967). Educational aspects of in loco parentis. *Journal of College Student Personnel, 8,* 231–233.

Callis, R. (1969). The courts and the colleges: 1968. *Journal of College Student Personnel, 10,* 75–86.

Carletta, C. F. (1998). Distinctions between the criminal justice system and the campus judicial process: Implication for public and private institutions. In B. G. Paterson & W. L. Kibler (Eds.), *The administration of student discipline: Student, organizational, and community issues* (pp. 43–54). Asheville, NC: College Administration Publications.

Carnegie Commission on Higher Education. (1971). *Dissent and disruption.* New York: McGraw-Hill.

Carnegie Foundation for the Advancement of Teaching. (1990). *Campus life: In search of community.* Princeton, NJ: Author.

Caruso, R. G. (1978). The professional approach to student discipline in the years ahead. In E. H. Hammond & R. H. Shaffer (Eds.), *The legal foundations of student personnel services in higher education* (pp. 116–127). Washington, DC: American College Personnel Association.

Caruso, R., & Travelstead, W. W. (Eds.). (1987). *Enhancing campus judicial systems* (New Directions for Student Services No. 39). San Francisco: Jossey-Bass.

Chickering, A. W. (1969). *Education and identity.* San Francisco: Jossey-Bass.

Chickering, A. W., & Reisser, L. (1993). *Education and identity* (2nd ed.). San Francisco: Jossey-Bass.

Consolvo, C., & Dannells, M. (2000). Disciplinary counseling: *Implications for Policy and Practice, 38,* 44–57

Cordner, P., & Brooks, T. F. (1987). Training techniques for judicial systems. In R. Caruso & W. W. Travelstead (Eds.), *Enhancing campus judicial systems* (New Directions for Student Services No. 39, pp. 31–42). San Francisco: Jossey-Bass.

Correnti, R. J. (1988). How public and private institutions differ under the law. In M. J. Barr & Associates, *Student services and the law* (pp. 25–43). San Francisco: Jossey-Bass.

Council for the Advancement of Standards in Higher Education (CAS). (2006). *The book of professional standards for higher education* (6th ed.). Washington, DC: Author.

Dalton, J. C., & Healy, M. A. (1984). Using values education activities to confront student conduct issues. *NASPA Journal, 22*(2), 19–25.

Dannells, M. (1977). Discipline. In W. T. Packwood (Ed.), *College student personnel services* (pp. 232–278). Springfield, IL: Charles C Thomas.

Dannells, M. (1978). *Disciplinary practices and procedures in baccalaureate-granting institutions of higher education in the United States.* Unpublished doctoral dissertation, University of Iowa, Iowa City, IA.

Dannells, M. (1990). Changes in disciplinary policies and practices over 10 years. *Journal of College Student Development, 31,* 408–414.

Dannells, M. (1991). Changes in student misconduct and institutional response over 10 years. *Journal of College Student Development, 32,* 166–170.

Dannells, M. (1997). From discipline to development: Rethinking student conduct in higher education. *ASHE-ERIC Higher Education Report, 25*(2). San Francisco: Jossey-Bass.

DeJohn v. Temple University, 537 F.3d 301 (3d Cir. 2008).

Dixon v. Alabama State Board of Education, 294 F.2d 150 (5th Cir. 1961).

Doe v. University of Michigan, 721 F.Supp. 852 (E.D. Mich. 1989).

Downs, D. A. (2005). *Restoring free speech and liberty on campus.* Oakland, CA: The Independent Institute.

Drinan, P., & Gallant, T. B. (2008). Academic integrity: Models, case studies, and strategies. In J. M. Lancaster & D. M. Waryold (Eds.), *Contemporary administration of student conduct and ethical development on college campuses* (pp. 258–278). Sterling, VA: Stylus.

Durst, R. H. (1969). *The impact of court decisions rendered in the Dixon and Knight cases on student disciplinary procedures in public institutions of higher education in the United States* (Doctoral dissertation, Purdue University, 1968). Dissertation abstracts, 29, 2473A–2474A. University Microfilms No. 69–2910.

Dutton, T. B., Smith, F. W., & Zarle, T. (1969). *Institutional approaches to the adjudication of student misconduct.* Washington, DC: National Association of Student Personnel Administrators.

Emmanuel, N. R., & Miser, K. M. (1987). Evaluating judicial program effectiveness. In R. Caruso & W. W. Travelstead (Eds.), *Enhancing campus judicial systems* (New Directions for Student Services No. 39, pp. 85–94). San Francisco: Jossey-Bass.

Esteban v. Central Missouri State College, 290 F. Supp. 622 (W.D. Mo. 1968), aff'd, 415 F.2d 1077 (8th Cir. 1969).

Family Educational Rights and Privacy Act, 20 U.S.C. §1232g (1974).

Fenske, R. H. (1989). Evolution of the student services profession. In U. Delworth, G. R. Hanson, & Associates, *Student services: A handbook for the profession* (2nd ed.) (pp. 25–56). San Francisco: Jossey-Bass.

Fenske, R. H., & Johnson, E. A. (1990). Changing regulatory and legal environments. In M. J. Barr, M. L. Upcraft, & Associates, *New futures for student affairs* (pp. 114–137). San Francisco: Jossey-Bass.

Fischer, W. M., & Geist Giacomini, N. G. (2006). Managing student conduct & conflict through mediation and other alternative dispute resolution processes. In J. Lancaster (Ed.), *Exercising power with wisdom–The bridge from legal to developmental practice* (pp. 49–62). Asheville, NC: College Administration Publications.

Fisher, T. C. (1970). *Due process in the student-institutional relationship.* Washington, DC: American Association of State Colleges and Universities.

Fitch, E. E., Jr., & Murry, J. W., Jr. (2001). Classifying and assessing the effectiveness of student judicial systems in doctoral-granting universities. *NASPA Journal, 38,* 189–202.

Fley, J. (1964). Changing approaches to discipline in student personnel work. *Journal of the National Association for Women Deans, Administrators, and Counselors, 27,* 105–113.

Fley, J. A. (1974). Student personnel pioneers: Those who developed our profession. *NASPA Journal, 17*(1), 23–39.

Foley, J. D. (1947). Discipline: A student counseling approach. *Educational and*

Psychological Measurement, 7, 569–582.

Footer, N. S. (1996). Achieving fundamental fairness: The code of conduct. In W. L. Mercer (Ed.), *Critical issues in judicial affairs: Current trends in practice* (New Directions for Student Services No. 73, pp. 19–33). San Francisco: Jossey-Bass.

Frederickson, J. (1992). Disciplinary sanctioning of impulsive university students. *NASPA Journal, 29,* 143–148.

Gallagher, R. P., Harmon, W. W., & Lingenfelter, C. O. (1994). CSAOs' perceptions of the changing incidence of problematic college student behavior. *NASPA Journal, 32,* 37–45.

Garland, P. H., & Grace, T. W. (1993). *New perspectives for student affairs professionals. Evolving realities, responsibilities and roles* (1993 ASHE-ERIC Higher Education Report No. 7). Washington, DC: George Washington University, School of Education and Human Development.

Gehring, D. D. (1995, April/May). Abreast of the law: Academic and disciplinary dismissals. *NASPA Forum, 6.*

Gehring, D. D. (2000, September/October). New revisions clarify FERPA rules. *NASPA Forum, 22*(1), 6–7.

Gehring, D. D. (2001). The objectives of student discipline and the process that's due: Are they compatible? *NASPA Journal, 38,* 466–481.

Gehring, D. D., & Bracewell, W. R. (1992). Standards of behavior and disciplinary proceedings. In W. A. Bryan & R. H. Mullendore (Eds.), *Rights, freedoms, and responsibilities of students* (New Directions for Student Services, No. 59, pp. 89–99). San Francisco: Jossey- Bass.

Georgia, R. T. (1989). Permissiveness and discipline in the higher education setting: A prolegomenon. *NASPA Journal, 27,* 90–94.

Gibbs, A. (1992). *Reconciling the rights and responsibilities of colleges and students: Offensive speech, assembly drug testing, and safety* (1992 ASHE-ERIC Higher Education Report No. 5). Washington, DC: George Washington University, School of Education and Human Development.

Gometz, L., & Parker, C. A. (1968). Disciplinary counseling: A contradiction? *Personnel and Guidance Journal, 46,* 437–43.

Gott v. Berea College, 156 Ky 376 (1913).

Greenleaf, E. A. (1978). The relationship of legal issues and procedures to student development. In E. H. Hammond & R. H. Shaffer (Eds.), *The legal foundations of student personnel services in higher education* (pp. 34–46). Washington, DC: American College Personnel Association.

Gregory, D. E. (1998). Student judicial records, privacy, and the press's right to know. In B. G. Paterson & W. L. Kibler (Eds.), *The administration of student discipline: Student, organizational, and community issues* (pp. 55–73). Asheville, NC: College Administration Publications.

Gregory, D. E., & Ballou, R. A. (1986). Point of view: In loco parentis reinvents: Is there still a parenting function in higher education? *NASPA Journal, 24*(2), 28–31.

Grossi, E. L., & Edwards, D. T. (1997). Student misconduct: Historical trends in legislative and judicial decision-making in American universities. *Journal of College and University Law, 23,* 829–852

Hammond, E. H. (1978). The consumer-institutional relationship. In E. H. Hammond & R. H. Shaffer (Eds.), *The legal foundations of student personnel services in higher education* (pp. 1–11). Washington, DC: American College Personnel Association.

Harper, S. R., Harris III, F., & Mmeje, K. C. (2005) A theoretical model to explain the overrepresentation of college men among campus judicial offenders: Implications for campus administrators. *NASPA Journal, 42,* 565–588.

Hawkes, H. E. (1930). College administration. *Journal of Higher Education, 1,* 245–253.

Hawkes, H. E., & Hawkes, A. L. R. (1945). *Through a dean's open door: A guide for students, parents and counselors.* New York: McGraw-Hill.

Hayes, J. A., & Balogh, C. P. (1990). Mediation: An emerging form of dispute resolution on college campuses. *NASPA Journal, 27,* 236–240.

Healy M. A., & Liddell, D. L. (1998). The developmental conversation: Facilitative moral and intellectual growth in our students. In D. L. Cooper & J. M. Lancaster (Eds.), *Beyond law and policy: Reaffirming the role of student affairs* (New Direction for Student Services, No. 83, pp. 39–48). San Francisco: Jossey-Bass.

Henning, G. (2007). Is in consortio cum parentibus the new in loco parentis? *NASPA Journal, 44,* 538–560.

Hentoff, N. (1992). *Free speech for me—but not for thee: How the American Left and Right relentlessly censor each other.* New York: HarperCollins.

Heumann, M., & Church, T. W. (Eds.) (1997). *Hate speech on campus: Case, case studies, and commentary.* Boston: Northeastern University Press.

Higher Education Amendments of 1992, Pub. L. No. 102-325, 106 Stat. 448 (1998).

Higher Education Amendments of 1998, Pub. L. No. 105-244, 112 Stat. 1581 (1998).

Higher Education Opportunity Act of 2008, Pub. L. No. 110-315, 122 Stat. 3078 (2008).

Hill v. Michigan State University, 182 F. Supp. 2d 621 (W.D. Mich. 2001).

Hodges, M. W. (1996). First Amendment and judicial affairs. In W. L. Mercer (Ed.), *Critical issues in judicial affairs: Current trends in practice.* (New Directions for Student Services No. 73, pp. 53–66). San Francisco: Jossey-Bass.

Hodgkinson, H. L. (1985). *All one system: Demographics of education–Kindergarten through graduate school.* Washington, D.C.: Institute for Educational Leadership.

Hoekema, D. A. (1994). *Campus rules and moral community: In place of in loco parentis.* Lanham, MD: Rowan & Littlefield.

Holmes, R. C., Edwards, K., & DeBowes, M. M. (2009). Why objectivity is not enough: The critical role of social justice in campus conduct work. In J. M. Schrage & N. G. Giacomini (Eds.), *Reframing campus conflict: Student conduct practice through a social justice lens.* Sterling, VA: Stylus.

Howell, M. T. (2005). Students' perceived learning and anticipated future behaviors as a result of participation in the student judicial process. *The Journal of College Student Development, 46,* 374–392.

Inter-Association Task Force on Alcohol and Other Drug Abuse. (n.d.). *Parental notification.* Retrieved from www.iatf.org/parent1a.htm

Janosik, S. M. (1995). Judicial decision-making and sanctioning: Agreement among students, faculty, and administrators. *NASPA Journal, 32,* 138–144.

Janosik, S. M., & Riehl. J. (2000). Stakeholder support for flexible due process in campus disciplinary hearings. *NASPA Journal, 37,* 444–453.

Janosik, S. M., & Stimpson, M. (2009). Improving outcomes assessment in student conduct administration. *Journal of Student Conduct Administration, 2,* 46–56.

Jendrek, M. P. (1989). Faculty reactions to academic dishonesty. *Journal of College Student Development, 30,* 401–406.

Kaplin, W. A., & Lee, B. A. (1997). *A legal guide for student affairs professionals.* San Francisco: Jossey-Bass.

Kaplin, W. A., & Lee, B. A. (2000). *Year 2000 cumulative supplement to the law of higher education* (3rd ed.). Washington, DC: National Association of College and University Attorneys.

Kaplin, W. A., & Lee, B. A. (2006). *The law of higher education* (4th ed.). San Francisco: Jossey-Bass.

Karp, D. R. (2004). Introducing restorative justice to the campus community. In D. R. Karp & T. Allena (Eds.), *Restorative community justice on the college campus: Promoting student growth and responsibility, and reawakening the spirit of campus community* (pp. 5–15). Springfield, IL: Charles C Thomas.

Karp, D. R., & Allena, T. (Eds.). (2004). *Restorative community justice on the college campus: Promoting student growth and responsibility, and reawakening the spirit of campus community.* Springfield, IL: Charles C Thomas.

Keller, M. L. (1985). Shall the truce be unbroken: New Jersey v. T.L.O. and higher education. *Journal of College and University Law, 12,* 415–427.

Kibler, W. L. (1993a). Academic dishonesty: A student development dilemma. *NASPA Journal, 30,* 252–267.

Kibler, W. L. (1993b). A framework for addressing academic dishonesty from a student development perspective. *NASPA, 31,* 8–18.

Kibler, W. L. (1998). Addressing academic dishonesty & promoting academic integrity. In B. G. Paterson & W. L. Kibler (Eds.), *The administration of student discipline: Student, organizational, and community issues* (pp. 161–175). Asheville, NC: College Administration Publications.

King, P. M. (1990). Assessing development from a cognitive-developmental perspective. In D. G. Creamer & Associates, *College student development: Theory and practice for the 1990s* (pp. 81–98). Alexandria, VA: American College Personnel Association.

Knock, G. H. (1985). Development of student services in higher education. In M. J. Barr, L. A. Keating, & Associates, *Developing effective student services programs* (pp. 15–42). San Francisco: Jossey-Bass.

Kohlberg, L. (1969). Stage and sequence: The cognitive-developmental approach to socialization. In D. Goslin (Ed.), *Handbook of socialization theory and research* (pp. 347–380). Chicago: Rand McNally.

Kors, A. C., & Silvergate, H. A. (1998). *The shadow university: The betrayal of liberty on America's campuses.* New York: Free Press.

Krasnow v. Virginia Polytechnic Institute, 551 F.2d 591 (4th Cir. 1977).

Kuh, G. D. (1990). The demographic juggernaut. In M. J. Barr, M. L. Upcraft, &

Associates, *New futures for student affairs* (pp. 71–97). San Francisco: Jossey-Bass.

Lake, P. F. (2009, April 17). Student discipline: The case against legalistic approaches. *Chronicle of Higher Education,* pp. A31, A32.

Lamont, L. (1979). *Campus shock.* New York: Dutton.

Lancaster, J. M., & Cooper, D. L. (1998). Standing at the intersection: Reconsidering the balance in administration. In D. L. Cooper & J. M. Lancaster (Eds.), *Beyond law and policy: Reaffirming the role of student affairs* (New Direction for Student Services, No. 82, pp. 95–106). San Francisco: Jossey-Bass.

Lancaster, J. M., Cooper, D. L., & Harman, A. E. (1993). Current practices in student disciplinary administration. *NASPA Journal, 30,* 108–119.

Lancaster, J. M., & Waryold, D. M. (2008). Finding our voice as a profession. In J. M. Lancaster & D. M. Waryold (Eds.) *Contemporary administration of student conduct and ethical development on college campuses* (pp. 279–294). Sterling, VA: Stylus.

Lederman, D. (1995, February 3). Colleges report rise in violent crime. *Chronicle of Higher Education,* pp. A3 1, 42.

Leonard, E. A. (1956). *Origins of personnel services in American higher education.* Minneapolis: University of Minnesota Press.

Leslie, D. W., & Satryb, R. P. (1974). Due process on due process? Some observations. *Journal of College Student Personnel, 15,* 340–345.

Lopez-Philips, M., & Trageser, S. P. (2008). Development and diversity: A social justice model. In J. M. Lancaster & D. M. Waryold (Eds.), *Contemporary administration of student conduct and ethical development on college campuses* (pp. 119–134). Sterling, VA: Stylus.

Lowery, J. W. (1998a, Fall). Balancing students' right to privacy with the public's right to know. *Synthesis: Law and Policy in Higher Education, 10,* 713–715, 730.

Lowery, J. W. (1998b). Institutional policy and individual responsibility: Communities of justice and principle. In D. L. Cooper & J. M. Lancaster (Eds.), *Beyond law and policy: Reaffirming the role of student affairs* (New Direction for Student Services, No. 83, pp. 15–27). San Francisco: Jossey-Bass.

Lowery, J. W. (1998c). The Silent Generation makes some noise: Student protest at Bowling Green State University (October 1949 and May 1957). *Ohio College Student Development Journal,* 1, 9–26.

Lowery, J. W. (1999, Fall). Understanding and applying the Campus Security Act. *Synthesis: Law and Policy in Higher Education, 11,* 785–787, 799-800.

Lowery, J. W. (2000, Fall). FERPA and the Campus Security Act: Law and policy overview. *Synthesis: Law and Policy in Higher Education, 12,* 849–851, 864.

Lowery, J. W. (2004). Battling over Buckley: The press and access to student disciplinary records. In D. Bakst & S. Burgess (Eds.), *Student privacy review: An annual review and compendium for higher education leaders* (pp. 40–45). Palm Beach Gardens, FL: Council on Law in Higher Education.

Lowery, J. W. (2005). Legal issues regarding partnering with parents: Misunderstood federal laws and potential sources of institutional liability. In K. Keppler, R. H. Mullendore, & A. Carey (Eds.), *Partnering with the parents of today's college students* (pp. 43–51). Washington, DC: NASPA–Student Affairs Administrators in Higher Education.

Lowery, J. W. (2006). The intersection of law and alternative practice: Current due process requirements. In J. Lancaster (Ed.), *Exercising power with wisdom–The bridge from legal to developmental practice* (pp. 17–32). Asheville, NC: College Administration Publications.

Lowery, J. W. (2007). Legal implications of campus crime. In J. F. L. Jackson & M. C. Terrell (Eds.), *Creating and maintaining safe college campuses: A sourcebook for enhancing and evaluating safety programs* (pp. 205–220). Sterling, VA: Stylus Publishing.

Lowery, J. W. (2008). Laws, policies, and mandates. In J. M. Lancaster & D. M. Waryold (Eds.), *Contemporary administration of student conduct and ethical development on college campuses* (pp. 71–96). Sterling, VA: Stylus.

Lowery, J. W., & Dannells, M. (2009, March). *Change & challenges: A longitudinal study of student conduct policies and procedures.* NASPA Conference, Seattle, WA.

Lowery, J. W., Palmer, C., & Gehring, D. D. (2005). Policies and practices of parental notification for student alcohol violations. *NASPA Journal, 42,* 415–429.

Mager, T. R. (1978). A new perspective for the First Amendment in higher education. In E. H. Hammond & R. H. Shaffer (Eds.), *The legal foundations of student personnel services in higher education* (pp. 12–23). Washington, DC: American College Personnel Association.

Martin, J. E., & Janosik, S. M. (2004). The use of legal terminology in student conduct codes: A content analysis. *NASPA Journal, 42,* 36–50.

May, D. L., & Lloyd, B. H. (1993). Academic dishonesty: The honor system and students' attitudes. *Journal of College Student Development, 34,* 125–129.

McBee, M. L. (1982). Moral development: From direction to dialog. *NASPA Journal, 20*(1), 30–35.

McCabe, D. L., & Bowers, W. J. (1994). Academic dishonesty among males in college: A thirty-year perspective. *Journal of College Student Development, 35,* 5–10.

Miller, T. K., & Prince, J. S. (1976). *The future of student affairs.* San Francisco: Jossey-Bass.

Mueller, K. H. (1961). *Student personnel work in higher education.* Boston: Houghton-Mifflin.

Mullane, S. P. (1999). Fairness, educational value, and moral development in the student disciplinary process. *NASPA Journal, 36,* 86–95.

National Education Association Task Force on Student Involvement. (1971). *Code of student rights and responsibilities.* Washington, DC: National Education Association.

Nuss, E. (1998). Redefining college and university relationships with students. *NASPA Journal, 35,* 183–191.

O'Neil, R. M. (1997). *Free speech in the college community.* Bloomington, IN: Indiana University Press.

O'Neil, R. M. (2003, August 1). . . . But litigation isn't the wrong response. *Chronicle of Higher Education,* p. B9.

Ostroth, D. D., Armstrong, M. R., & Campbell, T. J., III. (1978). A nationwide survey of judicial systems in large institutions of higher education. *Journal of College Student Personnel, 19,* 21–27.

Ostroth, D. D., & Hill, D. E. (1978). The helping relationship in student discipline.

NASPA Journal, 16(2), 33–39.

Paine v. Bd. of Regents, 355 F. Supp. 199, 203 (W.D. Tex. 1972), aff'd, 474 F.2d 1397 (5th Cir. 1973).

Palmer, C. J., Lohman, G., Gehring, D. D., Carlson, S., & Garrett, O. (2001). Parental notification: A new strategy to reduce alcohol abuse on campus. *NASPA Journal, 38,* 372–385.

Palmer, C. J., Lowery, J. W., Wilson, M. E., & Gehring, D. D. (2003). Parental notification policies, practices, and impacts in 2000 and 2002. *Journal of College and University Student Housing, 31*(2), 3–6.

Parr, P., & Buchanan, F. T. (1979). Responses to the law: A word of caution. *NASPA Journal, 17*(2), 12–15.

Parrish, B. W., Fern, M. S., & Dickman, M. M. (1998). Search and seizure considerations in university-owned housing: Implications for practice. *Journal of College Student Development, 39,* 264–272.

Paterson, B. G. (1994). Freedom of expression and campus dissent. *NASPA Journal, 31,* 186–194.

Paterson, B. G. (1998). Expression, harassment and hate speech: Free speech or conduct code violation. In B. G. Paterson & W. L. Kibler (Eds.), *The administration of student discipline: Student, organizational, and community issues* (pp. 113–126). Asheville, NC: College Administration Publications.

Paterson, B. G., & Kibler, W. L. (2008). Incivility on college campuses. In J. M. Lancaster & D. M. Waryold (Eds.), *Contemporary administration of student conduct and ethical development on college campuses* (pp. 175–201). Sterling, VA: Stylus.

Patton, L. D., Howard-Hamilton, M., & Hinton, K. G. (2006). Student development and student conduct practice. In J. Lancaster (Ed.), *Exercising power with wisdom—The bridge from legal to developmental practice* (pp. 77–95). Asheville, NC: College Administration Publications.

Pavela, G. (1985). *The dismissal of students with mental disorders.* Asheville, NC: College Administration Publications.

Pavela, G. (1992, July 19). Today's college students need both freedom and structure. *Chronicle of Higher Education,* pp. B1, B2.

Pavela, G. (2000, Spring). Applying the power of association on campus: A model code of student conduct. *Synthesis: Law and Policy in Higher Education, 11,* 817–823, 829–831.

Pavela, G. (2006a). Applying the power of association on campus: A model code of academic integrity. In J. Lancaster (Ed.), *Exercising power with wisdom—The bridge from legal to developmental practice* (pp. 151–158). Asheville, NC: College Administration Publications.

Pavela, G. (2006b). Model code of academic integrity. In J. Lancaster (Ed.), *Exercising power with wisdom—The bridge from legal to developmental practice* (pp. 159–170). Asheville, NC: College Administration Publications.

Pavela, G. (2006c). Model code of student conduct. In J. Lancaster (Ed.), *Exercising power with wisdom—The bridge from legal to developmental practice* (pp. 171–192). Asheville, NC: College Administration Publications.

Pavela, G. (2006d). Student ethical development and the power of friendship. In J.

Lancaster (Ed.), *Exercising power with wisdom–The bridge from legal to developmental practice* (pp. 117–128). Asheville, NC: College Administration Publications.

Pavela, G. (2008). Can we be good without god? Exploring applied ethics with members of student conduct hearing boards. In J. M. Lancaster & D. M. Waryold (Eds.), *Contemporary administration of student conduct and ethical development on college campuses* (pp. 112–118). Sterling, VA: Stylus.

Penney, J. F. (1967). Variations on a theme: In loco parentis. *Journal of College Student Personnel, 8,* 22–25.

People for the American Way. (1991). *Hate in the ivory tower: A survey of intolerance on college campuses and academia's response.* Washington, DC: Author.

Pitts, J. H. (1980). In loco parentis indulgentis? *NASPA Journal, 17*(4), 20–25.

Pruitt, D.A. (1996, May-June). The Carolinian's Creed. *About Campus, 1,* 27–29.

Ratliff, R. C. (1972). *Constitutional rights of college students: A study in case law.* Metuchen, NJ: Scarecrow Press.

Red & Black Publishing Company v. Board of Regents, 427 S.E.2d 257 (Ga. 1993).

Rhatigan, J. J. (2000). The history and philosophy of student affairs. In M. J. Barr, D. K. Desler, & Associates, *The handbook of student affairs administration* (2nd ed., pp. 3–24). San Francisco: Jossey-Bass.

Rhode, S. (1983). Use of legal counsel: Avoiding problems. In M.J. Barr (Ed.), *Student affairs and the law* (New Directions for Student Services, No. 22, pp. 67–80). San Francisco: Jossey-Bass.

Rhode, S. R., & Math, M. G. (1988). Student conduct, discipline, and control: Understanding institutional options and limits. In M.J. Barr & Associates, *Student services and the law* (pp. 152–178). San Francisco: Jossey-Bass.

Rudolph, F. (1990). *The American college & university: A history.* Athens, GA: The University of Georgia Press. (Original work published 1962).

Saddlemire, G. L. (1980). Professional developments. In U. Delworth, G. R. Hanson, & Associates, *Student services: A handbook for the profession* (pp. 25–44). San Francisco: Jossey-Bass.

Sandeen, A., & Rhatigan, J. J. (1990). New pressures for social responsiveness and accountability. In M. J. Barr, M. L. Upcraft, & Associates, *New futures for student affairs* (pp. 98–113). San Francisco: Jossey-Bass.

Schetlin, E. M. (1967). Disorders, deans, and discipline: A record of change. *Journal of the National Association for Women Deans, Administrators, and Counselors, 30,* 169–173.

Schrage, J. M. (2009). The Spectrum Model: Answering the call for a new approach to campus conflict and conflict work. *Journal of Student Conduct Administration, 2,* 20–25.

Schrage, J. M., & Giacomini N. G. (Eds.). (2009). *Reframing campus conflict: Student conduct practice through a social justice lens.* Sterling, VA: Stylus.

Schrage, J. M., & Thompson, M. C. (2009). Providing a spectrum of resolution options. In J. M. Schrage & N. G. Giacomini (Eds.), *Reframing campus conflict: Student conduct practice through a social justice lens.* Sterling, VA: Stylus.

Schuh, J. H., & Upcraft, M. L. (2001). Assessing an office of student conduct. In J. H. Schuh & M. L. Upcraft (Eds.), *Assessment practice in student affairs: An applications manual* (pp. 426–438). San Francisco: Jossey-Bass.

Schuster, S. K., Bird, L. E., & Mackin, M. B. (2008). First Amendment issues. In J. M. Lancaster & D. M. Waryold (Eds.), *Contemporary administration of student conduct and ethical development on college campuses* (pp. 202-215). Sterling, VA: Stylus.

Sebok, T. (2006). Restorative justice on campus: Repairing hamr and building community. In J. Lancaster (Ed.), *Exercising power with wisdom—The bridge from legal to developmental practice* (pp. 63–76). Asheville, NC: College Administration Publications.

Serr, R. L., & Taber, R. S. (1987). Mediation: A judicial affairs alternative. In R. Caruso & W. W. Travelstead (Eds.), *Enhancing campus judicial systems* (New Directions for Student Services, No. 39, pp. 73–84). San Francisco: Jossey-Bass.

Seward, D. M. (1961). Educational discipline. *Journal of the National Association for Women Deans, Administrators, and Counselors, 24,* 192–197.

Sherry, A. H. (1966). Governance of the university: Rules, rights, and responsibilities. *California Law Review, 54,* 23–39.

Shur, G. M. (1983). Contractual relationships. In M. J. Barr (Ed.), *Student affairs and the law* (New Directions for Student Services, No. 22, pp. 27–38). San Francisco: Jossey-Bass.

Shur, G. M. (1988). Contractual agreements: Defining relationships between students and institutions. In M. J. Barr & Associates, *Student services and the law* (pp. 74–97). San Francisco: Jossey-Bass.

Silverglate, H. A., French, D., & Lukianoff, G. (2005). *FIRE's guide to free speech on campus.* Philadelphia: Foundation for Individual Rights in Education.

Silverglate, H. A., & Lukianoff, G. (2003). Speech codes: Alive and well at colleges. *Chronicle of Higher Education,* pp. B7, B8.

Sims, O. H. (1971). Student conduct and campus law enforcement: A proposal. In O. S. Sims (Ed.), *New directions in campus law enforcement.* Athens, GA: University of Georgia, Center for Continuing Education.

Sisson, V. S., & Todd, S. R. (1995) Using mediation in response to sexual assault on college and university campuses. *NASPA Journal, 32,* 262–269.

Sloan, J. J. (1994). The correlates of campus crime: An analysis of reported crimes on college and university campuses. *Journal of Criminal Justice, 22,* 51–61.

Sluis, K. A. (2001). *An analysis of parent notification policy adoption in response to the Higher Education Amendments of 1998.* Unpublished master's thesis, Indiana University, Bloomington.

Smith, A. F. (1978). Lawrence Kohlberg's cognitive stage theory of the development of moral judgment. In L. Knefelkamp, C. Widick & C. A. Parker (Eds.), *Applying new developmental findings.* (New Directions in Student Services No. 4, pp. 53–67). San Francisco: Jossey-Bass.

Smith, D. B. (1994, Winter). Student discipline in American colleges and universities: A historical overview. *Educational Horizons,* 78–85.

Smith, G. P., & Kirk, H. P. (1971). Student discipline in transition. *NASPA Journal, 8,* 276–282.

Smith, J. M., & Strope, Jr., J. L. (1995). The Fourth Amendment: Dormitory room searches in public universities. *West's Education Law Quarterly, 4,* 429–440.

Snoxell, L. F. (1960). Counseling reluctant and recalcitrant students. *Journal of College Student Personnel, 2,* 16–20.

State ex rel The Miami Student v. Miami University, 680 N.E.2d 956 (Oh. 1997).

Steele, B. H., Johnson, D. H., & Rickard, S. T. (1984). Managing the judicial function in student affairs. *Journal of College Student Personnel, 25,* 337–342.

Stein, R. H. (1972). Discipline: On campus, downtown, or both, a need for a standard. *NASPA Journal, 10,* 41–47.

Stimpson, M. T., & Stimpson, R. L. (2008). Twenty-seven years of student conduct literature: Implications for practice, scholarship, and ASJA. *Journal of Student Conduct Administration, 1,* 14–31.

Stone, G. L., & Lucas, J. (1994). Disciplinary counseling in higher education: A neglected challenge. *Journal of Counseling and Development, 72,* 234–238.

Stoner, E. N., II. (1998). A model code for student discipline. In B. G. Paterson & W. L. Kibler (Eds.), *The administration of student discipline: Student, organizational, and community issues* (pp. 3–42). Asheville, NC: College Administration Publications.

Stoner, E. N., II, & Cerminara, K. (1990). Harnessing the "spirit of insubordination:" A model student disciplinary code. *Journal of College and University Law, 17,* 89–121.

Stoner, E. N., II, & Lowery, J. W. (2004). Navigating past the "spirit of insubordination:" A twenty-first century model student conduct code with a model hearing script. *Journal of College and University Law, 31,* 1–77.

Strickland, D. A. (1965). In loco parentis–legal mots and student morals. *Journal of College Student Personnel, 6,* 335–340.

Swinton, D. (2008). An analysis and overview of student disciplinary scholarship in higher education. *Journal of Student Conduct Administration, 1,* 45–60.

The Student Right-to-Know and Campus Security Act of 1990, 20 U.S.C. §1092 (1990).

Thelin, J. R. (2004). *A history of American higher education.* Baltimore: Johns Hopkins Press.

Thomas, R. (1987). Systems for guiding college student behavior: Growth or punishment? *NASPA Journal, 25,* 54–61.

Travelstead, W. W. (1987). Introduction and historical context. In R. Caruso & W. W. Travelstead (Eds.), *Enhancing campus judicial systems* (New Directions for Student Services No. 39, pp. 3–16). San Francisco: Jossey-Bass.

United States v. Miami Univ., 294 F.3d 797 (6th Cir. 2002).

U.S. Department of Education, Office of Postsecondary Education. (2001). *The incidence of crime on the campuses of U.S. postsecondary education institutions.* Washington, DC: Author.

U.S. Department of Education, Office of Postsecondary Education. (2005). *The handbook for campus crime reporting.* Washington, DC: Author. Retrieved from www.ed.gov/admins/lead/safety/handbook.pdf.

U.S. Department of Education, Final Rule 34 C.F.R. Part 99. 73 Federal Register 74806 (2008, December 9).

UWM Post v. Board of Regents, 744 F.Supp. 1163 (E.D. Wisc. 1991).

Van Alstyne, W. W. (1963). Procedural due process and state university students. *UCLA Law Review, 10,* 368–389.

Van Alstyne, W. W. (1966). The prerogatives of students, the powers of universities, and the due process of law. *Journal of the National Association for Women Deans, Administrators, and Counselors, 30,* 11–16.

Wagoner, J. L. (1976). *Thomas Jefferson and the education of a new nation.* Bloomington, IN: Phi Delta Kappa Educational Foundation.

Wagoner, J. L. (1986). Honor and dishonor in Mr. Jefferson's university: The antebellum years. *History of Education Quarterly, 26,* 155–179.

Warshaw, S., & Leahy, J. W., Jr. (1965). *The trouble in Berkeley: The complete history, in text and pictures, of the great student rebellion against the "new university."* Berkeley, CA: Diablo Press.

Warters, W. C. (2000). *Mediation in the campus community.* San Francisco: Jossey-Bass.

Warters, B., Sebok, T., & Goldblum, A. (2000). Making things right: Restorative justice comes to the campuses. *Conflict Management in Higher Education, 1*(1). Retrieved from http://www.campus-adr.org/cmher/reportarticles/Edition1_1/Restorative1_1.html.

Waryold, D. M. (1998). Increasing campus judicial board effectiveness: Are two heads truly better than one. In B. G. Paterson & W. L. Kibler (Eds.), *The administration of student discipline: Student, organizational, and community issues* (pp. 227–235). Asheville, NC: College Administration Publications.

Willenbrock, C. M. (2009, July/August). Courting change in judicial affairs: In a kinder gentler approach to judicial affairs the secret to improving student conduct. *Talking Stick, 26,* 36–43.

Williamson, F. G. (1956). Preventative aspects of disciplinary counseling. *Educational and Psychological Measurement, 16,* 68–81.

Williamson, F. G. (1961). *Student personnel services in colleges and universities.* New York: McGraw-Hill.

Williamson, F. G. (1963). A new look at discipline. *Journal of Secondary Education, 38,* 10–14.

Williamson, F. G., & Foley, J. D. (1949). *Counseling and discipline.* New York: McGraw-Hill.

Wilson, J. M. (1996). Processes for resolving student disciplinary matters. In W. L. Mercer (Ed.), *Critical issues in judicial affairs: Current trends in practice* (New Directions for Student Services No. 73, pp. 35–52). San Francisco: Jossey-Bass.

Wrenn, C. G. (1949). Student discipline in college. *Educational and Psychological Measurement, 9,* 625–633.

Young, D. P. (1970). *The legal aspects of student dissent and discipline in higher education.* Athens, GA: University of Georgia, Institute of Higher Education.

Young, D. P. (1972). The colleges and the courts. In L. J. Peterson & L. O. Garber (Eds.), *The yearbook of school law 1972* (pp. 201–260). Topeka, KS: National Organization on Legal Problems of Education.

Zacker, J. (1996). Evaluation in judicial affairs. In W. L. Mercer (Ed.), *Critical issues in judicial affairs: Current trends in practice.* (New Directions for Student Services No. 73, pp. 99–106). San Francisco: Jossey-Bass.

Zdziarski, E. L. (1998). Alternative dispute resolution: A new look at resolving campus conflict. In B. G. Paterson & W. L. Kibler (Eds.), *The administration of student discipline: Student, organizational, and community issues* (pp. 237–252). Asheville, NC: College Administration Publications.

Zdziarski, E. L., & Wood, N. L. (2008). Forums for resolution. In J. M. Lancaster & D. M. Waryold (Eds.), *Contemporary administration of student conduct and ethical development on college campuses* (pp. 97–111). Sterling, VA: Stylus.

Zelna, C. (2002). *Student portfolios.* Unpublished report. Office of Student Conduct, North Carolina State University, Raleigh, NC.

Zelna, C., & Cousins, P. (2002, May 30). Assessing judicial affairs at NC State University: Processes, techniques, and impact. NASPA NetResults. Retrieved from www.naspa.org/netresults.

Chapter 8

MULTICULTURAL AFFAIRS

Bettina Shuford

CULTURE AND MULTICULTURALISM

[We] have been entrusted with the difficult task of speaking about culture. But there is nothing in the world more elusive. . . . An attempt to encompass its meaning in words is like trying to seize the air in the hand when one finds that it is everywhere except within one's grasp. (Lowell, cited in Kuh & Whitt, 1988, p. 10)

There may indeed be as many different definitions of the term "culture" as there are people attempting to define it. However, there appears to be agreement regarding the various elements constituting culture. Generally, these include shared histories, languages, foods, dress, artifacts, symbols, traditions, customs, rites, rituals, ceremonies, other practices or patterns of behavior, belief systems, assumptions, philosophies or ideologies, values, norms, moral standards, ethical principles, and other common understandings (Kuh & Whitt, 1988). College students have many ties that bind them to their families, friends, home communities, religious institutions, and other aspects of their precollege lives. They arrive on campus with expectations, needs, and aspirations that have, to varying degrees, been shaped by their cultural experiences.

Once on campus, students begin to encounter other students that are different from themselves. Some students will embrace that diversity, while other students will seek out others whose cultural characteristics are similar to their own. Relationships with individuals that are similar to one's self provide social support and foster a sense of identity with and commitment to groups or subgroups where students feel welcome and comfortable. Depending on the extent to which broader institutional cultures support truly

245

inclusive campus communities, within which all members feel they genuinely "belong" or "matter," students may or may not develop similar identity with and commitment to their colleges or universities. Nevertheless, cultural experiences before and during college undoubtedly provide "a frame of reference within which to interpret the meaning of events and actions on and off campus" (Kuh & Whitt, 1988, p. 13).

Given this admittedly incomplete, but hopefully sufficient introduction to culture, what is multiculturalism and how are multicultural institutions to be defined? A multicultural organization as defined by Jackson and Hardiman (1994) in their Multicultural Organization Development (MCOD) Developmental Stage Model "reflects the contributions and interests of diverse cultural and social groups in its mission, operations and products or services. It acts on a commitment to eradicate social oppression in all forms within the system; includes the members of diverse cultural and social groups as full participants, especially in decisions that shape the system. Finally, it follows through on broader external social responsibilities, including support of efforts to eliminate all forms of social oppression and to educate others in multicultural perspectives" (Jackson, 2005, pp. 10–11). The model has six developmental stages that range from an exclusionary system on one end of the continuum to a multicultural system on the other end.

Depending on where campuses fall on the MCOD Developmental Stage Model, the cultural experiences and expectations that students bring with them to college may not be embraced in the same way by all students, particularly for students of color (Harper & Hurtado, 2007; Hurtado, Milem, Clayton-Pedersen, & Allen, 1999). Multicultural affairs offices and centers were established to reconcile the inconsistencies in students' experiences by creating a space on campus where students that were marginalized because of their culture could feel affirmed and connected to the institution.

Although the roles of multicultural affairs offices and centers have evolved overtime in terms of who gets served and program focus, the essential components of negotiating culture have remained at the core of their mission and purpose. A mono-cultural model was used during the first wave of these offices where the focus was on support for single identity groups. In the 1980s and 1990s, the scope of services was changed to a multicultural model to address the increasingly competing needs of other underrepresented groups on campus. In addition to providing direct services to underrepresented groups, these offices and centers also promoted cross-cultural awareness through programs and workshops for all students. The focus on culture in the current millennium has moved towards an intercultural model that advances a climate of inclusion where individual and group differences are valued.

THE BLESSINGS AND CHALLENGES OF INCLUSION

Willer (1992) quoted an ancient Chinese saying "May you be blessed with the opportunity to live in interesting times" (p. 161). Student affairs professionals have been blessed with opportunities to work with increasingly diverse student populations. Of course, this blessing is also a challenge. Simply stated, diversity often increases the potential for conflict. For example, when students of many races, religions, social backgrounds, sexual orientation, value systems, and sensibilities live together in "concentrated proximity" in residence halls, it becomes "inevitable that interpersonal tensions, misunderstandings, incivilities, and disharmonies will arise" (Amada 1994, p. 39). Consequently, higher education needs professionals that possess the knowledge skills and awareness needed to foster cross-cultural understanding and engagement among diverse student populations on campus.

Creating inclusive campus environments is challenging, but there is also great personal reward to be gained from helping create a campus "laboratory for learning how to live and interrelate in a complex world" (Spees & Spees, 1986, p. 5) and to prepare students to make significant contributions to that world. Pickert (1992) emphasized the need for college graduates to be "familiar with other cultures and their histories, languages, and institutions. . .[and] willing to consider perspectives held by people whose cultures differ from their own" (p. 61). Thus, opportunities for student affairs professionals to increase awareness and sensitivity, foster cross-cultural communication skills that contribute to human understanding and human development, and in other ways help make "the university experience the universal experience it should be" (Thielen & Limbird, 1992, p. 124) are perceived by many as "blessings."

Although many of the concepts addressed in this chapter apply to many diverse groups, page limitations clearly prohibit adequate discussion of issues pertaining to women (Jones, 1997; Whitt, Edison, Pascarella, Nora, & Terenzini, 1999); commuter students (Likins, 1991); and students with disabilities (Hitchings, Luzzo, Retish, Horvath, & Ristow, 1998; Hodges & Keller, 1999; Jones, Kalivoda, & Higbee, 1997). Therefore, the remainder of the chapter focuses on American underrepresented ethnic groups; biracial and multiracial students; lesbian, gay, bisexual, and transgender (LGBT) students; international students; religious diversity; and adult learners.

RACIAL/ETHNIC MINORITIES: DIVERSITY WITHIN
UNDERREPRESENTED ETHNIC GROUPS

In the 2008 report on Minorities in Higher Education, Ryu (2008) reported that in the last ten years, there has been substantial growth in the number of students enrolled in colleges and universities, particularly the number of students from underrepresented racial/ethnic groups. The rate of growth for these students increased from 24 percent to 29 percent between 1995 and 2005. During this same time period, the enrollment rate went from 10 percent to 12 percent for African American students, 7 percent to 10 percent for Latino students, 5 percent to 6 percent for Asian students and a steady enrollment for Native American students. The diversity found in the general population is now surfacing into higher education.

Although African Americans, Asian Pacific Americans, Latino Americans, and Native Americans comprise four broad racial/ethnic groups, there is considerable diversity within each of these groups. For example, Asian Pacific and Latino Americans have cultural heritages within many different countries, represent different ethnic or religious groups, speak different languages, wear different clothing, eat different foods, share different value systems, honor different traditions, and celebrate different holidays (Chan & Wang, 1991; Chew & Ogi, 1987; Kodama, McEwen, Liang, & Lee, 2001; O'Brien, 1993; Quevedo-Garcia, 1987; Torres, 2004). Similarly, American Indian tribes have "language differences and custom variations" (LaCounte, 1987, p. 66), and African Americans do not comprise a monolithic group within which all members share the same backgrounds, belief systems, expectations, aspirations, behavioral norms, or other cultural characteristics.

Even though many members of a specific cultural group may share certain experiences or perspectives, there are often exceptions that differentiate individual members of the group. Discussion of commonalities within and among groups may foster understanding of many group members, but should never be used to stereotype all members or to prejudge or make unfounded assumptions about a particular individual.

The History of Underrepresented Ethnic Groups in American Higher Education

Cultural groups are, to varying degrees, affected by their histories. What have been the histories of underrepresented racial/ethnic groups within American higher education?

African Americans

Although some African Americans were self-educated, served apprenticeships, and, to a limited extent, studied abroad (Thomas & Hill, 1987), only 28 African Americans received baccalaureates from American colleges prior to the Civil War (Bowles & DeCosta, 1971). Their pre-Civil War experiences with American higher education were limited to a few predominately White institutions (PWIs) that would accept African Americans, and a few historically Black institutions (HBIs) in existence at the time. Additional HBIs were founded during the years between the Civil War and 1890 (Bowles & DeCosta, 1971), after the second Morrill Act of 1890 provided the "funds for black education be distributed on a 'just and equitable basis'" (Ranbom & Lynch, 1987/1988, p. 17), and after the United States Supreme Court, in the case of *Plessy v. Ferguson,* ruled on the constitutionality of the "separate but equal" doctrine in 1896.

It was not until 1954 that the Supreme Court ruled, in *Brown v. Board of Education* and other cases, that separate but equal (or racial segregation within public education) was unconstitutional (Bowles & DeCosta, 1971; Ogletree, 2004). Still, some states continued to operate dual educational systems for African Americans and Whites (Williams, 1991) until Title VI of the Civil Rights Act of 1964 indicated that "no person in the United States, on the grounds of race, color, or national origin, be excluded from participation in, or be denied the benefits of, or be subjected to discrimination under any program or activity receiving federal financial assistance" (Malaney, 1987, p. 17). This legislation was largely responsible for opening the doors of PWIs to African Americans, and HBIs to whites. Although HBIs represented only about 3 percent of all colleges and universities in the United States, they enrolled approximately 12 percent of all African American college students in 2008 and awarded 19 percent of the total bachelor's degrees that year (Ryu, 2008).

Asian Pacific Americans

Asian Pacific Americans are the most recent group to immigrate to the United States in formerly unprecedented numbers. As a result of many military, economic, and political events (Min, 2006; Spring, 2007; Wright, 1987), between 1970 and 1980, the United States received "a steady stream of Asian immigrants and refugees" (Hsia & Hirano-Nakanishi, 1989, p. 22). The Asian American population more than doubled during this time period or grew at a rate "more than ten times that of the U.S. population as a whole" (Chew & Ogi, 1987, p. 40). Between 1987 and 2006, enrollment among Asian Pacific Americans in higher education increased by 61%, with nearly 61% enrolled in four-year colleges (Ryu, 2008).

Poverty, unemployment, and undereducation are not uncommon in some Asian Pacific American communities (Chan & Wang, 1991). Like other minority group members, Asian Pacific Americans are strongly connected to their communities and particularly to their families. The influence of traditional values is often dependent on environmental and contextual factors (Kodama, McEwen, Liang, & Lee, 2001). Factors such as generational status, immigration experiences, and acculturation add to the diversity and complexity of the Asian Pacific student populations (Kodama, McEwen, Liang, & Lee, 2001). Like some Latinos and Native Americans, some Asian Pacific Americans have difficulties with English, in part because English is seldom or never spoken in their homes.

Although campus racial incidents are often described in terms of African Americans and whites, "other students of color, including those of Hispanic and Asian origins, have likewise been affected by rising racial tensions in colleges and universities" (Chan & Wang, 1991, p. 43). Asian Pacific Americans are sometimes victimized or ostracized by their non-Asian peers. A given student may be the "only" Asian Pacific American (or one of very few) in the classroom, residence hall, or other campus environments.

As a result of many commonalities, Asian Pacific Americans have often joined with other underrepresented ethnic groups to request or demand campus programs and services for students of color. For example, Asian American Studies programs were developed following student protests in 1968–69 seeking "ethnic studies programs that would highlight the history and contemporary experiences of nonwhite groups in the United States, in order to counter the existing Eurocentric curriculum that either failed to include any information about people of color, or worse, badly distorted the latter's history" (Chan & Wang, 1991, p. 46).

One rather unique challenge faced by Asian Pacific American students is that they have been characterized as the "model minority" (Chan & Wang, 1991; Suzuki, 2002), in part because many Asian Pacific Americans do well in school. This stereotype, however, minimizes the fact that, like many other students, they must struggle with their academic endeavors. Further, it discounts the hard work many have done in order to succeed. Despite success in college, Asian Pacific students report a lower level of satisfaction with the college experience (Tan, 1994). High levels of enrollment and persistence of Asian Pacific students should not override the fact that special assistance is still needed by these students.

Latino Americans

MacDonald and Garcia (2003) in their essay on Latino access provided a historical view of Latinos in higher education from 1848 to 1990. They described five major eras of access into higher education for Latinos. The first period occurred between 1848 and the1920s where participation in college came from the privileged classes in the new territories following the Treaty of Guadalupe Hidalgo in 1848. During this period, the University of California admitted forty Latino students in 1869. The second era occurred between 1898 and 1920 following the imperial conquest of Puerto Rico and the creation of the University of Puerto Rico where the emphasis was on teacher training and industrial education. In the period between the 1920s and 1950s (the third stage), the first generation of working class Latino students entered higher education as a result of the GI bill and other philanthropic organizations. Latinos started entering into higher education in larger numbers between 1960 and 1980 (the fourth stage), following the era of civil rights demands. According to Wright (1987), "the collegiate history of Hispanics had scarcely begun before World War II. Even when they were admitted, Hispanics often had to deny or restrict their cultural identity in order to matriculate" (p. 7). Not until 1968, primarily as a result of the Civil Rights movement, particularly the "La Raza" movement, and the Civil Rights legislation described earlier in this chapter, did large numbers of Latino students participate in American higher education, primarily at two-year colleges (Wright, 1987). The last era described by MacDonald and Garcia occurred in the 1980s and 1990s. Through lobbying efforts, the federal government began to set policies that supported Latino access. Latino serving institutions were also designated during this period.

More recently, Latinos experienced the largest growth rate for college enrollment among the four major underrepresented ethnic groups with a gain of 66 percent between 1985 and 2005 (Ryu, 2008). In 2005, Latinos received 6.8 percent of all bachelor's degrees and 10.7 percent of the associates degrees awarded in the United States (Ryu, 2008). Although Latinos are the fastest growing underrepresented ethnic group in the U.S., they still remain underrepresented in higher education (Llagas & Snyder, 2003).

HSIs, HBIs, and tribal colleges have been successful in recruiting, retaining, and graduating substantial numbers of underrepresented ethnic students, many of them from lower socioeconomic backgrounds and with admissions credentials suggesting that they may be academically marginal college students. This success may be related to the extent to which these colleges and universities provide academic programs, student services, and psychosocial support systems that are congruent with the cultural identities of their students.

Native Americans

Native American tribal nations undoubtedly socialized, acculturated, trained, and educated their own members throughout their history. The education of Native Americans by non-Native Americans began at least as early as 1568, when Spanish missionaries established schools to Christianize Native Americans in what is now Florida. For many years thereafter, European settlers made sporadic efforts to train or educate Native Americans (Ranbom & Lynch, 1987/1988). For example, special facilities for Native

American students were provided at William and Mary in 1723, and "the Continental Congress approved $500 in 1773 for the education of Indians at Dartmouth College" (LaCounte, 1987, p. 65). Despite these early efforts, "only in very recent years have white institutions, with any fervor, sought Indian students" (Wright, 1987, p. 7).

Tribal colleges have played a significant role in the education of Native American students. The first tribal college opened in 1968. Currently, there are 32 tribal colleges with the majority being community colleges (National Center for Education Statistics, 2008a). These colleges are located in twelve states, ranging "from California to Michigan, and from Arizona to North Dakota" (Boyer, 1997, p. 3). Like many other two-year institutions, tribal colleges are attempting to increase their communication with four-year institutions in order to enable more of the students who begin college in familiar surroundings (e.g., on their own reservations) to continue their education (LaCounte, 1987).

Native Americans continue to be underrepresented in higher education (Darden, Bagakas, Armstrong, Payne, 1994). Their low matriculation rates, particularly at off-reservation four-year institutions, are related to a high school dropout rate of approximately 45 percent, underpreparation for college, limited financial resources, and inadequate assistance when they apply for financial aid. Strong ties to family and community, culture shock in moving away from primarily Native American environments, low participation in orientation programs, insufficient personal and academic support systems for Native American students on campus, and lack of Native American professionals serving as role models also affect their adjustment to the college environment (LaCounte, 1987).

Summary

Although historically black institutions (HBIs) and a few almost all-white institutions have provided undergraduate education for relatively small numbers of students of color over the course of many years, it was not until the 1960s and later, well over 300 years after the founding of Harvard, that substantial numbers of students of color entered American higher education. Many are currently enrolled at HBIs, HSIs, tribally-controlled institutions, urban commuter institutions, and two-year community colleges. For many reasons related to both historical and current realities, racial/ethnic minorities continue to be underrepresented in higher education, particularly at predominantly white, residential, four-year, and graduate/professional institutions.

MINORITY STUDENT SERVICES AND MULTICULTURAL AFFAIRS

Historical Overview

When large numbers of diverse students, particularly African Americans, began to appear on predominantly white campuses during the 1960s, little was done to address their special needs (Pounds, 1987; Young, 1986). A laissez-faire attitude on the part of faculty and administration may have been based on the naïve assumptions that underrepresented ethnic students would simply assimilate into the institutional culture with no effort by the institution to meet the needs of these students (Gibbs, 1973). According to Quevedo-Garcia (1987), assimilation requires "relinquishing one's cultural identity" (p. 52) and developing a new identity that coincides with the new or dominant culture. These underrepresented ethnic students, most of whom had no desire to sacrifice their cultural identities in order to "fit into" the campus culture, "felt isolated, lonely, alienated, and disenfranchised" (Fleming, 1984; Gibbs, 1973; Young, 1986). They realized they were "in these universities but not of these universities" (Stennis-Williams, Terrell, & Haynes, 1988, p. 74) or as a guest in someone else's house (Turner, 1994). Many responded with apathy or anger (Young, 1986).

In response to student protests and community pressure, along with court orders enforcing new laws emanating from the Civil Rights movement, institutions developed offices of minority student services (Wright, 1987), which many students of color considered "safe havens in an alien environment" (Young, 1986, p. 18). At approximately the same time, black houses and cultural centers were established (Patton, 2005) and functioned in a similar manner to minority student services offices. Minority student services were not limited to only serving undergraduate students. Similar offices were established in professional schools (Ballard, 2003). TRIO and Upward Bound programs were also established in this same time period in response to government mandates (Pounds, 1987). These offices were designed to prepare students from low-income or disadvantaged families for college, recruit them to college, and assist them once they were in college (Shuford, in press). Many of the participants in theses special service programs were first-generation underrepresented ethnic students. Today, some of these earlier programs, along with newer endeavors, continue to identify talented individuals; provide pre-college enrichment programs, which may include daylong or summer-long experiences on college campuses; and offer valuable services to students once they are enrolled in higher education (J. A. Taylor, Jr., personal communication, November 28, 1995).

Although some professionals within offices of minority student services assisted with or were responsible for precollege enrichment and minority student recruitment programs, most were charged with responding to the needs of already-enrolled students of color. Many provided leadership develop-ment and advising for increasing numbers of diverse student groups (e.g., Latino Student Union, Native American Student Associations, Black Greek Letter Organizations) and offered academic and financial aid advising, tutor-ing services, personal counseling, career development and placement servic-es, student activities, and cultural programs (J. A. Taylor, Jr., personal com-munication, November 28, 1995). In some ways, these offices served as mini-student affairs divisions for minority students. These offices also focused their work from a mono-cultural model where the emphasis was on targeting serv-ices towards the most disadvantaged group(s) on campus. The targeted groups varied by geographic difference, in the south, African Americans were the primary target group and in the southwest, Latinos and Native American students were the primary receivers of service (Shuford, in press).

Gradually, over the course of several years, many offices of minority stu-dent services evolved into offices of multicultural affairs, "due, in part, to an increased demand of services from other underrepresented groups and a heightened awareness of these groups in the greater society" (Shuford, in press). Although most of these offices still provided many valuable services to underrepresented ethnic students, their missions began to include a num-ber of outreach projects within the broader institutional community and to serve other underrepresented groups on campus (Shuford, in press; Sutton, 1998). For example, many staff in minority student services began to help their colleagues in other student affairs units to recognize, be sensitive to, and respond appropriately to cultural issues so that, for example, those in the Academic Advising Center could be effective academic advisers for diverse students. As the transition from minority student services to multicultural affairs offices began to take place, the mission of these offices expanded to include programs and services for LGBT students, international students, religious diversity, biracial students, first-generation students, and adult stu-dent learners. With the expansion of services to a broader community, mul-ticultural affairs offices began to shift to a multicultural model that included cross-cultural learning for all students.

Student affairs professionals who worked in offices of minority student services or multicultural affairs helped to develop major programs (e.g., those associated with Black History Month) and campus cultural centers (e.g., La Casa Latino Cultural Centers), which were designed to address the educational needs of both underrepresented groups and majority students. In addition, they often assisted their faculty colleagues in developing individual courses (e.g., Asian American History), departments (e.g., Black Studies), and interdepartmental programs related to ethnic studies, which emerged on many campuses in the late-1960s and 1970s (Chan & Wang, 1991) and expanded during the1980s and 1990s.

Expansion of Services

Other social justice movements came on the heel of the civil rights movement. As other underrepresented groups began to have a stronger voice in society and on campus, multicultural affairs offices moved away from the monocultural model that included work with single identity groups to a multicultural model that began to focus on individual and group differences. Partial listings of these groups are identified in this section.

Biracial/Multiracial Students

In the 2000 census, more than 6.8 million people selected more than one racial or ethnic category to identify themselves. Of that number, 40 percent were under the age of 18, which has significant implications for higher education (Jaschik, 2006). The focus on biracial individuals became more prominent in recent years due to individuals such as Tiger Woods and President Barack Obama being open to talk about their mixed race heritage. In his book, "Dreams of My Father," Barack Obama talked about the fear of not belonging and remaining an outsider (Obama, 2007). The feeling of being an outsider is not uncommon among biracial/multiracial individuals. In a study conducted by Talbot (2008), the participants had difficulty expressing what it is like to be a biracial student in a mono-cultural world.

On the college campus, biracial/multiracial students are sometimes confronted with having to choose one aspect of their identity over another (Talbot, 2008), or not feeling accepted in monoracial spaces on campus (King, 2008; Renn, 2003). Biracial students, similar to other underrepresented students, need to have a space on campus where they can feel safe and supported (Renn, 2003). Multicultural affairs offices and centers can create such support by acknowledging biracial/multiracial students in their mission statement, establishing a biracial/multiracial student organization, and providing programs that have a multiracial focus (Wong & Buckner, 2008).

Lesbian, Gay, Bisexual, Transgender Students (LGBT)

On many campuses, LGBT students have added their voice to the multicultural playing field. Support for LGBT issues within colleges and universities has increased within the last decade as "more faculty, staff, and students take the risk of openly identifying as lesbian, gay, bisexual, or transgender and actively work to increase the awareness of institutions about the needs and concerns of LGBT people" (Evans & Wall, 2000, p. 390). The range of support varies from institution to institution, from recognition of a LGBT student organization, support and educational programming from multicultural affairs offices or cultural centers, to specific offices designated to address GLBT issues (Sanlo, 2000).

Some multicultural affairs offices provide support services to LGBT students; however, the support and services needed by these students are often times different from the needs of other underrepresented groups (McRee & Cooper, 1998; Rankin, 2005). LGBT students not only face the range of typical developmental issues of college students, but must also cope with developmental issues related to their sexual identity (Bilodeau & Renn, 2005; Wall & Evans, 1991). While "most lesbian and gay adults acknowledge their affectional orientation to themselves during adolescence" (p. 140), the coming-out process does not usually begin until they reach college (D'Augelli, 1991). Additionally, LGBT students must also deal with harassment, homophobic attitudes, religions backlash, family and social relationships (D'Augelli, 1991; Levine & Love, 2000; Rhoads, 1997).

Multicultural affairs programming should target both LGBT students and heterosexual students (Evans & Wall, 2000). Support services for LGBT students should include social networks for students who may be struggling with identity, role models who can offer insights and share experiences on the coming out process, special interest housing, social events, and programs about coming out and LGBT identity development (Evans & Wall, 2000; Herbst & Malaney, 1999; Rhoads, 1997). The provision of programs and services for LGBT students should also recognize the diversity within the LGBT community (Evans & Wall, 2000).

International Students

The presence of international students in American higher education is growing in significant numbers. There are over six hundred thousand international students studying in U.S. colleges and universities representing 3.5 percent of the U.S. higher education enrollment (Institute of International Education, 2008a). The international exchange of students has transformed many American campuses (Ping, 1999). International students have begun to integrate into campus life and have been instrumental in educating American students about global life (Ping, 1999). International students are very open to sharing information about their countries, national histories, and cultures (McIntire, 1992). The challenge is creating forums where American and International students can engage in information sharing about their cultural backgrounds. In addition to the cultural diversity that international students bring to campus, the recruitment of international students has been used to enhance enrollment on campuses (Dalton, 1999). Although, such efforts have become more challenging due to the requirement by the federal government to maintain and update student information in the Student and Exchange Visitor Information System (SEVIS) by campus officials (Starobin, 2006). An international student presence on U.S. campuses has an economic impact on individual campuses and to the economy as well. According to the Open Doors report, "international students contribute over 15.5 billion dollars to the U.S. economy, through their expenditures on tuition and living expenses" (Institute of International Education, 2008b, p 3).

Despite the benefits of having an international presence on campus, international students face some distinct challenges when transitioning to a new environment that include difficulties related to psychological issues, academic issues and needs, sociocultural issues, residential transition challenges, counseling and health services, tuition costs, documentation issues, safety threats, dietary restrictions, and career development issues (Anderson, Carmichael, Harper, & Huang, 2009). Therefore, a variety of support services are needed to assist international students with their transition to their new environment.

On many campuses, there is a designated office or staff person to work with international students. Multicultural affairs offices are also beginning to provide support for international students and international programming. On campuses where there are several hundred international students, international student services offices serve as a mini-student affairs division (McIntire, 1992). Some best practices for effectively engaging international students on campus whether it is coordinated in an international student services office or in a multicultural affairs office include providing cross-cultural mentoring programs; family-style peer mentoring; hiring international residence hall staff; providing international focused programs in the residence halls; expanding dietary options on campus and in the community; providing a pre-orientation prior to their arrival on campus, as well as an ongoing orientation; increasing the awareness of domestic students about international students' needs; creating a one-stop-shop where international students can go to lounge, interact and address their problems; publicizing campus events in different languages; hiring culturally competent mental and physical health professionals; providing career center services to assist international students with employment opportunities; employing international students to tutor domestic students in learning other languages; and conducting assessment and evaluation of support services for international students (Anderson, Carmichael, Harper, & Huang, 2009).

International-focused programs can also be provided for all students on campus. For example, International Education Week occurs in the month of November and was established by the U.S. Department of State and the U.S. Department of Education to prepare Americans for a global society (U.S. Department of State and U.S. Department of Education, 2009a; Starobin, 2006). Suggested activities for International Education Week include hosting an international career day, organizing a symposium with an international theme, inviting individuals with an international experience to give a talk on the importance of international education and exchange, or organizing an international festival (U.S. Department of State & U.S. Department of Education, 2009b). Multicultural Affairs staff can play an important role in sponsoring or co-sponsoring these events, as well as providing support for international student organizations.

Religious Diversity

Throughout the history of this country, religion has played an important role in the lives of many of its citizens. Religious beliefs are an essential element of cultural diversity in America. "[The] United States has always had a number of different religions" (Uphoff, 2001, p. 106) that have long been underestimated (Griffith, 2008). For example, "[t]he religions of Native Americans were in place when Europeans arrived" (Uphoff, 2001, p. 106). Religious diversity expanded in the U.S. following the Immigration and Nationality Act of 1965 (Griffith, 2008). "New arrivals–particularly from Asia, Africa, Latin American, and the Middle East–generated an upsurge of religions that were outside the historical American mainstream" (Griffith, 2008, p. 26). The U.S. is now a "spiritual mirror of the world's religion" (Griffith, 2008, p. 25).

An awareness of religious diversity on college campuses is essential in that it helps us understand the human diversity that exists within our learning communities. Although many college campuses have increasingly become more secular in their orientation, spirituality and religion are still valued by many students. In a national study conducted by the Higher Education Research Institute (HERI) at UCLA in early 2004, entering students reported having high spiritual interest and involvement. They also reported having high involvement in religion. Eighty-one percent of the students indicated they attended a religious service within the last year or discussed religion and spirituality with their friends. Despite their religious values, students also reported a high level of religious tolerance and acceptance for students that are non-religious. Liberal students rated higher on the ecumenical worldview scale (reflects interest in different religious traditions) than conservative students. Eight percent of the respondents identified themselves as Jewish, Buddhist, Hindu, Islamic, or from other non-Christian religions (Astin & Astin, 2005).

Problems occur when religious beliefs, customs, and traditions are not understood by other groups (Uphoff, 2001). Similar to underrepresented racial/ethnic groups, religions underrepresented groups also face feelings of marginalization on campus (Mahaffey & Smith, 2009). Some issues faced by underrepresented religious groups include feeling isolated, dietary restrictions (lack of kosher and halal options), scheduling exams and major campus events on religious holidays, inadequate campus spaces for living accommodations and worship, and lack of sufficient role models and support (Mahaffey & Smith, 2009).

Multicultural Affairs offices can play an important role in helping to educate the campus about the customs and beliefs of different religious groups on campus. For example, Mahaffey and Smith (2009) identified the following strategies to create an inclusive and engaging community for students from underrepresented religious groups.

1. Initiate dialogues with students where you simply ask them about their experiences.
2. Collaborate with others on campus to provide support services for students, including outside organizations that can meet their religious needs.
3. Raise awareness by distributing a calendar of religious holidays and establish policies and procedures to accommodate religious observances and other special needs.
4. Help new students find religious groups during orientation.
5. Support religious organizations by providing support and advisement from campus officials and leadership training to aid members in sustaining the organization.
6. Encourage mentoring with faculty, staff and alumni.
7. Offer alcohol-free environments (housing and social events).
8. Sponsor theme housing that serves specific religious groups.
9. Be conscious of religious diversity.
10. Be cognizant of intersecting identities (race, culture, gender, sexual orientation and religion). The same holds true within the Christian faith as well (Stewart & Lozano, 2009).
11. Develop multifaith programming.
12. Provide campus spaces to meet religious needs.
13. Consider layout and scheduling options at fitness facilities.

Adult Students

Although students eighteen and over are considered adults, the adult student is distinguished from the typical traditional student based on age, maturity, and competing roles and responsibilities (Kasworm, 2003). Some of the characteristics of adult students include delayed enrollment from high school to college, part-time attendance, financially independent, dependents other than a spouse or partner, single parent, completed high school with a GED (Horn, 1996) or stopped out of college for a period of time (Palmer, 2008).

The adult student population began to see significant increases on college campuses between 1971 and 1991. During that period, adult students increased from 28 percent to 43 percent of the total undergraduate enrollment. The rate of increase began to decline in the 1990s due to the increase of traditional college age students going to college. In recent years, the growth rate for adult students has begun to shift again. In 2006, 34.9 percent of traditional college-age students had earned at least an associates degree compared to 34.3 percent of the adult students (Ryu, 2008). According to the National Center for Education Statistics (2008b), adult students are projected to increase by 21 percent between 2005 and 2016, while traditional students are only expected to increase by 15 percent for this same time period.

The characteristics that separate adult students from traditional age students require a different set of services and support systems that aren't addressed in traditional higher education models. Some unique services for adult students might include an orientation session that addresses their unique needs; access to resources about child care and elder care, study skills and other support services; activities that include the family; support and discussion groups; and extended office hours for student services (Rice, 2003).

THE ROLES OF MULTICULTURAL AFFAIRS OFFICES AND CENTERS TODAY

Although the titles and organizational placements of offices focusing on multicultural affairs and/or centers, the clientele served by these offices, and the breadth and depth of their programs vary by institution (Shuford, in press; Stewart & Bridges, in press; Wright, 1987), professionals in these offices generally serve as educators and advisers for their colleagues across their campuses and coordinate multicultural endeavors for their institutions, while at the same time providing valuable services, programs, and role models for underrepresented groups on campus.

Missions

The mission of a multicultural affairs office or center should be threefold.

- The office should provide support to underrepresented cultural groups. This support should include assessment and other efforts designed to identify the psychosocial, academic, and other needs of underrepresented students; communication of these needs, along with recommendations for meeting them, to other units on campus; programs and services that enhance students' personal, social, educational, and cultural development; and efforts to encourage underrepresented cultural groups to participate in and contribute to the life of the campus.

- The office should provide multicultural education for all students. Educational endeavors should assist majority and students from under-represented populations to identify their commonalities and recognize, understand, accept, respect, and value their differences. Students should learn to relate to members of diverse groups, communicate effectively across racial or cultural lines, and transfer these skills to a variety of settings (Hoopes, 1979).
- The office should promote systemic change that fosters a multicultural perspective across the campus. As change agents, multicultural/inter-cultural affairs professionals should work with their colleagues across campus to develop a multicultural organization described elsewhere in this chapter that incorporates diverse perspectives into every facet of the institution, including its admissions and hiring practices, adminis-trative policies and procedures, academic curriculum, and co-curricular activities (Jackson, 2005). Only when every unit on campus and the institution as a whole address multicultural issues in an optimal manner, will multicultural affairs offices no longer be needed.

Professional Standards

Council for the Advancement of Standards in Higher Education (Dean, 2006) emphasized that multicultural student programs and services must include the following goals:

- Promote academic and personal growth,
- Create a just community,
- Promote access and equity for underrepresented populations, and offer programs that educate the campus about diversity.

The standards further state that the programs and services offered through a multicultural student program unit must promote student learning and devel-opment that is purposeful and holistic (Dean, 2006).

ADMINISTRATION AND ORGANIZATION STRUCTURE

The Council for the Advancement of Standards (Dean, 2006) provides a set of general guidelines related to the organization and management of mul-ticultural affairs offices. According to the standards, multicultural affairs offices "must be structured purposefully and managed effectively to achieve stated goals" (p. 262), which include written policies and procedures, performance expectations of employees, and stated goals. Managers of these units must have accurate information to make decisions and to establish goals and objectives, which can be achieved through assessment of student learning outcomes. The standards further state that multicultural affairs offices must be in an organization structure that can support the achievement of their services and programs to students.

Until recently, there has been no published empirical data on multicultural affairs offices and services. Bridges, Cubarubbia, and Stewart conducted a survey of multicultural student services in 2008 that looked at institutional type, size of the institution, general program information, personnel information, range of services provided, and organizational effectiveness (Stewart & Bridges, in press). Shuford (in press) conducted a study on the history of multicultural affairs offices. The results from these two studies provided a glimpse of how these offices and centers function in a higher education setting and are highlighted throughout this section. When asked how they defined multicultural populations on their campus, all of the respondents indicated that race and ethnicity were a determining factor in who received services. Some multicultural affairs offices also indicated support for LGBT students, international students, disability students, reflection on faith and religion, social class, English as a second language, veteran status, first-generation status, foster youth, and geographic origin (rural or urban) (Stewart & Bridges, in press).

Organization Structure

Most of the respondents from both studies indicated that their offices were located organizationally in student affairs. A smaller segment of offices was located in academic affairs and reported to a provost or to the president of the institution where they worked with diversity from a broader institutional perspective. A senior level position might include titles such as vice president, associate or assistant president, dean, or special assistant to the president (Williams & Wade-Gordon, 2006). Many of these offices were developed within the last ten years (Shuford, in press).

Administrative Role

The role of the multicultural affairs offices varied based on where they were placed organizationally. Multicultural affairs offices located in student affairs had a primary focus on social, cultural, and academic support programs for students. The role in academic affairs included academic support functions for students (Stewart & Bridges, in press). In the case of the chief diversity officer, the administrative role often encompassed the entire campus and included functions such as the ones listed below.

1. Functional approach—the chief diversity officer provides leadership in conceptualizing, orchestrating and assessing institutional approaches to addressing diversity and inclusion.
2. Collaboration—The scope of developing a diverse and inclusive campus far exceeds the capabilities of a single person or office. The chief diversity officer serves as a boundary spanner across multiple areas on campus and works to integrate diversity initiatives through collaboration.
3. Leading through status and influence—Although the chief diversity officer has the mandate to lead diversity efforts, an individual in this position often does not have the formal authority to punish or reward individuals outside his or her authority. However, due to the visibility of the position, the chief diversity officer is able to use the power of the position to influence outcomes and to keep the diversity agenda moving forward.
4. Promoting change—The chief diversity officer also serves as a change agent in leading the efforts for diversity and inclusion on campus (Williams & Wade-Golden, 2006).

Programs and Services

Respondents in the multicultural student services survey indicated that the range of services offered on their campuses fell into three categories. The majority of the respondents offered cultural and social programming through their office or center. Less than half of the respondents offered academic programs.

The Council for the Advancement Standards for Higher Education identified a broader set of programs and services that should be offered by a multicultural affairs office. According to the standards, the programs and services in a multicultural affairs office must be intentional, based on student development theory, reflective of the demographic profile, and responsive to the needs of the targeted population (Dean, 2006). The program and service expectations for multicultural affairs offices should include the following.

1. Educational programs and services that focus on cross-cultural awareness
2. Promoting the academic success of students
3. Promoting personal growth and self-awareness
4. Advocating for opportunities for student engagement with leadership development and access to mentors and role models

5. Promoting a just community
6. Offering programs that increase multicultural awareness, knowledge and skills; and serve as a resource for multicultural training and development
7. Assisting students holistically across the range of their experiences on campus (Dean, 2006, p. 261).

Staffing

The staffing levels in multicultural affairs offices, as reported by respondents in the multicultural student services survey, ranged from a low of one full-time professional to a high of 35 professional staff at one institution. Most offices had on average, two or four staff members beyond the director. When the respondents were asked about the title and educational level of the senior staff member in the office, most of them indicated that they were at the director level and had a master's degree (Stewart & Bridges, in press).

The Council for the Advancement of Standards (Dean, 2006) has a set of guidelines for professional staff working in a multicultural student services office. According to the standards, a multicultural student service office must be staffed by individuals that can move forward the mission and goals of the office. It further states that the professional staff in the office must hold a graduate degree in a relevant field or possess a combination of relevant education and experience (Dean, 2006). Specific experiences needed for the position include:

1. Multicultural knowledge, awareness, and skills
2. Knowledgeable about identity development and the intersection of multiple identities on development
3. Ability to identify and assess campus climate issues
4. Possessing a commitment to social justice and change (Dean, 2006).

PROFESSIONAL DEVELOPMENT

Professional Associations

The following list of professional associations, conferences, and training institutes provides opportunities for networking and collaboration, professional development, and a forum for sharing and shaping best practices for individuals that work with diversity and social justice issues in a higher education setting.

1. Association of Black Cultural Centers (ABCC) was established in 1987 to provide a forum to celebrate, promote, and critically examine the African American culture. The ABCC provides support through professional development opportunities, programming support, curricular and cocurricular enrichment, and community outreach. (http://provost. ncsu.edu/oldsite/offices/diversity/abcc/).
2. California Council of Cultural Centers in Higher Education (CaCC CHE) was established in 1994 for the purpose of exchanging information and discussing common issues among multicultural/cross-cultural centers. The organization has three goals: advocacy networking and support, and development (http://www.caccche.org/about_us. html).
3. National Association of Diversity Officers in Higher Education (NADOHE) held its first national conference in 2007. The mission of NADOHE is to produce and disseminate empirical evidence through research to inform diversity initiatives, identify and circulate exemplary practices, professional development for current and inspiring diversity officers, inform and influence national and local policies, and create and foster networking opportunities (http://www.nadohe.org/mc/ page.do?sitePageId=92823&orgId=nadohe).
4. Ohio Consortium of Multicultural Centers in Higher Education (OCM CHE) was established in 2008 for the purpose of bringing multicultural affairs offices and centers together to share resources, to make connections with other centers, to promote and enhance the diversity work in the state, and to create professional development opportunities. (http://www.ocmche.org/index.html).

Conferences

1. National Conference on Race and Ethnicity (NCORE)
   Training
2. A World of Difference Institute–Anti-Bias Education and Diversity Training
   http://www.adl.org/education/edu_awod/default.asp
3. National Coalition Building Institute (NCBI)
   http://ncbi.org/
4. Social Justice Training Institute
   http://www.sjti.org/home_professional.html
5. Southern Poverty Law Center–Teaching Tolerance
   http://www.splcenter.org/center/tt/teach.jsp

Journals

1. Diverse Issues in Higher Education
2. Journal of Diversity in Higher Education

MULTICULTURAL AFFAIRS TECHNOLOGY

Multicultural affairs offices and centers, like other functional areas in student affairs, are finding ways to embrace technology in the provision of services to students. According to Junco and Mastrodicasa (2007), "the net generation (also known as millennials) is the most technologically advanced group of students ever to enroll in college" (p. 17) and they surpass adults 29 and over in their internet and cell use (Pew Research Center, 2010), although gaps in technology use among older adults and the net generation continue to decline with each passing year (Pew Research Center, 2010). For example, the median age of Facebook and Twitter users is now 33 and 31 respectively (Fox, Zickuhr, & Smith, 2009).

Differences in technology use have also been found with regard to race and gender. In a Pew Research Center Report on the computer usage of millennials (2010), Latinos reported using the internet less often than other racial groups. Women used social networking sites more often than men and were less likely to post a video of themselves online than men. In a study conducted with college students, men used the computer for academic work more often than women, and women scored significantly different than men in the following areas: use of Facebook, the cell phone for talking and text messaging, and blogs. Significant differences in computer usage between students of color and white students were also found. Students of color used the computer for academic work, internet surfing, instant messaging, cellular phone use and watching TV more often than white students in the survey (Lloyd, Dean, & Cooper, 2009).

As students continue to adopt new and emerging technologies into their everyday lives, there is an expectation on their part that student affairs professionals will also incorporate current and emerging technologies in the provision of services to students (Junco & Cole-Avent, 2008; Junco & Mastrodicasa, 2007). Net generation students expect to stay connected and interact with student affairs staff and services beyond the traditional work-day hours though the connection is not limited to face-to-face interactions (Heiberger & Harper, 2008; Junco & Cole-Avent, 2008). Net generation students make little distinction between "real-world" and online communication, and they see face-to-face and online communication as meaningful forms of communication (Junco & Cole-Avent, 2008). Since technology is such an important part of all students' lives, multicultural affairs professionals need to embrace the different modes of technology to help students connect and engage with their services and the university. Some of the more common technologies used by students include social networking sites, blogs, YouTube, instant messaging, text messaging, file sharing, and virtual worlds. Some examples for how multicultural affairs offices and centers can incorporate technology into the provision of services are listed below.

Interactive Websites

- There are a number of features that can be incorporated into a departmental website to make it more interactive and interesting for students. New content should be posted on a regular basis to keep students coming back to the site. Electronic newsletters, podcast of lectures and performances, student testimonies, online resources, online workshops, and videos can be posted on the website or through a Wiki link on the website. Presenting educational resources via the web reaches more students and provides 24-hour access to information.
- Some multicultural affairs offices and centers host a Virtual Diversity Resource Center through the department's website. These sites serve as an interactive virtual community that promotes awareness, appreciation, understanding and skill building around all issues of human diversity. Such sites can include interactive awareness activities, such as simulation games, videos, podcast of campus events, blogs, quizzes, definitions, etc. Examples of online resources that could be included in a virtual resource center are listed under the Online Resources heading.
- Many multicultural affairs offices and centers sponsor diversity dialogues following campus events and/or facilitate monthly discussion topics on some aspect of diversity. Hosting an on-line blog or discussion board can serve the same purpose as the diversity dialogues, except that it is done virtually. For campuses that list some aspect of diversity as a university learning outcome, students can use their blog reflections as an artifact in a developmental e-portfolio to ascertain the achievement of the learning outcome. Campuses that work with Second Life can create a virtual world for students to explore the many intersections of personal identity with themselves and others in a safe, virtual environment.

Alternative Modes of Service

- With the proliferation of online communication modes, personal interactions with students are no longer limited to face-to-face interaction. As noted earlier in this section, net generation students do not make a distinction between electronic and face-to-face communication, which creates opportunities for alternative modes of service to students. Some student affairs practitioners have created virtual office hours using instant messaging and other forms of technology to connect and engage with students. Multicultural affairs offices and centers can look at creative ways to use electronic and online resources to supplement face-to-face communication with students.

Marketing and Communication

- Social networks such as Facebook are used daily by a large majority of students on campuses (Pew Research Center, 2010). Since traditional modes for reaching students such as email are becoming less effective, student affairs professionals are looking at alternative ways to outreach to students (Junco & Cole-Avent, 2008). Facebook and text messaging are some of the more popular alternative modes student practitioners are using to reach students and promote programs and services. Some students see an administrative presence on Facebook as intrusive. The reality is the online social world is a part of the campus culture for students, staff and faculty (Martínez-Alemán & Wartman, 2009). So, an administrative presence is inevitable. However, administrators should be mindful of their boundaries when interfacing on Facebook and other social networks with students. Multicultural affairs and center staff can play a role in helping students effectively manage their online profiles to foster identity and promote community and engagement on campus.
- Twitter is also an effective way to promote programs on campus. Facebook and Twitter can also be used as a tool for gathering real-time feedback of students' experiences at campus events. Tweets and Facebook postings by students during presentations and events can serve as a gauge for how students are engaging with the material presented.

Below is a partial list of online resources that promote multicultural awareness and understanding among college students.

Online Diversity Resources

1. Be American College Personnel Association (ACPA) Commission for Social Justice Educators
http://www.myacpa.org/comm/social/
2. American College Personnel Association (ACPA) Standing Committees—standing committees on disability, LGBT awareness, men, women, multicultural affairs

http://www.myacpa.org/sc/sc_index.cfm
3. Diversity Web–an interactive resource hub for higher education advancing campus diversity work
   http://www.diversityweb.org/
4. Interfaith Calendar
   http://www.interfaithcalendar.org/
5. Multicultural Pavilion–a clearinghouse of multicultural awareness quizzes, awareness activities, definitions, quotations, etc.
   http://www.edchange.org/multicultural/index.html
6. National Association of Multicultural Education–a clearinghouse on multicultural resources on social justice
   http://nameorg.org/
7. National Association of Student Personnel Administrators (NASPA) Knowledge Committee–Resources for African American concerns; Asian Pacific-Islander concerns; disability; Gay, Lesbian, Bisexual and Transgender issues; Indigenous Peoples, Latino American concerns, women in student affairs.
   http://www.naspa.org/kc/default.cfm
8. Race the Power of Illusion–an online companion to California Newsreel's 3-part documentary about race in society, science, and history.
   http://www.pbs.org/race/000_General/000_00-Home.htm
9. Social Justice Training Institute - an on-line resource link related to social justice issues
   http://www.sjti.org/student_resources.html
10. Social Justice Training Institute–a listing of social justice readings
    http://www.sjti.org/suggested_reading.html
11. Teaching Tolerance–a Test for Hidden Bias
    http://www.tolerance.org/activity/test-yourself-hidden-bias
12. Understanding Prejudice–interactive exercises offering unique perspectives on prejudice, stereotyping, and discrimination
    http://understandingprejudice.org/

STUDENT DEVELOPMENT THEORY AND STUDENT LEARNING

Student development theory serves as a guide in helping student affairs professionals make sense of individuals and groups on campus (McEwen, 2003; Pope & Reynolds, 2004). However, it has been noted that many of the early theories did not include the perspectives of gender and race in the development of the theory (Patton, McEwen, Rendón, & Howard-Hamilton, 2007; Pope, Reynolds, & Mueller, 2004; Torres, Howard-Hamilton, & Cooper, 2003).

To fill this void, identity development models related to race, gender, and sexual orientation were introduced in the 1970s and 1980s to address the development of diverse student populations (Patton, McEwen, Rendón, & Howard-Hamilton, 2007). Some theorists, such as Chickering and Reisser later revised their original theory to be more responsive to diverse student populations. However, some scholars thought the theories still fell short in capturing the experiences of diverse student populations and in turn developed new theories (Kodama, McEwen, Liang, & Lee, 2001; 2002) that more adequately addressed the experiences of diverse students or added diverse components to an existing theory (McEwen, Roper, Bryant, & Langa, 1990). More recently, critical race theory (CRT) that looks at how race is grounded in society has been used "as a framework in which issues of racial and social and educational inequities are foregrounded" (p. 43) in higher education settings, which has an unintentional effect on the development of diverse student populations (Patton, McEwen, Rendón, & Howard-Hamilton, 2007).

Understanding student development theory, including its shortcomings, has been useful in guiding the practice of student affairs practitioners for many years. In recent years, there has been a shift in how student development is viewed in the educational process of the student. The transformative education model described in the document "Learning Reconsidered" (Keeling, 2004), redefines learning as a "comprehensive, holistic, transformative activity that integrates academic learning and student development" (p. 4), where the student's personal development contributes to the learning process. This new paradigm changes the way student affairs practitioners contribute to the success of students. There is a greater emphasis on intentionality, in terms of learning outcomes of programs and services within student affairs, as well as opportunities for connecting in and out-of-classroom experiences for students (Keeling, 2004)

CHALLENGES FACING MULTICULTURAL AFFAIRS IN THE FUTURE: ISSUES AND TRENDS

The demographics of diverse student populations on college campuses are steadily increasing as noted elsewhere in this chapter. On some campuses the minority is now the majority and diverse populations are expected to continue to grow in the future. With the noted change in structural diversity, some individuals may question whether direct support for targeted identity groups is still needed on campuses. Studies on the perception of campus climate have consistently shown the following: differential perceptions by underrepresented racial/ethnic groups and White students (Harper & Hurtado, 2007; Hurtado, Milem, Clayton-Pedersen, & Allen, 1999), a lesser sense of belonging by African American, Latino American, and Asian American students than White American students (Johnson, Alvarez, Longerbeam, Soldner, Inkelas, Brown-Leonard, & Rowan-Kenyon 2007) and quality of life issues for LGBT students (Rankin, 2005), which indicates that campuses are not where they need to be in creating a multicultural organization as described by Jackson and Hardiman (1994). Should multicultural affairs offices and centers continue to use their resources to support targeted identity groups on campus or should they focus their attention and resources on creating change at the organization level or at increasing cross-cultural understanding among all students? The question does not require an either-or response. Multicultural affairs offices and centers can and have been doing it all (see the three-part mission listed elsewhere in the chapter). The implementation for how this work gets done is now shifting to an intercultural model that embraces a climate of inclusion where individual and group differences are valued.

In an intercultural model approach, there is a greater focus on creating opportunities for cross-cultural engagement among all students. Research has shown that these types of interactions have a "positive effect on a range of educational outcomes" (Chang, 2007, p. 28). Having an intercultural focus does not preclude multicultural affairs offices or centers from providing support or direct services to the various identity groups they have traditionally served. The research on campus climate shows there is still a need for such support for these students. The intercultural model focuses on changing the climate through interactional diversity experiences (experiences with other cultures) and cocurricular diversity experiences (cultural awareness programs) (Hurtado, Milem, Clayton-Pedersen, & Allen, 1999).

The programs and services offered in an intercultural model should be purposeful and intentional and should allow students to engage in meaningful learning experiences (Keeling, 2004). A structure for making multicultural programs more intentional was developed by Jenkins and Walton (2008). In their model, multicultural programs are organized around three critical spheres: cultural education, cultural engagement, and cultural development. Cultural education programs "allow for students to interact with the critical knowledge needed to fully understand and focus on the history, practices, and infrastructure of various cultures" (p. 94). Cultural engagement programs fall in the social realm and include performances and other forms of entertainment. Cultural development programs address the holistic development of students as it relates to their own cultural understanding and the cultures of individuals that are different from themselves. The model works more effectively when programs are offered as a collection or series as opposed to a single, "one size fits all" event (Jenkins & Walton, 2008).

An example of an intercultural model in practice can be found at the Ohio State University (OSU). In 2008, the OSU Multicultural Center (MCC) transformed its delivery model for programs and services to an intercultural model. In this new model, the center has a team of intercultural specialists that works with all students. Although, the center staff still provide support to all cultural and identity groups, its new directive is to promote and increase intercultural understanding among all students. The mission of the multicultural center is to "facilitate the inclusive shared learning experiences of students where all can engage in dialogue, challenge barriers, and build collaborative relationships" (OSU Multicultural Center website, 2008, Vision, Mission, and Values section, ¶2). The values for the center include:

1. TRANSFORMATIVE EDUCATION: We contribute to the academic mission of the university by facilitating thought-provoking and participatory learning experiences;
2. COMMUNITY: We actively build an inclusive and positive environment for all members of The Ohio State University community;
3. COLLABORATION: We recognize that this important work on behalf of students is most effective when we pool our collective wisdom and resources;
4. INNOVATION: We continually enhance our services and vision by being open to, seeking and creatively implementing new ideas;
5. SOCIAL JUSTICE: We inspire individuals and groups to examine systems of privilege and oppression; and
6. EMPOWERMENT: We engage individuals and groups to develop their own sense of power in order to bring about social change (OSU Multicultural Center website, ¶3).

The language used in their mission and value statements reflects the transformative educational approach described in the "Learning Reconsidered" document discussed elsewhere in this chapter. The values statements presume a shared partnership in the educational process of students. The model also empowers all students to take personal and social responsibility in developing an inclusive campus climate. In this model, the MCC continues to celebrate and support identity groups previously served by the unit, but also welcomes all students to their events (OSU Multicultural Center website). For more information on the intercultural model at Ohio State University visit their website at http://multiculturalcenter.osu.edu/.

In an intercultural model approach, multicultural affairs offices and centers must work collaboratively with other areas on campus in "creating spaces and opportunities for meaningful cross [cultural] engagement" (Harper & Hurtado, 2007, p. 14). These offices and centers must also work at making systemic change at the institutional level. When campuses have truly become more inclusive at all levels of the institution, then these offices and centers will have worked themselves out of a job (Shuford, in press). In the mean time, there is still much work to be done around issues of inclusion and social justice.

CONCLUSION

Increasing the structural diversity on campuses has not guaranteed the full involvement of diverse student populations in the college or university experience. Student affairs professionals in multicultural affairs and all other functional areas must continue to identify the barriers that inhibit the inclusion of underrepresented group members and eradicate the barriers by addressing the specific needs of diverse students and by creating conditions that encourage communication and collaboration among diverse groups. Opportunities to create multicultural campus communities that maximize social integration and cross-cultural understanding, while honoring and celebrating individual and group differences, represent both challenges and blessings to today's student affairs professionals.

REFERENCES

Amada, G. (1994). *Coping with the disruptive college student: A practical model.* Asheville, NC: College Administration Publications, Inc.

Anderson, G., Carmichael, K. Y., Harper, T. J., & Huang, T. (2009). International students at four-year institutions. In S. R. Harper & S. J. Quaye (Eds.), *Student engagement in higher education: Theoretical perspectives and practical approaches for diverse populations* (pp. 17–37). New York: Routledge.

Astin, A. W., & Astin, H. S. (2005). The spiritual life of college students: A national study of college students' search for meaning and purpose. Retrieved from *Higher Education Research Institute Graduate School of Education & Information Studies University of California* http://www.spirituality.ucla.edu/spirituality/reports/FINAL%20REPORT.pdf.

Ballard, B. R. (2003). The establishment of minority affairs offices in schools of dentistry: Pros and cons. *Journal of Dental Education, 67*(9), 1046–1047.

Bilodeau, B. L., & Renn, K. A. (2005). Analysis of LGBT identity development models and implications for practice. In R. L. Sanlo (Ed.), *Gender identity and sexual orientation: Research, policy, and personal perspectives* (New Directions for Student Services, No. 111, pp. 25–39). San Francisco: Jossey-Bass.

Bowles, F., & DeCosta, F. A. (1971). *Between two worlds: A profile of Negro education.* New York: McGraw-Hill.

Boyer, P. (1997). *Native American colleges.* Princeton, NJ: Carnegie Foundation.

Chan, S., & Wang, L. (1991). Racism and the model minority: Asian Americans in higher education. In P. G. Altbach & K. Lomotey (Eds.), *The racial crisis in American higher education* (pp. 43–67). Albany, NY: State University of New York Press.

Chang, M. J. (2007). Beyond artificial integration: Reimagining cross-racial interactions among undergraduates. In S. R. Harper & L. D. Patton (Eds.), *Responding to the realities of race on campus* (New Directions for Student Services, No. 120, pp. 25–37). San Francisco: Jossey-Bass.

Chew, C. A., & Ogi, A. Y. (1987). Asian American college student perspectives. In D. J. Wright (Ed.), *Responding to the needs of today's minority students* (New Directions for Student Services, No. 38, pp. 39–48). San Francisco: Jossey-Bass.

Dalton, J. C. (1999). The significance of international issues and responsibilities in the contemporary work of student affairs. In J. A. Dalton (Ed.), *Beyond borders: How international developments are changing student affairs practice* (New Direction for Student Services, No. 8, pp. 3–11). San Francisco: Jossey Bass.

Darden, J. T., Bagakas, J. G., Armstrong, T., & Payne, T. (1994). Segregation of American Indian undergraduate students in institutions of higher education. *Equity & Excellence in Education, 27*(3), 61–68.

D'Augelli, A. R. (1991). Gay men in college: Identity processes and adaptations. *Journal of College Student Development, 32,* 140–146.

Dean, L. A. (2006). *CAS professional standards in higher education* (6th ed.). Washington, DC: Council for the Advancement of Standards in Higher Education.

Evans, N. J., & Wall, V. A. (2000). Parting thoughts: An agenda for addressing sexual orientation issues on campus. In N. J. Evans & V. A. Wall (Eds.), *Toward acceptance: Sexual orientation issues on campus* (pp. 389–403). Alexandria, VA: American College Personnel Association.

Fleming, J. (1984). *Blacks in college.* San Francisco: Jossey-Bass.

Fox, S., Zickuhr, K., & Smith, A. (2009). Twitter and status updating, fall 2009. *Pew Research Center's Internet and American Life Project.* Retrieved from http://www.pewinternet.org/Reports/2009/17-Twitter-and-Status-Updating-Fall-2009.aspx.

Gibbs, J. T. (1973). Black students/white university: Different expectations. *Personnel and Guidance Journal, 51*(7), 465–469.

Griffith, R. M. (2008). Beyond diversity and multiculturalism: Pluralism and the globalization of American religion. *Organization of American Historians Magazine of History, 32*(1), 24–27.

Grund, N. (2009, Fall). Does your student affairs operation twitter? *NASPA Leadership Exchange,* 30–31.

Harper, S. R., & Hurtado, S. (2007). Nine themes in campus racial climates and implementations for institutional transformation. In S. R. Harper & L. D. Patton (Eds.), *Responding to the realities of race on campus* (New Directions for Student Services, No. 120, pp. 7–24). San Francisco: Jossey-Bass.

Heiberger, G., & Harper, R. (2008). Have you facebooked Astin lately? Using technology to increase student involvement. In R. Junco and D. M. Timm (Eds.), *Using emerging technologies to enhance student engagement* (New Directions for Student Services, No. 124, pp. 19–35). San Francisco: Jossey-Bass.

Herbst, S., & Malaney, G. D. (1999). Perceived value of a special interest residential program for gay, lesbian, bisexual, and transgender students. *NASPA Journal, 36*(2), 106–119.

Hitchings, W. E., Luzzo, D. A., Retish, P., Horvath, M., & Ristow, R. S. (1998). Identifying the career development needs of college students with disabilities. *Journal of College Student Development, 39,* 23–32.

Hodges, J. S., & Keller, M. J. (1999). Perceived influences on social integration by students with physical disabilities. *Journal of College Student Development, 40,* 678–686.

Hoopes, D. S. (1979). Intercultural communication concepts and the psychology of intercultural experience. In M. D. Pusch (Ed.), *Multicultural education: A cross cultural training approach* (pp. 10–38). La Grange Park, IL: Intercultural Network.

Horn, L. (1996). *Nontraditional undergraduates, trends in enrollment from 1986 to 1992 and persistence and attainment among 1989–90 beginning postsecondary students* (NCES 97-578). U.S. Department of Education, NCES. Washington, DC: U.S. Government Printing Office.

Hsia, J., & Hirano-Nakanishi, M. (1989, November/December). The demographics of diversity: Asian Americans and higher education. *Change, 21*(6), 20–27.

Hurtado, S., Milem, J., Clayton-Pedersen, A., & Allen, W. (1999). *Enacting diverse learning environments: Improving the climate for racial/ethnic diversity in higher education, ASHE-ERIC Higher Education Report, 26*(8). Washington, DC: The George Washington University, Graduate School of Education and Human Development.

Institute of International Education. (2008, November 17a). *Open doors.* Retrieved from http://www.opendoors.iienetwork.org/?p=131533.

Institute of International Education. (2008, November 17b). *Open doors 2008: International students in the United States.* Retrieved from http://www.opendoors.iienetwork.org/?p=131590.

Jackson, B. W. (2005). The theory and practice of multicultural organization development in education. In M. L. Ouellett (Ed.), *Teaching inclusively: Resources for course, department & institutional change in higher education* (pp. 3–20). Stillwater, Oklahoma: New Forums.

Jackson, B. W., & Hardiman, R. (1994). Multicultural organization development. In E. Y. Cross, J. H. Katz, F. A. Miller, & E. W. Seashore (Eds.), *The promise of diversity: Over 40 voices discuss strategies for eliminating discrimination in organizations* (pp. 231–239). Arlington, VA: NTL Institute.

Jaschik, S. (2006). An end to picking one box. *Inside Higher Ed.* Retrieved from http://www.insidehighered.com/news/2006/08/08/race.

Jenkins, T. S., & Walton, C. L. (2008). Student affairs and cultural practice: A framework for implementing culture outside the classroom. In S. R. Harper (Ed.), *Creating inclusive campus environments* (pp. 87–101). Washington, DC: NASPA.

Johnson, D. R., Alvarez, P, Longerbeam, S., Soldner, M, Inkelas, K. K., Brown-Leonard, J., & Rowan-Kenyon, H. (2007). Examining sense of belonging among first-year undergraduates from different racial/ethnic groups. *Journal of College Student Development, 48*(5), 525–542.

Jones, S. R. (1997). Voices of identity and difference: A qualitative exploration of the multiple dimensions of identity development in women college students. *NASPA Journal, 38,* 376–385.

Jones, G. C., Kalivoda, K. S., & Higbee, J. L. (1997). College students with attention deficit disorder. *NASPA Journal, 34,* 262–274.

Junco, R., & Cole-Avent, G. A. (2008). An introduction to technologies commonly used by college students. In R. Junco & D. M. Timm (Eds.), *Using emerging technologies to enhance student engagement* (New Directions for Student Services, No. 124, pp. 3–17). San Francisco: Jossey-Bass.

Junco, R., & Mastrodicasa, J. (2007). *Connecting to the net generation: What higher education professionals need to know about today's students.* Washington, DC: National Association of Student Personnel Administrators.

Kasworm, C. E. (2003). Setting the stage: Adults in higher education. In D. Kilgore & P. J. Rice (Eds.), *Meeting the special needs of adult students* (New Directions for Student Services, No 102, pp. 3–10). San Francisco: Jossey-Bass.

Keeling, R. P. (2004). *Learning reconsidered: A campus-wide focus on the student experience.* Washington DC: ACPA and NASPA.

King, A. R. (2008). Student perspectives on multiracial identity. In K. A. Renn & P. Shang (Eds.), *Biracial and multiracial students* (New Directions for Student Services. No 123, pp. 33–41). San Francisco: Jossey-Bass.

Kodama, C. M., McEwen, M. K., Liang, C. T. H., & Lee, S. (2001). A theoretical examination of psychosocial issues for Asian pacific American students. *NASPA Journal, 38,* 411–437.

Kodama, C. M., McEwen, M. K., Liang, C. T. H., & Lee, S. (2002). An Asian American perspective on psychosocial student development theory. In M. K. McEwen, C. M., Kodama, A. N. Alvarez, S. Lee, & C. T. H. Liang (Eds.), *Working with Asian American college students* (New Directions for Student Services, No. 97, 45–59). San Francisco: Jossey-Bass.

Kuh, G. D., & Whitt, E. J. (1988). *The invisible tapestry: Culture in American colleges and universities (ASHE-ERIC Higher Education Report, No. 1).* Washington, DC: Association for the Study of Higher Education.

LaCounte, D. W. (1987). American Indian students in college. In D. J. Wright (Ed.), *Responding to the needs of today's minority students* (New Directions for Student Services, No. 38 pp. 65–79). San Francisco: Jossey-Bass.

Levine, H., & Love, P. G. (2000). Religiously affiliated institutions and sexual orientation. In N. J. Evans & V. A. Wall (Eds.), *Toward acceptance: Sexual orientation issues on campus* (pp. 89–108). Alexandria, VA: American College Personnel Association.

Likins, J. M. (1991). Research refutes a myth: Commuter students do want to be involved. *NASPA Journal, 29*(1), 68–74.

Llagas, C., & Snyder, T. D. (2003). *Status and trends in the education of Hispanics.* National Center for Education Statistics. Retrieved from http://nces.ed.gov/pubs 2003/2003008.pdf.

Lloyd, J. M., Dean, L. A., & Cooper, D. L. (2009). Students' technology use and its effects on peer relationships, academic involvement, and healthy lifestyles. *NASPA Journal, 48*(4), 695–709.

Mahaffey, C. J., & Smith, S. A. (2009). Creating welcoming campus environments for students from minority religious groups. In S. R. Harper & S. J. Quaye (Eds.), *Student engagement in higher education: theoretical perspectives and practical approaches for diverse populations* (pp. 81–98), New York: Routledge.

Malaney, G. D. (1987). A review of early decisions in Adams v. Richardson. In A. S. Pruitt, (Ed.), *In pursuit of equality in higher education* (pp. 17–22). Dix Hills, NY: General Hall.

MacDonald V., & Garcia, T. (2003). Historical perspectives on Latino access to higher educations, 1848–1990. In J. Castellanos & L. Jones (Eds.), *The majority in the minority: Expanding the representation of Latina/o faculty, administrators and students in higher education* (pp. 15–43). Sterling, VA: Stylus.

Martínez-Alemán, A. M., & Wartman, K. L. (2009). *Online social networking on campus: Understanding what matters in student culture.* New York: Routledge.

McEwen, M. K. (2003). Nature and use of theory. In S.R. Komives & Associates, *Student services: A handbook for the profession* (4th ed.) (pp. 153–178). San Francisco: Jossey-Bass.

McEwen, M. K., Roper, L. D., Bryant, D. R., & Langa, M. (1990). Incorporating the development of African American students into psychosocial theories of student development. *Journal of College Student Development, 31,* 429–436.

McIntire, D. (1992). Introduction. In D. McIntire & P. Willer (Eds.), *Working with international students and scholars on American campuses* (pp. xi–xx). Washington, DC: National Association of Student Personnel Administrators.

McRee, T. K., & Cooper, D. L. (1998). Campus environments for gay, lesbian, and bisexual students at southeastern institutions of higher education. *NASPA Journal, 36*(1), 48–60.

Min, P. G. (2006). Asian immigration: History and contemporary trends. In P. G. Min (2nd ed.), *Asian Americans: Contemporary trends & issues* (pp. 7–31). Thousand Oaks, CA: Pine Forge Press.

National Center for Education Statistics. (2008a). *Status and trends in the education of American Indians and Alaska Natives: 2008.* Retrieved from http://nces.ed.gov/pubs2008/2008084.pdf.

National Center of Education Statistics. (2008b). *Digest of Education Statistics 2007. NCES 2008-022.* Retrieved from Office of Educational Research and Improvement, US Department of Education: http://nces.ed.gov/fastfacts/display.asp?id =98.

O'Brien, E. M. (1993). *Latinos in higher education (Research Briefs, Vol. 4)* (No. 4). Washington, DC: American Council on Education, Division of Policy Analysis and Research.

Obama, B. H. (2007). *Dreams from my father: A story of race and inheritance.* New York: Random House.

Ogletree, C. J. (2004). *All deliberate speed: Reflections on the first half century of Brown vs. board of education.* New York: W. W. Norton.

Ohio State University Multicultural Center. Retrieved from http://multiculturalcenter.osu.edu/about-us/vision-mission-and-values/.

Palmer, C. (2008). An introduction to serving adult learners. In C. J. Palmer, J. L.

Bonnet & J. L. Garland (Eds.), *Serving adult learners: A handbook for effective practice* (pp. 3–4). College Park: National Clearinghouse for Commuter Programs.

Patton, L. D, (2005). Power to the people! Black student protest and the emergence of black cultural centers. In F. L. Hord (Ed.), *Black culture centers: Politics of survival and identity* (pp. 151–163). Chicago: Third World Press.

Patton, L. D., McEwen, M. K., Rendón, L, & Howard-Hamilton, M. F. (2007). Critical race perspectives on theory in student affairs. In S. R. Harper & L. D. Patton (Eds.), *Responding to the realities of race on campus* (New Directions for Student Services, No. 120, pp. 39–53). San Francisco: Jossey-Bass.

Pew Research Center. (2010). Millennials: A portrait of generation next. *Confident. Connected. Open to Change.* Retrieved from http://pewsocialtrends.org/assets/pdf/millennials-confident-connected-open-to-change.pdf.

Pickert, S. M. (1992). *Preparing for a global community: Achieving an international perspective in higher education (ASHE-ERIC Higher Education Report, No. 2).* Washington, DC: The George Washington University, School of Education and Human Development.

Ping, C. J. (1999). An expanded international role for student affairs. In J. A. Dalton (Ed.), *Beyond borders: How international developments are changing student affairs practice* (New Direction for Student Services, No 8 pp. 13–21). San Francisco: Jossey Bass.

Pope, R. L., Reynolds, A. L., & Mueller, J. A. (2004). *Multicultural competence in student affairs.* San Francisco: Jossey-Bass.

Pounds, A. W. (1987). Black students' needs on predominantly white campuses. In D. J. Wright (Ed.), *Responding to the needs of today's minority students* (New Directions for Students Services, No. 38 pp. 23–38). San Francisco: Jossey-Bass.

Quevedo-Garcia, E. L. (1987). Facilitating the development of Hispanic college students. In D. J. Wright (Ed.), *Responding to the needs of today's minority students* (New Directions for Students Services, No. 38 pp. 49–63). San Francisco: Jossey-Bass.

Ranbom, S., & Lynch, J. (1987/1988). Timeline: The long hard road to educational equality. *Educational Record, 68*(4)/69 (1), 16–22.

Rankin, S. R. (2005). Campus climate for sexual minorities. In R. L. Sanlo (Ed.), *Gender identity and sexual orientation: Research, policy, and personal perspectives* (New Directions for Student Services, No. 111, pp. 17–23). San Francisco: Jossey-Bass.

Renn, K. A. (2003). Understanding the identities of mixed-race college students through a developmental ecology lens. *Journal of College Student Development, 44*(3), 383–403.

Rice, P. J. (2003). Adult student services office. In D. Kilgore & P. Rice (Ed.), *Meeting the special needs of adult students* (New Directions for Student Services, No. 102, pp. 53–57). San Francisco: Jossey-Bass.

Rhoads, R. A. (1997). Implications of the growing visibility of gay and bisexual male students on campus. *NASPA Journal, 34*(4), 275–286.

Ryu, M. (2008). *Minorities in higher education 2000–2001: Eighteenth annual status report.* Washington, DC: American Council on Education.

Sanlo, R. L. (2000). The LGBT campus resource center director: The new profession in student affairs. *NASPA Journal, 37*(3), 485–495.

Shuford, B. C. (in press). Historical and philosophical development of multicultural student services. In D. L. Stewart (Ed.), *Building bridges, re-visioning community: Multicultural student services on campus.* Sterling, VA: Stylus.

Spees, E. C., & Spees, E. R. (1986). Internationalizing the campus: Questions and concerns. In K. R. Pyle (Ed.), *Guiding the development of foreign students* (New Directions for Student Services, No. 36, pp. 5–18). San Francisco: Jossey-Bass.

Spring, J. (2007). *Deculturalization and the struggle for equality: A brief history of the education of dominated cultures in the United States* (5th ed.). New York: McGraw-Hill.

Starobin, S. S. (2006). International students in transition: Changes in access to U.S. higher education. In F. S. Laanan (Ed.), *Understanding students in transition: Trends and issues* (New Directions for Student Services, No. 114, pp. 63–71). San Francisco: Jossey-Bass.

Stennis-Williams, S., Terrell, M. C., & Haynes, A. W. (1988). The emergent role of multicultural education centers on predominantly white campuses. In M. C. Terrell & D. J. Wright (Eds.), *From survival to success: Promoting minority student retention* (NASPA Monograph Series, No. 9, pp. 73–98). Washington, D.C.: NASPA.

Stewart, D. L., & Lozano, A. (2009). Difficult dialogues at the intersections of race, culture, and religion. In S. K. Watts, E. E. Fairchild, & K. M. Goodman (Eds.), *Intersections of religious privilege: Difficult dialogues and student affairs practice* (New Directions for Student Services, No. 125, pp. 23–31). San Francisco: Jossey-Bass.

Stewart, D. L., & Bridges, B. K. (in press). A demographic profile of multicultural student services. In D. L. Stewart (Ed.), *Building bridges, re-visioning community: Multicultural student services on campus.* Sterling, VA: Stylus.

Sutton, M. E. (1998). The role of the office of minority affairs in fostering cultural diversity. *College Student Affairs Journal, 18,* 33–39.

Suzuki, B. H. (2002). Revisiting the model minority stereotype: Implications for student affairs practice and higher education. In M. K. McEwen, C. M. Kodama, A. N. Alvarez, S. Lee, & C. T. H. Liang (Eds.), *Working with Asian American college students* (New Directions for Student Services, No. 97, pp. 21–32). San Francisco: Jossey-Bass.

Talbot, D. (2008). Exploring the experiences and self-labeling of mixed-race individuals with two minority parents. In K. A. Renn & P. Shang (Eds.), *Biracial and multiracial students* (New Directions for Student Services. No 123, pp. 33–41). San Francisco: Jossey-Bass.

Tan, D. L. (1994). Uniqueness of the Asian American experience in higher education. *College Student Journal, 28,* 412–421.

Thielen, T., & Limbird, M. (1992). Integrating foreign students into the university community. In D. McIntire & P. Willer (Eds.), *Working with international students and scholars on American campuses* (pp. 119–135). Washington, DC: National Association of Student Personnel Administrators.

Thomas, G. E., & Hill, S. (1987). Black institutions in U.S. higher education: Present roles, contributions, future projections. *Journal of College Student Personnel, 28*(6), 496–503.

Torres, V. (2004). The diversity among us: Puerto Ricans, Cuban Americans, Caribbean Americans, and Central and South Americans. In A. M. Ortiz (Ed.),

Addressing the unique needs of Latino Americans (New Directions for Student Services, No. 10, pp. 5–16). San Francisco: Jossey-Bass.

Torres, V., Howard-Hamilton, M. F., & Cooper, D. L. (2003). *Identity development of diverse populations: Implications for teaching and administration in higher education. ASHE-ERIC Higher Education Report, 29*(6). San Francisco: Jossey-Bass.

Turner, C. S. V. (1994). Guest in someone else's house: Students of color. *Review of Higher Educations, 17*(4), 355–370.

Uphoff, J. K. (2001). Religious diversity and education. In J. A. Banks & C. S. McGee Banks (Eds.), *Multicultural education: Issues and perspectives* (pp. 103–121). New York: John Wiley & Sons.

U.S. Department of State & U. S. Department of Education. (2009a). *International Education Week.* Retrieved from http://www.iew.state.gov.

U.S. Department of State and U.S. Department of Education. (2009b). *International Education Week.* Retrieved from http://www.iew.state.gov/sug-colleges.cfm.

Wall, V. A., & Evans, N. J. (1991). Using psychosocial development theories to understand and work with gay and lesbian person. In N. J. Evans & V. A. Wall (Eds.), *Beyond tolerance: Gays, lesbians and bisexuals on campus* (pp. 25–38). Alexandria, VA: American College Personnel Association.

Whitt, E. J., Edison, M. I., Pascarella, E. T., Nora, A., & Terenzini, P. T. (1999). Women's perceptions of a "chilly climate" and cognitive outcomes in college: Additional evidence. *Journal of College Student Development, 40,* 163–177.

Willer, P. (1992). Student affairs professionals as international educators: A challenge for the next century. In D. McIntire & P. Willer (Eds.), *Working with international students and scholars on American campuses* (pp. 161–167). Washington, DC: National Association of Student Personnel Administrators.

Williams, D. A., & Wade-Golden, K. (2006). What is a chief diversity officer? *Inside Higher Ed.* Retrieved from http://www.insidehighered.com/lauout/set/print/work place/2006/04/18/williams.

Williams, J. B. (1991). Systemwide Title VI regulation of higher education, 1968–88: Implications for increased minority participation. In C. V. Willie, A. M. Garibaldi, & W. L. Reed (Eds.), *The education of African-Americans* (pp. 110–118). New York: Auburn House.

Wright, D. J. (1987). Minority students: Developmental beginnings. In D. J. Wright (Ed.), *Responding to the needs of today's minority students* (New Directions for Student Services, No. 38, pp. 5–21). San Francisco: Jossey-Bass.

Wong, M. P. A., & Buckner, J. (2008). Multiracial student services come of age: The state of multiracial student service in higher education in the United States. In K. A. Renn & P. Shang (Eds.), *Biracial and multiracial students* (New Directions for Student Services. No 123, pp. 43–51). San Francisco: Jossey-Bass.

Young, L. W. (1986). The role minority student centers play on predominantly white campuses. In C. A. Taylor (Ed.), *The handbook of minority student services* (pp. 15–22). Madison, WI: National Minority Campus Chronicle, Inc.

Chapter 9

ORIENTATION

WANDA I. OVERLAND, AUDREY L. RENTZ AND MARGARET L. SARNICKI

INTRODUCTION

For as long as new students have experienced a period of transition to the educational environment, orientation programs have been a part of American higher education. Whether formally or informally organized, their purpose has been to assist entering students during the initial adjustment to the collegiate environment. Young men starting classes at Harvard in the 1640s were assisted by the shared efforts of dons and a graduate student or tutor whose job was "to counsel and befriend the young lads" (Morison, 1936, p. 253). According to Upcraft, Gardner, and Associates (1989), Harvard faculty, recognizing the importance of assisting students entering the academy, created a system in which current students aided new students in their transition. In the nineteenth century, a growing number of institutions began to assign faculty responsibilities for activities outside of the classroom, including the orientation of new students (Upcraft, Gardner, & Associates, 1989).

Increased enrollments in higher education institutions following World War II along with the rapidly changing composition of the student body resulted in modifications to orientation programs (Strumpf, Sharer, & Wawrzynski, 2003). Over time, orientation programs have become more comprehensive in nature, using multiple approaches and strategies to introduce new students to an institution's academic learning community from admissions through the first year. Creating intentional learning environments has resulted in greater collaboration between academic affairs and student affairs (Kezar, 2009; Miller, 2005; Strumpf & Wawrynski, 2000).

While orientation's presence within the academic community has remained constant, the focus of the program has evolved and changed over the decades. Many of the recent changes are a result of new technologies, changing needs of a diverse student population, increased family and parent involvement, emerging institutional trends, and greater national accountability (Mullendore & Banahan, 2005a). The national focus on creating integrated and seamless student learning experiences has brought a greater sense of purpose to orientation programs. Higher education institutions will need to continue to become more sophisticated and intentional with recruitment, retention, and student success initiatives in response to changing student demographics and service delivery options (Kezar, 2009; Mullendore & Banahan, 2005a; Murdock & Hoque, 1999). Today, orientation programs are recognized as effective retention strategies and viewed as pivotal programs in the enrollment management process (Gardner & Hansen, 1993; Hadlock, 2000; Penn, 1999). Research has documented a positive relationship between participation in orientation with student satisfaction and persistence (Kuh, 2001; Tinto, 2000). The competition for college applicants and the increasing diversity of today's student population have provided orientation professionals with opportunities and challenges never before encountered. Viewed as having a significant campus influence on student retention, as well as students' educational and personal development, many orientation directors are members of their college's or university's enrollment management team. This team concept has allowed orientation professionals to draw upon their rich and broad history of program successes to help an institution foster a holistic and developmental view of the students' collegiate experience.

In the 1920s, undergraduate students were viewed as a homogeneous group. On most campuses today, the undergraduate student body is recognized as diverse. There are an increasing number of students who are not traditional-aged, 18–24 years old, and who attend college part-time or take classes on-line. The National Center for Education Statistics predicts a rise of 19 percent in enrollments of people 25 and over between 2006 and 2017 and a 10 percent increase in enrollments of people under 25 (U.S. Department of Education, 2009). To be effective, orientation professionals no longer can assume that a single, general, broad-based program can meet the needs of all entering students.

To help the reader understand the dynamic nature of orientation, this chapter examines eight major themes. These themes are: (a) introduction; (b) history; (c) definitions, purpose, and goals; (d) administration and organizational structure; (e) program models; (f) diverse student needs; (g) parent and family orientation; (h) technology; and (i) issues and trends. In each section, whenever possible, the material is presented in chronological sequence to allow the reader to become familiar with the changes in response to shifts in philosophy and societal events.

HISTORY

Two distinct programmatic emphases have been identified within orientation's history. The first emerged in 1888 at Boston University, when an orientation day for new students was offered. These one-day programs were designed to concentrate on students' personal adjustment to college rather than an introduction to specific academic disciplines or the world of higher education (Butts, 1971; Drake, 1966). As faculty responsibilities expanded outside the classroom, they also were expected to orient students to the academic environment. This shift of responsibility from parent to faculty served as the impetus for *in loco parentis* (Johnson, 1998).

The second programmatic emphasis was developed at Reed College in 1911, with the introduction of a freshman course for credit entitled *The College Life Course* (Brubacher & Rudy, 1958). Within several months, both the University of Washington and the University of Michigan sponsored weekly meetings for entering students and rewarded attendance with academic credit (Butts, 1971). These early courses, usually scheduled in a series of 25 sessions, were designed to teach students how to succeed academically, including how to use the library, study skills, career counseling, and campus involvement (Fitts & Swift, 1928). National acceptance of these structured for-credit courses was quickly achieved. Interest in this program format grew dramatically from six institutions in 1915–1916 to 82 sponsoring institutions only a decade later (Brubacker & Rudy, 1958).

In *Advice to Freshmen by Freshmen,* University of Michigan President M. L. Burton described expectations for this time of transition:

> Remember that the change from high school to college is tremendous. You are no longer a high school boy or girl. You are a college man or woman. The University is a place of freedom. You are thrown upon your own resources. You are independent. But do not forget, I beg of you, that independence and freedom do not mean anarchy and license. Obedience to law is liberty. (Crocker, 1921, p. 1)

The dramatic rise in college enrollments after World War I changed who attended college and shifted responsibility for orientation from faculty to staff. Student personnel professionals accepted the orientation function as a specialized responsibility within their administrative domain. By 1930, nearly one-third of all higher education institutions offered credit courses (Mueller, 1961). During the 1930s, under the direction of E. G. Williamson, the University of Minnesota sponsored an orientation program for entering students that addressed the following areas on perceived student concern: personal living, home life, vocational orientation, and civic orientation

(Bennett, 1938). By the early 1940s, these credit courses were required for 90 percent of all new students (Mueller, 1961). Studies completed by the late 1940s revealed that 43 percent of higher education institutions had implemented orientation courses. While the majority of the courses centered on transitional and adjustment issues, some focused on the academic experience (Bookman, 1948; Strang, 1951). The courses typically were lecture style and often included a convocation program, which served as the formal induction into the academic community.

Although these two models played a crucial role in the development of contemporary orientation programs, they were not without their critics. Some argued about their length. For example, since the mid-1920s, the most effective length of an orientation program has been at times the subject of intense debate: ". . . some personnel workers have recommended that a really effective program will continue through the subsequent years to help students avoid difficulties–scholastic, health, social, economic, vocational and emotional" (Doermann, 1926, p. 162). Thirty years later, Strang (1951) and subsequently Mueller (1961) expressed their belief that an orientation program should not be a one-day or two-day event, but rather should be a continuous and dynamic process beginning in high school and ending after college graduation. Some 80 years later, Mullendore & Banahan (2005a) indicated that a multifaceted orientation approach that begins at the point of admission through the first year was essential to achieve student success. According to these beliefs, orientation is a developmental process assisting entering students with specific tasks associated with their transition and the subsequent goals of self-direction and interdependence.

As the number of orientation professionals on campuses increased, they sensed a need to come together to share ideas and discuss common problems. Twenty-four orientation directors met in Columbus, Ohio, in 1948 and convened the first conference of the professional association now known as the National Orientation Directors Association (NODA). In 1976, the association was chartered. The association goals are to provide services for orientation professionals and institutions and to encourage dialogue and discussion on orientation related topics. As the association grew, regional networking structures were created to support the exchange of ideas through newsletters, conferences, and drive-in workshops. Services and programs are now offered throughout the United States and Canada. The core values of the association are community, diversity, integrity, learning, scholarship, and services (National Orientation Directors Association, 2009).

Formal recognition and widespread support of orientation was achieved in 1943, when the Council of Guidance and Personnel Associations recommended that orientation programs be sponsored at the high school level as well as by higher education institutions. The Council recommended three major program goals: (a) increasing the understanding of occupational and social problems; (b) personal adjustment; and (c) increasing the awareness of the importance of physical fitness, including social hygiene (Council of Guidance and Personnel Associations, 1943). Responses from all 123 institutional members of the North Central Association of Colleges and Secondary Schools verified commitments to offer orientation programs that would include general lectures, testing, social activities, campus tours, religious activities, counseling, details of registration, establishment of faculty-student relationships, and academic success courses (Bookman, 1948; Kamm & Wrenn, 1947).

In the 1960s, in the midst of student activism and a new wave of accountability in higher education, orientation programs once again became the subject of scrutiny and criticism. Freshman Week was labeled "disorientation week" (Riesman, 1961). Orientation courses would no longer be included in the institution's curriculum unless documentation could be provided that these programs served a utilitarian and meaningful purpose on campus (Caple, 1964). Few research studies had been undertaken that could identify and assess the specific educational outcomes associated with participation in orientation activities. Involvement, let alone its relationship to student satisfaction and retention, had not yet appeared in the professional literature. Additionally, the lack of a theoretical foundation that supports orientation programs led to the criticism that these activities were "made of hopes, good will, educated guesses and what we fondly believe to be the needs of new students" (Grier, 1966, p. 37). Nevertheless, orientation programs became more prevalent and were recognized as effective retention initiatives (Mann, 1998).

From 1966 to 1976, modifications in programs included the creation of two-day or three-day overnight programs not only for new students, but also for their parents and family members. Some small institutions developed mini-courses taught by freshman faculty advisors during the five- to ten-day period before classes to provide a brief preview of academic life. Other campuses used small group sessions to teach T-group and other human relations skills, and Friendship Days emerged with an emphasis on social needs (Cohen & Jody, 1978; Foxley, 1969; Hall, 1982; Klostermann & Merseal, 1978). During the 1960s, upper-class students were selected to participate in the orientation program as student orientation leaders. They served in a variety of capacities, including helping new students become familiar with the institution, facilitating the transition into the academic environment and serving as peer mentors.

A projected decline in the number of college applicants provided additional value and significance to the efforts of orientation professionals in the 1960s and 1970s. Added to this was the shift in the 1970s from a homogeneous student population to a diverse population that necessitated changes in orientation programs (Barefoot & Gardner, 1993). Student satisfaction and retention became issues of major importance to many collegiate administrators. Consequently, orientation programs came to be viewed as contributing significantly to the economic stability of many colleges and universities. Support for the relationship between participation in orientation programs, student satisfaction and persistence appeared with greater and greater frequency in the research literature (Beal & Noel, 1980; Feldman & Newcomb, 1969; Hossler, 1999; Pascarella & Terenzini, 1991; Ramist, 1981).

The number of orientation programs grew significantly during the 1980s. Many institutions created first year programs to extend the transition of new students into the academy (Miller, 2005; Strumpf & Wawrzynski, 2000). The greatest increase was seen in first-semester courses. Two-thirds of four-year institutions provided a freshman course by the beginning of 1990 (Pascarella & Terenzini, 1991). In their article, Pascarella & Terenzini (2005) stated, "first-year seminars appear to benefit all categories of students" (p. 401).

Today, the trend on campuses is to provide a multifaceted orientation program, as well as a semester or full academic year freshman course. It is common practice today for institutions to provide a number of specialized programs for specific populations in a variety of pre-enrollment, entry and post-matriculation formats. However, the need still exists for congruence between student and institutional "fit" and the necessity to balance program components that address academic needs as well as issues outside of the classroom (Miller, 2005; Pascarella & Terenzini, 1991; Perigo & Upcraft, 1989).

As parents and family members have become more engaged in the educational experience, separate parents programs have been added to orientation. These sessions include components focused on their transition as family members and information about the institution. An outgrowth of this interest has resulted in the creation of parent and family programs on many college and university campuses.

Since the First Year Experience movement began in the 1970s at the University of South Carolina, programs have become more visible and dominant. Convocation and living-learning communities are examples of initiatives implemented to foster student learning and to integrate the out-of-class and in-class academic experience. This focus can be attributed to shifts in enrollment patterns, public accountability, retention initiatives, and a philosophical shift from teaching to the creation of holistic learning environments (Cutright, 2002).

Beginning in the 1990s, attention and resources were placed on incorporating technological advancements such as computerized databases, video-conferencing, and data management systems into orientation programs (Byrant & Crockett, 1993; Mullendore & Banahan, 2005a). For many students, the online, *virtual* campus is a reality.

A number of publications and resources have been developed or reintro-
duced during the last decades (Ritchie, 2001). *The Journal of College Orientation
and Transition* was re-established during the late 1990s and is published twice
a year along with *The Orientation Review,* a quarterly newsletter. A listserv was
created in 1996 to provide National Orientation Director Association members with an electronic vehicle to share ideas and information. In early 2000,
the Parent Services Network was created to provide information on parent
and family initiatives as well as a publication entitled *Helping Your First-Year
College Student Succeed–A Guide for Parents.* Building on this publication, *A
Guide for Families of Commuter Students: Supporting Your Student's Success* was
published in 2004. Recent publications for parents include *Empowering Parents
of First-Year College Students: A Guide to Success* published in 2007. A monograph, *Designing Successful Transitions: A Guide for Orienting Student to College,
Second Edition,* was published in 2003 jointly with the National Resource
Center for the First-Year Experience & Students in Transition. The fiftieth edition of the First-Year Experience Monograph Series, *Graduate Students in
Transition: Assisting Students through the First Year,* was published in 2008.

Mention the term *orientation* to most individuals and, depending on their
age, one or more images appear in their mind's eye. Raccoon coats, yellow
pompoms, football banners, and the swallowing of goldfish were prevalent
in the 1920s and 1930s; the freshman "beanie" was a rite of passage symbol
during the 1950s; and college blazers, T-shirts, and buttons were mandatory
in the 1960s. All of these helped entering students maintain a visible profile
on campus. Such adornments differ dramatically from the distinguishing
lengths of the black academic robes worn by faculty and students at Harvard
to denote the levels of status within the academic community; ankle-length
for faculty, knee-length for upperclassmen, and mid-thigh for freshmen.
Throughout the years, specific wardrobe items, customs, and rituals helped
identify entering students to others on campus and were required elements
of a process of both adjustment and socialization. While these traditions are
part of the history of higher education, new traditions and symbols have
been built into first year programs that affirm the mission and values of the
institution.

DEFINITIONS, PURPOSE, AND GOALS

In its broadest sense, "orientation can be defined as a collaborative institutional effort to enhance student success by assisting students and their families in the transition to the new college environment" (Mullendore &
Banahan, 2005a, p. 393). Consider the following representative goals statements gathered from a review of thirty years of literature:

1. To gain perspective, a sense of purpose and balance between the demands and opportunities of college life (Strang, 1951).
2. To increase student's receptivity to the total higher education experience (McCann, 1967).
3. To complete enrollment procedures in a humane manner (Butts, 1971).
4. To foster development of a peer group, creating an atmosphere of comfortableness and reduced anxiety (Krall, 1981).
5. To gather information that provides the institution with a better understanding of its student population (Smith & Brackin, 1993).
6. To provide opportunities for informal interaction and discussions with faculty (Mullendore, 1998a).
7. To acclimate students to the facilities, services and members of the institution's community (Hadlock, 2000).
8. To find a programmatic balance within orientation programs for both academic success components and topics related to the out of class experience (Miller, 2005).

Responding to a perceived exaggerated emphasis on students' social and personal needs in orientation programs of the 1950s, subsequent writers argued persuasively for a return to a focus on academic disciplines and the mission of higher education (Drake, 1966; Miller, 2005). In 1960, the American Council of Education provided an authoritative definition of orientation, viewing it as the process of integrating students into the campus learning community (Brown, 1972). However, Levitz and Noel (1989) believed that orientation programs must help students make the transition to college both socially and intellectually. During the past decades, a greater emphasis has been placed on a stronger academic focus in orientation programs. Research has documented that successful orientation programs have a "powerful influence on first-year social and academic integration" (Rode, 2000, p. 3). Thus, the goals of orientation programs have been expanded to include the integration of student learning and critical thinking of values across the curriculum both in and outside the classroom. This perspective recognizes the opportunity to achieve complementary learning outcomes and integrate all of the aspirations that the institution holds for its students. Programs should take a holistic perspective of student learning: "orientation should give newcomers the impression that they are about to start an important, qualitatively different chapter in their lives" (Kuh, 1996, p. 142).

Four goals for orientation program planners, echoing past practice, were proposed in an effort to respond to different institutional missions and the growing variety of programs offered. All programs should (a) aid students in their academic adjustment, (b) provide assistance with personal adjustment, (c) help entering students' families understand the collegiate experience, and

(d) assist the institution in gathering data about its entering students (Perigo & Upcraft, 1989; Upcraft & Farnsworth, 1984).

Attempts were made to develop a generic mission or purpose statement and common goals that might apply to all programs regardless of the institution. The most recent effort is documented in the seventh edition of The Book of Professional Standards for Higher Education produced by the Council for the Advancement of Standards in Higher Education (CAS). In this document, the Council stated:

> the mission of orientation programs must include facilitating the transition of new students into the institution; preparing students for the institution's educational opportunities and student responsibilities; initialing the integration of new students into the intellectual, cultural, and social climate of the institution and supporting the parents, partners, guardians, and children of the new student. (Council for the Advancement of Standards in Higher Education, 2009, p. 324)

The CAS Professional Standards for Higher Education noted the importance of identifying student learning and developmental outcomes when designing a comprehensive orientation program. Student orientation programs must be:

> integrated into the life of the institution; intentional and coherent; guided by theories and knowledge of learning and human development; reflective of developmental and demographic profiles of the student population; responsive to needs of individuals, diverse and special populations, and relevant constituencies. (Council for the Advancement of Standards in Higher Education, 2009, p. 324)

To fully achieve programmatic goals, institutions have developed a variety of programs that span from admission through the first year. Program characteristics may include courses, adventure or outdoor programs, summer reading programs, bridge programs, learning communities, on-line and web-based programs. Some of these programs may be for credit or noncredit; offered for one-day or multiple days in the summer or at the beginning of the academic year; and may be considered pre-entry programs, entry programs, and postmatriculation programs. Furthermore, program components may be offered by various departments across the institution.

Lastly, the CAS Professional Standards for Higher Education recommended a list of 13 goals to help orientation professionals design programs and activities. The list implies a broad institutional role for orientation. The student orientation program must:

1. be based on stated goals and objectives.
2. be coordinated with the relevant programs and activities of other institutional units.
3. be available to all students new to the institution, as well as to families.
4. assist new students as well as their families in understanding the purposes of higher education and the mission of the institution.
5. articulate the institution's expectations of students . . . and provide information that clearly identifies relevant administrative policies and procedures and programs to enable students to make well-reasoned and well-informed choices.
6. provide new students with information and opportunities for academic and personal self-assessment.
7. use qualified faculty members, staff, or peer advisors to explain class scheduling, registration processes, and campus life.
8. provide new students, as well as their families, with information about laws and policies regarding educational records and other protected information.
9. inform new students, as well as their families, about the availability of services and programs.
10. assist new students, as well as their families, in becoming familiar with the campus and local environment.
11. assist new students, as well as their families, in becoming familiar with the wide range of electronic and information resources available and expectations for their use.
12. provide time for students to become acquainted with their new environment.
13. provide intentional opportunities for new students to interact with fellow new students as well as continuing students and faculty and staff members. (Council for the Advancement of Standards in Higher Education, 2009, pp. 324–325)

ADMINISTRATION AND ORGANIZATIONAL STRUCTURE

As the diversity among entering students increases, orientation professionals must be able to design programs that meet specific needs of various student populations (Habley, 2004; Harbin, 1997; Johnson & Miller, 2000). This requires professional staff to be familiar with the needs of student subgroups and enrollment patterns (Eimers & Mullen, 1997). The type of program offered should be informed by desired learning outcomes, an analysis of institutional research, assessment, and institutional resources.

Research on student satisfaction emerged during the 1960s and 1970s. Several studies focused on measuring student satisfaction in purely academic terms by assessing when majors were chosen or by looking at students' years in school (Schmidt & Sedlacek, 1972; Sturtz, 1971).

As enrollments in the late 1970s began to decline at some colleges and universities, the retention of students became even more critical. A new significance was attached to the freshman year, particularly, the initial months during which new students' attitudes, values, and adjustment to higher education were influenced the most (Butts, 1971; Chickering & Havighurst, 1981; Feldman & Newcomb, 1969; Lowe, 1980). Administrators became aware of the link between the freshman year, student satisfaction, and student retention.

Early retention research efforts identified factors contributing to student attrition. One such conclusion was that attrition was most severe during or at the end of the freshman year (Sagaria, 1979). At four-year institutions, factors related to attrition were gleaned from student questionnaires: (a) course work requiring student study habits many students did not possess; (b) large classes; (c) an impersonal, uncomfortable campus environment; and (d) academic and social regulations (Beal & Noel, 1980; Hall, 1982). This information justified a new role for orientation as an aid to student persistence. Retention became so strongly linked with orientation programs that it was almost viewed as the primary reason for their existence. However, Tinto (1985, 1997), a respected author of retention literature, suggested that the most important goal of new student orientation experiences should be education and not simply retention. This discussion remains active as on-going conversations continue relative to student success, persistence, and student learning (Mullendore & Banahan, 2005a; Rode, 2004). Rode spoke of the importance of orientation programs:

> Orientation programs stand at the intersection of an institution's recruitment efforts and its retention strategies. A well-designed program will help solidify a student's decision to attend the school while assisting the student in making a good personal adjustment to college and learning how to be successful academically. (Rode, 2004, p. 1)

The organizational reporting of orientation programs has received more attention because of the recognition that orientation programs make a difference in retaining students and the strong linkages to academic success (Abraham, Nesbit, & Ward-Roof, 2003; Mullendore & Banahan, 2005a). Traditionally, orientation activities have been the sole responsibility of student affairs professionals. According to the National Orientation Directors Association (NODA) Data Bank, the majority of orientation programs are housed in student affairs divisions (Strumpf & Wawrynski, 2000). The CAS Professional Standards for Higher Education recommend that "the size, nature, and complexity of the institution should guide the administrative scope and structure of orientation programs" (Council for the Advancement of Standards in Higher Education, 2009, p. 328).

Staffing Models

Staffing patterns also reflect changing times and perspectives. During the years when the value ascribed to academic concerns was high, faculty members shared in planning and staffing programs. The re-emergence of faculty involvement in planning and implementing orientation programs has resulted in opportunities for enhanced student engagement partnerships (Council for the Advancement of Standards in Higher Education, 2009; Miller, 2005).

Generally, programs are the responsibility of a director of orientation, of first-year experience, or of new students. Depending on the size and mission of the institution, individuals responsible for orientation may have additional responsibilities (Strumpf & Wawrynski, 2000). An important factor in the delivery of an effective program is the role of the support staff. They are often the first individual that students and parents meet and the ones who respond to questions about orientation. Their interactions with students and their family members and ability to make decisions can make a significant difference in the quality of the experience for students and their families (Abraham, Nesbit, & Ward-Roof, 2003). To facilitate the collaborative nature of orientation, university-wide orientation committees provide assistance in shaping the program goals, learning outcomes, and program components.

Program implementation is made possible by a largely volunteer staff comprised of university constituents, including students. In the mid-1960s, undergraduates assumed new roles as coparticipants and collaborators in planning and as peer facilitators. In addition to the economic benefits of student paraprofessionals, these student leaders gained significantly from the experience themselves (Holland & Hubba, 1989). This type of student involvement was studied in 1989, and student paraprofessionals reported significantly higher gain scores on the developmental tasks of interdependence and tolerance than their control group peers (Holland & Hubba, 1989).

An effective student orientation leader program requires intentional planning and coordination. The identification of desired learning outcomes and the assessment of learning are valuable and important program components. Effective selection, training, and mentoring strategies are needed to provide a quality experience for the student orientation leader as well as the new student participating in the program (Abraham, Nesbit, & Ward-Roof, 2003; Mullendore & Banahan, 2005a).

Many professionals gained their initial experience as undergraduate student participants or leaders. While pursuing graduate work, some graduate students hold assistantships in departments that house orientation or first year programs that are comparable to entry-level positions. Full-time directors generally possess a master's degree (Strumpf & Wawrzynski, 2000). Some institutions, particularly on smaller campuses, place responsibilities for orientation programs under a full-time professional staff member who may also supervise other areas within student affairs or academic affairs.

Student affairs professionals specializing in orientation need to have a skill base that allows them to plan and implement programs that are educationally purposeful. Obviously, communication skills, programming abilities, leadership and administrative skills are needed in addition to sensitivity to the complex issues associated with students' growth and development. The professional who directs an orientation program must have the ability to work with a variety of constituents and stakeholders; have credibility and respect across the institution; be able to juggle multiple tasks, projects, and decisions; and remain calm and enthusiastic (Mullendore & Abrahamn, 1993; Mullendore & Banahan, 2005a). Given the changing dynamics of the campus, the professional staff must have a strong understanding of the diversity of today's students.

Funding Models

The CAS Professional Standards for Higher Education (Council for the Advancement of Standards in Higher Education, 2009) recommended that institutional funding be provided for the administration of orientation programs. Registration fees, student fees, contributions, sales, and donations are other potential sources of funding. It is critical that staff have the skills to develop and manage budgets, administer multiple funding streams, and advocate for funds from other sources. Lastly, a mechanism to support students who are unable to afford the costs of an orientation program should be developed and implemented.

Assessment and Evaluation

The dialogue regarding outcomes based assessment is occurring in accrediting bodies and state and national government entities (U.S. Department of Education [DOE], 2006). A number of landmark student affairs publications, such as *Student Learning Imperative* (ACPA, 1996) and *Learning Reconsidered: A Campus-Wide Focus on the Student Experience* (Keeling, 2004) reframed discussions among student affairs professionals on the importance of student learning in all functional areas. This philosophical shift necessitates intentional emphasis on learning outcomes in the design of orientation programs.

The utilization of institutional research data and orientation assessment results can be beneficial in gaining knowledge about the institution and emerging student trends and concerns. Data that should be examined include basic demographic trends as well as specific information such as full-time or part-time employment, full-time or part-time students, and characteristics that distinguish them from other students. Additional data on retention, class registration, persistence and attrition and student demographics can be helpful in making decisions about orientation program components. Historically, orientation programs were fine-tuned or modified to reflect results from previous year evaluations. Zis (2002) suggested that changing student demographics and trends in higher education calls for a different approach. Staff will need to be more aggressive in evaluating and assessing program effectiveness and learning outcomes as well as involving campus constituents in decision-making processes.

Mullendore and Banahan (2005a) recommended both qualitative and quantitative methods of data collection. In addition to institutional and national survey information that is collected by the college and university, staffs should consider conducting focus groups with new students during their first year to assess program effectiveness and orientation outcomes. Utilizing data from benchmarking studies and the CAS Professional Standards for Higher Education provides valuable information in evaluating various aspects of a program.

Program evaluation is critical and should be completed by all stakeholders and constituents involved in the program. All aspects of orientation should be regularly evaluated, including, but not limited, to the timing and duration of the program, program components, faculty and staff involvement, balance of challenge and support for students and family members, attention to transitional and developmental stages, the mix of academic and social activities, and information disseminated. The program design should be carefully scrutinized, and questions should be raised about issues such as "retention, the technical aspects of course registration and campus life, and social integration. First and foremost, orientation programs . . . will benefit greatly from basic planning, and thinking about what the intended outcomes of their experience should be" (Zis, 2002, p. 67).

Program Models

Three prototypes or models of programs serve as the foundation for many of today's orientation programs; the pre-enrollment or orientation model, offered during the summer months; the freshman day or week model, scheduled during the first semester of academic classes; and the credit course model, scheduled during the first semester or the entire academic year (McCann, 1967; Strang, 1951; Upcraft, Gardner, & Associates, 1989).

In addition, two philosophical viewpoints emerged during the 1960s that influenced the content of orientation programs. The first viewpoint was known as "microcosmic" and stressed testing, campus tours, informational meetings, and course registration activities. The second viewpoint, called "macrocosmic," emphasized issues associated with the intellectual challenges of academic life, cognitive development, and the mission of higher education (Fitzgerald & Evans, 1963). Elements of these two viewpoints continue to dictate most orientation programs.

The orientation structure should complement the mission and values of the institution, reflect the needs of the entering student body, and comprise aspects of the collegiate environment that enhance student success (Smith & Brackin, 1993). Today, many campuses incorporate a variety of models and it is not uncommon for a campus to have pre-enrollment programs, extended orientation sessions, freshman or orientation courses, and specialized programs for targeted populations, including summer bridge programs.

The Pre-Enrollment or Orientation Model

The Pre-College Clinic, established in 1949 at Michigan State University, was a summer program, two to four days in length, that included testing, counseling, information dissemination, and social events (Goodrich & Pierson, 1959). The value of the program as a public relations tool quickly became apparent as an aid to personalizing large college and university environments and as a means of improving students' initial adjustment and their grades.

Preadmissions or pre-enrollment programs typically are coordinated by the admissions office and involve particular aspects of the campus community. As part of the strategic enrollment plan, these programs are designed to market the institution and attract students to campus. Programs can vary from large campus visitation events to small group sessions that include appointments with faculty, campus tours, and presentations (Upcraft, Gardner & Associates, 1989).

Pre-enrollment orientation programs may also be designed for students who have applied and been admitted. These programs serve (a) to introduce students and family members to services on campus; (b) to assist students with their academic and social adjustment and integration; (c) to provide opportunities for formal and informal conversations and discussions with faculty, staff, and current students; and (d) to advise students in choosing a major and their academic courses for the first semester or quarter system (Rode, 2000).

The program implemented is dependent on the type of institution and its mission. For example, some large institutions with significant numbers of students from out-of-state will hold orientation sessions in central locations around the country. Colleges and universities with commuter or older student populations create programs, such as evening events, that accommodate their schedule. Regardless of the nature of the program, orientation programs are campus-wide recruitment and retention initiatives.

The Freshman Course Model

The traditional Freshman Course model was developed to introduce new students to available fields of study and to assist them in coping with concerns associated with their freshman status (Drake, 1966). These courses sprung from the counseling movement in higher education and were motivated by the perceived need to help entering students during their initial adjustment to a new institutional setting. Prior to 1960, slightly more than half of all institutions sponsored programs that emphasized freshman adjustment issues. However, by the mid-1960s, in the midst of student activism, this model was viewed as obsolete (Drake, 1966). Faculty voiced strong opposition to its perceived emphasis on *fun and games,* social events, and personal adjustment. They argued strongly and persuasively for a return to an orientation program that centered on academic concerns and the mission of general education (Dannells & Kuh, 1977). Orientation directors responded by designing an academic course to meet students' academic, personal, and social needs.

During the 1960s and 1970s, three forces merged, causing administrators to seek new programs that would teach entering students how to effectively navigate the institution's system. First, campuses were faced with many first-generation students who knew little about "the skills of studenthood" (Cohen & Jody, 1978, p. 2). Second, because of revisions in curricula and changes in regulations, the choices for freshmen became more complex. Finally, peer culture, with its great potential for assistance to freshmen, "seemed to have lost much of its potency in helping students to adapt" (Cohen & Jody, 1978, p. 2). It was less likely that an administrator would observe among freshmen, as Kingman Brewster had done at Yale in the 1960s, a single year's "progress from arrogance, to self-doubt, to self-pity, to rediscovery, and finally to mature ambition" (Brewster, 1968, p. viii). Out of this context, John Gardner established the influential Freshman Seminar program at the University of South Carolina, which in 1986 became the National Research Center for the Freshman Year Experience, and in 1995 obtained its current name of National Resource Center for the First Year Experience and Students in Transition.

The Freshman Seminar meshes two major elements in a small class format cotaught by a faculty member and an upper-class student: (a) shared information to help students understand their initial transition period, and (b) establishment of an environment that is socially supportive (Gordon &

Grites, 1991). The 2006 National Survey on First-Year Seminars reports that the three most important course objectives were (a) to develop academic skills, (b) to provide an orientation to campus resources and services, and (c) to focus on self-exploration and personal development (National Resource Center for The First-Year Experience and Students in Transition, 2006). The First Year Experience Seminar is probably the most popular model in use on campuses today. The nature and content of the courses vary, however, the overarching purpose of the seminar course is to help students make necessary academic and social adjustments as well as to assist them in developing critical thinking skills (Upcraft, Gardner, & Associates, 1989). They provide a broad view of the institution as well as focus on personal and academic skill development. Some institutions offer theme or academic discipline courses that concentrate on similar topics, but from a specific discipline or interdisciplinary perspective.

DIVERSE STUDENT NEEDS

Higher education institutions attract not only traditional students, but also diverse student populations (Edmondson, 1997; National Center for Educational Statistics, 2007). This requires colleges and universities to examine their orientation programs to assure that the specific needs and perspectives of students from diverse backgrounds are incorporated into planning, implementation and assessment activities. Providing specialized orientations, as a complement to a comprehensive program, allows for unique perspectives and needs to be addressed.

Commuter Students

In the past, less attention has been paid to students who commute to campus than residential students (Pascarella, 2006). They spend less time on campus, have increased off-campus responsibilities, and have fewer opportunities to make campus connections (King, 2004). Commuter students have unique challenges with respect to transportation, child care, connecting with faculty, staff, and peers, and being aware of and accessing campus resources. For some students, access and use of technology is a concern. Because commuter students represent significant diversity, our knowledge of their experience remains incomplete. However, orientation programs tailored to the needs of specific commuter student populations at an institution is essential.

Nontraditional Students

While the definition has varied, a nontraditional student has been defined by the National Center for Educational Statistics as someone who (a) delays enrollment, (b) attends part-time, (c) works full-time, (d) is considered financially independent, (e) has dependents other than a spouse, or (f) does not have a high school diploma (National Center for Educational Statistics, 2002). According to this definition, approximately 75 percent of undergraduate students meet at least one of these criteria, far different from the stereotype of the typical new college student (National Center for Educational Statistics, 2002). Orientation activities geared toward traditional students may not appeal to nontraditional students, but the need for peer and faculty connections, information on academic and cocurricular resources, and an introduction to both the culture of the institution and academic success remains. Intentional programming concerning issues such as scheduling, child care, and use of technology should be considered.

Transfer Students

National trends indicate that a growing number of students begin their postsecondary experience at a community college, with the expectation of transferring to another institution to complete a bachelor's degree. The transferability of credits, adjustment to a new campus, and an introduction to campus culture are topics that could be effectively addressed in a transfer student orientation. Krause (2007) found that students looked to orientation as a way to meet other students, and noted "the importance of peers as both friends and associates, the later being a particularly significant function in managing the *business* of university study" (p. 35). An orientation program can assist transfer students as they assimilate into the new collegiate culture, particularly if the size, mission, or type of institution being transferred to is vastly different from their previous one (Townsend & Wilson, 2006).

Students of Color

As the United States becomes more diverse, colleges have also become more racially and ethnically diverse (Rendon, Garcia & Person, 2004). Students of color may be defined as (a) members of racial/ethnic groups that have been historically underrepresented and underserved in American education, and (b) minorities (Rendon, Garcia & Person, 2004). During the transition to college, students of color need to gain confidence in their academic abilities, to negotiate between the differing expectations of college life and their home reality and to develop self-esteem as they create a college identity (Rendon, Garcia, & Person, 2004). Jalomo and Rendon (2004) identified "three critical processes involved in moving from one's former reality or home life to a new context that focuses on the college . . . experience: (a) separation, (b) validation, and (c) involvement" (p. 39). Separation begins when students identify with the college experience and learn how to manage two potentially different worlds or life experiences. Validation occurs when students learn the essential skills and information needed to navigate the collegiate environment. Support and affirmation from peers, faculty and staff increase the confidence of students. Lastly, involvement is when students begin to find a place for themselves academically and socially. Orientation programs can give students support during this transitional process as well as introducing them to services and resources for student success.

International Students

Over half a million international students attend American colleges and universities (Hoppenjans & Semenow, 2007). They bring diverse perspectives, contribute to the academic richness of a campus, encourage cross-cultural understanding, and return to their countries with a better understanding of the United States. In an orientation program,

> Many of the issues facing international students are similar to those facing domestic students. They need to navigate campus, literally and figuratively; learn about campus services; make connections with other students; establish feelings of safety; find a job; and establish communications with friends and family. (Hoppenjans & Semenow, 2007, p. 17)

However, international students also have unique needs. For example, the language barrier can complicate aspects of the collegiate experience. Government regulations and requirements add another layer of complexity. Thus, the cultural adjustment for many international students poses significant challenges. Orientation staff should work closely with the campus international student office to assure that these issues are being addressed in either the standard orientation program, or as an additional component. "The goal should not be to simply duplicate or replicate the programs offered to domestic students, but rather, to enhance and broaden existing programs so that they appeal to a wider range of students" (Hoppenjans & Semenow, 2007, p. 17).

On-line Learners

Distance learners or on-line students are defined as those who engage in a formal education process in which the students and instructor are not in the same place (National Center for Educational Statistics, 2007). In 2006–2007,

66 percent of the two-year and four-year Title IV degree-granting postsecondary institutions in the nation offered college-level distance education courses (National Center for Educational Statistics, 2007). Research has shown that retention rates are significantly lower for on-line courses than for traditional ones, but orientation has been identified as an effective strategy. Specifically, orientating students not only to the institution, but to the expectations of on-line learning is critical to student success (Harrell II, 2008; Nash, 2005). This dual-focused approach develops realistic expectations for on-line education while increasing the student's connectivity to the institution. Orientation can also serve as the foundation to create an on-line community of learners.

Veterans

Veterans have always had a presence on campus, but with increased veteran educational benefits and the influx of an estimated two million military personnel returning from overseas duty, a large numbers of veteran students are returning to college to pursue an academic degree (Cook & Young, 2009). This has, and will continue to, propel postsecondary institutions to expand the services they offer specifically for this population. In a 2009 survey of 763 postsecondary institutions, more than 55 percent reported that they offered veteran's services, with 65 percent of those indicating they have increased their focus on those programs since 2001 (Cook & Young, 2009). Institutions that previously provided an office dedicated exclusively to veteran's issues are most likely to be able to respond faster in offering specialized services for veterans, such as re-integration programs as well as orientation programs. This study found inadequacies in assisting military students with their transition to college, with only 22 percent of postsecondary institutions offered specialized transition programs for veterans (Cook & Young, 2009). Orientation programs can assist veteran students in having a positive transition from a military experience to a student civilian experience. Lastly, orientation programs can be helpful in assisting veteran students find a community of peers.

Graduate Students

Emphasis has traditionally been placed on orientating undergraduate students to the collegiate experience. Recently, however, there has been a recognition that graduate students can also benefit from an orientation process. Some of their needs are the same as undergraduates, such as locating housing, accessing campus health care, and securing financial aid. Graduate students may also have a greater need for services such as child care resources and community information. By partnering with other units on campus, orientation staff can assist graduate students in adjusting to the campus culture and accessing support services within the early days of their education. Since graduate students are enrolled in a specific academic program, departmental orientations that address specific information and requirements for their intended degree are helpful (Gansemer-Topf, Ross & Johnson, 2006). Graduate orientation programs serve a twofold purpose in assisting students' socialization into the institution as well as their academic department. This is achieved most effectively by offering both an institution specific orientation and a department or program-specific orientation (Poock, 2008).

Community College Students

While every campus has a range of student backgrounds, needs, and challenges, community colleges traditionally have more students who are older, work full-time, have families, and attend school part-time (Center for Community College Student Engagement, 2008). Orientation programs at these institutions are typically shorter in duration, offered at various times to accommodate work schedules, and are optional. Recent research has pointed to increased benefits for mandatory orientation, but found that one out of every five community college students surveyed was not aware of an orientation program, and only 44 percent indicated that they had attended an on-campus orientation. Furthermore, less than one third of new students knew about key college resources after three weeks of taking classes (Center for Community College Student Engagement, 2008). Programs that can assist community college students in learning how to navigate an academic community and how to access services will become necessary. As community colleges experience rapid growth, it is essential for institutions to create effective programs, such as orientation, to transition new students into the collegiate experience (Younger, 2009).

PARENTS AND FAMILY ORIENTATION

Orientation programs are clear opportunities to include, engage, and partner with parents and family members in their student's educational process and assist the student, parent, family members, and campus staff in establishing expectations for involvement. (Ward-Roof, Heaton, & Coburn, 2008, p. 43)

The growing participation of parents and family members throughout the collegiate experience can be attributed to the changing structures of families and campus environments, consumer orientation, increased parent and student communication (Merriman, 2007), perceived government support of parental involvement (Carney-Hall, 2008), and the encouragement of students themselves (Howe & Strauss, 2007). While the label *Helicopter Parent* has gained popularity as a symbol of parental intrusion, Wolf, Sax, and Harper (2009) define parental involvement as a "multidimensional construct, involving engagement in various aspects of the college environment including academics and co-curricular activities as well as expressed interest in the day-to-day well-being of college students" (p. 328).

Orientation programs for parent and family members are important for a number of reasons. First, students who feel supported by their families and the institution are more likely to be successful and satisfied with their academic experience (Cabrera, Nora, Terenzini, Pascarella, & Hagedorn, 1999; Hatch, 2000; National Survey of Student Engagement, 2007; Sandeen, 2000). Second, parents and family members are important partners in the education of their students. "Long before and long after attachments are made to new classmates, friends, roommates, faculty and staff, students rely on family/extended family members for feedback, reassurance, and guidance" (Austin, 1993, p. 97). Third, orientation programs acknowledge and convey the message that parents and family are valued partners in the educational process. Orientation also provides institutions with an opportunity to inform parents on restrictions to student information as defined by federal laws, most notably, the Family Educational Rights and Privacy Act (FERPA). Introducing parents to the institution's expectations for parental involvement is also an important facet of parent orientation.

In a recent national survey, 95 percent of institutions reported they offered a parent and family orientation program (Savage, 2007). Parent orientations address the academic experience and the emotional transitions that occur for both students and family members (Jacobs & With, 2002; Mullendore, 1998b). Mullendore and Banahan (2005b) encouraged an institution's early involvement with parents in an effort to positively influence student engagement. Because parents can affect student success and persistence, their understanding of the institution and the college experience are critical. Studies have confirmed that students communicate with their parents on a frequent basis (College Parents of America 2006; National Survey of Student Engagement, 2007), and when parents are knowledgeable concerning institutional services and programs, they are better able to assist when students encounter personal and academic challenges.

Family support has been shown to be even more essential in the persistence and success of students of color. Researchers have noted that family support has been a significant factor in the collegiate experience of Filipina Americans (Maramba, 2008), Cambodian Americans (Chhuon & Hudley,

2008), Native Americans (Okagaki, Helling, & Bingham, 2009), and African Americans (Love, 2008). Parents of first-generation students benefit from an introduction to the fundamentals of college, so they can better understand and support their student's experience. Nontraditional students are more likely to have spouses, partners, and children as members of their family system. Consideration must be given to the expanded concept of family that today's diverse students bring to campus, with programming and language appropriate for a broad definition of supportive partners.

Ward-Roof (2005, p. 32) offered the following 12 guidelines for developing a parent orientation.

1. Program goals should be aligned with the mission of the institution and the division where the program is organizationally located.
2. Faculty, staff, and administrators should assess the institutional parent population to best understand its demographics. . . .
3. Orientation professionals should not only be aware of the developmental issues of students but also those of parents. . . .
4. Include current students and parents of current students in the parent orientation program. . . .
5. Use faculty, staff, and administrators who are going through the college transition process with their own students to assist with the delivery of the parent program.
6. Regardless of the size of the institution and the orientation program, keep the experience personal. . . .
7. Set boundaries for the parents. Be candid with them about what they can and cannot access at the institution . . .
8. Develop and communicate to the parents how the college faculty and staff plan to interact with them on a long-term basis. Discuss where they can find information, who they can contact, and what to do if they have questions.
9. Address the tough campus issues. Discuss issues such as alcohol and other drugs, sexual assault, and campus safety.
10. Include unique aspects of the institution, academic expectations, and the components of campus life outside the classroom . . .
11. Provide parents with resource material in written form . . .
12. Have participants evaluate the orientation program.

TECHNOLOGY

The 2009 Horizon Report documented that "information technologies are having a significant impact on how people work, play, gain information, and collaborate" (Johnson, Levine, & Smith, 2009, p. 5). The authors identified a number of key trends and challenges for the present and future. Certainly one of the significant challenges is that technology changes rapidly. This creates pressure on financial budgets, staying current with technological trends, and accessibility as well as appropriate training for faculty, staff, and students.

Within higher education, the trends indicate that students want to be active participants in the learning environment. Many have grown up playing online games, are involved in multiple social networks, and expect digital access to information. If there is some certainty, it is that the expectations of students to communicate with mobile devices will only increase. There are significant opportunities for orientation program staff to use these technologies to reach students in new and interesting ways, even before they matriculate to campus. For example, some institutions are using games as learning and communication tools to reach students. Others are offering on-line components to their orientation programs (Moltz, 2009).

Facebook, with over 30,000,000 subscribers, along with other social networks have become part of the social and cultural mainstream. A number of reports (Arrington, 2005; HERI Research Brief, 2007) have documented that 85 percent to 94 percent of students, in participating college surveys, had Facebook accounts, and nearly 60 percent checked their accounts daily. Students who are entering higher education institutions today have joined online campus communities prior to coming to orientation. For many, they have established circles of friendships, had conversations with their roommates, and explored other social network sites associated with the institution. Campus departments and programs have established Facebook accounts to share information with new and current students. While e-mail has been the general mode of communication with students, it has become less effective. According to Lenhart, Madden, and Hitlin (2005), "When asked about which modes of communication they use *most often,* on-line teens consistently choose instant messaging over email in a wide array of contexts" (Kruger, 2009, p. 586). Several authors (Bugeja, 2006; Eberhardt, 2007; Farrell, 2006) have provided recommendations on how to incorporate technology into orientation programs. The recommendations are: (a) to incorporate information regarding social network groups into orientation sessions as a topic related to safety and future career implications; (b) to serve as a model for students in how to use social networks, such as Facebook; and (c) to assess the nature of campus wide use and the impact on the environment and culture.

A challenge with emerging technologies is the growing need to provide formal instruction in areas such as information literacy, visual literacy, and technological literacy (Johnson, Levine, & Smith, 2009). While some students are comfortable with technology, others may be uncomfortable or have limited access to technology. An added complexity is that many staff and faculty are not skilled or trained in these technologies (Junco, 2005).

The use of technology for administrative purposes can reduce administrative costs and human resource time, provide opportunities to visually highlight aspects of the institution and enhance the delivery of services and programs. For example, individuals participating in orientation can register and pay for the program electronically. Students can become more familiar with the institution through virtual tours, on-line programs, and CD-ROMS focused on specific topics. Additional technological services may include online placement tests, degree audit software programs, and web-based class scheduling. Departments and programs at institutions have created internet-based information programs. Programs such as Go Ask Alice!, Columbia University's health services program, are becoming common forms of providing students with valuable information (Columbia University, 2007).

Online orientation programs are another example of how institutions are delivering services and programs to ease students' transition. Many of these programs supplement on the ground programs. Examples of programs include online student profiles with customized information, virtual advisors, and online courses (Kruger, 2009).

The possibilities of how to utilize technology to better serve students is only limited by the creativity and imagination of orientation staff. However, ". . .conversations about technology ought not to be about the actual technology itself but about the process of using technology and how it does and might affect student learning and the delivery of services to students" (Kruger, 2009, p. 587).

ISSUES AND TRENDS

A review of the higher education literature documented the value of orientation programs in welcoming new students into the collegiate experience and providing them with tools to be successful academically and socially. Now more than ever, professionals must have a familiarity with the research literature that describes the new student. The following trends or issues will be a part of the orientation professional's agenda for the next few years:

1. With the emphasis on student learning, greater collaboration and partnerships across the institution will be needed, especially between student affairs and academic affairs.
2. The trend toward more academic focused orientation programs will increase to support student academic success and student learning outcomes.

3. Faculty involvement will continue to increase as orientation programs place a greater emphasis on academic expectations and an understanding of the academic environment.

4. A shift from planning enrollments to managing and designing the enrollment will impact orientation and first year programs.

5. Concerns regarding access to higher education will result in increased efforts to create summer bridge programs, collaborative programs with high schools and school districts, as well as programs designed for specific student populations prior to matriculation.

6. Given rising costs and diminishing support for higher education, retention and student success initiatives will be more critical, beginning with admission through the first year.

7. The changing nature of the student body and the diversity of the population will require orientation staff to examine programmatic and institutional practices to facilitate campus environments that are responsive to all students.

8. The increased involvement of parents and families in the education of family members will require attention to programs that meet their needs.

9. Growing concern regarding the funding of higher education will require intentional collaboration and funding models to support orientation programs. Collaboration across campus and sophisticated enrollment management models and initiatives will become standard and expected practices.

10. While the increasing use of technology helps make procedures such as registration easier for students and their families, its use can remove the opportunity for personal interaction. Professionals will need to put greater emphasis on the concepts of mattering and belonging as cornerstones of future programs.

11. The need for extended programs of support through small groups facilitated by peers and staff and/or faculty beyond the first few weeks seems to be evident. Such programs may be needed beyond the first year.

12. With increased attention on assessment, accountability, and learning, institutions will expect orientation professionals to utilize skills to implement more strategic and intentional assessment, evaluation and research activities than ever before. These activities should be designed to inform practice and to assist the institution in learning more about its students.

13. Identified learning outcomes will be critical components of strong orientation programs. These outcomes will be used to measure learning and identify subsequent programmatic opportunities to enhance stu-

dent reflection and academic integration.

14. Technology will increase the opportunity to incorporate electronic tools for communication, online programs, and create new ways to deliver orientation programs, including videoconferencing. New methods of communication will be necessary to assist entering students in building a sense of identity and a commitment to learning.

REFERENCES

Abraham, J. W., Nesbit, B. G., & Ward-Roof, J. A. (2003). Organization and administration of orientation programs. In J. A. Ward-Roof & C. Hatch (Eds.), *Designing successful transitions: A guide for orienting students to college* (2nd ed.). [Monograph] (Series No. 13). (pp. 67-81). Columbia, SC: University of South Carolina, National Resource Center for The First-Year Experience and Students in Transition.

American College Personnel Association. (1996). *The student learning imperative: Implications for student affairs.* Washington, DC: American College Personnel Association.

Arrington, M. (2005). *85% of colleges use facebook.* Retrieved from http://www.tech crunch.com/2005/09/07/85-of-college-students-use-facebook.

Austin, D. M. (1993). Orientation activities for the families of new students. In M. L. Upcraft, R. H. Mullendore, B. O. Barefoot, & D. S. Fidler (Eds.), *Designing successful transitions: A guide for orienting students to college.* [Monograph] (Series No. 13). Columbia, SC: University of South Carolina, National Resource Center for The First-Year Experience and Students in Transition.

Barefoot, B. O., & Gardner, J. N. (1993). The freshman orientation seminar: Extending the benefits of traditional orientation. In M. L. Upcraft, R. H. Mullendore, B. O. Barefoot, & D. S. Fidler (Eds.), *Designing successful transitions: A guide for orienting students to college.* [Monograph] (Series No. 13). Columbia, SC: University of South Carolina, National Resource Center for The First-Year Experience and Students in Transition.

Beal, P. E., & Noel, L. (1980). *What works in student retention.* The American College Testing Program and the National Center for Higher Education Management Systems. Iowa, IA: ACT.

Bennett, M. E. (1938). *The orientation of students in educational institutions.* Thirty-seventh yearbook (pp. 163–166). NSSE, Part I, Public-School.

Bookman, G. (1948). Freshman orientation techniques in colleges and universities. *Occupations, 27,* 163–166.

Brewster, K. J. (1968). Introduction. In O. Johnson (Ed.), *Stover at Yale.* New York: Collier Books.

Brown, R. (1972). *Tomorrow's higher education: A return to the academy.* Washington, DC: The American College Personnel Association.

Brubacher, J. S., & Rudy, W. (1958). *Education in transition.* New York: Harper.

Bryant, P., & Crockett, K. (1993, Fall). The admission office goes scientific. *Planning for Higher Education, 22*(1), 1–8.

Bugeja, M. (2006). Facing the facebook. *The Chronicle of Higher Education, 52*(21).

Butts, T. H. (1971). *Personnel service review: New practices in student orientation.* Ann Arbor, MI. (ERIC Document Reproduction Service No. ED 0570416).

Cabrera, A., Nora, A., Terenzini, P., Pascarella, E., & Hagedorn, L. (1999). Campus racial climate and the adjustment of students to college: A comparison between white students and African-American students. *Journal of Higher Education, 70*(2), 134–150.

Carney-Hall, K. C. (2008, Summer). Understanding current trends in family involvement. In Hall (Ed.), *Managing parent partnerships: Maximizing interference, and focusing on student success* (New Directions for Student Services, No. 122, pp. 3–14). San Francisco: Jossey-Bass.

Caple, R. B. (1964). A rationale for the orientation course. *Journal of College Student Personnel, 6,* 42–46.

Center for Community College Student Engagement. (2008). *Imagine success: engaging entering students* (2008 SENSE Field Test Findings). Austin, TX: The University of Texas at Austin, Community College Leadership Program.

Chhuon, V., & Hudley, C. (2008). Factors supporting Cambodian American students' successful adjustment into the university. *Journal of College Student Development, 49*(1), 15–30.

Chickering, A., & Havighurst, R.J. (1981). The life cycle. In A. Chickering & Associates (Eds.), *The modern American college* (pp. 16–50). San Francisco: Jossey-Bass.

Cohen, R. D., & Jody, R. (1978). *Freshman seminar: A new orientation.* Boulder, CO: Westview.

College Parents of America. (2006). *Survey of Current College Parent Experiences.* Retrieved from http://www.collegeparents.org/files/Current-Parent-SurveySummary.pdf http://www.collegeparents.org/files/Current-Parent-SurveySummary.pdf.

Columbia University (2007). *"Go Ask Alice!"* Retrieved from http://www.goaskalice.columbia.edu.

Cook, B. J., & Young, K. (2009). *From solider to student: Easing the transition of service members on campus.* Washington, DC: American Council on Education.

Council for the Advancement of Standards in Higher Education. (2009). *CAS professional standards for higher education* (7th ed.). Washington, DC: Author.

Council of Guidance and Personnel Associations. (1943). Recommendations. *Occupations, 21,* 46–48.

Crocker, L. G. (Ed.). (1921). *Advice to freshmen by freshmen.* Ann Arbor, MI: G. Wahr.

Cutright, M. (2002, September-October). What are research universities doing for first-year students. *About Campus, 7*(4), 16–20.

Dannells, M., & Kuh. G. D. (1977). Orientation. In W. T. Packwood (Ed.), *College student personnel services.* Springfield, IL: Charles C Thomas.

Doermann, H. J. (1926). *Orientation of college freshmen.* Baltimore: Williams & Wilkins.

Drake, R. W. (1966). *Review of the literature for freshman orientation practices in the United States.* Fort Collins, CO: Colorado State University. (ERIC Document Reproduction Service No. ED030 920).

Eberhardt, D. (2007, September/October). Facing up to Facebook. *About Campus, 12*(4), 18–26.

Edmondson, B. (1997, March). Demographics: Keeping up with change. *College Board Review, 180,* 25–30.

Eimers, M., & Mullen, R. (1997). Transfer students: Who are they and how successful are they at the University of Missouri? *College and University, 72*(3), 9–19.

Farrell, E. (2006). Judging roommates by their Facebook cover. *The Chronicle of Higher Education, 53*(2), p. A63.

Feldman, K. A., & Newcomb, T. M. (1969). *The impact of college on students.* San Francisco: Jossey-Bass.

Fitts, C. T., & Swift, F. H. (1928). *The construction of orientation courses for freshmen, 1888–1926.* Berkeley, CA: University of California Press.

Fitzgerald, L. E., & Evans, S. B. (1963). Orientation programs: Foundations and framework. *College and University, 38,* 270–275.

Foxley, C. H. (1969). Orientation or dis-orientation. *Personnel and Guidance Journal, 48,* 218–221.

Gansemer-Topf, A. M., Ross, L. E., & Johnson, R. M. (2006). Graduate and professional student development and student affairs. In M. J. Guentzel & B. E. Nesheim (Eds.), *Supporting graduate and professional students: The role of student affairs* (New Directions for Student Services, No. 115, pp. 19–30). San Francisco: Jossey-Bass.

Gardner, J. N., & Hansen, D. A. (1993). Perspectives on the future of orientation. In M. L. Upcraft, R.H. Mullendore, B. O. Barefoot, & D. S. Fidler (Eds.), *Designing successful transitions: A guide for orienting students to college.* (Monograph Series No. 13). Columbia, SC: National Resource Center for The Freshman Year Experience.

Goodrich, T. A., & Pierson, R. R. (1959). Pre-college counseling at Michigan State University. *Personnel and Guidance Journal, 37,* 595–597.

Gordon, V., & Grites, T. (1991). Adjustment outcomes of a freshmen seminar: A utilization-focused approach. *Journal of College Student Development, 32,* 37–41.

Grier, D. G. (1966). Orientation-Tradition or reality? *NASPA Journal, 3,* 37–41.

Habley, W. (2004, January 14). *What works in student retention?* Workshop presented by the ACT Office for the Enhancement of Educational Practices, Naperville, IL.

Hadlock, H. L. (2000, Spring). Orientation programs: A synopsis of their significance. *The Journal of College Orientation and Transition, 7*(2), 27–31.

Hall, B. (1982). College warm-up: Easing the transition to college. *Journal of College Student Personnel, 23*(3), 280–281.

Harbin, C. E. (1997). A survey of transfer students at four-year institutions serving a California community college. *Community College Review, 25*(2), 21–40.

Harrell II, I. L. (2008). Increasing the success of online students. *Inquiry, 13*(1), 36–44.

Hatch, C. (2000). Parent and family orientation. In M. J. Fabich (Ed.), *Orientation planning manual 2000.* Pullman, WA: National Orientation Directors Association.

HERI Research Brief. (2007, September). *College freshmen and online social networks.* Retrieved from http://www.gseis.ucla.edu/heri/PDFs/pubs/briefs/brief-091107-

SocialNetworking.pdf.

Holland, A., & Hubba, M. E. (1989). Psychosocial development among student para-professionals in a college orientation program. *Journal of College Student Development, 30,* 100–105.

Hoppenjans, J., & Semenow, L. (2007). Welcoming international students: Orientation for citizens of the world. *The Orientation Review, 36*(4), 17.

Hossler, D. (1999, Winter). Effective admissions recruitment. In G. H. Gaither (Ed.), *Promising practices in recruitment, remediation, and retention* (New Directions in Higher Education, No. 108, pp. 15–30). San Francisco: Jossey-Bass.

Howe, N., & Strauss, W. (2007). *Millennials go to college.* Great Falls. VA: LifeCourse Associates.

Jacobs. B. C., & With, E. A. (2002). Orientation's role in addressing the developmental stages of parents. *The Journal of College Orientation and Transition, 9*(2), 37–42.

Jalomo, R. E. Jr., & Rendon, L. I. (2004). Moving to a new culture: The upside and downside of the transition to college. In L. I. Rendon, M. Garcia, & G. Person (Eds.), *Transforming the first year of college for students of color.* (Mongraph Series No. 38, pp. 37–52). Columbia, SC: University of South Carolina, National Resource Center for The First-Year Experience and Students in Transition.

Johnson, L., Levine, A., & Smith, R. (2009). *The 2009 horizon report.* Austin, Texas: The New Media Consortium.

Johnson, M. J. (1998, Spring). First year orientation programs at four ycar public institutions: A brief history. *The Journal of College Orientation and Transition, 5*(2), 25–31.

Johnson, D. B., & Miller, M. T. (2000). Redesigning traditional programs to meet the needs of generation Y. *The Journal of College Orientation and Transition, 7*(2), 15–20.

Junco, R. (2005). Technology and today's first-year students. In M. L. Upcraft, J. N. Gardner, B. O. Barefoot, & Associates (Eds.), *Challenging & supporting the first-year student: A handbook for improving the first year of college* (pp. 391–409). San Francisco: Jossey-Bass.

Kamm, R. B., & Wrenn, C. G. (1947). Current developments in student-personnel Programs and the needs of the veteran. *School and Society, 65,* 89–92.

Keeling, R. P. (Ed.). (2004). *Learning reconsidered: A campus-wide focus on the student experience.* Washington, DC: American College Personnel Association and National Association of Student Personnel Administrators.

Kezar, A. (2009). Supporting and enhancing student learning through partnerships with academic colleagues. In G. S. McClellan, J. Stringer, & Associates (Eds.), *The handbook of student affairs administration* (pp. 586–601). San Francisco: Jossey-Bass.

King, T. A. (2004). Developing effective orientation programs for special populations. In M. J. Fabich (Ed.), *Orientation planning manual 2004* (pp. 31–37). Flint, MI: National Orientation Directors Association.

Klostermann, L. R., & Merseal, J. (1978). Another view of orientation. *Journal of College Student Personnel, 19*(3), 86–87.

Krall, J. K. (1981). New student welcome day program. *Journal of College and University Housing, 11*(2), 320–333. Baltimore, MD: John Hopkins University Press.

Krause, K. J. (2007). Social involvement and commuter students: The first-year student voice. *Journal of the First-Year Experience & Students in Transition, 19*(1), 27–45.

Kruger, K. (2009). Innovations and implications. In G. S. McClellan, J. Stringer, & Associates (Eds.), *The handbook of student affairs administration* (pp. 586–601). San Francisco: Jossey-Bass.

Kuh, G. (1996). Guiding principles for creating seamless learning environments For undergraduates. *Journal of College Student Development, 37*(2) 135–148.

Kuh, G. (2001). College students today: Why we can't leave serendipity to chance. In P. Altbach, P. Gumport, & B. Johnstone (Eds.), *In defense of American higher education.*

Lenhart, A., Madden, M., & Hitlin, P. (2005, July 27). *Teens and technology: Youth are leading the transition to a fully wired and mobile nation.* Pew Internet and American Life Project, Washington, DC,

Levitz, R., & Noel, L. (1989). Connecting students to institutions: Keys to retention and success. In M. L. Upcraft, J. N. Gardner, & Associates (Eds.), *The freshman year experience* (pp. 65–81). San Francisco: Jossey-Bass.

Love, K.M. (2008). Parental attachments and psychological distress among african American college students. *Journal of College Student Development, 49*(1), 31–40.

Lowe, I. (1980, April). *Preregistration counseling: A comparative study.* Paper presented at the California College Association Conference, Monterey, CA.

Mann, B. A. (1998). Retention principles for new student orientation programs. *The Journal of College Orientation and Transition, 6*(1), 15–20.

Maramba, D.C. (2008). Immigrant families and the college experience: Perspectives of Filipina Americans. *Journal of College Student Development, 49*(4), 336–350.

McCann, J. C. (1967). Trends in orienting college students. *Journal of the National Association of Women Deans, Administrators and Counselors, 30*(2), 855–889.

Merriman, L. (2007). Managing parents 101: Minimizing interference and maximizing good will. *Leadership Exchange, 5*(1), 14–19.

Miller, T. E. (2005). Student persistence and degree attainment. In T. E. Miller, B. E. Bender, J. H. Schuh, & Associates (Eds.), *Promoting reasonable expectations: Aligning student and institutional view of the college experience* (pp. 134–135). San Francisco: Jossey-Bass.

Moltz, D. (2009). Reorienting themselves. *Inside Higher Education.* Retrieved from www.insidehighered.com/layout/set/print/news/2009/08/19/orientation.

Morison, S. E. (1936). The histories of the universities. Lectures delivered at the Rice Institute, April 3–4, 1935. The Rice Institute Pamphlet, 1936(b), 23, 211–282.

Mueller, K. H. (1961). *Student personnel work in higher education.* Boston: Houghton-Mifflin.

Mullendore, R. H. (1998a). Orientation as a component of institutional retention efforts. In R. H. Mullendore (Ed.), *Orientation planning manual.* Bloomington, IN: National Orientation Directors Association.

Mullendore, R. H. (1998b). Including parents and families in the orientation process. In R. H. Mullendore (Ed.), *Orientation planning manual.* Bloomington, IN: National Orientation Directors Association.

Mullendore, R. H., & Abrahamn, J. (1993). Organization and administration of orientation programs. In M. L. Upcraft, J. N. Gardner, & Associates (Eds.), *The fresh-man year experience* (pp. 61–77). San Francisco: Jossey-Bass.

Mullendore, R. H., & Banahan, L. A. (2005a). Designing orientation programs. In M. L. Upcraft, J. N. Gardner, B. O. Barefoot, & Associates (Eds.), *Challenging & supporting the first-year student: A handbook for improving the first year of college* (pp. 391–409). San Francisco: Jossey-Bass.

Mullendore, R. H., & Banahan, L. A. (2005b). Channeling parent energy and reaping the benefits. In K. Keppler, R. H. Mullendore, & A. Carey (Eds.), *Partnering with the parents of today's college students* (pp. 35–41). Washington DC: National Association of Student Personnel Adminstrators.

Murdock, S. H., & Hoque, M. N. (1999, Winter). Demographic factors affecting higher education in the United States in the twenty-first century. In G. H. Gaither (Ed.), *Promising practices in recruitment, remediation, and retention.* (New Directions for Higher Education, No. 108, pp. 5–14). San Francisco: Jossey-Bass.

Nash, R. D. (2005). Course completion rates among distance learners: Identifying possible methods to improve retention. *Online Journal of Distance Learning Administration, 8*(4).

National Center for Educational Statistics. (2002). Retrieved from http://www.nces.ed.gov/fastfacts/.

National Center for Educational Statistics (2007). Retrieved from http://www.nces.ed/gov/fastfacts/.

National Orientation Directors Association. (2009). http://www.nodaweb.org/about-noda/mission-a-core-values.html.

National Resource Center for the First-Year Experience and Students in Transition. (2006). *Preliminary summary of results from the 2006 national survey on first-year seminars.* Retrieved from http://www.sc.edu/fye/research/surveyfindings/surveys/survey06.html.

National Survey of Student Engagement. (2007). *Experiences that matter: Enhancing student learning and success* (Annual Report 2007). Bloomington, IN: Indiana University Center for Postsecondary Research.

Okagaki, L., Helling, M. K., & Bingham, G. E. (2009). American Indian college students' ethnic identity and beliefs about education. *Journal of College Student Development, 50*(2), 157–176.

Pascarella, E. (2006). How college affects students: Ten directions for future research. *Journal of College Student Development, 47*(5), 508–520.

Pascarella, E. T., & Terenzini, P. T. (1991). *How college affects students: Findings and insights from twenty years of research.* San Francisco: Jossey-Bass.

Pascarella, E. T., & Terenzini, P. T. (2005). *How college affects students: Volume 2: A third decade of research.* San Francisco, CA: Jossey-Bass.

Penn, G, (1999). Enrollment management for the 21st century: Institutional goals, accountability, and fiscal responsibility. *ASHE-ERIC Higher Education Report, 26*(7). Washington, DC: The George Washington University.

Perigo, D., & Upcraft, L. (1989). Orientation programs. In M. L. Upcraft, R. H. Mullendore, B.O. Barefoot, & D. S. Fidler (Eds.), *Designing successful transitions: A guide for orienting students to college* (Monograph Series No. 13). Columbia, SC:

University of South Carolina, National Resource Center for The First-Year Experience and Students in Transition.

Poock, M. C. (2008). Orientation programs for graduate students. In K. A. Tokuno (Ed.), *Graduate students in transition: Assisting students through the first year.* (Monograph Series No. 50, pp. 91–105). Columbia, SC: University of South Carolina, National Resource Center for The First-Year Experience and Students in Transition.

Ramist, L. (1981). *College student attrition and retention.* College Board Report, No. 80–81. Princeton, NJ: College Entrance Examination Board.

Rendon, L. I., Garcia, M., & Person, G. (Eds.). (2004). *Transforming the first year of college for students of color* (Mongraph Series No. 38). Columbia, SC: University of South Carolina, National Resource Center for The First-Year Experience and Students in Transition.

Riesman, D. (1961). Changing colleges and changing students. *National Catholic Education Association Bulletin, 58,* 104–115.

Ritchie, J. (Ed.). (2001). *New member handbook.* Pullman, WA: National Orientation Directors Association.

Rode, D. (2000). The role of orientation in institutional retention. In M. J. Fabich (Ed.), *Orientation planning manual 2000.* Pullman, WA: National Orientation Directors Association.

Rode, D. (2004). The role of orientation in institutional retention. In M. J. Fabich (Ed.), *Orientation planning manual 2004.* Flint, MI: National Orientation Directors Association.

Sagaria, M. A. (1979). Freshman orientation courses: A framework. *Journal of the National Association of Women Deans, Administrators, and Counselors, 43*(1), 3–7.

Sandeen, C. A. (2000). Developing effective campus and community relationships. In M. J. Barr, M. K. Dresler, & Associates (Eds.), *The handbook of student affairs* (pp. 377–392). San Francisco: Jossey-Bass.

Savage, M. (2007). *National survey of college and university parent programs.* Minneapolis, MN: University of Minnesota. Retrieved from http://www.parent.umn.edu/ParentSurvey07.pdf.

Schmidt, D. K., & Sedlacek, W. E. (1972). Variables related to university student satisfaction. *Journal of College Student Personnel, 13,* 233–237.

Smith, B. F., & Brackin, R. (1993). Components of a comprehensive orientation program. In M. L. Upcraft, R. H. Mullendore, B. O. Barefoot, & D. S. Fidler (Eds.), *Designing successful transitions: A guide for orienting students to college.* (Monograph Series No. 13, pp. 39–54). Columbia, SC: University of South Carolina, National Resource Center for The First-Year Experience and Students in Transition.

Strang, R. (1951). Orientation of new students. In C. G. Wrenn (Ed.), *Student personnel work in college* (pp. 274–292). New York: Ronald.

Strumpf, G., & Wawrzynski, M. (Eds.). (2000). *National Orientation Directors Association data bank.* College Park, MD: National Orientation Directors Association.

Strumpf, G., Sharer, G., & Wawrzynski, M. (2003). 20 years of trends and issues in orientation programs. In J. A. Ward-Roof & C. Hatch (Eds.), *Designing successful transitions: A guide for orienting students to college* (2nd ed., Monograph Series No. 13, pp. 31–38). Columbia, SC: University of South Carolina, National Resource Center for The First-Year Experience and Students in Transition.

Sturtz, S. A. (1971). Age differences in college student satisfaction. *Journal of College Student Personnel, 12,* 220–222.

Tinto, V. (1985). Dropping out and other forms of withdrawal from college. In L. Noel, R. Levitz, D. Saluri, & Associates (Eds.), *Increasing student retention* (pp. 28–43). San Francisco: Jossey-Bass.

Tinto, V. (1997). Universities as learning communities. *About Campus, 1*(6), 2–4.

Tinto, V. (2000). Linking learning and leaving. In J. Braxton (Ed.), *Reworking the student development puzzle.* Nashville: Vanderbilt University Press.

Townsend, B. D., & Wilson, K. (2006). A hand hold for a little bit: Factors facilitating the success of community college transfer students to a large research university. *Journal of College Student Development, 47*(4), 439–456.

Upcraft, M. L., & Farnsworth, W. M. (1984). Orientation programs and activities. In M. L. Upcraft (Ed.), *Orienting students to college* (New Directions for Student Services, No. 25, pp. 27–39). San Francisco: Jossey-Bass.

Upcraft, M. L., Gardner, J. N., & Associates. (1989). *The freshman year experience.* San Francisco: Jossey-Bass.

U.S. Department of Education. (2006). *The Commission on the future of higher education draft report of 8/9/2006.* Retrieved from http://www.ed.gov/about/bdscomm/list/hiedfuture/reports/0809-draft.pdf.

U.S. Department of Education. National Center for Education Statistics. (2009). *Digest of Education Statistics, 2008* (NCES 2009–020), Chapter 3.

Ward-Roof, J. (2005). Parents' orientation: Begin with the end in mind. In K. Keppler, R. H. Mullendore, & A. Carey (Eds.), *Partnering with the parents of today's college students* (pp. 29–33). Washington DC: National Association of Student Personnel Administrators.

Ward-Roof, J., Heaton, P., & Coburn, M. (2008, Summer). Capitalizing on parent and family partnerships through programming. In K. C. Carney-Hall (Ed.), *Managing parent partnerships: Maximizing interference, and focusing on student success* (New Directions for Student Services, No. 122, pp. 43–55). San Francisco: Jossey-Bass.

Wolf, D. S., Sax, L. J., & Harper, C. E. (2009). Parental engagement and contact in the academic lives of college students. *NASPA, 46*(2), 325–358.

Younger, T. K. (2009, Summer). Students share how four year institutions can help them succeed. *Leadership Exchange, 7*(2), 19–21.

Zis, S. L. (2002, Fall). Changing student characteristics. Implications for new student orientation. *The Journal of College Orientation and Transition, 10*(1), 64–68.

Chapter 10

RESIDENCE HALLS

CATHY AKENS AND JEFF NOVAK

INTRODUCTION

Student housing at colleges and universities is being transformed by a paradigm shift in higher education that is stimulated by a convergence of issues including a recognition that learning happens outside the classroom, an emphasis on student engagement, exploding enrollment in higher education, the need to renovate or replace existing residence halls, the consumerism of today's college student and parent, and institutional concerns over student retention. (Luna & Gahagan, 2008, p. 1)

These shifting forces impact the role of housing in American higher education. Their purpose within the institution is evolving as universities examine student learning and the potential for residence hall programs to have a significant impact on desired outcomes. As Schroeder and Mable (1994) stated, "By focusing on student learning, residential hall programs can become interwoven with the fabric of the academy, bringing integration and coherence to a traditionally fragmented, compartmentalized, and often random approach to achieving important educational outcomes" (p. 302).

This chapter examines a number of issues related to residence hall programs, including history, mission and purpose, administration and organizational structure, staffing patterns, entry level requirements, programs and services, influence of residence halls on students, select legal issues, professional development, the future, and technology resources. The administration of residence hall operations is complex in nature, so it should be noted that there are aspects of the operation that are not addressed within the scope of this chapter, but are examined in other resources on the topic.

THE HISTORY OF RESIDENCE HALLS

Since the inception of America's higher education system, student housing, in one form or another, has existed. Residence halls, originally referred to as dormitories, were rooted in English universities, the system on which American higher education was modeled (Winston, Anchor, & Associates, 1993). As the number of American colleges and universities grew, students needed places to live and parents expected their children to be cared for while they were away from home. As student housing became more prevalent through the years on college and university campuses, its function began to have a major role in the overall campus development and facilities.

Higher educational institutions and facilities for housing students in the United States can be best traced by examining three distinct time periods throughout history: (1) the colonial period, (2) the mid-to-late nineteenth century, and (3) the twentieth century. From the beginning, American higher education was modeled after the well-known and established English universities, Cambridge and Oxford (Frederickson, 1993; Winston, Anchors, & Associates, 1993).

The Colonial Period

In England, residential facilities were constructed to meet logistical needs of students who often traveled long distances from homes to their respective campuses. In addition, the local housing market provided less than favorable conditions. Residence halls were designed to bring faculty and students together, both intellectually and morally, and were looked at as an essential aspect of the collegiate experience. Schuh (1996) stated that this structure attempted to meld learning both inside and outside of the classroom into an inclusive living/learning environment. Facilities were small in size with relatively few students. Students shared common areas, advisors, and curriculum, leading to an increased partnership between students and faculty (Henry, 2003). In England, professors were responsible for instruction, while staff such as porters and other officials, focused on supervision and the discipline of the students. With formal education of students as their main focus rather than the monitoring of behavior, faculty formed meaningful relationships with students.

Administrators of colleges and universities in the United States wanted to emulate English models of residential facilities, with the goal of bringing faculty and students together both intellectually and morally (Schuh, 2004). However, many factors made this effort difficult. As with their English counterparts, students often traveled long distances to attend school in the United States. Rudolph's (1990) research revealed that this allowed many regions of the country to be represented in the student population instead of drawing solely on the geographical area or local town. Parents of students sending their children far from home expected institutions to provide an appropriate living and learning environment (Henry, 2003). Unlike Cambridge and Oxford, where faculty were free from the parental role, a lack of funding in the United States required that faculty were charged with both the responsibility of instruction and discipline of students (Schroeder, Mable & Associates, 1994). This spawned the beginning of *in loco parentis,* whereby universities and colleges exercised parental control over all aspects of academic policy and many other phases of student life beyond the classroom, preparing students for civic and religious leadership. Upcraft (1993a) asserted:

> From the beginning of higher education in America, college administrators and professors have known that a student's education occurs as a result of what occurs both inside and outside of the classroom. Early American colleges educated students outside the classroom through the concept of *in loco parentis* whereby colleges acted on behalf of parents, assuming that they must exercise total control over students both inside and outside the classroom if students were to develop good moral character and become truly educated. (p. 319)

Residential facilities struggled to create a system equivalent to Cambridge and Oxford. Hampered financially, facilities were established more as dormitories, where students ate and slept separately from academic infusion and semblances of a living/learning environment. Henry (2003) stated that instead of melding the academic and social lives of students, the crux of the English system of residential facilities, few meaningful relationships between students and faculty were formed in the American models. As a result, rowdiness and poor behavior, often stereotypically associated with the characteristics of a dormitory, emerged. Connections between residence halls and the academic mission of the institution became increasingly unclear. Disciplinary issues, less than adequate living conditions, and adversarial relationships between faculty and students did not mirror those facilities in England as originally intended (Schuh, 2004).

Middle to Late Nineteenth Century

The second phase of American residential facilities occurred during the nineteenth century. Many presidents of colleges began to devalue the importance of student housing as their focus shifted toward research and instruction. It was during the period following the Civil War that many Americans went to Germany, further developing their education. In Germany, institutions primarily focused on teaching and research, with little or no attention paid to the collegiate way of life (Frederiksen, 1993). Students were responsible for finding their own living arrangements as universities focused on structures to house classrooms and laboratories. Graduates and faculty of these institutions brought this concept to America, which resulted in a widening of the gap between the classroom and the out-of-classroom and residential experiences (Frederickson, 1993; Schroeder et al., 1994). This separation continued as faculty members spent more time developing research in their respective disciplines. Student housing was no longer seen as a vital component of the collegiate experience and the responsibility of housing students was not a part of the institutional mission. Housing facilities that were built during the Colonial Period continued to house students, however, few resources were dedicated toward their upkeep (Schuh, 2004). Of the numerous colleges established during the nineteenth century, residential facilities were not included in construction of these campuses (Henry, 2003). The financial assistance through endowments and other donations institutions received was earmarked for academic buildings, while students had the responsibility to secure their own housing. This was consistent with the German model, which proposed that students were adults who should be able to find housing on their own (Frederickson).

During the latter half of the nineteenth century, housing stock in local communities was inadequate to accommodate students attending nearby institutions. . This period also marked the implementation of colleges just for women and parental concern for appropriate housing. University presidents responded by re-emphasizing the importance of construction of residential facilities on campus. Due to the influx of students and a new focus on campus life outside of the classroom, including intercollegiate sports and debating societies, campus housing became more attractive. Residential facilities for both women and men were developed to allow greater ease of participation in campus activities (Schuh, 1996).

Twentieth Century

The third period in collegiate housing was marked by major developments late in the nineteenth century and throughout the twentieth century. This was manifested by the increasing number of women and minorities entering higher education, the Great Depression, and the greatest expansion occurring as a result of the G.I. Bill and Title IV. These trends eventually led to the simultaneous expansion of residence halls.

As college presidents continued the push for the development of residential facilities, the goal was met with financial constraint as a result of the Great Depression. Henry's (2003) research indicated that states enacted laws that allowed for the issuance of bonds for residence halls. Additionally, the Federal Emergency Administration of Public Works (PWA), established in

1933, enabled many colleges and universities to obtain additional monies through loan and grant programs to construct low-cost housing (Frederickson, 1993). Between 1900 and 1940, construction of new institutions and enrollments flourished. Though there was a marked decline during World War II, the greatest expansion of American Higher Education prospered with the passage of the G.I. Bill and the Housing Act of 1950. According to Schroeder et al. (1994):

> This period witnessed the enrollment of women and blacks, the rise of extracurriculum, and the rapid proliferation of public higher education. These trends contributed to the expansion of residence halls, with the most rapid expansion occurring as a result of the G.I. Bill and Title IV of the Housing Act of 1950. (p. 7)

Residential facilities, primarily developed through business and finance divisions of an institution, were obtained with the sole purpose of housing and feeding students. The 1950s saw an even greater demand for campus housing. The United States Department of Housing and Urban Development (HUD) created the College Housing Program to aid in the construction of new residential facilities and renovations of existing halls, student unions and other cocurricular support buildings (Henry, 2003). Low interest loans and long amortization schedules allowed for greater affordability and construction of new facilities and renovation of existing ones (Fredericksen, 1993).

Housing was constructed quickly and at low cost, with little attention paid to the personal development of students. Facilities were often large, with structures having a cold and impersonal feel. Additionally, the construction process gave little thought to educational and developmental needs and opportunities for students within the halls that were being constructed (Schroeder et al., 1994). Lacking study rooms, common areas, and community space, the facilities were built with little attention to developing living/ learning environments. Rules were often strict, and students questioned authority. It was also during this time that faculty members were being distracted from instruction and research by what they saw as nonacademic functions, such as registration, advising, and counseling. At the same time, students showed an increased interest in extracurricular activities. Literary groups, intramural sport teams, and student clubs and organizations formed by the dozens (Miller, Winston, & Associates, 1991). Komives et al. (2003) suggested extracurricular activities arose from the students' desire to break away from the strict and traditional course of study.

In the latter part of the 1930s, as enrollments increased due to unemployment, student affairs was again becoming an important component in the

structure of colleges and universities. One of the most significant and landmark events affecting the professionalism of students affairs during the time,
was the development and codification of the *Student Personal Point of View*
(SPPV) (Delworth, Hanson, & Associates, 1989; Guthrie, 1997; Komives et
al., 2003). The report discussed the fragmentation that had occurred in higher education and encouraged institutions to give equal emphasis to the development of the person and the mind. Guthrie (1997) stated that the *Student
Personal Point of View:*

> Imposes upon educational institutions the obligations to consider the student
> as a whole—his intellectual capacity and achievement, his emotional make up,
> his physical condition, his social relationships, his vocational aptitudes and
> skills, his moral and religious values, his economic resources, and his aesthetic
> appreciations. It puts emphasis, in brief, upon the development of the student
> as a person rather than upon his intellectual training alone. (p. 23)

The report urged colleges and universities to consider the education of the
whole student and the many other entities that encapsulate complete development.

In 1949, the American Council of Education revised the original *Student
Personal Point of View*. This new report reaffirmed the development of the
whole student, while outlining goals and conditions for student growth, fundamental elements of a student personnel program, and the administrative
and governance functions of a student affairs program (Komives et al., 2003).
The document was written to stimulate a greater understating of student
affairs among higher level administrators of colleges and universities.

The *Student Personal Point of View* of 1937 and 1949 helped legitimize, provide vision, and offer guidance within higher education for student affairs.
During the next fifty years, the field of student affairs, which had evolved
from the early deans of men and deans of women, became a major administrative area in higher educational institutions, headed by vice-presidents
charged with directing the various campus programs and services for students (Sandeen, 1991). During these years, several significant events shaped
the development of both higher education and the student affairs profession.
Federal support and involvement, landmark legal challenges, increased
research and theory, and the development of professional standards helped
mold current institutions. Consequently, residence halls and their staffing
models were structured to reflect this new expansion and paradigm shift to
the education of the whole student.

The latter part of the 1960s and early part of 1970s paved the way for
increased focus on creating more of a living and learning environment within residential facilities. By 1980, the demand for on-campus housing surged

with many institutions allocating a percentage of their bed space for incoming freshmen and lottery processes for those students wanting to return to campus housing each year (Henry, 2003). In the 1990s, institutions began to construct smaller facilities, with more emphasis on common space, community centers, computer labs, and other increased amenities to compete with traditional apartments in the off-campus housing market (Grimm & Dunkel, 1999).

Many campus housing facilities are now more than 50 years old, and a large portion of a housing department's budget is earmarked for repair, ongoing and preventative maintenance, and upgrades to current residential facilities. Housing facilities are in desperate need of renovation, both inside and out (Ryan, 2003; Smith, 2000). Enrollment increase is coming at a time when funding for higher education had never been a bigger challenge. New enrollees look to campus housing for their accommodations, thereby placing great demand on colleges and universities to increase and renovate current facilities. In order to meet the changing demands of the student population, including higher quality programs, services and activities, college and universities will be forced to respond or students will seek housing elsewhere (Schuh, 2004). Residential facilities of the 2000s incorporate technological advances in security systems, swimming pools, tutoring centers, classrooms, high-speed data connection, and many other amenities to cater to the student demand and need (Grimm & Dunkel, 1999).

MISSION AND PURPOSE

Before a housing operation can begin to formulate its mission, the department would be wise to examine where its overall role in the institution lies. Most often, the housing and residence life program plays a vital role in the institution, and residence hall staff should be structured to support the academic goals and mission of the institution through the services and programs they provide. The Council for the Advancement of Standards (CAS) described the contribution of student housing on college and university campuses to the institution's mission: "The housing and residential life program is an integral part of the educational program and academic support services of the institution. The mission must include provisions for educational programming and services, residential facilities, management services, and where appropriate, food services" (CAS, 2001, p. 143).

According to the *ACUHO-I Standards and Ethical Principles for College and University Housing Professionals* (2007), the mission of a housing and residence life department should include:

1. Providing reasonably priced living environments that are clean, attractive, well maintained, comfortable, and which include contemporary safety features supported by systematic operations;
2. Ensuring the orderly and effective administration of the program through sound management;
3. Providing an environment, including programs and services, that promotes learning in its broadest sense, with an emphasis on academic support, success and enhancement;
4. Providing, in programs that include food services, a variety of nutritious and pleasing meals, in pleasant surroundings, at a reasonable cost;
5. Providing a service that satisfies the needs of the housing and food service customer in a courteous, efficient and effective manner. (p. 3)

Colleges and universities that are large and state-supported compared with those that are small and independent may place completely different emphasis on what the role of a housing and residence life program will play in its overall institutional mission. Schuh (2004) stated that in a small liberal arts college where most students live in campus housing, the programs and services offered by the housing department will be interwoven into the educational experience of residential students. In institutions that have a residential college focus, the mission often reflects the importance of a living-learning environment. Institutions that are largely commuter in nature with a small number of housing facilities may not place much emphasis on the role of on-campus living for students.

As noted in the previous section, the role that college and university housing plays in the lives of campus students has changed considerably through the years. In turn, the missions of housing and residence life departments have reflected these changes. Most missions of housing and residence life programs start with the basic premise of providing students living in on-campus housing with a safe and secure environment that is conducive to academic and personal growth. According to Abraham Maslow, humans possess five basic needs that are arranged in a hierarchy. These are physiological, safety, belongingness and love, esteem, and self-actualization (Bolman & Deal, 1997). Lower order needs, physical and safety, must be met and satisfied in order for individuals to be motivated by the higher order needs such as belongingness and love, esteem, and self-actualization.

Many housing and residence life programs are structured on the tenets of Maslow's developmental model. Student's basic needs are met by providing proper shelter and food through well-maintained facilities and options for dining. Safety needs can be met by ensuring that residence hall staff are properly trained in emergency response, safety and security measures and policies are constantly reviewed, and physical maintenance of residential facilities is a continuous focus. The challenge for residence hall staff is to keep the atmosphere focused on student learning and development, both inside and outside of the classroom, to meet Maslow's needs of belongingness and love, esteem, and self-actualization. Winston et al. (1993) suggest that residence halls should provide a living/learning environment, programs and services that enhance individual growth, and development of students as whole persons. Schroeder et al. (1994) proposed that residence halls emphasize skills that challenge a student's ability to use knowledge in work and leisure. Many of the programs and services that are undertaken in the residence halls are aimed at creating environments that celebrate diversity by bringing students together in a community where differences are celebrated, respected, and appreciated, providing for optimal learning (Rentz & Saddlemire, 1988). These environments aid in students' academic and career pursuits.

Though considerably more emphasis is often placed on the programmatic and educational aspects of living in on-campus housing, housing and residence life departments must not forget the important effect that physical facilities and student comfort levels with respect to safety can have on a student's overall experience. Novak (2008) found that students who reported lower levels of satisfaction with safety and security measures being taken in the residential environment and timeliness in which maintenance requests were responded to, felt less connected to the campus community, less satisfied with their residential experience, and had lower levels of academic achievement.

The missions of colleges and universities have changed over the years to reflect the needs of all stakeholders. Consequently, the role and corresponding missions of housing and residence life programs on campuses have been altered as well. Though all functions of a housing department are of importance, some have had more prominence than others. Schuh (2004) stated:

> The physical environment and programmatic offerings are interrelated, and each contributes substantially to the advancement of the residence hall system. Students cannot be expected to be interested in learning opportunities unless they live in adequate physical facilities. If guidelines for community living are not established, it is possible that facilities will not be respected and, in fact, may be abused. (p. 275)

Housing and residence life departments are a fundamental component of a student's collegiate experience and should be committed to providing a qualified and diverse staff dedicated to the mission. Staff should foster a welcoming environment where individual differences are shared and explored.

Opportunities for holistic education through individual and community development, the establishment of intentional and purposeful relationships among students and staff, the advocacy of personal responsibility, accountability, and sound ethical decision-making should be a continual focus. As discussed in the next section, all housing and residence life staff members contribute to the success of the department. From the front line student employee to the director, all should be focusing on supporting the intuitional mission, while operating under the contextual framework of their own departmental mission. Failure to do so can have profound impacts on departmental effectiveness, possibly resulting in program ineptitude and unsuitable services for students (Barr, 2000).

ADMINISTRATION AND ORGANIZATION

Housing and residence life programs throughout the United States share overwhelming similarities in appearance, structure, and philosophy. However, they are also quite different in both subtle and obvious ways (Winston et al., 2003). Upcraft (1993a) identified the importance of looking at the contextual factors that influence the organizational structure of a housing and residence life program. The first factor is institutional size. Housing departments with thousands of students on large campuses will organize their system much differently than the housing departments with only a few hundred students on small campuses. With larger operations, more staff for specialized areas is needed. In a smaller system, staff may take on many different roles from day to day. The second factor focuses on the institutional mission and the supportive role that housing and residence life programs play. The third factor spotlights the characteristics of the student body. Colleges and universities that are liberal arts in nature may structure and organize their residential facilities differently than institutions that have strong specialized academic majors. The fourth component of departmental structure takes into account the grade level of students who reside in the residence halls. A campus with a majority first-year population living in on-campus housing may be structured to meet transitional and other associated needs of first-time-in-college students compared with upperclass students. Fifth, organizational structure may be affected by campus policies with respect to mandatory housing. Some institutions require students to live in campus housing for part, if not all, of their academic career. Lastly, the racial and ethnic make-up of the residents can play a large role in the services offered and staff provided.

These six components taken together strongly influence the structure and organization of housing and residence life departments. Dunkel (2010) stated that most housing organizations can be categorized in one of two broad structures, integrated and split structures. In an integrated or comprehensive model, one organization is responsible for all programs and services under the direction of a Chief Housing Officer (CHO). Often comprehensive models are structured into common units such as: (1) Residence Life or Education, (2) Business Services and Technology, (3) Administrative Services, and (4) Facilities Management. Together, under the supervision of the Chief Housing Officer, these units are typically responsible for:

- Recruitment, selection, training, and supervision of student and professional staff
- Living-learning communities and academic initiatives
- Residential student conduct
- Assessment
- Safety and security
- Accounts receivables and payables
- Purchasing
- Personnel and payroll
- Postal operations
- Technology, including computer hardware, software, networks, databases, and web design
- Food service
- Application and contractual processes
- Room assignments and preferences
- Marketing and corresponding publications
- Facilities management, including grounds

In the comprehensive model, it is most desirable to have the chief housing officer report to the vice-president of student affairs (Upcraft, 1993a). The CHO, however, may report to both the vice-president of student affairs and vice-president of administration and finance with matters that pertain to typical residence life functions and budgetary/business functions respectively.

Split or bifurcated housing organizational structures often separate residence life services and programs from the other units (business services and technology, administrative services, and facilities management). In this model, it is not uncommon for the different unit heads to report to different supervisors. Residence life and education may report to the vice-president of student affairs while business services and technology reports to the vice-president for administration and finance. Administrative services and facilities management may yet report to another area within senior leadership of the institution.

Factors including whether the institution is state supported or independent and if the housing department is a comprehensive or split system can influence budgetary structures. Housing and residence life programs at many state-assisted institutions function as an auxiliary service. As an auxiliary unit of the institution, housing and residence life departments are self-supporting entities that derive their budgets from the revenue generated through room rent paid by students and other revenue sources. The generated funds are then expended through salaries, maintenance operations, residential life programming, telecommunications, reserves for future projects, current debt service, and all other expenses associated with their operation. At an independent institution, operating expenses for housing and residence life departments may be administered by the general operating fund of the institution, and funds are allocated just as they would be to other departments on the campus (Schuh, 2004).

Dunkel (2010) proposed some rationales to support a comprehensive model over a split system. First, comprehensive housing operations possess a common mission that enhances program quality and effectiveness by sharing resources, services, staff, and materials. Second, staffs are shared among units, and it is not uncommon for a department to share staff when a task requires it. Third, comprehensive housing operations can often eliminate unnecessary staffing, while split systems with their differing reporting lines can often become convoluted. Institutional priorities will ultimately determine if a comprehensive or bifurcated model is the best fit.

STAFFING PATTERNS

As previously discussed, following the expansion of colleges and universities, the corresponding increase in the diversity of students during the mid-twentieth century, the proliferation of student affairs, and student activism and protests during the 1960s, roles of residence halls and their staff members changed dramatically (Frederiksen, 1993). Prior to the 1960s, staff was mainly responsible for counseling and advising students. There was little emphasis on non-academic skill development, as staff struggled to keep up with the ever-increasing demands placed on them by soldiers returning from war. Institutions experimented with many different staffing patterns to meet the diverse needs of their changing populations.

As the 1960s progressed and early evidence suggested that there was value to living in on-campus residential facilities versus commuting, staffing patterns began to mirror this philosophy (Schroeder et al., 1994). Administrators of institutions began to focus on positions in residence halls that provided student services and educational and personal development opportunities within the residential environment. Housemothers, counselors, and advisors were replaced by residence educators with advanced college degrees, who were responsible for coordinating a large number of organizations, services, and programs (Winston et al., 1993). The notion of *in loco parentis* shifted to a student-institution relationship.

In the 1960s and 1970s, with substantial increases in student enrollment and further expansion of residence halls, student affairs and housing divisions became more specialized to serve the needs of a diverse student population. Residence hall staffing reflected the current trend of educating the whole student (Fenske, 1989). As a result, living-learning communities were formed. As the 1960s continued, the student development perspective emerged, calling for changes in academic and student affairs programs. This had a profound impact on the roles and functions of residence halls. Residence halls now took on the roles of educators, counselors, and managers, meeting the diverse needs of the student culture. Programs were implemented to meet these needs and enhance the students' total development.

Titles of many positions within housing programs may vary from institution to institution; however, the functions these roles perform are relatively consistent (Schuh, 1996). Perhaps there is no other department within the university setting that relies so heavily upon paraprofessional staff, commonly called residents assistants or resident advisors, to meet the diverse needs of students programmatically and organizationally (Conlogue, 1993). Resident assistants are most often undergraduate staff who live on a residence floor with other students and provide direct services to the students. Resident assistants serve as role models, counselors, and teachers while being students themselves. Blimling (1995) proposed that resident assistants must serve as effective role models to the students they serve by exhibiting proper behavior and effective student practices. Resident assistants act as facilitators of student development in their community, helping students live together in a way that is conducive to personal, social, and academic growth. Resident assistants frequently plan and implement programs and activities for the residents of their floor, building, or entire community. Resident assistants create and post educational bulletin boards or other resources. Residents seek resident assistants in times of personal or community crises and emergencies.

Resident assistants often have the most difficult role of any student affairs member. They live where they work, are always on call, and often are on the front lines of emergencies occurring in the residential facilities. Resident assistants are usually the first responders to the scene, comforting residents in times of crisis. They work with students individually and in groups, tailoring programs to meet the needs of the students they serve. They often deal with issues of suicide, assaults, and building maintenance, while also confronting policy violations in these same students they are there to serve. Meeting all the roles that the position requires can be quite daunting for undergraduate students, as they strive to balance their own academic, social, and personal needs (Boyer, 1987). Across campuses, resident assistants receive extensive and exhaustive training in student development theory, procedures and policies, counseling skills, confrontation, as well as many other functional areas needed to perform their roles. Supervisors of these student staff positions, graduate staff or professionals who often begin their own careers as resident assistants, are charged with guiding programs and services aimed at meeting the educational missions of university housing programs (Schuh, 1996).

As mentioned in the Administration and Organization section, the size of the institution and corresponding housing department, whether the institution is state-assisted or independent, and core missions, both institutional and departmental, can have profound impacts on the staffing patterns. Typically in larger housing programs, graduate students seeking an advanced degree, known as graduate directors or graduate assistants, supervise resident assistants, advise hall councils, oversee hall programming, enforce and adjudicate student conduct, and are often the first point of contact in departmental escalation procedures, to respond to emergency and crisis situations. Depending on the structure of the department, graduate assistants may directly oversee a smaller residential facility or help in the administration of a larger building. In both instances, graduate assistants most often report to an entry-level professional. These entry-level professionals, commonly referred to as hall directors, residence life coordinators, or residence directors, typically have a master's degree in student affairs, counseling or a related field. Hall directors are full-time professionals who implement the residence life program and supervise the staff in their respective communities. Often these positions require living in a provided on-campus apartment. They usually live within the community or area that they are responsible for, allowing for greater opportunities to interact with students and staff, while being able to appropriately respond to incidents in a timely manner.

In a larger institution, the next level of staffing may be an area coordinator, complex director or assistant director who has several years of full-time experience. These positions may oversee a number of buildings, graduate assistants, or entry-level professionals. In a smaller system, graduate assistants may report directly to an assistant director, director, or assistant dean for residential life (Schuh, 2004). Some larger departments may have specialized positions that help achieve their mission. These positions may focus on: (1) living/learning communities; (2) program assessment and creation; (3) recruitment, selection and training of student, graduate, and professional staff; and (4) advising the residence hall association. In smaller schools, entry and mid-level professionals may oversee all aspects of a residence life program. Typically, the next staffing level at larger institutions is the associate director, who ultimately reports to the director of the department. The director provides leadership in the management and administration of the housing operation. They are responsible for budget oversight, facilities planning, deferred maintenance and renovation schedules, and capital projects for new and existing campus residential facilities.

Though the focus of this chapter resides heavily on the residence life side of a housing program, it is important to note that many departments, particularly in larger institutions, have a myriad of positions focused on the operations side. These staff members are often responsible for: (1) the administrative aspects of marketing and recruiting to new and current students, (2) room assignments, (3) budget preparation and management, (4) technology needs for both students and staff, (5) accounting of payables and receivables, (6) facilities planning and maintenance operations, (7) summer conferences, and (8) postal operations. Additionally, some departments are responsible for the provision of food services to students, both living on or off campus.

ENTRY-LEVEL REQUIREMENTS

Many student affairs professionals begin their career in an entry-level residential life position. Typically this position requires a professional to live in and manage a residence hall. As previously noted, the title of this position is usually called hall director, residence life coordinator, or residence director. In a study done with housing directors, it was found that most institutions require a master's degree as the basic requirement for an entry-level housing position (McCluskey-Titus, 2002). Some require the degree be in student personnel or higher education, but degrees in other field are also considered at many institutions. "Although a majority of directors prefer student personnel/student development training, there is recognition that some training in business and management principles is needed" (McCluskey-Titus, p. 8).

Entry-level housing positions typically require some practical work experience as well. A master's degree in student personnel without the practical experience is not as desirable as a combination of both (McCluskey-Titus, 2002). Working as a graduate assistant in a residence hall is a common experience among those hired into entry-level positions. Many also have been a resident assistant or have other experiences working with students. Some graduate students also take advantage of practicum opportunities, or internships, such as through the ACUHO-I internship program, to gain experience (McCluskey-Titus).

Residence hall professionals perform a variety of roles, so it is important to understand the types of skills necessary in those roles. A study was conducted with housing directors, who were asked to rank 49 competencies, which were identified in research literature. The study then produced a list of the top 15, rank-ordered competencies, according to the respondents. Directors identified the following as the 15 most important competencies for entry-level professionals in housing: interpersonal communication skills, ability to work cooperatively with a range of different people, supervision of staff, decision-making, training, crisis management, staff selection, goal-setting, conflict mediation, policy development, ethics, discipline, legal implications, motivation, and evaluation (Dunkel & Schrieber, 1992).

PROGRAMS AND SERVICES

Most educators would agree it is important for campuses to have an intentional, comprehensive residential program that creates an environment in which students can learn and grow (Schuh & Triponey, 1993). Housing professionals can impact student development "simply because of the opportunities for extended, substantive contact with students where they live" (McCluskey-Titus, 2006, p. 4). Kuh, Schuh, and Whitt (1991) found that almost 75 percent of what a student learns in college results from experiences gained outside of the classroom. For students who reside on campus, it is safe to assume that many of these experiences will take place in the residence halls.

Much has been written about best practices for providing enriching learning environments for students (Kuh, Kinzie, Schuh, & Whitt, 2005; Kuh, Schuh, & Whitt, 1991). In an era of greater accountability, residential programs, like all student services, need to be able to demonstrate that their programs add value to the student experience, and contribute to the educational mission of the institution. Housing officers will, in the future, continue to be called upon to provide data that demonstrates the positive effects of the residential experience (Schuh, 2006).

There is typically a broad range of opportunities for residence hall students to engage in programming (Schuh, 2004). A program can be defined as any intentional event designed to enhance students' learning and development (Dude & Shepherd Hayhurst, 1996). On many campuses, planning these programs is part of the job responsibilities of both paraprofessional and professional staff living in residence halls. Most campuses provide programming as a way of enhancing the university's overall learning objectives, and providing a sense of community for resident students. Research findings support the fact that undergraduate learning is enhanced when activities outside of the classroom complement formal instruction in class (Astin, 1993; Boyer 1987; Kuh, Schuh, & Whitt, 1991; Terenzini & Pascarella, 1994). "When residence halls are designed as purposeful educational settings, they can promote effective undergraduate education" (Schroeder et al., 1994, p. 1).

Schroeder (1993), in arguing that there are too few connections between the academic priorities of the institution, and residence hall programs and services, suggested that residence life programs must do the following: "Contribute to the quality of students' academic experiences; foster the creation of authentic residential communities; contribute to institutional enrollment management initiatives; prudently utilize limited resources; and demonstrate the value of programs and services" (p. 520). All elements of the residence hall operation have to be planned with these goals in mind, if they are to be achieved. Universities that create an intentional plan for programming and support services in residence halls should focus on creating an educational and enriching environment.

Community

The Boyer Commission published a report in 1998 regarding the status of undergraduate education. The report stated:

> Research universities should foster a community of learners. Large universities must find ways to create a sense of place and to help students develop small communities within the larger whole. . . . The campus must be a purposeful place of learning in which every student feels special connections, [as] shared rituals play a powerful role in creating the larger university community which smaller, personalized communities of learners can coalesce. . . . Commuters and residential students alike need to know that they are needed and valued members of the community. (pp. 34–35)

The importance of community in a residential setting has been emphasized by many researchers. "For students in residence halls, community is the sense of belonging with other members of the group and a set of shared experiences that bind them together and make them a mutually identifiable group" (Blimling, 1995, p. 472). Residence life professionals have long focused on the development of community as a vehicle for developing cohesive, integrated and effective living environments. Only recently has there been more of a shift to thinking about community development as a means to a greater end of student learning and development. Communities can promote a learning-focus by reinforcing strong academic expectations and helping students to create an academic identity (Minor, 1999). Initially much of the emphasis was on how a community environment helps students with their transition. Schlossberg (1989) and others have discussed how important it is for an individual to feel that he or she "matters" and the negative impact they experience when they do not believe that others care about them. The benefits of community, we now know, are greater than just assisting the individual student with adjustment. A well-planned community, one that is tied into the institution's academic mission, can have a positive influence on a student's academic achievement and personal development in many different dimensions (Minor). Living in a residence hall alone does not necessarily ensure these positive benefits. Small student groupings structured around students' academic major, common interests or service interest help to break down student isolation and anonymity, and increase the likelihood that students will engage in academic work that ultimately leads to greater student learning (Kuh, Douglas, Lund, & Ramin-Gyurnek, 1994). Resident assistants, the paraprofessional "front-line" staff members in residence halls, are often told that creating a sense of community is their main priority. Programming is just one approach to fostering community.

Programming Models

A number of conceptual models exist that can be used in the development of programs for residential students. These models include student development theories, intervention models, and campus ecology models (Schuh, 2004). A criticism has often been that residence hall programming is not intentional, or it is often carried out without a theoretical foundation. Therefore, it is important for educators to consider the best approach to programming on their own campus. Schuh and Triponey (1993) suggest that regardless of the model that residence hall programmers choose to adopt, there are some elements that programmers should always consider. They include:

1. Be aware of the institution's mission and ensure that programs are consistent with and supportive of the mission.
2. Plan programs with the model in mind. While there is not one best programming model, finding one that is most effective for a particular setting and using it as a guideline is important.
3. Conduct periodic assessments to understand the needs of residents.
4. Involve students in the planning and delivery of programs so they can also learn from the experience.
5. Provide a balance of different types of programs so students have the opportunity to develop in a variety of areas.
6. Provide adequate resource support to those who carry out programming. This includes budgetary and staff support.
7. Include an evaluation component to ensure that established objectives are successfully met.

Morrill, Hurst, and Oetting (1980) developed a framework that describes three dimensions of interventions for student development. This model identified three types or purposes for programming: (1) remedial programming, (2) preventive programming, and (3) developmental programming. According to these authors, first, a remedial intervention, or program, generally occurs after something has occurred and there is damage, or something in need of a response. In a residence hall setting, this may be planning an alcohol program in response to a high number of policy violations, addressing homophobic remarks in a community through an educational program, or implementing an academic development plan for those who did not succeed their first semester.

Second, a preventive intervention, or program, is one that is planned in anticipation of certain student needs or concerns that are fairly predictable. Typically these are needs that can be stress-producing for students. For students new to campus, the residence hall staff would help ease the anticipated transition from high school to college by planning programs on study skills, homesickness, and time management. Another example of a preventive program is one that deals with educating students about campus crime and safety.

Finally, a developmental intervention or program is, unlike the other two, not focused on addressing current or potential problems, but is instead intended to foster student growth. Developmental programs are then, more proactive in nature. Residential life staff might plan programs in the areas of leadership development, global awareness, or career planning. Most educational programs fit into one of these three categories (remedial, preventive, or developmental programming). Using this framework as a guide, staff can plan programs to meet the needs of students.

In addition to programming, many institutions have integrated support services into the residence halls to enhance the academic success of resident students. Examples of this include tutoring, Supplemental Instruction (SI), academic advising, career support, learning communities, counseling, and peer mentors (Hyman & Haynes, 2008). These kinds of services in residence halls enhance the academic culture of the community and the convenience of the services to students makes them more accessible. Such academic initiatives are most successful when formed out of a partnership between student affairs and academic affairs, and when they are consistent with institutional mission and culture (Whitt & Nuss, 1994).

Trends and Issues in Programming and Community Development

Given the varied institutional missions and priorities for different campuses, it would be difficult to provide a list of best programs. However, there are enough commonalities among institutional goals and students' needs across campuses to identify some common trends and issues in residence hall programming.

Safety and Security

A safe campus is a basic expectation of all members of the campus community, including students, faculty, staff, and parents and families (Perrotti, 2007). For students, this need must be met if they are to be comfortable and thrive in a learning environment. Recent campus tragedies (i.e., at Virginia Tech in April, 2007 and at Northern Illinois University in February, 2008) serve as reminders of the need for campus safety plans and educational programs (Grimm, Day, & Atchley, 2008). Additionally, legislation such as the Campus Safety Act, later renamed the Jeanne Clery Disclosure of Campus Security Policy and Campus Crime Statistics Act (Clery Act) in 1998 (Grimm et al.), has also heightened the focus on safety. This federal law, which requires colleges and universities to disclose information annually about campus crime, has also heightened students' and especially parents' attention to campus safety. Students' personal safety has become a focus for programming on many campuses. Often, educational messages are shared through prearrival mailings to students, during orientation, upon moving into the residence halls, and during initial meetings convened by the resident assistant of each community. Residence hall staff members often work in conjunction with other campus departments, such as Campus Police and Victim Advocacy, to provide residents with educational programs, aimed at preventing crime and instilling good habits for personal safety.

Technology

Many current students are members of the Net Generation, also referred to as Millenials. Millenials are those born from 1982 to 2000, and comprise the largest generation in history (Howe & Strauss, 2003). Members of this Net Generation are heavily "deviced" and typically fluent in technology (Holeton, 2008). This significant influence of technology and students' reliance upon it as their preferred means of communication requires a reexamination of traditional programming and community-building efforts. Residence hall staff has the added challenge of determining how to best foster community among students who are so well-connected to others' through technology and virtual communities. "Long associated with the residential college experience is the establishment of a core friendship group that supplants the high school peer group" (Anderson & Payne, 2006, p. 27). These groups, often associated with one's floor or residence hall building, were regarded as separate and distinct from earlier affiliations (Anderson & Payne).

Current students have access to technology, such as mobile phones, instant messaging, social networking, text messaging, and more, that facilitates immediate interaction among individuals, regardless of their distance from one another. While residence hall staff continues to focus on building community among students who live in close proximity to each other, many of those students are devoting a significant amount of time and energy to preserving previously established relationships. Additionally, in today's residence halls, community building among the residents begins long before students arrive on campus. When students get their acceptance notices, they form social networking groups and begin discussion about college. Similarly, residence hall social networking groups are formed when entering students learn where they will live (Holeton, 2008).

There are a number of examples of institutions that have effectively used technology to enhance community development efforts, even before students arrive on campus. Holeton (2008) suggests that these newer tools allow institutions to encourage student learning and development in new ways.

> To take advantage of these tools, student affairs and residence life professionals should be proactive, not merely reactive. They should plan together—in staff training, workshops, and retreats—how to use student-owned devices, residence websites, multimedia production, electronic discussion, social networking, and immersive environments to serve their goals. (Holeton, p. 44)

Living and Learning Communities

Campus educators have found that one of the best ways to integrate the goals of undergraduate education into out-of-class activities is through the development of residentially based learning communities (Zeller, 2006). These communities are places where "innovative curricular and pedagogical practices can be implemented by creating connections between students' experiences inside and outside the classroom" (Zeller, p. 60). Such programs are based on the belief that so much of learning occurs in students' daily living (Pascarella, Terenzini, & Blimling, 1994). When universities create small communities where students are clustered together as part of some educational program, students benefit from a learning experience that integrates their in-class and out-of-class activities (Shapiro & Levine, 1999). Examples of residential learning communities include residential FIGs (Freshman Interest Groups), residential colleges, theme-centered living communities, and major-based living communities (Shapiro & Levine).

First-Year/Students in Transition Programs

The "first-year experience" is intended to create an institutional environment that supports students' transition to college and helps to ensure persistence to graduation. Many of the programs and services previously discussed are specially designed to support first-year students, or those in transition (transfers). Luna and Gahagan (2008) stress that residential learning initiatives support the first-year experience because they "(a) provide a vehicle to front-load academic resources to help students succeed, (b) can create intentional supportive communities, and (c) can effectively incorporate peer leadership for first-year students" (p. 3).

A primary emphasis of many residential learning communities is to assist first-year students with their transition to university life. Often first-year students are assigned to live together and benefit from special programs, services, classes, and staffing in place to help foster their success (Upcraft & Gardner, 1989).

Applying Student Development Theory

Residential Life professionals have the opportunity to shape the learning environment for students living on campus. Their ability to do this is dependent, in part, on their understanding of how students grow and develop, and how the environment impacts that process. Developmental theories address the "nature, structure and processes of individual human growth" (Pasarella & Terenzini, 2005, p. 18). Student development theories "help residence hall staff understand how students change and grow, and serve as a guide in structuring interventions. Whether the presenting circumstance is simple or complex, student development theory can be extremely useful in framing educational responses in helping students learn" (Schuh, 2004, p. 283). Professionals should be familiar with various developmental theories, and how they are used in practice.

> Student development professionals who understand theory can use it to guide their every day practice of staff supervision, advising groups and individuals, program planning policy decisions, and counseling with few additional resources. Those who are unfamiliar with theory have an obligation to become familiar with it to enhance their practice. Practitioners must not only use theory in practice but must demonstrate its values to the campus community. (Baxter Magolda, 1993, pp. 127–128)

Existing developmental theories can be grouped into several categories, including psychosocial theories, cognitive-structural theories, typology theories, and person-environment theories (Evans, Forney, & Guido-DiBrito,

1998). Psychosocial theories examine individuals' personal and interpersonal lives (Evans, 1996). Cognitive-structural theories describe changes in the way people think, but not what they think (Evans). Typology theories "examine individual differences in how people view and relate to the world" (Evans, p. 179). Person-environment theory consists of interaction models that describe the interaction of the student with the environment (Evans, 1996). Additional theories, such as transition theory and student persistent theories, while not focusing on student growth in the same way as the others, do have valuable application in the residential setting. Each group of theories can be useful to professionals in better understanding students and creating environments in the residence halls that foster greater learning and development.

Yet, there is skepticism about whether theory is used enough ". . . by practitioners as they develop policy, make decisions, solve problems, deliver services and programs, manage budgets, and in general, do their jobs" (Upcraft, 1993b, p. 260). This may be in part because of the belief that many of the "mainstream" developmental theories often apply best to white males between the ages of 18 and 22 (Upcraft, 2005), the population on which many of these older theories were based. Practitioners often question whether the older theories apply to contemporary students, who reflect a greater diversity than the populations that attended college when many of the student development theories were first developed. Fortunately, there has been progress in developing theories that reflect the diversity of current students. There are more theories emerging in the literature that fit individual underrepresented groups: older students; women; gay, lesbian and bisexual students; students with disabilities; and others (Upcraft, 2005).

Residential living can be an ideal setting for students' personal development to be nurtured and supported, but this can only happen when residence hall staff are intrusive and intentional in all aspects of their interactions with students (Winston & Anchors, 1993).

> The research . . . clearly indicates that simply living in residence halls has little direct effect on students' academic or personal development. More intrusive and systematic interventions in the residential environment are called for if this environment is to make a meaningful difference in students' lives. (Winston & Anchors, p. 55)

Winston and Anchors (1993) offer a number of recommendations for housing programs committed to addressing student development goals. In part, they recommend:

1. Purposefully structure residence halls in ways that clearly communicate to residents and potential residents that living in residence halls is intended to be an extension or enhancement of classroom learning. One of the most effective ways to address these goals is to create living units that have a sense of community and whose residents have a transcending common interest.
2. Carefully focus attention on the needs of students from underrepresented populations, such as people of color and first-generation college students. The housing staff should clearly articulate a commitment to creating communities that are hospitable to students from varied backgrounds.
3. Develop means of providing recognition to individuals and groups who show commitment to and achievements in out-of-class learning.
4. As Kuh, Schuh, Whitt, and Associates (1991) note, "know your students, how they learn, and the conditions that affect their development" (p. 348). This can be done only when the professional staff has frequent informal contacts with residents and develops schemes for systematically collecting meaningful information from and about students.
5. A clearly stated expectation of students who choose to live in college residence halls should be active citizenship. This citizen involvement can be expressed in numerous ways, such as participation in hall or campus government and program development or involvement in community service activities (p. 54).

INFLUENCE OF RESIDENCE HALLS ON STUDENTS

Activities and opportunities associated with residence hall living have the potential to challenge and educate students (Schroeder et al., 1994). They can help form connections between what is learned in the classroom and everyday living. Well-defined and structured residence hall living can promote effective educational opportunities when structured to promote and encourage the examination of individual values, cultural understanding and appreciation, and many other outcomes associated with effective undergraduate education (Fenske, 1989). Residence hall living may meet the diverse needs of residents by providing support and fostering environments conducive to student learning. Residence hall communities are often designed to focus on what and how students learn and what motivates them to do so. Although many areas within a university setting offer educational opportunities for students, none have the potential to influence as many students as do housing and residence life departments (Winston et al., 1993).

Residence hall facilities, staff, and programs can influence the quality of students' educational and personal development (Blimling, 1999; Chickering, 1974; Murray, Snider, & Midkiff, 1999; Zheng, Saunders, Shelley, & Whalen, 2002). Research has been conducted to determine if students who live in residence halls perform better academically than those who live at home or commute to college (Blimling, 1999; Chickering, 1974; Pascarella & Terenzini, 1991; Tinto, 1993). This research revealed that students who live in residence halls consistently persist and graduate at higher rates than students who have not had this experience. Astin (1993) reported that the positive effects of living in residence halls during the freshman and sophomore years increased the probability that college students would complete their college programs and increase students' feelings of self-confidence. Chickering's (1974) studies on resident versus commuter students consistently showed that resident students took more credit hours, had higher grade point averages, and persisted and graduated with higher frequency. He found that these differences still exist, even when controlling for initial differences such as socioeconomic status, academic ability, and past academic performance. Ballou, Reavill, and Schultz (1995) found that students who had lived in university housing during their first year were 12 percent more likely to complete their undergraduate education. Additionally, Astin (1993) stated that by far the most important environmental characteristic associated with college persistence is living in a residence hall during the freshman year.

Perhaps one of the greatest factors of student success in college is involvement in extracurricular activities and other kinds of campus involvement by those who live in residence halls (Astin, 1993). Living on campus maximizes opportunities for social, cultural, and extracurricular involvement, and this increased involvement accounts for residence hall living's impact on student development. In comparison with commuters, those living in residence halls often report being more satisfied with the institution and their educational experiences. Chickering's (1974) research indicated that residence hall students had significantly more social interaction with peers and faculty and were more likely to be involved in extracurricular activities and to use campus facilities. Given the students' greater social and extracurricular involvement, it is not surprising that residence hall students, as compared to those who live off-campus, have different perceptions of the social climate of their institution and express different levels of satisfaction with college (Schroeder et al., 1994).

Although there is not an abundance of evidence, some studies suggest that students residing in residence halls make greater positive gains in psychosocial development compared with those students living off campus. Chickering (1974) stated that commuter students showed lower positive self-ratings at the end of the freshman year on academic self-confidence, public speaking ability, and leadership skills when compared with students living in residence halls. Hughes (1994) postulated that residential living is a powerful environment for encouraging openness to diversity with opportunities and programs that provide interaction with peers and staff dealing with multicultural issues. There have also been some studies that have found that students living on campus often report higher levels of self-esteem when compared with off-campus students (Winston et al., 1993). This may be due to the fact that those students living on campus have greater interaction with faculty, administrative staff, and peers. The research of Schroeder et al. (1994) found evidence indicating that students living in residence halls may experience greater value changes than their counterparts who live off campus and commute to college. The strongest evidence seems to be in the areas of aesthetic, cultural and intellectual values, social and political liberalism, and secularism.

Residence hall staff should support the academic goals and mission of the institution through the services and programs that enhance individual growth and development of students as whole persons. Schroeder et al. (1994) proposed that residence halls emphasize skills that challenge a student's ability to use knowledge in work and leisure. Many of the programs and services that are undertaken in the residence halls are aimed at creating environments that celebrate diversity by bringing students together in a community where differences are celebrated, respected, and appreciated (Rentz & Saddlemire, 1988).

Staff members in residence halls assist students in forming connections between what is learned in the class and everyday living. Well-defined residence halls are structured to promote and encourage the examination of individual values, cultural understanding and appreciation, and many other outcomes associated with effective undergraduate education. Residence hall staff promote student learning while keeping the educational goals of the institution at the forefront, contributing to the overall development of students. Perhaps most importantly, freshman students residing in private off-campus apartments were least satisfied with their college experience and were less likely to return to school the following term when compared to their counterparts living in on-campus housing (Chickering, 1974). Pascarella and Terenzini (2005) concluded after reviewing earlier research:

> Our earlier review pointed to the remarkably consistent evidence that students living on campus are more likely to persist and graduate than students who commute. The relationship remains positive and statistically significant even when a wide array of precollege characteristics related to persistence and educational attainment are taken into account, including precollege academic performance, socioeconomic status, educational aspirations, age, and employment status. (p. 421)

Over the last twenty years, few issues across American colleges and universities have garnered as much attention by administrators as student retention (Barefoot, 2004). Major publications that rank colleges and universities have added retention and graduation rates to their published statistics. Previously considered a badge of honor for institutional status on selectivity, the inclusion of these figures with respect to institutional quality has reversed this notion (Barefoot, 2004). Retention is often cited as an indicator of student success. If students are able to persist from their first year in college to the second, there is increased likelihood they will ultimately be successful and graduate. As colleges and universities continue to use retention as a measure of success, the importance of living on campus during one's first year will continue to play a pivotal role.

SELECT LEGAL ISSUES

The management of on-campus housing requires an awareness of the legal issues that pertain to the daily operation of residence halls. Gehring (1993) warns of the great potential for legal liability in residence halls, stating that it is probably far greater than any other area in student affairs. Gehring further stated:

> Student affairs professionals working in housing must deal with the physical aspects of buildings, student government, activities and programming, discipline, interpersonal conflicts, and a variety of personal problems. Each of these responsibilities is fraught with potential legal issues. However, these risks can be managed. To minimize potential liability, housing professionals must be familiar with the legal parameters involved in daily housing operations. The best way to manage risks is to identify potential dangers before they become problems. (p. 344)

While it is difficult to be familiar with all laws pertaining to on-campus housing, a general understanding of the most pertinent issues can help staff identify potential risks and implement policies and practices that minimize legal liability. Naturally, staff should consider seeking input from their campus legal counsel, when time permits such consultation (Gehring, 1993). However, because staff members are often in situations where they must act immediately, this general understanding of legal parameters is imperative (Gehring).

This section cannot possibly cover all legal issues related to housing operations, but other resources and guides are available to provide a broader overview. The issues that impact housing operations are numerous. First, the nature of the housing agreement, which typically defines the terms and conditions of the housing assignment, creates a unique relationship between students and their institutions. Generally, courts accept this relationship as contractual in nature (Gehring, 1993). The Family Educational Rights and Privacy Act of 1974, popularly known as the Buckley Amendment or FERPA, relates to the protection of student records (Kaplin & Lee, 1995). This law is pertinent to a housing operation because of the type of information collected or maintained about students. Housing and residence life staff must also be familiar with the Americans with Disabilities Act (ADA), in order to ensure that proper housing accommodations are available to students in need of them, as stipulated by law. There are numerous issues that impact housing operations, but perhaps three significant issues worthy of further discussion are fire and safety procedures, physical facilities, and program supervision. These three areas were identified earlier by Schuh (1994) and remain relevant today.

Fire and Safety

One area of concern for housing and residential life staff is fire and safety. Schuh (1994) identified fire as one of the greatest dangers for students living on campus, and emphasized the importance of staff having an understanding of fire safety and the potential for liability when proper procedures are not in place.

> Most states have laws and regulations regarding firefighting equipment, smoke detectors, fire drills, and the like, so it is critical that residence life staff become conversant with these laws and regulations—and follow them explicitly. Routine inspections should be held and staff should work closely with physical plant personnel to ensure that all equipment is functional. Failure to engage in these safety procedures will result in tremendous legal exposure to the campus. (p. 285)

As noted in a previous section, student safety on campus is a growing issue of concern, and one which presents potential liability for a university. The Campus Safety Act, later renamed the Jeanne Clery Disclosure of Campus Security Policy and Campus Crime Statistics Act (Clery Act) in 1998 (Grimm et al., 2008), requires colleges and universities to disclose information annually about campus crime. Housing and residential life staff must continually assess the safety procedures in place for the residence halls, and educate students about ways to minimize risks to their own personal safety. Students should also receive instruction about such things as how to leave the building in case of a fire, how to operate fire extinguishers, and what to do in different types of emergencies (Gehring, 1993).

It is also important to note that on July 31, 2008, Congress completed re-authorization of the Higher Education Act (HEA) by passing the Higher Education Opportunity Act, and the bill was signed into law on August 14, 2008. This new law provides guidelines related to the reporting of fires in the residence halls and procedures for handling reports of missing persons in the residence halls. An analysis of the law written by the American Council on Education (2008) states that institutions with on-campus housing are required to publish annually a fire safety report that details such information as the number of fires, deaths, injuries, fire drills, fire-related property damage, and the type of fire detection systems in each building. The act also requires institutions that both participate in any federal higher education programs and maintain on-campus housing to establish a missing student notification policy for students who reside in on-campus housing and have been determined after an investigation by campus security officials to be missing for 24 hours.

Physical Facilities

Housing operations have responsibility for maintaining the physical facilities and its equipment in a way that serves students' needs, and provides for a reasonably safe environment. Yet often at inopportune times, ". . . something will happen to render the physical facilities inoperative or dangerous. This could be anything from an elevator breaking down to a violent act of weather resulting in making the physical facility unusable" (Schuh, 1994). Residence hall staff then has the responsibility to act in a way to protect the residents from harm. Procedures must be in place so that problems are immediately reported and addressed in a timely manner. In addition to the buildings being maintained in a reasonable manner, periodic inspections to uncover defects must also be conducted (Gehring, 1993). "Documented, periodic inspections with follow-up maintenance requests are essential in avoiding negligence" (Gehring, p. 363).

Program Supervision

On most campuses, there is a variety of events held in the residence halls or sponsored by the staff. While most of the programs do not pose risk to the participants, there are some, especially those that require a certain amount of participant skill or involve the consumption of alcoholic beverages, which do pose greater risk to participants (Schuh, 1994).

Higher-risk activities that involve participant skill are often expected to adhere to institutional event planning and risk management policies. Personnel in risk management or legal counsel can often serve as resources in program planning to help staff ensure that risk is minimized. Dunkel and

Schuh (1998) also recommend that planners follow "industry standards" when available. This might pertain to athletic and recreational events, events with specialized equipment, or water sports events.

Activities involving alcohol consumption are typically regulated by university alcohol policies. Some universities or housing programs have policies that prohibit alcohol at student events; that is certainly the best way to minimize risk. However, if events are planned where alcohol is served, staff must be cautious about the risk they assume. Schuh (1994) offers the following suggestions regarding planning events with alcohol:

> To minimize risk, be knowledgeable about state laws. If students are under the legal drinking age, they should not be allowed to consume alcoholic beverages. The institution should never be a part of sponsoring illegal activities. . . . The amount of alcohol purchased should be realistic. Planners should purchase an amount that will be commensurate with the number of participants anticipated. Food and alternative beverages should be provided. Before planning an event at which alcoholic beverages will be available, the campus alcohol information center or health center should be consulted for information about program planning with alcohol. (p. 287)

Dunkel and Schuh (1998) also recommend that an organization employ the use of a commercial vendor for events, allowing professional bartenders to manage the alcohol aspect of the event.

Residence hall staff has a tremendous responsibility to act in a manner that minimizes risk and harm to students. Knowledge of pertinent legal issues and the consultation with legal counsel and other professionals on campus can aid in minimizing the potential for liability.

PROFESSIONAL DEVELOPMENT

Well developed professionals are a key resource in any successful organization. Much has been written about the need for the continuous development of professionals, development that extends beyond the initial educational preparation.

> Even though we student affairs professionals understand better than most people the importance of continuous learning and co-curricular experiences for students, we often overlook the value of such activities for ourselves. In this changing global society, it is imperative to keep pace with changes, maintain cutting-edge knowledge, and stay mentally and physically healthy in the process. (Batchelor 1993, p. 378)

Investment in the development of residential life professionals should be viewed as an investment in the experience offered to students. Failure to provide professionals with strong supervision and ongoing development can mean mediocrity in the service that is offered to students (Barr, 1993).

Learning is best achieved when there is a clear set of objectives that serve as a foundation for action. Professionals who develop specific goals and demonstrate a commitment to achieving them, are more likely to be successful in achieving their goals. Just as there has been a shift from focusing on teaching to learning as it relates to students' education, professionals also need to think in terms of their own learning objectives when creating a professional development plan. This plan should encompass what the professional intends on learning, doing, or experiencing, in order to build upon already developed skills and knowledge. Professional development plans are often completed annually, and serve as a tool for planning and discussion among staff members and their supervisors.

Professional development can consist of mentoring, reading, formal classroom education, staff development activities, volunteer and committee work, involvement in professional associations, networking, and conference attendance. Professional involvement is one important aspect of professional practice. Individuals engaged in managing residential life programs on their campuses will benefit from involvement in professional associations. Professional organizations serve multiple purposes. Nuss (1993) identified several reasons individuals and institutions belong to professional associations:

> . . . opportunities for professional growth, a means to benefit from the services and programs provided, a chance to test professional competencies, a desire to join with others of similar interest to influence the future direction of the association or profession, and a professional sense of obligation to help advance the status of the profession and fund programs that assist it. (p. 368)

There are several professional associations with which many housing professionals are involved. These, like most professional associations, are volunteer-driven organizations with elected officers, supported by a central office staff. Decisions about professional association involvement should be based upon one's professional goals, talents, and institutional needs (Nuss, 1993). The Association of College and University Housing Officers–International (ACUHO-I) is the primary professional organization that serves housing professionals. Its main purpose is to encourage high-quality residential programs on college and university campuses. ACUHO-I membership is by institution, so any professionals within a housing department that holds a membership, may access membership benefits and resources. The association also recognizes 14 regional associations (some of which are international regions), many of which sponsor an annual conference, which is in addition to the annual ACUHO-I Conference and its many other professional institutes, workshops, and conferences. The Association of College and University Housing Officers–International also published a set of standards in 2005. The document, "Standards for College and University Student Housing," identifies standards for residence hall operations in areas including business and management, physical plant, education and programming, food service, ethics, and qualifications for professional staff.

Residential life professionals often belong to larger and more comprehensive student affairs organizations, such as the American College Personnel Association (ACPA) or the National Association of Student Personnel Administrators (NASPA). Both organizations, through their professional development programs, publications, and annual conferences, seek to address the professional needs of individuals working in student affairs. ACPA's structure includes commissions, which are designed to represent the job/functional areas or professional specializations in which ACPA members are employed or have an interest. There is a Commission for Housing and Residential Life, made up of those who work in or have an interest in the areas of housing and residence hall programs.

THE FUTURE

As housing and residence life professionals attempt to formulate strategic, five-year, and ten-year plans, they do so with a certain level of uncertainty in what the future may hold for residence halls. College and universities are facing tough economic challenges both at the federal and state level. Severe budget cuts, layoffs, and furloughs are just some of the ways institutions are coping to offset financial burdens. Planning for the future becomes increasingly difficult as housing and residence life professionals delve into these evolving issues. Current and future staff will be kept busy confronting: (1) consumer needs and community development, (2) financial challenges, (3) technological improvements, and (4) staffing challenges.

Consumer Needs and Community Development

Booming enrollments are predicted for the next ten years and competition for students grows larger (DeCapua, 2006). Administrators are recognizing the importance of how much residential facilities are weighed in one's decision to attend or not attend a particular institution.

> Today's students have a very different background from students 30 and 40 years ago. The majority of today's incoming freshmen grew up in single-child or two-child families and have had their own bedrooms since an early age. They are more consumer oriented, and are very likely 'shopping' several colleges and universities. Where a student will live is beginning to have a major impact on the college selection process. Today's students may be required to share a room during their freshman year, but they are unlikely to stay on campus as upperclassmen unless the campus can provide such options as an apartment or private rooms similar to off-campus housing. What used to be considered luxuries such as kitchens, private bathrooms, study lounges, and social spaces, are now considered basic necessities. (schoolfacilities.com, 2002)

As students demand greater amenities that incorporate technological advances, academic initiatives, and recreational facilities that match the competition of the off-campus housing market, housing and residence life programs will need to respond.

Increasingly, students are coming to colleges and universities with greater needs, both emotionally and physically. Housing and residence life programs are bombarded with requests for special accommodations. Some students making the requests are registered with campus disability offices, while others are not. Requests include private rooms, private bathrooms, pet therapy animals for emotional stability, first floor rooms, and a multitude of others. Housing and residence life professionals must become knowledgeable about what is required to accommodate and what is not. Given the increased demand for private accommodations, it is important to know that compared with the traditional residence hall experience, students living in private bedrooms tend to isolate themselves more, decreasing their opportunities for social interaction. According to a 2008 American College Health Association survey, within the last year, 30 percent of college students reported feeling so depressed that it was difficult to function and 49 percent felt overwhelming anxiety. Additionally, 10 percent of students also reported being diagnosed or treated for depression and more than 6 percent seriously considered suicide (www.healthyminds.org, 2010).

The notion of only supplying a bed for a student to sleep in is long gone. Housing and residence life professionals have to be familiar with students' interests and future standards for new construction. One of the initiatives designed to help professionals in collegiate housing identify and meet consumer demand for the future, is the 21st Century Project of the Association of College and University Residence Halls-International (ACUHO-I). The 21st Century Project aims to set the standard for higher educational institutions with regards to construction of new, state-of-the-art residential facilities that incorporate the tenets of sustainability, flexibility, community, and technology in meeting "the ever-changing roles residences play in the collegiate experience" (ACUHO-I, 2008).

Financial Challenges

On-campus residence halls in the early years of higher education were not built until they could be completely funded. Dormitories were never built on borrowed money (Bartem & Manning, 2001). Increasingly, within the last ten years, higher education administrators have utilized and implemented common business practices, such as outsourcing of services, to obtain lower costs by looking to the private sector to build and ultimately pay for new residence halls.

Residence halls continue to age and departmental budgets are increasingly focused on repair, on-going and preventative maintenance, and upgrades to current residential facilities. In order to meet the changing demands of the student housing market through construction of new facilities and renovation of existing ones, college and universities are looking for new ways to finance projects.

Traditionally, rent increases and reduction of residence life program expenditures have been seen as ways to help defray costs of renovation and new construction of residential facilities (Stoner & Cavins, 2003). As colleges and universities continue to search for alternative funding sources in current economic conditions, many dip into the reserves of auxiliaries. Departments, such as housing, are forced to raise rent to meet financial obligations and fund new projects. In an effort to cut living costs and still build additional housing, some colleges and universities find solutions in the form of privatized housing. In 1997, there was virtually no privatized housing (Van Der Werf, 1999). In 2000, approximately $500 million in privatized college housing contracts existed, and in 2007, it became much more popular, with privatized housing contracts exceeding billions of dollars and 214 privatized student housing projects on college and university campuses in the United States alone (Bekurs, 2007). Perhaps the largest increase in outsourcing with collegiate housing can be linked to what Moneta and Dillon (2001) term "Collaboration." Collaboration, another form of private partnering, exists when an institution and outside provider partner together in the provision of a service or activity. These imaginative arrangements, real estate development projects, are often established to provide housing, dining, retail and commercial facilities.

Prior to the privatization boom, the most frequent method of financing collegiate housing was in the form of debt finance through bond issuance. In this structure, college and universities issue bonds for sale to gather revenue for the construction of new projects or renovation of current facilities. In this arrangement, the institution retains the greatest amount of control, yet bears the maximum quantity of risk and additional debt load (Henry, 2003). As colleges and universities struggle financially while considering existing debt capacity and bond ratings for new construction, they have explored other avenues of financing new student housing. As a result, many campuses have chosen to partner with private developers to design, develop, construct, finance, and in some cases, manage all aspects of new residential facilities. While enrollments skyrocket, partnering with private developers can expedite construction schedules, avoid bureaucratic roadblocks, preserve debt capacity, and overcome restrictions with existing debt covenants (Bekurs, 2007; Cirino, 2003; Short & Chisler, 2006). Though fairly new in growth, privatization of residence halls can trace its roots to a private firm which, using equity capital from Northwestern Mutual Life Insurance Company, developed, built and managed a residential facility on the University of North Carolina at Chapel Hill campus (Short & Chisler, 2006). Many private developers are offering the ability to customize housing and minimize risks while maximizing rewards.

An essential principle of the privatized housing model is the existence of a ground lease transaction, whereby the college or university leases institutionally-owned land to a private developer or nonprofit organization for the purpose of constructing new housing (Henry, 2003; Short & Chisler, 2006). There are a handful of well-financed real estate investment trusts (REITs) that have cornered the market of partnering with college and universities to build residential housing. These major companies are well-funded and publicly traded organizations that are eager to partner with institutions that are seeking creative ways to finance and construct their housing needs (Zaransky, 2006). After selecting a developer, an institution generally agrees to lease the land used for the housing project to the company. The level of control and oversight that the institution wants to ultimately retain determines the depth of this public-private relationship.

A major benefit that state institutions have over private developers is that the college or university is able to use tax exempt debt and pay no property taxes (Bekurs, 2007). The arena of public-private partnering has enabled private developers to be able to capitalize on the advantages held by state institutions, with savings to all. Often termed the tax-exempt corporation model, public-private partnerships have been structured with the aid of an institution's foundation as it helps arrange for tax-exempt bonds to be issued for the project (Henry, 2003; Van Der Werf, 1999). Institutions set up housing projects through the Internal Revenue Code 501 (c) (3) corporation policy. Through a 501 (c) (3), a nonprofit organization is not a taxable entity as long as its activities are charitable, religious, educational, scientific, literary, testing for public safety, fostering national or international amateur sports competition, or preventing cruelty to children or animals (Internal Revenue

Service, 2003). The type of funding and how it is obtained are often predicated on the relationship of the public-private partnership. Institutions may establish off-balance-sheet financing, whereby the cost of any new housing project is not included on the overall institutional debt capacity (Henry; Short & Chisler, 2006). Ryan (2003) stated:

> Terms and conditions of these partnerships vary from campus to campus. For example, the location of housing (on or off campus), management arrangements, length of the agreement, and occupancy requirements (if any) are often unique to each campus. Lease arrangements or management agreements between the developer and the college or university are carefully negotiated. Some campuses treat public-private housing as part of their inventory for purposes of student application, assignment, and payment for the space and in some cases provide a residential life program in the facility. Other campuses keep the housing at arm's length in terms of all of the management functions. (p. 65)

The amount of control that the institution retains, such as policy formulation, budget oversight, and daily management in the project, increases the likelihood the debt will be included in the overall debt capacity of the college or university (Short & Chisler, 2006). As budget cutbacks and financial shortfalls continue to afflict institutions of higher education, college and university administrators must engage in creative ways to secure increased funding and provision of services. While some institutions directly provide all services including staffing, others will choose outsourcing. Higher education continues to see the financial benefits of outsourcing as contracts with vendors are often written with monetary provisions. These provisions include guaranteed improvements to be made to existing facilities, new construction of facilities, and annual payments back to the institution.

Technological Improvements

With each passing day, the use of technology is changing the landscape of how services are offered and how students learn. These changes impact the future of residence halls. Immediate access to information is paramount. The use of the World Wide Web and cable television continues to increase as modalities for teaching. Construction of new residential facilities and renovation of current buildings, must take into account these technological advances. New residence halls are being constructed with wireless internet in both common and individual spaces. Whether television should be delivered through traditional methods of cable lines or internet protocol based lines remains an issue for new construction projects. It is no doubt that colleges and universities that place a high emphasis on living/learning communities will pave the way for the inclusion of academic facilities, such as smart class-rooms, in residence halls.

As students push for increased privacy and independence, they also expect a high degree of safety and security. "Residence life professionals must move campus security to a higher priority within their organizations and attack the problems aggressively" (Janosik, 1993, p. 514). Housing and residence life departments are and will continue to increase their use of tech-nologically advanced security systems that incorporate cameras, electronic locking methods, and emergency notification protocol.

STAFFING CHALLENGES

Recruitment and retention of entry-level staff remains an issue that requires great attention in housing and residence life, and student affairs in general. The "live-in" requirement is often associated with the entry-level position in the housing and residence life department. Living and working in the same location tends to limit privacy and suppress the independence that comes with separating personal and professional demands. Although there is no empirical data, recruitment and retention of new professionals can be a challenge for many institutions. Candidates for entry-level positions in hous-ing are often interested in institutional policies that address certain aspects of the live-in experience, including whether partners and family can reside with the staff member, whether pets are permitted, and the inclusion of meal plans and other benefits for the live-in staff member. These issues often play a contributing role in a candidate's decision about whether to apply for a res-idence hall director position at a particular institution. Geographic location and the condition of living accommodations can also affect the quality of an applicant pool for live-in positions. The recruitment of staff remains a chal-lenge for many institutions, requiring increased efforts to be made in recruit-ing highly qualified candidates for their entry-level positions.

Despite the many issues outlined here that face the future of the housing and residence life profession, there remains a strong need for professionals to perform the important function of on-campus living on college and uni-versity campuses. This aspect of the collegiate experience will remain an important component in the students' overall educational experience. Housing and residence life staff will need to continue to adapt to the ever-changing needs of the students they serve in the provision of services and res-idential facilities. Upcraft (1993a) stated:

The bottom line, however, is that institutions that are committed to quality must develop residence halls that are efficiently managed, affordable, safe, and well maintained, and most important, that contribute to the personal and academic development of all residents. Residence halls that do not proactively address students' developmental needs may well be at a major competitive disadvantage in comparison to local apartment complexes. Attention to students' needs and interests from well-qualified, caring professionals can be an excellent "selling point" to students and parents alike. (p. 201)

TECHNOLOGY RESOURCES

The following websites provide useful information related to residence halls:

1. ACUHO-I (Association of College and University Housing Officers International): http://www.acuho-i.org
2. NASPA (National Association of Student Personnel Administrators/ Student Affairs Administrators in Higher Education): http://www.naspa.org
3. ACPA (American College Personnel Association): http://myacpa.org
4. NACURH (National Association for College and University Residence Halls): http://www.nacurh.org

REFERENCES

ACUHO-I. (2008). *The 21st century project.* Retrieved from www.21stcenturyproject. com.

American Council on Education. (2008, August). *ACE Analysis of Higher Education Act Reauthorization Analysis.* Retrieved from http://www.acenet.edu/e-newsletters/p2p /ACE_HEA_analysis_818.pdf.

American Psychiatric Association. (2010). Healthy Minds. Healthy Lives. Retrieved from http://www.healthyminds.org/More-Info-For/College-Age-Students.aspx

Anderson, C., & Payne, R. (2006). Understanding students today and tomorrow. In B. M. McCluskey & N. W. Dunkel (Eds.), *Foundations: Strategies for the future of collegiate housing* (pp. 22–40). Columbus, OH: Association of College and University Housing Officers International.

Association of College and University Housing Officers–International. (2007). ACUHO-I Standards and Ethical Principles for College and University Housing Professionals. Retrieved from http://www.acuho-i.org.

Astin, A. W. (1993). *What matters in college: Four critical years* (Rev. ed.). San Francisco: Jossey-Bass.

Ballou, R. A., Reavil, L. K., & Schultz, B. L. (1995). Assessing the immediate and residual effects of the residence hall experience: Validating Pace's 1990 analysis of on-campus and off-campus students. *Journal of College and University Housing, 25,*

16–21.

Barefoot, B. O. (2004). Higher education's revolving door: Confronting the problem of student drop out in U.S. colleges and universities. *Open Learning, 19,* 9–19.

Barr, M. J. (1993). Becoming successful student affairs administrators. In M. J. Barr (Ed.), *The handbook of student affairs administration* (pp. 522–529). San Francisco: Jossey-Bass.

Barr, M. J. (2000). The importance of institutional mission. In M. J. Barr, M. K. Desler, & Associates (Eds.), *The handbook of student affairs administration* (2nd ed.) (pp. 25–36). San Francisco: Jossey-Bass.

Bartem, R., & Manning, S. (2001). Outsourcing in higher education: A business officer and business partner discuss a controversial management strategy. *Change, 33,* 42–47.

Batchelor, S. W. (1993). Mentoring and self-directed learning. In M. J. Barr (Ed.), *The handbook of student affairs administration* (pp. 378–389). San Francisco: Jossey-Bass.

Baxter Magolda, M. B. (1993). Intellectual, ethical and moral development. In R. Winston & S. Anchors (Eds.), *Student housing and residential life* (pp. 95–133). San Francisco: Jossey-Bass.

Bekurs, G. (2007). Outsourcing student housing in American community college: Problems and prospects. *Community College Journal of Research and Practice, 31*(8), 621–636.

Blimling, G. S. (1995). *The resident assistant: Working with college students in residence halls* (4th ed.). Dubuque, IO: Kendall/Hunt.

Blimling, G. S. (1999). A meta-analysis of the influence of college residence halls on academic performance. *Journal of College Student Development, 40,* 551–561.

Bolman L. G., & Deal T. E. (1997). *Reframing organizations: Artistry, choice, and leadership* (2nd ed.). San Francisco: Jossey-Bass.

Boyer Commission on Educating Undergraduates in the Research University. (1998). *Reinventing undergraduate education: A blueprint for America's research universities.* State University of New York at Stony Brook: Author.

Boyer, E. L. (1987). *College: The undergraduate experience in America.* San Francisco: Jossey-Bass.

Chickering, A. W. (1974). *Commuting versus resident students.* San Francisco: Jossey-Bass.

Cirino, A. M. (2003). Outsourcing student housing: Is privatized housing the right option for your campus? *NACUBO Business Officer, 32,* 33–35.

Conlogue, J. A. (1993). Resident assistant perceptions of their roles and responsibilities. Ed.D. dissertation, University of Pittsburgh, United States–Pennsylvania. Retrieved from ProQuest Digital Dissertations database. (Publication No. AAT 9406339).

Council for the Advancement of Standards for Student Services/Development Programs. Standards and Guidelines for Housing and Residential Life Programs. (2001). College Park, MD: Council for the Advancement of Standards for Student Services/Development Programs.

DeCapua, R. J. (2006) Outsourcing student services: Perceptions of college administrators at four-year institutions in Connecticut. Ed.D. dissertation, Johnson &

Wales University, United States–Rhode Island. Retrieved from ProQuest Digital Dissertations database. (Publication No. AAT 3234448).

Delworth, U., Hanson, G. R., & Associates. (1989). *Student services: A handbook for the profession.* San Francisco: Jossey-Bass.

Dude, K., & Shepherd Hayhurst, S. (1996). Residence life programming and the first-year experience. In W J. Zeller, D. S. Fidler, & B. O. Barefoot (Eds.), *Residence life programs and the first-year experience* (2nd ed.) (pp. 125–134). Columbia, SC: University of South Carolina.

Dunkel, N. W. (2010). *Comprehensive versus split housing organizational structures.* Manuscript in preparation.

Dunkel, N. W., & Schrieber, P. J. (1992). Competency development of housing professionals. *Journal of College and University Student Housing, 22*(2), 19–23.

Dunkel, N. W., & Schuh, J. H. (1998). *Advising student groups and organizations.* San Francisco: Jossey-Bass.

Evans, N. J. (1996). Theories of student development. In S. R. Komives & D. B Woodard Jr. (Eds.), *Student services: A handbook for the profession* (3rd ed.) (pp. 164–187). San Francisco: Jossey-Bass.

Evans, N. J., Forney, D. S., & Guido-DiBrito, F. (1998). *Student development in college: Theory, research, and practice.* San Francisco: Jossey-Bass.

Fenske, R. H. (1989). Historical foundations in student services. In U. Delworth, G. R. Hanson, & Associates (Eds.), *Student services: A handbook for the profession.* San Francisco: Jossey-Bass.

Frederiksen, C. F. (1993). A brief history of collegiate housing. In R. B. Winston, Jr., S. Anchors, & Associates (Eds.), *Student housing and residential life: A handbook for professional committed to student development goals.* San Francisco: Jossey-Bass.

Gehring, D. D. (1993). Legal and regulatory concerns. In R. B. Winston, Jr. & S. Anchors (Eds.), *Student housing and residential life* (pp. 344–269). San Francisco: Jossey-Bass.

Grimm, J. C, Day, J., & Atchley, L. (2008). Safety and security: An important element of first-year residence education. In W. J. Zeller (Ed.), *Residence life programs & the new student experience* (Monograph no. 5, 3rd ed.) (pp. 173–187). Columbia, SC: University of South Carolina, National Resource Center for The First-Year Experience and Students in Transition.

Grimm, J. C., & Dunkel, N. W. (1999). *Campus housing construction and renovation: An analysis of cost and design.* Columbus, OH: The Association of College and University Housing Officers–International.

Guthrie, D. S. (1997). *Student affairs reconsidered: A Christian view of the profession and its contexts.* Latham, MD: University Press of American, Inc.

Henry, C. S. (2003). The history of campus housing in the United States. In N. W. Dunkel & J. C. Grimm (Eds.), *Campus housing construction* (pp. 1–13). Columbus, OH: The Association of College and University Housing Officers–International.

Holeton, R. (2008). New students, emerging technologies, virtual communities, and the college residential experience. In W. J. Zeller (Ed.), *Residence life programs & the new student experience* (Monograph no. 5, 3rd ed.) (pp. 31–52). Columbia, SC: University of South Carolina, National Resource Center for The First-Year

Experience and Students in Transition.

Howe, N., & Strauss, W. (2003). *Millenials go to college: Strategies for a new generation on campus*. Washington DC: American Association of College Registrars.

Hughes, M. (1994). Helping students understand and appreciate diversity. In C. C. Schroeder, P. Mable, & Associates (Eds.), *Realizing the educational potential of residence halls* (pp. 190–217). San Francisco: Jossey-Bass.

Hyman, R., & Haynes, M. (2008). Academic support services in the residential setting. In G. Luna & J. Gahagan (Eds.), *Learning initiatives in the residential setting* (Monograph No. 48, pp. 43–54). Columbia, SC: University of South Carolina, National Resource Center for the First-Year Experience and Students in Transition.

Internal Revenue Service. (2003). *Charities & non-profits*. Retrieved from http://www.irs.gov/charities/article/0,,id=96099,00.html.

Janosik, S. M. (1993). Dealing with criminal conduct and other deleterious behaviors. In R. B. Winston, Jr., S. Anchors, & Associates (Eds.), *Student housing and residential life: A handbook for professionals committed to student development goals* (pp. 501–516). San Francisco: Jossey-Bass.

Kaplin, W. A., & Lee, B. A. (1995). *The law of higher education* (3rd ed.). San Francisco: Jossey-Bass.

Komives, S. R., Woodard, D. B., & Associates. (2003). *Student services: A handbook for the profession*. San Francisco: Jossey-Bass.

Kuh, G. D., Douglas, K. B., Lund, J. P., & Ramin Gyurmek, J. (1994). *Student learning outside the classroom: Transcending artificial boundaries*. ASHE-ERIC Higher Education Report No. 8. Washington, DC: The George Washington University, Graduate School of Education and Human Development.

Kuh, G. D., Schuh, J. H., Whitt, E. J., & Associates. (1991). *Involving colleges: Successful approaches to fostering student learning and personal development outside the classroom*. San Francisco: Jossey-Bass.

Kuh, G. D., Kinzie, J., Schuh, J. H., Whitt, E. J., & Associates. (2005). *Student success in college: Creating conditions that matter*. San Francisco: Jossey-Bass.

Luna, G., & Gahagan, J. (2008). Residence halls–the classroom expanded. In G. Luna & J. Gahagan (Eds.), *Learning initiatives in the residential setting* (Monograph No. 48, pp. 1–6). Columbia, SC: University of South Carolina, National Resource Center for The First-Year Experience and Students in Transition.

McCluskey-Titus, P. (2002). Getting ready for the first job. In J. F. Conneely (Ed.), *Planning a career in college and university housing* (pp. 2–12). Columbus, OH: Association of College and University Housing Officers–International.

McCluskey-Titus, P. (2006). Programmatic philosophies in residence life. In B. M. McCluskey & N. W. Dunkel (Eds.), *Foundations: Strategies for the future of collegiate housing* (pp. 3–15). Columbus, OH: Association of College and University Housing Officers International.

Miller, T. K., Winston, R. B., & Associates. (1991). *Administration and leadership in student affairs: Actualizing student development in higher education*. Muncie, IN: Accelerated Development Inc.

Minor, F. D. (1999). Community development. In J. H. Schuh (Ed.), *Educational programming and student learning in college and university residence halls (pp. 97–123). Columbus, OH: Association of College and University Housing Officers International.

Moneta, L., & Dillon, W. L. (2001). Strategies for effective outsourcing. *New Directions for Student Services, 96,* 31–49.

Morrill, W. H., Hurst, J. C., & Oetting, E. R. (1980). A conceptual model of intervention strategies. In W. H. Morrill, J. C. Hurst, & E. R. Oetting (Eds.), *Dimensions of intervention for student development* (pp. 85–95). New York: John Wiley & Sons.

Murray, J. L., Snider, B. R., & Midkiff, R. M. (1999). The effect of training on resident assistant job performance. *Journal of College Student Development, 40,* 744–747.

Novak, J. M (2008). A comparative analysis of differences in resident satisfaction, retention, and cumulative grade point average between University of Central Florida owned and affiliated housing. Ed.D. dissertation, University of Central Florida, Orlando, FL.

Nuss, E. M. (1993). The role of professional associations. In M. J. Barr (Ed.), *The handbook of student affairs administration* (pp. 364–377). San Francisco: Jossey-Bass.

Pascarella, E. T., & Terenzini, P. T. (1991). *How college affects students.* San Francisco: Jossey-Bass.

Pascarella, E. T., & Terenzini, P. T. (2005). *How college affects students: A third decade of research* (volume 2). San Francisco: Jossey-Bass.

Pascarella, E. T., Terenzini, P.T., & Blimling, G. S. (1994). In C. C. Schroeder & P. Mable (Eds.), *Realizing the educational potential of residence halls* (pp. 22–52). San Francisco: Jossey-Bass.

Perrotti, J. A. (2007). The role of the campus police and security department in the 21st century. In J. F. L. Jackson & M. Cleveleand Terrell (Eds.), *Creating and maintaining safe college campuses: A sourcebook for evaluating and enhancing safety programs* (pp. 173–187). Sterling, VA: Stylus.

Rentz, A. L., & Saddlemire, G. L. (Eds.). (1988). *Student affairs functions in higher education.* Springfield, IL: Charles C Thomas.

Rudolph, F. (1990). *The American college and university: A history.* Athens, GA: The University of Georgia Press.

Ryan, M. R. (2003). Contemporary issues in student housing finance. *New Directions for Student Services, 103,* 59–71.

Sandeen, A. (1991). *The chief student affairs officer: Leader, manager, mediator, educator.* San Francisco: Jossey-Bass.

Schlossberg, N. K. (1989). Marginality and mattering: Key issues in building community. In D. C. Roberts (Ed.), *Designing campus activities to foster a sense of community* (New Directions for Student Services, No. 38, pp. 5–15). San Francisco: Jossey-Bass.

SchoolFacilities.com. (2002). *New trends in student housing.* Retrieved from http://www.schoolfacilities.com/_coreModules/content/contentDisplay_print.aspx?contentID=124.

Schroeder, C. C. (1993). Conclusion: Creating residence life programs with student development goals. In R. B. Winston, Jr., S. Anchors & Associates (Eds.), *Student housing and residential life: A handbook for professionals committed to student development goals* (pp. 517–534). San Francisco: Jossey-Bass.

Schroeder, C. C., Mable, P., & Associates. (1994). *Realizing the educational potential of residence halls.* San Francisco: Jossey-Bass.

Schuh, J. H. (1996). Residence halls. In A. L. Rentz & Associates (Eds.), *Student affairs practice in higher education* (pp. 269–297). Springfield, IL: Charles C Thomas.

Schuh, J. H. (2004). Residence halls. In F. J. D. MacKinnon (Ed.), *Rentz's student affairs practice in higher education* (pp. 268–297). Springfield, IL: Charles C Thomas.

Schuh, J. H. (2006). Accountability in student housing and residential Life. In B. M. McCluskey & N. W. Dunkel (Eds.), *Foundations: Strategies for the future of collegiate housing* (pp. 3–15). Columbus, OH: Association of College and University Housing Officers International.

Schuh, J. H., & Triponey, V. L. (1993). Fundamentals of program design. In R. B. Winston, Jr. & S. Anchors (Eds.), *Student housing and residential life* (pp. 423–442). San Francisco: Jossey-Bass.

Shapiro, N. S., & Levine, H. H. (1999). *Creating learning communities.* San Francisco: Jossey-Bass.

Short, J., & Chisler, C. R. (2006). Privatized and off-campus housing relationships. In N. W. Dunkel & B. M. McCuskey (Eds.), *Foundations: Strategies for the future of collegiate housing* (pp. 121–133). Columbus, OH: Association of College and University Housing Officers–International.

Smith, J. J. (2000). Great expectations: College use housing as student draw. *Buildings, 94,* 28–32.

Stoner, K. L., & Cavins, K. M. (2003). New options for financing residence hall renovation and construction. *New Directions for Student Services, 101,* 17–27.

Terenzini, P. T., & Pascarella, E. T. (1994). Living with myths: Undergraduate education in America. *Change, 25*(6), 28–32.

Tinto, V. (1993). *Leaving college: Rethinking the cause and cures of student attrition* (2nd ed.). Chicago: The University of Chicago Press.

Upcraft, M. L. (1993). Organizational and administrative approaches. In R. B. Winston, Jr., S. Anchors & Associates (Eds.), *Student housing and residential life: A handbook for professionals committed to student development goals* (pp. 189–202). San Francisco: Jossey-Bass.

Upcraft, M. L. (1993). Translating theory into practice. In M. J. Barr (Ed.), *The handbook of student affairs administration* (pp. 260–273). San Francisco: Jossey-Bass.

Upcraft, M. L. (2005). The dilemmas of translating theory into practice. In M. E. Wilson & L. E. Wolf-Wendel (Eds.), *ASHE reader on college student development theory* (pp. 647–653). Boston: Pearson.

Upcraft, M. L., & Gardner, J. (Eds.). (1989). *The freshman year experience.* San Francisco: Jossey-Bass.

Van Der Werf, M. (1999). Colleges turn to private companies to build and run student housing. *The Chronicle of Higher Education, 45*(40), pp. 37, 39.

Whitt, E. J., & Nuss, E. M. (1994). Connecting residence halls to the curriculum. In C. C. Schroeder & P. Mable (Eds.), *Realizing the educational potential of residence halls* (pp. 133–164). San Francisco: Jossey-Bass.

Winston, R. B. Jr., Anchors, S., & Associates. (Eds.). (1993). *Student housing and resi-*

dential life: A handbook for professional committed to student development goals.* San Francisco: Jossey-Bass.

Zaransky, M. H. (2006). *Profit by investing in student housing: Cash in on the campus housing shortage.* Chicago: Kaplan.

Zeller, W. J. (2006). Academic integration & campus transformation. In B. M. McCluskey & N. W. Dunkel (Eds.), *Foundations: Strategies for the future of collegiate housing* (pp. 59–66). Columbus, OH: Association of College and University Housing Officers International.

Zheng, J. L., Saunders, K. P., Shelley, M. C., & Whalen, D. F. (2002). Predictors of academic success for freshman residence hall students. *Journal of College Student Development, 43,* 267–283.

Chapter 11

STUDENT ACTIVITIES

Edward G. Whipple and Keith B. O'Neill

HISTORY

Student activities have always been a part of college life; however, "student activities" themselves have taken different forms since the beginning of the American higher education. Students can choose from a variety of activities: lectures and films, social events, fraternity and sorority life, student organization involvement, student government participation, cultural programs, and artist or musical series. Most students can find something to inspire their interests through involvement in student activities on their campuses.

Early American higher education did not offer students a wide array of extracurricular activities. Colonial-era colleges, which focused on religious service as the foundation of student life, offered students extracurricular activities that included regular prayer, church attendance (especially on the Sabbath), and other religious activities shaped for those preparing to enter the clergy. As early as 1719 at Harvard University, groups of youths gathered to read poetry, discuss life issues, and enjoy beer and tobacco. A movement away from more pious activities was attributed to the academic class system, a unique feature of American higher education that encouraged competition among students and hazing within certain types of activities.

Horowitz (1987) described the beginning of college life, which evolved in the late eighteenth and early nineteenth centuries as follows:

All over the new nation, colleges experienced a wave of collective student uprising, led by the wealthier and worldlier undergraduates. College discipline conflicted with the genteel upbringing of the elite sons of Southern gentry and Northern merchants. Pleasure-seeking young men who valued style and open-

ly pursued ambition rioted against college presidents and faculty determined
to put them in their place. In every case, the outbreaks were forcibly sup-
pressed; but the conflict went underground. Collegians withdrew from open
confrontation to turn to covert forms of expression. They forged a peer con-
sciousness sharply at odds with that of the faculty and of serious students and
gave it institutional expression in the fraternity and club system. (p. 11)

Among early student activities, the literary society played a major role in
campus life until the latter part of the nineteenth century. The original purposes of these societies were to provide opportunities for public speaking and
discussions of literature, politics, and history. These groups became competitive among each other and developed strong student loyalty within each
organization. As the societies grew, they demonstrated different characteristics depending on the students' families' social statuses and ranks. As more
students joined societies, college and university administrators recognized
their importance to student life, and societies were correctly recognized as
being more than mere extracurricular gatherings. They became the center of
interest on campus, powerful student-financed and student controlled educational enterprises that paralleled, and even threatened, the narrow and traditional classical academic program of the old-time college (Sack, 1961).

Some literary societies evolved into Greek-letter social organizations; the
first was Phi Beta Kappa, founded in 1776 at the College of William and
Mary. Men's Greek-letter social organizations (fraternities) began with the
Union Triad: Kappa Alpha Society (1825), Sigma Phi (1827), and Delta Phi
Society (1827) (Anson & Marchesani, 1991). Increasing numbers of Greek-
letter social organizations appearing on college campuses led to feelings of
antagonism on the part of many members of the campus community but
eventually lessened after the Civil War. The period immediately preceding
the Civil War and after saw the rise of women's Greek-letter social organizations (sororities) and the rise of professional societies in academic disciplines
such as medicine, law, and engineering; these professional societies also used
Greek letters in their names, similar to their socially-oriented counterparts.

Student government associations and governing boards developed during
the early days of Greek-letter social organizations in the nineteenth century.
At the University of Virginia, Thomas Jefferson believed that students should
be motivated by pride and ambition, rather than by fear and penalty. He supported a student governing board to enforce university regulations, a function that had previously been a faculty responsibility. His plan was unsuc-
cessful due to the state legislature's failure to establish the proposed governing board, the inability of the Virginia students to handle the responsibility,
and the honor code that bound many of the students from providing evidence against each other (Brubacher & Rudy, 1976, 1997).

After the Civil War, as student organizations and athletics became popular, literary societies declined in importance as institutions' curricula expanded. More pronounced after the Civil War was the emergence of a "different" America:

> Students came to represent a broader group than heretofore and some of them were lacking in any serious intellectual or pre-professional interest. Others were coming to college mainly as a prelude to an active career in business and finance. This was the era of the emergence of modern America, when strong-willed entrepreneurs were constructing a vast industrial plant and creating the economic basis for a complex urban society. The goals that were being pursued by the ambitious young men of the country were, more than in antebellum times, predominantly materialist, tangible, pragmatic ones. The attitude of such young people was very often likely to be one of profound anti-intellectualism. (Brubacher & Rudy, 1976, p. 120)

This anti-intellectualism quickly created an atmosphere on campus for the emerging prominence of clubs, fraternities and sororities, intercollegiate athletics, and student publications. In many cases, these activities were based on a philosophy antithetical to the institution's academic mission. In addition, a more radical student government movement was emerging at various campuses. At Vanderbilt, Pennsylvania, and Chicago, student committees were created to maintain order in the dormitories. At Princeton, Vermont, Virginia, Wesleyan, and Bates, groups of student advisors were formed to consult with the faculty on a variety of matters. The Universities of Illinois and Maine even delegated responsibilities for disciplinary concerns to groups of students. These served as the catalyst for the student council movement of the twentieth century (Brubacher & Rudy, 1976, 1997).

Also after the Civil War, faculty tended not to concern themselves as much with student life outside the classroom, thereby encouraging the fraternity to become a natural place for student socialization. These organizations tried to meet students' developmental needs that were not being met by literary societies, and toward the end of the nineteenth century, they also provided living accommodations. For students who attended strict religious institutions, Greek-letter social organizations provided a release from rules and regulations pertaining to student behavior. Also, the secretive nature of fraternities and sororities was appealing to students who sought to challenge college authorities (Brubacher & Rudy, 1976).

As the nation moved into the twentieth century, students who were not interested in fraternity or sorority life (or who could not afford it) established other types of student organizations. Campus life took on a new focus with the emergence of nonsecret organizations like academic clubs that focused on the disciplines (English, foreign language, history, and so on) and which included faculty membership. Other student clubs, focusing on religion, music interest, and sports, were also started.

The first student-center facility was constructed at the University of Pennsylvania in 1896. This building offered a central, physical location for fellowship among students, and allowed their activities and resources to be unified for practical and convenience purposes. Such buildings became known as "unions" in recognition of the fellowship they encouraged, as well as the unifying symbol of student life on campus. As the campus community saw the importance of student union buildings and the activities associated with them, the number of unions built after World War I increased rapidly (Stevens, 1969). Along with the buildings came various programming efforts designed to meet the needs of the institution and surrounding community, and campus unions developed these activities, and tied them to the academic mission of the institution. They included cultural events, speakers' series, lectures, and musical events. The union truly became, on many campuses, the "living room" or "hearthstone" of the institution (Packwood, 1977).

After World War I, administrators were concerned about the disconnection between extracurricular student life and the institution's academic mission. The administration and faculty made a concerted effort to integrate the two:

> As administrators shifted from confrontation to accommodation, they officially recognized student organizations. . . as deans of men and women cooperated with leaders of student societies in planning events and enforcing codes of conduct, the apparent distinctions between institutional goals and those of college life faded. (Horowitz, 1987, p. 119)

Prior to World War II, administrators worked to more clearly define the goals of students' activities on campus. They began to recognize the importance of the college environment, particularly as it impacted the students' education. With the return of military personnel ("G.I.s") from World War II, the complexion and landscape of college and university campuses changed dramatically. Increases in the number of women and older men provided new opportunities and expectations for student activities. Fraternity and sorority life rose to dominance once again as it reclaimed its commitment to leadership and achievement in college life (Horowitz, 1987).

During the 1960s, with the decline of *in loco parentis,* institutional priorities changed the relationship between the institution and its students. Extreme cultural currents, the Civil Rights Movement, and new radical political groups all influenced student life on the college campus. These movements shaped an atmosphere of student independence on campuses, and students became more autonomous in choosing their programs, both within and outside the classroom. For example, the personal need to socialize and associate with peers through traditional student activities (such as in Greek life or student government) became unpopular; consequently, membership in these types of organizations declined nationally, particularly in the Greek-letter social organizations.

The evolution of graduate student personnel preparation programs in the late 1960s and early 1970s also influenced student activities. Professionally-prepared student affairs staff members worked with students to create campus environments with more positive working relationships among faculty, staff, and students. During this period of change, faculty became involved in student organization advising, special-interest clubs flourished, dormitories became more attuned to the residential living-learning idea, and student unions provided space for well-designed programs to address a variety of extracurricular areas. Leadership development and volunteerism also emerged as popular out-of-class activities for students.

During the 1980s, student populations became more diverse than ever before. Increased numbers of older students, international students, students of color, women, and veterans changed the nature of student activities on campuses. Since the 1990s, and into the twenty-first century, higher education has faced continual challenge in changing student demographics that were first apparent in the 1980s. After the conservative movement of the 1980s and increased student focus on career and financial success, more students attempted to balance their collegiate experience with non-career involvement.

Higher education, in general, has experienced a shift in focus inside the classroom from teaching towards student learning. This new emphasis extends into the nature of cocurricular activities as evidenced by such landmark statements on student success as the *Student Learning Imperative* (ACPA, 1994), NASPA's *Reasonable Expectations* (Kuh et al., 1995), and *Learning Reconsidered* (Keeling, 2004) and *Learning Reconsidered 2* (Keeling, 2006). These documents became signposts for student affairs professionals in creating conditions to improve student learning, and in shaping cocurricular campus life in its evolution to advancing learning, supported by all resources available to higher education. Student affairs professionals and faculty counterparts continually explore collaborative ways to enhance the overall educational experience for an increasingly diverse student population (Komives et al., 1996), and new approaches to successive generations will continue to accommodate the changing college student population.

Today, as in the past, employers value student participation in extracurricular activities, and they see such involvement as important to future success in the job market. For many reasons, students seek ways to enhance their academic experience through active participation in student activities.

DEFINITION

Student activities are out-of-class, cocurricular programs, events, or occasions on a college campus that support students' academic, professional, social, physical, spiritual, or emotional development. These activities include leadership development, student union programming, student organization participation, campus governance, fraternal organizations, and special institutional events (e.g., homecoming, family weekends, and so on). In addition, many campuses have student-run programming organizations, often connected with a student union facility, that plan events like concerts, speakers' series, or cultural celebrations. Program variety is wide and unique to each campus.

Higher education literature does not provide for a definition of student activities. Rather, it identifies specific objectives for a student activities program. Mueller (1961) suggested that student development is enhanced by activities that are successful in "complementing classroom instruction or enhancing academic learning; developing social interaction; providing for a profitable use of leisure time; and encouraging better values and higher standards" (p. 275). Miller (1982) suggested the primary responsibility of student affairs professionals is to assist students in their personal growth, development, and education, much of which includes learning how "to learn, cope, lead, follow, solve problems, make decisions, relate to others, handle stress, and otherwise effectively function in an increasingly complex world" (p. 10–11). Today's successful student activities programs still encompass these objectives, which enhance learning outside the classroom, facilitate relationship and community building, encourage social interaction, and promote a value-based developmental experience; these are among the most central outcomes required for a successful collegiate experience (Keeling, 2004).

Student participation in personal activities and in special-interest groups continues to grow, sometimes at the expense of involvement in more traditional, organized activities such as student government, Greek-letter social organizations, and in student union programming. More students are engaged in activities that have a direct impact on their job opportunities and future careers.

The magnitude and variety of today's campus programming requires a more comprehensive definition of student activities and student life. Pike (2000) suggested that "student life focuses on all students and is committed to having them learn, among other things, university traditions through which they develop a sense of community and commitment to the university" (p. 16), and that institutions enhance student learning by making connections between what students learn and the communities (including campus, local, national, and international) in which they live.

Programs like these help to ground student learning in something tangible that students experience each and every day. Such programs can be both student-run and sponsored in conjunction with faculty, administration, and community members. Recent trends have focused students' interest more toward service and volunteer work, on the campus and in the community, and technological advances have opened a new dimension of engagement with the rise of online social networking. Student affairs professionals must find ways to accommodate and collaborate in such dynamic dimensions of student life to ensure that student activities retain their original purpose of supporting student learning and promoting student success.

Need

Involvement in student activities is crucial to the development and growth of students. According to Miller and Jones (1981), student activities are an essential part of educational development for college students. Through participation in student organizations, students acquire a variety of skills that are transferable from one setting to another. Dunkel and Schuh (1998) defined transferable skills as being "related to people, data, and things in a generalized or transferable fashion (for example, from one field, profession, occupation, or job to another)" (p. 119). Pascarella and Terenzini (1991, 2005) concluded that personal development and learning are enhanced when students are involved in educationally purposeful extracurricular activities. These might include situations where students utilize their conflict mediation and time management skills to effectively complete a task.

Overall, the impact of involvement in such activities, including athletics, Greek life, or other structured participation, can be complex (Pascarella & Terenzini, 2005). Chickering and Reisser (1993) stressed the importance of the development of the whole student and of supporting the formation of their intellectual, social, emotional, and physical dimensions. A thorough understanding of students, their developmental needs, and the value of their involvement is crucial.

Staff must be knowledgeable and aware of students' needs and dimensions of development in order to offer meaningful programs. They must have the resources to assess and enhance programs. In addition, an identified educational philosophy should define the thematic rationale of activities, not a single activity or program. Within that rationale, activities should be designed to meet the programming goals of a variety of populations (Mills, 1989). With a renewed focus on defined learning outcomes (Keeling, 2004), goal-oriented student activities will help to focus student learning outside the classroom to help students develop practical skills to complement their own professional preparation.

Purposes

The Council for the Advancement of Standards (CAS) offered professional guidelines ("standards") for use when structuring student activities programs at colleges and universities. According to CAS (2009), the campus activities program must "enhance the overall educational experience of students through development of, exposure to, and participation in programs and activities that improve student cooperation and leadership while preparing students to be responsible advocates and citizens" (p. 96). CAS encouraged student activities programs to operate in an environment that assists students to: participate in cocurricular and governance activities; develop leadership abilities and healthy interpersonal relationships; explore activities individually and in groups to encourage learning, to appreciate a diversity of backgrounds, values, and ideas; and contribute to the educative mission of a campus community (CAS, 2006).

Research has focused on a "learning purpose" of involvement in student activities. For example, student activities can aid in values development, and programming strategies can be designed to provide students with values and growth opportunities (Brock, 1991). Student activities can also assist students in clarifying ethical decision-making, and ethical systems, which reflect different leadership values and contents, may be integrated into leadership training modules and used as a basis for what students need to learn while practicing ethical leadership (Boatman & Adams, 1992).

Astin (1993) found that student involvement inside and beyond the classroom yielded greater student satisfaction in the college experience, and a firmer belief in the efficacy of undergraduate education. It is clear that student activities are not merely a respite from the classroom, as effective activities programming provides its own classroom through the construction of a comprehensive campus community. "When we talk about community in higher education, we are usually referring to a broad vision for campus life that allows students to learn, grow, and develop to their best potential in a challenging yet safe environment" (Maul, 1993, p. 2). Student learning, leadership development, and campus and community involvement are all enhanced when student activities are understood, designed well, and incorporated into a comprehensive undergraduate program.

ADMINISTRATION

The administration of student activities can take many forms, depending on an institution's mission, history, size, student demographics, funding levels, and control status as a public or private college or university. However, common emphases are found among many activities programs, including student organization advising, leadership education, student union programming, concerts, speakers' series, Greek affairs, and many campus special events. Also, student government advising functions are often found within the student activities administrative organization.

There is no common or preferred model for administering student activities (McKaig & Policello, 1979), but it is necessary to design a structure that works well to serve a particular campus student population and culture. An activities program, broad in scope and with a variety of offerings, can be among "central elements in the persistence decision-making process" (Pascarella & Terenzini, 2005, p. 427), and the key to providing such programs is the ability to effectively administer them.

Student activities staff members must offer programs that reflect the priorities of the student affairs organization and of the institution. Styles (1985) indicated that effective program planners should pay particular attention to specific areas that impact effective programming: current research, assessing special populations' needs, balancing bureaucracies, managing power and influence, internal evaluation, and accountability. Further, student activities staff must advocate for external program resources from well-informed perspectives to help guide institutional officers in making educated decisions that affect program design and delivery. Staff must have a voice among those without such knowledge in deciding the organizational status and resource allocation of student activities staff, as the consequences for the profession and for the education of students could be quite serious otherwise (Sandeen & Barr, 2006).

A major factor that determines the focus of a student activities program is whether or not the program is tied to the institution's student union facility. If such a link exists, the administration of the student activities program would likely feature a central staffing pattern. If no link exists, specific programs may be the responsibility of other student affairs offices, such as a dean of students office or office of student life. Depending on the size of the institution, the staff member responsible for directing student activities may report to the senior student affairs officer. In cases where the activities program is part of the union facility operation, the student activities director may report to the director of the union. Structure designs can vary as widely as do student populations, resource conditions, or institutional profiles. Sandeen (1989) wrote about the issue of administrative responsibility for activities programming and the student affairs staff's need to seek a balance between control and freedom. He advised program planners to be sensitive to issues of important campus constituencies, including the president, students, faculty, external groups, and other student affairs staff. In formulating policy for campus activities, administrators should consider the following:

- The educational mission of the institution;
- The priorities of the president;
- The social and educational needs of the students;
- Legal considerations pertinent to the institution;
- The willingness of faculty to participate;
- The support of the student affairs staff;
- Student participation in establishing and revising the policy;
- The establishment of a faculty-student policy council to review the policy and its application; and
- The needs (e.g., concerts, child care, cooperative living groups) of special student groups (Sandeen, 1989, p. 67).

Another key to successful administration of student activities is the staff's ability to work with different constituencies, particularly with diverse students. Successful staff members must understand clearly the context in which student activities are housed at an institution. They must be globally aware and sensitive to the many variables that affect students in a campus environment. Successful staff members work collaboratively with other student affairs personnel to ensure a comprehensive student activities program. According to Newell (1999), "If students get consistent, reinforcing messages from classroom, residence hall, collaborative learning groups, service-learning and the like, they validate one another" (p. 19). Once the campus community identifies high-priority learning initiatives or learning outcomes, students can receive a consistent message from a variety of sources.

Finally, the ability to assess and evaluate student engagement in activities and programs which involve them to develop skills in effective leadership, management, communication, decision-making, and problem-solving is integral, not only to adjust the institutional approach to student learning, but also to advocate for the resources necessary to continue the administrative ability to provide such experiences. Demonstrated proof (quantitative or qualitative data) of a program's effectiveness is often required when justifying requests for resources, and when personnel must show advances in student learning. Recent trends in building a culture of assessment throughout student affairs have included ways to quantify and qualify program quality. Student activities can easily demonstrate student learning (and administrative success in supporting learning) through responsible assessment and evaluation (acting upon data received). Assessment helps to make meaning of how, what, when and where student learning takes place, often to answer the call to accountability from external demands or from internal commitments to improvement (Keeling et al., 2008).

STUDENT DEVELOPMENT AND STUDENT ACTIVITIES

Importance

It is imperative for student activities staff to have adept knowledge of student development theory, as it demonstrates the importance of the educational process of the whole student. If an intended outcome of higher education is to graduate informed, responsible citizens, then curricular and cocurricular experiences are equally important. Research shows the tremendous impact of the extracurricular experience. Since students spend the vast majority of their day outside of the classroom, the emotional, social, moral, physical, and mental impact of campus activities are significant (Astin, 1993; Chickering & Reisser, 1993; Feldman & Newcomb, 1969; Pascarella & Terenzini, 1991, 2005). In addition, the influence of the student peer group is also significant. Astin (1993) stated that

> Perhaps the most compelling generalization from the myriad of findings summarized . . . is the pervasive effect of the peer group on the individual's development. Every aspect of the student's development—cognitive and affective, psychological and behavioral—is affected in some way by peer group characteristics, and usually by several peer characteristics. Generally, students tend to change their values, behavior, and academic plans in the directions of the dominant orient of their peer group. (p. 363)

Astin's (1993) research indicated that student satisfaction with campus life (including academics) is influenced directly by the degree of cocurricular involvement. For example, students who were involved in activities with other students (e.g. sports, student organizations, attending campus events, socializing) were more pleased with their collegiate experience. This impact of association makes a dramatic difference in students' success in college and their retention. "There is considerable evidence, however, that active participation in the extracurricular life of campus can enhance retention" (Upcraft, 1985, pp. 330-331). Types of student activities that have a positive impact on retention include establishing close friendships, participating in orientation programs and activities, joining student organizations, involving oneself in social and cultural activities, attending lectures, actively using campus facilities, and generally participating in cocurricular activities (Upcraft, 1985).

According to the 2007 National Survey on Student Engagement (NSSE), almost 40 percent of senior students indicated they had engaged in "enriching educational experiences." These experiences included participating in cocurricular activities, community service or volunteer work, and conversations with students of a different race or ethnicity. Kuh and associates (1991) investigated what students learn through participation in cocurricular activities, and concluded the following:

- Orientation participation positively impacts social integration and institutional commitment and indirectly impacts the student's satisfaction with the institution and his or her desire to persist;
- Involved students are more positive about their undergraduate experience, including their social life, living environment, and academic major. College participation, according to the research, is important to the student's job success after graduation;
- Participation in extracurricular activities allows for the opportunity to gain leadership, decision-making, and planning skills, which are transferable to the job market;
- Involvement allows for learning about mature, intimate interpersonal relationships;
- The opportunity for leadership work in activities translated to more active community and civic leaders after graduation; and
- The research indicates that the only factor that predicts adult success is participation in extracurricular activities. (pp. 8–9)

Later research at a number of institutions whose students continually scored above average on subsequent NSSE administrations found that "engagement has been shown to be the best predictor of student success, after controlling for past academic performance and preparation" (Kinzie & Kuh, 2004, p. 4). This engagement, especially in cocurricular realm of student learning and development, suggests that involvement in student activities is paramount. A continual challenge (and opportunity) remains for the activities-based student affairs professional to provide appropriate and relevant experiences that are necessary for positive student growth and development. Student activities, when based on an understanding of student development theory, become crucial.

Using Student Development Theory

In order to facilitate student learning and development effectively, student activities staff members must be aware of development theory and how to translate theory into practice. Student learning and development are dependent upon the type of environment in which an action or activity takes place (e.g., workshop, meeting, program, policy) and the desired outcomes.

As leaders in higher education, student affairs professionals accept the challenge and the responsibility to create learning environments that encourage student development, since "the primary goals of student affairs professionals are to facilitate students' development . . . it is our responsibility, both professionally and ethically, to know and understand the individuals, groups, and institutions with whom we work" (McEwen, 2003, pp. 154-155). Intentional interventions take place through a variety of activities both in and out of the classroom, and interactions among students potentially represent "labs for learning to communicate, empathize, argue, and reflect" (Chickering & Reisser, 1993, p. 392). Interactions that encourage student development take place through active participation in various activities created intentionally by student affairs professionals, and are designed so that students can create connections between learning that takes place in the classroom with other experiences, events, and individual people that affect their daily lives.

In discussing the relationship between involvement, retention and student learning, Tinto (1987) suggested that:

> Though the research is far from complete, it is apparent that the more students are involved in the social and intellectual life of a college, the more frequently they make contact with faculty and other students about learning issues, especially outside the class, the more students are likely to learn. (p. 69)

Involvement with various components of campus life can increase students' probability of learning, both in and out of the classroom (Tinto, 1987).

Astin (1993) offered a comprehensive analysis of the effects of involvement on student learning. Living in a campus residence hall exhibited direct positive effects on self-reported growth in leadership and interpersonal skills. Student-faculty interaction demonstrated a positive correlation with all self-reported areas of intellectual and personal growth. Student-student interaction correlated positively with self-reported growth in leadership ability, public speaking, interpersonal skills, analytical and problem-solving skills, and critical thinking skills.

Historically, student affairs has been criticized for not basing program development on student development theory. The lack of a theoretical or conceptual foundation may be due to the personal interests, skill, or knowledge levels of professional staff, emerging crises, professional trends, political expediency, influence of special-interest groups, administrative culture, and local tradition (Hurst & Jacobson, 1985).

Given the importance of students' extracurricular experience and the time devoted to it, it is critical that student affairs staff use student development theory to facilitate student learning and development. Those involved in student activities programming must be knowledgeable of appropriate development theory and related issues. These include learning theory, group dynamics, student demographics, educational philosophy, institutional governance, supervision, and organizational development (Marin, 1985). An understanding of various student development theories and theory families will provide for more effective program design and delivery. Theory is "particularly helpful, especially when it comes to understanding why students do the things they do; without some theory, this would often be incomprehensible" (McIntosh & Swartwout, 2001, p. 25). Personnel must never underestimate the power and purpose of theory in certain situations.

Finally, how might student activities programs meet the needs of the 45-year-old, divorced mother of three who is returning to college to complete a degree, while at the same time accommodate the 18-year-old, first-year college student? Student activities staff must be aware of the developmental needs of both students, who hold very different expectations for a co-curricular program. Institutions must respond to different needs of students, and student development theory can aid program planning to help students refine skills in areas such as self-direction, social relations, leadership, volunteer services, and cultural preparation (Miller & Jones, 1981).

PROGRAMS

Types of programs offered for student learning are varied. Whether through sponsorship by student organizations, a student programming board, a student union, or student affairs staff, student activities programs include a wide variety of opportunities designed to support extended education outside the classroom. Such programs focus on the arts, speakers, politics, diversity awareness, community service, and leadership development.

Many programs are common to most college and university campuses: student government advising, student organization services, Greek affairs, student union programs, multicultural programs, leadership development, and volunteer activities.

Student Government

Student government is an important part of campus life, but for many student affairs staff members, student government poses a problem that centers on the relationship between the institution and the student government organization. If student affairs staff members do not understand this important relationship, which is different than the institution's relationship with any other student organization, serious difficulty can ensue. In many cases, the student government president has direct access to the institution's president; thus, it is crucial that the senior student affairs officer and the staff liaison to student government are aware of this special relationship. Student affairs staff should act in a strong supportive capacity with student government, ensuring that appropriate educational opportunities are available, such as leadership training and special workshops, to assist student government members' development. In addition, staff should continually keep the student government leadership aware of its role as the official, representative voice of the students and its legal, moral, and ethical responsibilities to represent their student constituencies to the administration in a timely, constructive, and mature manner.

In a survey of student government advisors, Boatman (1988) found six characteristics of a strong student government: (a) student leaders' understanding of the institution's structure and the relationship of other student groups to student government; (b) the direct and regular access of student government leaders to top institutional administrators and faculty in both professional and social settings; (c) a mutual respect and common view of the institution by student government leaders, their advisors, and institutional representatives; (d) a positive working relationship between the student government and the student press; (e) a high degree of student participation and retention in student government elections, activities, and meetings; and (f) training student government leaders to analyze the institution's structure and implementing needed change and appointing student leaders to institutional committees.

Boatman (1988) also noted that the qualities of a student government advisor should include those of honesty, openness, strong interpersonal communication skills, and the ability to deal with a range of opinions and feelings. In addition, advisors should be resources for students with regard to the institution's history, campus culture, policies, politics, and current issues, and should have credibility with (and access to) administrators.

Research has demonstrated that participation in student government has favorable, demonstrated effects on students. These effects include a significantly greater reported development of social and practical competencies and workplace skills that employers find valuable, and the development of self-confidence, self-esteem, and an interest in civic engagement after college (Kuh & Lund, 1994).

Student Organization Services

With ever-changing membership of student organizations, and at times, the lack of consistent advising, staff support is important to help support students through organizational transitions and changes in leadership. Other than student governing bodies and Greek-letter social organizations, student groups on campus may not receive much direct attention; such groups as honor societies, religious organizations, academic clubs, sports clubs, and special interest groups may not have direct staff advising support. For many students who belong to these organizations, membership is their link to student life. According to Terenzini and Pascarella (1997), "If individual effort or involvement is the lynchpin for college impact, then a key matter becomes how a campus can shape its intellectual and interpersonal environments in ways that do indeed encourage student involvement" (p. 178). Student organizations provide a wealth of opportunities for student involvement that can match any student's interests.

Institutions should provide student organizations with meeting space, resource and supply centers, and office space, depending on the goals of the particular student organization and whether the institution is able to provide such resources. Centrally-located mailboxes can aid in communication and support efforts at community-building among students and student groups.

Staff must be instrumental in providing educational training programs for student organization leaders and their members. These may include sessions on resources available at the institution, financial management, membership recruitment, publicity, motivating members, and fundraising techniques. Many campuses feature a student organization information fair, which allows for new and current students to learn more about the opportunities for involvement and leadership outside the classroom.

Because of the wealth of faculty talent, student affairs staff should invite faculty to assist in providing programs and advising services to students. Besides engaging their academic expertise, faculty members can work with students outside the classroom to strengthen the ties between academic and student affairs, and to help the student take part in a more seamless learning experience.

Not all institutions enjoy an adequate supply of financial and human resources, and student organizations may often benefit from cosponsorship of events and programs. This collaborative practice can include sharing funds, personnel, and communication resources to plan or implement a program. Advantages of cosponsorship are that the potential for programming variety is enhanced, student leadership and programming skills are developed, publicity for all involved groups can strengthened, and a positive synergy develops between the cosponsoring organizations. Student activities staff must encourage such community-building efforts whenever possible, and particularly when financial resources dictate the need for such partnerships.

Greek-Letter Social Organizations (Greek Affairs)

Greek-letter social organizations are among the most controversial student activities programs. Since their beginning, there has been continual debate over the value of fraternities and sororities on college campuses. Critics have claimed that these organizations are exclusionary, sexist, and gender-specific and that their existence is contrary to the values colleges and universities hope to convey to students (Maisel, 1990). Administrators have questioned these groups' relevance to campus life as well as the relationship between the Greek community and the institution.

Institutional emphasis on and influence of fraternity and sorority life varies from campus to campus. Fraternity and sorority members can be integral stewards of campus traditions and tend to hold many student leadership roles. Members tend to provide important community service, but at the same time may promote activities that are seen as demeaning, discriminatory, and even dangerous. Hazing, a criminal offense, is often associated with Greek-letter social organizations, and is sometimes employed as a new member's rite of passage upon entry into Greek life. The value of fraternity and sorority life remains the subject of debate and research. "Blue ribbon" committees have been established to review Greek life, recommending either its elimination from campus or a significant change in the relationship between the host campus and fraternities and sororities. The University of Southern California, the University of Alabama, Bowling Green State University, Denison University, and Gettysburg College are a few institutions that have studied the role of Greek life on their campuses. It is common for administrative support for Greek affairs to come from the offices of student activities, the dean of students, student life, housing, or residence life.

Faculty has been particularly critical of common perceptions of anti-intellectualism among fraternity and sorority members. While a Greek chapter may have some of the most outstanding scholars on campus, it also may have some members experiencing grave academic difficulty (Winston & Saunders, 1987).

Values and attitudes of students impact their view of learning. In a study of Greek values and attitudes, Baier and Whipple (1990) found that the Greek system appears to provide a "safe harbor" for those who seek conformity, family dependence, social apathy, and extensive involvement in extracurricular activities. The Greek system also "provides a 'legitimate' campus subculture for students to associate with others who are affluent, have relatively undefined academic and vocational goals, and place a higher priority on social life than intellectual pursuits" (p. 52).

Because of the debate on many campuses regarding the value of fraternities and sororities, it is important that staff have a well-defined plan for working with students affiliated with these organizations. When groups fail to meet expectations and stated goals, actions must be taken on the part of university officials and the organization's national leadership to realign students' actions with their standards (Maloney, 1998). A thorough understanding of the value of fraternity and sorority life as it relates to an institution's academic mission is crucial for students to realize, if Greek-letter social organizations are to succeed.

According to the Council for Advancement of Standards in Higher Education (2006), in order to accomplish its mission, an effective Greek advising program must:

1. Promote holistic student wellness (intellectual, spiritual, social, moral, civic, professional, and physical);
2. Provide leadership training and knowledge of group dynamics and management;
3. Promote involvement in cocurricular activities;
4. Encourage community service and philanthropic engagement;
5. Develop student awareness of human diversity; and
6. Highlight learning opportunities that exist among diverse group experiences.

To be effective, student affairs staff must help Greek organization members understand their roles and responsibilities on campus (Whipple & Sullivan, 1998). Programs should encourage a sense of community among Greek members and the greater community. The Greek advisor must establish effective lines of communication among the chapter leadership, alumni, institutional administration, and the national/international Greek organizations. Communication and partnerships among these constituencies are invaluable when working through issues that arise.

Greek organizations are traditionally and continually associated with particular issues, including substance abuse, hazing, poor community relations, and a lack of sensitivity to diversity issues. Alcohol abuse and hazing are often linked, and provide a continual challenge to student affairs staff in curbing illicit behavior. Institutions often can develop healthy partnerships with local law enforcement authorities and with the organizations themselves to create strategies for healthy living. When Greek organizations are housed outside of the institution's residential system, neighborhood associations often become a partner in these efforts as well. Some Greek governing boards have established human relations committees that work to promote, through programming, more sensitive and tolerant communities. Students must understand that positive behavior, role modeling, and appreciation of diverse backgrounds can lead to the strengthening of their own groups. Student affairs staff should continually look for educational opportunities to model healthy behaviors and to create a sensitive and understanding community among all members.

Many colleges and universities seek to create learning communities for their students, faculty, and staff (Whipple & Sullivan, 1998). Institutions should expect all programs, both inside and outside of the classroom, to contribute to student learning in some manner. Fraternities and sororities offer excellent opportunities to cultivate seamless learning, where students are active participants in the learning process and assume a large part of the responsibility for their own learning (Kuh, 1996).

Fraternity and sorority life can add much to campus life and provide a positive experience for many students. However, it is important that student affairs staff establish procedures whereby the institution can evaluate the positive campus contributions Greek-letter social organizations can make. Evaluation of support services provided by the institution and national/international organization is also necessary.

Student Union Programs

On many campuses, the student union or student center facility is the "community center of the college, for all members of the college family—students, faculty, administration, alumni and guests" (Packwood, 1977, p. 180). Depending on the student affairs administrative organization, much of the student activities advising for campus programming may come from student union staff members. In any case, the student union should be an important gathering place for students and afford an array of activities that contribute to the overall campus community.

The CAS Standards (2009) for student unions stated that the primary goals of the college union must be "to bring campus constituents together, build campus community, support and initiate programs, provide services, and maintain facilities that promote student learning and development" (p. 154). In addition, campus unions must offer students opportunities to "learn and practice leadership, programming, management, social responsibility, and interpersonal skills. As a center for the academic community, the union provides a place for increased interaction and understanding among individuals from diverse backgrounds" (CAS, 2006, p. 117). These activities can offer an important link to all facets of student life and strengthen the ties to academic pursuit.

Union activities programming must meet the needs of today's student. Levitan and Osteen (1992) suggested that programming changes can be the result of dynamic media and advancing technology, creative new leadership programs, the need for interpersonal relationships and skill building, an increased emphasis on volunteerism and service, and increased diversity and changing student demographics. Trends of particular importance to student union activities include adapting physical space to accommodate activities that extend classroom learning and academic dialogue, embracing programmatic opportunities brought about by changing student populations and their patterns of involvement, and current media and technological advances that facilitate social interaction and networking, both in a virtual world and "live."

Multicultural Affairs and Diversity Programming

As the student population on campuses becomes more diverse, the need for multicultural programming increases. Multiculturalism may be the most unresolved issue on campuses today (Levine & Cureton, 1998). Students, faculty and staff demand programs that meet the diverse needs of all members of the campus community. This diversity stems from uniqueness of background or origin, and celebrated with regard to race, ethnicity, religious identity, ability, age, orientation, and along many other dimensions. Student affairs staff increasingly will be called upon to provide the expertise to promote diversity programming. They must be able to define multiculturalism and create appropriate learning outcomes to expand students' understanding of diversity and to build a culture of appreciation and celebration of differences. Hu and Kuh (2003) discovered that "experiences with interactional diversity have positive effects for virtually all students in all types of postsecondary institutions with a wide range of desirable outcomes" (p. 331). A multicultural dialogue that features students, faculty, staff, and other members of the campus community can not only benefit students' academic learning, but can heighten student civic engagement and citizenship development. "More programs and activities are needed to bring together people with different political views and religious traditions and from different countries of origin to engage in productive dialogue" (Hu & Kuh, 2003, p. 331).

Through the variety of interactions with students and the learning that occurs within a group, student activities programs can promote multiculturalism and an appreciation of diversity. Students can learn from opportunities, structures, and strategies for replacing stereotypes with personal knowledge to view differences for their qualities, importance, and potential to create growth. Staff should avoid the common mistakes of (a) trying to program for diverse constituencies without including input from the target groups, (b) assuming that all members of a particular culture are alike, (c) making multicultural programming the responsibility of one committee only, and (d) assuming that certain artists hold the greatest appeal for their particular identity group.

Student affairs staff must look at ways to redefine campus norms that have served as barriers to the integration of underrepresented students into campus life. Hurtado and associates (2003) suggested that institutions "must bring diverse students together . . . and must create opportunities and expectations for students to interact across racial and other social divides" (p. 152). Intercultural learning has become integral to student engagement in global learning. As students become more familiar with other cultures, they find participation in diversity programming easier and more interesting. Arminio and associates (2000) warned that student affairs professionals must "continue to seek means by which the racial identity of students of color is not sacrificed when students of color participate in predominately White groups" (p. 506). No one should sacrifice aspects of his or her identity in order to be involved in campus life.

Student affairs staff must partner with student leaders and student organizations to change campus structures in order to eliminate barriers to inclusion, to modify hierarchies that perpetuate majority viewpoints, and to recreate programming and advisory boards that encourage diverse representation.

Leadership Development

Leadership development directly impacts the quality of student life on a campus. When student leaders are well-versed in the basics of leadership, student activities can be more organized and developed. In many cases, that development will impact organization members positively, and often a student's effectiveness to lead an organization depends on the success of the student organization. The campus is the student's laboratory for successful experimentation and learning about leadership.

> Teaching leadership skills is an important element of civic responsibility and can occur through experiences in student organizations . . . and classroom settings. Repeated exposure through course work, community work, activity management, student research, interaction with senior university administrators, and management of campus and system-wide elected student leadership posts creates community leadership skills. (McDonald, 2002, pp. 28-29)

Leadership is a much-researched and complex phenomenon. A shift in the leadership paradigm has taken place in the last two decades; most prior research was centered on the individual as leader rather than the process of leadership (Komives et al., 1998). Educators must redefine their understandings of leadership to reflect that "leadership is not something a leader possesses so much as a process involving followership" (Hollander, 1993, p. 29). When designing future programs and activities to foster leadership, student affairs staff members should consider the concept of followership (both recruiting and maintaining qualified followers) into consideration.

Current definitions of leadership describe a social, relational process with a level of interaction between leaders and followers who work together to accomplish the same goal (Komives et al., 1998, 2007). Leadership also includes a socially responsible component defined as "purposeful and intentional . . . practiced in such a way as to be socially responsible" (Komives, et al., 1998, p. 14). The role of change is also prevalent in current definitions of leadership. Matusak (1996) defined leadership as "initiating and guiding and working with a group to accomplish change" (p. 5). Rost (1991) defined leadership as an "influence relationship among leaders and their collaborators who intend real changes that reflect their mutual purposes" (p. 99). This shift affects how leadership development activities should be designed, promoted, and implemented in the campus setting.

Some institutions assign a staff member to work solely to leadership development activities. Other institutions may incorporate leadership training into various program offerings, with staff members responsible for each program addressing the leadership education components.

Leadership development can take place in different environments. Seminars and workshops can be offered on specific topics. For example, a session on how to recruit members may be offered to all student organizations, or a program on improving communication skills may be provided for fraternity and sorority executive officers. Leadership development programs should take a variety of forms, as formal and informal activities, and should be presented across a variety of program formats (i.e., training, workshops, service-learning, and so on). A leadership advisory committee can be beneficial in assessing student needs and the resources available to address those needs (Nolfi, 1993).

On some campuses, student affairs staff may instruct credit and noncredit courses. For example, specific for-credit leadership training courses may be available to fraternity and sorority presidents and student government leaders. First-year students and sophomores often benefit from introductory leadership courses that focus on basic skill-building to prepare them to assume future roles of campus leadership.

Recognizing changing student demographics, student affairs staff members may develop student leadership programs that acknowledge students' on-campus involvement, and that also reflect the overlapping needs of traditional and nontraditional students

Community Service

Community service can be a vital part of a student activities program. Participation in a service organization helps prepare students for volunteerism in their community after graduation. "Many institutions of higher education have become active members of their local communities in a variety of ways, with both sharing their human, educational, technical, and fiscal resources" (Gugerty & Swezey, 1996, p. 92). Student affairs staff can aid in supporting service by explaining the civic responsibility it supports. These activities teach students about their roles in the world around them.

Some student organizations exist with a sole focus on service, and others incorporate "service" as one part of their missions. These organizations include fraternities and sororities, honor societies, and student government. Given the nature of volunteer or service organizations, staff must help members establish clear goals and expectations for participation. Also, they should communicate continually the goals and benefits of the organization to the campus community. These groups can lose focus if strong student leadership and committed advising are not present. The rewards of a group's efforts are sometimes not easily seen, and members who desire instant gratification may lose interest in participation.

Service organizations are valuable to a campus culture because of the positive impact of student participation. Astin (1993) found that "participation in volunteer work also has a positive correlation with a variety of attitudinal outcomes: commitment to developing a meaningful philosophy of life, promoting racial understanding, and participating in programs to clean up the environment" (p. 392). Research on college students has demonstrated that peer involvement ranks among the most significant influences on student learning and development (Astin, 1993; Chickering & Reisser, 1993; Pascarella & Terenzini, 1991, 2005). Peers helping peers, in a volunteer or service setting, can be extremely beneficial for all involved.

Higher education has been called to renew its historic commitment to service and the learning that takes place as a result of service (Jacoby, 2003; Jacoby & Associates, 1996). Not only should students be encouraged to volunteer and serve others, but initiatives should be in place to use service as a "teachable moment" for students as well. This new relationship between service and learning was defined as, "a form of experiential education in which students engage in activities that address human and community needs together with structured opportunities intentionally designed to promote student learning and development. Reflection and reciprocity are key concepts of service-learning" (Jacoby, 1996, p. 5).

Service-learning can also be integrated into leadership and student activities. Linking community service and leadership development opportunities helps student organization members to develop as "servant-leaders."

> Moving a student from an understanding of charity to an understanding of justice often requires a parallel move from the group to a sense of individualism that then translates back to the group and community. It is through this movement that students mature and develop as "whole people" committed to the betterment of the society of which they are a part. (Delve & Rice, 1990, p. 64)

This integration of service with leadership and campus activities may occur through retreats and workshops, credit and noncredit leadership courses, orientation programs, and recognition. CAS (2009) suggested that the "primary mission of service-learning programs is to engage students in experiences

that address human and community needs together with structured opportunities for reflection intentionally designed to promote student learning and
development" (p. 351).

STUDENT ACTIVITIES ISSUES AND TRENDS

At the close of the first decade of the twenty-first century, higher education continues to be influenced by external factors, including the international economy, political landscapes, changing student demographics, technology upgrades, and new demands for knowledge and workplace skills.
These influences often require that students seek higher levels of engagement
than ever before, and student affairs staff must be aware of current issues and
trends that shape students' experiences on college and university campuses.

Changing Student Demographics

Adult Learners

At many institutions across the country, the impact of changing demographics is affecting the focus of student activities programs. "Nontraditional" students are fast becoming "traditional" students, as colleges and universities continue to admit students who are outside of the "traditional" age
range of 18 to 22 years of age. According the U.S. Department of Education
(2007), by 2010, 38 percent of all college students will be over age of twen-
ty-five, almost 60 percent of students will be females, and about 40 percent
will attend parttime. Only about two in five of all college students will fit the
traditional stereotype of the American college student: 18 to 22 years of age,
attending college full time and living in a campus residential unit. The
increase of adult learners, and particularly females, continues to change the
nature of student affairs programs and services. As a result, student affairs
staff must be aware of adult learners' needs and motivations. Specific services like childcare and focused programs that match adult learners' (and their
families') interests are integral to building a comfortable environment for
their participation. Ringgenberg (1989) suggested that:

> Returning students and women students need child-care facilities, support
> groups for themselves and their families, a common gathering ground, and
> social, recreation, cultural, and educational programs that meet their interests.
> Programming for a family is a great deal different from programming for the
> traditional age student. For example, tastes in music and comedy can be
> extremely different. However, failure to provide family programming could
> isolate these students from campus. (pp. 33-34)

Most adults who return to college, or who attend college for the first time, matriculate to accomplish specific objectives, to develop social contacts and relationships with others, or to learn for the pleasure of acquiring knowledge. However, the recent international economic downturn has also encouraged people to consider returning to higher education to refine skills and to prepare them for new employment opportunities, especially if their employment situation had been directly affected by economic influences.

The developmental needs of returning adults differ, according to their stage of early or middle adulthood, a midlife transition, or a later-life phase. Among these stages are different levels of development of the ego, the intellect, and of morals and ethics. Student affairs staff must be aware of these phases and provide appropriate support for each. From the transition of arrival to college, through achievement of student success throughout a degree program, and preparations for departure and professional placement, staff must be aware of the unique experiences adult learners bring to campus, and must prepare them adequately to re-enter the workplace with new and updated professional knowledge and skills.

Lesbian, Gay, Bisexual, Transgender, Queer, and Questioning (LGBTQ) Students

On many campuses, student organizations exist for students who identify as lesbian, gay, bisexual, transgender, queer, questioning, or with another orientation or sexual identity. Unfortunately, given many campus climates, these students do not feel a part of the mainstream of student life. Student affairs staff can improve the quality of life for LGBTQ students by developing programs to meet their needs, and should advocate for institutional policies to include protection from discrimination against sexual orientation. Staff should be educated on LGBTQ issues and on strategies to address potential harassment that is often associated with the LGBTQ student experience.

Campus environments are different in their acceptance of LGBTQ students. Good (1993) described five programming stages for the student affairs staff, depending on the institution's level of readiness. The first stage is programming focused on reducing hate crimes and teaching students to appreciate diversity. The second stage develops programs to promote a positive student self-identity. The third stage aggressively establishes a place for students on campus and allows them to share their experiences with the college community. Stage four moves from the external environment faced by the students to personal adjustment issues. Finally, the fifth stage should provide for an environment where students can feel comfortable within the campus community and that helps them affirm who they are. In recent years, staff training programs such as Safe Space, Safe Zone, and ally development activities have become common as student affairs staff members use this stage approach as a framework for designing programs that include and celebrate the LGBTQ student experience on campus.

Students with Disabilities

The number of disabled students entering postsecondary education is rising (Weeks, 2001). A 2006 report of fall-semester postsecondary enrollment indicated 12 percent of all college students reported having at least one disability. This is an increase from a 1978 survey where only 3 percent of freshmen claimed a disability (Weeks, 2001).

> Section 504 of the Rehabilitation Act of 1973 states, ". . . no otherwise qualified handicapped individual in the U.S. . . . shall solely, by reason of his handicap, be excluded from participation in, be denied the benefits of, or be subjected to discrimination under any program or activity receiving federal financial assistance." Under Section 504, provisions must be made for students with disabilities when planning and executing university programs and activities. These programs include any "physical education, athletics, recreation, transportation, other extracurricular, or other postsecondary education program or activity." Colleges and universities must not only provide interpreters for lectures and wheelchair access to facilities, but also must create programs (e.g., recreational and educational) that support the special needs of students with disabilities.

International Students

As more international students arrive at institutions across the country, they must be accommodated academically and socially. It is not the sole responsibility of an international student services office to care for international students; rather, it is everyone's responsibility to ensure that international students are successfully being integrated into the campus community.

International students provide a great benefit to American institutions through their efforts to educate all students for living in a global society. "International students bring with them rich experiences and unique cross-cultural perspectives that help to internationalize the campus and give host country students first-hand opportunities to share learning with individuals from around the world" (CAS, 2006, p. 220).

Student affairs professionals should work closely with the staff responsible for administering international student programs on campus. Activities can be planned for international students and for American students in order to promote common goals. All students can benefit from such interactions and relationships. The challenge for staff is to acknowledge and balance the activities that are important to promoting international students' cultural, ethnic, or religious backgrounds with those activities that help assimilate them into the culture of the campus, and to create an environment where students share a sense of purpose and unity while still accepting and appreciating diversity.

Other Special Student Populations

Students seek higher education from many different backgrounds with a wide range of life experiences, talents, and interest. One goal of student affairs staff must be to make students' experience on campus relevant and supportive of their academic progress. Regardless of ability level, interest area, or resources available, creative programming and advising can help to make an extraordinary learning experience for a student.

First-generation students, whose parents did not attend college, may be less likely to be fully academically and socially prepared for higher education, and may be less functionally aware of how a college or university operates. Specific orientation programs or services can be designed to engage these students beyond the classroom to help create a seamless learning environment. Targeted activities, student organizations, or other intervention efforts may help first-generation students find success in assimilating to the college environment.

Students who have served in the military are returning to campuses in increasing numbers, especially after the Servicemen's Readjustment Act ("G.I. Bill") was expanded in 2008. This recent development expanded the benefits traditionally provided through the G.I. Bill to qualified veterans of the armed forces, and offered many former servicepersons the ability to gain a college degree. However, the move away from military service to a college or university environment suggests an intense change in lifestyle, in physical environment, in daily activity, and in academic engagement, and this can be a difficult transition for veterans. Student affairs staff can aid in such a transition and in veterans' continued success through strategic and intentional design of activities and programs that engage them and invite the sharing of their unique experiences among other members of the campus community.

Student affairs professionals have learned extensively about how generations have shaped higher education and broader society. Most recently, there has been significant literature on how students of the millennial generation have approached and graduated college. As Millennial alumni begin to enter the workforce, higher education must be prepared for the next generation (sometimes labeled "Generation Z," the "Net Generation," or the "iGeneration") and find creative, innovative ways to engage students through technological and strategic methods of instruction. Student affairs staff members must consider ways to adapt programs and services to accommodate future students' unique worldview.

Legal Issues

Like the university at-large, staff members in student activities are faced with a myriad of legal issues when developing student programs outside the classroom. While it is clearly not possible to discuss all the legal relationships and implications in depth, institution officials must be aware of potential legal ramifications that exist when implementing certain decisions relating to student activities.

Four primary legal relationships exist between students and their respective institutions. These four relationships are (a) constitutional, (b) torts, (c) statutory, and (d) contractual (Gehring, 1993). All four relationships can involve students, activities, and the institution as a result of decisions made by college officials and student leaders.

For public institutions and those private institutions where state action is involved, the First Amendment must be taken into account before authorizing or denying a student organization the opportunity to plan an event on campus. A decision to invite a controversial speaker to lecture on campus, to show an X-rated movie at the university theater, to deny a student group the opportunity to march on campus, or to hold a meeting at a campus building will typically force the institution to balance the interests of the First Amendment with college officials' and students' desires to have a campus free of offensive, obnoxious, or disrespectful speech. The First Amendment protects most speech, but not all. If speech is obscene, represents a clear and present danger, constitutes fighting words, or will incite others to panic or imminent, lawless action, the institution may be able to restrict a person's speech. While restrictions on a student's freedom of expression may be considered under only the most extraordinary of circumstances, student leaders and college officials should provide constructive outlets to contrary opinions or activities when certain controversial events occur on campus.

As for tort liability and statutory concerns, universities will often find that such a relationship will exist with students, employees, and guests of the University. A tort is broadly defined "as a civil wrong, other than a breach of contract, for which the courts will allow a damage remedy" (Kaplin & Lee, 1995, p. 89). In the collegiate setting, tort law has been most often applied in negligence cases relating to personal injury sustained while attending an activity sponsored by a student group or the institution, or while being physically present on campus. Higher education institutions have a duty to protect their students and other invited guests from known or reasonable foreseeable dangers.

Fraternity and sorority problems associated with hazing, alcohol, and physical destruction of university premises have resulted in civil lawsuits brought by students or their families for tort behavior. Colleges must regularly check to see that (a) hazing or violent relationships among groups are not occurring, (b) university premises (e.g., fraternity and sorority houses and residence halls) are safe from physical defects, and (c) no minor incidents have occurred that forewarn the university of possible future, larger accidents (Gulland & Powell, 1989).

Criminal statutes relating to uses of alcohol (e.g., social host liability and underage drinking) and proscribing hazing will create legal relationships not only between the students and the institution, but students and the state as well. Thus, institution officials and students must be cognizant of the criminal and civil statutes that may apply to them.

In addition, federal mandates, such as the Student Right to Know and Jeanne Clery Disclosure of Campus Security Policy and Campus Crime Statistics Act (the "Clery Act"), create special relationships between students and particular employees of the university. Campus authorities (institutional officials who hold significant responsibility for student and campus activities, but who do not act in a counseling capacity) are required by the Clery Act to report all occurrences of crime specified in the legislation (homicide, sexual offenses, robbery, aggravated assault, burglary, arson, and motor vehicle theft). While many leaders in the higher education community voiced their opinions that this definition was too broad as written, administrators who work with student and campus activities are considered campus authorities and are mandated by law to report all instances of crime. This responsibility may require that confidentiality cannot be maintained. Student activities staff members should consult their campus legal counsel for additional information and questions about a particular situation.

Finally, the relationship between an institution and a student is contractual in nature, and such contracts may be explicit or implicit, written or oral. Institutions must be careful in drafting information and policies contained within student handbooks, brochures, and catalogues, because courts may view these documents as supporting or defining a contractual relationship between the institution and the student. It is clear that the law pervades the entire college campus, and significantly shapes action relative to student activities. Where appropriate and when possible, competent legal counsel and advice should be solicited to guide staff and students away from incident and liability.

Funding Issues

On many campuses, funding of student activities programs comes from nonstate dollars. The most common terms for a funding source are a "student activity fee" or "general fee." On some campuses, student activities may be funded from both state dollars and nonstate dollars, depending upon which administrative office coordinates the programs. With the increasing scrutiny of state budgets and public calls for institutional accountability in the educational enterprise, there is continual assessment and evaluation of institutional expenditures. This requires staff to remain aware of changing budget situations. One of the student benefits of extracurricular involvement is the opportunity to work with budgets, and staff should educate students about federal and state budget issues, sources, and the impact these have on student activities programs.

Working with volatile budgets is a problem for all student affairs programs, including student activities. However, many options exist to help save resources and maximize their use. These options include cosponsorship and collaboration, using local talent and technology, emphasizing student and staff skills development, and seeking support from creative outlets other than traditional sources (state, foundations, and agencies). Students themselves can often benefit from increased publicity and community engagement through creative fundraising activities; whether through a student organization-sponsored event, service offered, or other endeavor, it is possible to gain exposure, visibility, and resources through creative means of engagement with one's campus community.

PROFESSIONAL ORGANIZATIONS

Student affairs staff members who work in student activities have the opportunity to join several national/international organizations that promote activities programming. These include the Association of College Unions-International (ACUI) and the National Association of Campus Activities (NACA). Both provide professional development and student activities programming ideas.

The Association of College Unions-International was founded in 1914 as a collaborative conference among Midwestern colleges and universities in the United States. The purpose of ACUI is to help college unions and student activities improve their programs and services and to contribute to student growth and development. There are currently 536 member institutions from urban and rural, two-year and four-year, large and small, public and private colleges and universities. Association members are also located in Canada, Australia, Great Britain, New Zealand, and Japan. The Association is divided into 15 geographical regions. At the regional level, there are opportunities for student participation as well as opportunities for union and activities staff to participate in ACUI programs, activities, and leadership positions. In addition to regional activities and conferences, ACUI sponsors an international conference and national workshops and seminars.

ACUI publishes a magazine, *The Bulletin,* six times a year during odd-numbered months and provides updated information on trends in union and student activities work. An online newsletter, the *Union Wire,* is also published six times a year during even-numbered months. The association's headquarters are in Bloomington, Indiana, and more information can be found online at www.acui.org.

The National Association of Campus Activities (NACA) was founded in 1960 to provide its members with educational and informational benefits related to activities programming: cooperative buying, membership-education programs and services, talent showcases, trade publications, and national and regional conferences and workshops. Over 1,000 institutions of higher education and 650 associate agencies from all 50 states and Canada are members. NACA hosts a national convention, regional conferences, summer and winter workshops, state meetings, educational projects, a resource library, numerous publications, and professional development opportunities.

Eight times a year NACA publishes a magazine, *Campus Activities Programming,* containing educational articles, news, reports, evaluations, and advertising of interest. Headquarters for NACA are located in Columbia, South Carolina, and additional information can be found online at www.naca.org.

Other associations and resources of interest to student activities staff may include:

- The Association of Fraternity Advisors (www.fraternityadvisors.org), located in Indianapolis, Indiana, serves as a clearinghouse for resources for fraternity and sorority advisors nationwide. The organization holds an annual conference each fall, and provides avenues for discussion among Greek advisors, campus administrators, and representatives from inter/national fraternity and sorority headquarters.
- DiversityWeb (www.diversityweb.org), sponsored by the American Association of Colleges and Universities, provides resources for diversity initiatives and education.
- College Student Educators, International (www.myacpa.org), also known as the American College Personnel Association (ACPA); and Student Affairs Educators in Higher Education (www.naspa.org), also known as the National Association of Student Personnel Administrators (NASPA) are both headquartered in Washington, DC, and serve as two national "umbrella" associations for professionals in all functional areas of student affairs.
- StudentAffairs.com (www.studentaffairs.com), an online guide to college student affairs, serves as a clearinghouse for a broad spectrum of

information about higher education, including job listings and additional web sites of interest to student affairs professionals.
- The *Chronicle of Higher Education* (www.chronicle.com) is the primary news sources for many aspects of higher education. Available either in print or electronic editions, the *Chronicle* is recognized as a leading voice to report academic news, issue development, education politics and legislative updates, funding updates, and ideas pertinent to the field.

TECHNOLOGY RESOURCES

Especially through numerous technological advancements made in the last decade alone, higher education has been transformed in the ways it delivers instruction, programs, and services to students. The demands of modern college life require the use of personal computer workstations or laptops, and many campuses have invested in the creation of computer labs and the use of software that enables all students to access the Internet, e-mail, and online coursework facilitation. With current proliferation of social-networking websites and similar online communities, student affairs staff must strategize to use these technological abilities to students' greatest advantages.

Technology can also help in maintaining membership and involvement records within student organizations. Some institutions feature cocurricular transcripts, which can be generated from periodic collection of updated student organization rosters. E-mail lists can facilitate mass communication among several members, and webpage design can share news and information online through a unique, stylized, and graphic approach. Software packages are available to help organizations assess strengths and weaknesses of programs, and to track data for later use. These advances in technology have facilitated effective and efficient management of student organizations over the past several years.

ENTRY-LEVEL EMPLOYMENT QUALIFICATIONS

While there are no prescribed requirements for student affairs staff who work in student activities, there are preferred qualifications for candidates who wish to apply for positions in this area. An active undergraduate experience marked by involvement and leadership in student activities is important. This involvement may include membership in a fraternity or sorority, service as a representative on student government, experience with programming or event management for activities like Homecoming, or participating in special-interest organizations. Past experience working with faculty and administrators on a regular basis is also beneficial.

When recruiting student activities staff, many institutions prefer candidates with degree credentials from an accredited graduate preparation program. At the master's level, a generalist background is important. Potential staff should take advantage of the breadth of courses available to them through graduate work. Assistantships in areas of student activities, student unions, event programming, Greek affairs, or in group advising can be valuable. In addition, a prospective student activities staff member should try to gain shorter-term practicum experience in a variety of student activities settings. Preferred candidate qualifications also include excellent organizational and communication skills, and the ability to relate well with a variety of populations (students, families, faculty, staff, alumni, and community members).

Throughout the history of American higher education, student activities have been useful tools that have assisted faculty and staff to enhance the learning environment for students. Student affairs staff members' knowledge, skills, and dispositions, combined with the emerging process of student development create a truly seamless, challenging, and supportive learning environment. For these reasons, student activities are viewed as an integral tool for student affairs staff to reach a primary goal of educating students. Such programs and activities can help in "transmitting knowledge, affecting skills development, changing attitudes, and helping students reach their potential. This may be the heart of student affairs work and, indeed, the soul of the student affairs educator (Liddell, Hubbard, & Werner, 2000, p. 21).

REFERENCES

American College Personnel Association. (1994). *The student learning imperative: Implications for student affairs.* Alexandria, VA: Author.

Anson, J. L., & Marchesani, R. F. (Eds.). (1991). *Baird's manual of American college fraternities.* Indianapolis, IN: Baird's Manual Foundation.

Arminio, J. I., Carter, S., Jones, S. E., Kruger, K., Lucus, N., Washington, J., Young, N., & Scott, A. (2000). Leadership experiences of students of color. *NASPA Journal, 37,* 496–510.

Astin, A. W. (1993). *What matters in college?* San Francisco: Jossey-Bass.

Baier, J. L., & Whipple, E. G. (1990). Greek values and attitudes: A comparison with independents. *NASPA Journal, 28,* 43–53.

Boatman, S. (1988, April). Strong student governments and their advisement. *Campus Activities Programming, 20,* 58.

Boatman, S., & Adams, T. C. (1992, April). The ethical dimension of leadership. *Campus Activities Programming, 24,* 62–67.

Brock, C. S. (1991, December). Ethical development through student activities programming. *Campus Activities Programming, 24,* 54–59.

Brubacher, J. S., & Rudy, W. (1976). *Higher education in transition.* New York: Harper & Row.

Brubacher, J. S., & Rudy, W. (1997). *Higher education in transition: A history of American colleges and universities.* New Brunswick, NJ: Transaction.

Chickering, A. W., & Reisser, L. (1993). *Education and identity* (2nd ed.). San Francisco: Jossey-Bass.

Council for the Advancement of Standards (CAS) in Higher Education. (2006). *CAS professional standards for higher education* (6th ed.). Washington, DC: Author.

Council for the Advancement of Standards (CAS) in Higher Education. (2009). *CAS professional standards for higher education* (7th ed.). Washington, DC: Author.

Delve, C. I., & Rice, K. L. (1990, Summer). The integration of service learning into leadership and campus activities. In C. I. Delve, S. D. Mintz & G. M. Stewart (Eds.), *Community service as values education* (pp. 55–64). San Francisco: Jossey-Bass.

Dunkel, N. W., & Schuh, J. H. (1998). *Advising student groups and organizations.* San Francisco: Jossey-Bass.

Feldman, K. A., & Newcomb, T. M. (1969). *The impact of college on students.* San Francisco: Jossey-Bass.

Gehring, D. D. (1993). Understanding legal constraints on practice. In M. J. Barr & Associates (Eds.), *The handbook of student affairs administrators* (pp. 274–299). San Francisco: Jossey-Bass.

Good, R. T. (1993, Summer). Programming to meet the needs of the lesbian-gay community. *Campus Activities Programming, 26,* 40–44.

Gulland, E. D., & Powell, M. E. (1989, May). Colleges, fraternities and sororities: A white paper on tort liability issues. Research report, Covington & Burling.

Gugerty, C. R., & Swezey, E. D. (1996). Developing campus-community relationships. In B. Jacoby & Associates (Eds.), *Service-learning in higher education: Concepts and practices* (pp. 92–108). San Francisco: Jossey-Bass.

Hollander, E. P. (1993). Legitimacy, power, and influence: A perspective on relational features of leadership. In M. M. Chemers & R. Ayman (Eds.), *Leadership theory and research: Perspectives and directions* (pp. 29–47). San Diego, CA: Academic Press.

Horowitz, H. L. (1987). *Campus life.* Chicago: University of Chicago Press.

Hu, S., & Kuh, G. D. (2003). Diversity experiences and college student learning and personal development. *Journal of College Student Development, 44,* 320–334.

Hurst, J. C., & Jacobson, J. K. (1985). Theories underlying students' need for programs. In M. J. Barr, L. A. Keating, & Associates (Eds.), *Developing effective student services programs* (pp. 113–136). San Francisco: Jossey-Bass.

Hurtado, S., Dey, E. L., Gurin, P. Y., & Gurin, G. (2003). College environments, diversity, and service learning. In J. C. Smart (Ed.), *Higher education handbook of theory and research* (vol. 18, pp. 145–188). New York: Springer.

Jacoby, B., & Associates. (1996). *Service learning in higher education: Concepts and practices.* San Francisco: Jossey Bass.

Jacoby, B. (2003). *Building partnerships for service-learning.* San Francisco: Jossey-Bass.

Jeanne Clery Disclosure of Campus Security Policy and Campus Crime Statistics Act, 20 U.S.C. § 1092.

Kaplin, W. A., & Lee, B. (1995). *The law of higher education: A comprehensive guide to legal implications of administrative decision making* (3rd ed.). San Francisco: Jossey-Bass.

Keeling, R. P. (Ed.). (2004). *Learning reconsidered: A campus-wide focus on the student experience.* Washington, DC: American College Personnel Association and National Association of Student Personnel Administrators.

Keeling, R. P. (Ed.). (2006). *Learning reconsidered 2: A practical guide to implementing a campus-wide focus on the student experience.* Washington, DC: ACPA, ACUHO-I, ACUI, NACA, NACADA, NASPA, & NIRSA.

Keeling, R. P., Wall, A. F., Underhile, R., & Dungy, G. J. (2008). *Assessment reconsidered: Institutional effectiveness for student success.* Washington, DC: International Center for Student Success and Institutional Accountability (ICSSIA).

Kinzie, J., & Kuh, G. D. (2004). Going DEEP: Learning from campuses that share responsibility for student success. *About Campus, 9*(5), 2–8.

Komives, S. R., Lucas, N., & McMahon, T. R. (1998). *Exploring leadership for college students who want to make a difference.* San Francisco: Jossey-Bass.

Komives, S. R., Lucas, N., & McMahon, T. R. (2007). *Exploring leadership: For college students who want to make a difference* (instructor's guide, 2nd ed.). San Francisco: Jossey-Bass.

Komives, S. R., Woodard, D. B., & Associates. (1996). *Student services: A handbook for the profession* (3rd ed.). San Francisco: Jossey-Bass.

Kuh, G. D. (1996). Guiding principles for creating seamless learning environments for undergraduates. *Journal of College Student Development, 37*(2), 135–148.

Kuh, G. D., & Lund, J. P. (1994). What students gain from participating in student government. *New Directions for Student Services, 66,* 5–17.

Kuh, G. D., Lyons, J., Miller, T. K., & Trow, J. (1995). *Reasonable expectations.* Washington, DC: National Association of Student Personnel Administrators.

Kuh, G. D., Schuh, J. H., Whitt, E. J., & Associates. (1991). *Involving colleges.* San Francisco: Jossey-Bass.

Levine, A., & Cureton, J. S. (1998). *When hope and fear collide.* San Francisco: Jossey-Bass.

Levitan, T., & Osteen, J. M. (1992). College union activities and programs. In T. E. Milani & J. W. Johnston (Eds.), *The college union in the year 2000* (pp. 11–25). San Francisco: Jossey-Bass.

Liddell, D. L., Hubbard, S., & Werner, R. (2000). Developing interventions that focus on learning. In D. L. Liddell & J. P. Lund (Eds.), *Powerful programming for student learning: Approaches that make a difference, 90,* p. 21–33.

Maloney, G. W. (1998). Disciplining student organizations. In B. G. Paterson & W. L. Kibler (Eds.), *The administration of campus discipline: Student organizational and community issue* (pp. 129–148). Asheville, NC: College Administration Publications.

Marin, J. (1985, February). The college union's role in student development. *ACUI Bulletin, 53,* 22–23.

Masiel, J. M. (1990, Fall). Social fraternities and sororities are not conducive to the educational process. *NASPA Journal, 28,* 8–12.

Matusak, L. R. (1996). *Finding your voice: Learning to lead . . . anywhere you want to make a difference.* San Francisco: Jossey-Bass.

Maul, S. Y. (1993). *Building community on campus: A compendium of practical ideas.* Bloomington, IN: Association of College Unions-International.

McDonald, W. M. (Ed.). (2002). *Creating campus community: In search of Ernest Boyer's legacy.* San Francisco: John Wiley & Sons.

McEwen, M. K. (2003). The nature and use of theory. In S. R. Komives & D. B. Woodard, Jr. (Eds.), *Student services: A handbook for the profession* (4th ed., pp. 153–178). San Francisco: Jossey-Bass.

McIntosh, J. G., & Swartwout, D. (2001). Lights on, lights off. *About Campus, 6*(3), 25–27.

McKaig, R. N., & Policello, S. M. (1979). Student activities. In G. D. Kuh (Ed.), *Evaluation in student affairs* (pp. 95–103). Washington: American College Personnel Association.

Miller, T. K., & Jones, J. D. (1981). Out-of-class activities. In A. W. Chickering & Associates (Eds.), *The modern American college* (pp. 657–671). San Francisco: Jossey-Bass.

Miller, T. K. (1982). Student development assessment: A rationale. In G. R. Hanson (Ed.), *Measuring student development* (pp. 5–15). San Francisco: Jossey-Bass.

Mills, D. B. (1989). Campus activities coordination. In D. C. Roberts (Ed.), *Designing campus activities to foster a sense of community* (pp. 39–48). San Francisco: Jossey-Bass.

Mueller, K. (1961). *Student personnel work in higher education.* Boston: Houghton-Mifflin.

Newell, W. H. (1999). The promise of integrative learning. *About Campus, 4*(2), 17–23.

Nolfi, T. (1993, November). Designing a student leadership program. *ACUI Bulletin, 61,* 4–10.

Packwood, W. T. (Ed.). (1977). *College student personnel services.* Springfield, IL: Charles C Thomas.

Pascarella, E. T., & Terenzini, P. T. (1991). *How college affects students.* San Francisco: Jossey-Bass.

Pascarella, E. T., & Terenzini, P. T. (2005). *How college affects students: A third decade of research.* San Francisco: Jossey-Bass.

Pike, G. R. (2000). Rethinking the role of assessment. *About Campus, 5*(1), 11–19.

Rehabilitation Act of 1973, § Section 504, as amended U.S.C.A. § 794.

Ringgenberg, L. J. (1989). Expanding participation of student subgroups in campus activities. In D. C. Roberts (Ed.), *Designing campus activities to foster a sense of community* (pp. 27–37). San Francisco: Jossey-Bass.

Rost, J. C. (1991). *Leadership for the twenty-first century.* New York: Praeger.

Sack, S. (1961). Student life in the nineteenth century. *Pennsylvania Magazine of History and Biography,* 270–273.

Sandeen, A. (1989). Freedom and control in campus activities: Who's in charge? In D. C. Roberts (Ed.), *Designing campus activities to foster a sense of community* (pp.

61–68). San Francisco: Jossey-Bass.

Sandeen, A., & Barr, M. J. (2006). *Critical issues for student affairs: Challenges and opportunities.* San Francisco: Jossey-Bass.

Stevens, G. (1969). The college union–past, present, future. *NASPA Journal, 7,* 16–21.

Styles, M. (1985). Effective models of systematic program planning. In M. J. Barr, L. A. Keating & Associates (Eds.), *Developing effective student services programs* (pp. 181–211). San Francisco: Jossey-Bass.

Terenzini, P. T., & Pascarella, E. T. (1997). Living with myths: Undergraduate education in America. In E. J. Whitt (Ed.), *College student affairs administration* (pp. 173–179). Needham Heights, MA: Simon & Schuster.

Tinto, V. (1987). *Leaving college: Rethinking the causes and cures of student attrition* (2nd ed.). Chicago: University of Chicago Press.

Upcraft, L. (1985). Residence halls and student activities. In L. Noel, R. Levitz, D. Saluri & Associates (Eds.), *Increasing student retention: Effective programs and practices for reducing the dropout rate* (pp. 319–344). San Francisco: Jossey-Bass.

U.S. Department of Education, National Center for Educational Statistics. (2007). *Digest of educational statistics 2006.* Washington, DC: U.S. Government Printing Office.

Weeks, K. M. (2001). *Managing student disability compliance.* Nashville, TN: College Legal Information.

Whipple, E. G., & Sullivan, E. G. (1998). Greek letter organizations: Communities of learners? In E. G. Whipple (Ed.), *New challenges for Greek letter organizations: Transforming fraternities and sororities into learning communities* (pp. 7–18). San Francisco: Jossey-Bass.

Winston, R. B., & Saunders, S. A. (1987). The Greek experience: Friend or foe of student development? In R. B. Winston, W. R. Nettles, & J. H. Opper (Eds.), *Fraternities and sororities on the contemporary college campus* (pp. 5–20). San Francisco: Jossey-Bass.

Chapter 12

STUDENT FINANCIAL AID PRACTICE

R. Michael Haynes and V. Barbara Bush

INTRODUCTION

As federal and state support of public higher education continues to dwindle, students and their families are being asked to bear more of the cost of attending postsecondary institutions. Subsequently, the availability of financial assistance in the form of grants, work study, loans, and scholarships is playing an increasingly prominent role in the college selection process. The literature contains myriad examples of research related to the importance of financial aid in the college selection process (Carreras, 1998; Chapman, 1981; St. John, Paulsen, & Starkey, 1996; Zarate & Pachon, 2006). What was once a resource which provided the opportunity of a low or no-cost college education to the neediest of students is now a college selection variable which is evaluated by most prospective students regardless of economic status.

This chapter begins with a brief examination of the history of student financial assistance and the varying institutional philosophies that impact the administration of an aid office. Next to be addressed are institutional and student eligibility criteria, sources of funding, a description of the federal programs, and the administrative capabilities and regulations related to administering an aid office. The authors believe that a brief review of the historical and philosophical context of student financial assistance is relevant as a depiction of the evolution of programs over time and the shift in societal beliefs regarding who should pay for college.

Note: The authors would like to acknowledge the contribution of Dr. Vickie Ann McCoy, Assistant Professor in the Department of Counselor Education at West Chester University, to this chapter.

Philosophies related to the administration of student financial assistance are as varied as the number of postsecondary institutions which participate in aid programs. Therefore, it is not the authors' intention to encourage or dissuade one particular philosophy in favor of another, but rather to provide current and future practitioners with guidelines by which they can administer a financial aid office. Standards set forth by the United States Department of Education, the National Association for Student Financial Aid Administrators, and the Council for the Advancement of Standards in Higher Education provide the framework for these guidelines.

HISTORY OF FINANCIAL AID

Although the earliest roots of financial aid can be found in scholarships awarded at Harvard in 1643 (Center for Higher Education Support Services, 2009), financial aid in its modern form originated in the years immediately following World War II (WWII). The Servicemen's Readjustment Act, or the GI Bill, was passed in 1944 in an effort by the U.S. Federal Government to assist returning WWII veterans and to avoid a public outcry similar to the one that occurred after the government failed to keep its promises to returning World War I servicepersons. The GI Bill was managed by the Veterans Administration, and it offered returning WWII servicepersons payments for education or guaranteed loans for home or farm ownership (U.S. Department of Veterans Affairs, 2009).

In 1947, veterans accounted for 49 percent of all college admissions, and by the expiration of the original bill in 1956, nearly one-half of all WWII veterans had participated in some form of higher education (U.S. Department of Veterans Affairs, 2009). Undoubtedly, more than any other single event in U.S. history, the enactment of the GI Bill of the 1940s made higher education a possibility for the average citizen. Access to colleges and universities was no longer dependent on a mastery of the classical requisites or social standing. The GI Bill opened the doors of the academy to an entire generation of new students who became college eligible due to their service to their country and not through their personal wealth or legacy (Wilkinson, 2005).

Post WWII, the federal government assumed an even greater role in removing financial barriers for college-going veterans. Before the GI Bill, the majority of federal financial assistance came in the form of direct institutional budgetary support. However, as the number of non-traditional college students demanding their opportunity for higher education increased, so did the need for student-directed federal financial assistance (Center for Higher Education Support Services, 2009).

A global phenomenon analogous to WWII brought about additional federal support. The Cold War of the 1950s, specifically the Russian government's launching of the Sputnik satellite, prompted the U.S. Congress to pass the National Defense Education Act (Wilkinson, 2005). Citing the need to increase the number of U.S. college students enrolling in the sciences and mathematics (Advisory Commission on Intergovernmental Relations, 1981), the National Defense Student Loan program offered a federally subsidized option for financing a college education. This program evolved into the National Direct Student Loan program in 1972 and is currently known as the Federal Perkins Student Loan program. The Perkins Loan program continues to offer low-interest financial assistance with generous repayment terms and conditions for those students desiring occupations in public service (Center for Higher Education Support Services, 2009).

It was also in the 1950s that a small group of colleagues, primarily representing the well established Ivy League schools of the northeastern US, met to share their concerns for providing for the needs of a growing number of applicants for whom the costs of college attendance were viewed as discouraging. These Ivy League officials envisioned a growing demand from a new group of first generation college aspirants whose financial resources would be limited. It was John Monro, the Dean of Admissions for Harvard, who would share his relatively simple philosophy of attempting to provide adequate student assistance to the extent it would be needed for an individual student to reasonably meet the annual expenses of a Harvard education. He shared some basic principles and guidelines as well as a rather simple formula to help roughly determine an individual family's ability to pay. After some further refinement, his concepts and rationale were published by the College Board (Monro, 1994). Initiatives of President Johnson's Great Society movement, the Economic Opportunity Act (EOA) of 1964 and the Higher Education Act (HEA) of 1965, provided the impetus for shifting even greater amounts of monetary assistance to low-income, typically first-generation college students (Office of Student Financial Assistance, 1988). The financial aid programs authorized in the HEA are listed in the Title IV section of the bill, and are often referred to by aid professionals as Title IV assistance. The HEA established the Federal College Work Study (FCWS) and Supplemental Education Opportunity Grant (SEOG) programs and consolidated these with the National Defense Student Loans to create what would become known as Campus Based Programs (Office of Postsecondary Education, 1996). Although they are funded at the federal level through capital contributions requiring an institutional match, awarding and administration of the Campus-Based Programs occur at the institutional level (U.S. Department of Education, 2009c). The HEA also generated the Guaranteed

Student Loan program as an additional subsidized, low-interest option for students demonstrating need.

It is important to recognize the Federal TRIO Programs as another important outcome from the Economic Opportunity and Higher Education Acts of the 1960s. The first TRIO initiative, Upward Bound, was created in 1964 to help low socioeconomic, first-generation students complete their secondary education and transition to higher education (Laws, 1999). In 1965, Talent Search emerged with programming designed to inform disadvantaged students of the resources available for college admission and completion. The third component of TRIO, Student Support Services, was created in 1968 to provide postsecondary institutional grants meant to increase persistence to graduation for academically, financially, or physically disadvantaged students (U.S. Department of Education, 2009f).

The 1972 re-authorization of the Higher Education Act saw the creation of the Basic Educational Opportunity Grant (BEOG), currently known as the Pell Grant, and the State Student Incentive Grant, currently known as the Leveraging Educational Assistance Program. The enactment of the BEOG program introduced a new concept to Title IV aid and the college choice process. Unlike the Federal Work Study and Supplemental Educational Opportunity Grant programs in which federal aid funds were allocated to institutions for the selection process, BEOG awards could be used by students at any Title IV eligible post-secondary institution (Center for Higher Education Support Services, 2009).

In 1978, passage of the Middle Income Student Assistance Act removed family income as a criterion for participation in the federally-subsidized Guaranteed Student Loan program and immediately expanded the number of students eligible for Title IV assistance. Two years later, the passage of the Higher Education Amendments provided for Parent Student Loans, which allowed families to borrow at levels up to the entire cost of attendance; an option not offered by other forms of aid (Center for Higher Education Support Services, 2009). The significance of the Middle Income Student Assistance Act and the Higher Education Amendments was monumental because for the first time, based upon cost of attendance, students and their families theoretically could receive sufficient financial assistance in the form of work study, grants, and/or loans to pay the full cost of attendance at any Title IV eligible institution.

The Higher Education Amendments of 1992 marked the implementation of a single application, the Free Application for Federal Student Aid (FAFSA) which students could complete to be considered for any Title IV and most state programs (Center for Higher Education Support Services, 2009). With financial information from the student and his/her family the FAFSA is also used to generate an Expected Family Contribution (EFC), or estimation of how much they should be able to contribute to the annual educational expenses. By utilizing the FAFSA to generate EFC minus the institution's published cost of attendance budget, financial aid professionals were able to evaluate student eligibility in a more uniform and consistent manner.

Another substantial change brought about by the 1992 Higher Education Amendments was the creation of a federally-insured student loan program that expanded Title IV participation to any student regardless of family income or need. The Federal Unsubsidized Stafford Loan Program provided students, with little or no need, a mechanism for obtaining additional educational funding (Center for Higher Education Support Services, 2009).

The 1992 Amendments authorized the William D. Ford Federal Direct Loan Program, a new Title V program that offered students a federally administered program analogous to the Family Federal Education Loan Program (FFELP) (Center for Higher Education Support Services, 2009). The Ford Direct Loan is gaining prominence in the current aid environment because of legislative inquiries into the fiscal viability of the FFELP and commercial banks' inability to secure adequate capital for payments to students. This program allows the federal government to serve as the lender thereby not only eliminating subsidized interest payments to commercial banks, but also assuaging the anxiety of postsecondary institutions and students who rely on guaranteed student loan funds (General Accounting Office Washington D.C., 1997).

At a 2005 conference held at the University of Virginia, which convened a number of highly respected researchers attempting to address whether or not the U.S.'s "flagship public" universities truly supported increased educational opportunity, a key question was raised. The researchers wondered whether these leading institutions could resist the ruthless competition for top students which seemed to be the driving force for so much of the spending causing tuition to increase. The hope was expressed that these institutions would work together to reduce some of the wasteful aspects of such competition. It was noted that this effort could not be undertaken solely by any one institution, but could be achieved by cooperation (College Board, 2006). Participants at the conference were challenged to test the antitrust climate and to do so aggressively in the public interest. Such effort was encouraged to include the possibility of public/private collaboration, similar to those prevailing at the high-water mark of collaboration with the Keppel Commission, which had directed student aid policies in the 1970s. Indeed, such collegial discussion on difficult topics whose resolution would benefit the greater common good, further enhanced by quality research and analysis, was and will always be the grounds for truly professional problem solving (King, 1999).

PHILOSOPHY AND PURPOSE

Compliance

According to the Council for the Advancement of Standards (CAS) (2006), the mission of a Financial Aid Office (FAO) should include attention to the stewardship of student financial assistance funds and service to the institutional student body. Specifically, good stewardship is defined as assuming institutional responsibility for the administration of aid programs from all levels and ensuring that all compliance requirements and reporting schedules are met. In some institutions, the FAO is also charged with the administration of scholarship programs that are typically awarded on academic or talent merit, not financial need.

As the cost of college attendance continues to rise and participation in higher education becomes more of a user's market, compliance with federal and state regulations is paramount (Scott & General Accounting Office, 2007). Increasing numbers of students are depending on some form of federal and/or state assistance; subsequently, these funds are becoming a larger component of the institutional budget. Loss of eligibility, due to mismanagement of funds or failure in reporting requirements, can lead to catastrophic consequences for both students and the institution.

Services to Students

In many instances, the Financial Aid Office also provides holistic financial counseling for the student body. This holistic financial counseling includes providing students with educational resources in the form of budgeting, alternative assistance options, and sound postgraduation loan debt management (Recommendations for Financial Aid Counseling, 2007). However, ethical standards prevent aid officers from recommending student loan providers. With increases in educational costs, the student financial assistance office must become an on-campus financial information resource for both students and their families and not simply processors of aid and scholarship applications.

Enrollment Management

While the purposes and duties of the student aid office are often presented as altruistically motivated to serve only the needs of the students, in reality, student financial assistance is often the mechanism by which various institutional purposes are accomplished, thus creating a dovetail between financial aid and enrollment management. For example, many private institutions possess significant endowments that alleviate their need to participate in federal and state student assistance programs. Not only are these institutions exempt from the task of administering sometimes arduous programs with restrictive criteria, but they are also free to pursue an enrollment management strategy which achieves a specific institutional mission such as greater diversity (Hossler, 2000).

Ultimately, the mission and philosophy of the Financial Aid Office is bound only by codified federal and state regulations and can vary as greatly as the institution's mission and philosophy. The FAO may follow practices where students are packaged, or awarded, on a first-come, first-served basis, with need as the only one criterion considered. Such a practice might support an institutional strategy to secure early admission commitments from students thereby allowing better projection of actual enrollments. Other strategies might include awarding priority to the students with the greatest financial need, which is the original purpose of student financial assistance. Although the federal and state regulations may dictate who is eligible for consideration of aid programs and how program allocations are awarded, financial assistance can still mirror blind admissions practices in order to attract a more diversified student body while maintaining more stringent academic requirements.

INSTITUTIONAL ELIGIBILITY

To be considered for participation in Title IV and other Federal Student Assistance programs, an institution must provide evidence that it meets the U.S. Department of Education's eligibility criteria. The U.S. Department of Education Student Financial Aid Handbook (2009c) offers three definitions of an eligible institution: (1) an institution of higher education, (2) a proprietary institution of higher education, and (3) a postsecondary vocational institution.

Institutions of higher education may be either public or private but must always be classified as nonprofit. Postsecondary vocational colleges may also be public or private, but they must maintain nonprofit status for FSA participation purposes. However, some postsecondary vocational institutions are for-profit proprietary institutions and are always considered private and for-profit. These profit postsecondary vocational institutions are not qualified for FSA participation. The Universities of Texas and Michigan, as well as Mississippi State University and the State University of New York, are examples of public, higher education institutions. These types of institutions receive varying percentages of their annual budgets from state allocations which, historically, have assisted in keeping costs to students lower than their private counterparts. Examples of private higher education institutions include Harvard, Stanford, Baylor, and the University of Southern California. These institutions are primarily funded by private sources such as foundations and donors, meanwhile, they also benefit from the Title IV assistance that their eligible students receive (U.S. Department of Education, 2010e). Both types of institutions offer what Hambrick, Evans, and Schuh (2002) define as distinct cultures consisting of campus artifacts and/or landmarks, student perspectives or norms unique to the particular institution, and values reflective of the institution's students, faculty, and staff.

Vocational colleges may also be public or private, but they must maintain nonprofit status for FSA participation purposes. These institutions may offer bachelors, associates, or certification degrees, but typically do not provide as many of the cocurricular services and programming as do their traditional counterparts. Examples of public vocational colleges are Texas State Technical College, ITT Technical Institute, and DeVry University (U.S. Department of Education, 2010e).

For-profit, proprietary institutions usually offer a narrowly-tailored degree or training plan for students wanting to acquire a unique skill set for a specific market in a shorter time period than traditional colleges offer. Examples of for-profit proprietary institutions include Arizona Automotive Institute, California Culinary Academy, and The Fashion Institute of Design and Merchandising (U.S. Department of Education, 2010e).

Eligible institutions must also be legally authorized by the state in which they operate and be accredited by a nationally or regionally recognized accrediting association. The following are examples of accrediting associations approved by the U.S. Department of Education:

- Middle States Commission on Higher Education
- New England Association of Schools and Colleges
- North Central Association of Colleges and Schools
- Northwest Association of Schools and Colleges
- Southern Association of Colleges and Schools
- Western Association of Schools and Colleges
- New York Board of Regents
  (U.S. Department of Education, 2010b)

For a complete listing of accrediting bodies approved for participation in Title IV funding, the reader is referred to the U.S. Department of Education Web site: http://www2.ed.gov/admins/finaid/accred/accreditation_pg10.html#TitleIVRecognition.

Eligible institutions must only admit students who have received a high school diploma or the equivalent. Students who were home schooled and thus do not possess a high school diploma or the equivalent must demonstrate the ability to benefit from college attendance criteria as outlined by the U.S. Department of Education (U.S. Department of Education, 2009d). A complete listing of institutional eligibility criteria is available in the volume and chapters related to *Institutional Eligibility* in the current edition of the Student Financial Aid Handbook (U.S. Department of Education, 2009d).

STUDENT ELIGIBILITY

There are many criteria which institutions must consider before determining a student's eligibility for Title IV assistance. The following criteria are of primary importance: the student must be a U.S. citizen or permanent resident; enrolled in coursework leading toward a degree or certificate; and not in default on a FSA loan or owe a repayment of FSA grant funds (Scott & U.S. Government Accountability, 2009). These data and other information related to eligibility requirements are collected when the student completes the Free Application for Federal Student Aid (FAFSA).

In the early days of financial aid, students completed the FAFSA in paper format and submitted it to the Department of Education which created two reports: the Student Aid Report (SAR) which provided the student with his/her expected family contribution (EFC) used to determine need; and the Institutional Student Information Record (ISIR), which provided the institution with information related to the student's family's financial profile. In the past, financial aid professionals spent hours manually reviewing ISIRs to calculate each student's EFC and specific program eligibility. Today, students have the capability of completing the FAFSA via a Department of Education Web site, and the information is transmitted to both parties electronically.

According to the U. S. Department of Education (2006), the Expected Family Contribution (EFC) is an estimate of the amount which students and/ or their families should be able to pay toward their annual educational expenses based upon the student's financial status and family size. The EFC is calculated solely on information provided on the FAFSA and includes such factors as income, assets, number of persons in the household, and other family members attending college. For EFC purposes, students are classified as either dependent or independent. Dependent students are those under the age of 24 who have not received their first bachelor's degree, are unmarried, and have no children. Dependent students must include parental information on the FAFSA for use in calculating their EFC. Independent students are defined as those over the age of 24, who have received a bachelor's degree, are married, and/or have children. Independent students are not required to include their parents' financial information for calculation of their EFC (U.S. Department of Education, 2009d).

The electronic records provided to schools contain information that is verified through several U.S. Federal Agencies. First, aid eligibility related to United States citizenship is verified through the databases maintained by the Department of Homeland Security; second, FAFSA information is also verified through Social Security Administration records to insure the applicant's name and date of birth are accurate; and finally, FAFSA records from male students between the ages of 18 and 25 are verified for registration with the U.S. Selective Service System (U.S. Department of Education, 2009d).

The ISIR also contains information related to financial aid received by the student at current and past institutions of attendance. The FAFSA record is verified against National Student Loan Data System (NSLDS) records to determine if the student owes a repayment of federal grant funds received erroneously or has defaulted on a federal student loan. Comment codes related to specific eligibility questions alert the Financial Aid professional that additional research is needed before determining the student's eligibility. Financial aid professionals can access the NSLDS for information related to repayments and/or defaults or to obtain contact information for an institution the student may have previously attended. The NSLDS system also maintains comprehensive enrollment and aid payment history for every student receiving funds from the Federal Pell Grant program, Supplemental Educational Opportunity Grant program, Federal Perkins Loan program, Family Federal Education Loan Program, and William D. Ford Federal Direct Loan Program (U.S. Department of Education, 2009d).

Although the requirements presented so far are related to initial eligibility, it should be noted that the U.S. Department of Education (2009d) also dictates academic progress criteria related to continuing eligibility. The 1976 Higher Education Amendments established the requirement that students must be evaluated academically, both quantitatively and qualitatively, to ensure progress is being made toward successful completion of a degree plan. Specifically, financial aid professionals are required annually to evaluate students' grades to: (a) ensure that they are maintaining at least a C or equivalent cumulative average, and (b) ensure that they are following an institutionally-determined policy regarding the number or percentage of courses completed within an academic period. Students are ineligible for aid when their enrollment time-frame exceeds 150 percent of the published length of their program of study. They may, however, regain eligibility for FSA at the time the financial aid professional determines they are meeting institutional policy requirements. The complete listing of student eligibility requirements can be found in volume 1, chapter 1, *Student Eligibility,* of the current SFA Handbook (U.S. Department of Education, 2009d).

STUDENT FINANCIAL ASSISTANCE PROGRAM FUNDING SOURCES

In recent years, there has been a shift toward higher tuition rates in higher education and a corresponding shift toward larger percentages of student using loans more heavily than grants. These trends have fostered great discussion about the end result of what has evolved as an "expectation that someone else will pay." Indeed, the proliferation of student aid programs and options now available are seen by some as adding to such a view (Vedder, 2004). Student financial assistance programs are funded from myriad sources including federal and state agencies, institutional revenue sources, and private benefactors. In fiscal year 2009, $180 billion was expended for student educational assistance from all sources. When this $180 billion is adjusted for inflation, it represents a 90 percent increase from fiscal year 1999.

However, the federal government contributes the largest share of all funding by far in the form of Title IV and Title VII allocations. For fiscal year 2009, the federal government allocated over $116.7 billion for grant, loan, and work-study student assistance. With inflation adjustment, this represents a 91 percent increase over a ten-year period (College Entrance Examination Board, 2009). For fiscal year 2010, the Obama administration presented a proposed federal budget of $129.4 billion for student assistance (U.S. Department of Education, 2009e). This amount represents an increase of nearly 11 percent in just one year from 2009.

The majority of federal funding is allocated to the Federal Perkins and Stafford programs with $83.9 billion in 2009. Over a ten-year period, after adjusting for inflation, funding for these programs has increased nearly 100 percent, while funding for work-study and grant programs has remained basically flat. Of the $24.8 billion allocated to grant programs in 2009, 73.3 percent was directed to the Federal Pell Grant program. Federal Work Study allocations actually decreased over the past decade by 5 percent from $1.2 billion to $1.1 billion (College Entrance Examination Board, 2009). One might argue that the increase in loan funding is reflective of the increasing societal and political philosophy that higher education is a users' commodity and the decreasing belief that everyone benefits from an educated populous.

All 50 states allocate resources to some form of student financial assistance. In 2009, states allocated $8.5 billion and $900 million to grant and loan programs, respectively (College Entrance Examination Board, 2009). Unlike federal allocations that are typically funded by tax revenues, state financial aid programs are financed in a variety of ways. Some programs are funded through allocations to the institutions, much like the bulk of the Title IV programs, while others may be funded by the institution via state mandated legislation. For example, some states mandate that a portion of tuition paid at public institutions be set aside for need-based grant and loan programs.

Institutionally funded programs may be awarded based on student need or merit or a combination of both criteria. Typically, need-based programs are grants while merit based awards are termed scholarships. The actual funding for these programs may come from institutional discretionary funds, or most likely, from private donors, such as alumni or foundations. The criteria of institutional programs can vary as many ways as there are to assess student demographics. For example, an institutional grant program may be strictly based upon need as demonstrated by completion of the Free Application for Federal Student Aid, or it may contain a course of study component while institutional scholarships may be awarded based upon some predetermine level of performance on a college entrance exam or high school grade point average.

Grant and scholarship programs funded by private sources become even more complex as they typically reflect the wishes, interests, and background of the donor. For example, an alumnus may fund a scholarship for a student from his/her high school or home town, majoring in a particular field of study, or demonstrating a specific academic or athletic talent. Most athletic scholarships are termed as "grants-in-aid" and are funded by private sources in the form of booster or alumni associations. Additionally, some privately funded scholarships may also include a need component, making their criteria analogous to most grant programs. In some states, public institutions are restricted from making institutionally or privately funded awards based on race or ethnicity; however, private institutions are usually exempt from these concerns (Heller, 2000). Unlike institutionally funded grants and scholarships, funds donated by private source are typically highly restricted to honoring the donors' wishes and cannot be reallocated for other institutional purposes.

FEDERAL STUDENT AID PROGRAMS

Loan Programs

While there is an array of federal student aid programs, they all may be classified under one of the following categories: loans, grants, or work-study. While programs within each category may share common institutional and student eligibility criteria, the nature of each category is inherently unique. Loan programs, need-based or not, require either a repayment or a service agreement from the student borrower. Programs in this category would be classified as "debt" financing of educational expenses. Grants typically require no repayment on behalf of the recipient and are often referred to as "gift aid." Some exceptions include grant programs that revert to a loan if certain academic and/or postgraduation services are not fulfilled. Work study is considered "self-help" as students earn their financial assistance through institutionally related employment during their periods of enrollment. The Title IV student loan programs are:

- Federal Family Education Loan Program (FFELP)
- William D. Ford Federal Direct Loan Program (DL)
- Federal Perkins Student Loan Program
- Federal Family Education Loan Program

Institutions may elect to participate in any or all of the Title IV programs. In 2009, the majority of guaranteed student loans have been funded through the Federal Family Education Loan Program (FFELP). This is due primarily to the ease of managing a program in which private banks are the primary administrators. The federal government guarantees the bank through interest payments and prevention of defaulted loans, while the private fiduciaries assume responsibility for administering the application process, obtaining completed promissory notes, and collaborating with servicing departments to manage the repayment process. Placing this responsibility in the hands of experienced entities allows students and postsecondary institutions to benefit from millions of dollars in guaranteed loan payments in an expeditious and efficient manner (Schachter, 2009).

There are three products offered under the FFELP umbrella: (1) Subsidized Stafford Loans, (2) Unsubsidized Stafford Loans, and (3) Federal Parent Loans. Varying interest rates are offered for each product, with the subsidized loans having the lowest interest and the unsubsidized and Parent products having substantially higher rates. Also, there are annual and aggregate limits in the subsidized and unsubsidized programs with each having a repayment grace period of six months following graduation, withdrawal, or falling below half-time enrollment. The Parent Loan has no such grace period, and generally repayment begins shortly after disbursement. Additionally, Parent Loans are based on the applicant's creditworthiness, which is not a consideration for student loans (U.S. Department of Education, 2009d).

William D. Ford Federal Direct Loan Program

The William D. Ford Federal Direct Loan Program (DL) is a viable alternative to the Family Federal Education Loan Program (FFELP) that is becoming more prominent in the financial aid environment. The DL program offers products analogous to those of FFELP; however, the U.S. Department of Education, instead of a commercial bank, serves as the lender and servicer (U.S. Department of Education, Direct Loans, 2009b). As with the FFELP program, the interest rate is determined by the U.S. Department of Education, and each loan also incurs a principal percentage origination fee. Direct Loans have the same annual and aggregate limits associated with the FFELP, and students may not borrow in excess of their cost of attendance in conjunction with other forms of aid.

Federal Perkins Student Loans

The Federal Perkins Student Loan Program originated as the National Defense Student Loan Program (NDSL) enacted in 1958 as a result of the National Defense Education Act. As a member of the Campus Based Programs, the Perkins program is administered at the institutional level, including application, award, and collection. The interest rate for Perkins loans is fixed at 5 percent, and students are offered a nine-month repayment grace period following graduation, withdrawal, or falling below half-time enrollment. The program offers several forgiveness options for students interested in the health, education, or civil service professions.

Grant Programs

Grants are a form of financial aid that is often referred to as "gift aid," indicating that the recipient is not required to repay the award. There are several federal grant programs and a myriad of state offerings. The primary federal grant programs are:

- Federal Pell Grant Program
- Supplemental Educational Opportunity Grant Program (SEOG)
- Leveraging Educational Assistance Partnerships (LEAP)
- Academic Competitiveness Grants (ACG)
- National Science and Mathematics Access to Retain Talent (SMART) Grants
- Teacher Education Assistance for College and Higher Education (TEACH) Grants

Federal Pell Grant Program

The origins of the Pell Grant can be found in the 1972 reauthorization of the Higher Education Act that created the Basic Educational Opportunity Grant (BEOG). The Higher Education Amendments of 1980 renamed the BEOG program to the Pell Grant program to honor Senator Claiborne Pell, a long-time advocate of federal assistance for students pursuing higher education (U.S. Department of Education, 2009c).

Aside from the general Title IV eligibility requirements, Pell Grant eligible students must not have received a bachelor's degree and must demonstrate an expected family contribution (EFC) below the federally mandated threshold. For the aid year 2009–2010, the maximum EFC to be considered for Pell eligibility was $4,617. Award amounts for fiscal year 2010 vary from $200 to $5,550 and are a function of the student's EFC, enrollment status (full, half, or three-quarter time) and the institutional cost of attendance (COA) budget as calculated by the Financial Aid Office (U.S. Department of Education, n.d.).

Historically, the U.S. Department of Education provided individual Pell Grant payment grids that included the possible combinations of enrollment status, COA, and EFC in order to assist aid officers in identifying the appropriate award amount. However, today's technology is capable of maintaining databases that are updated annually to accommodate changes in federal regulations and automatically package Pell Grants based on the current requirements.

Though educational costs and enrollment status can vary across institutions and students, the Federal Pell Grant uses a student's EFC to determine his/her entitlement to funds, thereby assuring that it is portable. Therefore, eligible students are free to use their Pell Grant award toward payment for attendance at any of approximately 5,400 Title IV eligible institutions (U.S. Department of Education, 2009c). Additionally, as an entitlement, some institutions allow Pell Grants combined with non-Title IV or state aid to exceed the student's cost of attendance.

Supplemental Educational Opportunity Grant Program

The Supplemental Educational Opportunity Grant (SEOG) was created by legislation stemming from the Higher Education Acts of 1965. It is the gift aid component of the Campus Based Programs and awarding priority is given to Pell Grant Eligible students (U. S. Department of Education, 2009a). Similar to the other Campus Based Programs (Federal Perkins Loans and Federal College Work Study), the federal government allocates funds directly to institutions which are required to provide a 25 percent match for each award.

Leveraging Educational Assistance Partnership

The Leveraging Educational Assistance Partnership (LEAP) program sanctioned by the U.S. Department of Education allows for the allocation of federal funds to states, which in turn make grant awards to substantially needy students. All 50 states and the United States territories receive LEAP funding, which requires at least a dollar-for-dollar match in making student awards. As the programs are administered at the state level, the acronym

"LEAP" may or may not be included in the title of an individual state's program (U.S. Department of Education, 2009d).

Academic Competitiveness Grant and National Science and Mathematics Access to Retain Talent Grants

In 2006, the Academic Competitiveness Grant (ACG) and National Science and Mathematics Access to Retain Talent Grant (National SMART Grants) were created to encourage students to take the necessary high school preparatory courses that would enable them to pursue degrees in the sciences and technology (U.S. Department of Education, 2010a). The two programs act in concert with eligible students receiving ACG funding in their first and second year of postsecondary enrollment and SMART grants in years three and four.

Students eligible for ACG awards must be Pell Grant eligible, must have completed an academically rigorous secondary course of study as outlined by the U.S. Department of Education, and must enroll subsequently in a postsecondary discipline related to mathematics, science, engineering, or technology (U.S. Department of Education, 2010a). The maximum ACG award is $750 annually, and students must also have earned a cumulative grade-point average of 3.0 on a 4.0 scale at the conclusion of their first college year (U.S. Department of Education, 2010a).

To be eligible for a National SMART grant in years three and four, students must maintain half-time enrollment, a cumulative grade point average of 3.0, and be Pell Grant eligible. Additionally, students must be enrolled in a degree plan related to the following fields: physical, life, or computer sciences; engineering; technology; mathematics; or a foreign language with critical shortages (U.S. Department of Education, 2009a).

Teacher Education Assistance for College and Higher Education Grants

To address the shortage of elementary and secondary teachers in low-income and/or high need areas, the College Cost Reduction Act of 2007 authorized the Teacher Education Assistance for College and Higher Education (TEACH) Grant Program. Eligible students may receive up to $4,000 per year and must be enrolled in a course of study that will prepare them to assume elementary/secondary instructor positions upon graduation. In return, a recipient must agree in writing to serve as an instructor in a qualified school for four academic years within eight calendar years (Federal Student Aid, 2010d).

Federal College Work Study

Federal College Work Study (FCWS) is considered a self-help program because students earn this form of financial aid through jobs on-campus or with agencies associated with the institution. Created by the Higher Education Acts of 1965, FCWS is administered by participating institutions as part of the Campus Based Programs. Eligible students must demonstrate need and the ability to work up to 20 hours per week. Departments who employ FCWS recipients are reimbursed for 75 percent of the wages and, in some instances such as tutoring and literacy programs, 100 percent of the salary is covered.

The FCWS program is unique in that it is beneficial to both the student and the institution. The student can earn financial assistance through on-campus employment which, in most instances, is more "student friendly" than some off-campus jobs. Typically, college employers are more flexible in scheduling work around class schedules and are more amenable to time-off requests for tests or class assignments. Another benefit is that students gain valuable work experience which can be used as the foundation for their post-graduation resumes. Furthermore, many institutions incorporate intentional learning outcomes into job duties, thereby solidifying experiential learning opportunities.

From an institutional perspective, departments may gain valuable part-time assistance at a fraction of the cost associated with full-time, benefit eligible employees. Student workers could allow departments to temporarily redirect resources as needed due to work volume, special projects, and staff shortages and outages. Additionally, the presence of student workers in the department might lend the opportunity for permanent staff to serve as mentors, which can be a source of job satisfaction for institutional employees.

ADMINISTERING STUDENT FINANCIAL ASSISTANCE

Sound Financial Aid Practice

The Financial Aid Office is accountable to many constituents: the federal and state governments that establish student eligibility and program reporting criteria; the institution that utilizes the FAO in achieving enrollment management strategies; and the students whose primary interest is the amount of financial assistance they can receive and the time frame. However, regardless of which purpose it is serving at what time, the FAO must demonstrate sound practices with equity and access for all students requesting their services.

Two associations that provide guiding principles for all financial aid offices (FAO) regardless of institutional type or governance are The National Association of Student Financial Aid Administrators (NASFAA) and The Council for the Advancement of Standards (CAS) in Higher Education. Both NASFAA and CAS offer guidelines for the professional and ethical behavior of financial aid professionals; moreover, CAS provides additional standards for the logistics of operating a FAO.

In 1999, the National Association of Student Financial Aid Administrators' (NASFAA) Board of Directors established a 12-point statement of ethical principles as standards of conduct for financial aid administrators. Specifically, the *Statement of Ethical Principles* recommends that financial aid professionals shall:

1. Be committed to removing financial barriers for those who wish to pursue postsecondary learning.
2. Make every effort to assist students with financial need.
3. Be aware of the issues affecting students and advocate their interests at the institutional, state, and federal levels.
4. Support efforts to encourage students, as early as the elementary grades, to aspire to and plan for education beyond high school.
5. Educate students and families through quality consumer information.
6. Respect the dignity and protect the privacy of students, and ensure the confidentiality of student records and personal circumstances.
7. Ensure equity by applying all need analysis formulas consistently across the institution's full population of student financial aid applicants.
8. Provide services that do not discriminate on the basis of race, gender, ethnicity, sexual orientation, religion, disability, age, or economic status.
9. Recognize the need for professional development and continuing education opportunities.
10. Promote the free expression of ideas and opinions, and foster respect for diverse viewpoints within the profession.
11. Commit to the highest level of ethical behavior and refrain from conflict of interest or the perception thereof.
12. Maintain the highest level of professionalism, reflecting a commitment to the goals of the National Association of Student Financial Aid Administrators.

(National Association of Student Financial Aid Administrators, 1999).

Financial Aid Officers are bound by The Statement of Ethical Principles which serves as a guideline to practice and covers a wide array of the responsibilities held by financial aid professionals. The role of the financial aid office is much more complex than its stereotype and does not stop with the tasks of accepting applications and awarding funds to students. Financial aid professionals must participate in outreach to both enrolled and prospective students and their families with the intent of informing them about resources which can make a college degree possible through the various financial aid programs (U.S. Department of Education, 2009d). Furthermore, financial aid professionals must always be cognizant of their role as aid program stewards and ensure that all business activities are beyond reproach.

Sound financial aid practice and federal regulations require financial aid professionals to command a firm understanding and fair application of need analysis guidelines. Need analysis is the process by which financial aid administrators determine exactly how much assistance a student requires to meet his/her educational expenses for a one-year period (National Association of Student Financial Aid Administrators, 2007b). Student cost of attendance (COA) budgets should include all reasonable educationally-related expenses such as tuition, mandated fees, room and board, and an allowance for transportation and living expenses (National Association of Student Financial Aid Administrators, 2007a).

Financial aid offices typically follow the federal methodology (FM) in determining student need and subsequent award amounts. Following the FM, a student's need is calculated as follows:

Cost of Attendance (as calculated by the attending institution)
  minus
Expected Family Contributions (as calculated by completion of the FAFSA)
  minus
Other Sources of Assistance (institutional/external scholarships, third party payments such as employers, etc.)
  equals
Unmet Financial Need

Financial aid administrators must exercise great care to ensure that students' financial aid packages do not exceed their calculated COA in conjunction with EFC and other sources of assistance. When a student receives more financial assistance than for which he/she was eligible, an over award has occurred. If the over award is detected prior to the disbursement of financial assistance, the aid must be canceled or reduced to rectify the issue. However, in many cases, if the over award occurs due to a post-disbursement change in COA or other financial resources such as a scholarship, the disbursed aid in some instances may be exempt from reduction or cancelation (U.S. Department of Education, 2009d).

The federal government provides financial aid administrators latitude to make adjustments in the need analysis formula based upon extenuating circumstances. Professional judgment may be used to increase the cost of attendance component, recalculate the expected family contribution, or both. When considering a professional judgment action, the aid professional may review the student's FAFSA information, his/her parent's tax return, and/or documents supporting a financial burden unique to the student. All professional judgments should be made judiciously, and supporting information needs to be well documented in the student's financial aid file (National Association of Student Financial Aid Administrators, 2007b).

Responsibilities and Roles

According to a document created by the Washington Consulting Group and the Office of Student Financial Assistance (1988) the roles and responsibilities of higher education financial aid officers include: (1) recognizing the basic areas of responsibility within the aid office; (2) understanding the points of interaction with other administrative offices; and (3) identifying professional organizations for support and development within the field.

The major responsibilities of the financial aid office include monitoring institutional compliance, counseling students, monitoring student eligibility, determining financial need, administering the grant programs, administering the loan programs (for both students and parents), managing the campus-based programs, and using outside consultants and service agencies. In addition to these responsibilities, Financial Aid Officers must work closely with the campus community including institutional offices such as those of the President, admissions, business, registrar/academic records, counseling, placement, veterans, academic dean, data processing, development, and special programs. In working with these offices, Financial Aid Officers are responsible for developing a financial aid committee, and a network of connecting and overlapping responsibilities with these offices. It is also the responsibility of Financial Aid Officers to create relationships with outside agencies and professional associations (Washington Consulting Group & the Office of Student Financial Assistance, 1988).

The financial aid office (FAO) serves in many capacities both within and outside of the institution. FAO staffs serve as financial counselors, student advocates, outreach coordinators, and institutional leaders and managers. While there are no federal and/or state guidelines related to the reporting structure of the FAO, there are distinct regulations separating the functions of receiving Title IV funds and disbursing those funds to students. While the FAO administers the awards and authorizes the payment of funds, a separate office without affiliation or shared staff (typically the business office), disburses the funds to the student's account or directly to the student (U.S. Department of Education, 2009d).

Financial aid administrators must also be advocates for increased aid programs. As governmental support of higher education continues to dwindle, the expenses that students and their families are asked to bear continue to increase. Aid administrators must use both data analysis and reports related to enrollment and unmet needs to convey to these students how current trends cause this inverse relationship which may negatively impact current and potential aid awards. In short, the FAO must assume a role of "checks and balances" in relation to tuition and fee increases which may ultimately be passed on to students.

Structure and Staffing

There are no regulations that stipulate to which administrative unit the FAO must report. In many institutions, the FAO reports to student affairs as its functions are deemed to contribute to the holistic development of students. In other institutions, however, the FAO reports to the dean/vice president for enrollment management for a more direct connection to recruitment efforts. There are also those institutions that consider student financial assistance to be a business function, aligning the office with fiscal affairs. In a survey of FAOs, 37.7 percent reported to student affairs, 19.0 percent to enrollment management, 18.5 percent to general administration, 10.7 percent to fiscal affairs, and 7.3 percent to academic affairs (Williams, 1999; as cited by Coomes, 2004).

The Council for the Advancement of Standards in Higher Education (CAS) (2006) provides explicit guidelines for the organization and management of a FAO. According to these guidelines, the FAO must ensure that policies related to aid administration are current and accessible to interested parties. Job duties and performance expectations must be documented and reviewed with FAO staff on a routine basis. The financial aid industry is not only heavily regulated but it is also at the heart of most students' participation in higher education. Therefore, workflows for processing applications and awarding assistance and the processes for addressing student appeals must be intentional, systematic, and well documented.

As the work level of a FAO is directly correlated with the number of students receiving aid, it is difficult to provide steadfast guidelines as to the number of staff needed to accomplish stated mission and goals adequately. However, the U.S. Department of Education (2009d) clearly states that the aid office must be staffed by an adequate number of professional and clerical personnel subject to institutional audits and program reviews. While the number of staff required to accomplish adequate service varies by institution,

CAS does offer several standards related to proper staff selection. According to CAS, staff members should possess a minimum of a bachelor's degree or equivalent relevant experience. They must have a working knowledge of aid regulations and be judicious in applying these regulations in a fair and equitable manner. Additionally, staff members must understand that financial aid rules and regulations change requiring intentional, periodic reviews of federal and state policies (Council for the Advancement of Standards in Higher Education, 2006).

Though FAO staffing patterns vary from institution to institution, a 2002 study conducted by Redd and Miller contained a survey summary of FAO staffing patterns. The authors of this study reported that the average FAO consisted of 5.6 full-time staff members. It is no surprise that the larger four-year public institutions had the largest FAO staffs (an average of 10.7 full-time staff members) while the smaller two-year private colleges had the smallest FAO staffs (an average of 1.4 full-time staff members). Of the Chief FAO administrators who responded to the Redd and Miller survey, 54 percent indicated that their highest level of educational attainment was a master's degree, while 34 percent reported holding only a bachelor's degree, and a mere 4 percent reported completion of a doctoral degree (Redd & Miller, 2002; as cited by Coomes, 2004). Additionally, a 2006 study by Byrne examined FAO's in Texas and identified 14 model institutions in terms of FAO services. The average staffing in these model FAO offices was 22 full-time equivalent (FTE) staff members. Of the average 22 members, nine were professional staff, eight were support staff, and five were student workers (Byrne, 2006).

The FAO staff must receive training and periodically review federal education privacy laws. The Family Educational Rights and Privacy Act (FERPA) prohibit educational institutions of all levels from disclosing certain educational and financial information without the student's permission. However, the privacy rights are transferred from the parents to the student upon the student's eighteenth birthday (U.S. Department of Education, 2010c). This required transference is complicated as the majority of undergraduate students must include parental financial information on their FAFSA. A complete understanding of what can and cannot be disclosed to the family of aid recipients is critical to avoiding compliance issues.

FAO leadership must understand laws and institutional policies related to human resources and managing an operating budget. Administrators must ensure the professional development of staff through effective evaluation techniques and, as appropriate, participation in industry conferences and training seminars (Council for the Advancement of Standards in Higher Education, 2006).

As mentioned earlier, student workers can be of invaluable service in the operation of campus departments and offices. However, due to the confidential nature of student financial assistance, student workers must be carefully selected and highly trained in not only FAO operation, but in aspects of customer service, including training in FERPA (Council for the Advancement of Standards in Higher Education, 2006). FAO student workers must be highly cognizant that they are privy to personal financial information of their peers and, in some instances, friends and acquaintances. Disclosure of financial aid information in an inappropriate setting could result in an embarrassing situation or, at worst, a legal matter.

FAO staff must be provided the resources necessary to conduct business in an efficient and effective manner. Office logistics should be periodically reviewed to ensure compliance with federal and state access and safety laws. The FAO should provide for offices and/or conference areas where staff and students can meet privately when discussing confidential information. The FAO should be allocated sufficient and secured space for federally required document retention. This area should be able to be locked, and file cabinets should be fireproof (Council for the Advancement of Standards in Higher Education, 2006).

TECHNOLOGY

Technology has been instrumental in facilitating and accelerating the financial aid application and awarding process. Students can complete the Free Application for Federal Student Aid on line in a fraction of the time required to complete the hard-copy form. Processed information is transmitted to FAOs electronically where mainframe computer systems can review thousands of students' eligibility and award accordingly with overnight batch processes. The National Student Loan Data System, the clearinghouse of federal student loan and grant information, can be accessed in real time by aid administrators to resolve conflicting information or update enrollment statuses. Incorporating and advancing technology into the financial aid industry was a logical initiative as so many processes are decision tree based and progressive in nature.

It should be noted that although technology has proven invaluable in managing the highly complex regulatory environment associated with financial aid, it has also commanded a large portion of the time resources of aid administrators. The allocation of time to information technology is often at the sacrifice of personalized service to students. Furthermore, financial aid systems are many times merely components of a more holistic and comprehensive Student Information Management System (SIMS) that may require a highly technical skill set to comprehend technological interfaces (National Association of Student Financial Aid Administrators, 2005).

The National Association of Student Financial Aid Administrators (NAS-FAA, 2005) offers the following questions for aid professionals to consider when researching software systems. Does the system:

1. Enhance student services?
2. Increase the quality and quantity of student services without substantial increases in personnel?
3. Alleviate FAO staff from routine activities and allow them to become more accessible to students?
4. Demonstrate flexibility, adaptability, and the ability to be customized without major and/or substantial modifications to the soft and/or hardware?

NASFAA also recommends contacting personnel at other institutions which are using the software currently being considered. On-site visits provide a wonderful opportunity to hear user evaluations. However, the decision rarely rests solely with the aid administrators; and in some institutions, the decision has little to do with how well software performs student services but, instead, its capacity to manage fiscal and human resource functions (National Association of Student Financial Aid Administrators, 2005).

Government Websites

U.S. Department of Education (USDOE) http://www.ed.gov/. This is the home link to the USDOE from which information about education at any level can be accessed. Information specific to financial aid administrators can be accessed at the Information for Financial Aid Professionals (IFAP) web site, http://www.ifap.ed.gov/ifap/. IFAP is often viewed as the single most important source of information for aid administrators by providing access to training opportunities, current and past issues of the Student Financial Aid Handbook, codified federal regulations, and federal updates in the form of "Dear Colleague" letters. Familiarity and regular review of this site is highly encouraged for the sound administration of a financial aid office. In addition to detailed financial aid information, the USDOE provides links to research topics, educational statistics, governmental policy, and organizational structure.

National Center for Education Statistics (NCES) http://nces.ed.gov/. This federal website is a dedicated repository for educationally related data at the state, national, and international level. In addition to administering data systems, such as the Integrated Post-Secondary Education Data System (IPEDS), the NCES also produces reports related to US education for use by federal, state, educational, and business agencies.

Advisory Committee on Student Financial Assistance http://www2.ed.gov/about/bdscomm/list/acsfa/edlite-index.html. Created in 1986 by the Higher Education Amendments, this agency is a member of the U.S. Department of Education. Its 11 member board serves in a bipartisan capacity as a source of information and advice-related student financial assistance to the Secretary of Education and Congress. Membership is by appointment from the Speaker of the House of Representatives, the President pro-tempore of the Senate, and the Secretary of Education. Appointees are representative of higher education administration, educational agencies, and the financial aid industry.

National Student Loan Data System (NSLDS) https://www.nslds.ed.gov/nslds_FAP/secure/logon.jsp. This secure website was developed for financial aid professionals in an attempt to alleviate the paper burden associated with financial aid transcripts. The site contains detailed federal student loan, Pell and SEOG program, and institutional enrollment information. The implementation of NSLDS freed FAOs from the labor-intensive task of reviewing paper financial aid transcripts provided by transfer students. It also allows student information systems to programmatically review annual and aggregate loan limits and issues related to ineligible Pell and SEOG receipts. Students can access their personal federal student loan information at the student portal http://www.nslds.ed.gov/nslds_SA/.

Nongovernmental Organizations and Professional Associations

National Association of Student Financial Aid Administrators (NASFAA) http://www.nasfaa.org/Home.asp. NASFAA is the national professional organization of financial aid administrators. Its mission is to promote "the professional preparation, effectiveness, support, and diversity of persons and organizations involved in the administration of financial aid. . . ." Founded in 1966, NASFAA is a member-driven organization with more than 20,000 members representing over 3,000 postsecondary institutions. The organization is governed by a Board of Directors, three commissions, and 18 committees. Located in Washington, D.C., the day-to-day operations of NASFAA are managed by 38 permanent staff members (National Association of Student Financial Aid Administrators, 2010).

National Association of State Student Grant and Aid Programs (NASSGAP) http://www.nassgap.org/. The NASSGAP is dedicated to the promotion and improvement of state assistance programs. The organization is also committed to lobbying governmental leaders and agencies as to additional resources needed to improve higher education. Its membership includes single agency representation from every US state and territory that offers loan, grant, and/or work study programs. The organization also promotes and serves as the repository for scholarly research on state-administered assistance programs.

National Council on Higher Education Loan Programs (NCHELP) http://www.nchelp.org/. This organization is comprised of national representatives from the student lending industry, guaranty agencies, loan repayment servicers, and postsecondary institutions. The primary goal of NCHELP is to promote access to higher education through the Federal Family Education Loan Program. Leadership is provided by an elected board and officers physically located in Washington, DC.

The College Entrance Examination Board http://www.collegeboard.com. The College Entrance Examination Board, or College Board, was founded in 1900 as a nonprofit organization dedicated to providing students and their families with the necessary resources for access to and potential success in college. Its 5,700 member schools, colleges, universities, and educational organizations provide students, families, and educational institutions with information related to college choice, financial aid, and teaching and learning. Its products include the SAT (formerly the Scholastic Aptitude Test), the PSAT, and the Advanced Placement Program (College Entrance Examination Board, 2010).

General Information Sites

FinAid http://www.finaid.org/. FinAid was launched in 1994 by Mark Kantrowitz as a holistic financial aid information resource. The site offers information on loans, grants, and scholarship opportunities as well as resources related to the college-choice process. FinAid has received acclaim from its counterparts for its comprehensive, yet objective, service to students, their families, and financial aid administrators. In fact, many FAOs provide a link to FinAid on their institutionally-maintained home pages.

FastWeb http://www.fastweb.com/. Also founded by Mark Kantrowitz, FastWeb provides users with information related to scholarships, internships, financial aid, and college choice. Users create an account and enter personal demographic data that FastWeb uses to correlate individuals with scholarship criteria.

PROFESSIONAL DEVELOPMENT

Professional Associations

The National Association for Student Financial Aid Administrators (NAS-FAA) was founded in 1966, and is the largest professional association for aid administrators and staff. The association's goal is to promote maximum funding and effective aid delivery methods to assist needy students in their pursuit of postsecondary education (National Association of Student Financial Aid Administrators, 2010). NASFAA maintains headquarters in Washington D.C. and is directed by a board of directors and 38 permanent staff members.

The NASFAA website serves as a repository of legislative, training, and technology resources. NASFAA's site is updated daily to reflect practically "real-time" congressional activity related to financial aid legislation. The organization's training link includes resources for outreach activities, processing aid, and program self-reviews. The technology section provides FAO professionals with direct links to the various U.S. Department of Education processing sites for FAFSAs, Pell Grants, and Direct Loans. Additionally, discussion lists ranging from general financial aid to default prevention are provided.

NASFAA also publishes several periodicals related to current events, position papers, and scholarly research. The *Student Aid Transcript* is published quarterly with a circulation of approximately 5,500 readers. The NASFAA monograph series provides financial aid professionals with applicable information related to administering financial aid offices and programs. NASFAA's *Journal of Student Financial Aid* provides members with refereed articles related to research, policy, or position issues in student financial assistance (National Association of Student Financial Aid Administrators, 2010).

NASFAA holds an annual conference in July of every year to which upwards of 1,800–2,000 of its 30,000 members attend (National Association of Student Financial Aid Administrators, 2010). The conference allows members from all strata of financial aid to come together to share best practices, hear from legislators, and receive additional practical training.

NASFAA provides professional development and training to its members. There are four types of NASFAA membership: Institutional Membership, Affiliate Membership, Student Membership, and Constituent Membership (companies and organizations). Additional information and requirements for membership can be found at http://www.nasfaa.org/redesign/JoinNASFAA.html.

Regional Associations

In addition to NASFAA, financial aid administrators may join the numerous regional and state associations. Currently there are six regional associations: The Eastern Association of Student Financial Aid Administrators http://www.easfaa.org/; the Midwest Association of Student Financial Aid Administrators http://www.masfaaweb.org; the Rocky Mountain Association of Student Financial Aid Administrators http://www.rmasfaa.org; the South-

ern Association of Student Financial Aid Administrators http://www.sasfaa.
org; the Southwest Association of Student Financial Aid Administrators http:
//www.swasfaa.org; and the Western Association of Student Financial Aid
Administrators http://www.wasfaa.org.

Each organization is similar in structure to NASFAA with a board of directors or executive council and officers elected by the membership. Each association also holds an annual conference with workshops, training, and professional development opportunities. All 50 states and the District of
Columbia and Puerto Rico have member organizations with similar governance structures.

ISSUES AND TRENDS

As Financial Aid Offices, like all modern institutions, continue to struggle
in an ever changing society, the zeitgeist often dictates the newest direction.
Some salient issues in the field of Higher Education Financial Aid Administration include, but are not limited to, the following: escalating costs, financial aid programs, and student aid in a post 9/11/01 climate.

Escalating Costs

From the period 2000 to 2010, tuition and fees at public four-year colleges
and universities increased by an average annual rate 4.9 percent beyond cost
of living increases. Furthermore, these increases are substantially greater for
four-year public and not-for-profit private institutions, 15 percent and 20 percent respectively, when considered only from 2005 to 2010 (College Entrance Examination Board, 2009). In fact, over the past decade, college tuition
has increased at greater rates than any other consumer product (Draeger,
2008).

The cause for these increases can be linked to dwindling federal and state
support of higher education over the past few decades. For the majority of
states, it is the postsecondary institutions' boards of regents which regulate
tuition rates. Over the past decade, these boards have more or less permitted
the market to set the price (Field, 2007). Although state reductions in higher
education appropriations continue to be the popular culprit for rising tuition
and fee costs, a 2003 congressional report offers contrary evidence. Many
states have reduced higher education appropriations, but for fiscal year
2002–2003, 38 states increased or held flat appropriations for higher education while all 50 states increased tuition at public four-year institutions
(Boehner & McKeon, 2003). Once the boards of regents swallowed the
unpalatable idea of placing a larger percentage of cost increases upon students
and their families, the riches they gained made the idea more palatable.

Even if governmental regulations of public institutions' tuition were enacted, or in some states reinstated, it can be hypothesized that the pursuit of a college degree is now a market commodity. Housing and other auxiliary services are priced at the institution's discretion and can be increased to impact revenue streams as well. Once colleges and universities experience the benefits of supply and demand, like any other consumer good, the cost of public higher education will continue to rise.

Financial Aid Programs

In a partial effort to eliminate federal expenditures in the form of interest subsidies to private banks, the 2010 Congress is considering legislation that will eliminate the Family Federal Education Loan Program and require all postsecondary institutions move to the William D. Ford Federal Direct Lending Program. This action would establish responsibility with the federal government for the lending, servicing, and collecting of guaranteed student loans. There are long-term benefits associated with this proposed move, such as student loans no longer being subject to shortages in the capital market and all students receiving the same loan benefits. However, in the short-term, the logistics associated with a governmental agency assuming the disbursement and collection of billions of dollars in loans could prove problematic. Additionally, the repercussions of such a wholesale change in student loan policy could be disastrous at the private bank level, where thousands of account representatives are employed to serve as liaisons to universities and colleges. Pending legislation could mandate that institutions enroll in the Direct Lending program as soon as the fall of 2010.

During the 2000s, the federal administration has also proposed the elimination of various components of the Campus Based Programs, specifically loan cancellation aspects of the Federal Perkins Student Loan Program and the Supplemental Educational Opportunity Grant (SEOG). Officials have cited that these programs have accomplished their original purpose, such as loan cancellation benefits for Federal Perkins borrowers who enter public service, or are allocated to institutions and awarded to students in an outdated manner, such as SEOG (U.S. Department of Education, 2009e).

Student Aid Post-September 11, 2001

Higher education was not exempt from the impact of the events of September 11, 2001. While the federal coffers would obviously be strained by the nascent war effort, the public responded in benevolent fashion as millions of dollars were donated for relief and postsecondary scholarships for the dependents of those lost during the terrorist attacks. As of 2009, 23 organizations/foundations and over 50 colleges and universities had established higher education assistance programs for the victims and/or dependents of the September 11, 2001 events (National Association of Student Financial Aid Administrators, 2010).

The September 11 events also brought about changes to the financial aid system at the federal level. By September 14, 2001, the federal government had issued guidelines on the management of student loans for persons immediately summoned for military duty. Lenders and guarantors were to extend in-school deferments and offer forbearances for those serving active duty. Even students who had defaulted on their students loans were granted a reprieve from collection activity during their service time (National Association of Student Financial Aid Administrators, 2001). The Higher Education Act extension bill signed into law in 2006 authorized student loan forgiveness benefits for the spouses and families of those who died or were disabled as a result of the attacks (National Association of Student Financial Aid Administrators, 2006).

Although U.S. military veterans have benefited from educational provisions since the mid 1940s, new bills have emerged in the 2000s to provide additional benefits for those serving post September 11, 2001. The Post-9/11 GI Bill and Yellow Ribbon program provide financial support in the form of tuition and housing payments to veterans with a minimum of 90 days service on or after September 11, 2001. The key difference between these programs and other veteran assistance initiatives is that benefits are based on individual state tuition rates and not a predetermined monthly allowance from the federal government (U.S. Department of Veterans Affairs, 2010).

SUMMARY

The intent of this chapter was to provide current and future higher education administrators, student affairs personnel, and financial aid professionals with a working knowledge of the history of student financial assistance, institutional and student eligibility requirements, federal student assistance programs, and the sound administration of a financial aid office (FAO). It was not the authors' intent to assume a philosophical position on the purposes and roles that the FAO serves in institutional missions and goals. However, it is reasonable to predict that an increasing number of students are and will continue to require federal, state, and institutional financial assistance in order to participate in higher education.

All students approach college with varying goals, desires, and levels of academic and social preparation. Although it may be true that not all will benefit from participating in higher education, it may be equally true that financial aid administrators are bound to ensure that President Lyndon Johnson's wishes that ". . . a high school senior in this great land can apply to any college or university in any of the 50 states and not be turned away because his family is poor" (Johnson, 1965) be upheld.

REFERENCES

Advisory Commission on Intergovernmental Relations. (1981). *The federal role in the federal system: The dynamics of growth. The evolution of a problematic partnership: The feds and higher ed.* Washington, DC. Retrieved from http://www.eric.ed.gov/ERICDocs/data/ericdocs2sql/content_storage_01/0000019b/80/33/11/6d.pdf.

Boehner, J.A., & McKeon, H.P. (2003). *The college cost crisis.* Congressional Report. Retrieved from http://cssp.us/pdf/CollegeCostCrisisReport.pdf.

Byrne, D. K. (2006). *Relationships between financial aid policies, practices, and procedures at Texas public colleges and universities.* Unpublished doctoral dissertation, The University of Texas at Austin.

Carreras, I. E. (1998). *Institutional characteristics of importance at the college search stage among Latino high school students.* Unpublished dissertation, Boston College, Boston, MA.

Center for Higher Education Support Services. (2009). *History of financial aid.* Retrieved from http://www.chessconsulting.org/financialaid/history.htm.

Chapman, D. W. (1981). A model of student college choice [Electronic version]. *Journal of Higher Education, 52*(5), 490–505.

College Board. (2006). *College access: Opportunity or privilege?* New York.

College Entrance Examination Board. (2009). *Trends in college pricing.* Retrieved from http://www.collegeboard.com/html/trends/.

College Entrance Examination Board. (2009). *Trends in student aid 2009.* Retrieved from http://www.collegeboard.com/html/trends/.

College Entrance Examination Board. (2010). *About us: The college board.* Retrieved from http://www.collegeboard.com/about/index.html.

Coomes, M. D. (2004). Student financial aid. In F. MacKinnon & Associates, *Rentz's student affairs practice in higher education* (pp. 337–368). Springfield, IL: Charles C Thomas.

Council for the Advancement of Standards in Higher Education. (2006). *CAS self-assessment guide for financial aid programs.* Council for the Advancement of Standards in Higher Education, Washington, DC.

Department of Education. (2006). *Federal Student Aid Handbook, 2006–2007. Application and verification guide.* Washington, DC: US Department of Education. (ERIC Document Reproduction Service No. ED494725). Retrieved from EBSCOHost ERIC database.

Draeger, J. (2008). No such thing as a free lunch, but what about college? *Student Aid Transcript, 19*(2), 44–51.

Field, K. (2007). *Congress may seek to punish states that cut higher-education budgets.* The

Chronicle of Higher Education. Retrieved from http://chronicle.com/article/Con
gress-May-Seek-to-Punish/39876/.

General Accounting Office, Washington, D.C. (1997). *Student financial aid: High risk series* (Report No. GAO/HR-97-11). Washington, DC: General Accounting Office. (ERIC Document Reproduction Service No. ED404950). Retrieved from EBSCOHost ERIC database.

Hamrick, F.A., Evans, N.J., & Schuh, J. H. (2002). *Foundations in student affairs practice.* San Francisco: Jossey-Bass.

Heller, D. (2000, April). The role of race and gender in the awarding of institutional financial aid. Paper presented at the Annual Meeting of the American Educational Research Association, New Orleans, LA.

Hossler, D. (2000). The role of financial aid in enrollment management. *New Directions for Student Services, 89,* 77.

Johnson, L. B. (1965). Remarks at Southwest Texas State College upon signing the Higher Education Act of 1965. Lyndon Baines Johnson Library and Museum, Austin, TX. Retrieved from http://www.lbjlib.utexas.edu/johnson/lbjforkids/edu_whca370-text.shtm.

King, J. E. (1999). *Financing a college education: How it works, how it's changing.* Phoenix, AZ: American Council on Education/Oryx Press.

Laws, J. (1999). The influence of upward bound on freshman grade point average, drop-out rates, mathematics performance, and English performance. *The Western Journal of Black Studies, 23*(3), 139–143.

Monro, J. U. (1994). Helping the student help himself. *Journal of Student Financial Aid, 24*(2), 9–16.

National Association of Student Financial Aid Administrators. (1999). *NASFAA's statement of ethical principles and code of conduct for institutional financial aid professionals.* Retrieved from http://www.nasfaa.org/subhomes/MediaCenter/NAS FAACodeofConduct.pdf.

National Association of Student Financial Aid Administrators. (2001). *Gen 01-13: Recent terrorist attacks-persons affected by military mobilization.* Retrieved from http://www.nasfaa.org/publications/2001/GEN0113.html.

National Association of Student Financial Aid Administrators. (2005). *E-aid office 2005: Systems, features, functionality, and integration.* Washington, D.C. Retrieved from http://www.nasfaa.org/Redesign/NASFAACatalog.html#Publications.

National Association of Student Financial Aid Administrators. (2006). *Details on changes made by the HEA extension law.* Retrieved from http://www.nasfaa.org/pub lications/2006/gheaextdetails100406.html.

National Association of Student Financial Aid Administrators. (2007a). *Developing the cost of attendance.* Washington, D.C. Retrieved from http://www.nasfaa.org/Re design/NASFAACatalog.html#Publications.

National Association of Student Financial Aid Administrators. (2007b). *Professional judgment in eligibility determination and need analysis.* Washington, D.C. Retrieved from http://www.nasfaa.org/Redesign/NASFAACatalog.html#Publications.

National Association of Student Financial Aid Administrators. (2010). *About NAS-FAA.* Retrieved from http://www.nasfaa.org/redesign/AboutNASFAA.html.

Office of Postsecondary Education. (1996). *34 codified federal regulations: Part 673*. Retrieved from http://edocket.access.gpo.gov/cfr_2007/julqtr/pdf/34cfr673.1. pdf.

Office of Student Financial Assistance (ED) Washington, D.C. (1988). *The federal student financial aid handbook. 1988–1989*. Washington, DC: Office of Student Financial Assistance. (ERIC Document Reproduction Service No. ED298823). Retrieved from EBSCOHost ERIC database.

Recommendations for Financial Aid Counseling. (2007). *Recruitment & Retention in Higher Education, 21*(11), 6. Retrieved from Academic Search Complete database.

Schachter, R. (2009). The state of student aid. *University Business, 12*(7), 61–66.

Scott, G., & General Accounting Office. (2007). *Federal family education loan program: Increased Department of Education oversight of lender and school activities needed to help ensure program compliance report to congressional requesters*. (Report No. GAO/07-750). Washington, DC: U.S. Government Accountability Office. (ERIC Document Reproduction Service No. ED497650). Retrieved from EBSCOHost ERIC database.

Scott, G., & U.S. Government Accountability (2009). *Proprietary schools: Stronger Department of Education oversight needed to help ensure only eligible students receive federal student aid*. (Report No. GAO/09-600). Washington, DC: U.S. Government Accountability Office. (ERIC Document Reproduction Service No. ED506753).

St. John, E. P., Paulsen, M. B., & Starkey, J. B. (1996) The nexus between college choice and persistence. *Research in Higher Education, 37*, 175–220.

U.S. Department of Education. (2009a). Federal student aid. *Grant programs fact sheet*. Retrieved from http://studentaid.ed.gov/students/attachments/siteresources/ Grant_Programs_Fact_Sheet_04_2009.pdf.

U.S. Department of Education. (2009b). *Direct loans: The William D. Ford direct loan program*. Retrieved from http://www.ed.gov/offices/OSFAP/DirectLoan/index. html.

U.S. Department of Education. (2009c). *Federal Pell Grant Program*. Retrieved from http://www.ed.gov/programs/fpg/index.html.

U.S. Department of Education. (2009d). *Federal student aid handbook*. Washington, DC. Retrieved from http://ifap.ed.gov/ifap/byAwardYear.jsp?type=fsahand book&awardyear=2008-2009.

U.S. Department of Education. (2009e). *Fiscal year 2009 budget summary: Section III. Programs proposed for elimination*. Retrieved from http://www2.ed.gov/about/over view/budget/budget09/summary/edlite-section3.html#seog.

U.S. Department of Education. (2009f). *Fiscal year 2010 budget summary–May 7, 2009*. Retrieved from http://www.ed.gov/about/overview/budget/budget10/summary/ edlite-section3d.html.

U.S. Department of Education. (2009g). *Office of postsecondary education: History of the Federal TRIO programs*. Retrieved from http://www.ed.gov/about/offices/list/ope/ trio/triohistory.html.

U.S. Department of Education. (2010a). *Academic competitiveness and national SMART grants*. Retrieved from http://www2.ed.gov/about/offices/list/ope/ac-smart.html.

U.S. Department of Education. (2010b). *Accrediting agencies recognized for title IV pur-

poses. Retrieved from http://www2.ed.gov/admins/finaid/accred/accreditation_pg10.html#TitleIVRecognition.

U.S. Department of Education. (2010c). *Family educational rights and privacy act.* Retrieved from http://www2.ed.gov/policy/gen/guid/fpco/ferpa/index.html.

U. S. Department of Education. (2010d). *Federal Student Aid. TEACH grant program.* Retrieved from http://studentaid.ed.gov/PORTALSWebApp/students/english/TEACH.jsp.

U.S. Department of Education. (2010e). *IPEDS executive peer tool and peer analysis system.* Institute of Education Sciences, National Center for Education Statistics. IPEDS Data Center. Integrated Postsecondary Education Data System. Retrieved from http://nces.ed.gov/ipeds/datacenter/InstitutionByGroup.aspx.

U.S. Department of Education. (n.d.). *Federal Pell grants: Fiscal year 2011 budget request.* Retrieved from http://www2.ed.gov/about/overview/budget/budget11/justifica tions/p-pell.pdf.

U.S. Department of Veterans Affairs. (2009). *GI Bill history.* Retrieved from http://www.gibill.va.gov/GI_Bill_Info/history.htm.

U.S. Department of Veterans Affairs. (2010). *What is the post-9/11 GI bill?* Retrieved from http://www.gibill.va.gov/GI_Bill_Info/CH33/Post-911.htm

Vedder, R. (2004). *Going broke by degree: Why college costs too much.* Washington, D.C.: American Enterprise Institute.

Washington Consulting Group, & Office of Student Financial Assistance. (1988). *A self-instructional course in student financial aid administration. Module 4: The roles and responsibilities of the financial aid office.* Washington, DC: Washington Consulting Group, & Office of Student Financial Assistance. (ERIC Document Reproduction Service No. ED307826). Retrieved from EBSCOHost ERIC database.

Wilkinson, R. (2005). *Aiding students, buying students: Financial aid in America.* Nashville, TN: Vanderbilt University Press.

Williams, M. S. (1999). *Staffing issues in student financial aid: A report on the NASFAA 1998 staff and salary survey.* Washington, DC: National Association of Student Financial Aid Administrators.

Zarate, M. E., & Pachon, H. P. (2006). *Perceptions of college financial aid among California Latino youth.* The Tomas Rivera Policy Institute, University of Southern California School of Policy, Planning, and Development, Los Angeles. Retrieved from http://www.eric.ed.gov/ERICDocs/data/ericdocs2sql/content_storage_01/0000019b/80/3e/53/43.pdf.

Chapter 13

STUDENT HEALTH

RICHARD P. KEELING, TREY AVERY,
JENNIFER S. M. DICKSON, AND EDWARD G. WHIPPLE

HISTORY

Student health care has a long tradition in American higher education. From the 1660s until the mid-1850s, students were generally seen as responsible for their own health, though. In most universities, students were expected to seek aid from medical personnel in surrounding communities. (Farnsworth, 1965, as cited in Saddlemire, 1988)

At Amherst College in 1859, Dr. Edward Hitchcock, labeled "the father of college health" (Boynton, 1962), a professor of hygiene, was the first formal provider of student health services. The philosophy that guided his practice and treatment of students was that the "body and mind should work together harmoniously" (Saddlemire, 1988, p. 185). Later, in 1861, Amherst created the first comprehensive department of hygiene and physical education. The college provided for annual examinations, instruction on hygiene, and regular physical exercise, and collected data on student illness and treatment (Boynton, 1971).

Faculty concern over campus living conditions, the threat of epidemics of infectious diseases and increased interest in promoting mental health led to measures such as the inspection of student living quarters. As athletic programs grew in size and stature, some colleges provided what is known today as a "team doctor." Student infirmaries were created to serve students who were unable to care for themselves; the first of these was created at Princeton University in 1893, followed by the first formally organized student health service in 1901 at the University of California (Boynton, 1962).

Until the 1960s, students frequently sought care off campus for information and help with sexually transmitted infections, alcohol and other drug use, mental health concerns, and contraception. In 1977, the American College Health Association recommended that college health programs include: "(1) outpatient and inpatient services; (2) mental health; (3) athletic medicine; (4) dental services; (5) rehabilitation and physical medicine; (6) preventive medicine; (7) health education and promotion; (8) environmental health and safety; and (9) occupational health" (Saddlemire, 1988, p. 187). Bridwell and Kinder (1993) summarized these changes as follows:

> The mission for health centers remained relatively unchanged until the late 1960s and early 1970s, when the social and cultural revolution sweeping out nation altered forever the way colleges and universities dealt with students. The sexual liberation movement, the popularization of drug and alcohol use on campuses, and an aggressive new student activism brought change to the student health agenda. These new issues demanded new approaches: drug and alcohol treatment and education programs; specialized services, such as women's clinics offering gynecologic and contraceptive services; and many others. And during this period, students became much more vocal in expressing their discontent with campus agencies or services that were not meeting their needs. All of these forces served as catalysts leading to the health centers that we see on today's campuses. (Bridwell & Kinder, 1993, pp. 481-482)

Prescott (2007) also provided a rich, comprehensive, and detailed history of college health programs.

TODAY'S COLLEGE HEALTH PROGRAMS

College health during the first decade of the twenty-first century encompasses a broad array of services to students, including: health promotion and prevention; mental health, counseling, and psychotherapy; consumer services (students' rights and responsibilities and insurance); immediate/urgent medical and nursing care; pharmaceutical, laboratory, diagnostic, and therapeutic imaging; emergency, surgical, and anesthesia services; inpatient/infirmary; athletic, sports, and recreational medicine; dental health; environment health and safety; and occupational health services (American College Health Association, 1999).

Today, student health services are often called *college health programs* to acknowledge these programs' comprehensive scope in promoting students' holistic growth and development. While most college health programs provide services only for students, a significant minority also offers health care for students' dependents, and, less often, for faculty and staff. With changing college student demographics, health programs are revising their focus to meet a greater diversity of health needs. Many health programs provide leadership to the campus community about health issues and have responsibility for managing responses to epidemics and other community and public health emergencies.

Colleges and universities have designed their health programs to respond to the particular needs of their student population. Within the constraints of available resources, and in relation to the availability and accessibility of other sources of health care in the community, the organizational structure and the service patterns in college health programs vary extensively. Their history, however, reflects common themes (Keeling, 2005).

Institutions of higher education usually commissioned student health services to respond to public health challenges (notably, epidemics of infectious disease), to ensure that students had access to basic health care, regardless of their health insurance status; to assess and remedy students' illnesses expeditiously (to avoid lost time from class); and to compensate for the perceived shortcomings of other sources of health care nearby (Keeling, 2000; Prescott, 2007; Turner & Hurley, 2002). Campus health centers today, particularly on four-year campuses, have evolved as practical solutions to real problems in students' lives. They focus on providing timely, cost-effective health services, dictated by the immediate context and circumstances. Community colleges and urban commuter institutions less often provide comprehensive clinical services because their students are more likely to have a source of health care off-campus, and because they are less likely to identify the college as their primary community. Alternatively, universities with academic medical centers may provide especially robust service options. Health services were planned, or have gradually evolved, to address local needs within locally defined parameters; therefore, college health programs are as varied as the institutions that provide them, and as different as the communities in which they are located.

Within this text, counseling centers are addressed in a separate chapter, even though in practice many counseling programs are now structurally and programmatically integrated components of a larger campus health program. Psychiatric care, which historically was provided through student health service centers (because psychiatrists shared the medical model) may now also be offered through counseling centers. Multidisciplinary mental health care has become more widespread, whether or not it is provided through a consolidated campus health program. In this chapter, the medical, nursing, ancillary (i.e., diagnostic testing, pharmacy, and specialized therapies such as physical therapy), and prevention services associated with traditional student health centers will be addressed. However, the intersections of medical and mental health care, regardless of the administrative or physical organization of those services on any particular campus, will be noted. Attention to these intersections reflects the growing support for a holistic and integrated model for college health programs (Silverman, Underhile, & Keeling, 2008).

MISSION AND PURPOSE

First and foremost, college health programs are learning support services that help students achieve their academic, intellectual, and personal potential by strengthening health and well-being and removing barriers to learning. Good campus health programs provide convenient access to competent, high-quality health care in a format and pattern that responds to students' lifestyles and to accommodate academic assumptions and patterns. For example, college health programs allow for more walk-in care than in other practice settings to accommodate ways in which most students are learning to assess their own symptoms, to determine whether professional care is needed, and to access the necessary care. At the same time, campus health-related programs prepare students to be effective, issue-literate health care consumers.

However, colleges and universities are not primarily in the health care business. Their mission is educational, and their goal is to advance student learning. Institutions of higher education provide health care in support of their mission and goals by caring for students as "whole people." In this way, they support students' capacity to learn, and they reveal a dual purpose to health care on campus: to prevent or treat illness and injury and to preserve or strengthen students' performance and potential as learners. College and university health programs, then, should be focused on student success, which is at the heart of the mission of higher education (Keeling, 2000; Silverman et al., 2008).

This dual purpose commits college health programs to function as something more than a campus clinic. A sound student health center is not simply a freestanding urgent-care center. Clinical services for students with illnesses and injuries do not comprise all of college health. To preserve and strengthen students' performance and potential as learners, college health programs must inevitably address the health needs of students who seldom, or never, come seeking clinical care. They also must address the quality of the learning environment and the overall health of the student community. Effective college health programs are not purely clinical operations, no matter the quality of their reactive, reparative services; offering clinical services alone misses the point of college health (Swinford, 2002).

Any discussion of the design, organization, operations, delivery, and outcomes of student health programs must account for national trends in the expectations and responsibilities of college health, changes in the patterns of funding for college health programs, the significance of health and health-related programs and services to student learning, and the importance of health programs in the achievement of broad institutional effectiveness in promoting student engagement, learning, and success. The addition of data from the neurosciences about manners of learning has provided critical evidence in support of a more integrative, developmental, and holistic approach to personal, social, and academic success (Haier, 2009). From this perspective, college health programs must effectively and successfully support students as learners. Student affairs professionals must be aware of the many factors affecting a student's total health status and well-being. Understanding these factors will enable professionals to help and support students to be successful, both in and out of the classroom (Keeling, 2004a).

HEALTH AND LEARNING

From a theoretical understanding of student health, it is helpful to note that students are neither as endangered psychologically or emotionally nor as untroubled physically as the popular media might suggest. The common portrayal of health among students suggests that most undergraduates of traditional age are deeply troubled, few are resilient, and all are otherwise basically healthy. A more balanced view, and one strongly supported by available data, suggests that: traditional undergraduates have generally positive health status, but a significant minority have chronic health conditions, such as asthma and diabetes, that require monitoring and treatment; the illnesses and injuries experienced by most students are of relatively low intensity and seriousness and will resolve by themselves, with good self-care, or after simple interventions or treatments; the interference that routine primary-care problems cause to academic functioning and progress is slight; but as many as 10 percent to 20 percent of students have some degree of symptoms of depression or other mental illness, and many require psychotropic medications (ACHA, 2009b).

The most pressing and fundamental conclusion arising from recent research on the neurophysiology of learning is simply that the learning process is a brain-based, physical, organic process that requires work. The mind is not some ephemeral, abstract entity; it is inherent in the work of a living organ (the brain). In fact, there is an extensive and growing scholarly literature that explores learning using both neuroscientific tools, such as brain imaging, and the philosophy of science (Bechtel, Mandik, Mundale, &

Stufflebeam, 2001; Churchland, 1989; Sousa, 2006). Thinking, learning, and creating are energy-dependent, oxygen-consuming processes that occur in a living, physical person. Learning, as the process of meaning-making, is not simply content-comprehension, but is the perceivable representation of actual changes in brain microanatomy and function. Learning depends on the documented plasticity of brain cells and networks (Mareschal, Johnson, Sirois, Spratling, Thomas, & Westermann, 2007). The quality and effectiveness of learning depend on the state of the brain of the learner. Conditions in the learner that affect the brain, from depression (common) and insufficient sleep (more common) to fever (very common in association with upper respiratory infections) influence students' readiness and capacities to learn. These observations then provide tremendous opportunities for college health programs to support and commit to student learning, engagement, and success all within the broader institutional learning environment (Keeling, 2004a).

Survey data from NCHA indicate that, according to students themselves, the health concerns that impede academic success (e.g., incomplete, tardy, or poor performance on assignments, low or failed academic performance in coursework) stem primarily from psychological, psychosocial, or stress-related sources. Data suggest that health concerns can undermine the ability of students to learn as effectively and flexibly as possible (ACHA, 2009b).

Research further suggests that, given a more holistic understanding of health, students have *health* problems far more often and more intensely than they have *medical* problems. Students' most common health concerns (those that impact academic success, the formation of strong relationships, long-term health status and even survival) are seldom witnessed or addressed in standard medical or health-care settings; these concerns include drinking, use of recreational drugs, smoking, at-risk sexual behavior, physical risk-taking, interpersonal violence, and eating disorders. The scope of each of these health problems far exceeds the prevalence of its associated medical manifestations. For example, many more students binge drink than receive medical or mental-health services for alcohol abuse (Keeling, 2000).

These findings have meaning for university and college leaders charged with shaping and administering college health programs on campus. In order to fully address students' health, staff must provide a balance of healthy recreation opportunities, prevention programs, health education, mental health, and clinical health services. What was once the norm–centering health efforts in a clinic and presenting health programs as responsive to clinical demand rather than being proactive in advancing the health of students and strengthening the learning environment–is no longer sufficient in addressing the health needs of college students.

Students' decisions about their health can support or impede their academic success and their level of educational attainment. Attrition can be due to health problems like stress, lack of social connectivity, depression, striving to balance work and school, substance abuse, and other challenges. The role of health promotion (which addresses the whole community of students) and health education (which focuses on individual students with clinical problems) is to support students in learning to make healthy decisions. As students try to make these decisions, there are clear interactions of stress, depression, and distraction with readiness and capacity to learn. These interactions can be exacerbated by poor choices in coping, such as the use of substances like alcohol or marijuana to mask stress or treat depression. Engagement with academic work is both a function and indicator of health status. The more able students are to engage successfully in learning, the more likely they are to engage in healthy behaviors. On the other hand, those students who are less engaged often exhibit higher health-risk behaviors (ACHA, 2009b). With regard to health and learning, research has proven the following:

- The learner matters in the learning process. Each student's literal state of mind (state of the brain) influences the efficiency, effectiveness, and outcomes of learning experiences.
- Learning is a brain-based, organic process. Health and learning are deeply linked and integrated.
- Learning involves the "whole" person. Trying to distinguish classroom "learning" from the "learning" reflected in personal and social maturation is an over-simplification of the real process of learning.

Health is increasingly appreciated as a broad quality of well-being that constantly, intentionally, and unintentionally affects student learning. Students who understand this connection may seek out health and recreation activities that promote learning. These activities include getting enough sleep, eating well, avoiding excessive alcohol and caffeine, engaging in regular vigorous physical activity, nurturing healthy friendships and avoiding or discounting the influence of unhealthy peers. Students often intuitively or experientially come to appreciate the positive activities, and they learn lessons about how excessive alcohol consumption interferes with sleep and comfort and compromises academic performance. They learn that "all-nighters" are seldom academically effective. Just as students experience health and learning as interconnected, so too must administrators and faculty at colleges and universities.

HEALTH IN HIGHER EDUCATION

Although health is broadly defined as "a state of complete physical, mental, and social well-being, and not merely the absence of disease or infirmity" (World Health Organization, 1947), the concept of health is often limited in modern society to clinic-based prevention and treatment of illness. This meaning of *health*–a broad, integrated and holistic quality–often is reduced to *health care*–an important and much needed service provided by a group of specially-trained professionals whose expertise prepares them to assess, describe, and treat certain parameters of health and its problems. While health is essential to intellectual growth, mental flexibility, and the development of empathic, engaged, and moral relationships, health care has a definitively fixed and restricted scope (Keeling, 2000). These understandings are especially relevant to the traditional-aged college population if campuses are to ensure their health programs contribute effectively to student learning and success.

Campus health programs have too often operated in organizational silos in which individual departments with discrete responsibilities (student health center, wellness center, counseling center) respond to or try to prevent physical or mental illness. Moreover, by their usual administrative placement in a typical student affairs organization, health services are located outside of the academic curriculum. In addition, the organization of institutions into major administrative units such as academic affairs and student affairs allows faculty members to focus on research, scholarship, and the teaching of disciplinary content, rather than on active development of the student as a whole person with a spectrum of needs (Keeling, 2000; Keeling, Underhile, & Wall, 2007). College health programs are sometimes marginalized as sideline or auxiliary consumer services, as though health itself were unrelated to learning and student success, and health-related programs are consequently rendered as secondary to the central mission of the institution. The distinction between health and health care regularly manifests itself on campuses through two significant, and problematic, organizing principles: the separation of body and mind (health remains apart from learning and the learner), and the segregation of student life (including health) and academic programs into distinct functional and organizational entities. Without a nuanced appreciation of the connections between health and learning, such dichotomies continually reinforce the separations within and between themselves. These separations inhibit maximum student learning (Keeling, 2005).

These limited ways of understanding and addressing health ignore the well-documented linkages between the health of students and their personal, social, and academic success. They additionally neglect important opportunities to strengthen student engagement and promote student success by removing or ameliorating health-related barriers to learning, and to create healthy environments in campus communities that improve student-learning outcomes. Addressing and investing in students' health is essential for success in effectively educating the whole student.

HEALTH ON CAMPUS

Current thinking about campus health and its challenges emphasizes its influence on the quality of the learning environment and campus culture. As is true of student learning, student health must be collectively owned across the campus (Keeling, 2002). This interpretation, which explicitly links health to learning and environment, suggests broad responsibility for health across campus and has implications for service delivery.

Campus health programs should actively work toward making the environment a safe and healthy one and should share information, including assessment and outcome data, to help inform institutional policies and practices that were not previously thought to have an impact on health. Campus health programs must invest energy and resources into public health and community-level programs that affect large groups of students, and should invite students, student groups, and other campus constituencies to be part of this community-wide collaboration (Keeling, Kantor, Cruse, & Roper, 1995). This campus ecology model advocates linking clinical and public health services in college health programs. It calls for a level of intentional design that was

> often missing in typical campus programming efforts. . . . Too often health education programs are isolated as single random efforts and not well-integrated to meet the needs of students as they grow and mature over the course of their collegiate experience. The overall effect of providing the links that connect learning across the years and facilitating integration with other curricular and co-curricular learning experiences to create a comprehensive health education program is a model of ecological health services. (Banning & Kuk, 2005)

This approach broadens the targets for interventions for a healthy campus. Students, faculty, curricula, and organizational and physical structures all play a part:

> Individual health does not occur in a vacuum and health intervention must be multi-dimensional, holistic, and include the entire milieu in order to be successful and lasting. In other words, a focus on students within an illness paradigm cannot effectively produce a healthy campus environment. (Banning & Kuk, 2005)

These links among health, learning, and environment inform higher education policy and practice in important ways that can promote and sustain student engagement and success.

Rethinking programs can highlight the ineffectiveness of compartmentalized approaches to student health. Student health is inseparable from the context that defines the manifestation of illness, and most certainly the treatment of such illness. For example, to appropriately treat students for diabetes, it is essential to know how and where they make, buy, and eat their meals, when their class schedules allow time to eat, and whether the health service will cover the cost of testing supplies. Alternatively, to efficiently contain a meningitis outbreak, one must take into account the configuration of student residences, social networks, and the means for disseminating educational information, vaccines, and treatment. A greater understanding of the impact of an individual or community-health episode will lead to minimized duration and effect of the episode. This knowledge helps institutions to deliver relevant services that use campus resources within structural organization and limitations.

ADVANCING THE HEALTH OF STUDENTS: COLLEGE HEALTH MODELS

Given the known influences of health on learning and the frequency with which health concerns affect academic engagement and achievement, many institutions of higher education have begun to adopt an ecological and developmental view of health on campus. In that framework (a framework we have witnessed repeatedly in our work in higher education across many campuses), *health* is understood to be:

- *Multidimensional,* rather than segregated into categorized components (i.e., physical, mental, spiritual) or assumed to be one-dimensional (usually physical, as in the presence or absence of physical illness and injury). From this perspective, health (as a positive quality of well-being), is not simply the condition experienced by a person who is not ill or uninjured;
- *Integrated;* the elements of health are all related, each to all of the others;
- *Community-based and community-oriented,* rather than purely individual; that is, the health of others affects the health status, health behaviors, and overall well-being of each member of the community (the ecological perspective);

Table 13.1. Changing Perspectives on Campus Health.

Past	Emerging
☐ Owned by specific health disciplines	☐ Shared by health and other disciplines
☐ Organized discretely	☐ Diffused organizationally
☐ Treated in isolation	☐ Integrated
☐ Illness-focused	☐ Attention to prevention
☐ Understood by purely private and personal	☐ Community influence and effects recognized

- *Organizationally diffused and multicentric,* like learning, rather than assigned to or located in a specific facility or program. Health is not the property or the sole responsibility of the health center, and the counseling center does not hold ownership or responsibility for mental health. There is a difference between *leadership* in matters of health (which is appropriately vested in professionals working in health programs) and *ownership* of health as a campus concern (which is shared broadly across the institution);
- *Sensitive to context,* and influenced by intrapersonal, interpersonal, social, cultural, environmental, institutional factors; and
- *Central to the ability of colleges and universities to achieve the goals of their mission,* rather than peripheral, secondary, or ancillary, because it affects student learning, engagement, and success.

This more humane and holistic vision of health on campus, linked with a growing recognition of the extraordinary prevention opportunity that college provides, has led to significant shifts in the theory and practice of health (in all of its dimensions) on campus. Those changes are summarized in Table 13.1.

These concepts increasingly guide institutions in strategic planning processes to meet the multi-faceted health and wellness needs of today's students. The emerging principles of college health tend to reunite students' minds and bodies, recognize them as whole people, and broaden the responsibilities of college health programs. Table 13.2 summarizes current trends by comparing historical and emerging operational comparisons.

While there is no uniform, universally accepted model for college health programs, the general direction of the field is certainly toward making campus health programs and services the destination of choice for students in regard to health questions and concerns. Rather than counting clinical visits as a burden, health centers now see them as opportunities to educate students and maximize their ability to learn.

Table 13.2. Historical and Emerging Operational Comparisons.

Historical	*Emerging*
Emphasis on clinical services; major focus is on individual work with patients or clients	Balanced clinical and preventive (including outreach and community mental health) services; increasing focus on population-based, or campus-wide, health concerns
Secondary prevention: addressing the consequences of already-established problems or behaviors	Primary prevention: avoiding the development of behaviors or conditions that will weaken or compromise health
Some interdisciplinary work, but primarily parallel practice	Intentionally interdisciplinary practice
Allocation of resources based on traditional patterns, including history, power, and status; incremental budgeting	Data-driven and mission-centered practice and allocation of resources
Traditional counseling services; often, a separate mental health section established in the student health service. Counselors may resist integration with mental health services because of fear of "medicalization" of their practice	Systematic, contextual, community-based mental health service

The Council for the Advancement of Standards (CAS) in Higher Education set guidelines for clinical health programs (the traditional student health services):

> the model . . . is not as important as the assessment and decision process through which leaders responsible for the connection of health and student learning came to a conscious choice and an intentional design for the services offered. The most important aspect of any clinical health service will be its ability to create and maintain necessary, non-duplicate, responsive services, as well as collaborative relationships with the larger community, the faculty, and the student affairs staff. These relationships are essential in maintaining an emphasis on assisting in a student's academic success and a focus on the population's needs for a healthy and safe campus community. (Jackson & Weinstein, 1997, as cited in CAS, 2009, p. 136)

ADMINISTRATION OF COLLEGE HEALTH PROGRAMS

Campus health programs must be organized, structured, and operated within the context of the mission, priorities, and resources of each institution.

Still, as tailored as these organizations must be for individual colleges and universities and the needs of their respective student bodies, there are core commonalities in the ways in which they approach the complicated tasks of keeping students well while in school and supporting their success as learners. Though the details vary, most college health programs, though varied, tackle the same broad issues, including finding the right organizational and functional home for student health within the administrative structure of the institution, making sure systems and facilities meet the growing expectations of today's students, ensuring the quality of care, providing a coordinated continuum of services that includes primary medical care, access to long-term medical management through health insurance, mental-health services, and health education and promotion, and promoting cross-disciplinary and cross-campus collaboration to achieve these goals (Keeling, 2000; Keeling et al., 2007).

At many institutions, there are separate health and counseling centers with their own directors, usually reporting to the same administrator. For both practical and theoretical reasons, though, an increasing number of colleges and universities have chosen to merge, or integrate, health and counseling programs into a single larger organization led by a shared executive director. Prevention (health education, health promotion, health protection, and wellness) programs may be located within either or neither. At some institutions, these programs are part of a general student life department, such as a dean of students office, because of their focus on student development. On other campuses, prevention programs may be part of the recreation program, with the focus on health and wellness.

The great majority of campus health programs are placed within divisions of student affairs. Separate health and counseling centers generally report to assistant or associate vice presidents except in smaller institutions, where they may report directly to the vice president or other senior student affairs officer. The executive director of large, comprehensive, integrated campus health programs may carry a second title as assistant or associate vice president reporting to the senior student affairs officer. Institutional, personnel, and operational factors contribute to the effectiveness of the structure in place at any individual institution.

FUNDAMENTAL COMPONENTS OF COLLEGE HEALTH PROGRAMS

Programs and Services

Though the configuration and details vary from campus to campus, college health programs consistently include at least two essential components:

Table 13.3. Essential Components of College Health Programs.

Primary Medical Care	*Health Education, Promotion, Prevention, and Public Health*	*Mental Health and Counseling Services*
Medical and Nursing Services provide *basic primary care* for *minor illness and injury,* routine and prevention-oriented *well women's and men's care, chronic illness, sexually transmittable infection screening, immunizations, travel health consultation, laboratory and dispensary services. Secondary prevention,* including individual health counseling and instruction in self-care, is also part of the clinical encounter. *Emergency services* should be accessible to students as needed.	Health Education Services include *education* and *primary prevention programs* centered on *risk behavior areas* such as *alcohol, drug and tobacco use, sexual health, social/emotional health, stress, nutrition, assault, and injury.* Public Health Surveillance and Infrastructure should address *data collection, identification and reporting of communicable diseases,* as well as *environmental health and safety issues.*	Psychiatric and Counseling Services provide consultations for faculty, staff and students, in *individual and group settings,* on challenges and concerns, including *depression and anxiety, eating disorders, stress management,* and *violence. Education* on effective *self-care and coping skills, psychiatric evaluation,* and *medication management* should be available. Mental health services should strive to be *community-based, contextually appropriate, easily accessible and barrier-free.*

primary medical care and health education (promotion, prevention, and public health). As noted earlier in this chapter, mental health/counseling services are incorporated into college health programs with increasing frequency, and psychiatry services have often been located in them even when counseling services were not. Brief explanations of these components are outlined in Table 13.3.

In the table, services are broken up into distinct components, yet the boundaries between these components are never so clearly configured on campus. Usually, more overlap between these service areas and greater coordination among them leads to more effective and holistic programming to meet students' needs. The administrative organization of these components varies. Those features of structure and placement are less important than the effective provision of sound basic services.

The definition of a basic *primary care* service formula is not universal. The level of services provided in college health centers varies extensively. In most cases, however, primary care includes office visits for routine, emergent, and urgent medical problems, routine women's health care (including both annual examinations and assessment and treatment of minor gynecological conditions), limited follow-up visits, care for acute exacerbations or complications of chronic illnesses (e.g., asthma, diabetes), and referral of students with unusual or complex chronic illnesses to specialists.

While *medical and nursing services* and *psychiatric and counseling services* are mostly self-explanatory, the concept of *health education,* which, as an umbrella term, includes both wellness and health promotion, takes unique form at colleges and universities. A primary role of the college health program is to provide health education that informs students of the effects of current behavior on future health status. There should be an emphasis on how current behavior affects students' learning environment, their performance at the institution, and their ultimate quality of life. Providing a healthy environment that supports wellness behaviors, promotes healthy lifestyle choices, and provides health education is consistent with the mission and goals of higher education.

The discipline of *health promotion* is primarily one of student development, and, therefore, it has become increasingly common to link health promotion more directly to other student development programs, and to place it organizationally with those programs, rather than with clinical services and clinical colleagues (Keeling, 2005; Keeling & Engstrom, 1993). On the other hand, patient education or disease management education should take place within the scope of medical and clinical services. Examples of the former include providing instruction to a student on how to use over-the-counter medication, take his or her temperature, or monitor for early sign of influenza, while examples of the latter include teaching a student about how to manage asthma, diabetes, or human immunodeficiency disease.

But health promotion and wellness efforts traditionally differ in ways that locate these programs outside the purview of the clinical encounter. Like most other student development activities, health promotion focuses more on the community of students than the individual student. Clinical efforts are typically one-on-one efforts, while health promotion efforts seek to engage the entire community (Keeling, 2000). Health promotion and wellness efforts must be provided strategically where students have easy and regular access to them, typically in a student union, the recreation center, or in satellites located in residence halls with additional locations for commuter students. Traditional medical practice requires that patients come to a clinic, while health promotion and wellness efforts are more likely to be woven into campus life. Locating health promotion programs with student health centers encourages health promotion to adopt a model of formality that limits its ability to develop positive rapport with students. Finally, medical practice devotes most of its resources to helping an individual, while health promotion and wellness devote resources to broader community needs (Keeling,

2005). Health promotion works from a philosophy that most individuals have an innate desire to be healthy. Therefore, while data inform health educators about the needs and strengths of populations, health educators strive to provide thoughtful, planned, developmentally appropriate programs that will bring the greatest good to the greatest number.

Public health, which includes environmental health, takes a distinctive shape on college campuses. Each institution's health service should play a role in addressing the core functions of public health, including assessing the health-related needs of the campus, supporting policies that promote and protect the health of the campus community, and collaborating with other institution departments to assure that needs are addressed. The director of the health service and staff should have strong collaborative relationships and agreements with local city and county public health agencies. Each institution's health and counseling services should be active participants in the institution's crisis-response planning. Protecting the health of members of the institution's community requires a mechanism, such as a committee or crisis team, that will address communicable disease surveillance/prevention through disease identification and reporting, epidemiologic investigations, screening programs, immunization programs, and plans/procedures for quickly responding to disease outbreak situations, and issues of environmental health and safety including food safety, air quality, waste disposal, pest control, and water quality (Keeling, 2004b).

Human Resources

College health programs depend upon several types of professional and support staff to provide health care and prevention programs, administer the organization, and make it operate effectively.

- *Health care providers:* Depending on the scope and range of services offered, college health programs may require physicians, mid-level providers (nurse practitioners and physician assistants), registered nurses, professional counselors (including clinical, counseling, and educational psychologists, clinical social workers, and marriage and family therapists), physical therapists, and/or athletic trainers. Most physicians in college health are generalists who provide primary care, such as internists, family physicians, and pediatricians. Some are psychiatrists, and a few, usually in part-time roles, are specialists in dermatology, otorhinolaryngology, orthopedics, or sports medicine. Mid-level providers have important roles in most student health centers. Nurse practitioners, especially, provide the majority of routine women's health care in many centers, and they are the *only* full-time primary care providers in many others. The training and preparation of nurse practitioners make them especially well-suited to the character of college health practice, which emphasizes a holistic approach to students whose medical problems are often self-limited. Registered nurses not only provide essential support to other health care providers, but also perform triage; practice independently within specific guidelines (especially for high-volume, low-intensity problems such as upper-respiratory infections); and manage immunization, allergy, and travel medicine services. The presence of professional counselors in student health services depends on the organizational model.

- *Prevention professionals:* Health centers that have responsibility for health promotion, health education, wellness, public health, and environmental health require appropriately trained professionals in each area. As noted earlier, most commonly, campus health programs include health education. The work includes educating the student for self-management of chronic illness or change in health behaviors. Also, health promotion (which is more broadly focused on the campus community, and the work is community-based change in culture, norms, and behaviors) is included. Professional health educators are employed for most of these roles. In some institutions, nutritionists or registered dietitians address eating, dietary, and weight management issues for students as well.

- *Administrative staff:* There is no single recommended or proven leadership and administrative model for campus health programs. Until the 1980s, most directors were physicians. Today, diversification in leadership has brought nurse practitioners, health care administrators, mental health professionals, and health educators into directorships (Prescott, 2007). Few physicians are trained as administrators. A physician, who has been intensively trained to be a clinician, often does *not* have the experience necessary to manage a college health program today. If the director is *not* a clinician (usually a physician or nurse practitioner), there is usually a medical director who is accountable for clinical services and practice. In larger health centers, the director may be a clinician and still have a medical director. In health centers with large and moderately large staffs (in the experience of the authors, those with 20 or more people), there is often an assistant director for administration, whose portfolio includes human resources, physical plant, technology, budget, financial administration, and planning. More complex health centers will also employ accountants, billing clerks, information technology specialists, medical records specialists, and registration and reception staff.

- *Support and ancillary staff:* College health programs, like other outpatient primary-care organizations, generally employ medical or nursing assistants, administrative assistants, and laboratory or pharmacy technicians.

Expected Performance and Productivity

It is important to note the differences between the roles and goals of college health programs and those of community health care providers. While one would hope that all clinical encounters in any setting would provide an opportunity for one-on-one health education, in college health this is an intended and integral component of the clinical service. Students often are learning how to manage their own health care for the first time. They are just beginning to understand their own bodies, symptoms, and health behaviors. Health care visits in college health are supposed to be developmental and educational. Each encounter is expected to be a learning experience (Keeling, 2005).

Not only do students receive education about wellness, self-care, and healthy behaviors, but they also acquire the knowledge and experience to become informed health care consumers, a set of transferable skills that they will need and use well beyond their years on campus. Traditional-aged college students benefit most from educational opportunities that allow them to develop and refine personal and social skills, including goal-setting, stress management, communication, and decision-making. These basic skills form the foundation of classic health education and are consistent with professional literature on resiliency, youth development, student development and brain research. Health programs are in the unique position to teach students how to navigate and utilize health care systems and provide information about their rights as patients. In addition, health services can explain the complexities of confidentiality, control of personal health information, health insurance, and payment systems. Interactions within student health programs should ultimately educate students to be informed and active participants in their own health care decisions. Most of those learning opportunities will occur in association with clinical encounters.

It is, therefore, not appropriate to use the same indicators of professional productivity when assessing the use of human resources in student health services as would be the case with community providers. Each clinical encounter is meant to be longer and more involved, because teaching and learning are part of that encounter. In college health, Figure 13.1 illustrates how a physician or mid-level provider might complete 3,200 clinical encounters per year, on an annualized basis. Their peers in community health centers would be expected to provide 3,500 or more, and, in productive group medical practices, 4,400 (MGMA, 2008).

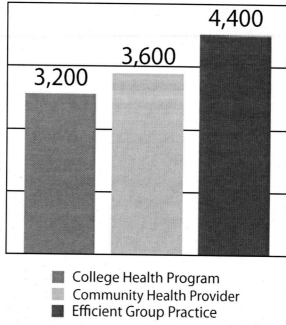

Figure 13.1. Patients per Provider (Annual).

Financial pressures on college health centers have, unfortunately, often increased demand for greater productivity, and, accordingly, reduced the length of clinical visits and stripped them of much of their developmental and educational potential.

ROLE OF STUDENTS IN COLLEGE HEALTH PROGRAMS

Physicians, mid-level providers, nurses, social workers, counselors, administrators, and students themselves are responsible for the design and delivery of health-related programs and services to the campus community. The most effective colleges and universities take into account not only students' needs, but also their perspective in shaping their college health programs. The campus ecology model and decades of good practice in college health suggest that students have an obligation to the campus community, as the community does to them, to participate in the design of health programs (Banning & Kuk, 2005). To provide a sound and sustainable structure for student involvement, many college health programs establish student health advisory boards or committees, chaired by and composed of students from various academic programs and organizations, to provide regular advice and give voice to students' needs or concerns. The fact that participation in and the quality of student leadership of such groups vary extensively does not invalidate the importance of maintaining and investing in them.

Students also serve key roles as peer health educators in many campus health programs. Trained peer educators are in a unique position to increase the number of student referrals to health professionals. Frequently, peer educators have more access to a greater number of students (especially underserved or high-risk groups) due to their peer identity and role in campus outreach programming. During campus outreach presentations, peer educators not only provide education on health and wellness issues, but also promote essential campus health services. Santelli, Kouzis, and Newcomber (1996) found that peers who were familiar with campus health services significantly affected other students' attitudes about campus-based health centers. In the future, peer education programs should and likely will continue to be an integral part of wellness programming (Keeling & Engstrom, 1993).

Outreach should be intentional and measured to match the goals of campus health services. Therefore, continual recruitment, selection and training of diverse cohorts of peer educators will be required. Moreover, potential peer educators will need to be carefully assessed to determine if their existing traits, experiences and academic preparation are appropriate to the specific health promotion activity and/or program (Keeling & Engstrom, 1993). Assessment data from student health centers and assessments of peer health programming should be used to continually improve the quality of programs and demonstrate effectiveness, especially in times of financial turmoil when the programs are often targeted for reductions or discontinuation.

Students' Sources of Health Information

Students receive their health information from a variety of sources. Not surprisingly, the Internet currently tops the list of resources students access the most, though it is not the most believed. Student health center staff and health educators (including peer health educators, who likely have far greater credibility than friends) continue to be regarded as reliable references and authorities when students seek information. Online research may provide useful and easily available facts, but it supplements (and does not replace) traditional sources of health information. Figure 13.2 shows ACHA (2009a) data on student sources of health information.

These student data reflect trends seen in the general population. According to the Pew Internet Project, the vast majority of people with a health question want to consult a health professional. The second most popular choice is friends and family, and the third, is the Internet and books (PEW Internet & American Life Project, 2006).

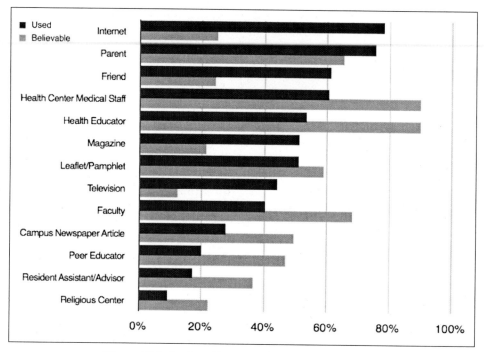

Figure 13.2. Student Sources of Health Information.

STANDARDS AND ACCREDITATION

The Council for the Advancement of Standards (CAS) in Higher Education has established standards for clinical health, health promotion, and counseling services that inform the structure and content of college health programs today. In describing the basis for the most current iteration of the guidelines, CAS states:

> [The] perception of the factors and influences that contribute to the health and well-being of an individual and affect the quality of student learning and engagement has changed in the past four decades; the nature and character of health-related services should change in parallel. The criterion against which to assess the continued value of any health-related service is its relationship to supporting student learning and creating a healthy campus community. . . . A public health model or an ecological model with an emphasis on primary prevention, societal intervention, and community creates a golden gateway to a future foundation. (CAS, 2009)

The guidelines for clinical health practice are summarized in Table 13.4.

Table 13.4. CAS Standards and Guidelines for Clinical Health Services (2009).

The following characteristics exemplify clinical health services that are consistent with the environment of healthcare delivery and the environment of higher education:

- Access to multiple data sources on the characteristics and health status of the population.

- A spectrum of services that supports the learning mission of the campus community and health in its broadest sense.

- Easy and equal access to services by all students.

- Advocacy for a healthy campus community by providing leadership on policy issues regarding health risks of the population in the context of the learning environment.

- Evidence of measures of quality, such as accreditation of services, the use of recognized standards, and data on service delivery and effectiveness.

- Significant student involvement in advising the program's mission, goals, services, funding, and evaluation.

- Providing leadership during a health-related crisis.

Both CAS and the American College Health Association (ACHA) have additional published standards for the practice of health promotion on campus. The tenets by which these organizations operate are generally in agreement: health and learning are inextricably connected; therefore, health services are a learning support service. Health is not purely a biomedical quality measured through individual clinical indicators, but includes cultural, institutional, socioeconomic, and political influences that affect both individuals and communities. Furthermore, social justice is inextricably linked to health, whereby advocating for equal access to resources and services (and against health disparities) leads to better health for all (ACHA, 2005; CAS 2009).

ACHA described its standards as a measure to "guide daily efforts, assess individual skills and capacities, and assist in decisions to improve practice through professional development" (ACHA, 2005). Through the pursuit of these ideals health promotion professionals support student learning and address larger institutional issues (and barriers) to building capacity of individuals and communities. The standards explicitly encourage health services staff, as well as students, to participate in planning and decision-making for the care of themselves, their community and their environment. It is through this type of structure that student health services and programs continue to foster such ideals in the next generation of health care consumers and professionals. ACHA standards are summarized in Table 13.5.

Table 13.5. The ACHA Standards for Health Promotion Practice (2005).

- Integration with the learning mission of higher education;
- Collaborative practice (through campus and community partnerships);
- Cultural competence;
- Theory- and evidence-based practice; and
- Continuing professional development and service.

College health programs may seek formal accreditation through either the Joint Commission on the Accreditation of Healthcare Organizations (JCAHO) or the Accreditation Association for Ambulatory Health Care (AAAHC). For colleges and universities, accreditation is not required by any federal or state law, but it provides external validation of the quality of programs, services, policies, and operations (ACHA 1999; MGMA, 2008). Accreditation especially is helpful when health centers seek to bill third parties, such as insurance companies, for professional or ancillary services. Being accredited provides objective validation that a campus health program's health care programs and services, infrastructure, organization, leadership, policies and procedures, health records, peer-review and quality-improvement programs and facilities meet usually accepted standards applied to other ambulatory health care operations. Preparation for accreditation is a demanding process that includes a detailed self-study. Campus health programs may invest two years in that process before hosting a site visit by a team of health professionals and administrators from other institutions. Accreditation generally must be renewed every three years (Terms of Accreditation, 2009, www.aaahc.org/).

Protection of Health Information

As health care providers, health centers on college campuses must generally comply with regulations and policies designed to protect the privacy of student health information and to allow students to have (and control access to) that information. These laws assume that upon age 18 or with matriculation in college, students become eligible to manage their own educational and health records, and authority to do so is transferred to them from their parents.

The Health Insurance Portability and Accountability Act (HIPAA) protects the privacy of patient records and identifiable health information. The law requires health care entities to enact appropriate safeguards to protect privacy by setting limits on the uses and disclosures of such information. The Family Education Rights and Privacy Act (FERPA) protects the privacy of students' education records and applies to educational agencies and institutions that receive funds under any program administered by the U.S. Department of Education.

HIPAA and FERPA give students the right to inspect, amend, and control disclosure of their health and education records, respectively. Schools cannot disclose these records, to anyone including parents, without the consent of the student, unless in very specific situations, such as when students have broken the law, or when there is a health or safety emergency that requires it.

The intersection of HIPAA and FERPA on campus can often be complicated. The disclosure of individually identifiable information usually warrants a case-by-case determination, in accordance with these laws as they apply to particular institutions, as well as state laws governing the release of health information.

FINANCING COLLEGE HEALTH PROGRAMS

In the long experience of the authors, college health programs depend on revenue from one or more of these sources:

Student fees: Especially in public and larger institutions, the primary source of revenue for college health programs is a student fee, charged in addition to tuition. In some cases, this is a segregated fee, collected and designated exclusively for the purpose of supporting health-related programs and services. In others, the "health fee" is an identified or unidentified component of a larger student fee. Many student health centers operate as auxiliary enterprises, as their budget is derived entirely from revenue they generate from health fees and other sources; they do not receive institutional funds collected in tuition or received from governments. Until recent years, health fees supported *only* medical (sometimes including psychiatry), ancillary, and prevention services. Today, student fees often contribute to revenue for mental health services (counseling centers and counseling components of comprehensive health centers) as well. The level of student health fee charged varies extensively with the scale of the service, scope of programs, and student enrollment.

Institutional allocations: In small colleges, whether public or private, health services are sometimes supported by allocations of institutional funds derived from tuition or governmental appropriation. This is *usually* the case for counseling services, except when counseling services are integrated in comprehensive health programs.

Retail and fee-for-service revenue: Many student health centers collect additional revenue from students in the form of: per-visit charges (analogous to copayments required by insurance companies; to avoid creating barriers that would discourage students from accessing services, campus health programs and counseling centers generally do not impose per-visit fees for mental health services); specific service charges, such as for copying medical records; fees for ancillary diagnostic or therapeutic services, such as laboratory tests or medications; fees for medical supplies, such as crutches and bandages; retail transactions for prescription pharmaceuticals, over-the-counter medications, condoms, etc.; and 6) selected professional services, such as specialist visits or mental-health care beyond a defined number of visits. In an effort to diversify revenue beyond fees and institutional allocations, many health services now collect as much as 30% to 40% of their revenue from these sources (Keeling & Heitzman, 2003).

Third-party reimbursements: Many college health services collect third-party reimbursements from insurance companies for ancillary care provided to students, especially laboratory tests, imaging procedures, specialty visits, and pharmaceuticals. In some cases, students must pay for these services out-of-pocket and then seek reimbursement from their own insurance carriers. Third-party reimbursements for professional services, typically physician and mid-level provider visits, have been implemented in a growing number of health centers, as well. Most students are at least somewhat familiar with using health insurance to get health care, and doing so in the campus health center is not surprising to them. Significant infrastructure is required to process third-party bills and reimbursements, and institutions that wish to do insurance billing must require that all students have health insurance. The experience of most health centers that conduct third-party billing is that the revenue derived from reimbursements relieves pressure on further increases in the student health fee and may allow stabilization of the fee (or of institutional funding), but third-party billing has not eliminated the need for continuing institutional funding nor allowed the discontinuation of health fees.

Grants and contracts: Health centers with substantial resources may augment their revenue by receiving government or foundation grants and contracts, especially for specific health promotion programs and activities.

It seems unlikely that college health programs will be able to sustain their historical basic funding models without modifications in the future. Although demands for more and better services are increasing, existing resources likely will not increase, especially at state institutions. Institutions that fund health programs (especially the medical delivery) directly from central funds likely will reevaluate the wisdom of that strategy as competition for limited funds increases. To prevent losing essential prevention programs, some health centers will turn to grants, contracts, discretionary funds, and research projects. Effective college health directors in the future will be agile managers of funding streams, careful stewards of what institutional or fee-based funds they still have, and competent overseers of the increasingly complex business operations conducted in their program centers (Keeling & Heitzman, 2003).

Health Insurance

Since college health programs provide a selected range of programs and services and do not, in general, offer emergency, specialty, or hospital care, the access to the full range of health care services that students might need during their academic experience demands that they also have adequate health care insurance coverage. Many undergraduates may be covered by their parents' health care insurance plans throughout the period of enrollment, but graduate and professional students, international students, nontraditional undergraduates, and traditional-age undergraduates whose parents are unemployed or uninsured must purchase their own health insurance. Even students who are covered by parental plans may discover that those plans do not provide sufficient coverage in the area in which the campus is located (Keeling & Heitzman, 2003).

To address these needs, institutions usually provide access to a college- or university-sponsored health insurance plan that is reasonably priced and customized to meet the most likely needs of students. These plans emphasize emergency care, specialty visits, short-term hospitalization, mental, and prescription drug coverage. The plan must cover services that complement the health services provided by the institution. College health administrators seek to use the institutionally-sponsored health insurance plan as a way to offer students a relatively seamless package of services that blends on-campus and off-campus providers. When feasible, collaboration among institutions to develop a common plan is beneficial and productive. Many state-based systems of institutions have lowered costs by employing that strategy.

All students should have health insurance; however, this is not an easy requirement to meet given today's escalating health care costs. The Immigration and Naturalization Service (regulation 62.14) requires that all international students have health insurance. Many institutions now require the same of all students in any category. In those cases, students may be able to waive purchase of the institutional health insurance plan if they can show definite proof of comparable coverage (hard waiver) or if they claim such coverage (soft waiver).

TRANSFORMING COLLEGE HEALTH PROGRAMS

Today's vibrant and successful campus health programs demonstrate the following features:

- Reorganization and restructuring of health-related resources, especially the broad integration of health-related programs and services under **central leadership and direction**. The convergence of data on brain development, learning, the impact of physiological changes in the brain on cognition, and health behaviors of college and university students has resulted in the reorganization and restructuring of many campus health-related programs and services. This reconsideration of service delivery "helps to identify key relationships and linkages that now exist and suggests locations for new learning opportunities in the future" (Haier, 2009; Keeling, 2004a);
- As a consequence of this restructuring, leadership of health-related programs and services is commonly **centralized in the position of one high-level administrator** who may be a clinician. Many of the most important challenges facing campus health programs in the coming decade are financial, managerial, and administrative rather than clinical;
- Universal access with basic services covered by a **mandatory student health fee** is popular along with revenue diversification with fee-for-service (primarily for ancillary services, supplies, and pharmaceuticals) and third-party billing;
- Justification of both current and new resources by **alignment with demonstrated student needs and service demands**;
- Development of **comprehensive, integrated, campus-wide mental health systems and services** including crisis, outreach, surveillance, case-finding, and clinical programs;
- **Close linkage of primary care and mental health services to improve case-finding and access** for recognizing psychological and mental health concerns, especially depression;
- **Balanced clinical and outreach services. Increased accountability** for the use of resources, operational efficiency, and demonstration of effectiveness;
- **Data-driven, evidence-based practice, and resource allocation**;
- General **responsiveness to diversity** of today's college students. This includes sensitivity to different socioeconomic backgrounds, ability levels, and personal and family health histories;
- Creativity in **educational outreach** on health and wellness;

- **Leadership in prevention** of, or response to, local or national health emergencies; and
- Ability to **plan strategically** to allocate resources effectively in light of **economic challenges**.

ADDITIONAL SOURCES OF INFORMATION

The following are useful sources of information on college health programs.

- American College Health Association (ACHA). ACHA National Office, P.O. Box 28937. Baltimore, Maryland 21240-8937. (410) 859-1500; Fax (410) 859-1510. www.acha.org
- National College Health Assessment Survey (latest results), www.acha-ncha.org/
- Healthy Campus 2010, www.acha.org/info_resources/hc2010.cfm
- HIPAA information, U.S. Department of Health and Human Services www.hhs.gov/ocr/privacy/index.html
- FERPA information, U.S. Department of Education, www.ed.gov/policy/gen/guid/fpco/ferpa/index.html
- National Association of Student Personnel Administrators (NASPA). 1875 Connecticut Avenue, NW, Suite 418, Washington, DC, 20009. www.naspa.org
- Exemplar websites for campus health programs that offer significant resources for student health information:
- Student Health Center, New York University: www.nyu.edu/shc
- "Go Ask Alice" service, Columbia University: www.goaskalice.columbia.edu
- Center for Health, Bowling Green State University: www.bgsu.edu/health

REFERENCES

American College Health Association (ACHA). (1999). *Guidelines for a college health program.* Baltimore: Author.

American College Health Association (ACHA). (2005). *Standards of practice for health promotion in higher education* (2nd ed.). www.acha.org/info_resources/SPHPHE.cfm.

American College Health Association (ACHA). (2009a). American College Health Association–National College Health Assessment II: Reference group executive summary, Fall 2008. Baltimore: Author.

American College Health Association (ACHA). (2009b). National College Health Assessment Spring 2008 Reference Group Data Report. *Journal of American College Health, 57,* 477–488.

Banning, J., & Kuk, L. (2005). Campus ecology and college student health. *Student Health Spectrum,* 9–15.

Bechtel, W., Mandik, P., Mundale, J., & Stufflebeam, R. S. (Eds.). (2001). *Philosophy and the neurosciences: A reader.* New York: Wiley-Blackwell.

Boynton, R. E. (1962). Historical development of college health services. *Student Medicine, 10,* 354–359.

Boynton, R. E. (1971). The first fifty years: A history of the American College Health Association. *Journal of the American College Health Association, 19,* 269–285.

Bridwell, M. W., & Kinder, S. P. (1993). Confronting health issues. In M. J. Barr & Associates (Eds.), *The handbook of student affairs administration* (p. 481–492). San Francisco: Jossey-Bass.

Churchland, P. S. (1989). *Neurophilosophy: Toward a unified science of the mind-brain.* Cambridge, MA: MIT Press.

Council for the Advancement of Standards (CAS) in Higher Education. (2009). *CAS Professional Standards for Higher Education* (7th ed.). Washington, DC: Author.

Farnsworth, D. L. (1965). *College health services in the United States.* Washington, DC: American College Personnel Association (Student Personnel Monograph Series #4).

Haier, R. K. (2009, November-December). What does a smart brain look like? *Scientific American Mind,* 26–33.

Jackson, M., & Weinstein, H. (1997). The importance of healthy communities of higher education. *Journal of American College Health, 45,* 237–241.

Keeling, R. P. (2000). Beyond the campus clinic: A holistic approach to student health. *American Association of Colleges and Universities Peer Review,* 13–18.

Keeling, R. P. (2002). Why college health matters. *Journal of American College Health, 50,* 261–265.

Keeling, R. P. (Ed.). (2004a). *Learning reconsidered.* Washington, DC: National Association of Student Personnel Administrators.

Keeling, R. P. (2004b). Population level prevention in practice. *Leadership Exchange, 2,* 14–17.

Keeling, R. P. (2005, November). *Prevention in higher education: What is college health about?* Student Health Spectrum (Chickering Group), Cambridge, MA: Aetna Student Health.

Keeling, R. P., & Engstrom, E. L. (1993). Refining your peer education program. *Journal of American College Health, 41,* 259–263.

Keeling, R. P., & Heitzmann, D. (2003, Fall). Financing health and counseling services. *New Directions for Student Services, 103,* 39–58.

Keeling, R. P., Kantor, L. M., Kruse, K., & Roper, V. (1995). Enhancing peer education programs in special campus environments. In E. L. Engstrom (Ed.), *Enhancing peer education programs.* Baltimore: American College Health Association.

Keeling, R. P., Underhile, R., & Wall, A. F. (2007, Fall). Horizontal and vertical structures: The dynamics of organization in higher education. *Liberal Education, 93,* 22–31.

Mareschal, D., Johnson, M., Sirois, S., Spratling, M., Thomas, M., & Westermann, G. (2007). *Neuroconstructivism: How the brain constructs cognition.* Cambridge: Cambridge University Press.

Medical Group Management Association (MGMA). (2008). *MGMA physician compensation and production survey.* Washington, DC.

PEW Internet and American Life Project. (2006). *Online health search 2006.* Washington, DC. www.pewinternet.org/.

Prescott, H. M. (2007). *Student bodies: The influence of student health services in American society and medicine.* Ann Arbor, MI: University of Michigan Press.

Saddlemire, G. (1988). Health services. In A. L. Rentz & G. Saddlemire (Eds.), *Student affairs practice in higher education* (p. 185–202). Springfield, IL: Charles C Thomas.

Santelli, J., Kouzis, A., & Newcomer, S. (1996). Student attitudes toward school-based health centers. *Journal of Adolescent Health, 18,* 349–356.

Silverman, D., Underhile, R., & Keeling, R.P. (2008, June). *Student health reconsidered: A radical proposal for thinking differently about health-related programs and services for students.* Spectrum. Cambridge, MA: Aetna Student Health.

Sousa, D. A. (2006). *How the brain learns.* Thousand Oaks, CA: Sage.

Swinford, P. (2002). Advancing the health of students: A rationale for college health programs. *Journal of American College Health, 50,* 309–312.

Turner, H. S., & Hurley, J. L. (2002). *The history and practice of college health.* Lexington, KY: University Press of Kentucky.

World Health Organization. (1947). Constitution. New York: www.who.int/governance/eb/who_constitution_en.pdf.

Chapter 14

AFTERWORD

FIONA J. D. MacKINNON

The thesis of this book centers on the changing nature of higher education and the opportunity for student affairs to contribute in a consequential way to the education of all students. Stress within the academy has resulted in a lack of attention to the learning agenda for individual students and for the community. Student affairs has the opportunity to seize the moment, reflect and refocus on both curricular and cocurricular cultures, and build an engaging learning environment.

The changing backdrop for higher education over the past 50 years has provided a unique opening for student affairs professionals to shape the learning environment for students—without battling the status quo. Dramatic societal changes such as the pervasiveness of the business market model, ever-present technology, the global perspective, the shelf-life of information, continuous influence of the media, and access and affordability of higher education, to list but a few variables, have taken the attention of administrators and faculty leaving no campus entity in charge of the college learning community. These changes have diluted the college experience for students. Focus on "what is the easiest way for me to amass credits" and "how can I get a well-paying job when I complete my degree" places emphasis on the form and not the substance of the learning experience. This change in the perception of education has swept students, parents, state legislators and college administrators along with the tide.

Student services in any college or university has to be configured to meet the unique needs of the campus. Two-year colleges have distinctive student affairs pressures that are different from those of small private institutions and from mega-sized land grant institutions; East Coast colleges differ from Midwest and western institutions, large and small. Each institution has to consider its own heritage, tradition, and goals resulting in a distinctive organization of student affairs. The commonality of student affairs work in all colleges is that student learning and student success take precedence to all other agendas.

CHALLENGE FOR ADMINISTRATORS

Problems with the financial "bottom line" as well as student enrollment and retention have required administrators to seek the advice of the marketers and business consultants rather than holding firm to standards and educational principles (Ross, 2009). In the race for scarce resources, administrators have turned to business models relegating the quality of education to the sidelines (Wilson, 2009). Monies from tuition and state reimbursement have greater consequence on the sustainability of the institution than the integrity of the curriculum. Acquiescing to parent and student petitions, as well as threatened lawsuits, has more significance than holding students accountable for quality coursework and curricular content. Accumulation of credits has become a substitute for the learning experience. Too often, administrative expedience becomes the dominant problem solving modus operandi in market-oriented higher education.

CURRENT FACULTY PRESSURES

In the past four decades the upwardly mobile aspirations and financial concerns of colleges have placed priority on the number of graduate and professional programs offered rather than the quality of undergraduate education. The aim has been to achieve a higher notch in the Carnegie classification of colleges or the ranking of the day. This has caused a disproportionate emphasis on faculty research, even at colleges and universities that had strong reputations for undergraduate education. The introduction of the *U.S. News and World Report* rankings in the 1980s, mimicking college football and basketball polls, placed even more emphasis on faculty publications and ratings rather than the quality of undergraduate teaching (Sperber, 2005). The proliferation of graduate programs, and complicity between institutions of higher education and the professions have led to higher levels of credentialing that also place undergraduate education in a secondary position of importance. As a result of pressure to publish, an uneasy and not necessarily welcomed agreement between students and faculty has emerged that says that faculty will not place too much pressure on students if students will agree not to place too many demands on faculty. Inflated grades of A and B are the currency of the educational agreement. This dilutes the academic experience for both faculty and students, and leaves the learning community without structure or support.

STUDENTS' READINESS FOR COLLEGE

Students today need help in understanding what a college degree means. The high school experience frequently colors expectations for college; the common media portrayals of the fancy-free college life lead to unrealistic assumptions at both two- and four-year colleges. Matriculating students who complete college credit in high school often confuses college with a continuation of high school. This is the reality of their academic experience. Indeed at least 60 percent of students transfer from one or more colleges to fulfill degree requirements, resulting in a patchwork of learning experiences and reinforcing the notion that college is simply an accumulation of course credit (Schneider, 2005). Students entering college need coaches and mentors to help them frame their college goals–both short- and long-term. Student affairs professionals can fulfill that role.

A subtle, societal disdain for college students has appeared in the culture. The academic and social expectations for college students are low. When the term "kids" is used to describe college students, a false and demeaning perspective emerges for young adults who may have been in the military in Iraq or Afghanistan fighting for their country, for young adults who certainly vote and marry, probably drink alcohol responsibly, who have seen friends commit suicide, who work one or two jobs to make ends meet, and know what it is like to have family members laid off from work (Ashburn, 2009). Students in this generation have varied backgrounds and experiences from which to draw wisdom. The label "kid" connotes irresponsibility rather than accountability, and makes certain unwarranted, derogatory assumptions about young adult behavior.

Most students in high school have not had the opportunity to engage in the intensity of "deeper or deep learning" that is necessary for a transformational college experience (National Learning Infrastructure Initiative, 2009). Most students do not value their own ideas, never mind the ideas of faculty. College students who do not experience intellectually engaging learning experiences are being short-changed by the institution and by the professionals who are responsible. Many of the students attending college in the current generation have been poorly equipped for college level work, and assuredly need direction when embarking on the college experience.

While administrators are preoccupied with raising finances and bolstering enrollment and faculty are focused on research and publication, student affairs professionals are the only authority left that has the opportunity to shape the entire community of learning for the campus. This is an influential role. Student affairs professionals, unlike the rest of the campus, are not necessarily driven by the marketing philosophy that has resulted in the shaky status of higher education (Bok, 2006; Hersh & Merrow, 2005).

EXPECTATIONS FOR STUDENT AFFAIRS

The common element in the student affairs philosophy has always been to assist learners with the intellectual challenge and the fulfillment of academic goals. As the first campus administrators to meet with students during the orientation period, student affairs alone drives the expectations for the college experience no matter the students' intellectual competence, appropriateness of life stage, social background and maturity, quality of previous educational experience, or readiness for the critical developmental tasks that will be encountered during the college years. Student affairs professionals with understanding of meta-cognition and learning have the keys to coach matriculating students to become motivated, engaged, and successful learners. Like athletes accustomed to competing at the high school level learners in college must be coached to develop more complex learning skills for participation in college learning. In this way student affairs professionals build the community of learners by focusing on "deeper or deep learning," short- and long-term learning goals, and complex learning strategies. Student affairs can assume responsibility not only for the cocurriculum but also for the intellectual and cognitive aspects of college in partnership with students—because no one else on campus can.

RUBRIC FOR RENEWING AND EXPANDING
PROFESSIONAL COMMITMENT

Renewal is critical in the press for doing more with less caused by reduction in personnel and other resources. Economy of effort has to be strategically calculated for outcomes that matter most. In order to reenergize periodically Howard Gardner provided a course of action, a framework, utilized by the GoodWork Project (2005) that leads professionals through four areas of reflection. The first area of professional reflection focuses on refining the Mission and the essential nature of the goals to be achieved. This is not the well-worn mission of the unit, the division, or the university but the special tasks that must be accomplished at this particular time and place for these specific students (Gardner, 2005). The second area of reflection for professional renewal involves revisiting potential Models in the literature or from other disciplines that shed light on the responsibilities at hand. Consider the influence of positive mentors, or even, in Gardner's words, "tormentors" whose dark ways have left a negative imprint. Seek a path that leads to positive accomplishment and outcomes for students.

The third component of renewal explores one's personal reflection in the Mirror Test of Personal Commitments. With this component Gardner (2005) suggests the following question, "If we look at ourselves clearly and transparently, are we doing the best job that we can?" Are we helping students to get the best college education possible? Are the criteria used to appraise success appropriate? The personal searching process may yield cracks in the mirror that lead to the resolution of questions and shed light on different options and actions. Confidence for moving forward evolves from the soul-searching process.

And the fourth component for professional renewal examines the broader profession as it appears in the mirror, the Profession-wide Mirror Test. This is the reflection of professional commitments, policies and procedures for supporting college student success. According to Gardner the question to ask about professional standards and practices comes from Moliere's saying, "You are responsible not only for what you do but for what you fail to do." Is the profession moving with the times to support college student learning, potential and success? This is the professional question of consequence.

SOME EXAMPLES OF THE RUBRIC IN ACTION

The past 50 years have seen great change in the setting for student affairs; consequently, the Gardner GoodWork rubric is a handy checklist for generating topics for reflection. What follows is a limited list of topics that hopefully stimulate reflection from a variety of perspectives: from that of the individual student affairs professional, the student affairs profession, the literature of the profession, and the individual institution.

First of all, consider the Mission of the student affairs profession that has evolved from the "specialist" and "generalist" orientations following World War II (Caple, 1998). The focus has always been on assisting students develop their potential and succeed with their academic goals. Clearly the essence of the professional mission must take into consideration the academically underprepared college students of this generation. Student affairs professionals at the primary level of intervention need to be the learning specialists in the academy.

Since the 1950s, the "in loco parentis" stance of student affairs has increased in spite of, or perhaps because of, student development theory. In the 1950s the student affairs mission promoted student responsibility and accountability for individuals and for student communities. Student affairs professionals mentored students in leadership, follower-ship and decision-making in all areas of student life. Housemothers and graduate interns were not necessary in residence halls. Students supported the mores and guidelines that they themselves set for their communities, as they would at home. Setting expectations and standards for appropriate behavior is key. Success in college requires breaking from the past and stepping into a mature, personally directed future.

The second step of the GoodWork rubric calls for examination of constructive Models that provide professional direction. Gardner suggests Plato's Academy, Alverno College, or Berea College as interesting models for the academy. Even models, such as lifespan development and lifelong learning, for example, offer alternative exemplars to college student development models. Maximizing optimal development is very much in keeping with the student affairs point of view, but operates within a framework of potential rather than deficiency.

The dilemma with college student development theory is that it is an extension of adolescent psychology that, of necessity, looks at what is lacking in behaviors, skills, and attitudes. This viewpoint casts the spotlight on deficiencies, not on the capabilities that under gird potential. In young adults the reservoir of untapped strengths provides the basis for untapped potential. Without a complete understanding, deficiency models influence professionals in practice by focusing on the inchoate student rather than responsible young adults who have the capabilities to meet high expectations. Deficiency also tempers multicultural understanding by focusing on difference and what is not there rather than the commonalities that can override differences and draw us together as human beings. Language and frameworks matter.

Another model that deserves scrutiny is the functional areas model that has served as the backbone of student affairs work since the 1930s. Most students would prefer continuity and one professional to provide them with problem solving and support services. As in the medical field, one physician who can attend to all physical needs is preferable to four different specialists, each of whom sees the patient as a different organ. So too for students, continuity is preferable to four different advisors, each with a different specialty. Technology now makes answers available to professionals and students obviating the need for some functional area offices until later in the college sequence. The continuity of a "guide on the side," especially for matriculating students, may help to answer the retention problem. Simplifying the organizational structure of student services for the ease of student use would be a worthwhile objective.

Implementing the concept of the "guide on the side" would support matriculating students by creating continuity in a semester long, small seminar of about 10 to 12 students, led by a student affairs professional that would lay out the process for managing the academic work of college. The seminar would demonstrate the difference between high school learning and college learning. Starting with goal setting each student would have an opportunity to discuss (a) long term, post-college goals; (b) semester goals; and (c) goals for each class that week given the content to be covered. Strategies for learning would be shared. The deep approach to learning that links the student's personal understanding to classroom learning could be demonstrated: building on students' prior knowledge, focusing on main ideas and underlying principles related to students' lives, and inspiring curiosity and motivation (Biggs, 1999). Topics such as preferred learning styles, self-management for learning, motivation, lifelong learning, careers, majors, and creativity would be discussed. Plans for cocurricular activities could be woven into goal-setting as students accomplish the academic standards that ensure their continuation in school. Students would have an opportunity to monitor their grades and continue meeting with the seminar until that time when they were able to achieve success on their own.

The third component of the Gardner model concentrates on the Mirror Test of Personal Commitments. The mirror test reflects the individual persona. Both positive and negative feedback deserve attention. For example, some student affairs professionals are known for their "camp counselor" approach to the college experience. College cannot be equated with camp; the desire to help students by making things fun or finding shortcuts run counter to the purpose of college. College is the equivalent of the work assignment for young adults. Just as that everyone starts a job needs help with conceptualizing specialized assignments, so too young adults need help with the tools and infrastructure that will allow them to stay in college.

Graduate preparation programs cannot possibly cover all the academic coursework and experiential learning necessary to prepare professionals for practice. Whether anticipating a position in academic advising, residence life, or the career center, professionals must expect to prepare extensively to develop a comfortable philosophy for practice. For students of all ages who are making life-altering transitions, educational decisions involve high-stakes concerns. These concerns cannot be taken lightly. The personal reflection in the mirror provides insight into strengths and shortcomings.

The fourth component of the rubric centers on the totality of the profession as it is reflected in the mirror, Profession-wide Mirror Test. As the student affairs profession has moved away from umbrella organizations like the American Counseling Association it has become more internally focused. In fact, the professional organizations have become insular, quite narcissistic, and overly concerned with their own structures and welfare, rather than the membership, and the science and practice related to college student success.

Furthermore, the professional organizations have been more troubled about their own existence than being of service to the professionals who belong– two organizations ostensibly covering the same territory are burdensome for the membership. Indeed the marketing philosophy has had a definite effect on the tone and climate of the annual conferences. One illustration, for example, concerns the distribution of stickers at the conferences ensuring marketing attention for the graduate programs, the state associations, the functional area associations, and prospective graduate students. Even list-procs in the field reflect the problems that faculty have preserving their graduate student programs at the doctoral and master's level. The topics of undergraduate student success, unleashing student potential, and academic success are lost in the shuffle.

The literature of the student affairs profession has become limited to just a few journals, books, and authors in spite of the importance of the range of disciplines such as counseling, sociology, life-span development, ethnic studies, and so on. The dominant point of view stresses that student affairs is responsible for out-of-class, cocurricular experiences, and not for the character and tone of the campus learning agenda. At this time, no one on campus is responsible for the learning agenda. With the plethora of ill-equipped students appearing on every college campus, the importance of the learning ethos becomes ever more critical. Student affairs has an important role to play to help colleges and universities succeed in their undergraduate mission. The seriousness of the issue may be measured by the data on persistence, retention, or college dropout rates (inconsistent as they may be). According to ACT (2004), 63 percent of students from the 1995–1996 cohort attending college achieved a college degree within six years. A study of the 1972, 1982, and 1992 cohorts attending college found that 53 percent completed degrees at four-year public or private colleges (National Center for Education Statistics, 2004). These data raise troubling questions about the role of student affairs in the drop-out process. Surely student affairs professionals are the responsible professionals who help students examine their options. The data do not instill confidence in the efforts of student affairs personnel to support individual learning goals.

Student affairs professionals walk a fine line in accepting the symbolic hold of parents on students, but attesting to the students' right to be in control of their own educational journey. Newly matriculated college students need to know that the important adults in their lives have confidence in their abilities to resolve problems as they emerge into their newly earned status as college students. Young adults come to college with the capacity to handle their own transitions just as any person enlisting in the military, getting married, or moving to begin a new job would be expected to do. Reinforcing independence is the best thing that colleges and parents can do for students.

At this time, student affairs has the ability to influence campus attitudes and values as well as policy, process, and procedures. With administrators and faculty otherwise preoccupied, the profession has an open door for creating positive change. This is the time for student affairs to act with confidence and creativity to revive the vitality of the learning environment and the higher education experience for all.

CONCLUSION

Reflection helps with renewal. Renewal is vital in these austere times when higher education is no longer attracting the financial resources that create a secure future, and state and private coffers provide only limited support. In these precarious times, it is critical that student affairs provide leadership and concrete evidence of the value added contribution of the profession. The Gardner rubric presents one comprehensive framework for examining the broad spectrum of contributions that the profession—adds to the higher education experience for students.

Student affairs has important insight and a role to play as guardian of the learning environment on the campus. Neither faculty nor administrators are able to fill the void. In the 1960s, counseling psychology and student affairs were very much involved in the nuances of student learning and persistence. More is known today about meta-learning, deep learning and learning strategies, as well as cognitive sciences, than ever before. This area of expertise should be provided as the first level of graduate student preparation to help graduate students understand their own learning agenda. For matriculating students, the practicalities of learning would provide the infrastructure for a successful college experience.

Higher education is under scrutiny, and the value of student affairs may also be questioned. Providing a value-added component to the lives of each student is what really matters. Student affairs' central goal is helping students learn the skills, attitudes, and motivation that allow them to participate fully in their education, to achieve their goals in higher education, to expand their potential as human beings, and to contribute as citizens of the democracy.

REFERENCES

ACT. (2004). *The role of academic and non-academic factors in improving college retention.* ACT Policy Report. Iowa City, IA: Author. www.act.org/research/policymakers/pdf/college_retention.pdf.

Ashburn, E. (2009, December 13). Why do students drop out? Because they must work at jobs too. *The Chronicle of Higher Education,* p. 1. Retrieved from http://chronicle.com/article/Why-Do-Students-Drop-Out-/49417/?sid=pm&utm_source=pm&utm_medium=en.

Biggs, J. (1999). *Teaching for quality learning at university: What the student does.* Philadelphia: Society for Research into Higher Education and Open University.

Bok, D. (2006). *Our underachieving colleges: A candid look at how much students learn and why they should be learning more.* Princeton, NJ: Princeton University Press.

Caple, R. B. (1998). *To mark the beginning: A social history of college student affairs.* Lanham, MD: American College Personnel Association, University Press of America.

Gardner, H. (2005). Beyond markets and individuals. In R. H. Hirsch & J. Merrow (Eds.), *Declining by degrees: Higher education at risk* (pp. 97–112). New York: Palgrave Macmillan.

Hersh, R. H., & Merrow, J. (Eds.). (2005). *Declining by degrees: Higher education at risk.* New York: Palgrave Macmillan.

National Center for Education Statistics. 2004. http://nces.ed.gov.

National Learning Infrastructure Initiative, 2009. Arizona State University: EDCAUSE.http://www.west.asu.edu/nlii/learningtable.htm.

Ross, J. (2009. December 6). Fund raisers' bonuses: A moral hazard for higher education. *The Chronicle of Higher Education,* p. 1. Retrieved from http://chronicle.com/article/Fund-Raisers-Bonuses-a-Moral/49330/.

Schneider, D. (2005). Liberal education–Slip-sliding away? In R. H. Hirsch & J. Merrow (Eds.), *Declining by degrees: Higher education at risk* (pp. 61–76). New York: Palgrave Macmillan.

Sperber, M. (2005). How undergraduate education became college lite–and a personal apology. In R. H. Hirsch & J. Merrow (Eds.), *Declining by degrees: Higher education at risk* (pp. 131–143). New York: Palgrave Macmillan.

Wilson, R. (2009, February 6). Downturn threatens faculty's role in running colleges. *The Chronicle of Higher Education,* p. 1 Retrieved from http://chronicle.com/article/Downturn-Threatens-the/10586.

AUTHOR INDEX

A

Aaron, R., 220
Abes, E. S., 17, 25
Abraham, J. W., 291, 293
Abrahamson, T. D., 76
Adams, Abigail, 36
Adams, John, 36
Adams, T. C., 366
Adler, Mortimer, 15, 16
Affsprung, E. H., 187
Albright, R. L., 56
Allen, R. D., 182
Allen, W., 246, 270, 271
Allena, T., 208, 209
Alvarez, P., 271
Amada, G., 181, 221, 247
Anchors, S., 316, 323, 324, 337, 338, 340
Anderson C., 334, 335
Anderson, Edward, 134
Anderson, G., 257
Anson, J. L., 360
Antonio, A. L., 70
Appleby, D. C., 111, 112
Appleton, J. R., 198, 200, 201
Aquinas, St. Thomas, 10, 13
Arceneaux, C., 175
Archer, J., 155, 156, 158, 159, 164, 165,
        168–169, 170, 173, 174, 176, 178, 179,
        180, 181, 182, 183
Ardaiolo, F. P., 199, 202, 203, 204, 205,
        209, 211, 215, 217
Aristotle, 9, 10, 13
Arminio, J. I., 378
Armstrong, M. R., 210
Armstrong, T., 252
Arndt, J. R., 204

Aros, C., 157, 160, 161, 162, 166, 180, 184,
        185
Arrington, M., 304
Ashburn, E., 462
Ashby, J. S., 169
Astin, A. W., 258, 331, 339, 366, 369, 371,
        381
Astin, H. S., 258
Atchley, L., 334, 342
Atkinson, D. R., 182
Atkinson, R. C., 87
Aulepp, L., 154, 178
Austin, D. M., 302

B

Bagakas, J. G., 252
Baier, J. L., 163, 375
Baker, D. B., 122, 124
Baker, T. R., 211, 213, 220
Bakken, C. J., 203, 204
Baldizan, E. M., 216
Ballard, B. R., 253
Ballou, R. A., 201, 339
Balogh, C. P., 209
Banahan, L. A., 282, 284, 286, 287, 291,
        292, 293, 294, 302
Banning, J. H., 178, 438, 448
Barbaro, M., 90
Barefoot, B. O., 80, 82, 286, 341
Baron, A., 177, 182
Barr, M. J., 56, 59, 201, 324, 345, 367
Barr, R., 102
Barr, V., 157, 160, 161, 162, 166, 180, 184,
        185
Barron, Barbara, 133
Bartem, R., 348

471

Delve, C. I., 381
Delworth, U., 154, 178, 320
DeMers, S., 176
Demetriou, C., 113
Demos, G. D., 158
Dewey, John, 7, 10, 16
Dey, E. L., 378
Dickman, M. M., 206
DiGeronimo, T. F., 152, 168, 170, 182
Dillion, W. L., 348
Dixon, D., 169
Doermann, H. J., 184
Domokos, L. S., 12–13
Donnay, D. A. C., 33
Douce, L. A., 155, 159
Douglas, K. B., 332
Downs, D. A., 222
Draeger, J., 423
Drake, R. W., 283, 288, 296
Dressel, J. L., 185
Drinan, P., 220
Drum, D. J., 176, 185
Dude, K., 330
Dungy, G. J., 368
Dunkel, N. W., 321, 324, 326, 329,
    343–344, 365
Dunkel-Schetter, C., 167, 168
Dupuis, V. L., 5, 10
Durst, R. H., 197, 198, 209, 212
Durtschi, J., 162
Dutton, T. B., 209, 212

E

Eberhardt, D., 304
Edison, M. I., 247
Edmondson, B., 297
Edwards, D. T., 201
Edwards, K., 208
Ehrlich, Thomas, 144
Eimers, M., 290
Eliot, Charles, 42
Emmanuel, N. R., 226, 227
Endres, J., 157
Engstrom, E. L., 444, 449
Erickson Cornish, J. A., 170
Erskine, C., 155, 157, 158, 159, 160, 162,
    163, 164, 165, 166, 167, 170, 171, 172,
    174, 175, 177

Evans, N. J., 24, 255, 256, 336–337, 403
Evans, S. B., 295
Ewing, M. J. M., 155

F

Farnsworth, D. L., 430
Farnsworth, W. M., 289
Farrell, E., 156, 157, 304
Feldman, K. A., 286, 291, 369
Feller, R., 133
Fenichel, A., 156
Fenske, R. H., 197, 226, 327, 338
Fern, M. S., 206
Field, K., 423
Finney, Charles, 37
Fischer, W. M., 228
Fisher, T. C., 203, 206
Fitch, E. E., Jr., 212, 228
Fitts, C. T., 283
Fitzgerald, L. E., 295
Fitzgibbon, M., 182
Fleming, J., 38, 253
Fley, J. A., 198, 200
Floyd, S., 162
Foley, J. D., 206, 215, 220–221
Folsom, B., 139
Footer, N. S., 203
Forest, L., 153
Forman, M. E., 153
Forney, D. S., 336–337
Fox, R., 105
Fox, S., 266
Foxley, C. H., 285
Franklin, Benjamin, 14
Frederickson, C. F., 316, 317, 318, 319, 326
Frederickson, J., 207
Free, J. E., 154
Freeman, J., 124
Frost, S. H., 97, 98, 101

G

Gahagan, J., 315, 336
Gallagher, R. P., 155, 160, 161, 162, 163,
    166, 168–169, 170, 171, 172, 174, 175,
    176, 180, 181, 182, 184, 186, 206–207,
    164–165
Gallant, T. B., 220

Wang, L., 248, 249, 250, 254
Ward-Roof, J. A., 291, 292, 301, 303
Warman, R. E., 154
Warnath, C. F., 153
Warshaw, S., 199
Warters, W. C., 208
Wartman, K. L., 268
Waryold, D. M., 200, 210
Washington, Booker T., 39
Washington, J., 378
Wawrzynski, M., 281, 291, 293
Weaver-Graham, W., 155, 161, 162, 164–165, 168–169, 171, 175, 176, 181, 185, 272
Webb, R. E., 155
Weeks, K. M., 384
Weigel, R. G., 172, 173
Weinstein, H., 441
Weiscott, G. N., 169
Welch, I. D., 168
Wellman, Jane, 144
Werner, R., 391
Wessel, R. D., 120, 121, 122, 123, 124, 140
Westermann, G., 435
Whalen, D. F., 339
Whipple, E. G., 375, 376
Whiston, S., 131
Whitaker, L. C., 155, 178
White, E. R., 98, 107, 109
White, K., 179
Whitehead, Alfred North, 16
Whitehead, D. M., 79, 81
Whiteley, J. M., 17, 153, 172, 173, 178
Whiteley, S. M., 157, 164
Whitfield, E. A., 133
Whitt, E. J., 247, 276, 330, 331, 333, 338, 369
Whitt, Elizabeth, 22, 23–24, 79, 82
Widseth, J. C., 155
Wiesen, F. A., 179
Wilkenson, R., 397, 398
Willenbrock, C. M., 208
Willer, P., 247
Williams, A., 168
Williams, D. A., 262, 263
Williams, J. B., 249
Williams, M. S., 416
Williams, S., 113
Williamson, E. G., 39, 151, 167, 283

Williamson, F. G., 206, 211, 215, 220–221
Wilson, J. M., 212
Wilson, K., 298
Wilson, M. E., 214
Wilson, R., 461
Wilson, S. B., 155
Winston, R. B., 375
Winston, R. B., Jr., 54, 55, 112, 240, 316, 319, 323, 324, 327, 337, 338
With, E. A., 302
Wolfe, D. S., 302
Wolff, M., 139
Wong, M. P. A., 255
Wood, A., 179
Wood, C., 133
Wood, N. L., 204, 208
Woodard, D. B., 31, 319, 320, 363
Woolston, D., 106
Wrenn, C. G., 200, 206, 220–221, 285
Wrenn, R. L., 178
Wright, D. J., 249, 251, 252, 253, 260

Y

Yamashita, M., 162
Yarris, E., 151, 152, 158, 163, 166, 168, 173, 174, 175, 176, 177, 178
Young, D. P., 203, 206
Young, K., 300
Young, L. W., 253
Young, N., 378
Young, R. B., 16, 24
Younger, T. K., 301

Z

Zacker, J., 227
Zaransky, M. H., 349
Zarate, M. E., 396
Zarle, T., 209, 212
Zdziarski, E. L., 204, 208
Zeller, W. J., 335
Zelna, C., 227
Zhang, B., 155, 161, 162, 163, 165, 166, 169, 174, 182, 185
Zheng, J. L., 339
Zickuhr, K., 266
Zis, S. L., 294
Zunker, V. G., 135

SUBJECT INDEX

496 *Rentz's Student Affairs Practice in Higher Education*

and student relationships, 200–202
utilitarian, 35
for women, 33–34, 37
instruction, 210–211
insurance billing, 454
insurance reimbursements, 181
integrated model, 325
integrative approach, 123–124
intellectualism, 40–41, 42, 44
intentional interventions, 371
interactional diversity experiences, 271
interactional technologies, 184
interactions, 378–379
interactive cube, 174 (*see also* cube model)
interactive virtual community, 267
Interactive websites, 267
Inter-Association Task Force on Alcohol
    and other Substance Abuse Issues,
    214, 225
intercollegiate athletic programs, 41
intercultural model, 246, 271–273
interdependence, 74
Interfolio, 130
internal environment, 78
internal strengths, 78
internal weaknesses, 78
International Association of Counseling
Services, Inc. (LACS), 155, 156–157, 175
    International Education Week,
    257–258
international-focused programs, 257–258
international students, 256–258, 299,
    384–385, 455
Internet, 90, 107–109, 449
resources for enrollment management (*see*
    online resources)
Internet addiction, 179
Internet-based information programs, 305
internship coordinators, 140
internships, 139–140, 146–147, 155, 172, 175
interventions, 371
interviewing schedule, 142
involvement
    definition, 299
    providing opportunities for, 374
    quality of campus life, 81–82
    relationship to retention and learning,
    371
    in student health, 448–449

and student success, 339, 370
irrevocable expulsion, 207

J

Jackson State University, 154
job postings system, 141
John Hopkins University, 34, 41, 98, 101
Joint Commission on the Accreditation of
    Healthcare Organizations (JCAHO),
    452
Joint Statement on Rights and Freedoms of
    Students, 218
Joint Task Force on Student Learning, 22
Journal of College Orientation and Transition,
    287
Journal of College Student Personnel, 99
journals, 99, 175–176, 266, 287
judicial affairs, 226–230
judicial systems, 211–213
jurisdiction and institutions, 202–203

K

Kent State University, 154
Kings College, 32
knowledge, 6
Krasnow v. Virginia Polytechnic Institute, 202

L

land grant act, 35
land grant colleges, 38–39
land grant universities, 14
lateral expansion, 34
Latino Americans, 250–251
Laws of Nature, 9, 10–11
lawsuits, 180
leadership advisory committee, 380
leadership development, 379–380
leadership skills, 139
learning, definition of, 23
learning and health, 434–437, 451
learning communities, 335
learning outcomes, 100, 111–112, 293–294,
    365, 368
learning outcomes assessment, 110
learning process, 434–435
learning purpose, 366

and student retention, 282, 285–286, 291
and technology, 303–305
traditions and symbols, 287
Orientation Review, 287
outcomes, 144, 146, 289, 293–294
outcomes based assessment, 293–294
outcomes perspective, 119
outcomes report, 145
outreach programs, 162, 165, 449
outreach projects, 254
outsourcing, 155, 185, 348
over award, 414

P

Paine v. Board of Regents, 203
paraprofessional staff, 327
parental involvement, 302
parental notification policies, 214
parent and family programs, 286, 301–303
parent loans, 408
Parent Services Network, 287
Parent Student Loans, 399
partnerships, 22
paternalism, 201, 226 (*see also in loco parentis*)
pathological behavior, 206–207
patient education, 444
patients per provider, 447–448, 448t
pedagogy, 100
peer advisors, 104–105
peer group influences, 369
peer health educators, 449
People for the American Way, 222–223
periodicals, 175–176
permissions, 295
personalization, 76–77
personalized communication techniques, 68–69
personal searching process, 464
person-environment interaction theories, 55, 337
"Perspective on Student Affairs," 56
Pew Internet Project, 449
philosophical history, 12–15
philosophical influences, 12–15, 15–17
philosophical methodology, 4
philosophical schools (*see* philosophy)
philosophy
    Aristotelian realism, 13

and axiology, 6–7, 10
current thoughts/challenges, 23–25
definition of, 4–5, **7**
and epistemology, 6
existentialism, 11–12
idealism, 8–9
neo-thomism, 10
and ontology, 5, 8
pragmatism, 10–11
realism, 9
religious idealism, 13
physical facilities maintenance, 343, 348
physicians, 445, 446
placement model, 120, 121–124
placement offices, 155
placement tests, 81
planning, strategic, 77–78
Poesy v. Freemason, 39, 249
positive environments, 57
positive outcomes, 216–217
poverty, 183–184
Powerful Partnerships, 22
pragmatism, 10–11, 15, 20, 22, 23
Pre-College Clinic, 295
predominately White institutions (Pais), 248–249
pre-enrollment model, 294, 295–296
preparation for college, 462–463
presidents of institutes, 41–42
preventative services, 158, 165
prevention programs, 442
preventive intervention, 333
preventive professionals, 446
primary medical care, 443–444
Princeton, 32
principles of good practice, 22
privacy issues, 89–90, 418, 452–453
privacy rights, 417
private accomodations, 347
private institutions and due process, 204–205
private sources funding, 407
privatized housing model, 348–350
privileged communication, 181
procedural due process, 203
proceduralism, 217
professional associations, 46, 264–265
professional commitment, 463–464
professional development, 174–176,